The Last Transport

To ~~[name]~~
with good wishes

[signature]

The Last Transport

The Holocaust in the Eastern Aegean

Anthony McElligott

BLOOMSBURY ACADEMIC

LONDON • NEW YORK • OXFORD • NEW DELHI • SYDNEY

BLOOMSBURY ACADEMIC
Bloomsbury Publishing Plc
50 Bedford Square, London, WC1B 3DP, UK
1385 Broadway, New York, NY 10018, USA
29 Earlsfort Terrace, Dublin 2, Ireland

BLOOMSBURY, BLOOMSBURY ACADEMIC and the Diana logo are
trademarks of Bloomsbury Publishing Plc

First published in Great Britain 2025

A catalogue record for this book is available from the British Library.

A catalog record for this book is available from the Library of Congress.

ISBN:	HB:	978-1-4742-2798-8
	PB:	978-1-4742-2799-5
	ePDF:	978-1-4742-2801-5
	eBook:	978-1-4742-2800-8

Typeset by Integra Software Services Pvt. Ltd.
Printed and bound in Great Britain

To find out more about our authors and books visit www.bloomsbury.com
and sign up for our newsletters.

For a 'lost community' whose names we know

When one speaks of the genocide of six million Jews, one can only be saddened by the massacre of a whole community of men and women, all innocent. But we don't know them. One is only truly amazed when one has known them personally and when they are constantly running through one's mind, even if these few people represent only a small part of the six million.

Elisa Franco Hasson, *Il Était Une Fois l'Île Des Roses*
(Éditions Clepsydre: Nivelles, 1996, repr. 2012), p. 77

Contents

DODECANESE 1944

Agathonission

Arki
Arki

Patmos
Kambos
Patmos
Lipsi
Lipsi
Farmakonission

TURKEY

Milas

Leros

Kalolimnos

Emborios
Telendos

Kalymnos

Bodrum

Kinaros

Levitha

Piramos

Kalymnos

Liadi

Kos
Asfendiu

Kos
Kardamäna

Marmaris

A e g e a n   S e a

Kefalos

Vathy

Gyali
Mandrakion
Nissyros
Nikia

Symi
Pedion
Symi

Astypalä
Astypaläa

Megalon Chorion
Tilos
Livadia

Rhodes Town
Kremasti

Soroni
Afandou

Salakos

Dodecanese
1923–1943 to Italy;
from November 1943 German occupation

Syrna

Alimia

Chalki

Arhangelos
Rhodes

Monolithos
Istrios
Lindos

N

W   E

S

Mesanagros

Katavia

Saria
Saria

Diafanion

Karpathos
Spoa

Pyla
Arkassa
Karpathos

Armathia
Fry
Kassos

M e d i t e r r a n e a n
S e a

Crete
Italian zone
(German zone since Sept. 1943)

0   10   20   30 km

© Peter Palm

RHODES ISLAND 1944

A e g e a n   S e a

Kahal Shalom
Synagogue
Cape Zonari

Rhodes Town

Trianta Beach

Kremasti • ● Ialisos • Triánta
Paradisi ● ● Sgourou • Kalithea
● Pastida

Theológos ● ○ Temple
● Soroni ★ **Maritsa** • Maritsa

*Jewish
Cemetery*

Prison camp

*Kalithea
Beach*

Kalavarda ● Fanes ●
Psito (Psinthos) HQ ◇
Ancient Kamiros ○
Psinthos ●

Kalithies ● ● Faliraki

Ladiko Bay

Mandriko ● Salakos ●
Cape Kopria
Mount Profitis Ilias HQ ◇
Apollona ●

Dimilia ● ◇ **Colonia Campochiaro HQ**
Eleousa ●

● Afandou

Mandou Bay

● **Colonia
San Benedetto**

Alimia
Makry
Island

Kritinia ●

Stroggylo
Island

● Ebonas

Tragoussa
Island

Kolimbia ●

*Glyfada
Beach*
● Ialisos
Attavyros

Arhangelos Bay

Malona ● ● Arhangelos

Cape
Armenistis

Ag. Isidoros ●

Massari ●

Malonus Bay

Siana ●
Cape
Ag. Georgios

Tharri ● ● Laerma

Háraki ●

Haraki Bay

● Monolithos

Istrios ●

Profilia ●

Lardos ●

◀ ★ **Gaddura**
Kalathos ●
Vliha Bay

● Pilona
● Lindos

Lindou Beach

Marmari
● Apolakkia
Arnitha ● Vati ●

Asklipio ▢
(Asklipieio)

*Lardou
Bay*

● Pefkoi (Pefki)

*Cape Lardos
(Pokos)*

Apolakkias Bay

● Genadi
(Gennádio)

● Mesanagros

Genadi Bay

*M e d i t e r r a n e a n
S e a*

Katavia ◀ ★
Colonia San Marco
Katavia ●

Lahania ●

*Karavolas
Island*

Plimiri ●

Ag. Georgios ●

Prasonisi

0   5   10 km

◀ Italian
▢ German
★ Air Base
■ Internment and prison camp

© Peter Palm

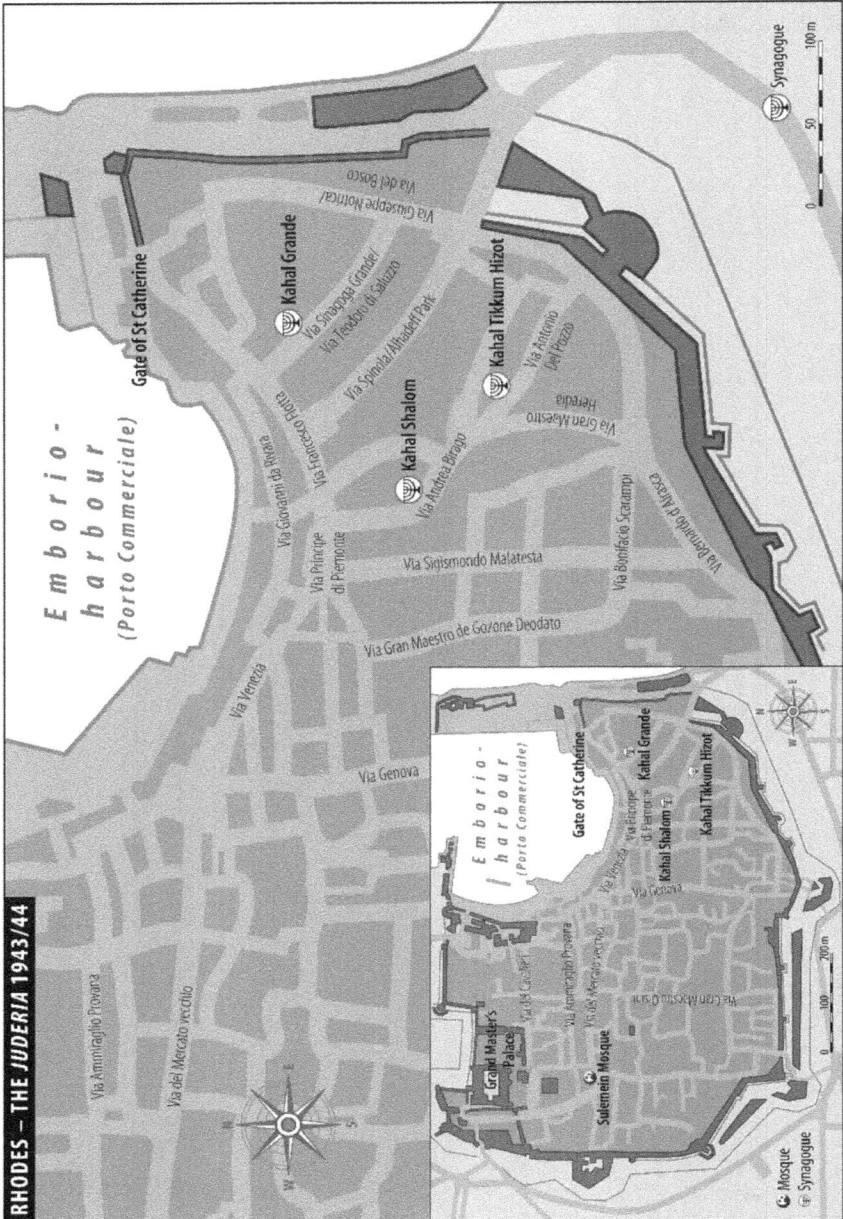

RHODES – THE *JUDERIA* 1943/44

Emborio-harbour
(Porto Commerciale)

Gate of St Catherine

Kahal Grande
Via Sinagoga Grande
Via Teodoro di Saluzzo
Via Spinola/Alhadeff Park

Via Giuseppe Nicroa/
Via del Bosco

Kahal Tikkum Hizot
Via Antonio
del Pozzo

Kahal Shalom
Via Andrea Bragio

Via Gran Maestro
Heredia

Via Francesco Paira

Via Giovanni da Rivera

Via Principe
di Piemonte

Via Sigismondo Malatesta

Via Bonfacio Scadampi

Via Bernardo d'Alseca

Via Gran Maestro de Gozone Deodato

Via Venezia

Via Genova

Via Ammiraglio Provana

Via del Mercato vecchio

© Peter Palm

Synagogue

50   100 m

Emborio-
harbour
(Porto Commerciale)

Gate of St Catherine

Kahal Grande
Via Principe
d'Piemonte

Kahal Tikkum Hizot

Kahal Shalom

Via Venezia

Via Ammiraglio Provana

Via del Mercato vecchio

Via Genova

Grand Master's
Palace

Suleimen Mosque

Via Gran Maestro G. rani

0   100   200 m

Mosque
Synagogue

Illustrations

Maps

Tables

Acknowledgements

My thanks go first and foremost to the former president of the Jewish Community of Rhodes and Kos, Bella Angel Restis; she has benevolently followed the progress of this book from its inception. The current president, Claudia Restis, continues to show the same warm support as her mother. From the very beginning of my research, the Community's administrator Carmen Cohen has been a patient interlocutor, sharing her infinite knowledge. She has made her office at the Synagogue in Rhodes my go-to office when in Rhodes, and with her husband, Moises, has extended the warmest of friendships. It is not often that scholars develop a close relationship with archivists, but that has been the case with Eirini Toliou, the director of the Hellenic State Archives of the Dodecanese. As with Carmen and Moises, Eirini and her husband Stefanos have made Rhodes my second home. A special thanks and a debt of gratitude go to Marcel Danon and the Danon family in Cape Town. They generously sponsored my early effort to bring together scholars working on the Aegean and the Holocaust. Marcel has continued over the past decade to encourage my research and has extended his and his family's warmth and friendship to me.

This is a book about families that perished in the Holocaust and some that survived through good fortune. I have been honoured that some of their descendants have shared with me their stories: Joe Elkana (Florida); his cousin Shoshanah Alcana (Israel-Rhodes); Henry Franco (Texas); Ruben Amato Lee (London); Bettina Benatar Luetgerath (Hamburg). I am grateful to them for their trust. From his home in Los Angeles, Aron Hasson has spearheaded the Rhodesli archive of memory. He curates a veritable collection of photographs, artefacts and memorabilia documenting facets of Rhodian Jewish life before its destruction. He has kindly shared both this and his vast knowledge of Jewish Rhodes. In the later stages of my work, I came to know Michael Frank (New York), whose 'conversations' with a centenarian survivor are an inspirational study in the excavation of memories. In Rhodes at the beginning of my research, I met the Italian scholar Professor Marco Clementi (University of Calabria) and since then we have forged a close collegial friendship, making the study of a dark period of history bearable.

No scholarly work is possible without the aid of the gatekeepers of the archive and fellow scholars. In addition to the Dodecanese archive, I wish to record my thanks to the archivists and librarians without whose assistance this book would not have been possible: The Wiener Holocaust Library London; London School of Economics Special Collections; the National Archives, Kew; Bundesarchiv Berlin, Freiburg and Ludwigsburg; the Archive of the Committee of the International Red Cross, Geneva; the International Tracing Service, Bad Arolsen. I have benefitted too from the endeavours of other researchers – above all, Liliana Picciotto at the Centro di Documentazione Ebraica Milan – as I have from the work of Jacqueline and Miriam Benatar (Yad Vashem). The filmmaker Ruggero Gabai, Milan, kindly provided me with a copy of his film, *The Longest Journey*, allowing me to quote from it in this book. The curators at the Yad Vashem Archives, the Fortunoff Archive and the Holocaust Visual Archive of the Shoah Foundation facilitated access to survivor interviews, which have been so vital to this study. A special thanks goes to Michael Singer of the Cape Town Holocaust Centre (CTHC) for granting permission to use material from the South African Union of Jewish Students, 'Student Holocaust Interviewing Project' and the South African Holocaust and Genocide Foundation Archive. I am grateful to my former student Milena Callergi Cosentino who facilitated contact to the CTHC. Dr Maayan Hillel (now at Northwestern University Chicago) secured and translated for me the account in Hebrew by Moses Surmani of his escape from Rhodes in 1943. She and my former colleague, Dr Roberto Mazza, have been both scholarly partners and friends over the years.

Meanwhile, as well as Marco Clementi, the following scholars have been selfless in sharing their research with me: Professor Aron Rodrigue, Stanford University, kindly obtained documents from the World Jewish Congress, Cincinnati; Vadim Altskan, United States Holocaust Memorial Museum, made available digitalized material from the USHMM's vast digital collection; Professor Renée Hirschon, St Peter's College, Oxford, shared her ongoing research into Jewish life in the Aegean; Professor Steven Bowman, University of Cincinnati, shared the affidavit of Rino Merolle, a rare document that was otherwise inaccessible; with the help of Jordan Goodman, Professor Jon Agar, University College London, kindly obtained for me a file I had overlooked from The National Archives Kew, at a time I was unable to travel. I am indebted to each of them. My former colleagues in the history department at the University of Limerick were a great support in the early days of this research. The university provided some of the funding for me to conduct research trips in the early days; and its wonderful humanities librarian, Pattie Punch, moved mountains to obtain vital reading material, as well as giving good craic! The late Professor Tom Lodge, as dean of faculty was constantly encouraging, intellectually engaging, and a close friend. He is missed. As too is my successor as the chairholder in history at the University of Limerick, the late Professor Jan Plamper. Despite his illness, Jan took time to read and comment on a paper I gave to an incredibly stimulating group of scholars at the Berkeley conference on 'Italy's Aegean Possessions' organized by Aron Rodrigue and Valerie McGuire. The fruit of that meeting is now available to read. Over a decade ago, I co-edited a book with the distinguished scholar Jeffrey Herf on antisemitism before and since the Holocaust. That collaboration has blossomed into a warm friendship – and I have benefitted from our conversations ever since.

Writing can be a lonely business, and once immersed in the material, there is a danger of losing sight of the argument. This is when a different pair of eyes becomes vital to establishing a coherent and critical narrative. Who better to do this than old friends and new ones? Throughout my career I have been lucky to have been supported by Professors Elizabeth Harvey, Nottingham-Berlin, Alan Kramer, Dublin-Hamburg, and Sir Richard Evans, Cambridge. They have read parts or all of the manuscript in its early and later iterations; offered their wisdom and insights, steering me away from errors. They have simply been the best judges of my work. Among my newer friends and acquaintances reading earlier versions of chapters, Vadim Altskan and Ludmila Gordon (USHMM Washington), offered astute insights; Ruben Amato Lee made me think carefully about crafting sentences (and their content), and Bettina Benatar Luetgerath offered kind encouragement. I have also benefitted from different audiences listening to me speaking about Jewish Rhodes. Toby Simpson at the Wiener Holocaust Library organized my first talk on the subject to a public audience; a more specialist audience comprising my former student Professor Nadine Rossol and her colleagues in the history department of Essex University discussed my early exploration of the topic and helped to expand its scope. As the book took shape, Professor John O'Brennan and Dr Paul Newman at the National University Maynooth allowed me to introduce to an Irish audience this little-known story. Similarly, my good friend Lynn Jackson, the CEO of Holocaust Education Ireland (HEI), gave me the opportunity to bring the story of the Jewish community and its brutal ending in the summer of 1944 to an Irish audience when she invited me to deliver the guest lecture on the deportation from Rhodes as part of HEI's annual summer school in Dublin. The lecture eventually appeared in print form in a collection on the Holocaust in Greece edited by Giorgos Antoniou and Dirk Moses, I am grateful to both scholars for including my work. More recently in Berlin, a group of retired doctors gave me the benefit of their own well-informed insights into German history and the Holocaust at a special event organized by my longstanding friends Frauke Tedsen and Sebastian Ufer, in which my Berlin 'Aegean neighbours' Renate and Eberhard Lott participated with their inimitable enthusiasm. Ecki 'Johny Outlaw' Schweppe, Hamburg, who with Alan Kramer is a member of the 'Glücksbataillon Rhodos', has accompanied me on my various trips to Rhodes, offering a welcome distraction from the dark history that occupied my attention most of the time. He, Alan Kramer, Claudia Unruh, Renate Ahrens, Alison Kraft, Liz Harvey, Tim Kirk, Roger Newbrook, Jordan Goodman, Dallas Seeley, John O'Brennan and Catherine 'Diva' Lawless, have been important staging posts in this book's journey.

Back in Rhodes, Professor John Sakkas, University of the Aegean, has been a collegial interlocutor over the years and helped to facilitate an international symposium I organized in summer of 2014, when I was able to enjoy the company of the staff of the International Writers' and Translators Centre, Rhodes (IWTC). The IWTC has continued to offer its cooperation since that summer. My research in Geneva was eased considerably by Catherine Cossy and her husband Urs Stoecklin, whose photographic skills are evident in some of the illustrations in this book. I am also grateful to their friend, the journalist Pietro Boschetti, who kindly loaned me his apartment during my research trip to the International Committee of the Red Cross (ICRC). Latterly, I have had the benefit of getting to know scriptwriters Kaan Turgay, Wiesbaden, and Cristina Contes, Zurich, who have graciously listened and then shared their own ideas. Peter Palm, Berlin, drew the splendid maps – my apologies that he has had to wait so long to see them in print. A paragon of patience is my editor at Bloomsbury, Emily Drewe, who commissioned the book (too) many years ago. She has remained enthusiastic, taking a special interest in its final version. A very special thanks to her and her team.

A lot has happened in the time it has taken me to research and write this book: not least three beautiful grandchildren: Amelia on the cusp of young adulthood, Lucy who reached her first decennial milestone, and Demetrios who arrived in time for the book's postscript. Anna, Sophie, and Max have accompanied this book from its first outing at the Wiener Holocaust Library in 2013 to its completion. As the text expanded, Gavin Esler offered good advice ('authors never finish a book, they just stop writing'). Serg Sergiou was not only there to help with computing issues if these arose, but latterly he has cooked some splendid meals. Finally, Wiltrud Lamersdorf has patiently lived with this project. She has shared in the story's poignancy, while being a constant reminder that there is life beyond the study of death.

For the past decade I have immersed myself in a world needlessly and cruelly cut short. It would be remiss of me not to dedicate this work to the lives I have studied so closely.

Rhodes/Berlin, winter 2023

Abbreviations

ACICR	Archives Internationale Croix Rouge/Archives of the International Committee of the Red Cross
AJDC	American Joint Distribution Committee
BArch	Bundesarchiv Berlin-Lichterfelde
BA-L	Bundesarchiv-Ludwigsburg
BA-MA	Bundesarchiv-Militärarchiv
BMA	British Military Administration
CDEC	Centro di Documentazione Ebraica Contemporanea
DELASEM	Delegazione per l'Assistenza degli Emigranti Ebrei/Delegation for the Assistance of Jewish Emigrants
FP	Feldpolizei
GAKR	Genika Archia tou Kratous/Archia Dodekanisou Rhodos
GFP	Geheime Feldpolizei
HIAS	Hebrew Immigrant Aid Society
HICEM	Acronym: Hebrew Immigrant Aid Society, Jewish Colonization Association, & Emigdirect
IRO	International Refugee Organization
NARA	United States National Archives and Records Administration
PNF	Partito Nazionale Fascista
RSHA	Reichssicherheitshauptamt (Reich Security Main Office)
SAHGF	South African Holocaust and Genocide Foundation

SS   Schutzstaffel

TNA   The National Archives Kew

UNRRA   United Nations Relief and Rehabilitation Administration

USHMM   United States Holocaust Memorial Museum

WJC   World Jewish Congress

WL   Wiener Holocaust Library

YVA   Yad Vashem Archives

Preface

From the first moment, when it had not yet become known to the wider world but, rather, unfolded day by day in the hidden recesses of nameless, obscure places and was the secret of the accomplices, victims and henchmen, from that first moment the Holocaust brought with it a horrible dread – a dread that it might be forgotten.[1]

The impetus to write a book on the Holocaust originated with Emily Drewe, my editor at Bloomsbury. However, she had in mind a very different type of book, and I was initially reluctant to embark on the project.

At the time I was still teaching a Holocaust class at the University of Limerick and relied on an array of different types of sources that covered perpetrators, victims, onlookers and so on. Included in these sources was the photograph of the boy that fronts the cover of this book. The original caption accompanying the image told us that the boy's name was Alessandro Angel from the island of Rhodes, and that the photograph was taken sometime in 1943, the year before the Jews of Rhodes and Kos were deported to Auschwitz. The more I thought about my editor's proposal, the more I became attracted to the idea of writing about this boy. I had in mind the book by the German historian Götz Aly about a young girl, Marion Samuel, whose life was also brutally cut short by the Holocaust.[2] The boy in the photograph was maybe a year or two younger than Marion, but their fates – like those of the circa 1.6 million children killed in the Holocaust – coincided 3,000 kilometres apart.[3] The community to which he belonged was the last under the German Occupation of Greece and the islands to be deported to Auschwitz in the summer of 1944.

Thus inspired by Götz Aly's account of Marion Samuel, I got started on the research following up my lead – the photograph of the boy identified as 'Alessandro'. I began by looking for information on his family, and this meant tracking down census files. I travelled to Rhodes, the former jewel in the crown of Italian colonialism in the Eastern Mediterranean (1912–47), first to explore the state archives of the Dodecanese and to enquire into the collection of the Jewish Museum itself. I also contacted the Fondazione Centro di Documentazione Ebraica Contemporanea (Foundation Centre for the Documentation of Contemporary Jewry, CDEC) in Milan where Liliana Picciotto had headed a team of researchers compiling lists of Italian victims of the Holocaust.[4]

My search for census material in the state archives of the Dodecanese proved fruitless. The census files could not be located; they seemed to have simply vanished.[5] I contacted the social anthropologist Renée Hirschon of St Peter's College, Oxford who, many years earlier, had come across a household census (presumably 1940 or 1941) of Jews on Rhodes. Luckily, Professor Hirschon had come into possession of the registration cards with the intention of working on Jewish family structure at a future date. However, there was some difficulty locating Alessandro's family because the cards were in no order and, subsequently, they were misplaced.[6] Meanwhile, back in Rhodes the Jewish Community's administrator, Carmen Cohen, kindly brought down from its storage in the attic an old and worn large ledger of households of the Jewish community, begun around 1920. The entries were written in Hebrew, Soletreo (the written form of Ladino, the spoken vernacular Judeo-Spanish of Sephardi Jews) and with later entries in Italian; they were in no particular order and were sporadic. Indeed, this large volume of many hundreds of pages was organized neither alphabetically nor otherwise. Names and details were entered haphazardly, possibly reflecting the period heads of household registered as taxpayers with the community. Nonetheless, after a while, at entry #424, I found Alessandro's family, but I also made an unexpected discovery.

The father, Samuele Angel (born 1880) had a previous family by Bulissa Coen. Together they had six children. When Bulissa died in 1924, Samuele, in keeping with Jewish tradition, remarried in August 1925, bringing his youngest daughter Gioia (1921–44?) into the marriage. Together with his second wife, Rebecca Alhadeff (1889–1944), there were four more children born between 1926 and 1936. Alessandro was the eldest, having been born on 10 July 1926. This discovery regarding the second family and the ages of the children was quickly corroborated by checking the database of the CDEC on the deportees from Rhodes. Even though I had still not accessed the household census, it was clear to me that the original premise for my project, the story of the young boy identified as Alessandro Angel, had been demolished by just a fragment of the source evidence.[7]

These initial forays into 'Alessandro Angel', with their surprising discovery, did not bring the project to a halt, but rather they changed its direction. For meanwhile, I had been following leads in other archives, as one source led to another, taking me either physically or virtually to archives in Greece, Germany, the United Kingdom, Switzerland, the United States and South Africa. These archives and their holdings in turn led me onto different paths of inquiry. The lists of victims compiled by Liliana Picciotto allowed me to create a demographic of those deported from Rhodes and Kos. Sources in Rhodes combined with those of the World Jewish Congress in Cincinnati opened the way to establishing the socio-economic structure of the community and provided other valuable information, as did the files of the International Committee of the Red Cross in Geneva. However, the recently discovered files of the Italian *Carabinieri* did two things. First, these files documenting everyday life opened a window into the inner world of the Jewish community, allowing a more nuanced picture to emerge than that found in much of the memorialist literature stemming from the diaspora. Second, the files showed degrees of Italian collaboration and complicity in the persecution, deportation and spoliation of Jews, and were suggestive of the multi-layering of motivation. They are, by all measures, the most important source for reconstructing (albeit only in part) Jewish life before the deportation.

Maurice Soriano, in his capacity as post-war president of the remnant community, was unaware of their existence when he wrote to Yad Vashem in 1978 stating 'With great regret we have to tell you that the entire archive of our Community at the time of the mass deportation of all its members has been destroyed, stolen or looted and consequently no documentation exists concerning the tragedy of our co-religionists, except for an outline written by ourselves setting out the tragic circumstances of the deportation.'[8] But the *Carabinieri* had monitored and photographed the official correspondence of the Community, thus in part replicating the archive Soriano alludes to. Moreover, mundane files concerning ordinary individuals cast a light onto families who would otherwise have remained obscured. Not only do these files augment survivor accounts of their lives before the deportation, they sometimes challenge the post-war narrative of a harmonious Jewish community popular among the diaspora.

Meanwhile, British and German military sources complicated the issue of the role of contingency in the Aegean as a motive for the deportation. The files that spoke least about the deportation were those of Himmler's men responsible for the deportation – although these too had their usefulness. Their reticence was counteracted by the detailed reports generated by post-war investigators into war crimes, whose findings are held in the Bundesarchiv Zentrale Stelle der Landesjustizverwaltungen Ludwigsburg and in the Staatsarchiv in Bremen. The book in its current form would not have been possible without documentation from the above archives.

*

Alessandro had just turned 18 years old when he was deported on 23 July 1944 along with 1,761 other Jews from the two islands, and therefore could not have been the boy in the photograph if its dating was correct. As a result of this fact, my original intention to write about the boy in the photograph changed course, guided by the sources that had emerged over the course of my preliminary research (and would change again over the course of subsequent research and writing).

The varied detail that emerged from my early archival searches suggested a richer and fuller landscape than originally envisaged. Unlike his parents and younger siblings, the older Alessandro survived the initial selection at Auschwitz only to die in the notorious concentration camp of Mauthausen in the spring of 1945, shortly before liberation.[9] For the small number of those who survived, roughly 12 per cent of those deported, the journey back to life after liberation was not an easy one. Nor would their story be widely known for a long period after 1945, only emerging into the light as methodological approaches in Holocaust studies and historiography more generally changed.[10] Nevertheless, the files of the World Jewish Congress, the American Jewish Joint Distribution Committee and the United Nations Rehabilitation and Recovery Administration provide rich insights into this 'hidden' post-war world of survivors.

There was a reason why the deportation from the Eastern Aegean remained 'hidden from history'. The deportations from Rhodes, Kos and Crete, as well as from the Ionian island of Corfu, and together affecting barely 4,000 Jews were obscured by the larger shadow of the Shoah in Eastern Europe. Small islands in the Aegean attracted little attention among scholars. Academic interest in the Mediterranean as a theatre of the Nazi genocide of the Jews, apart from brief references in older general works, remained scant.[11] It was only from the 1990s that attention shifted towards the Greek peninsula, exemplified by the studies of Steven Bowman, Mark Mazower, Kathleen Fleming and, latterly, Rena Molho.[12] But the Aegean islands still remained 'hidden' from view.

Thus, for many years after the war, the story of the community and its destruction remained the purview of the Rhodesli diaspora and was based on family stories gleaned from survivors. 'Tell me about your life on Rhodes.' So begin many of the interviews with survivors during the decade from the 1980s to the 1990s (with some outliers in the early 2000s). Taken together, there are well over a hundred interviews, but if we count by survivor rather than interview, the number reduces to around sixty-eight. The majority of interviews of Rhodes and Kos survivors are housed at the Shoah Foundation's Visual History Archive, University of Southern California, the Fortunoff Archive located at Yale University, the USHMM collections, and Yad Vashem Archives. In addition to these better-known collections is the South African Oral History Project that also is a rich repository of testimonies (again with some of the same survivors). There is a smaller collection of interviews in Brussels, a handful of documentaries, notably Ruggero Gabai's and Marcello Pezzetti's 2013 film, *The Longest Journey*, which focuses on a 'conversation' between three survivors in situ in the *Juderia*. At the time of their interviews, some of the survivors were in their fifties, and some were already in their seventh decade. Much water had passed under the bridge in the nearly five decades since their liberation from the camps in 1945, and memories can become blurred with the passage of time.

In the emerging narrative of life on Rhodes and Kos, much was left to conjecture, and sometimes to literary embellishment. For survivors and later generations the relevant archives containing the facts of Jewish everyday life in the Eastern Aegean and its subsequent destruction were largely unknown.

Indeed, the most important collection of documents to shed light onto Jewish life in Rhodes and its subsequent destruction was not discovered until the 2010s. The narrative of life on Rhodes and Kos and the events that overtook the community in the summer of 1944, thus was mostly based on a small number of chronicles from within the community's diaspora.[13] Together with the interviews of survivors, some of which were later transcribed as memoirs, *post facto* knowledge was added, and we discuss this dimension of memory in relation to the destroyed Jewish community in Chapter 9.

The scholarly landscape has changed radically during the last decade with important studies of Italian rule in the Dodecanese, and of Jewish life, emerging from a younger generation of scholars.[14] This transformation has been largely facilitated by the re-cataloguing of the holdings of the Dodecanese State Archives by its (then) new director, Mrs Irene Tolios. The hitherto labyrinthine and idiosyncratic character of the archive organized by its previous custodian has now given way to proper cataloguing and thus been made traversable for historians. Meanwhile, the discovery of the Royal *Carabinieri* archive a decade ago, with its pedantic recording of the minutiae of everyday life, has been an important source for those interested in studying the Jewish community, or indeed, all groups and people in the archipelago. For the first time, a window opened on the inner life of the Jewish community before its destruction.[15]

Nonetheless, in spite of these developments, our knowledge of the community and its destruction remains fragmented. There still has been very little 'integrative history' connecting 'the policies of the perpetrators, the attitudes of surrounding society, and the world of the victims' as suggested by the American-Israeli historian Saul Friedländer more than two decades ago.[16] The present study of the Aegean Jews is an attempt to follow Friedländer's example.[17] It has relied on a combination of building blocks of knowledge: an internationally far-flung and disparate range of archive sources, leavened by survivor accounts and family narratives to attempt an integrative picture of a given community and its fate in time and space, without claiming finality on the subject.

*

Set against the larger story of the Holocaust and its six million victims, the fate of the Aegean Jews, numbering less than 2,000, appears as a mere brush stroke on the broad canvas.

Nevertheless, there is a strong case for viewing the picture up close to pick out the detail that is often overlooked when looking at the larger landscape. How did Alessandro and his compatriots experience life in Rhodes and in Kos before and during the war? How did the Jews of Rhodes and Kos interact with other groups, notably the Italian colonizer after 1912 and the German occupier from 1943, not to mention Greeks and Turks? How did they face their fate in the summer of 1944? Why did some survive the camps and others not? What do we know about the survivors in the months following liberation? How is the 'lost world of Jewish Rhodes' remembered among the diaspora and how – if at all – does this memory correspond to the lived experience at the time?[18] Finally, who is the boy in the photograph?

These are some of the questions pursued in *The Last Transport*. My approach follows recent scholarly trends in Holocaust historiography that have leaned towards a micro-study of a person, a place or an event, rather than following a larger sweep of history.[19] It drills below the surface of the historical landscape to retrieve individual actors. Adopting a micro-historical approach has its dangers, not least that of lapsing into a form of latter-day antiquarianism, or what historian Sir Ian Kershaw once referred to as a 'so what' narrative in which historical examples accumulate on the page, but with no particular sense of direction or over-arching argument.[20] Nevertheless, a critical micro-history can lay bare in a more tangible fashion the dynamic of the Holocaust in its specific context of time and space, where not only its perpetrators are historical actors, but also the victims are present as subjects in their own right.[21] Explaining the Holocaust is aided by examining the context from the bottom up, as it is by looking from the top down. The fruitfulness of this 'integrated history' has been more than adequately demonstrated by Saul Friedländer.[22]

This case study of the Holocaust in a small corner of the Aegean and at the furthermost geographical point to Berlin seeks not only to bring to the fore the context of how something so terrible and unfathomable could occur. It also addresses a desideratum that became obvious to me during the course of my research, namely that of restoring to the victims their everyday humanity: their faces (hidden behind statistics), their names, their lives, their individual and collective histories in time and space. To quote Rabbi Shalom Fridmann, the Director of the Amud Aish Memorial Museum in Brooklyn, 'For too long, the story of the Holocaust has been from the perspective of the perpetrators. We owe it to the victims to present their narrative, too.'[23] Because without investigating the micro-contexts in which the persecution and destruction of Europe's Jewish communities took place, it seems to me at least, we miss one crucial point of studying the past: namely to understand, make sense of, and explain the past, while restoring the dignity of its victims.[24]

1

The Holocaust in its Aegean Context

The history of the Holocaust in Greece and in the Balkans is richly documented.[1] But the fate of the Jews of the Aegean islands is less well known. Even recent studies of the Holocaust in Greece barely glance at the tragedy that occurred on the islands of Crete, Rhodes and Kos.[2] Meanwhile, the fate of Jews on the Ionian island of Corfu seems to have been by-passed altogether by much of the scholarship. These small Jewish communities in the Aegean and Ionian seas were among the last – if not *the* last – of the hitherto unscathed Jewish communities of Europe to be seized and destroyed in the final months of the German occupation of Greece and the islands. Indeed, following the deportation of the Cretan and Corfiot Jews in June, those of Rhodes and Kos were the last to be transported from mainland Greece in the summer of 1944, bound for the gas chambers of Auschwitz. The Germans began their withdrawal from Greece barely six weeks later.[3]

By the spring of 1943, nearly half of the six million victims of Hitler's 'war against the Jews' were already dead.[4] However, there were still approximately a quarter of a million Jews alive in the Balkans at this date. If we include the Jews of Italy, Hungary and Romania, the total population comes close to two million (Table 1.1). Their fates too would be sealed as the tide of war turned against Germany, thus pushing the Nazis' 'Jewish Question' ever further into the foreground of Germany's war aims. The decision to turn the Nazi 'final solution of the Jewish question' (*Endlösung der Judenfrage*) into a continent-wide 'total solution' (*Gesamtlösung der europäischen Judenfrage*), had been broached by Reinhard Heydrich at the notorious Wannsee Conference in January 1942. Its extension to Greece began to take shape in the summer of 1942. At the beginning of 1943, Dieter Wisliceny, a 33-year-old SS-Captain and so-called 'advisor on the Jewish question' attached to the German Legation in Bratislava (referred to as Pressburg by the Germans), was sent to Salonica by Adolf Eichmann to organize the deportation of that city's Jews. It was estimated at the time that he would need 'six to eight weeks' to complete the task.[5]

At the time of the first deportation from Salonica in March 1943, and certainly by the last deportation from that city seven months later, the tide of war was turning against Germany and its continental empire was shrinking. From the point of view of the regime's radical bureaucrats in the various administrative departments concerned with implementing Hitler's war against European Jewry, time was running out.[6] As it did, the focus on Jews took precedence above all else. With reference to Rhodes, the historian Saul Friedländer made note of this ideological imperative:

> We speak of mid-August-1944: A few weeks beforehand a boat was sent from Athens to Rhodes to seize the Jewish community of the island – fishermen [*sic*] and their families; slowly, during ten days, the boat sailed to Athens. Those Jews who survived were put on trains to Auschwitz, and slowly, because of the bombings, they reached Auschwitz where they were immediately exterminated. At the very same time, the Reich was going to pieces. Most people were aware of the fact that the war was coming to an end and Germany would be utterly defeated. Yet, among the tasks which had to be completed as thoroughly as possible was the extermination of the Jews. Without a constant ideological prodding, there is no way of explaining this utter destruction.[7]

We will see in the course of this study that while the ideological impetus to murder circa 4,000 Jews of Rhodes, Kos, Crete and Corfu stemmed from Hitler and Himmler, its implementation was left to Eichmann's field operatives at the so-called 'Jewish Desk' (*Judenreferat*) IV B4, which Eichmann headed, who not only 'worked towards Hitler's will', but indeed, shared it.[8] However, the 'constant ideological prodding' Saul Friedländer refers to in the above quote does not exclude the importance of contingency, as once formulated by Hans Mommsen.[9] As the war turned against Germany, Jews as *the* enemy featured ever more strongly in Hitler's mental landscape.[10] Indeed, longstanding ideological intention and ad hoc imperatives contingent on the progress of war were the two sides of the same coin.[11]

In a prescient article published in 1941, the American sociologist Samuel M. Strong placed Nazi persecution of Jews (and others) into a wider context of desensitization towards mid-twentieth-century violence and barbarization.

> Prophets of doom in times of deep crises are not exceptional manifestations. During the past six years public opinion has been aroused continuously by a ceaseless stream of unfathomed human tragedies until it gradually became less squeamish, leaving behind the forebodings of hypersensitive minds. The annihilation of millions of Chinese made the brutal mutilation of thousands of defenseless Ethiopians seem less astounding; in turn, the blasting of the entire city of Guernica along with the bombing and destruction of several million lives in Spain prepared public opinion to view with somewhat decreasing alarm the ferocious 'baptism of fire' which engulfed city after city of the successively conquered countries. Human imagination is not lively enough to grasp the extent of decisive pulverizations of community life and the wanton dislocations of vast populations that followed in the train of the Axis horror. This holocaust [*sic*] is still continuing with such devastating fury that it is impossible to know the number of victims of warfare, starvation, civilian bombings, and of the Nazi scheme to exterminate certain populations which they consider inferior.[12]

Strong's analysis provides part of the answer to some of the questions raised in this study. Published in the USA at a time when the Holocaust in its fully fledged form was only just getting underway, it also reminds us that there was nonetheless contemporary knowledge of the murderous dimension to the persecution of Jews.[13] However, in the context of a brutalized and brutalizing war, 'special case' pleading took a backseat to that of prosecuting the war and defeating Hitler. The Allies, in other words, had other concerns.

Jews in Greece before the war formed a sizeable minority, about 10 per cent of the Greek population, with its greater majority domiciled in Salonica, before 1912 called the 'Jerusalem' of the Balkans, and until 1917 still part of the Ottoman Empire.[14] Even with the city's 'hellenization' after the arrival of Greek refugees from Smyrna [modern-day Izmir] in the early 1920s, coupled with the exodus of Muslims, Jews still constituted around a quarter of Salonica's population in 1939.[15] With one or two exceptions, in provincial Greece, Jews tended to be clustered mostly in semi-rural communities, not unlike the *shtetl* in Eastern Europe. In Athens, the city's Jews were integrated into the wider community to the point of 'invisibility'. In Rhodes, Kos, Corfu and Crete, they were often barely distinguishable from their Turkish and Greek neighbours in terms of outward appearance, even though they were concentrated in so-called Jewish neighbourhoods.

At the time of the German occupation of Greece in 1941, there were roughly 77,380 Jews spread across twenty-five communities, including the Aegean islands. The majority of Greek Jews lived in Salonica (58,000) followed by Athens (3,000). Most of the medium and larger towns of all the occupied zones had Jewish communities. These were mostly small-sized communities of between a few hundred Jews, as in the towns of Florina and Arta, or the Aegean islands of Crete (*c.* 350) and Kos (*c.* 100), to between 1,800 and 2,000, as in the provincial towns of Ioannina and Kavala, or on the Ionian island of Corfu and in Rhodes. By the end of the war, barely 10,000 of the Greek Jewish population, or 13 per cent of its pre-war total, had survived, according to the Jewish Board of Deputies of Greece. Moreover, the rate of attrition was much more severe in some localities.[16]

Numerically, the Jews of the Eastern Aegean constituted only a small part of this larger world. They were nonetheless at the centre of an important network of Sephardim linked to Salonica in northern Greece and to Antalya and Izmir in Turkey. They were integral to the Levantine trading world that stretched from Damascus in Syria to Jerusalem in Palestine, to Alexandria in Egypt, to Tripoli in Libya, to Tangier and Casablanca in Morocco.[17]

Their fate during the war was complicated by the fact that mainland Greece and the islands were divided among the Axis powers in a tripartite occupation in spring 1941 (Map 1.1).[18] Bulgaria gained the wheat belt of Thrace, from the Greek Macedonian cities of Sérres in the west to Kavala in the east, and most of northern Macedonia, notably Bitola with its large Jewish community. Albania, Croatia and parts of Macedonia, and some Greek islands, including Corfu and Kephalonia, came under Italian jurisdiction, as did Athens. The Germans took control of the strategically important port of Piraeus together with north-eastern Greece from the border town of Florina close to Yugoslavia to the three-fingered peninsula of Halkidiki, as well as of the slim belt of the Evros region bordering Turkey with the port city of Alexandropoúli in the south. They also occupied the north Aegean islands of Lemnos, Mytlilene (Lesbos) and Chios. At the heart of the German zone of occupation was Salonica.

Map 1.1 The tripartite occupation of Greece and the Aegean islands[19]; © Peter Palm

However, the twelve Eastern Aegean islands that formed the archipelago of the Dodecanese remained unaffected by the division of Greece, for they formed part of Italy's colonial possessions in the Eastern Aegean, from May 1925 known officially as *Il Possedimenti d'Egeo* and renamed four years later as *Isole Italiane d'Egeo*.[20]

The pace of Nazi persecution of Jews in Greece was slowed by what was perceived in Berlin as the uncooperative attitude of the Italian military authorities in Athens. Before the overthrow of Mussolini in July 1943 by the Grand Council and conservative elites led by Marshal Pietro Badoglio, who subsequently signed an armistice with the Allies, there were numerous reports to this effect. On one occasion in June 1943, Wisliceny allegedly was threatened with arrest by the Italian authorities if he again strayed into their jurisdiction in the hunt for Jews.[21] Meanwhile, the Bulgarian government appeared equally tardy in implementing persecutory measures when it came to Jews who were Bulgarian nationals (they were less concerned about the 11,000 Greek and Macedonian Jews from the Bulgarian-occupied territories deported to Treblinka).[22] Romania too had few scruples where the fate of foreign Jews was concerned, complying with Nazi genocidal policy. Thus Karl Klingenfuss, a key figure at the so-called Jewish Desk of the German Foreign Office, could report favourably to Eichmann in August 1942 on the carrying out of anti-Jewish policies in that country.[23] Nevertheless, even in Romania, as in Bulgaria and Hungary, national policy towards the Jews tended to be guided more by local opportunism than by entrenched antisemitic attitudes, although the latter were surely present.[24]

Although the systematic and continent-wide murder of Jews did not assume its final shape until the winter of 1941/42, there were already reports from military forces, as well as the German Foreign Office and SS officials, that point to the genocidal character of German policies towards Jews in the Balkans, beginning in Serbia in the late spring of 1941.[25] Initially, the killing of Jews in Serbia was mostly ad hoc and part of reprisal killings carried out by the *Wehrmacht*.[26] However, by the autumn, this policy had taken a sinister turn as it evolved into the systematic obliteration of Jewish life. Already in early November 1941 and well before the expansion of the Holocaust throughout the region, the legation counsellor in the German Foreign Office,

Franz Rademacher, who had travelled to Belgrade during the last week of October, reported to his superiors that the 'Jewish Question' in Serbia had been resolved.[27]

Altogether, between 1941 and 1944, the Holocaust claimed over a million Jewish lives in Southeastern Europe (Table 1.1), and thus well over half of the region's pre-war Jewish population. While the greatest number of Jewish victims were from Romania and Hungary, the greatest impact was in Macedonia and Thrace, with Greece, Yugoslavia and Croatia following in descending order.

In proportional terms, the Holocaust in the Balkans occupies the middle of the spectrum of Jews killed from Western to Eastern Europe. Italy, of course, is not part of the Balkans, although during the war it was closely linked to the region as an occupying power and from September 1943 its northern region

Table 1.1 Jews killed in the Balkans, Central-Southeastern Europe and Italy, 1941–44 (ranked according to impact)

Country	Estimated Jewish population 1939/41	Estimated numbers killed	Estimated as percentage of pre-war Jewish population
Macedonia	7,800	7,600	97.4
Thrace	5,100	4,850	95.0
Greece	77,380	63,500	82.0
Yugoslavia*	74,480	60,000	81.0
Croatia	37,000	30,000	81.0
Hungary**	795,000	502,000	63.1
Romania***	760,000	420,000	55.2
Italy	44,500	7,680	17.2
Bulgaria	50,000	6,000	12.0
Albania	200	5 (60)	2.5
Total	**1,851,460**	**1,101,635** [1,101,690]****	**59.5**

Notes: * Excludes Macedonia. **19.3.44. *** Includes Transylvania. ****It should be noted that the data varies according to source, and some data are approximate.

Sources: All figures are estimates compiled from the following sources: Yad Vashem, Holocaust Resource Center http://www.yadvashem.org/yv/en/holocaust/resource_center; Raul Hilberg, *Die Vernichtung der europäischen Juden* (Fischer Verlag: Frankfurt am Main, 1990 [1961]), p. 1280. Different data/calculations for individual countries can be found in Wolfgang Benz (ed.), *Dimension des Völkermords: Die Zahl der jüdischen Opfer des Nationalsozialismus* (dtv wissenschaft: Munich, 1996).

and its Aegean possessions as occupied territory. Meanwhile, the fate of Greek
Jewry under the Axis occupation varied considerably between the three zones.
Around 87 per cent (and higher according to some estimates) of Greek Jews
died during the Holocaust, but there was considerable variation across the
country depending on the policy of the zone of occupation. This ranged from
slack cooperation and outright resistance by the Italian military administration
to Nazi racial policy, to the opportunistic compliance of Bulgaria in occupied
Thrace and Macedonia, to the dogged meticulousness of the Germans in
Salonica and elsewhere in their occupation zone on the mainland.[28]

The trajectory of the war largely explains the relative lateness of the
Holocaust in the Aegean and in those parts of mainland Greece formerly
under Italian control. For it was only after Italy's withdrawal from the war
in September 1943 that any remaining obstacles to Jewish annihilation were
finally removed.[29] The timing of Italy's withdrawal, coupled to the wavering of
Hitler's allies in the Balkans, intensified the sense of urgency of mission for the
'uncompromising generation' of young men in the German Foreign Office and
at Eichmann's 'Jewish Desk'.[30]

*

In political terms, the Dodecanese islands were not part of Greece, although
the overwhelming majority of the 135,358 islanders (1936) were Greek
Orthodox.[31] Instead, the Dodecanese islands were part of Italy's colonial empire
in the Mediterranean after being seized from the Ottoman Turks during the
Balkan Wars in 1912, and then formally ceded to Italy in 1923 by the Treaty
of Lausanne, in spite of protestations from Greek Dodecanesian nationalists.
The tension between Italians and Greeks on the islands provides an important
context to the story, for this animus affected Jews. We explore this aspect in
later chapters. For the moment, it is perhaps useful to get a sense of the wider
geopolitical context that framed their lives before their destruction in 1944.

The larger islands of the Dodecanese had traditionally attracted the
attention of the great powers of the day. Their geographical location in
the Eastern Aegean, at the confluence of trade routes from continental Europe
to Asia Minor, spanning the Levant and Mediterranean basin bordering North
Africa and beyond, rendered them geopolitically important. It was for this

reason in ancient times that the Phoenicians had occupied them. Much later, the seafaring Venetians and the Genoese each in turn made Rhodes, Kos and Simi their strongholds for trade and buccaneering activities in the Eastern Mediterranean, challenging early Byzantium. The strategic importance of the islands of the Eastern Aegean remained a key consideration for all powers, great and small, well into the twentieth century. As one commentator put it in 1944: '[the] islands lie at the gateway to the East, constituting a key to a land route through Asia Minor and to the sea routes North through the Dardanelles and south through the Suez Canal.'[32]

The modern face of the archipelago was (and still is) a palimpsest of the various powers to claim sovereignty over it. The crusader Order of the Knights of St John of Jerusalem captured Rhodes in 1310 from the Byzantine emperor and built a series of major fortresses, overlapping the Hellenic and Byzantine structures, and sometimes destroying the latter. The Ottomans, who in 1522 seized the islands from the Knights, initially built magnificent mosques and bathhouses (*hamans*), but are alleged to have subsequently left much to benign neglect. They also conferred a degree of autonomy on the religious-ethnic communities through the *millet* system.[33] Italy, the new master from 1912, set about transforming the islands with an extensive programme of excavation of sites considered of archaeological importance, restoration of the knights' citadel and its medieval walls, and embarked on the construction of new buildings in neo-colonial and fascist styles over the next two decades. In addition, the Italians created a modern sewerage system, built arterial roads, and developed spa resorts as they developed the island's tourism, their construction programmes giving Rhodes, Kos and Leros their 'imperial' face.[34] Italy's occupation lasted until 1947, when Article 14 of the Treaty of Paris between Italy and the Allied Powers finally ceded the islands to Greece on 10 February.[35]

Throughout the modern period, the course of politics in the Dodecanese islands was contingent on many complex and converging factors that would come to a head during the war years. Acknowledging this restores a regional texture to the destruction of the Jews of the Aegean. The first thing we should consider was the utter powerlessness of the islands. The islands collectively were a subject entity and as such were pawns on a chessboard of 'big power' politics. There was a strong element of romantic Greek irredentism that sought union with the 'motherland' (*enosis*), mostly kept alive among the urban professional and elite families of the larger islands, such as Kalymnos, although many of their members lived in exile in Athens or in Alexandria in Egypt after 1912. This group remained vehemently opposed to Italian rule throughout the period and in every sense were the opposite of the Jews (and indeed, Muslims), who were said to have accommodated themselves to Rome.[36]

In very broad terms during the era of the Holocaust, there were three if not four powers asserting or claiming hegemony over the Dodecanese. The largest and probably the most influential of the powers was Great Britain. Throughout the period it played to a lesser or greater degree a key role as power broker but always with its own interests in view. Italy, described by historian Richard Bosworth as 'the least of the great powers', was after the Great War nonetheless the dominant regional power in the Eastern Aegean.[37] Until the mid-1920s, its foreign policy focused on expansion into Asia Minor as the Ottoman Empire crumbled, as well as securing its hold in Libya and later in the Horn of Africa. However, Britain and France limited Italy's geopolitical aspirations. For example, in 1919/20, London and Paris thwarted Rome's ambition to become a Mandate Power. Meanwhile, although the Ottoman Empire had collapsed alongside the Central Powers, an emergent modern Turkey under Kemal Ataturk in the decade after its triumph over the Greek expeditionary force in 1922, was able to assert itself. Its return to regional prominence mirrored Athens' decline. Greece remained for all intents and purposes a client state dependent on London.

By 1943, the picture had changed. Greece's commitment to the allied cause was in stark contrast to Ankara's ambivalence. Nevertheless, both London and Washington expected Turkey would eventually enter the war against Germany, which it did on 1 March 1945. However, London and Washington differed on what the reward should be, with the latter apparently contemplating the Dodecanese as the prize Ankara might expect, while the British inclined to recognizing the Greek case for *enosis*, albeit without offering a firm commitment.[38] Meanwhile, the German occupiers, having extinguished the Jewish presence, facilitated the removal of Turks from the island, ostensibly as a solution to famine on the islands, but in greater likelihood to garner the collaboration of Dodecanese nationalists in maintaining civil order.[39] The complex relationship between these countries forms the outer shell of our framework of the Holocaust in the Aegean. An inner second shell was formed by the tetchy relationship between Italians and Dodecanese nationalists.

Greek islanders had initially hailed Italy as a liberator when it seized the Dodecanese islands from Ottoman Turkey in 1912. Indeed, one of Rome's first announcements was that its presence would be temporary and that the islands would soon have their freedom from foreign powers. The Treaty of Ouchy (1st Lausanne Treaty) in 1912 formally ended the war between Italy and Turkey and foresaw the return of the islands to Ankara (at that time referred to as Angora), while Italy would receive Tripoli in return. As a consequence of the Treaty, the movement for *enosis* with 'Mother Greece' mobilized around well-organized and co-ordinated plebiscites throughout the Dodecanese between December 1912 and February 1913 protesting 'against the intentions of the Italian Government concerning the handing over to the Turkish yoke of the twelve islands' and demanding the transfer of the islands to Greece.[40] The first of these plebiscites took place on the island of Nisiro in December 1912 and the last one on Kalymnos the following February.

The outbreak of war in 1914 distracted 'Big Power' attention from the Eastern Aegean. Nevertheless, both Athens and irredentist nationalists in the Eastern Aegean were hopeful that Greek Prime Minister Eleutherios Venizelos' order for Greek mobilization on the side of the Entente would be handsomely repaid with the islands at the end of the war. But the fact that Greece had allied itself in 1917 to the Entente held little sway at the Paris Peace Conference. Woodrow Wilson's Fourteen Points and the principle of self-determination of peoples already before the end of the war had raised hopes in Athens. One of the principal leaders of the Dodecanese irredentist movement, Dr Skevos Zervos, an Anglophile who appears also to have been a confidant of Venizelos, made several appeals (couched in heady language) to the Great Powers, and travelled to the Paris Peace Conference in 1919 with Venizelos to make the case for *enosis*. His plea was in vain, despite widespread sympathy in some quarters in London, Paris and Washington for the Dodecanesian cause.[41] Because of a secret annex to the Treaty of London in April 1915 that brought Italy into the war on the side of the Entente in return for territorial gains including the Dodecanese, union with Greece was taken off the negotiating table for the foreseeable future.

The revelation of the secret agreement with Italy soured relations between irredentist Greeks in the Dodecanese and Italians for the next two decades. And Greek disdain for Italy was extended to those considered its collaborators in the islands. Matters were not helped by the unstable continental situation in the wake of the collapse of the Central European and Ottoman empires and the unsettled questions of borders that resulted from this. Meanwhile the volatile domestic situation in Italy that eventually led to Mussolini's rise to power injected a further unsettling factor into the mix. As Italian Fascism's star ascended with its pretensions to restoring imperial glory, that of Greek irredentism and a Greater Greece extending into Asia Minor waned in the wake of the debacle of the Asia Minor campaign. The Dodecanese Question thus remained in the balance for the next five years until the Treaty of Lausanne in 1923 appeared to settle the question of sovereignty over the Dodecanese archipelago in favour of Italy.

After the departure of Venizelos from the premiership in early 1924, the Dodecanesian movement lost a powerful ally. The governments in Athens that followed over the next four years were keen to seek rapprochement with Rome, and this meant sacrificing the interests of the twelve islands. Indeed, the Greek authorities actively sought to suppress Dodecanese irredentism through censorship and keeping close surveillance on its activists in Athens, now considered a thorn in the side of Italo-Greek relations. This position remained unchanged even after Venizelos' return to power in July 1928, when, within a year of the statesman's return, Mussolini declared in an interview that there was no longer a 'Dodecanese Question'. As Zervos observed in an appeal to the League of Nations in 1931, Greece remained 'small, weak, poor and out of favour' and the plight of the Greek Dodecanesians rendered 'invisible'.[42]

The response from the Italian authorities to the *enosis* plebiscites in the islands before the war had been swift: they banned further meetings and arrested and exiled the leaders drawn from the local intelligentsia, including priests, teachers, mayors, and councillors, if they had not already fled. The harsh response set the tone for the years to follow. After the Treaty of Lausanne, Senator Mario Lago was appointed civilian governor of the Dodecanese, now under Italian sovereignty. He remained in office until November 1936. With Lago's appointment, Mussolini's government began in earnest its programme of turning the islands, and Rhodes in particular, into the flagship of Italian colonialism.[43] This affected above all others the ethnic Greek majority whose representatives baulked at the policy of Italianization in schools that commenced in the mid-1920s. The Greek language, history and traditions were relegated secondary to Italian culture. Protests from some quarters within the Orthodox Church (without the approval of Apostolides, the Metropolitan of Rhodes), and from the liberal professions, were loud. As in 1912/13, the response of the Italian authorities was ruthless. Teachers were dismissed from their posts, trials were held, some nationalists were imprisoned, and many were exiled.[44]

Despite the tough repressive measures curbing irredentism, before the mid-1930s there was still a degree of Greek autonomy, successfully negotiated by the Metropolitan of the Orthodox Church and other conciliatory leaders of the Greek community. However, this changed radically with Lago's departure and the arrival of a staunch ally of Mussolini, Cesare Maria de Vecchi, who declared he had come to instil the 'fascist spirit' into the islands.[45] De Vecchi's arrival at the end of 1936 boded ill for the three ethnic-religious communities. Whereas Governor Lago had cultivated close and cordial relations with the Jewish community, if not necessarily with the Greeks, de Vecchi was a virulent antisemite determined to curb the Jews.[46] He appears to have shown little active interest in Muslims other than to encourage their repatriation to Turkey. Greeks were another matter. De Vecchi, who styled himself 'dictator' over the islands, intensified the process of Italianization to the detriment of Greek traditions. A British consular report of June 1940 noted that by the end of the 1930s, the Greeks on the islands were seething with discontent but unable to act because they were 'completely under the heel of the Italians'.[47]

After the commencement of hostilities between Italy and Greece at the end of October that year, de Vecchi was recalled to Italy out of fear that his oppressive and capricious rule would stir up a revolt among the Greek population, considered pro-British. His successors, briefly General Ettore Bastico and, until September 1943, Admiral Inigo Campioni, proved to be more diplomatic in their dealings with the Greeks. Nevertheless, British, and later German intelligence reports refer to the ongoing bitter relations between Greeks and Italians. Meanwhile, Campioni, an old-fashioned military man, displayed both courtesy and favour towards the Jews of Rhodes and Kos, who he considered Italian citizens.[48] It is likely that relations between Greeks and

Jews soured even further after the Jewish Community's pledge of support to the Italian cause in the early summer of 1940.

The advent of persecutory measures against Jews following the introduction of the Italian Racial Laws in November 1938 constrained Jewish life, and are dealt with in Chapter 3. As with the Germans, we shall see that the story is more complex than at first assumed. The Council of the Jewish Community, for instance, declared its allegiance to Rome when Italy entered the war, and this was in the wake of the passing of the Italian Racial Laws in 1938. Survivors have a memory of benign treatment from the Italians, and indeed, this was largely the case, despite fascist stipulations to the contrary. The precarious condition of the Jews of Rhodes and Kos during the intensification of war in the spring and early summer of 1944, especially during the severe allied aerial sorties against the island concludes the chapter. Here we shall see that the Italian administration did not distinguish between claimants for aid based on their religion or perceived race. Contemporaneous to the disbursement of social welfare were measures undertaken by the *Carabinieri* to register Jews as a separate group from the rest of the population. Later, this registration would play a central role in the deportation.

With Italy at war with Britain from June 1940, the expectation that there might be a decisive British intervention in the Eastern Mediterranean reinvigorated irredentist dreams of union with Greece. But any hope that a speedy end to the Italian occupation of the islands would see the restoration of the Dodecanese to Greece remained unfulfilled, especially once Germany entered the Balkan theatre of war in early 1941. Plans formulated in London to send an expeditionary force to seize the Dodecanese islands in 1940/41 did not translate into action. The reason for this was probably the difference in opinion between the War Office and other departments in Whitehall as to the best course of action to take.[49] Over the course of the following two years, doubts about Italy's commitment to the Axis cause rang alarm bells in Berlin. Should Rome lose control of the Dodecanese, that would expose Germany's position in North Africa and in Crete. In the early spring of 1943 a German force, initially a battalion and quickly upgraded to divisional strength, was sent to Rhodes to support the Italian Aegean force. Mussolini's demission in July 1943 and Italy's subsequent withdrawal from the war in September led to Germany seizing control of the archipelago.

Chapter 4 examines the German presence on Rhodes and the subsequent struggle between the erstwhile allies. The German seizure of the Dodecanese and of Rhodes and Kos in particular sealed the fate of the Jews. Nevertheless, for at least a year, the German military authorities fostered cordial relations with all inhabitants of the islands, including Jews. As we shall see, against a background of worsening conditions, German soldiers and Jews co-existed in relative harmony. Thus, Chapter 4 takes a closer look at the period between the German occupation of the island and the deportation in summer 1944, focusing on the garrison and concluding with a look at its relations to Jews.

Although the Eastern Aegean had not initially occupied a central place in German military strategy, this would change over the course of the war, and especially after Italy struck an armistice with the Allies. From late 1943 to the summer of 1944, the strategic importance of holding the Dodecanese, and of Rhodes and Leros as fortress islands, loomed large in military considerations in Berlin. However, by the late summer of 1944, the fortunes of war had moved against Germany, and a withdrawal from the Greek peninsula, including arrangements to abandon the Aegean, were in train.[50] By now, it became clear to some of Hitler's paladins, including the architect of the genocide of the Jews, Heinrich Himmler, that it was a matter of time before the Allies would bring the much vaunted 'Thousand Year Reich' to an inglorious end.[51] This realization altered the imperatives driving the war.

The 'war against the Jews' – in evidence already in mid-1941 – took on greater urgency. As territorial victory slipped Germany's grip, the racial war was propelled to the foreground, as we will see in Chapter 5. In this chapter, not only are the perpetrators and the practical measures for the deportation examined, but also the plight of the victims is narrated, mostly through their own voices as they were uprooted and sent to their deaths. The journey to Auschwitz remained indelibly printed in the memory of the survivors. They endured the horrors of the Nazi archipelago of camps, beginning with Auschwitz. The written documentation is sparse, but the testimonies of survivors offer an insight into their suffering and their struggle for survival during the ten months of incarceration. Less than half of those admitted to Auschwitz and then transferred to other camps survived. The cruelty towards and suffering of those admitted to the camp and later transferred to other camps is told in Chapter 6.

The hostility of Greeks towards Italians in general dovetailed with traditions of Christian *Judeophobia*. Younger Jews and Italians were integrated, sometimes through marriage, as we shall see in following chapters. But their close affinity cannot explain why, with a few exceptions, little was done by Greek (or Turkish) neighbours to save the Jews of Rhodes and Kos in the summer of 1944. There had been little overt antisemitism among Greeks outside the traditional religious-based anti-Jewish behaviour that usually reared up around Easter.[52] Nevertheless, Jews, especially Jewish merchants, were perceived by outsiders to be key beneficiaries of Italian rule at the expense of Greeks. According to the temporary British consul in 1936, 'the old Greek merchant class was being ruined owing to the official encouragement given by the Italians to Italian and Jewish merchants.'[53] Meanwhile, neighbourly bonds as well as common business interests cemented relations between Turks and Jews. After September 1943, the *Governatore*, while no longer a political factor in the Dodecanese, nonetheless remained the administrative authority working closely with the office of the German Military Administration and would oversee the dispersal of Jewish property. Members from all three communities – Greek, Turkish and Italian – and not just the German occupiers, would benefit from the disposal of Jewish property, which we examine in Chapter 7.

After liberation from the Nazi camps, some of the Jewish survivors returned to their homes on Rhodes. Before they returned, they gathered in Jewish safe houses in Rome, Bologna, Milan and Florence, waiting for news of family members before returning to the Aegean. We know little about this Italian interregnum. Yet, it was a formative period in the lives of the survivors, in some cases lasting up to five years, when the direction of their futures would be decided. While initially, some wished to return to Rhodes and Kos, and some did return, their plans soon changed. The majority, once they realized their community had been irrevocably destroyed, looked to relatives in the Congo, South Africa, and the United States or tried to enter Palestine to start new lives from under the shadow of the Holocaust. Both confusion and uncertainty among the wider Rhodesli diaspora in North America and in South Africa and the Belgian Congo characterized knowledge of what had happened to their kinfolk. We will examine this period between liberation from the camps and a return to life in Chapter 8. Much of what we know about Jewish life on Rhodes and Kos has come to us through the memories of the survivors.

Until recently, their story has mostly remained within the realm of diasporic family narratives. It is largely a story balanced between nostalgia for a lost world and the trauma of its destruction that has crystallized a particular memory of Jewish life before the deportation.[54] This dimension of remaking Jewish Rhodes is explored in the final chapter of this book.

2

Inside the *Juderia*

Rhodes was a small Jerusalem, a family, a community of innocent and pure people. [...] In the community, everyone knew each other, no one locked his door, and there were no Jews in prison. We lived together with the Greeks, Turks and Italians of the island. We had no contempt or distrust for one another.[1]

Following their expulsion from Spain in 1492, Spanish-speaking Jews (referred to by the Hebrew name 'Sephardim') settled in Rhodes in the early sixteenth century at the behest of the Ottoman Sultanate, allegedly because of their trading acumen.[2] Upon arriving on Rhodes, they were allocated quarters within the protective medieval walls of the Knights Citadel, to the south-east in an area of intersecting alleys leading off wider thoroughfares that became known in Ladino vernacular as the *Juderia* (Jewish quarter). Although there was not a formal demarcation between the Turkish and Jewish neighbourhoods of the old town, the *Juderia* was roughly bounded by the Via Turcheria, a long street to the north and by the southern gate of St Catherine leading to the harbour, an area described at the beginning of the twentieth century as the 'best quarter' of the old town (Map 2.1).[3]

How was life experienced by the descendants of these Jewish settlers in the *Juderia* prior to their deportation in 1944? In survivor recollections, in family histories, and in much of the diasporic depictions of life in Rhodes, an idyll emerges of communal innocence cruelly shattered by Nazi racial violence. This nostalgia for the 'lost world of Rhodes' dominates contemporary narratives of life before 1944. But it does not provide the whole story, for it is frequently contradicted by archive sources exposing the inner life of the *Juderia*. And yet, neither nostalgia for an idealized past, nor less-flattering contemporary

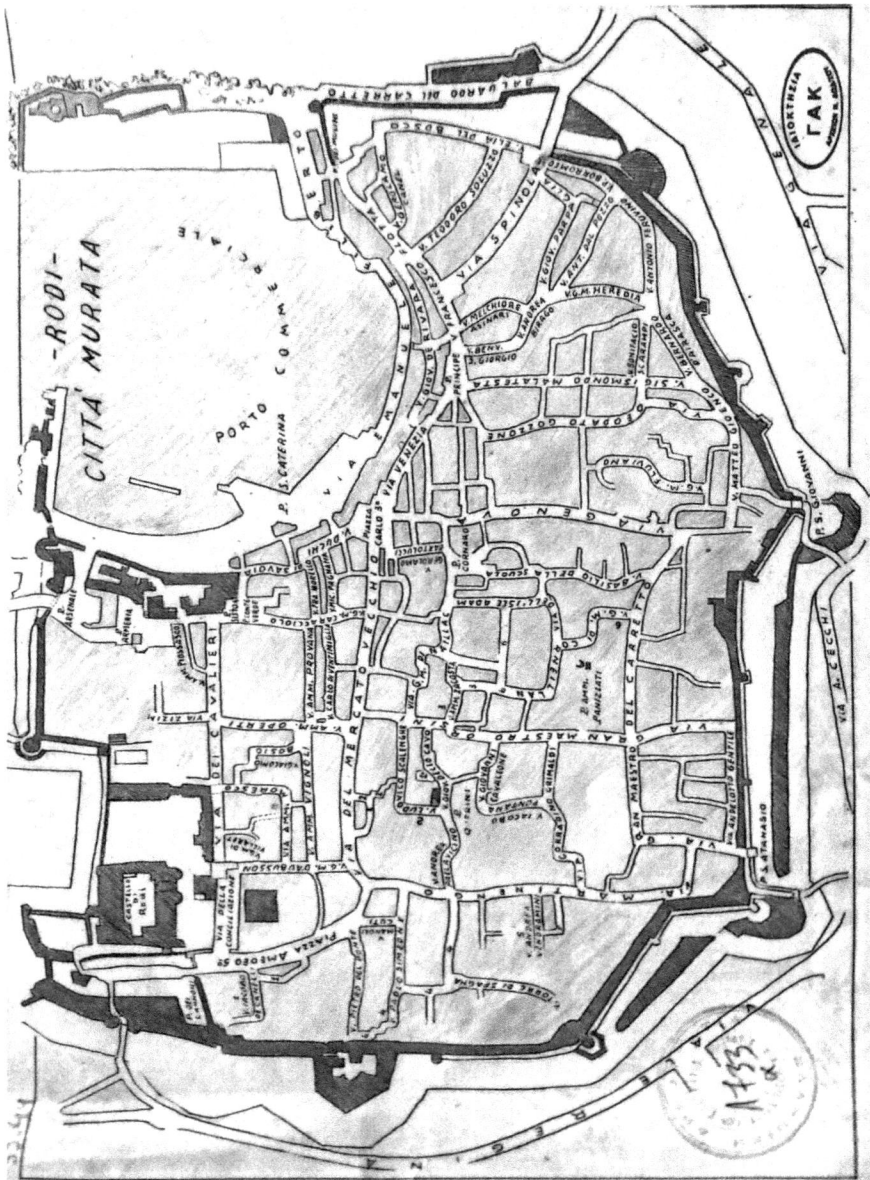

Map 2.1 Italian hand-drawn map of the Walled City, *c.* 1939 (undated)

Source: Courtesy Genika Archeia tou Kratous-Archeia Dodekanisou: Rodos, N. 39/44: Topography of the Old City (χάρτες #1733)

facts of the *Juderia*'s everyday life necessarily negate one another. Its everyday struggles, its tensions, as well as its mundane joys and sorrows, indeed, its ordinariness, provided the rich texture of the tapestry that constituted pre-deportation Jewish life. This chapter attempts to restore some of this texture. It explores the different social, cultural and political aspects of life inside the *Juderia*.[4]

*

There had been a Jewish presence on Rhodes before the arrival of Sephardim in the sixteenth century, composed of Greek-speaking Romaniote Jews who had settled, as their nomenclature suggests, during the biblical period under the Romans.[5] Over the centuries, there was a constant flow of Jewish travellers, traders and settlers to and from the islands of Rhodes and Kos. Jews from across the wider Ottoman Levant from the Middle East and North Africa also came. These Jews were eventually subsumed into the larger Sephardic community. In the modern period, Sephardic Jews came from Anatolia, notably from Smyrna, Bodrum and Antalya after the Greco-Turkish war, 1921/22.[6] As the anthropologist Renée Hirschon has shown, the Jews of Rhodes and Kos were part of a dense network based mostly on kinship ties and trade spread across the Ottoman and post-Ottoman Levant. Thus, the *Juderia*, while retaining the traditions of Ladino Sephardic culture, was also deeply embedded within a larger Levantine world that was infused with a strong Ottoman culture.[7]

Gauging the size of the Jewish community of Rhodes and Kos before the onset of Italian rule in 1912 is beset with problems; there is little in the way of reliable data.[8] It is likely that it stood at around 4,000 by the late nineteenth century. A census of 1917 put the overall population of Rhodes at 40,365, the majority of whom were Greek Orthodox Christians (31,715); aside from a small number of foreigners, Turks and Jews made up the rest, the former numbering just over 5,000, and the latter 3,295.[9] A census of 1921/22 put the Jewish population at just over 4,104, and this did not greatly alter over the decade, so that by the time of the 1931 census, Jews numbered 4,310 (comprising 2,198 males and 2,112 females) or 7.8 per cent of the island's total population of 54,818. The island of Kos had a much smaller Jewish community numbering a mere 169 (100 males and 69 females), or 0.8 per cent of that island's population (at the 1921/22 census, the community had numbered a mere 69 persons).[10]

The Jewish inhabitants of Kos were, in fact, related to the Jewish families of Rhodes. The most common family names on both islands were Hasson, Israel, Alhadeff, Capelluto and Menascé.[11] The increases in population on both islands were due to both births and inward migration, mostly from Anatolia after 1922. But by 1937, Jews in Rhodes were believed to have numbered 3,930 (roughly half the number of Muslims and Catholics, and a fraction of the Orthodox population).[12] Meanwhile, the surviving records of the Italian Race Census of 1938/39 and a further census of 1940 show there were between 525 and 544 Jewish families on Rhodes on the eve of their deportation.[13] By the time Italy opened hostilities against Greece, the Jewish population had suffered a significant decline, although exact figures are murky. It is widely known that many Jews left the island after the introduction of the Race Laws on 17 November 1938.[14] In that year, according to data provided in *Pinkus ha Kehillot*, there were 4,000 Jewish inhabitants of Rhodes and 166 in Kos. By 1944, the year of deportation, the figures of 1,900 and 94 respectively are cited.[15]

Whether poverty-induced or triggered by anti-Jewish measures, the reduction in numbers was not exclusive to Jews. The wider population of Rhodes had been declining since the later nineteenth century and was only halted in the mid-1920s when the Italian policy of settler-colonization began in earnest. While over half of the 13,000 Italian migrants who came to the Dodecanese islands in this period serviced the naval base on the island of Leros, possibly as many as 5,000 settlers – mostly from Sicily – came to Rhodes as farmers or as part of the administrative and military infrastructures, adding to the existing community of Levantine Italians (numbering about 1,200 in 1945). By 1942 British intelligence sources estimated that Italians in the Dodecanese numbered just over 60,000, of whom the majority were part of the expanded military presence.[16] In spite of this influx, the town of Rhodes suffered a population decline that lasted into the war years. In 1912, its population was said to be around 38,000; within two decades it had sunk to 17,466; after which it increased slightly, so that by 1942 it hovered around 25,000.[17] Thus, the Jews of Rhodes made up around 10 per cent of the town's population.

Until the abolition in 1938 of the religious courts that dated to the Ottoman *millet* system of religious-based communal self-administration, the Jews of Rhodes and Kos enjoyed a degree of autonomy over their internal affairs.[18] And even though by the 1930s the younger generation was integrated into wider Italian culture, the community, bounded by its spatial limits, still retained distinctive cultural and religious features. This, however, was not a Jewish peculiarity. As observers noted, 'every island, and in the larger islands – Rodi, Coo (i.e. Kos) and Scarpanto – every distinct natural and economic area, forms a distinct community.'[19] Indeed, the forty-five larger villages of Rhodes were distinguished by their religious-ethnic characteristics: rural villages with a few exceptions were Orthodox Greek. Whereas the southern half of the old town of Rhodes was dominated by Turks and Jews, the new suburb of *Neocorio* beyond the citadel walls to its north-west was inhabited mostly by Italians and well-off Greeks and a handful of wealthier Jews. New settlements were established in certain coastline areas, but these were for Italian settlers and military, such as Campochiaro (present-day Eleousa), St Benedetto (present-day Kolimbia) 25 kilometres south of Rhodes town, St Marco near Kattavia in the south of the island, and finally Villanova, close to the air base of Maritsa in the north-west (present-day Paradiso).[20] On Kos, the Jewish quarter was much smaller and located in the centre of the old town, congregating close to the Kahal Shalom synagogue, built in 1747. Before the influx of Jews from western Anatolia after the so-called 'Catastrophe' (debacle) of the Greek Asia Minor Campaign, the community on Kos had been reduced to barely ten families. It now expanded threefold but remained small up to the deportation.[21] The Hellenophile and former naval commander John Myres described the few 'Jewish families (and Turks) of Kos as bearing physical similarities of the townspeople of Bodrum (Greek Halicarnassus) as "easy-going cultivators, tradesmen, and merchants".[22]

Most accounts of the *Juderia* give only an impressionistic picture of life within the walled city and tend to concentrate on its folkloric aspects.[23] Frequently missing in these accounts is any firm information on the composition of the Jewish community, or of its interaction with either its immediate Turkish neighbours, or with the Greek majority, or with the Italian colonists. There are nevertheless ample sources that open a window onto life in the *Juderia*, not least the recently discovered archive of the *Carabinieri*, and of course, the testimonies of survivors.[24] Travellers to Rhodes also provide snippets of information, usually colourful descriptions of the Jewish and Turkish quarters, with their neighbourhoods dissolving almost imperceptibly into each other.

Thus Reverend Henry Fanshawe Tozer, an Oxford don who visited the Aegean three times in the last quarter of the nineteenth century, described the handsome, solid and elaborately decorated buildings of the broad thoroughfare and 'heart' of the Jewish quarter (popularly known as Calle Ancha among the Ladino-speaking Jews; in the later 1930s it was renamed by the Italians as Via Francesco Flotta), which 'is especially picturesque on a Jewish festival day, as in one of our rambles we saw it, when its occupants are dressed in their rich holiday costumes'.[25] Charles Booth, who visited Rhodes in the 1920s, alluded to a darker tradition when he referred to the burning of the Romaniot synagogue by the Knights in 1502, and the practice at Easter among Orthodox Greeks of burning an effigy of a Jew.[26] Antisemitism, where it existed among Greeks, tended to be rooted in traditional Christian folklore of the Crucifixion. Many survivors of the deportation from Rhodes and Kos recalled cordial relations with Greeks, but they also remembered the Orthodox Easter as a time to avoid passing through Greek neighbourhoods for fear of insults or stones being hurled at them. Latent antipathy was embedded in a perception among Greeks in some quarters that Jews were both 'fellow travellers' and economic beneficiaries of the Ottomans, and later of the Italians to the detriment of local Greek merchants.[27] And as we will see below, Jewish youth identified closely with Italy and Italian culture. Nevertheless, in spite of references by Jewish survivors to tensions around the Orthodox Easter, by and large Greek attitudes towards Jews were good.[28]

Nazi propaganda minister Joseph Goebbels visited the island on a Hapag Lloyd tour to mainland Greece and the Dodecanese in the early spring of 1939, when he was drumming up support for Hitler's increasingly belligerent stance vis-à-vis Britain.[29] Arriving in Rhodes on 2 April, a Sunday, Goebbels received a warm welcome from the Italian governor before settling in at the magnificent Albergo delle Rose, which he described in his diary as 'wonderful' because of its location 'direct on the sea'. Goebbels waxed lyrical about 'the unending surface of the water shimmering deep blue. It is so quiet and peaceful here', he wrote in his diary. 'The noisy world lies so far away. Evening walk through Rhodes. Took a look at the new district. The Italians have made something marvellous. They have a strong talent for colonisation.'[30] As one might expect, Hitler's propaganda minister had little positive to say about the *Juderia*, which he visited.

> Tour in a small horse-drawn coach through the town. Very interesting. A modern district, mainly built by fascism. A Jewish quarter, poor and stinking of rubbish and dirt. Ugh, hellish! A Turkish quarter, not much better. So these are the people who live here. There are indeed master races who must use them. If this does not happen, then all the filth would rise to the top.[31]

Despite Goebbels' predictable vitriol, travellers before and during the war revelled in the 'exotic other' of the old town, whose 'streets are narrow and winding, but are kept very clean'.[32] The celebrated German writer and First World War hero, Ernst Jünger, had visited the island the year before Goebbels and, like Fanshawe Tozer half a century before, and contrary to his own alleged antisemitic leanings, was beguiled by the Jewish quarter and its inhabitants, whose 'faces are very well chiselled'.[33]

Typically, the houses of the old quarter were one- and two-storey stone buildings, many of them constructed during the later Ottoman period after the earthquake of October 1856 destroyed 8,000 houses.[34] On Kos also, there had been an extensive rebuilding programme after the earthquake of April 1933 destroyed the old town killing five Jews. The eighteenth-century Kahal Shalom synagogue too, was destroyed.[35] On both islands the smaller, usually single-storey houses frequently, but not always, comprised a single large room with raised niches or platforms which were usually partitioned (*moní* in Greek and referred to as *sofas* in the vernacular) for sleeping. Sometimes these houses had an additional smaller inner room. Where there was an upper floor, this was reached by narrow, steep wooden stairs (or a ladder). Families might enjoy the flat roof as a terrace, using it to sleep in the hot summer, as Sylvia Berro, a survivor of the deportation and camps, recalled.[36]

The exterior of the houses was plastered and was often painted especially in the spring around Pesach. Small white and black pebbles forming an elaborate mosaic (*chochlakia*) decorated the interior floors of the houses, as in the courtyard. Heavy wooden or metal doors led from the street or alley to a courtyard where a few houses in the old quarter had a well, but this was not for providing drinking water. Eliezer Surmani, who also survived the deportation and camps, remembered how it was his task, like that of many children, to fetch water from the public fountain in the main square of the *Juderia*, probably in an earthenware jug.[37] Nor did many of the houses have ovens. Instead, as with the four or five water fountains of the *Juderia*, there were public ovens where the women could bake bread and prepare other foods. Some bakers, such as Rahamim Israel and his son Elia, rented out their ovens to the families of the *Juderia*.[38] Rebecca Amato Levy's family rented their home and were lucky in that their landlady had an oven she let her tenants and neighbours use.[39]

After the Lausanne Treaty formally ceded the Dodecanese islands to Italy on 24 July 1923, and with Mario Lago's appointment as civilian governor of the islands, Rhodes and the other larger Dodecanese islands underwent a veritable renaissance as the classical past was literally unearthed through archaeological digs. The Italians embarked on a restoration programme of ancient monuments and of the medieval Knights' Citadel.[40] Many visitors to the island were drawn by the classical heritage. This had already been true of travellers during the nineteenth century when philhellenism was at its height, and this continued well into the middle of the twentieth century. An imagined classical glory is evident in the writings of Ernst Jünger and his brother Friedrich who came to Rhodes in the 1930s; it permeates the works of Erhart Kästner, an NCO in the *Luftwaffe* who arrived on the Dodecanese islands in 1944 to research the 'natural history' of the islands as part of a propaganda assignment, and who remained on Rhodes until Germany's capitulation in May 1945. We see it also in the observations of the writer Lawrence Durrell (a Classicist) who arrived in May 1945 as part of the British military administration of the Dodecanese, and his contemporary, the French writer Raymond Matton. Both Durrell and Matton were effusive about the island's classical heritage and its medieval architecture. Like Kästner, however, neither appears to have spared a thought for the once thriving community of Sephardic Jews who had inhabited this space or asked what might have happened to them.[41]

Tourism was encouraged by the Italian authorities, who also promoted the 'orientalism' of the old town, and as a result commerce in the *Juderia* flourished.[42] By the end of the 1930s, Rhodes had a capacity of around 400 beds in the six large hotels, the most extravagant of them being the Albergo delle Rose with 200 beds. Another large hotel built by the Italians was Hotel Therme, which opened its doors in 1938. In addition to these large establishments there were at least five hotels with between twenty-five and sixty beds and numerous smaller hotels of twenty beds or less.[43] According to official statistics, in the region of 50,000 tourists visited Rhodes in 1934.[44] There was opportunity for Jews in such tourism, not only as 'figures in an oriental landscape', but also as traders selling items specific to the folk traditions of the island, and as tourist guides.[45]

Over the period, the number of cruise ships traversing the Aegean and halting at Rhodes had increased to such an extent that the island authorities had difficulty meeting the demand for authorized tourist guides. The Italian administration was conscious that the reputation of the island as a tourist destination also depended on the quality of its guides and the impression they made on visitors. There had been complaints, for instance from the manager of the grand hotel Albergo delle Rose, of tourist touts behaving in such a way as to make tourists feel uncomfortable. And this led to a demand for better trained and licensed guides. Indeed, tourism was heavily regulated by various ordinances that required guides to be adequately trained and licensed. The ordinances also fixed the prices that could be charged at visitor sites. Until 1939, when their licences were withdrawn, the best guides for the old city were its Jews.[46]

For the residents of the old quarter of Rhodes, life was intimate, not only because of the confined space, but also because of kinship. Miru Alcana, when asked many years later about life in Rhodes and specifically in the *Juderia*, recalled,

> The life in Rhodes was beautiful, beautiful. [...] Everyone very friendly like one family. No matter how many neighbors we have, everyone is just like family [...] In fact, we used to say Auntie Rosa, Auntie Straya, Auntie Rebecca, but we didn't know if they were relative[s] or not. Because our parents they say, say hello to Auntie Rebecca or say hello to Auntie Rifka. To everyone we have to say Auntie. So for us all neighbors was family.[47]

Calling an adult 'auntie' or 'uncle' did not necessarily denote kin, for it was also a mark of respect. Nonetheless, its usage among neighbours is suggestive of the close and extended family ties that underpinned the social cohesion of the *Juderia*.

Many of the streets within the walled city were little more than alleys barely allowing two or three adults to pass, some were slightly broader and longer than others; the smaller alleys frequently intersected the larger thoroughfares. Such propinquity of life in all its aspects could be bewildering to outsiders like the patrician Vittorio Alhadeff, who looked upon the *Juderia* as exotic and his co-religionists as quaint by virtue of their folk customs.[48] Accounts of everyday life in the *Juderia* paint a picture of an idyllic and close-knit community, with survivors of the Holocaust in later life recalling a happy childhood, one where families were caring and loving. For Rachel Hanan growing up on the island was 'like a paradise', while her older sister Diamante described life as one 'endless holiday'.[49] Clara Soriano was emphatic in an interview in 1996, when she declared, 'I was in a world of sunshine.'[50] Isaac Jack Lévy recalled in his memoir, 'All along our daily paths, whether going to school, to work, to the synagogue, or visiting a friend or relative, we walked amid familiar and smiling faces.'[51] Although he did not live in the *Juderia*, Sami Modiano nonetheless could recall the 'open door welcome' of the homes of its Jewish residents.[52]

Because Jewish households in Rhodes and Kos frequently comprised three generations, childhood is remembered by survivors as an idyll with loving grandparents. Indeed, it was often the grandparents, and grandmothers in particular, who played an important role in the children's lives. In the family of Sara Jerusalmi, her mother Miriam relied on grandmother Palomba to make the children's clothes and help with the household chores.[53] Laura Varon, whose family we will encounter at various points in this study, remembered,

> My grandmother for us was a second mother and after school we always (go) to see Grandma because she always had cookies for us and she had a window going through the park and we went to play with the children in the park and we alway came back through the window, so Grandma didn't worry about, to go to home.[54]

Grandparents could be humorous too in how they managed their grandchildren. The Surmani family lived at Via delle Ferittoie 24–26, close to the main square of the *Juderia*.[55] The head of the family, Giacobbe (who was 44 years old when deported), worked as a sales employee at the Alhadeff department store. His wife, Giovanna (née Hasson) died in childbirth in 1938.[56] The six children were cared for by their paternal grandmother Tamar who lived with them.[57] Tamar shared this task with her deceased daughter-in-law's mother, Rosa, who lived at the same property but to the front of it (Giacobbe's family lived at the rear). Rosa's husband had a store selling salt, pickles and tobacco, also at the front of the building. According to Eliezer Surmani, the two grandmothers were always bickering with each other, but showered the children with little gifts of sweets. When Eliezer's maternal grandmother Rosa looked after him and he became restless, she would send him on an 'errand' to her husband with a message in French that he could not understand. Eliezer would enter his grandfather's shop and repeat the message to Grandfather Hasson who would tell him to sit a moment on a trunk. Minutes would pass and his grandfather would continue to be 'absent mindedly' busy while little Eliezer sat still waiting for the errand to be completed. Eventually, bored, the boy would ask Grandfather Hasson if he had forgotten about the errand, at which point Eliezer would be sent back to his grandmother empty-handed. Years later, he realized this was a playful trick employed by his grandparents to keep him distracted from getting up to mischief.

As the Surmani children grew older, Eliezer's father endeavoured to inculcate good moral behaviour in his children, for family reputation was everything in the *Juderia*.[58] Eliezer's immediate family, like many families of the *Juderia*, did not have much money and it is likely they were partly supported by grandfather Hasson. Although they lived a materially modest life, they were respectable and proudly defended their family honour. When Eliezer's father found out that his son was consorting with a slightly older boy who allegedly had stolen money from his father's business, Eliezer was told, 'If you choose a friend make sure he is better than you.'[59]

Flora Fils' parents (the Hassons) and her Aunt Vida also would send her on bogus errands whenever Flora began to make a nuisance of herself with the message 'keep me here' in either Greek or Turkish, which she could not understand.[60] Her father too worked in the Alhadeff department store as manager of the chinaware section and presided over a large family of six girls and two boys at Via Grande Maestro Deodato Gozone Nr 3038 in the heart of the *Juderia*.[61] For Flora, as with her sister Stella, the only two survivors of the family, recalling their childhood and family intimacy provides a stark contrast to the brutal rupture that was to come in 1944.

Jewish festivals are remembered by survivors as especially vibrant occasions.[62] We noted above how Fanshawe Tozer on his visit to Rhodes had been beguiled by the 'rich holiday costumes' of the Jews. Above all else for survivors who were children at the time of the deportation, the two-day festival of Purim, celebrating Jewish deliverance under the ancient Achaemenid Empire, as recorded in the Book of Esther, is fondly remembered.[63] For the children of the *Juderia* Purim – third in the calendar of High Holy Days – was a time of carnival with the wearing of costumes, masks, and play-acting, with the role of Queen Esther being the most coveted among the girls. The highlight of the festival (apart from the re-enactment of Queen Esther) appears to have been rides in colourfully bedecked horse-drawn carriages in the 'Calle Ancha', which would be filled with throngs of people and loud with music-making. Purim was, as Jack Hasson recalled, a 'lovely, lovely time'.[64] Laura Varon remembered 'we used to sing and dance practically all day … until 10 or 11 o'clock at night'.[65]

For the festival of Pesach or Passover that soon followed Purim, families were kept busy with children helping to prepare for the eight-day festivity by baking and repainting and cleaning homes. Rebecca Amato Levy remembered how 'For the Sephardim of Rhodes, Pesah [*sic*] was a holiday filled with happiness, a gathering of family and friends and a time when no one in the Jewish Quarter or Juderia was left alone or hungry'. And she continued,

> The preparation began six to eight weeks prior to the Passover holiday. The first phase consisted of a thorough cleaning of the house. The interior of the house was washed with hot water and soap. For the deep scrubbing, they used what was called 'barro y arena'. Barro was sort of a clay and arena was sand from the sea. They were mixed to form an abrasive. Whatever woodwork was in the house was polished with a mixture of kerosene and oil and this made the woodwork really shine.

> The tapeties [*sic*] (oriental rugs) were picked up off the floor, taken to the seashore, immersed in the salt water and then scrubbed with stiff brushes and spread out on the rocks to dry. [...]

> Once a room was cleaned, it was used as little as possible. All the bedding had to be taken out, shaken and aired thoroughly, any of the bedding that needed fixing or replacing was done at this time. It was a time for 'kapleyando kolchas' which meant covering the quilts.

The interior walls in the homes of the *Juderia* had a whitewash finish. Every Pesah [*sic*], the families would whitewash these walls as well as the exterior of the house. The floors consisted of small smooth pebbles called 'sheshicos' and these were scrubbed with a brush, then scrubbed again with short brooms until they were absolutely clean and shiny. After the kitchen cupboards were cleaned, they were sealed by tying the knobs together with a white rag. None of the cupboards were opened until two days before Passover. The sidewalk right outside the entrance was scrubbed and the 'kortijo' (courtyard) was used for all the meals before Pesah. Everyone in the family helped clean for the holiday and many families helped each other.[66]

As far as survivor Stella Levi was concerned, Seder, the Holy Day following Purim, was the best holiday on Rhodes for her religious traditional family. It was then that the preparations for Passover began and 'there was a joy in the whole Jewish district'.[67] For the children of the *Juderia* one of the best moments of the feast of Sukkot (which was otherwise a more religious feast) was decorating the Sukkot booth with myrtle in the form of a Star of David. During the High Holy Day of Rosh Hashana, celebrating the Jewish New Year, Laura Varon 'could smell the holiday [spirit] in the air'.[68] For children, like Flora Fils, there was an added benefit to the high holidays for they were measured for new clothes by a dressmaker who would come to the home and new shoes were ordered from one of the *Juderia*'s many shoemakers, such as Rebecca Amato Levy's first husband, Moshe Hasson, whose shop was in the Via Turcheria.[69]

Kinship networks in the *Juderia* were large. Rachel Hanan's extended family could only meet on certain festival days 'otherwise there would be a hundred cousins'.[70] Because endogamy within the Jewish community was usual, the boundary between kinship and social networks was porous and underpinned what social historians refer to as a 'moral economy' of mutualism.[71] Alberto Israel, whose family were by tradition bakers to the community, recalled:

> We made bread. We made matzah for Passover. It was baked by the Israel family. On Fridays there was bread for the poor. This bread wasn't for sale. We made it especially for the poor. We did the same thing when we made matzah. We had two prices for the matzah. Those who could afford it paid a little more, so the poor would be able to get theirs without paying. This way everybody had matzah for Pesach. Everyone who had anything gave generously. Everybody helped each other.[72]

Despite kinship, Jewish Rhodes, even within the boundaries of the *Juderia*, was a society divided by disparities in wealth, social status, religious practice and politics, as Rebecca Amato Levy noted in her memoir.[73] According to Renée Hirschon, the community comprised a broad stratum of the 'middling classes' of mostly independent traders and artisans. Tailors, shoemakers, tinsmiths, grocers and other small-scale family-run crafts and trades make frequent appearances in the household census of 1941.[74] The strong presence of artisanal and small-scale tradesmen was typical of the Sephardic communities of the eastern Mediterranean, as Judith Humphrey also found in her study of the Jewish community of Chania in Crete.[75] But this stratum was by no means homogenous for even within it there were differences in social conditions. Nevertheless, for the majority, material life was modest.[76]

In many diaspora accounts of Jewish Rhodes, the wider island community is frequently absent from the picture with Jews appearing to live a hermetic existence outside island society in general. While it is the case that the community was close-knit, it was not inward-looking. Indeed, it was deeply integrated into the wider commercial life of Rhodes and Kos, either as merchant wholesale suppliers, or shopkeepers, or street vendors, or peripatetic hawkers, or artisan craftsmen, or as bankers. Looking back on her youthful years in the *Juderia*, Rachel Hanan recalled – with some exaggeration – how on *Shabbat* the island's commercial life, dependent as it was on the Jewish businesses of the old town, came to a standstill.[77] Moreover, commercial interests were not ethnically bounded, with Jews and Turks frequently in business together.

Co-existent with these small-scale family businesses were larger enterprises. Rhodes' economy was dominated by the typical activities of the larger islands of the eastern Mediterranean, influenced by location and climate. Until the Italian occupation, fishing and sponge-fishing had been staples of the island economy before the First World War, and so too were the production of olive oil, mostly for domestic consumption, or making soap. Some local products, such as onions, figs, sesame and wine were important export commodities already before the First World War.[78] Before the Second World War, the Italian tobacco concern, TEMI, manufactured cigarettes that were also exported, mostly to Italy.[79] The Italians also established a raw silk factory in the south of the island near Kattavia during the 1920s.[80] Aside from the commercial empire of the Alhadeff family that also included a large beer bottling factory, many of these larger enterprises were Italian and Greek owned. However, there was a thriving industry in ceramics and handwoven rugs organized on a large scale, which involved several Jewish merchants, such as Mosè Modiano, Nissim Benatar and Bension Menascé.[81]

The social differences within the Jewish community were, perhaps, also reflected in the size and value of properties in the *Juderia*. Nathan Hasson, for example owned three single-storey houses, each with one to three rooms and each valued between I£5,600 (lire) and I£11,000 (together with other property, his portfolio had an overall value of I£76,000). The house of Giuseppe Leon in the Via Elia de Bosco was valued at I£7,411, while that of Rahamim Alhadeff in Via Sigismondo Malatesta, built over two floors with six rooms, was valued at I£8,333; that of Mosé Sadi(s) in Via Venezia was valued at I£9,722.

Alongside these modest buildings were the more substantial homes and commercial properties of the *Juderia*'s wealthier merchant class such as Haim Tarica who, before his suicide in 1944, had owned two shops in the commercial quarter valued respectively at I£21,500 and I£55,000. Tarica also owned two further properties in the *Juderia*, one of which was a dwelling of five rooms over two floors, and the other a more substantial house of seven rooms over two floors. However, these buildings had relatively low values of I£7,800 and I£18,400. Similarly, Moise Alhadeff owned a large shop and warehouse in the old city, but also possessed at least a further five properties in the *Juderia*. The total value of his property portfolio came to well over I£100,000. Another warehouse, namely that owned by Bension Menascé at the confluence of Via Venezia and Piazza Principe, had five storage rooms and was valued at nearly I£74,000.[82] The large single-space warehouse of Celebi Turiel in the commercial quarter at the Piazza Carlos III (also known as Piazza del Fuocco) was valued at I£56,666. Turiel also had a shop at the same address and another storehouse in the market of Via Venezia. His house in the *Juderia* was in Via Benvenuto di San Giorgio (present-day Dosiadou and close to the Kahal Shalom synagogue); together these more modest properties were valued at around I£40,000.[83]

One of the most valuable commercial properties in the *Juderia* was the warehouse of Uriel Hasson in Via Andrea Birago (present-day Odos Simmiou), a street leading to the Piazza Principe, and where the Kahal Shalom synagogue is located. Hasson's property was a two-room building over two floors and was valued at I£106,200.[84] The Via Andrea Birago also had several substantial domestic buildings, such as Mosé Galante's house at Nr 12 valued at I£33,400; this had eleven rooms over three floors, and as such was one of the more prominent private properties of the *Juderia*. Galante's house was like that of Michele Menascé in the same street and valued at I£46,650. It stood next door to the Kahal Shalom synagogue.

Several wealthy families in Rhodes, however, built or bought large town villas in the modern neighbourhoods of Neocorio, to the north-west of the medieval city. In this new neighbourhood larger and more expensive properties could be found. For example, a wealthy member of the Menascé clan resided in a house that had ten rooms over two floors with a value estimated at I£63,430. Similarly, Sami Modiano's family lived in Via Santo Stefano, in a villa comprising thirteen rooms over three floors and valued at I£50,390. In 1924, the wealthy merchant Isaac Franco built a substantial house in what eventually became the Via Emmanuel III.[85] Not all houses in this street were of high-end value, but many of them were of considerable substance.[86] Possibly the most expensive house in the Neocorio was that owned by Signaru Capuia in Via Maria Pia di Savoia, which she shared with her mother-in-law. This had a valuation of I£138,000.

At the apex of the Jewish communities in Rhodes and on Kos was a comparatively wealthy cosmopolitan elite with financial and mercantile links (often underpinned by family ties) to the Levant. The Menascé and Alhadeff families, who were bankers to the community, were probably the wealthiest, and frequently donated to charitable causes. Of the nine banks in Rhodes, four were Jewish-owned: Salomon Alhadeff & Fils, Isaac Alhadeff, Notrica Menascé and Bension Menascé.[87] Within this elite stratum, numbering approximately two dozen families, the Menascé, Notrica, Franco, Soriano and Alhadeff families were pre-eminent.[88] They mostly lived in the 'smarter suburbs' outside the walled town, notably in the *Neocori* neighbourhood that extended to the Mandraki, as recalled by Alice Tarica (who lived in this privileged quarter of Rhodes) and Rachel Hanan (who did not).[89] On Kos, the family branch of the Menascés lived in an expansive villa purchased in 1916 by the paterfamilias Haim Celebi Menascé, located at a distance from the narrow streets close to the eighteenth-century synagogue where the majority of Jewish families lived before the earthquake of 1933.[90]

As well as close ties, there was long-standing rivalry between these elite families that surfaced from time to time. Sometimes, the fault-lines of conflict could appear within families too. When Isaac Alhadeff fell out with his cousins Jack and Ascer over the question of whether Isaac's son, also called Jack, might join the board of the Salomon Alhadeff & Fils bank, Isaac promptly left to establish his own rival bank. Isaac had extensive commercial and property interests in Turkey, Greece, Italy, the Belgian Congo, South Africa, and in the Egyptian port of Alexandria where the family also had a home. In 1938, after the introduction of the Italian Racial Laws the family transferred its Milan and later its Greek factories to Buenos Aires in Argentina. As with many well-connected Jews from Rhodes and Kos, Jack Alhadeff was able to recover most of his family's Rhodes-based assets after the war.[91]

The Alhadeff's position as 'banker to the community' brought them into potential and actual conflict with members of the community who had taken out credit with the bank. The Modiano family, for example, had moved to Rhodes from Salonica in 1912. The paterfamilias was Samuele Modiano, born in 1858 who established his stationery (*cancelleria*) business in the Piazza Principe, which was the main square of the *Juderia*.[92] Modiano had two children, Grazia (b. 1884) and Giacobbe (b. 1899). Grazia married a cousin Mosè Modiano in 1911, and they too arrived in Rhodes in 1912. Giacobbe, 13 years old at the time of moving to Rhodes, would in 1925 marry Diana Franco from a well-established family on the island; the couple would have two children, Lucia and Samuele (Sami). While the elder Samuele's material condition deteriorated to the point that in 1934 he was described in official documents as 'poor' (*miseri*), and he had to rely on his brother Isaaco to send him money each month, his son Giacobbe and son-in-law Mosè appeared to prosper, at least until the early 1930s, when the world economic depression overtook the islands and affected their fortunes.

Mosè (born in 1874) was a merchant of oriental rugs, whose business interests extended to military uniforms and haberdashery.[93] He was also a licensed broker and public notary (*mediatore sensale e scrivano pubblico*), and in this capacity he collected rents for the Dodecanese authorities. He was confident enough to have borrowed heavily between 1924 and 1932 in order to expand his business and to acquire a substantial plot of land beyond the walls of the old city, presumably to build a house. But by the beginning of the 1930s his fortunes altered radically, and he found himself in debt to the *Governatore* to the tune of I£514,449, allegedly the sum of collected rents that he had not transferred to the authorities. In addition he owed I£158,800 to seven local businessmen, including four prominent members of the Jewish community: the jeweller Isaaco Benveniste, Salomon Capelluto, Isaaco Menascé and Nissim Tarica.[94]

The *Governatore* closed Modiano's file in 1932, when he appears to have cleared his debt to the authorities by liquidating some of his property and by borrowing from the Alhadeff Bank.[95] Consequently, by the early 1930s he still had an outstanding debt on a loan of I£230,000 with unpaid interest (at 5 per cent) to the Alhadeff Bank, as well as the money he owed to his original creditors. Modiano had to rely on friends to support his family. His creditors together with the Alhadeff Bank now sought repayment through the courts. Finally, in 1936 the court in Rhodes ruled against Modiano and ordered the sale of seized assets (comprising a two-storey building valued at I£60,000 and a warehouse valued at I£241,675 as well as a smaller storage space valued at I£575, together totalling I£302,000).[96] The entire process must have amounted to a public humiliation, not least because his financial predicament appeared in the local gazette.[97] Possibly, this affair might explain why Mosè Modiano did not (or was unable to) join the exclusive 'club' of B'nai B'rith, dominated as it was by those same businessmen to whom he owed money. But like many of the island's Jewish businessmen, Modiano was also tenacious. By the end of the decade he had reapplied for (and was granted) the restoration of his trading licences enabling him to re-open his uniforms and haberdashery business in Via Grand Maestro Naillach. He was also granted a licence as an insurance broker for the National Insurance Company of the Italian Possessions of the Aegean.[98]

While the elite stratum of Rhodes Jews enjoyed a social calendar punctuated by theatre, dances and concerts, most of the Jewish community lived a life of long hours of toil.[99] As we saw above, many of the men were tradesmen with their own craft workshops, frequently in silver- and leather-working, such as the boot-maker Giuseppe Capelluto; or they were medium-sized merchants trading a variety of goods, for instance in grain, textiles or livestock, such as Celebi Alcana, who imported poultry from Turkey (see Illustration 9.1) and Baruch Avzaradel, a butcher who imported cattle, also from Turkey.[100] In an age before mass fabrication of clothing had spread in any meaningful way to the islands, families either made their own clothes or hired one of the many dressmakers or tailors in the *Juderia*. Clothes were often hand-sewn, nonetheless the spread of the Singer sewing machine transformed the tailoring sector, offering opportunities to those with an entrepreneurial spirit. Isaac Hugno, according to his daughters Diamante and Rachel, was a 'renowned' tailor on the island. Until the war, when his fortunes reversed as 'demand for suits fell', he had earned enough for the family to live in a substantial two-storey house with eight rooms at Via Grand Maestro Heredia Nr 16 in the heart of the Jewish quarter.[101] In the community, a successful businessman such as Hugno was seen as a man of substantial means, even though when compared to the upper stratum of Jews his wealth was modest. In terms of his background, Hugno was more aligned to the stratum of 'middling' class studied by Hirschon. He had been born into a poor family, orphaned early, and brought up by his grandmother. Isaac began working at an early age as a tailor's apprentice and through dint of his endeavours over many years had become successful.[102]

One of the community's popular garment makers employing at least a half dozen dressmakers on a putting out basis was Giuseppe Benatar (another tailor of 'renown') whose business at the Piazza Principe 34 specialized in *trousseaux de mariage*.[103] If married, most women of the *Juderia* remained at home engaged in domestic work (*casalinge*). Nonetheless there were opportunities for work, both within the home and outside. Some older and more experienced women, especially if single, sewed whole garments for individual customers, or put out work to teenage girls like Sylvia Berro, the daughter of Ruben Hasson. She recalled in the mid-1990s, how during the Depression, she lost her job in a ceramic factory and went to work as an apprentice to a 'stingy' dressmaker, enduring long hours 'from Sunday to Friday'.[104]

For many of the inhabitants of the *Juderia* striving to make ends meet was common and often a hand-to-mouth existence. Miriam (Maria) Na[c]hmias, the widowed mother of Stella and Rica, worked as a cook at the Rabbinical College until its closure in 1938, earning just enough for the family to scrape by.[105] It was also hard to eke out a living for those like Ruben Alhadeff, a peripatetic trader born in 1883 who sold his wares in the surrounding villages; or Sylvia Berro's father Ruben Hasson (b. 1874), a vegetable-seller who had to support a family of seven,[106] or Sadih[k] Amato, also a perambulatory trader who sold dried fruit and sweets, and who, like Alhadeff, was 60 years old at the time of the deportation. Described by the authorities as living in economically poor conditions, Amato had to support a wife and seven children ranging in age from 24-year-old Giuseppe to 4-year-old Maria, as well as taking care of his elderly father.[107] Meanwhile, the poverty of 40-year-old Bazzalel A. was such that the authorities in 1934 deemed him eligible for public welfare.[108]

But the authorities took a dim view of those driven by extreme poverty to beg, probably because this interfered with promoting Rhodes as an idyllic tourist destination. Thus, 58-year-old Hannah H. was censured after 'despite having been warned, asked for alms in a vexatious and petulant manner from some tourists passing by on the motorboat "Calitea"', near the Via delle Mure di Castiglio. She was taken into custody for breaching article 670 of the criminal code (*codici penali*), sentenced to a month's imprisonment suspended for two years and subsequently placed on the 'offenders' (*pregiudicate e sospetta*) register.[109]

The family of Avner Hanan (b. 1900), one of Rhodes' many perambulatory shoe polishers (*lustrascarpe*), lived in conditions like those of Amato. Avner had four young children and with his younger brother Ezra also supported elderly parents, Moreno and Bulissa, who lived with him. Described as being propertyless, Avner's family lived in Via Fasana Nr 11, a few doors from Ezra and his family.[110] Similarly, the family of Elia Levi residing in Via della Grande Sinagoga was described in a welfare report as 'living in straitened economic conditions'. Elia's parents did not possess assets, two of his five siblings were still in school (1935) and the three older ones were apparently without employment. Elia was described by the Italian authorities as 'sympathetic to the aims of the regime, and respectful of its institutions'. He worked for the public telegraphic company where he was said to be obedient and helpful. Elia was the breadwinner of the family. Three years later, in December 1938, he would attempt to tread the well-worn path for Rhodes' Jews and migrate to Africa, in the first instance without his wife Rachele (née Galante) and their little son, Isaaco, who had been born in 1936. He was granted permission to depart, but he did not leave.[111]

*

The younger generation of Jews was better educated than its parents' generation because of modern schooling through the Alliance Israélite Universelle and from the mid-1920s, through either the private *Scuola Italiano Israelite* or the Catholic Italian municipal school.[112] Better education opened opportunities in an expanding tertiary sector at home, as well as commercial opportunities in the Rhodesli diaspora, especially in the Congo. Education and training were thus greatly valued. Rhodes had three levels of schooling and training, aside from a nursery for infants and a Rabbinical College. In the academic year 1937/38, the year before Jewish children would be expelled from Italian public schools, there were 59 *scuola elementari* or elementary schools on Rhodes with a total of 6,004 pupils; of these students, 347 (or 5.77 per cent) were Jewish children, like Sami Modiano or Sara Hanan and her cousin, Ascer, all born in 1930. At the next level, were the three *scuola medie* or middle schools, with 577 pupils of whom 85 (14.7 per cent) were Jewish youngsters, like Alessandro Angel and Alberto Israel. The final level of educational provision was the commercial college. Attendance here was dominated by Jewish youngsters. Again in 1937/38, 71 (86.5 per cent) of the 82 students hailed from Jewish families and divided almost equally between boys and girls.[113] British observers noted that the courses at the commercial college on Rhodes were 'attended almost exclusively by Jews', eager to learn a trade that would be their passport to a better life overseas.[114]

In the absence of higher educational institutes, a very small number of youths, mostly from the leading families of the community, continued their education at university in Italy. The fascist government provided a total subsidy of I£100,000 to enable students from the islands to study at a *Università del Regno* on mainland Italy. Thus Nissim Alhadeff, the son of the banker Isaaco Alhadeff, and Alessandro Benatar, the son of a well-to-do wholesale merchant, were able to pursue their medical studies on the Italian mainland, eventually becoming stranded there with the outbreak of war.[115]

Rome's attempt to develop its cultural leadership in the Levant included promoting Jewish scholarship. Thus in 1928, a Rabbinical College was established with an annual subsidy of I£30,000 from the Italian Ministry of Foreign Affairs that made Rhodes a centre of Judaic learning in the Levant, albeit for a brief period until 1938.[116] The College achieved international renown in the ten years of its existence.[117] The president of its board was Vitalis Strumza, a long-serving career diplomat and administrator who had the full support of governor Lago, while the board itself consisted of the leaders of the Community. On the eve of its closure (1937/38), it had twenty students drawn from across the Levant and organized into three classes, and in 1936/37 graduated nineteen scholars.[118] The College, however, despite its excellent reputation, also quickly ran into financial difficulties in spite of its annual subsidy. Lago wrote to the Ministry in 1935 outlining some of the College's financial difficulties and stressed the necessity of continuing financial support to keep it open. For the elders of the Jewish community in Rhodes, the aim of the College was to revive Orthodox Judaism among Levantine Sephardim at a time when there was a perception that Jewry was weakening in the face of growing secularization and the onslaught of antisemitism.[119] But for governor Lago and for Rome, the College represented evidence of Italy's wide-ranging cultural mission in the Eastern Aegean.[120] Lago's successor, De Vecchi, was less enthusiastic about promoting and subsidizing Jewish institutions, and without adequate funding and plagued by internal conflicts, the college closed in 1938.[121]

In an era when education beyond middle school was the exception and not the rule, it is not clear to what extent the introduction in 1938 of the Laws for the Defence of Race (*Leggi per la difesa della Razza*) impacted on the educational careers and aspirations of Jewish youth.[122] Indeed, it was common for the *Juderia*'s youth to start employment after completing middle school at 14 years old, and sometimes they left earlier.[123] Many Jewish youth took practical courses at the commercial college in preparation for emigration. But others chose professions that would allow them to gain employment on the island. Diamante and Rachel Hugno's brothers, for example, studied accountancy, a useful profession that would stand them (and their family) in good stead through the difficult years of the war, until deportation.[124]

Diamante had dreamed of becoming a schoolteacher, but her father, the 'tailor of renown', insisted she cease her schooling at 14 and apprenticed her to a dressmaker, seeing this as a better opportunity for her. Indeed, many young women learned to sew in the home, a skill that could earn some money as a dressmaker, as we saw in Sylvia Berro's case. Meanwhile, when her mother died in 1936, 15-year-old Lucia Sciarcon (later Amato) began work in a cigarette factory to support the family (her two brothers immigrated to Palestine in 1938).[125] Finally, many young women worked in the family business, nevertheless appearing in official documents as *casalinghe* (*casalinga* singular) that is, as home-makers.

By the time of the deportation in 1944, there were broadly speaking four generational cohorts making up the community. The first cohort was that born from the middle to the last third of the nineteenth century (1850–79), this was the grandparent generation. The second cohort comprised those born in the three decades from 1881 to 1909, they constituted the parent generation by our period. The third cohort born in the decade from 1910 to 1929 made up the generation of youth. The final cohort was that of children born from 1930 until the date of deportation and ranging from toddlers to early teens under the age of 14 years old.[126]

While the grandparent generation continued to embrace the Ottoman-era Sephardic customs of their youth, the parent generation born in the final decades of the nineteenth century had already begun to adopt western dress. This change was aided by the establishment in Rhodes of the Alliance Israélite Universelle in 1899, whose mission was to improve Jewish identity and to enable social progress under Ottoman rule. The school did much to impart western culture.[127] By the time their children were born in the decade following the ending of the Great War, assimilation went further still under the Italian aegis, not least because of Rome's policy in the Dodecanese of Italianization.[128] Thus, education was important for opening up the cultural horizons of the Aegean Jews, as Stella Levi acknowledged to Marcello Pezzetti in Ruggero Gabbai's film *Longest Journey*, in contrast to (rural) Greeks, considered by Italians as backward.[129]

A portrait photograph of Rabbi Capuia's family partly captures this shift from Ottoman Jew to Westernized Jew (Illustration 2.1).[130] While the parents lived in the *Juderia*, their son Leon and his family resided at 19 Via Victor Emmanuel III in the upmarket suburb of Neocorio. In the photograph the patriarch Giacobbe (Yakov), born in 1854, who had served as chief rabbi and who had also taught at the Alliance Israélite Universelle, and his wife, Miriam Piha, sit flanked by their two sons and daughters-in-law, and grandchildren. Both elderly parents are wearing traditional dress. The patriarch with his long

Illustration 2.1 The Capuia family, 1935
Source: Courtesy Peppo Capuia Family Archive

beard wears the 'shalvar' – the wide Turkish trousers, and a 'sayo' – the long white shirt, over which he is wearing a long open coat, but he is also wearing a *fez*, which by the interwar years had replaced the turban traditionally favoured by rabbis. Miriam is dressed in the style typical of older Jewish women of the island: a long shift or 'breshin' covered by a heavy silk or velvet dress, also covered by a heavy fur-lined jacket made of velvet, the 'polka de samara'; a small cap of velvet with a brooch as centrepiece crowns her head and this is covered by a shawl.[131] By contrast their two sons Leon, a grocery merchant, and his wife Regina Menascé, and J[Y]uda and his wife Amalia, are dressed in western-style apparel typical of the interwar Mediterranean urban middle class. Leon's and Regina's 10-year-old son, Roberto, appears in another photograph from 1943 as a thoroughly westernized young man.[132]

The style of the grandparent generation by the 1920s had become a point of interest for folklorists in the 1930s keen to capture the culture of the 'old ways' of Ottoman Jewry before this was swept away by the forces of modernization, and by doing so, created an image of the 'Orient Jew' as exotic or quaint.[133]

As in any society there was a class and cultural distinction in the way one dressed. Rebecca Amato Levy provides a good description of this. 'At the turn of the century', she writes,

The middle aged rich men wore a shirt with a starched collar, with a tie and a tie clip of gold with a pearl in the middle. They wore a jacket, vest and modern pants. A gold pocket-watch with a gold chain was worn from the lapel of the vest to the vest pocket. The less well off men wore the same clothing, but with less ornamentation. The rich men wore short boots with buttons on the side and galoshes and carried canes in gloved hands. They grew mustaches and side-burns, and on their heads they wore red fezes. The rich fashionable men wore felt hats for everyday wear, and for special occasions derbies and top-hats. The poor men wore berets called 'kasketos' and 'giorginas'.[134]

Some of this style, particularly the buttoned boots, galoshes and side-burns, had disappeared or was disappearing by the 1920s. While felt hats had largely displaced the *fez* among the middle classes, the latter nonetheless remained an integral part of the dress of older men, as we saw with Rabbi Capuia. The flat cap or beret remained the preferred headwear of labouring men, but by the later interwar years the beret also had become favoured among young Jewish men and women and was also part of the uniform worn by younger students attending the Rabbinical College.[135]

Two surviving photographs of Sylvia Berro's father, Ruben Hasson and his family, also capture this transformation, but also the co-existence of the two cultures (Illustration 2.2).[136] The first photograph taken in 1924 when Ruben was in his mid-forties, shows him together with his family (they lived at Nr 6 Via Guiseppe Notrica). He is bareheaded and clean-shaven, save for a moustache. His shirt is buttoned at the collar beneath a waistcoat and western-style suit. His wife, Mazaltov appears in 'westernized' dress and the four pre-teen children, Vida (b. 1913), Vittorio (b. 1915), Bellina (b. 1917) and Sylvia (b. 1920), are dressed in a style typical of the Mediterranean urban classes (with the girls each wearing identical but individually made outfits). There is little in this photograph or in the children's later portraits, taken some time in the 1930s, to suggest an Ottoman world. Indeed, a decade later the teenage children are fully westernized in appearance. However, their father appears almost as a palimpsest of the changes taking place in the community: he wears a western-style jacket over the Turkish 'sayo', with the Ottoman *fez*, the sartorial ensemble giving him a look that straddled both Orient and Occident.[137]

The degree of cultural assimilation might have been a consequence of Jewish integration into a modernizing world of commerce and industry.[138] But

Illustration 2.2 The Hasson family, 1924 and *c.* 1930s

Source: Courtesy Aron Hasson, *Jewish Life in Rhodes 'Family Portraits'*, Rhodes Jewish Historical Foundation, Los Angeles (2022)

it also reflects the influence of Italianization mentioned earlier, a process that had been gathering pace since the mid-1920s, and which now breached the social, if not always the generational divide.

As might be expected, younger Jews found it easiest to integrate. A sizeable number of younger men and women found employment in the larger Italian commercial establishments or in the island's public administration. The arrival of the Italians in 1912 was in fact the beginning of a cultural and political kinship between Italians and young Jews. As Stella Levi, born a decade after the Italian arrival, later recalled, 'I always thought that Italy actually brought civilization, an opening towards the West that I found extremely appealing.'[139] After the Holocaust, Stella and other survivors continued to emphasize this Italian affinity when called upon to share their memory of life on Rhodes. Families sent their children to the Italian Roman Catholic secondary school

and the Roman Catholic Convent (from 1926 these schools superseded the
Alliance Israélite Universelle in the provision of secondary education).[140] Of
thirteen teachers listed at the Jewish Italian School for the academic year
1933/34, only two were from Rhodes.[141] Even the director of the Rabbinical
College Professor Rabbi Riccardo Pacifici and many of his nine staff came
from Italy.[142] Rather than Athens or Salonica or the Jewish enclaves of the
eastern Mediterranean, the younger generation thus looked to Rome and
further afield to Brussels and Paris, for its cultural references.

As we have seen, life in the *Juderia* is remembered by survivors as a time of
innocence; some also recalled the deep religious observance among families.[143]
Alberto Israel in his recollection spoke about how, 'On weekdays, people got
up at six o'clock to go to prayer, some came back at noon if work permitted,
but all were present for the evening prayer. This is a fervour that we don't see
anymore. Rhodes was a small Jerusalem.'[144] Regina Mazza (née Palombo) also
recounted to Jaqueline Benatar in 1988 how all members of the community
kept kosher and observed the dictates of religious holidays, with even little
children learning to fast at Yom Kippur. In between these festivals

> Every Saturday, the family, the children, they would go to the kehilla
> (i.e. synagogue) … we would come back, we would eat at the table like
> everybody else. Noche Shabbat (*Shabbat* eve), we would do kiddush, right?
> We were very modest families and everybody led their lives like in Israel
> [*sic*], didn't they? And that was the life of Rhodes, modest but … it was
> cheerful, it was good.[145]

And Stella Levi reminisced, 'Ours was a very particular religious spirit, it
virtually dictated the rhythm of our daily lives.'[146]

Some survivors recalled five or six synagogues serving the Community,
although this number possibly includes other religious institutions, such as the
yeshiva.[147] In fact, by 1940 there were just two synagogues recorded in official
records, the Kahal Shalom dating from the sixteenth century and the earlier
built Sinagoga Grande. However, there appears also to have been a small
privately financed synagogue that functioned only during the high holidays,
the so-called 'synagogue of the rich', located in the plush Via dei Ricci ('the
street of the rich'; present-day Odos Gavala).[148] There was also a school for
teaching the Talmud, a yeshiva, and it appears most youth attended classes to

learn Hebrew. It was not uncommon for students of the Rabbinical College to provide the lessons in Hebrew to school pupils. Matilde Levy (née Cohen), for example, remembered her teacher as a 'young man who had completed his studies at the Rabbinical College' and came for two or three hours a week to the Jewish school to instruct the pupils.[149]

Some survivors referred to daily attendance at the synagogue among the older generation. However, despite providing regular religious lessons in Hebrew, there is evidence to suggest that religiosity, especially among the young, was in fact waning. The two main synagogues had only three officiating rabbis and six assistant rabbis (*assistenti officianti rabbinici*) between them. Their number represents a much thinned out presence from earlier days, especially when compared to the ten mosques and twenty imams serving the Turkish community of roughly the same size.[150] The small number of rabbis and places of worship may thus not only mirror the decline in the size of the community, but possibly also reflect a loosening of religious commitment, if not a growing secularization among the young of the community. As Lucia Amato recalled, synagogue was attended mostly by the older generation.[151]

Until the 1930s, the religious communities were *quasi*-autonomous legal entities with the right to levy a religious tax and with their own arbitration courts.[152] The circa 200 male Jewish heads of household registered on the community roll in the early 1930s were entitled to elect a General Council, the Ben-Din, composed of rabbis from the two synagogues and the yeshiva, as well as community elders. The Ben-Din in turn elected the Grand Rabbi. After Chief Rabbi Reuben Eliahu Israel's death in 1932, this role appears to have been temporarily filled by Rabbi Michel Albagli until he left for the United States in 1939, after which the position remained vacant.[153] The Chief Rabbi of Alexandria in Egypt and the Italian Union of Jews headquartered in Rome took an active interest in the community's organized life. But probably of greater importance in terms of everyday life was the local General Council periodically elected by the registered heads of household.[154]

This body was dominated by the elite families of Rhodes and Kos, with key positions rotating among them. They furnished the community's council with its chief officers, including its presidents (see below). In addition to the council, there were welfare and charitable institutions such as B'nai B'rith, Bicur Holim, Ozer Dalim and Patronato Scolasitco designed to aid the community's poor. These too were dominated by the islands' elite families, with wives of prominent members taking on leading roles.[155] The social life of the elite Jewish families took place mostly outside the quotidian calendar of the majority of Jews, with the exception of religious holidays. Their members circulated freely among the islands' political classes of the Italian *Governatore*, the mayoralty, and the military, as well as associating with their wealthy Italian and Greek counterparts. Yehuda Tarica and his wife Renée Capelluto, for example, moved easily within Rhodes' high society, taking part in social events at Il Circolo d'Italia Touring Club and visiting the opera at the recently opened Puccini Theatre in the grand avenue Via Foro Italico leading to the Mandraki.[156]

Many survivors refer to the harmony of the community. But such a recollection masks the everyday petty, and sometimes more serious, conflicts within the Community and between Jews and their gentile neighbours. While most survivors recollect amicable relations with Turks and with Greeks, there were nevertheless tensions, notably with the Greeks, usually around Easter time when children were warned not to pass through Orthodox Christian neighbourhoods. Rhodes had not seen a recurrence of the notorious Blood Libel of 1840, but its memory persisted, and Jews remained wary of their Orthodox neighbours at this time of year.[157] Sometimes the source of tension might appear petty, but its impact could lead to a souring of communal relations. For example, Michele Menascé, who lived in the Sinagoga della Pace, wrote to the authorities in mid-September 1936, to complain about a Greek Orthodox family of ten who lived in the same street. Their boisterous behaviour was a continuous source of irritation during Friday prayers ushering in the Sabbath. Menascé wrote to the authorities demanding that the family be expelled from the neighbourhood.[158] Relations between individuals from the ethnically diverse communities of Rhodes might have soured over financial agreements that had turned bad. Nissim Tarica, like Menascé one of the community's leading men, took several of his Greek debtors to court (not just Modiano as we saw above). One might well speculate on how far such poor relations fed into a latent Judeophobia among Greeks.[159]

On other occasions, arguments might flare up and quickly subside rather like the Aegean's legendary storms without lasting impact on inter-communal relations. For example, on the morning of 31 October 1938, in the Via Mercato Vecchio (the long thoroughfare that stretched from the north of the old town and ended at the Piazza Venezia), 30-year-old Giuseppe Alcana (Miru Alcana's older brother) 'came to quarrel for futile reasons' with 30-year-old Panaioti Pacaci, a Greek with Italian citizenship originally from Castelorisso (Kastelorizo). The two men came to blows, with Alcana striking Pacaci on the mouth causing a wound to the lower lip. Pacaci attended the local hospital for treatment and the laceration healed within six days. By the time Lieutenant Franceso Terlizzi filed his report, the two had reconciled their differences.[160] Giuseppe's cousin, Isaaco, also was quick to resort to his fists to settle arguments. In 1934, he struck his neighbour, 19-year-old labourer Nissim Danon, again over a trivial matter.[161]

In a small island community of the eastern Mediterranean there was typically machismo among younger men, regardless of ethnicity or religion. The slightest provocation could result in blows being exchanged. Moses Israel, an employee in Hizkia Franco's shop in Via Vecchio Mercato, twice found himself the subject of a police report. In 1934, he intervened in an incident outside the shop involving a 14-year-old student from the Rabbinical College who had given a friendly punch on the arm of a passing Greek. Instead of apologizing, the boy had turned and made faces at the 21-year-old, who then slapped the boy twice and gave him a kick, whereupon Israel together with several other Jewish men intervened, punching and scratching the Greek in the face. The Greek's assault on the boy was not serious, but the contusions he received in return were severe enough to require medical attention. Three years later, Israel was again involved in a fracas in the street with another Greek man. When Alessandro Coen, a shop assistant, intervened to separate the two, Israel turned and punched Coen in the face, fracturing his nose. Coen reserved the right to press charges against Israel, who later applied to emigrate to the Congo.[162] In none of these incidents involving Jews and gentiles was there any evidence of antisemitism as a source of conflict. As we will see in the following chapter, this changed by the later 1930s, as fascists became increasingly brazen in verbal attacks upon Jews.

Tensions might also plague individual families. Although it is difficult to find widespread evidence for this, some sources cast a thin beam of light onto the inner life and woes of individual families. The correspondence between young Claire Barchi and her successful businessman uncle Ralph [Raphael] Capelluto in Seattle charts the difficulties Claire's family experienced during

the 1930s, culminating in their expulsion from Rhodes after the passing
of the Racial Laws and arrival in Tangiers in the summer of 1939.[163] Like
many families in the *Juderia* the family underwent a change in its financial
circumstances, and Claire (and sometimes her aunt Esther) wrote regularly
to Ralph in the hope he might be able to help them. Claire's father Avraham
Barchi (also spelt Barki), a shoemaker by trade, lost his licence in 1939. Their
situation was not made easier by a male relative by marriage, Nissim Levy, who
was married to Gioia, the younger sister of Claire's mother, Mazaltov.

Levy appears to have been a spendthrift, a financially reckless man, who was
also neglectful of Gioia. A month after arriving in Tangier on 2 July, Claire's
aunt Esther wrote to Ralph complaining about Nissim:

> Nissim has such a bad character that since the day he found out that you
> sent some money to Avraham, he has given us no rest, cursing us directly
> or behind our backs. After so many years of marriage, he [still] asks us for
> dowry. After all Avraham did for them, especially after each childbirth when
> we all would go to look after ... [Gioia] and would spend a lot of money to
> cover up for Nissim. And now ... [Avraham] has given them more than 1,000
> francs because he took pity on Gioia. And when we embarked, [Avraham]
> gave [Nissim] 600 francs ..., and when we reached Genoa, [Nissim] asked
> for more and he arrived in Tangier three weeks after us. We went to meet
> him, and dear Mazaltov found a house for them and paid one month in
> advance. But he did not even thank her.[164]

A few days later, Claire also wrote to her uncle, no less dismissive of this
awkward family member. 'We have near us Uncle Nissim who is Gioia's
husband, who from the day of his marriage has given us such a bad time', she
wrote. Nissim, it seems, while in Rhodes was forever demanding the I£2,000
dowry, stating he needed it because of the loss of his licence to trade. And
Claire continued, 'But a lot of people lost the permit and did not need anyone
because they had more brains than him, were thinking of tomorrow, and did
not squander their money.' Claire poured out a litany of complaints about her
uncle and added: [His] 'last name is "Levy", and as you may recall while in
Rhodes, the saying "Empty-headed Levy" ... fits him well.'[165]

Conflicts were not confined to the streets or to families. There were also
tensions within the organization of the community itself, suggesting all was
not well within its administration. One of the last acts of Governor Mario

Lago before his return to Italy in the winter of 1936 was to issue a fiat in mid-June dissolving the Jewish council, after Hizkia Franco stepped down from the role of president in November 1935.[166] Vitalis Strumza, the third most senior official in the Italian administration and a prominent member of the Jewish community, was given the task of executing the decree and organizing the election of a new eight-man Council, which was duly signed off by Lago on 28 June.[167] The new Council was composed of men the Italian civilian authorities referred to as 'of good standing' in the wider Jewish community and in Rhodes per se. Led by Giovanni (John) Menascé, who owned the family bank as well as a number of factories, the council was in fact again drawn from members of the wealthy mercantile elite, some of whom were related to one another either through blood or through marriage. Thus, three of the members were from the Menascé family, including the community's president John Menascé. Ruben Capelluto was a director of the Alhadeff department store and was married to Rebecca Alhadeff, Giacobbe Franco was a wealthy merchant and jeweller, Sami Notrica, like Michael Menascé and Isaaco Menascé, was a businessman of substantial means, as too was Giuseppe Algranti and the pharmacist Maurizio Soriano (who after the war would serve as president of the community).[168]

The catalyst for the dissolution and election of a new Council was a crisis of confidence in the governance and administration of the community. In the years before 1936, there appears to have been incompetent administration – if not *mis*-management – of the community's finances, including those of its various charitable organizations, notably Bicor Holim, a charity for the protection of moral life. The new council, it was believed, would restore both 'regularity and dignity' to the community after years of financial strife. It would also help to reform the *kehilot*, the institutional religious life of the community which some felt had been in decline. '[It is an] indisputable fact', *El Boletin*, the Ladino-language community newspaper reported, 'that our temples are in need of reform and reorganization'. It would appear that the organization of religious life had been in difficulty since the death of the Grand Rabbi in 1932, and attempts at reform faced entrenched resistance, possibly from the existing rabbinical council.[169] The nature of the problem was not explicitly articulated by contemporaries, but it appears that the leadership of the community, which was both assimilationist and conservative, was also facing a challenge from

Zionism, especially among younger teachers, as well as a general ebbing in religiosity among Jewish youth.[170]

Ever since his arrival in Rhodes, Governor Lago had shown himself to be well disposed towards the Jewish community, seeing its leaders as politically trustworthy, and he was undoubtedly also deeply appreciative of the vital role the community's traders played in the island economy. The new Council and its members also played a considerable role in the charitable organization of B'nai B'rith.[171] This organization comprising the largely socially conservative elements of Rhodes' Jewish community was devoted to the Italian state and opposed to the radicalism of the Zionist movement of Ze'ev (Vladimir) Jabotinsky and his Union of Zionist Revisionists (*Hatzohar*) that called for the immediate establishment of a Jewish state in Palestine, and which had a following in some sections of the Jewish community in Rhodes. The B'nai B'rith was not opposed to Eretz Israel (the Promised Land), indeed there was a close affinity with Jerusalem, but this was of a spiritual rather than political nature. The elders of the community in Rhodes were uncomfortable with what they considered the ideological extremism of Jabotinsky's movement. Moreover, B'nai B'rith members, such as Professor Pacifici, while not members of the National Fascist Party (*Partito Nazionale Fascista* – PNF) were nonetheless loyal to the regime in Rome, and frequently expressed this loyalty.[172]

However, this was a position not shared by some younger teachers in particular who foregrounded Jewish identity, espoused Zionism, and clearly made an impression on youngsters such as Rachel Hanon and Laura Varon, to name just two. The attraction of Jabotinsky's politics is almost, if not completely, invisible in popular accounts of Jewish Rhodes (in much the same way that fascism's attraction among some of the island's Jews is also overlooked). Nonetheless there is acknowledgement of the affinity between the revisionist Zionist *Hatzohar* and Jewish youth. Laura Varon recalled in an interview in 1997 how: 'after school ... we used to be very Zionist in Rhodes ... fervent Zionists, we were also revisionists'; although she admitted as a child, she did not know the meaning of the latter term.[173]

The appeal of Zionism among the Community's younger members led to friction between Zionist activists in the Jewish school and the Community elders, and this appears to have been behind the sudden departure of its director as well as some teachers from the School Board. Speaking on behalf of the Council, Hizkia Franco, formerly president of the community and now as editor of the Ladino-language newspaper *El Boletin*, declared that the role of the Jewish school was to serve the interests of the Italian state and to promote religious instruction, and not to spread Zionist ideology.[174] The Council clearly found these Zionist activists a thorn in its side. A month earlier, in May, Franco had prepared an article for *El Boletin* in which he accused Zionists of sowing 'discord and disunity in Judaism' by spreading a 'phantasmagorical ideology' among youth, and thus promoting 'indiscipline, insubordination and also revolt' in Jewish schools. Nevertheless, such Council initiatives to suppress Zionist influence among youth overstepped the boundary of what even the authorities found acceptable. The *Carabinieri* officer charged with vetting the newspaper believed Franco's article would provoke protest among Zionist youth. Indeed, it 'reveals the intransigent and intolerant mentality of the president [*sic*] of the community which could provoke incidents and reactions among the young revisionist Zionists. [Therefore] I have ordered unless otherwise advised by [Secretary General of the Governatore] that the Boletin is not published unless it suppresses the article.'[175] It appears that some young Zionists were antifascist and through diverse reports kept their comrades (and the Community) informed of the rising tide of antisemitism elsewhere in Europe, and in particular of developments in Nazi Germany.

When Israel Cohen, formerly a teacher at the Jewish school in Rhodes, published a pamphlet 'The Jews in Germany' in 1933, he and the Italian Union of Jews quickly fell afoul of the authorities, resulting in his temporary arrest in the spring of 1934. At least fifty copies of the pamphlet had been sent to Rhodes by the Italian Union of Jews, and the *Carabinieri* was keen to confiscate these. To this end *commissario* Crivallario sought the aid of Hizkia Franco to not only to locate the pamphlets, but also to ensure all Jewish journals refrained from publishing anti-German articles. For his part, Franco was willing to assist the authorities in Rhodes in the maintenance of social and political order. Similarly, when sailors from the British battleship *Revenge* played a soccer match with the Italian team in September 1933, it was reported that two or three young Jews cheered on the sailors instead of the home team. The reason for their apparent contempt of the Rhodes' side was the blatant antisemitic views of the *Il Messaggero di Rodi* sports editor. Franco assured the authorities that he would 'have a word' with the youths.[176]

Younger Jews especially were quick to challenge what they perceived as anti-Jewish behaviour or those considered as hostile to Jews. When it was reported that two princesses (one of whom was related to the queen of Holland) staying at the Hotel Savoy (in the old town's Jewish quarter) had been accosted by two young Jews who demanded to know their nationality and on learning it was German, 'made a gesture of contempt', Franco used the *Shabbat* service in the synagogue to denounce such behaviour and demanded the names of the offenders.[177] Evidently, underlying the outward harmony of the community (as remembered by survivors) were both inner and inter-communal frictions, sometimes captured in the reports of the *Carabinieri*. Thus, in late summer 1934, it was reported:

> during a visit to the walled city by groups of tourists on the liner 'Oceania', a few young Israelites, who usually tag along with the tourists and sneak in from everywhere, climbed the minaret of the 'Suleimani' mosque and from up there, they fired crackers and taunted passers-by on the street to the rhythm of the muezzin when he calls for prayer.[178]

But as revealing as the youths' behaviour of inter-communal frictions was the fact that the complainant, Mahmud H., did not wish his name to be made known to Vitalis Strumza, for fear of 'unpleasant' repercussions.

Quite apart from minor misdemeanours or lesser infringements of the law (discussed in the next chapter), there were more serious violations and criminal activity. As in any society, the *Juderia* harboured its own 'dangerous classes'. Alberto Israel's benign memory of Jewish Rhodes where the people were 'innocent and pure' and 'no Jews were in prison', glosses over the day-to-day existence of those on the margins of society. Some of them eked a living from prostitution, whether licensed or casual, as in the case of Stella L. (b. 1908), who lived in Via Antonio del Pozzo (present-day Gavalas Leontos).[179] Others made small returns from petty larceny. Ester C. (b. 1901), a washerwoman who lived in the heart of the *Juderia* (in 1934, she resided in Via della Castellania and prior to the deportation in Sigismondo Malatesta) and was described by the authorities as coming from an impoverished home, engaged in both casual prostitution and petty theft, the latter primarily from her neighbours. In 1934, she received medical treatment by the public health authorities after contracting gonorrhoea after engaging in casual prostitution.

Three years later she was before the court on a charge of theft of a linen blanket from an elderly neighbour's house, receiving a fine of I£500. In 1942, she was again charged with stealing, this time a hen from a neighbour's home and sentenced to twenty-eight days' confinement and a fine of I£700.[180]

Others lived lifestyles associated with the rougher side of 'the tracks'. The older brothers of Richetta L., Menascé and Salvo, had a string of convictions in the 1930s for drug dealing, trading explosives and using threatening and violent behaviour. Richetta's boyfriend, Moise R., also served a custodial sentence in 1934 for drug dealing (in fact, they appear to have met while she was visiting her brother Menascé in prison). With such a shared career, the authorities were dubious about allowing Moise R. to take up permanent residency in Rhodes prior to marrying Richetta.[181]

As in many societies, incidents of domestic violence perpetrated by males in Jewish families occurred from time to time, as too did sexual violence against neighbours and neighbours' children. We do not know if these were isolated or common acts, since it was only the most egregious ones that came to light. Thus, in May 1934, 29-year-old Israel H., an itinerant trader, attended hospital after sustaining an injury during a family quarrel. It is not clear what the cause of the conflict was, but three years later, his 19-year-old wife, Violetta B., lodged a complaint with the *Carabinieri* after Israel had beaten her up. As well as a proclivity to domestic violence, H. also appeared before the court in October 1934 for aggravated theft and was given a custodial sentence, as well as entered onto the offenders' register.[182]

Another case on the margins of society where the boundary between transgressive misdemeanours and sexual delinquency appeared to be either seamless or simply dissolved was that of Boaz B. As in the case of H., B. was known to the police, having been charged for contravening various regulations over a period of ten years, commencing in the early 1930s. B. was by profession a truck driver delivering mostly wood from the forests around the San Stefano, Monte Profeta and Campochiaro areas south of Rhodes. Until the later 1930s, he lived with his wife and son in the village of Apollona. His first brushes with the law were for minor misdemeanours, mostly driving offences and negligence.[183]

It is difficult to judge from a distance of eighty years, and when we only have police and court records to go on. Nonetheless, even a source-critical eye cannot escape the impression that B. lived with some disregard for the laws of respectable society. In 1936, his behaviour had transitioned from simple misdemeanour to aggravated misdemeanour when he came before the courts for breaking Art. 81-515 of the Criminal Code (Codice Penale). He received a hefty fine and his licence was suspended for five years. Two years later, in February, he and his family were expelled from Apollona by order of the prefecture.

The slippage from cavalier behaviour to serious crime came in July 1938, when B., together with two Italian settlers from Campochiari, 28-year-old Antonio W., originally from Bolzano and 16-year-old Bruno V., originally from Trento, was implicated in the gang-rape of a 14-year-old girl Bruna Z., from Campochiari, resulting in her contracting gonorrhoea. B. was sentenced to eight months' imprisonment but appealed. When his case came before the tribunal again in January 1940, the sentence was overturned for lack of hard evidence. Nevertheless, in February 1940, the *Carabinieri* ordered that B.'s name be filed in the register of criminal and dangerous persons.

His police record did not prevent him from continuing to chalk up offences and engage in illicit activities. By the time his five-year suspension was over in 1941, when he was applying for a licence to deliver coal, he was living in the *Juderia*, but later moved to Archangelos. But he was also interested in delivering goods other than mere coal. In 1942 for instance, together with two butchers (a Turk and an Italian) from Asguro and Coschino (Koskinou) he was involved in the illegal slaughter of a cow, with the intention of selling the 40 kg of meat, and in 1943 implicated in a haul of 85 kg of tomatoes and 76,000 kg of aubergines in Trianda intended for the black market. In March 1943, together with his younger brother Salvo and another acquaintance, he found himself before the courts again, this time for receiving stolen truck tyres from the army depot in Campochiari. B.'s file ends in mid-July 1944, with a hand-scrawled note stating that he was to be handed over into the custody of the German Secret Military Police (*Geheime Feldpolizei*), presumably for deportation.[184]

*

Even though the First World War had disrupted the economy of the Dodecanese islands, it was partly redressed by the Fascist construction boom and its accompanying benefits. If J.L. Myres noted in 1920, that Rhodes was the 'least-developed island of (......) all' the Dodecanese islands despite its trading links, this had certainly changed by the 1930s.[185] Nevertheless, by the latter period, the economic boom was slowing, if not coming to an end on the islands of Rhodes, Kos and Leros. The limited and precarious nature of economic life for many large families of all denominations on Rhodes meant that they traditionally 'exported' their offspring to those lands where economic opportunities appeared still to be abundant.[186] The pattern of pre-1914 migration took Jews from Rhodes and Kos to the United States, but principally to what was then the Belgian Congo and to Rhodesia where the opportunity to trade was greatest.[187]

Hardly a family in the *Juderia* remained unaffected by emigration, initially driven by the push of poverty and the pull of opportunity that a fresh start promised. Samuele Angel (b. 1880), had emigrated sometime at the turn of the century to Seattle where he appears to have had relatives.[188] The exact date of his arrival in the United States is uncertain, but tuberculosis drove him back to Rhodes a short time later. He returned to his homeland armed with an ice-making machine purchased in the United States and established himself in business. Samuele had married Bulissa Coen around the turn of the century, and with her had six children.[189] The sons from this marriage also emigrated, but to the Belgian Congo rather than North America. In 1937, his daughters Caden (Kitty) and Rica applied for passports to join their siblings in the Congo, and they subsequently departed. Following Bulissa's death in 1923, Samuele remarried bringing his youngest daughter Gioia (b. 1918) into the new marriage and with his second wife, Rebecca Alhadeff (b. 1889), had a further four children. The family remained very poor, and Samuele struggled to make ends meet in a modest house in Via Ammiraglio Bonaldi, a poor street in the *Juderia* close to the town walls.[190]

At the beginning of the 1930s, the Jewish population in Rhodes numbered 4,310, but over the course of the next decade it would drastically reduce in size, a consequence of economic pressure and of Italian racial policies that removed the right to stay of those who had come to Rhodes after 1919. Thus in the decade between the population census of 1931 and the onset of war between Italy and Greece in 1940, the Jewish population more than halved in size. However, ties to families and to Rhodes were never really cut. Many years later Alberto Israel gave an account to historian Marcello Pezzetti of the 'natural history' of courtship and marriage between those who had emigrated and those who remained.

> The Jews of Rhodes, when they left, acted like salmons [*sic*]. When it was time to get married, they would come back to find a wife and then they would take their wives away. The weddings were held at Kahal Grande, the great synagogue, which has since been destroyed. The photographer Pandeli was up on the terrace with his camera taking pictures of the weddings. They [composition of the photographs] were all exactly the same, only the bride and groom changed. Weddings were held on Fridays. On Saturday they would have a reception at home. On Sunday they were on the ferry heading back to Congo or America. The trip was their honeymoon.[191]

Indeed, Alberto's older brother Daniel, who had immigrated to the Congo in the late 1920s, returned in 1935 to marry Gioia Hasson.[192]

Gordon DeLeon, who was born in Rhodes in 1908 but left as a child with his family soon after the Italian occupation in 1912, remembered the strict informal rules governing courtship from afar.

> You know in the old country it didn't matter how much money you had. Just remember you must know what lineage, what family you came from. When the people came to America, we forgot about family. There were many engagements that were broken because the father and mother knew which family the man came from – wouldn't allow the daughter to get engaged with that because they came from a different family. It was very, very strict. Over here (America) there wasn't such a thing as what family came from, Many of the young boys and girls that came here were teenagers – 16, 15, 18 year old. Pretty soon they fell in love. If this young man fell in love with a girl whose family wasn't in the same class, the father (in Rhodes) would sent [*sic*] a letter over here calling bloody murder.[193]

The Jewish youth of Rhodes as in any community had their regular haunts where they socialized among themselves. Leisure activities were mostly innocent such as hiking, bathing at the Puerte del Mare outside the walls, and simply getting together with friends and cousins to sing and dance.[194] These mostly innocent encounters were sometimes underwritten by youthful desires, especially along the Mandraki, the palm-tree-lined boulevard bordering the harbour where at weekends a military band entertained the public. Here, the young and old alike gathered to meet and to socialize. They also met with members from the Italian garrison. As Rebecca Amato Levy recalled in her memoir, 'On Saturday and Sunday nights, the Jews, Greeks, Turks and Italians would gather to walk along the promenade and to sit at the outdoor cafes while listening to the military bands that performed at the nearby plaza.'[195] Sami Modiano recounted:

> Once a week, the Mandracchio was the young people's meeting place; they strolled up and down. The boys would exchange glances with the girls as they walked back and forth. In the middle of the Mandracchio there was a gazebo where a military orchestra, either from the navy, or the air force or the army, would set up. They would play magnificent music.[196]

The boys and girls may have 'glanced' at one another, but unsupervised contact was frowned upon and a marriage proposal still had to be approved by the parents. Stella Levi, seven years his senior (b. 1923) and strikingly beautiful, would have been among the older youth being ogled by their opposite sex and perhaps ogling in return. As Vittorio Alhadeff noted, such promenading 'was a spectacle at the same time amusing and touching to watch'.[197] The young women of the *Juderia* made an impact on Italian men, as Stella reminisced in *The Longest Journey*.

> We danced tango, foxtrot, and of course the waltz. They played Italian songs like 'Tornerai'. [She sings: '*Tornerai da me ...* '] Upon the arrival of the Jewish girls in the Mandracchio, there was almost a sigh of: 'Ah! There they are! They're here!' They were all gorgeous and glowing, as the Italians used to say. Loving. Colourful. They brought colour, an entirely fresh colour to the place.[198]

And as Stella De Leon remembered, 'It was happy! It was happy ... go out with the boys, with the girls, with the friends, go to cinema, you come home, you make little parties, it was a happy life.'[199] Although the character of these encounters was mostly innocent as this quote suggests, the 'glowing' young women of the *Juderia* fired the passion of some of the young Italian men (and vice versa!), for it was not uncommon for them to get together intimately.[200]

A particular feature of the Italian population was its gender imbalance: 3,085 males and 1,934 females in 1931, which in turn acted as a catalyst for further integrating Jews into the Italianizing landscape. Alberto Israel remembered how 'Many Jewish girls married Italian boys who were in the army or in the navy' and even though initially some Jewish parents and religious leaders disapproved of these youthful liaisons, the community soon became accustomed to them.[201] Two of Lucia Garzolini's sisters married Italians, one of whom was a sailor, as did Caden Sciarcon, the older sister of Lucia Amato.[202] Twenty-year-old Achille Da Fano, a Jew originally from Venice, arrived in Rhodes as a conscript attached to the 9th Infantry Regiment probably in 1925 or 1926. Here he met 21-year-old Gioia Arditi, herself a native of Milas in Turkey. The pair married on 16 December 1927 when Gioia was already pregnant. She gave birth to their daughter, Giuseppina, five months later in early May (they subsequently had three more daughters, Maria, Elsa and Annetta; see Illustration 2.3).[203]

Ten years later in 1936, another infantryman, Rino Merolle (b. 1915), also fell in love with a girl from the *Juderia*, Matilde Alhadeff (b. 1915), who lived with her widowed mother Bulissa in the Piazza Principe.[204] Unlike Da Fano, Merolle was a Catholic and a member of the PNF and appears to have been

Illustration 2.3 The Da Fano and Gioia Arditti family

Source: Courtesy Genika Archeia tou Kratous/Archeia Dodekanisou: GAKR Carabinieri 1.1.1042, Coll. Ufficio Centrale di Publica Sicurezza I/1, Da Fano

something of a 'wheeler-dealer' with an extensive network of contacts across the four communities.[205] It would appear that Italian fascist doctrine on Jews cut little ice with Merolle where his personal life was concerned.[206] Similarly, Vittoria Sidis married an Italian soldier, Ernesto Litrici in 1937, and converted to Catholicism.[207] Twenty-year-old Sara Coen cohabited with a young soldier, 23-year-old Duilio Bartoccini, who hid her in a Catholic monastery to save her from deportation, before himself being among the military internees deported from the island.[208] After the war, it was popularly believed that young girls from the *Juderia* were saved from the Nazis by marrying Italian soldiers, for they frequently converted to Catholicism and, as in the case of Teresa Buciuk and Vittoria Levi Balsamo, often moved to Italy.[209] Where the Italian also happened to be a Jew, as in Da Fano's case, but remained in Rhodes, there was little hope of escape.[210]

Not only Italian soldiers found the girls from the *Juderia* attractive. Local Greeks and later German soldiers did too. But amorous advances from the wrong type of suitor could prove risky. Eliezer Surmani humorously recalled an incident involving his older sister with a Greek man. 'One time somebody was whistling [at] my sister and she was walking down one of the shopping [streets] … you know …. She took off her slipper and hit this Greek on the head [Surmani laughs] because he was whistling at her and all that … you know, she felt offended.'[211]

The idyll of the *Juderia* as recalled by most if not all survivors would come to an end ten months after the Dodecanese islands were seized from the grip of the Italians. The arrival of Germans on Rhodes, the rupture with Italy, and the German garrison's relations to Jews, are dealt with in Chapter 4. The years preceding the arrival of the Germans, however, were not easy for Jews. Their hitherto benign situation under Italian rule worsened from the later 1930s because of growing antisemitism within the Italian administration of the islands. We examine this in the next chapter.

3

Italians and Jews

> *The Italian government were very good to the Jewish people. They didn't*
> *harm anybody ... or anything. They were very nice until the Germans came*
> *in ... they were allies and that's when the trouble started for the Jews.*[1]

Nearly fifty years after the deportation, Sara Gilmore (née Hanan) echoed the sentiment of her fellow islanders, when she recalled how before the deportation, life in the *Juderia* had been beautiful; how Jews and Italians had enjoyed close affinity; and how the German triumph had shattered this idyll. Memory, as we shall see in the final chapter of this study, plays tricks. The older Sara was recalling her life as a young teenager. A recollection filtered through the lens of her subsequent experience of deportation, the camps and *post facto* knowledge about the Holocaust in general.

For Sara and many of her compatriots, if the Germans were 'bad', then the Italians were 'good'.[2] Neither the passing of the Italian Racial Laws of 1938 nor Mussolini's declaration in November 1943 that all Jews were enemies of the Italian Fascist state altered this perspective.[3] Yet, as we shall see in this chapter, life for many Jews on Rhodes and Kos under the Fascist regime was very different from the nostalgic recollection of survivors. Whilst relations between Italians and Jews may have been for the most part close, elements within the administration sought their marginalization and eventual removal from island life.

*

The institution that took an active interest in Jews before the deportation in 1944 was the *Ufficio Centrale di Pubblica Sicurezza* (Central Office for Public Security) of the *Carabinieri*. This police department was established under

Lago's tenure at the beginning of the 1930s, and from 1932 it set about perfecting a system of total surveillance and regulation of the entire adult population that today would be the envy of many modern states. Its remit was to gather intelligence about the population and all organizations per se – not just Jews. According to Mr Wakefield-Harray, Britain's temporary consul in Rhodes, 'the informer system was rampant, secret police were ubiquitous, [and] the population were cut off from the outside world as no foreign broadcasts might be listened to'.[4]

After Marshal Pietro Badoglio signed an armistice with the Allies in September 1943, thus withdrawing Italy from the war (see following chapter), the *Carabinieri* in the Dodecanese (now under German control) was purged of Badoglio loyalists, and subsequently functioned in tandem with the German military police and Secret Military Police (*Geheime Feldpolizei*).[5] Notable among the collaborators was Colonel Ferdinando Mittino, the head of the *Ufficio Centrale di Pubblica Sicurezza*.[6] As we shall see in the following chapters, there were an estimated 1,662 Fascists collaborating with the Germans, about a third of whom were police officers.[7] The *Carabinieri* continued monitoring the population at large, but its focus on Jews altered by virtue of the proclamation of the Fascist Republic of Salò in December 1943 that cast Jews as de facto 'foreign enemies'.[8]

Italy's colonial presence in the Eastern Aegean was underpinned by territorial and cultural imperatives and not so much by racial considerations (unlike in the Horn of Africa where, incidentally, the new governor of the Dodecanese from 1936, De Vecchi, had previously governed in Italian Somaliland).[9] Until 1938, Aegean Jews were without discrimination integrated into the Italian sphere in the Levant. Indeed, until the introduction of the Racial Laws in the autumn of that year, Jews were present at all levels in the Italian colonial administration of the Dodecanese, even at its highest level, for example Vitalis Strumza, who, until his involuntary departure from Rhodes in 1939, was a senior member of the *Governatore*. Strumza had taken up his duties in 1921 at the behest of the Italian military governor at the time, Felice Maissa. Born in Ottoman Salonica in 1859, Strumza had been a career administrator under the Ottomans. Settled in Rhodes as chief of cabinet to the Italian governor, he was the third highest-ranking official in the Dodecanese administration. In recognition of his services the *Governatore* bestowed on him the honorific title of '*cavaliere*' (the English equivalent is 'knight'). Strumza had married Anna Bronstein in 1894 in Salonica. By the later 1930s, he was living alone as a widower (his adult son Maurizio lived in France). As an amateur scholar of the religious communities of the Aegean, Strumza published a small pamphlet on the history of the Jews in Rhodes in 1936, and served the Jewish Community, acting as President of the Board of the Rabbinical College until its closure in 1938.[10]

According to Guido Grassini, the head of the *Carabinieri* and a prominent figure in the *federazioni dei fasci di Combattimento di Rodi*, Strumza, who after 1923 had acquired the lesser Aegean citizenship, was awarded full Italian citizenship in February 1934, 'For [his] proofs of devotion and loyalty to our Government.'[11] Without becoming a member of the *Partito Nazionale Fascista* (PNF), or any of its related organizations, Strumza loyally served the regime, as he had previously loyally served the Ottomans, remaining the consummate diplomat 'above politics'. Indeed, until the implementation of anti-Jewish policies, this culture of accommodation was a common trait of the cosmopolitan Jewish elite in Rhodes and Kos, with the Menascés, Sorianos, Alhadeffs, Franco, and Pacifici families being examples of this. However, Jewish fealty to Mussolini and Fascist Italy was typical not just of Aegean Jews, but broadly reflected the values of a well-situated class throughout Italy at that time.[12]

Of the three indigenous communities cohabiting on Rhodes and Kos, the Jews were seen as the most assimilated into the culture and politics of Fascist Italy. Indeed, many Jewish youth joined the ranks of Fascist youth organizations, although there were by the later 1930s reports of increasing tensions between gentile and Jewish members (as we shall see). Surviving family photographs from the period show young boys and girls proudly attired either in the uniforms of the Fascist youth organization *Opera Nazionale Balilla* (1926–37) or its successor *Gioventù Italiana del Littorio* (1937), or its female equivalent *Piccole Italiane* for girls aged 8–14 years old.[13] Little is known about Jewish membership of these organizations, although in theory school children were obliged to join. Similarly, little is known about the *Giovane Italiane* for teenage girls up to the age of 18 years, whereas on the eve of the passing of the Racial Laws, at least fifty-four Jewish teenage boys were members of the *Giovani Fascisti*, the Fascist youth wing of the PNF. Moreover, there is little information

on possible male Jews as members of the Rhodes and Kos branches of the PNF
or of adult women joining the *Fasci Femminili*.[14]

Diamente (Hugno) Franco recalled how two of her four brothers belonged
to the *Giovani Fascisti* while at school. According to Diamente, they joined
because of peer pressure, although by the 1930s membership in a Fascist
youth organization had become compulsory for students.[15] However, many
male youths joined out of conviction and excitement. Boys in their mid-to-
late teens, like Giacomo Franco, the son of Hizkia Franco (at that point, still
president of the Community), eagerly joined the Fascist youth organizations
and attended Saturday classes on fascism.[16] So too did the two teenage friends
Giacomo Alhadeff and Nissim Hugno in June 1936. The young friends lived
in the same street in the *Juderia*, Via Ammiraglio Bonaldi. Nissim's father,
Giuseppe, was a butcher, and appears to have owned two properties at numbers
37–39 (the family lived at Nr 37, and presumably next door, Nr 39, was his
shop). Nissim worked at the shoe manufacturer, *Timaleo*. Giacomo worked
as a shop assistant and lived with his widowed mother, Rosa née Franco
and his two siblings, Sadoc and Ricca. They received glowing reports from
Grassini and thus joined the fascist ranks.[17] Sami Modiano's older cousins,
19-year-old Samuel, an engineering student, and 22-year-old Saul were also
eager members. Italian propaganda extolling the virtues of fascism seems to
have been particularly effective among youth, as Alberto Israel told Marcello
Pezzetti: 'My brother was an *avanguardista*. The other one was in the Fascist
Youth. We were all Fascists.'[18]

For youngsters such as Alberto there was also the thrill of simply *belonging*
to a group and demonstrating one's youthful enthusiasm for Mussolini and
imperialist Italy in equal measure. There was little extraordinary about
this positioning of Jews vis-à-vis Fascist Italy. As Alica Tarica-Israël with
hindsight recalled: 'In the context of the times, such a commitment was
not at all surprising: the population was fully committed to Mussolini's
cause and showed great patriotism towards him.'[19] And not only boys found
'belonging' exciting. As Diamante's sister, Rachele later recalled: 'we all
belonged … it was fun.'[20]

Among many families of the *Juderia*, enduring loyalty to Italy was
paramount. Alberto Israel recalled how loyalty to the regime was inculcated
at an early age. As is well known among child-psychologists, children's views

frequently imitate those of their family environment. When the call came from Rome to donate precious metals to raise finance for the Italian expedition in Ethiopia, Alberto Israel's parents, as loyal citizens, duly handed over their precious gold wedding rings. Nevertheless, politics also strained relationships among friends, as Stella Levi recalled when mentioning how one of her brothers failed to demonstrate to his peers a similar enthusiasm for Italian Fascism.[21] As we shall see, relations between Jews and gentiles became increasingly fraught as anti-Jewish attitudes surfaced in some quarters of the population by the end of the decade.

Viewed retrospectively, 1936 appears as a turning point in relations between Italian colonizers and Jews. According to Hizkia Franco in his post-war chronicle of the community's destruction, the 'origin and cause of all our woes' began with Mussolini's pact with Hitler and with the arrival at that point of Cesare Maria De Vecchi Count di Val Cismon as governor of the Dodecanese.[22] Whereas Lago had cultivated communal consensus and close relations with the leading Jews of the community in particular, De Vecchi, described by one historian as the 'Nero of the Dodecanese', exhibited a harsher outlook as far as the local communities of the Dodecanese were concerned.[23] Certainly conditions worsened for Jews with De Vecchi's arrival. However, Vecchi's hostile policies were not targeted solely at Jews and might be better understood as an intensification of the Italianization of the Dodecanese, inaugurated under Lago. Thus De Vecchi encouraged inward migration of poor peasants from Sicily to settle the newly established farming colonies of San Benedetto (present-day Kolimbia) in 1935–36, San Marco (present-day Agios Pavlos, near Kattavia) in 1936, and oversaw the completion of Campochiaro (the site also of a military base) by 1939.[24] Initially, those most affected by this form of Italianization were in fact rural Greeks. Nor was the Turkish community exempted from De Vecchi's plan to Italianize the islands.

There is little evidence to indicate a sudden change in policy directed exclusively at the Jews after De Vecchi's arrival in December. However, this would soon change.[25] In March 1938, the Cairo-based journal *Israel* reported that the governor had ordered the curtailing of lessons in Hebrew and that a number of Zionist teachers had been dismissed from the Jewish school, adding that Jewish businesses had been ordered to remain open on *Shabbat* and instead to close on Sunday, the Christian day of rest.[26] The dismissal of

Zionists from schools would not have gone amiss with Hizkia Franco, who saw these teachers as a thorn in the side of the community leadership. But the stricture curtailing instruction, religious or otherwise, in languages other than Italian while not aimed exclusively at Jews, nonetheless struck at the heart of Judaism. Lessons in Turkish and Greek suffered a similar fate. Nevertheless, there was a particular quality to the policies that sought to 'de-Jewify' the culture and traditions of the Jewish community. Perhaps more importantly, De Vecchi's virulent antisemitism provided a signal to those lower down the administrative hierarchy and in some quarters of the population to translate their own Jew-hatred into action, as we shall see.

The process of Italianization begun by Lago was intensified under De Vecchi, rekindling the smouldering resentment towards the Italian administration and towards those considered either its collaborators or its beneficiaries. Even after the passing of the Racial Laws, among Greeks, Jews were widely held to be beneficiaries. British sources noted 'it could be said, that the Jews were, of all the people of the Dodecanese, the best disposed towards the Italian regime'.[27] The Jewish community in Rhodes had fared well under Ottoman rule too, its leaders occupying positions of influence. The Jewish Community Council's good relations with Lago are well known. After Lago's departure, every effort was made by the Jewish leaders in Rhodes to conciliate De Vecchi – even holding a special memorial service in the Sinagoga Grande when the governor's mother died in December 1936.[28] On the eve of the announcement of the Racial Laws, in response to their ongoing acquiescence, De Vecchi signalled his contentment with the leaders of the Jewish community.[29] Even after the announcement in September of anti-Jewish measures (see below) targeting Jews who had arrived after 1919, the president of the community John Menascé sought conciliatory relations to De Vecchi, possibly in the hope that measures might be softened for those Jews with Aegean or full Italian citizenship.[30]

The result of such demonstrations of loyalty was that Jews were perceived in some quarters to be both a manipulator and beneficiary of Greeks' oppression. In spite of normally cordial inter-confessional relations, in periods of tension attitudes towards Jews gave way to antipathy as Greeks came to see themselves as victims of Italian aggression, especially after 28 October 1940 (the start of the Italo-Greek war).[31] Barely five months earlier, when Italy declared war against

Britain in June 1940, the Union of Italian Jewish Communities in Rome had issued a pledge of loyalty to the regime, which was enthusiastically endorsed by Giacobbe Franco, the vice-president of the Community in Rhodes.[32]

The deep intertwining of many Jews into the very fabric of Mussolini's Fascist project left them psychologically unprepared for the discriminatory measures introduced on the eve of Yom Kippur in early October 1938. As Rachel Hanan recalled, the community 'did not expect this treatment'.[33] In his memoir, the scholar of Sephardi customs Isaac Jack Lévy recalls the impact on his family when a month earlier the decree 'for the defence of the Italian race in schools' was announced in Rhodes on Friday 9 September (the law was passed on Monday 5 September): 'Having returned from the synagogue, all the members of the family were ready for the Sabbath meal. Suddenly the news dealing with the racial laws which appeared on the front page of the local paper spread throughout the Juderia [...]. As children, we could not grasp the agony of the moment.'[34] The local gazette, *Il Messaggero di Rodi*, published its own highly inflammatory comment declaiming 'to hell with all the Jews!' ('All 'inferno tutti gli Ebrei').[35] The school ban was followed in November by the promulgation of the Italian Racial Laws, which codified a panoply of anti-Jewish measures.[36] Henceforth, conditions for Jews would radically alter for the worse.

The Racial Laws for the Defence of the Italian Race (*le legge razziali per la difesa della razza italiana*) mirrored the German Nuremberg Racial Laws in a number of its clauses.[37] There were sweeping restrictions imposed on the Jewish community. For example, ritual slaughter (*shechitah*) was forbidden; and religious courts were abolished.[38] As in Germany, the laws excluded Jews from owning property, and forbade them from retaining Christian servants. Nissim Benatar, the father of the medical student Alexander, together with Nissim Capuia, Giuseppe Mallel and Yakir (Giacomo) Menascé, fell afoul of the new restriction and had to let go the Orthodox Christian women employed in their households.[39] Alice Tarica, a young girl at the time, remembered how in her house the Greek domestics and chauffeur had to be let go from their employment. Nevertheless, she noted too, that the family soon found Jewish replacements to work in the house.[40] Meanwhile, Jewish doctors in private practice, such as Dr David Gaon, as well as Jewish lawyers, were forbidden from taking on gentile clients. Jewish wholesale merchants, among them

Giacobbe Jerusalmi and Giuseppe Algranti, who held lucrative contracts with the Italian administration, now lost these. The laws excluded Jews from public service, affecting among others, Dr Haim Misrachi, a consultant at the public hospital, who, like Dr Gaon and his family, would be among those murdered in Auschwitz in August 1944.

The laws even engulfed Vitalis Strumza, who only a few years earlier had been praised for his 'fidelity to Italy and dedication to his work'.[41] Strumza's Italian citizenship was revoked, he was forced to relinquish his title of 'Cavalier', and he was removed from his post. On 26 November, he returned his Identity Card, stoically 'without suffering pain and bitterness'.[42] Stripped of his Italian citizenship, and denied restitution of Aegean citizenship and thus reduced to statelessness, Strumza left the islands in 1939. We last hear from him when he wrote to Bension Menascé from the Algerian town Oran in May 1939; it is possible that he eventually left for France to join his son.[43]

Notably those Jews who had hitherto enjoyed all the trappings of full citizenship now found themselves transformed into *quasi* outcasts. Alice Tarica, who was just 7 years old at the time the laws were passed, carried the memory of this over many decades, remembering how the laws diminished her father's standing in society. 'We never imagined the kind of things that would happen', she recalled.

> First, they seized my father's job. This was a huge blow. It wasn't that we didn't have enough money to get along … it was more a question of human dignity for my father. Next, we had to stop visiting with our social circle at the weekends. The parties, and all of that, came to an end for us. They took away our servants, and then finally they took away our schooling. Those were the four things that I really remember.[44]

She remembered in particular how her parents' social ties were not immediately ruptured, for friends 'came, but it wasn't like it was before. It was as if there was a barrier between them and us. We felt diminished in some way. My father, who had been such a social person, closed himself off […] he had a sadness about him … I think he realised what the life of a Jew had actually become.'[45] Those Jews who at one time had been at the centre of Rhodes' gilded society, now found themselves pushed to its margins and eventually completely isolated.

Finally, in December 1938, squares and streets with names or references relating to the Jewish community received new designations, memorializing Italian Fascist 'heroes'. Thus, Piazza Alhadeff became Piazza Amos Marmotti; Via della Sinagoga became Via Ugo Pepe della Paci; Via Giuseppe Notrica became Via Giovanni Beta and Via Sinagoga Grande briefly became Via Antonio Locatelli (before being renamed Dei Savi).[46] The fondly remembered 'Calle Ancha' ('wide street') in the Ladino vernacular that formed the 'spine' of the *Juderia* received its official designation as Via Francesco Flotta. Not only were traces of Jewish culture effaced: *Turcheria*, the road that bisected the eastern part of the old city referencing its Turkish legacy, and which acted as the northern boundary of the Jewish quarter, changed to Via Sigismondo Malatesta. Meanwhile a number of smaller streets in the Turkish quarter received names celebrating Italy's colonial conquests in North Africa. A further step in this prelude to destruction came in the winter and early spring of 1939 with the registration of Jews as a separate category of population in the Racial Census.

After the passing of the Racial Laws, those who had large assets or bank holdings moved these, or attempted to move these, to other jurisdictions. Yehuda Tarica began smuggling funds to his sister-in-law in Egypt and to a brother in Paris.[47] The banker Isaac Alhadeff had extensive commercial interests in Turkey, Greece, Italy, the Belgian Congo, South Africa, and in the Egyptian port of Alexandria where the family also had a residence.[48] In 1938, his cousins transferred their Milan and Greek mainland businesses to Buenos Aires in Argentina. As with many well-connected Jews on the island, his son Jack was able to recover most of the family wealth after the war.[49] Others transferred their commercial businesses to trusted friends in order to circumvent the clause in the Racial Laws forbidding Jews ownership or directorships of large commercial enterprises.[50] Following the passing of the laws, and over the course of 1939, some of Rhodes' leading Jewish business-owners were alleged to have clandestinely moved more than I£30 million of financial assets abroad, using the French Consul as a go-between. Not just the wealthy engaged in protecting their interests. The Guardia di Finanza (Customs and Excise) kept a close watch on all inhabitants of the Dodecanese, in particular on Jews, pouncing on anyone they suspected of currency violations, or of evading duty on imports, or of smuggling contraband.[51]

The tentacles of antisemitism reached out to every part of the Jewish community: no one was spared. As we saw above, persecutory measures included the expulsion of Jewish children from Italian public schools. In those families where education might be expected to last into young adulthood, exclusion from school was a heavy blow to both ambition and dignity. Sami Modiano, the son of Giacobbe Modiano, was just 8 years old in 1938 when he had to leave school. Until the war years his father had been a respected manager at the Alhadeff department store, and the family lived in a fine villa in Santo Stefano in the Neocorio. His older male cousins (Grazia's children) had been able to complete their secondary education with diplomas. Expulsion from school was for Sami the first experience of persecution that would remain indelibly printed in his mind. As he told the historian Marcello Pezzetti,

> When I was in third grade of elementary school, one morning the teacher called me to the front of the class. I thought he wanted to ask me questions. I was well prepared that day and I was glad to be called on, but when I got to his desk he seemed a bit uneasy, and he said to me under his breath: 'Sami Modiano, you have been expelled from school.' At that moment, I thought I had done something … wrong because the worst punishment was expulsion. Sadly, he reassured me: 'No, no, calm down, Sami.' He put his hand on my head, 'You didn't do anything wrong. Do not cry. Go home and your father will explain why you were expelled.' Crying I asked my father why I had been expelled. My poor father tried to explain. He spoke of racial laws that I didn't understand. I was only eight years old.

Sami reflected on this episode in his life with its lasting impact. 'I have to accept the fact that I am uncultured; I never got an education. It deeply troubles me to say that I was deprived of my education. So, what is this? Is this not pain?'[52]

As with Sami, Stella Levi at the age of 16 experienced the stigma that came with being denied education. 'The Racial Laws and our expulsion from school', she recalled to Pezzetti, 'were for me a humiliation and an insult from which I never recovered.'[53] Similarly, Rosa Israel's family was typical of the *Juderia*'s middling class. Her strictly orthodox father was a shoe manufacturer whose business premises were in the heart of the *Juderia*, and who supplied the islands with his products. Rosa's mother, described in official documents as a homemaker, also worked occasionally as a dressmaker. Rosa's great uncle had been the Grand Rabbi of Rhodes until his death in 1932, and the family was well-read. Rosa had wanted to continue her education beyond school, she was conversant in Italian literature and French, and had studied Hebrew. But for Rosa, the Racial Laws ushered in a 'dark time' when she found herself excluded from school at 15 years old and instead went to work as a trainee typist with the brokerage company, *Compania Commerciale Italiana*.[54]

The Racial Laws ended educational opportunities for most children, whether privileged or not. Nevertheless, for some of the Rhodes Jews there were still ways to get around this measure. During the early war years, Lina Amato was still a very small child (she was born in 1936) whose well-off family could afford to pay for a private tutor when she reached school-age. Her tutor was Miss Capelluto, who had in fact been a teacher at the Italian elementary school until her dismissal in 1938. She organized a curriculum mirroring that of the Italian school for Lina, her cousin Izzie Alhadeff (the son of the banker), and two other boys, Maurizio and Roberto. The four children wore uniforms, learned their lessons as if in a regular class, took music lessons and acted in plays. Miss Capelluto even organized an 'end-of-year' concert with the children performing for their families in the garden of Giacobbe Alhadeff's palatial house in Via Foro Italico. Lina later told how she would have liked to have followed in her mother's footsteps and become a concert pianist. However, after the exclusion of Jews from school and the interjection of persecution and war, her dream was never realized. She and her family escaped the deportation in 1944, unlike her tutor and Roberto and Maurizio. As we shall see later in this study, the family would return to Rhodes after the war had ended. Despite this relatively good fortune, Lina recalled 'my happy years were short'.[55]

The Racial Laws thwarted the ambitions of many youngsters for it banished them not only from Italian schools but also from universities, unless already enrolled. As a young girl, Rachel Hanan had hoped to study medicine, but the Racial Laws denied her the opportunity to attend university let alone complete her secondary schooling. Instead, she had to take up employment as a clerk in an office of the Italian administration.[56] For Miru Alcana from a working family, the law meant she had to abandon her training to become a midwife, and instead found work in a local perfume shop.[57] Traditionally for older children from less privileged backgrounds, the alternative to school was work, and for many, emigration.

The issues we have been discussing relate to persecutory measures arising from the Racial Laws. Before the later 1930s, the *Carabinieri* archives appear to be largely silent as far as recorded incidents of overt anti-Jewish behaviour among the population. There were occasions when religious insensitivity (if not hostility) towards Jews was displayed by those in a position of authority, such as the Mother Superior of the hospital who forbade Jewish rites when a patient died. And there were indeed antisemites who were keen to express their antipathy towards Jews – such as the sports reporter of *Il Messaggero di Rodi* we encountered in the previous chapter. While these examples from the early 1930s appear to have been the exception, there was nevertheless a popular racist tide already on the rise with De Vecchi's arrival at the end of 1936. The new governor's blatant antisemitism provided a green light to others who shared his prejudices against Jews. While concrete evidence to show how widespread this was is sparse, a number of individual episodes of anti-Jewish behaviour cast some light onto popular attitudes in some quarters of Rhodes society.

In February 1937, a complaint was lodged with the Schools Superintendent Professor Giulianini by the president of the Jewish Community John Menascé against 34-year-old Grazia Di Pierro, originally from Bari, and a teacher at the Jewish elementary school.[58] Di Pierro was notorious for being tardy when it came to being ready for the school bus that picked up the children and her in the morning. On 12 February, Di Pierro 'as usual' kept the children and the bus driver waiting. On this occasion, one of the pupils, 12-year-old Bension Menascé, muttered aloud: 'now we are late for school because of this damned woman', without having noticed that Di Pierro meanwhile had boarded the bus and had overheard his comment.[59] Bension's comment had been triggered by the thought of receiving punishment for their late arrival. Even though the repeated delays were not the fault of the children, the headmaster of the school, Scialom Gattegno had previously vented his anger at his pupils, threatening them with punishment the next time this occurred. Having arrived at school, Di Pierro demanded Gattegno punish the boy for his insolence but quickly found herself under the spotlight for her 'curse on the Jews'. According to Menascé's fellow pupils, including Maurizio and Alice Tarica, when questioned later, Di Pierro had responded: 'you are cursed because you have been cursed by God and for this you are without a country and you will always be beneath the Christians.'[60]

When questioned, Di Pierro did not deny she had said this, but she denied her comment was anti-Jewish. Instead, she claimed it was intended only for the boy and his family and not levelled at Jews per se. Nevertheless, against a background of growing antisemitism, Jewish sensibility to such abusive language was raw. John Menascé (no relation to the boy), who reportedly was not given to dramatizing small matters, felt compelled to take the matter further because of the racist overtones of her insult. Giulianini in turn passed the complaint to the *Carabinieri*. Guido Grassini, despite his own predilection for fascism, sought to de-escalate the conflict between an Italian Catholic and the Jewish community. In his report to the *Governatore*, Grassini depicted Di Pierro as 'a woman of good political conduct, but who morally seems to leave much to be desired since her frivolous conduct has been the subject of many comments in the past'. In this case, there was little doubt as to the substance of the accusation against her 'since Di Pierro is known as a woman with a long and coarse tongue, and it is more than likely that what the boys said is true'. Grassini recommended a rebuke and no further action. 'I think a word to the teacher Di Pierro could heal the incident without any further fuss.'[61]

Di Pierro had strenuously denied the charge of antisemitism. Nonetheless, her choice of words clearly indicate her hostility towards Jews. The incident reveals some ambivalence on the part of the authorities suggesting the drift to De Vecchi's antisemitic stance was not universal, nor would it become universal. At the same time, while this incident exposes a vein of anti-Jewish attitudes running through parts of the local Italian population, it also reveals a willingness among Jews to challenge and seek redress for incidents of antisemitism. The complaint against Di Pierro was not the only one to surface in 1937.

Relations between Jewish and gentile members of Fascist organizations were deteriorating before the announcement of the Racial Laws. Only a few records of this worsening are extant, but they are, nonetheless, instructive. On 25 July 1937, a group of thirty-one young Jewish Fascists (members of the local branch of the *Fasci Giovanili di Combattimento Federale dell'Egeo*) who had been on a traffic training exercise, found themselves close to a water

fountain.[62] At this time of the year, temperatures in Rhodes can soar to 90°
Fahrenheit or 32° Celsius and the humidity can reach the mid-80s. The youths
were sweating and clearly thirsty. However, their squad leader Dr Elvio Spano
stopped them from drinking the cold water, ostensibly 'in the interests of their
health'. In response, several of them led by Giacomo Franco, the 18-year-old
son of Hizkia Franco, and Raimondo Hasson, whose father owned a clothing
store, disobeyed Spano, and refused to move from the fountain, whereupon
Spano called the youths to attention in order to address them. According to a
note given to the *Carabinieri*:

> Dr Spano intervened, summoning the Fascist youths (including the officers)
> and gave them a lecture, saying, among other things, the following words:
> 'a young man who commits such a fault [of defiance or weakness] must be
> considered a hydrophobe (Idrofobo, *sic*) and must be treated as the British
> once treated the Arabs and people of inferior races, namely with the whip.'[63]

Whether this public chastisement had the desired effect upon the young men,
is unlikely, for the thirty-one Jewish Giovani Fascisti sent a complaint against
Spano to the regional command. What made matters worse for the troop is
that Spano allegedly exclaimed in response to Hasson's and Franco's refusal to
leave the fountain, 'Of course, only the Jews!'. In their complaint, the youths
claimed that Spano had intended them with his reference to 'inferior races'.

However, the complaint against the squad leader backfired. The youths
were accused of having 'a bad record' and thus capable of making a baseless
accusation against Spano. Their Christian compatriots in the *Fasci Giovanili
di Combattimento* who had witnessed the episode and who on earlier
occasions had brushed up badly against Spano, on this occasion vouched for
the squad leader's version of the incident. Spano came from a local family
of zealous Fascists who were not averse to waging campaigns of attrition
against those they despised.[64] A specially convened disciplinary committee
found the signatories of the complaint guilty of making a false accusation
and thus slandering Spano's name and reputation. It proceeded to expel six
of their number with immediate effect.[65] A further eleven were informed that
their membership would not be renewed in the New Year; while fourteen
were re-admitted by the Brigade commander Chiorandi on 21 October with a
formal reprimand. By the end of the year, 37 of 54 Jewish youths remained as

members of the *Giovani Fascisti*, and within a year of this incident, because of the Racial Laws, all were expelled.

Increasingly, Jews found it difficult to either defend themselves or seek redress against antisemitic slurs, especially where the offender was a member of a Fascist organization. Ezra Hanan, the father of Sara whom we cited at the beginning of this chapter, found this out to his cost. Despite increasingly difficult trade conditions in the 1930s, Ezra continued to ply his trade of sweets (*caramelle*), sweet foods (*dolcoumi*) and ice cream (*gelati*).[66] In June 1938, Hanan was again selling ice cream outside Gate 3 of l'Arena del Sol in San Giovanni (today, Diagoras football stadium) when he became involved in a verbal altercation that would cost him his licence. An 18-year-old Greek and member of the *Giovani Fascisti*, Nicola P., was checking tickets at the gate at six o'clock that evening when he approached a Turkish vendor for an ice cream. The vendor referred the sale to Hanan who prepared the ice cream for P., but the teenager refused to accept it because it had been 'prepared by a Jew'. P. had uttered these words in Italian, in response to which an offended Hanan told the youth to 'speak his father's tongue' – i.e. Greek, and not Italian. This comment landed Hanan in trouble with the authorities. Initially this was because only Italian was to be spoken in public, and by telling the youth to speak in Greek, he was undermining the policy of Italianization, according to the *Carabinieri*. Matters worsened in the course of exchanges with Mittino's office, and eventually Hanan was forced to sell his licence to another man, Filipo C. An attempt to emigrate to the Congo in June 1939 was thwarted (we do not know why), and, like his brother Avner, Ezra became a street shoe shiner (*lustracarpe*).[67]

Italian Fascists occupied positions within the administration and the police authorities that gave them a degree of power over Jews. The Italian historian Marco Clementi has estimated that after the capitulation of Italy in September 1943, and the subsequent purge of the Italian forces and administration of pro-Badoglio sympathizers, 500 members of the PNF remained in the administration and in the various offices of the *Carabinieri*, including its chief, Giudo Grassini, and the head of the Office for Public Security, Ferdinando Mittino.[68] With the passing of the Racial Laws, Jews found themselves at the mercy of anti-Jewish attitudes within the licensing department of the *Carabinieri*. In many cases, Jewish traders suffered a loss of income when their trading licences were either withdrawn or not renewed.

The administrative process of renewing annual trade licences became a weapon of discrimination against Jews, often with flimsy misdemeanours cited as grounds for rejection. In 1939, for example, Mittino looked into Giuseppe Alcana's background, when the latter's trade licence was due for renewal.[69] Giuseppe was a shoemaker and the older brother of Miru Alcana and had come to the attention of the judicial authorities investigating a case of petty theft. However, there was no tangible evidence and the charge against Giuseppe was dropped. In 1938, Alcana was in an altercation (see below), and in late 1939 he was stopped for riding his bicycle without lights.[70] The Alcanas were a large clan comprising three families and intertwined with a number of other well-known extended families of the *Juderia*, in particular the Hassons. The two paterfamilias Abramo (b. 1869) and Celebi were brothers and had a younger sister, Regine (b. 1894), a widow. They, like their spouses and children, were born in Rhodes, but of Turkish descent. Celebi Alcana (b. 1874) was a trader who owned a buoyant poultry and milk stall at the New Market (Nuovo Mercado). The family's home in the Jewish quarter was valued at I£15,000 and Alcana was described as being of good economic and social standing. Like many traders, he had a supply network that extended to Anatolia, from where his family originated. He also worked together with a Turkish trader from Trianda. The pair came under the spotlight in November 1934, accused of adulterating milk, and jointly received a fine of I£300, of which each paid half. On a previous occasion, Celebi was ordered to destroy two rancid milk vats by the public hygiene inspector. Four years later, in 1938, he was among a group of six traders fined for undercutting the regulatory price of eggs.[71]

The day-to-day conditions arising from persecution, and later from war, drove many traders to engage in activities in a grey zone between legality and illegality. Such activities might range from simply trading outside licensed hours to more serious transgressions. These were petty infractions and hardly amounted to a dangerous profile. Nevertheless, these minor transgressions were taken into account when considering applications for renewal of licences, in which the *Carabinieri* played a central part. It is not unreasonable to think Mittino was using any possible excuse to deprive Jews of their livelihoods, as we can see in the following case.

Samuele Angel, the perambulatory sweet-maker (*venditare ambulante di dolciumi*) we met in Chapter 2, lost his licence in early 1939, apparently after being caught buying hens on the black market.[72] The loss of the licence plunged him and his already impoverished family into utter destitution. The family's material condition was described by the licensing office as 'poor' (*misere*), with their home valued at a mere I£4,000. Angel pleaded in vain with Mittino for the restoration of his licence in order to maintain his family and five children. At the end of April, he appealed to the municipal authorities:

> From the day that my trading license was withdrawn, I felt the need to labour at any other work despite my already advanced years as long as I must provide bread for my five children, still at a tender age. However, my destiny falls on deaf ears, for I could only do my old job, carried on for more than 40 years. The need of my family, composed as mentioned above of five creatures, did not manifest itself until now, and it is precisely this reason that compels me to make this appeal, praying that I get back my license which is the most precious object to be eternally thankful for. With perfect observance. [signed: Samuele Angel].[73]

As a deaf man, Angel had little prospect of obtaining other employment. In desperation, he also wrote to his older son by his first marriage, who had emigrated to the Congo, for money. Fortunately for Samuele and his family, the municipal authorities eventually restored his licence after payment of the permit fee of I£6.[74]

Where a misdemeanour could not be found to deprive Jews of their licences, other grounds were found. Baruch [Bohor] Avzaradel, who we encountered briefly in Chapter 2, was one of fourteen butchers who by the beginning of the war traded at the Nuovo Mercado.[75] He had been born in Kos on 25 December 1875 and lived with his wife and four of his six children in their own house in Via Dei Savi. He originally traded various goods, but in 1934, he took over the meat stall from Hafiz Omer in lieu of an unpaid property debt.[76] As with all food traders, Avzaradel was subject to the strict hygiene inspections that occurred from time to time, and which he appeared to satisfy. His business appears to have thrived, for they lived comfortably, according to *Carabinieri* reports. The war was to have an impact on his fortunes. As part of an effort to maintain an orderly distribution of food, the authorities introduced rationing of meat and fish. A maximum of 4,800 kg of meat was all that could be traded at the Nuovo Mercado. As a result, the number of butchers in the market was too high, and consequently they were halved to seven. Among those who lost their market permit was Avzaradel. However, the loss of the permit cannot be ascribed to antisemitism, for his fellow butcher Giuseppe Cugno was permitted to continue trading. Nonetheless, the subsequent treatment of Avzaradel suggests at best some ambivalence towards Jews, and, at worst, downright hostility, on the part of the administration.

Avzaradel appealed the decision, stating he had a family to support and no other means by which he could do this. Two other butchers, a father and son, neighboured his stall at the market. In his letter, Avzaradel stated that the older man did not have a family, while the son had a wife and child. They also had income from property on Kalymnos, their home island. Avzaradel saw nothing wrong with depriving the two men of their business in order to retain his own. The matter was referred to Mittino's office. It transpired the son had been fined several times for petty misdemeanours dating back to the early 1930s (so he too subsequently lost his permit). Concluding his report, Mittino stated there were no grounds for restoring Avzaradel's market licence, but in compensation, he would be allowed to open a local butcher's stall (*rionale macellaria*) in the Jewish quarter. The process dragged on until January 1942, when further appeals were rejected in finality by Vice-Governor Farelli's office and the file closed. By this stage, the fact that Avzaradel was of 'Jewish race' had become a factor in the decision.[77]

Sometimes, no grounds were furnished for denying a trade permit. In 1939, Sadih[k] Amato's licence was not renewed by Mittino without explanation. In the same year, Mittino's office deprived eleven Jewish tourist guides of their licences, transferring these instead to so-called 'Aryans'.[78] Among the guides who lost their licences was 36-year-old Leone Israel, who lived with his parents and two younger sisters in the Piazza Principe. His father, Giuseppe, was a street sweet-seller, while his mother kept house. The family was poor; therefore, Leone's income was vital for the family's survival in difficult economic times. The insult of such discrimination must have cut deep for those who closely identified with the Italian state. Twenty-year-old Moise S. was a student who also worked as a guide and who lived with his parents in Via Dei Savi. Moise was the youngest of three children to 'old' parents (his father was 70 years old and his mother 60 years old, and neither worked).[79] Two years before, he had applied to join the Aegean branch of Mussolini's *federazione dei fasci di combattimento*, and now he was the target of an organization some of whose members had lately converted to antisemitism. The loss of their permits drove Leone and Moise to join many of the community's young men who emigrated in order to find work abroad. This was the only way that a family might stay afloat in difficult times because loved ones could be expected to send remittances back to Rhodes.[80]

Money and its lack moved to the forefront of daily struggles for many families in the *Juderia* during the war years, depriving many youngsters of a carefree youth because of grinding poverty. Nine-year-old Claire Barkey's (Clara Barkai) letters to her uncle in the United States bear witness to the distress of impoverishment and hunger upon the young. Not every youth had a wealthy uncle to help them. Understandably, to escape this condition, some of them resorted to behaviour which took them outside the law.[81] In 1940, 14-year-old A. was accused by his employer, Giuseppe C., of theft. According to C., I£893 had gone missing from a drawer in his shop's office over a period of two months and he accused A. of being the thief.[82] C. had casually employed A. over a period of eight years and thus had trusted him with keys to the office when he was absent. No one else had access to the office. In order to test his suspicion of A., the shopkeeper set a trap by leaving overnight I£120 in the office drawer. The following morning, the money was gone. Confronted by his employer, A. allegedly admitted the theft, stating that he had spent the money on 'billiards and for the purchase of foodstuffs (raisins, ice-creams, pasta, oranges, etc …)'.

An investigation followed, in the course of which we learn a lot about the teenager. He was described as of generally good character and well-behaved at home, but also, according to the *Carabinieri* officer who interviewed the family, A. was an impulsive boy 'with a tendency to commit property crime'. However, *Carabinieri* lieutenant Giuseppe Spano pointed out that A. was 'an intelligent and shrewd youth, of good background' and thus capable of understanding the difference between right and wrong.[83] This assessment implied he was criminally culpable. Eventually, after the reports were completed, the boy faced the magistrate in June 1942. There was little in the way of solid evidence, it was just C.'s word against that of the boy, and A. now disputed he had taken the money. The court discharged him because of lack of evidence of intent to steal or that he properly understood the implications of what he was alleged to have done.[84] Despite his discharge, the *Carabinieri* added the boy's name to the 'convicted and socially dangerous persons' ('*persone pregiudicate e socialmente pericoloso*') register.[85]

As we also saw in Chapter 2, brushes with the law existed in the Jewish community, as they did among other groups. But following the Racial Laws, targeting Jews created a climate of fear and uncertainty, which was probably the intention. For only thus would Jews be 'encouraged' to leave the Aegean.

*

Apart from the period of population exchanges following the Greco-Turkish War 1921/22, when the Aegean islands briefly became an inward migratory destination, the archipelago traditionally 'exported' its populations to other parts of the world where economic opportunity beckoned. Thus, Greeks and Jews as immigrant labour and traders formed diasporic communities across the globe. The intensification of Italianization coupled with poor economic opportunity encouraged the exodus of Greeks, whereas a decree of 1 September 1938 ordering the expulsion of non-Dodecanesian Jews (including those who had acquired either Italian or Aegean citizenship after 1919) and codified two months later in the Racial Laws, plunged the future of the Jewish community into doubt.[86] Already from September until the end of the year, there were between 104 and 161 permanent departures of Aegean and foreign national Jews, among them the former teacher of the Talmud at the Rabbinical College, Marcus Berger and his wife and daughter, who left for France. By March 1939, when the census of Jews had been completed, their number had reduced after nearly a decade of decline to around 1,902 in 525 households.[87]

Traditionally, the Jews of Rhodes and Kos migrated to the Belgian Congo and Rhodesia where members of their community had established businesses in the early years of the century. They also immigrated to the Americas, where they had existing networks. Some sought out Turkey or Palestine, and occasionally the Jewish enclaves of the African-Mediterranean coast.[88] There had been intermittent migration throughout the three decades prior to the announcement of the Racial Laws, and this was not unusual. But the worsening conditions for Jews in an increasingly difficult economic context triggered an upswing in applications for exit visas that also coincided with the laws. Between 1 September and 21 November 1938, the authorities in Rhodes issued 104 passports to Jews who had acquired Italian citizenship after 1919, many of them seeking their fortunes in the Belgian Congo and in Rhodesia.[89] The implementation of the Racial Laws accelerated the rate of departures and affected larger numbers.

The Racial Laws created three categories of Jewish 'outsider' whose residency on the island was made precarious: i) those of Turkish origin without documents; ii) those of Turkish origin with Aegean documents; and iii) foreigners (*stranieri*).[90] Article 24 of the Racial Laws stipulated that those persons who had arrived to the Dodecanese after 1919, and who were not Italian citizens but held Aegean citizenship, had now to return immediately to their place of origin. For many Jews on Rhodes this meant Turkey, but very often this route too, was barred to them. For example, Salomon Varon had been born in Turkey and arrived in Rhodes in 1919, where he met Regine Coen. When they married in 1924, he gave up his Turkish citizenship and became an Aegean citizen instead. With the passing of the Racial Laws, Varon was also deprived of his Aegean citizenship and thus became stateless and subject to the expulsion order.[91] His case would have been repeated cross the community. Ezra Hanan's wife, for example, had been born in Smyrna. It is not known when she came to Rhodes, but possibly following the population exchanges after 1923.[92] The pair married in October 1926, when she was 19 and he 24 years old. We also don't know if upon marriage she lost her Turkish nationality or if she became an Aegean citizen. Either way, she would have been affected by the expulsion order. Thus, in 1939, Ezra applied for a passport that would take them to the Belgian Congo via Italy, Tangiers and Palestine.[93] Others, who had acquired Italian citizenship, also faced the loss of rights, as we saw with Vitalis Strumza.

Jews originally from Anatolia were reduced to statelessness, since they were no longer in possession of Turkish documents having relinquished these on settling in Rhodes. In addition to those Aegean families whose rights to citizenship were now revoked (or never acquired in the first place, estimated by Giacobbe Franco at between 300 and 700 persons), there were a further 500 or so foreign Jews, mostly central European refugees stranded on Rhodes since July 1939 after their steamer *Rim* caught fire. They too would have to leave the island. In all, at the very least 700 persons, and at most, up to a thousand, were affected by the decree.[94]

The decree expelling non-Italian Jews had set a six-month deadline with threats of punishment for non-compliance. After representations from the Jewish Community Council, a short extension of the 28 February deadline for leaving the Dodecanese was agreed by the *Governatore*.[95] Meanwhile, Giacobbe Franco, in his capacity as vice-president of the Community, fired off a number of letters, including to the Chief Rabbi of Paris, the DELASEM Zionist refugee organization in Milan, to the French Consul in Rhodes and to the US ambassador in Rome, pleading for assistance or, in the latter case, for safe passage to the United States.[96] In his correspondence with the leaders of the Sephardi-Rhodesli community in Salisbury (Rhodesia, now Zimbabwe), Franco broadly gave the occupations of the expellees, thus emphasizing their potential contribution to the well-being of the ex-pat community.[97]

Departures quickly followed the completion of the Racial Census in March. In mid-April 1939, 142 Jews affected by the laws left Rhodes together with 68 Jews of Turkish origin and 15 foreign Jews. Departures accelerated over the summer and autumn. In July, 222 Jews were expelled (among them 30 Hungarian Jews), or left voluntarily (the single largest group numbering 81 Rhodian Jews). Up to the early spring of 1939 between 200 and 250 mostly young male Jews in their teens and twenties left Rhodes, many of them for the Belgian Congo and Rhodesia, where they had relatives and contacts offering employment.[98] Of this number, 113 had Italian passports, 31 were Turkish nationals, and just under a dozen were foreign nationals. In September, a group of 66 persons applied for exit visas for Palestine, and in October, a further 155 Jews departed. A conservative estimate of the total number of Jews, who left in 1939 because of the Racial Laws, stands well in excess of a thousand.[99]

Among the older cohort (those born before 1900) was a sizeable number who came from Western Anatolia, predominantly from Antalya or from Smyrna (Izmir), and Halicarnassus (Bodrum), many from the latter two towns arriving in the wake of the Greco-Turkish war.[100] Thus Moses Benaderet, originally from Smyrna, together with his wife and daughter, was among those who left on the ship *Erzorum* on 25 January 1939.[101] Although sizeable in number, they were not the bulk of leavers. Many of those who left after the introduction of the Racial Laws were young and single and had been born on Rhodes. There were a handful of unaccompanied children under the age of 13 among the expellees – 10-year-old Maria Aranoff was probably the youngest. She departed also on the steamship *Erzorum* on 7 February bound for the port of Mersin in Southern Turkey where she had been born, and presumably, where she still had family.[102] In addition to those with exit visas, a small number of Rhodes' Jews left without obtaining the necessary permission (*immigrazione clandestine*) on the Greek-registered ship *Ayios Nikolaos*, provoking administrative enquiries as to their whereabouts in Haifa, once they had landed.[103]

Maria Aranoff's journey was straightforward. For many expellees travelling further afield, the journey was more convoluted, progressing in fits and starts. Typically, and depending on where they were aiming for, they would travel first to Bari or Brindisi in Southern Italy, or to Genoa in the north-west. From there their journey would take them to Marseilles in France, or Barcelona in Spain, after which they might undertake a crossing on a passenger steamer to the Moroccan port city of Tangier, from where they hoped to carry on. The next leg of the journey, if to the Belgian Congo or Rhodesia, would be by a combination of ship and train. There was no trans-Africa railroad system to take them easily and thus the journey might take many weeks and sometimes months before reaching a destination. Not all of the expellees completed their journeys, especially once the war in Europe commenced. The Varon family, for example, only got as far as Italy before being forced to return to Rhodes.[104]

Hundreds of Jews were in the same position as the Varon family. For many, the timing of the expulsions in 1939 was unfortunate, for once war broke out in Europe at the beginning of September, movement between countries became curtailed. Only a small number of those seeking to join relatives in the Belgian Congo or Rhodesia got there. Instead, well over 150 Jews from Rhodes and Kos became stranded in Tangier – before 1940 and the fall of France, still a joint French and Spanish protectorate under international administration since 1923/24 – and an important staging post for those travelling further.[105] Thus the implementation of the Italian Racial Laws in Rhodes and Kos provoked a refugee crisis in the Aegean and Mediterranean basin, albeit one overshadowed by the contemporaneous displacement of thousands of Jews taking place in Greater Germany and Central Europe.[106]

After the political climate for Jews grew increasingly hostile with the passing of the Racial Laws, Rebecca Amato Levy and her husband Moise Hasson, a shoemaker, left Rhodes in April 1939 with exit passports in the hope of joining his sister in Casablanca. Instead, they found themselves stranded in Tangier, where they joined between 700 and 800 European Jewish refugees fleeing persecution.[107] They quickly accommodated themselves to their new situation and even opened a shop making shoes, with Rebecca sewing the leather uppers aided by her husband's nephew. However, life was hard as a stateless refugee, especially after Moise died of pneumonia aged 44 years in 1944. Rebecca recalled the social tensions as the war years dragged on, the squabbling among the refugees and between refugees and the host community, and the enforced idleness.[108] Most of the refugees were without means, and life in Tangier was by no means cheap. It was estimated that a family of between two and four persons needed the equivalent of I£850–1400 a month to survive, depending on where one lived (whether in the Moroccan or European quarters).[109] There were tensions over scarce resources even before the impact of war took hold. Already in early August 1939, the Jewish Refugees Council in Tangier had written to the Council in Rhodes outlining the social, economic and political problems caused by the influx of Aegean Jews.[110]

Leaving Rhodes was a costly business that made the prospect difficult for many families. Currency restrictions prohibited many of those leaving the islands from taking their savings (if they had any) with them. Thus, many of the expellees were destitute by the time they arrived at their destinations.[111] Depending on where they were heading to, an adult could expect to pay £15 and a child £8, including berth and subsistence on board ship. This was a substantial sum of money for ordinary people, especially where large families were concerned, at a time when the official rate of exchange stood at roughly I£20 to the sterling's pound. For example, assuming their teenage children would have been charged the child rate, the Varons would have had to pay around I£1,400. Moreover, shipping companies preferred payment in sterling.[112] In the case of the *Rim* refugees and those Rhodes Jews who sought passage to Palestine, the Rhodes Refugee Committee overseeing arrangements for the expellees, sought a fixed group price of £2,200 from a Greek shipping company, thus reducing the burden on individuals to between £5 and £8, or I£98 and I£146.[113] In addition to the price of a ticket, there were the associated costs in Rhodes of obtaining the exit visas (passports). Finally, there was also a risk of being defrauded by unscrupulous brokers.[114]

The Refugee Committee of the Rhodes Jewish Community petitioned various organizations and donors to fund the expellees, notably the Rhodesli diaspora, who proved to be generous.[115] Individual families also reverted to relatives abroad who had in the meantime established successful businesses to both sponsor them and furnish the capital needed to pay for the journey into exile. Thus, Isaac Jack Lévy's maternal uncle, David Mussafir, who had settled in Montgomery Alabama, paid for a first-class cabin for his sister Caden Mussafir (b. 1901 in Milas, Turkey) and their mother Sarota Amato Musafir on a passenger steamer bound for Tangier via Genoa and Barcelona. Even though they too became stranded in Tangier and thus prevented from sailing onwards to the United States, the early leg of the journey provided gastronomic delights. Isaac recalled:

> We were traveling in first class thanks to Uncle David because we couldn't take any money out of Rhodes, and the waiters used to bring antipasto. And my grandmother, mother and I used to eat it and we loved it! And they brought it to us every day. My grandmother used to say, '*Es Bueno esto! Es Bueno!* This is good! It's good!' But we never realized that we were eating ham: it was prosciutto, and we had kept a kosher home.[116]

For Isaac Jack Lévy's family, the changed circumstances of life stranded in Tangier included often going hungry in the four and a half years they spent there. During this period, Isaac grew accustomed to breaking kosher by eating ham.[117]

However, once arrived at their destination, expellees struggled to carve out an existence. Five weeks after arriving in Tangier, Claire Barkey again wrote to her Uncle Raphael telling him of the difficulties faced by the refugees.

> […] here you cannot do much if you don't have a trade and great capital. It is true that papa is very handy, but not enough to set up shop. Therefore, we are looking for a small store for items to be sold retail. But we must think before we go into business and not do things in a haphazard manner and eat up the money we brought with us. Stores like that cannot easily be found as they ask too much for the goodwill [lease]. And if we are to pay three or four thousand francs for the goodwill, we will have nothing left as capital. For this reason we have found nothing.[118]

A lack of mobility compounded the difficult material conditions, for refugees were confined to the International Zone, meaning they could not cross into the rest of Morocco where prices were cheaper. Like most refugees from the Aegean, the family, 'always thinking of the prospect of remaining penniless', led a hand-to-mouth existence.[119] Claire's father eventually acquired a new skill in leatherworking, but never obtained steady employment. By the family's third year in Tangier in July 1942, a particularly unstable period in the Free Zone, Claire wrote again to her uncle,

> Dear Uncle Raphael, you cannot imagine how difficult life is in Tangier. Everything is so expensive, and there is little of everything; especially clothing is out of reach. When we wear out some clothing, we think that we cannot afford replacement. Dear Uncle, food is so expensive that what Rachel [her sister] and I earn, as Papa is idle, is hardly enough for food. Life is impossible now.[120]

To be sure, these were small sacrifices made by many in the exiled community in Tangier when viewed in the context of what was unfolding across the European continent. Fortunate to have been inadvertently spared deportation; nonetheless, theirs was a hard and uncertain life in limbo.[121]

While the Belgian Congo remained by far the preferred destination, an increasing number of younger Jews, including Miru Alcana's 17-year-old cousin Salvo [Salvatore] sought out Palestine. Two of Lucia Amato's brothers were among '[the] many Jews of Rhodes who had Italian passports' and were among the 197 Rhodian Jews who joined the 550 refugees from the steamer *Rim* bound for Palestine in August 1939, probably on the M.S. *Fiume* and the M.S. *Constanza*.[122] Similarly, two of Lucia Garzolini's brothers had previously left Kos for Rhodesia in 1937, while a third brother was among those who left for Palestine the following year, leaving behind her and David, the youngest in the family.[123]

Preferred destinations remained the Belgian Congo and Rhodesia. Of those who left Rhodes in 1939, for example, the overwhelming majority of the 155 heads of household departing Rhodes between September 1938 and January 1939 were destined for the Belgian Congo (88), followed by Rhodesia (48) and Turkey (29). Only two were bound for Palestine and Haifa, and three for America.[124] The Belgian Congo and Rhodesia were natural choices, given the kin and communal networks. An exit to Palestine was a more complicated affair, given that it was under British Mandate and once Italy and Britain were at war with each other, passage to Palestine or beyond to central and southern Africa was effectively cut off. Thus, an application to allow Aegean Jews safe passage via Palestine to the Congo in 1942 was hindered by a British bureaucratic mind-set that placed all Italian passport holders into the one basket of 'enemy aliens' unless proven otherwise.[125]

The data is certainly incomplete, nonetheless, they both confirm our knowledge of destination preferences among Aegean Jews (the Belgian Congo), but also add an interesting corrective to the widespread view that it was mainly the younger people who left. While we can see that this holds true for those wishing to voluntarily leave for new pastures in Africa, those affected by the Racial Laws – that is involuntary leavers – tended to be families. Of 41 families listed in late 1938, they numbered 212 persons (the remaining 23 persons were lone individuals). These were families who had been part of the human flow traditionally moving between Western Anatolia and the Dodecanese or forcibly removed after the Lausanne Treaty and whose acquisition of either Italian or Aegean citizenship was now revoked, among them the Varon family we have already encountered.[126]

Thus, expellees counted many families among their number. Vittorio Levi left Rhodes with his wife and daughter in early October 1938 on the M.S. *P. Foscari* bound for the Belgian Congo. At the end of the same month, 34-year-old Gioia Gattegno departed for the Congo with her three sons on the M.S. *Lero*. In January 1939, 36-year-old Violetta Mussafir left for the Congo with her five children on the M.S. *Egeo*. Thirty-one-year-old Rachele Amato had left on the same ship the previous month (on Christmas Day) with her son, as did 47-year-old Sarah Notrica accompanied by her son. Some of the women who left were joining spouses already settled in the Congo, either in the capital Leopoldville or in Elisabethville or in the bush in Katanga. Rachele Mizrachi, who was 48 years old at the time, was hoping to join her husband, Moses Gabriele, a shoemaker/trader, when she applied for her passport.[127] Lea Israel applied for emigration in January 1939, a month before her 50th birthday. Described as of good moral and political conduct but without fixed assets, Lea was married to 56-year-old Abramo Hasson, a private employee who had emigrated to the Belgian Congo together with their son, 27-year-old Eliachim. Lea was granted her permit and subsequently left the island.[128]

Many of the younger women who left Rhodes for the Congo or for Rhodesia were single and were sponsored as domestic servants (*esklave*), although they would later become wives of those males from the community who had emigrated earlier. In the mid-1930s, Vittoria Alhadeff (b. 10 March 1915) left for Elisabethville in Belgian Congo to marry Rahamin (Racamin) Franco (b. 1902), an employee. The wedding took place on 20 August 1937. Vittoria was the daughter of Mosé (Mussani) Alhadeff and Rachele Soriano. Her father Mosé together with his brother Giacobbe had a grocery business at Piazza Principe 29 (he is described as an épicier) where the family also lived (the brother lived at Tramontana 4 with his sister Ester). As in Lea Israel's case, Vittoria's departure saved her life; her parents and her six younger siblings together with her uncle and aunt were murdered in Auschwitz.[129] On 27 November 1938, Caden (Ketty) Angel, a daughter from Samuele Angel's first marriage to Bulissa Coen, left too, also bound for the Belgian Congo to join her older siblings Vittoria and Alberto.[130] Voluntary and involuntary emigration spared these siblings of Samuel's first marriage the fate of their youngest sister Gioia and their four half-siblings.

These divergent and unpredictable fates ran through the Jewish community of Rhodes and Kos, as they did through individual families. Hanulla Israel (b. 29 December 1903[131]) had been living in Cairo since the end of April 1934 and almost a year later, 24 March 1935, married a French national Benjamin Chloms Maatouk Haddad, only to separate from him less than two years later in February 1937. The pair subsequently were granted a divorce by David Pareto, the Grand Rabbi of Alexandria. Meanwhile two of Hanulla's brothers, Vittorio (51 years old) a shoemaker and Giacomo (35 years old) a private employee, emigrated to the United States; while the middle brother Leon (49 years old) a private employee, remained in Rhodes. Her older sisters Bulissa (married to Bohor Israel),[132] Rebecca (married to Abramo Galante),[133] Estrea (45 years old) and married to Marco Amato,[134] and Mazaltov (married to Marco Scemaria),[135] remained in Rhodes. The family owned a house in its own grounds and the sisters between them had savings to the tune of approximately I£25,000. This family too, would be among those deported and murdered in 1944 and their property expropriated.[136]

It is difficult to determine if all applications for passports were for permanent emigration. For example, 19-year-old domestic servant Graziella Coen applied for her six-month passport in November 1938 for Egypt, Syria and Palestine to be able to visit her parents, Giuseppe and Diamante. The outbreak of war appears to have prevented her return to Rhodes for Grazielle does not appear in the deportation list compiled by the Italian authorities. It is possible, of course, that there never was an intention to return. When interviewed many years later in the 1990s, Rebecca Amato Levy recounted how she and her husband had applied for temporary passports to visit his sister in Casablanca, only to be refused because the authorities suspected they were intending to leave Rhodes permanently, which in fact they were. They had come to this decision because of the threat of violence by one of Hasson's customers who was a member of the PNF. They did eventually receive exit visas.[137]

While the implementation of the Italian Racial Laws forced the departure of hundreds of Aegean Jews and 'encouraged' emigration of those not immediately affected by the laws, it was not the *sole* driver as so often believed.[138] Indeed as already mentioned, emigration had long been part of Aegean culture. Nonetheless, unknown to the Jewish migrants at the time, emigration, whether voluntary or involuntary, whether motivated by economic pressures or the result of discrimination, proved to be a blessing in disguise. However, for some Jews expulsion from the *Possedimenti d'Egeo* had a devastating impact.

The *Governatore* had little room for manoeuvre when it came to implementing the provisions of the Racial Laws. All Jews, whose citizenship had been revoked by the laws, had to leave regardless of their previous good conduct or social standing, as 55-year-old Nissim Tarica, described by the *Carabinieri* as 'wealthy' (*benestante*), found to his tragic cost. Tarica was closely integrated into the upper echelons of Rhodes society. He lived with his 32-year-old Turkish-born wife Lina and 10-year-old son Sami in Via 4 Maggio, an exclusive street in the San Giorgio district (see Illustration 3.1). Tarica possessed an extensive portfolio of properties and factories; he was a regular visitor at the exclusive Il Circolo d'Italia Club of Rhodes where he gambled with Italian friends. In the same year as the discriminatory laws were passed, Tarica was granted a radio licence after Guido Grassini vouched he was 'not considered capable of using the concession for illicit purposes'.[139]

Because his wife had originally come from Smyrna and had acquired Italian citizenship after 1919 through her marriage to Tarica, they like many other Jews whose loyalty and affinity to Italy had hitherto been uncontested, were plunged into a state of despair by the revocation of Lina's citizenship and the ultimatum to quit Rhodes. Within the space of a few months, Tarica had gone from being considered a loyal citizen in the eyes of Guido Grassini to a 'notorious usurer', in the words of the commander of the Rhodes *Carbinieri* station, *Maresciallo* Giuseppe Multinu.

Tarica, who had been born in Rhodes and was an Italian citizen, applied for the provisions of the law to be waived on 6 February. This was refused. In his report of 8 February, *Carabinieri* captain Arnaldo Valentini referred to 'the Jew Tarica' who had appeared in his office in an extreme emotional state, according to Valentini.

> [Tarica] affected by the measures for the defence of race, was informed by me this morning that his appeal, directed to the government and aimed at obtaining a stay in Rhodes, had been turned down. He was deeply upset.
>
> After a quarter of an hour, he returned to the office with the application for a passport for himself, his wife, and his son. In handing in the application, he stated that the passport would then only serve for his wife and son, as he would make other arrangements these days. I urged him to calmness and reason, pointing out to him that he has a wife and child and that as a man he should not even think of suicide. Tarica replied evasively telling me that he could not bear the measure taken against him.[140]

Later that morning the banker Bension Menascé appeared at Valentini's office urging him to defer the decision until after Lina Tarica's visit to Secretary General Bazzani, the most senior official in the *Governatore*. This appeal to the highest level of the administration also failed on grounds that there could be no derogation from the application of the law. All parties concerned in the case were subsequently informed on 15 February.[141]

Tarica failed to return home at his usual time in the afternoon of the following day. The news that the appeal to the *Governatore* had failed despite Menascé's advocacy on the family's behalf had been the final straw. His body was discovered the following morning at the pier of San Nicola. It appears that he had thrown himself into the sea at the Foro Italico at the end of the Mandraki and his body had been carried north-west by the current. Interviewed by the *Carabinieri*, close family friends and his sister Flora concurred as to Tarica's fragile mental condition. In the week preceding his suicide, he had been in a state of extreme nervousness. The family doctor, Dr David Gaon, testified how

Illustration 3.1 Nissim Tarica, Lina and son Sami
Source: Courtesy Genika Archeia tou Kratous/Archeia Dodekanisou GAKR Carabinieri 1.1.264 (1934)

Tarica had in the past suffered a nervous breakdown (*esaurimento nervoso*), and now had been thrown into a state of 'constant agitation' at the prospect of undertaking a long journey into the unknown.[142]

Within the space of a few months, the Racial Laws had pushed Tarica from the centre of Rhodes society to beyond its periphery. His social standing had been taken from him and so too from his wife and son. Lina had lost her Turkish citizenship when she married Tarica and the laws reduced her to statelessness. Rather than face the humiliation that accrued to being categorized as 'the Jew Tarica' and joining his wife as a refugee deprived of nationhood and, in his eyes, honour, he took his own life while still (nominally) an Italian citizen.[143]

*

A new generation of Italian historians have challenged the post-war narrative of the 'good Italian' in respect of the Holocaust.[144] As we have seen in this chapter, until the summer of 1944, anti-Jewish measures on Rhodes and Kos were implemented by the Italian administration, and enforced by the

Carabinieri, and not by German occupation forces, who arrived only in early 1943.[145] Indeed, Hizkia Franco (in retrospect) drew a direct line from De Vecchi and the Racial Laws to the deportation and catastrophe in 1944. Moreover, as we shall see in the following chapter, elements within the Italian administration played a key role in the deportation.

However, we should caution against a one-dimensional portrayal.[146] As is often the case, the picture is grainier than a simple monochrome canvas depicting Italian Fascist antisemitism. In the same issue of *Israel* that reported on Italy's anti-Jewish measures, two 'corrections' written by John Menascé, the president of the Community, were also printed alongside the critical article pointing out that the community 'had never been so well-regarded and [well-] treated as now'.[147] It is possible that Menascé was being cautious, affirming a positive relationship rather than draw the new governor's ire. De Vecchi was an antisemite, but this did not mean his orders were always carried out with equal fervour. Indeed, anti-Jewish measures were implemented in Rhodes and Kos with a degree of foot-dragging and were viewed with ambivalence by some Italians, as Lucia Garzolini recalled.

> [...] the Italians were very apologetic to us. They told us that those were the rules that they had received and unfortunately, they had to apply them at some point in time. Not at the beginning, but at some point they were obliged to. And also some of the Jews belonged to clubs – you know, an Italian circle of clubs, and we were excluded from them at that time also. But the Italians were apologetic about that. They said they were obliged to do it because of some rules they had received from the mainland. Generally, we had a normal life even after the racial laws.[148]

Indeed, when Rachel Hanan faced dismissal from her job after the introduction of the Racial Laws, the women in her office (overwhelmingly from mainland Italy) threatened to strike unless Rachel was retained, which is what happened until her deportation in the summer of 1944.[149]

De Vecchi's volatile and sometimes bizarre reign finally came to an end in December 1940, when he was recalled to Italy and briefly replaced by General Ettore Bastico.[150] In July 1941, the Dodecanese islands received a new governor in the person of Admiral Inigo Campioni, who proved to be more conciliatory towards the Jews. Previously imposed restrictions on the community were now lifted or eased, with some customs, such as ritual slaughter (*shechita*), restored. Jewish cultural and social life did not diminish during the war years in any way that was specific to Jews. The community continued (or resumed) holding charity balls and lotteries to raise money for poor families; individual movement within the Dodecanese archipelago continued until 1943; licences to trade or carry out other commercial activities continued to be issued to Jews of 'good conduct' in spite of efforts by Mittino and his ilk to deprive Jews of their livelihoods. And Jewish rites were respected.[151] Thus, under Campioni's governorship, persecutory measures were softened, if not entirely ignored.[152] Before restrictions were tightened after the German seizure of the islands, movement between them was still permitted. For example, Samuele Angel's youngest daughter from his first marriage, Gioia, was granted permission to travel to Kos on health grounds in order to recuperate.[153]

Campioni's softer policy vis-à-vis Jews continued after the islands had been brought under the heel of the German Wehrmacht. To be sure, the rescinding in liberated Italy of the Racial Laws by a royal decree of 20 January 1944 held little sway in the Dodecanese where the post-Fascist government of Marshal Badoglio had no influence. Nevertheless, the positive administrative response to the plight of residents of the old town who suffered the impact of the severe aerial bombardment of the harbour in the spring and early summer of 1944 provides a case in point of curbing or simply ignoring persecutory measures against Jews, thus providing a modest challenge to revisionist claims about the 'bad Italian' under Fascism. In Rhodes at least, the Italian authorities granted relief without discrimination and without interference from the German military administration.[154]

The aerial bombardments against Rhodes from early 1944 were to have a profound effect on the civilian population of the *Juderia*, whose proximity to the harbour made it vulnerable. By now the tide of war had turned against the Germans, and Rhodes and the Dodecanese more generally were seen by Churchill as vital to Britain's long-term interests in the Eastern Mediterranean in any post-war settlement. The British timed the raids to coincide with the arrival of supply ships. As well as having the purpose of disrupting and destroying German supplies, these attacks were designed to spur the hitherto neutral Turkish government into joining the allied cause. As the war entered its final phase, the British carried out over 300 day and night sorties against the Dodecanese – targeting in particular, Rhodes, Kos and Leros.[155] Between February and the beginning of July, over a dozen sorties against the harbour and old town left a trail of destruction, leaving many houses and businesses either fully destroyed or badly damaged.[156] A devastating attack occurred on 8 April – at the beginning of *Shabbat* and during the service marking the beginning of Pesach festivity (see below). This attack destroyed the older of the two synagogues. British bombers returned in successive waves over the next three days, wreaking havoc upon mostly civilian targets (the Germans reported little damage to military installations).[157]

At the end of May, there was a further attack, but this time affecting those parts of the town with mainly Italian and Turkish residents. June saw a marked intensification. The attacks began on 3 June, a Saturday when Jewish businesses would be closed. A similar pattern to the April attacks appeared to be in play: the 3rd had been a single attack, but the following weekend a wave of attacks occurred, starting on *Shabbat* (10 June) and followed in succession on the 12th, 15th and 16th and finally on the 18th. This week-long bombing of the close quarters of the harbour, taking in the *Juderia*, had a devastating impact. The sortie on the 18th was by no means the last attack. This came on 28 June, a Wednesday, when the residents of the old quarter would have been going about their business. The bombers struck at the heart of the *Juderia*, wreaking havoc in Via Elia del Bosco, in Via Venezia, Via Giovanni de Rivera, and in the Piazza Principe di Piemonte. An attack a few days later on 1 July, again a Saturday, appears to have been the last before the deportation.[158] Not only were the neighbourhoods of the middling and poor families of the *Juderia* in the cross-hairs of British bombers, but also some of the more elegant neighbourhoods of the wealthy beyond the citadel. It was during these attacks (probably in May) that the offices of the Turkish Consul Selahattin Ülkümen, located near the Mandraki, were hit, with at least two fatalities among his staff, and apparently injuring his pregnant wife.[159] The Turkish consulate building was not the only casualty during these later bombardments. Substantial properties of some of the elite families, including that of the banking brothers Joseph and Ascer Alhadeff, were also damaged.[160]

The one attack that has remained deeply etched into the collective memory of survivors is that of April 1944, occurring on the first day of the feast of Pesach. At least sixty-one homes, the majority belonging to Jewish families in the heart of the *Juderia*, were affected during this attack spanning 8–10 April. Thus homes in Via Grande Maestro Fluviano, Via Generale Boniface Scarampi, Via Deodata Gozzoni, Via Sigismondo Malatesta and Via Bernardo d'Airasca, which were heavily populated with Jewish families, were hit. During the raid on 8 April, Iscia Benun, his wife Sara Alcana – the daughter of Celibi Alcana and Rachele Soriano – together with their 10-year-old son, Mordechai, were killed. Twelve-year-old Stella, who had been injured, was fostered by her maternal grandparents and Aunt Miru.[161] Subsequent bombardments spread to properties just beyond the medieval walls close to the old cemetery, damaging properties in Via Ogaden, Via Addis Ababa, Via Mogadiscio, Via Bernardo San Giorgio and Via Matteo Gicenco, where Turks, Greeks and Italians lived. According to Hizkia Franco the two aerial attacks of February and April left between 28 and 34 dead among the Jewish community, with the attack at the commencement of Pesach producing the highest single death toll of twenty-six Jewish victims from forty-six dead.[162]

According to official reports, the three days of aerial strikes destroyed or badly damaged at least eighty-four buildings; thirty-six residences belonged to Jewish families. Official figures put the number of persons affected by the three days of aerial attacks at ninety-seven. However, as the attacks extended into the early summer, the numbers of Jewish victims decreased because of an exodus to nearby villages. Thus, the later attacks in mid-June (on 12th, 15th, 16th and 18th) claimed the lives and properties of mostly Greeks, Turks and Italians residing within the old walls of the citadel. Nevertheless, some Jewish homes in Via Francesco Flotta collapsed during the attack on 18 June, including that of Marco Scemaria, who we will encounter again in Chapter 7.

Even though the aerial raid in late June resulted in fewer Jewish victims, it nonetheless claimed the lives of thirteen residents of the old quarter and left twenty-one injured, as well as completely destroying 110 houses, and a further 153 buildings severely damaged.[163] Some Jewish homes in Via Venezia were destroyed in this raid, but now the bombers were targeting areas either to the north in the old town or outside the citadel. This attack had come barely ten days after the attacks in mid-June when most of the victims had been Greek and Turks. The last attack on 1 July destroyed homes in Via Venezia Mastia and Via Sigismondo Malatesta.[164] By this time many of the Jewish families who could do so had left the area, and the few that remained suffered the consequences along with their Turkish and Greek neighbours. The devastation was still very much in evidence when a party of officials of the International Red Cross arrived in early 1945. It found 'the Jewish quarter had been in part razed to the ground by the bombs'.[165] These raids, but especially that of April, prompted many families of the *Juderia* to leave their homes and to seek refuge in the villages of Trianda (Ialyssos) and Cremasto (Kremasti), and in some of the outlying semi-rural settlements. For this reason these early aerial attacks prompting the exodus to the villages have remained etched in the collective memory of Rhodes Jews, whereas later bombardments are rarely recalled. A few weeks after the deportation, there was no reference by the Germans to what had once been a Jewish quarter. In his report on the attacks in June for the division's war diary, Lieutenant Herpich observed:

> The last month has given the town of Rhodes, the economic centre of the island of Rhodes, a completely different face. The many aerial attacks caused panic and led to a mass exodus of the population to the countryside. The majority of the bombs fell in the densely populated Turkish [*sic*!] quarter, where a total number of 110 houses were destroyed and 153 were heavily damaged. 13 civilians were killed and 21 were injured.[166]

As in the case of British bombs that fell on the old quarter of Rhodes, the Italian authorities made no distinction between ethnicity and religion when considering claims for compensation. Instead, the economic status of the claimant was the sole determinant.

Where feasible, the Italian authorities repaired and re-allocated those dwellings and buildings that had suffered minor to moderate damage. These homes would be made available to the homeless, who thus counted among the beneficiaries from the reallocation of Jewish-owned property after the deportation. The surviving files show at least a third of the ninety or so claimants were Jewish. Among the non-Jewish claimants was Rino Merolle, the infantryman and member of the PNF we encountered briefly in the previous chapter, but who was also claiming on behalf of his partner Matilde Alhadeff and their baby son.[167] Their home in Via Boniface Scarampi 54 had been hit during the Pesach raid on 11 April 1944. However, they were lucky to have escaped the brunt of the attack, since we learn that much of their household goods remained unscathed. The Italian Rino Merolle, who by now was married to Matilde Alhadeff and was working as a baker, was described as being in 'good economic condition' and for this reason they did not qualify for aid. Nor did Ezra Hanan, whose home in Via Bernardo D'Airasca (until 1939: Via della Fasana; today Odos Irinas) had been made uninhabitable during one raid, receive compensation.

Why Hanan was denied compensation is unclear from the records. However, this seems to have had little to do with his being a Jew, for his brother's house, two doors away, was also badly damaged during the same raid, and Allegra Hanan, Ezra's sister-in-law, was granted compensation. Allegra's family was lucky not to have suffered any loss of life during the raid. Theirs was a large and impoverished household with six young children and dependent parents living with them. Allegra's husband Avner was suffering from depression and unable to work as a licensed shoe polisher. The two older children, girls in their mid-teens, participated in a public works scheme. These circumstances may have qualified the family for support. These examples suggest that within the Italian administration there was still some degree of humanity at play.

Thus, even though the discriminatory Racial Laws were technically in force, Jews per se were not excluded from hardship support, and they frequently received it. The key criterion was not ascribed to race, but the material condition of the claimant. For example, when the home of poverty-stricken Nissim Alcana, the cousin of Miru, was destroyed, his family qualified for a subsidy of I£500. When the house of impoverished widow Mazaltov Amato was destroyed, along with her belongings, in Via Sigismondo Malatesta in the raid of 8 April, she too was granted a hardship subsidy of I£500. Similarly, the home of 65-year-old Giuseppe Franco at Via Sigismondo Malatesta 54 was destroyed during the third and last raid during Pesach festivities. He lost all his worldly goods. With six dependants relying on him, and facing destitution, the authorities granted him a subvention for food and accommodation.

His namesake, Giuseppe Franco, also lived in Via Sigismondo Malatesta. A dyestuff company had employed Franco, but it is not clear if he was still working in 1944. Disaster struck this large family in February 1944 when one of the first aerial sorties against the port by the British destroyed a large part of the *Juderia*. During this raid a bomb struck their home and destroyed it, killing Giuseppe's wife Mathilda and five of his seven children. Two daughters survived, as did his 'old and suffering' (*sic*) mother-in-law, Rebecca Hanan.

The severity of his loss obviously moved the authorities to double Franco's award for compensation from the usual I£500 to I£1,000. Giuseppe and the two surviving daughters, Rachele and Stella, would be among those deported in July. Of this family, only Stella would survive.[168]

Thus in some cases the loss of life appears also to have been a criterion. Nissim Sciami, a private employee residing at Via Deodato Gozzone 19, who was described by the welfare authorities as living in 'not lavish conditions' but not in extreme poverty, was granted aid after two of his children were killed in the raid. After 15-year-old Matilde, the daughter of Celebi C[H]asson, a shoe shiner by trade and his wife Maria Alcana (the sister of Miru Alcana), from Via Sigismondo Malatesta, were killed during the same raid of 8 April, the family received aid.[169]

Ultimately, it is hard to say what additional criteria officials took into account when determining a case. We also do not know how much leeway an individual officer had in coming to a decision. It is likely that most officials followed regulatory guidelines. For instance, while death or injury might be considered a reason for making an award, this was not necessarily a decisive criterion. There were tragic cases of loved ones killed during these aerial attacks where no award was made. This is what happened to the sweet-maker Isacco Israel, who lived in Via Sigismondo Malatesta, and whose daughter Desirée was killed. His application for support was rejected. Similarly, the circumstances of Bohor Russo, whose daughter was killed and his house and belongings in Ben San Giorgio, as well as his shop on the island of Leros, were destroyed, held little sway with officialdom and he, too, was rejected. Indeed, the authorities only compensated to the tune of I£17,800 around a third of the families affected by the devastation wreaked by allied bombs in April.[170]

The files of the Italian administration open a window through which we can chart the extent of material poverty in the *Juderia* on the eve of deportation. The terms used repeatedly by the welfare authorities to describe the impoverished conditions of many families included descriptions such as: '*trovasi in non floride condizione economiche*', or '*precarious*'.[171] However, there were hidden costs that inflicted a toll on the Jewish population. In addition to the daily struggle in the face of albeit low-level but grinding persecution, the repeated attacks, especially during the night, scarred a less-visible landscape than that of the stones and mortar of buildings. Historical scholarship has revealed much about the trauma of 'shell shock' because of persistent heavy artillery fire in the trenches during the First World War.[172] Recently, scholars have expanded their attention to the experiences of civilian populations in the wake of war.[173] However, little is known about the mental impact of the repeated aerial attacks on Rhodes, or Kos for that matter. And yet aerial bombardments by British planes in a densely populated neighbourhood must have been devastating in sensory terms, as well as in terms of the sheer destruction to life and limb, and homes. The psychological impact of these raids was profound, especially for those who were children at the time. Alice Tarica whose family home was close to the Mandraki, recalled 'when the evening came, we were always trembling and had no appetite … we would huddle up against our mother'.[174] Her father had created a type of bomb-shelter in the basement of the house, as Alice recalled:

> The attacks – terrible ones – took place mainly at night. As soon as the sirens sounded, papa and mama dragged us out of bed and into the cellars. Papa had turned the basement into a shelter, reinforcing the structure with beams and sandbags … In this shelter, we felt safe. We stayed there until the end of the alert. Sometimes we even spent the night there.[175]

Perhaps the impact of these aerial attacks was all the more traumatic, not least because Rhodes' civilian community hitherto had been mere witnesses to the conflict. Now they were situated at its frontline.

Just one example of the devastating experience of war is offered by the story of Avner Hanan, the husband of Allegra and brother of Ezra, mentioned above. Avner was born in 1900, and by 1944 had been married to Allegra (b. 1902) Alhana (Alcana) for seventeen years.[176] Together they had five children, Lea, born in 1928, was the oldest, followed by Asher, a year younger than Lea, and then three more siblings born in the early and mid-1930s: Laura (1932), Bulissa (1933), and the youngest, Abramo (also known as Alberto), born in 1936. As we saw above, they lived together with his parents Moreno and Bulissa in Via Bernardo D'Airasca, a street close to the harbour that housed many poor families. Ezra also lived in this street with his wife Maria Ventura and their six children, all roughly the same ages as those of Avner and Allegra, barring the two youngest children, Giacobbe and Salva. Avner, as mentioned above, had held a licence as a shoe shiner since 1931, but his pitch was in one of the squares of the old town affected by the aerial raids.[177]

While life for many in the *Juderia* could be financially tough, including for
Ezra who, as we saw earlier, made and sold sweets, it appears to have been a
particularly hard struggle for Avner for trade had never been reliable, and the
war had severely curtailed it. As a result the family lived in straitened conditions.
Their proximity to the harbour meant that they and their neighbours were
at constant risk from British sorties against Rhodes. And indeed, their house
was hit on more than one occasion. To escape the bombardments, Avner
and his family sought safety at an inherited farm in Candilli near Trianda.
Deprived of an income, Avner had progressively sunk into depression. On
20 June, he summoned his children, instructing 14-year-old Ascer to go and
buy cucumbers, Lora [Laura] to find and play with friends in the village,
and Alberto to fetch cigarettes. Once the children had left on their errands,
Avner went into the garden with some rope, which he threw around a branch
of an old carob tree next to the house. Allegra discovered him on her return
from work at 1.30 pm, and sent the eldest child, Lea, to report the suicide to
the authorities.

Avner was cut down from the tree by the *Carabinieri* officer and a local
doctor from Trianda, Michele Petridi who arrived on the scene at around 7.00
pm. Petridi established Avner had died from asphyxiation, but also believed
death had been quick for the vertebrae had snapped. Avner left behind a note
in which he stated simply: 'It would be better to end it – I'm tired of enduring
this life.' According to the *Carabinieri* officer writing the death report, 'these
phrases referred to the sorrow felt by him for the almost complete demolition
of his home [which] happened several times in succession'. Avner was also
depressed by the fact that, as a result of the continual bombing, not only had
his home been destroyed, but also the square in the *Juderia* where he once
plied his trade. He thus lost the means to support his family. In a society where
males were traditionally the sole breadwinner and this defined a 'man', the
consequences were devastating to selfhood.[178]

The marginalization of Jews after De Vecchi's arrival at the end of 1936,
codified in the Race Laws two years later, wrought immeasurable psychological
damage upon many parts of the Jewish community. We saw how Nissim
Tarica's suicide was a desperate response to his family's expulsion from a
society where he had enjoyed recognition and social standing. His namesake,
Yehuda Tarica, underwent a similar transformation from socialite to outcast,

albeit without the same tragic result (his fate, however, would be sealed by the deportation). In spite of the stoicism displayed by Vitalis Strumza, stripped of his title of *cavaliare* and his citizenship, one cannot but get a sense of the underlying pain this must have caused him. Sami Modiano, too, recalled as a child the pain of exclusion when he had to leave school. The impact was no less among those who occupied less-exalted positions. Laura Varon recalled her father's withdrawal from life around him as he sank into depression. Who knows how many more were similarly affected by these unremitting measures of oppression by the Italian administration. Avner's suicide bore similar hallmarks. The loss and uncertainty brought about by displacement through repeated aerial bombardments was a shared one for the inhabitants of the *Juderia* that spring and early summer. A month later, this tragedy would be overshadowed by the greater tragedy of the deportation when Avner's widow and children were rounded up and deported to Auschwitz together with Ezra and his family and the elderly grandparents Moreno and Bulissa. Fourteen-year-old Ascer and his two siblings would survive the camps. His cousin Sara, just one month older, and whose recollection of life under the Italian regime opened this chapter, also would survive, but she would be the sole survivor from Ezra's family of six children.[179]

4

The Germans on Rhodes

seen strategically … [Rhodes] was the most important element in the defence of the Greek zone (griechischen Raumes).[1]

The occupation of Greece after its surrender to the Germans in April 1941 initially had little relevance for the Dodecanese. The archipelago remained an Italian sphere of control, while the larger strategic prize of Crete came under German military command. However, the changing tide of war in North Africa, coupled with a growing unease in Berlin over Italy's resolve to remain a steadfast Axis partner, had shifted Berlin's focus to the Aegean islands by early 1943.[2] The extension of German military hegemony over the Dodecanese islands in September following the Italian surrender that year eventually paved the way for the destruction of Jewish life in the Aegean. For at the very moment in 1944 when Berlin was preparing its military withdrawal from Greece, the Aegean islands of Rhodes and Kos (together with Corfu and Crete) were briefly propelled to the frontline in the Nazis' 'war against the Jews'[3] with devastating consequences.

The persecution of Jews in Greece was already underway from early spring 1943, when the first German detachments arrived in Rhodes. However, their arrival had less to do with Jews than with strategic military goals. The German garrison on Rhodes was small. Its role initially was to provide a support to the Italian force in the event of an Allied attack, and thus to keep a flight-path open for German troops withdrawing from the North Africa theatre of war, and eventually, from Crete. For much of the time from March 1943 to summer 1944, the German garrison focused on conventional military matters, such as supplies, troop discipline, liaising with the Italian command (prior to 8 September), and securing Rhodes' defences. With Italy's withdrawal from the war on 8 September, Berlin gave Army Group E the order for the military occupation of the Italian zones of occupation in Greece and the seizure of the Dodecanese archipelago, the latter achieved by November.

Some commentators believe Britain's failure to secure the islands of the Eastern Aegean constituted the turning point as far as the fate of the Jews is concerned.[4] This argument has the benefit of hindsight and overstates British competence. As we shall see, policy divisions and poor resourcing hampered a British military initiative in the Eastern Aegean. Moreover, in autumn 1943, after the Germans seized the islands, and indeed, until mid-July 1944, there was no indication that Aegean Jews were in danger. The first part of this chapter examines the pros and cons of military contest in the Aegean. It then goes on to look at the deteriorating rapport between the German and Italian forces, leading to the battle for Rhodes. It concludes with a sketch of the German garrison and its relationship to the Jewish community.

*

As we saw in Chapter 1, because of their strategic position in the Eastern Mediterranean, the larger islands of the Dodecanese featured strongly in British Mediterranean policy.[5] Before the war, London's priority had been that of maintaining a balance of power in the region, in order to protect British vital interests in the oilfields of Iran as well as keeping open the Suez Canal, Britain's gateway to India and the Far East.[6] Even though this position changed once Britain found itself at war with Italy from the early summer of 1940, London still had to consider Greek interests since the two Mediterranean countries were not yet at war with each other. Therefore, the British minister in Athens, Sir Michael Palairet, urged caution in numerous dispatches to the Foreign Office in London, so as not to draw Greece into conflict with Italy.[7]

When Britain declared war against Germany, Rome began preparing defences in the archipelago against a possible British and Turkish attack. A diplomat from the British mission in Belgrade who visited Rhodes with his wife in early February 1940 observed how the arrival of troop reinforcements and the strengthening of defences had transformed Rhodes into a 'sort of fortress'.[8] As soon as Greece found itself at war with Italy in October 1940, the War Office in London considered sending an expeditionary force to seize the islands. London dispatched a naval flotilla with a landing force of 200 commandos to the island of Castellorizo, close to the Anatolian coast, at the end of February 1941. However, this expedition, codenamed *Abstention*, had to be aborted in the face of an Italian counteroffensive.[9] There were bigger concerns in the southern Aegean with the battle for Crete looming. Instead, London fell back on a strategy of propaganda broadcasts via the BBC to stoke further Greek hostility in the Eastern Aegean towards the Italians.[10]

There were constraints on British policy, not least, the question of available resources for military operations in Greece and in the Aegean. After the fall of France in the early summer of 1940, Britain 'stood alone' in Europe and logistically was overstretched.[11] In some quarters of the political and military establishment in London, a fully blown military commitment to Greece was unwelcome and some viewed intervention as an unnecessary diversion of vital land and naval resources. The British position vis-à-vis the Dodecanese in the period before the Italian attack on Greece (and even before Italy's declaration of war against Britain in June) can be characterized as cautious at best, and at worst, one of prevarication. While some in Whitehall were at pains not to exacerbate tensions with Italy, there were also disagreements over the entire issue of sovereignty of the Dodecanese islands that harked back to the early days of dealing with Dodecanese nationalism and Greece's Mediterranean aspirations. Whitehall mandarins such as Orme Sargent, the deputy under-secretary at the Foreign Office, were cautious for they feared an entanglement in Greece would revive irredentist claims in the Dodecanese that might spill over to challenge British power in Cyprus.[12] Hence, emphasis was placed on fighting 'Italian fascism' in the Dodecanese and not Italian colonialism. At the same time, London, like Berlin later in the war, was assiduous in its efforts not to alienate Turkey (with its revived interest in the Dodecanese), as a potential ally.[13]

Germany's successful campaign in Crete in May 1941 curtailed British military operations in the Eastern Mediterranean. The fall of Crete was a debacle for London and its loss to Germany exposed British forces in Egypt. It was a mere 452 miles from Chania to Alexandria and 564 miles to British headquarters at Cairo, and thus in striking distance of the German *Luftwaffe*. Until the course of the war began to turn against Berlin (notably after abandoning the siege of Tobruk), Britain's role in the Eastern Mediterranean remained constrained by German air superiority. German successes brought home to Prime Minister Winston Churchill's military commanders that any frontal engagement with Hitler's forces at that point was doomed to fail without American air support. Nevertheless, the Royal Navy continued to rule the Aegean waves.[14] British policy therefore shifted to 'hit and run' missions by commandos from Special Operations Executive (SOE) operating out of Egypt. Their mission was to harass German positions on the islands, gather vital intelligence and, later in the war, to spread propaganda among enemy troops with the aim of undermining fighting morale. These tactics remained characteristic of British operations in the Dodecanese until the end of the war.[15]

Following the decision to abandon the siege of Tobruk, German reversals in North Africa mounted, notably its defeat at El Alamein in November 1942 and culminating in the destruction of the Afrika Korps during the Tunisia Campaign of May 1943.[16] These reversals not only ended Berlin's ambitions in North Africa, but they also pushed the Aegean into the forefront of Hitler's Mediterranean strategy. The timing was important, for the scales of power within Italy were tipping against Mussolini. Himmler had undertaken a journey to Rome in mid-October 1942 to meet with Mussolini and his foreign minister (and son-in-law) Count Ciano. The meeting lasted nearly two hours and ranged widely, including the fate of Italy's Jews. In a memorandum to Hitler and to Ribbentrop, Himmler stated that the Axis would remain firm only as long as Mussolini remained in power.[17]

Italy's performance in North Africa had been lacklustre, to say the least, with evidence of widespread war-weariness among its troops.[18] The growing doubt in the German High Command about Italy's commitment to the war resulted in a contingency plan being drawn up, initially codenamed *Alarich* and then *Konstantin*, by July 1943 it had become *Unternehmen Achse* (*Operation Axis*).[19] In the event of Itay's withdrawal from the war, this plan foresaw the disarming of Italian garrisons, the seizing of war materiel, and the occupation of the Italian zone of Greece and the Dodecanese islands.[20] The success of the Allied landing in Sicily, triggering Mussolini's removal from power on 25 July 1943, injected an urgency into German strategic planning in the Aegean.

Of particular concern to Germany was the question of the security of Crete and the potential loss of a backdoor for the retreat of the remaining Afrika Korps.[21] To the south of the island, the British in Palestine and Egypt now posed a reinvigorated threat to the German occupation of the island; as did Allied air bases to its east in Cyprus. Meanwhile, to the west Malta provided an important base for an Allied naval offensive in the south Mediterranean, and notably for an invasion of Italy via Sicily, or of Greece through the Peloponnese. From Berlin's perspective in early 1943, the strategic importance of Crete and the Dodecanese to its north as a 'defensive corridor' for troops disengaging from the North African theatre of war in order to regroup in the Balkans became paramount as Hitler's empire shrank over the following months.[22]

Thus, from early 1943, the Dodecanese islands, and notably Kos with its airfields, Leros with its deep-water naval base and Rhodes, the largest and most important island, assumed strategic importance for Berlin. They would continue to be of vital importance until Germany concluded its withdrawal from Greece in autumn 1944. Rhodes in particular assumed key significance for the German forces in the region. The supreme commander of German forces in the Balkans, Field Marshal Maximilian von Weichs, together with the commander of Army Group E, General Alexander Löhr, as well as the Commander of *Luftwaffenkommando Südost* General Martin Fiebig, held the view that 'seen strategically ... [Rhodes] was the most important element in the defence of the Greek zone (*griechischen Raumes*)'.[23] Should it fall, then the British would close off the path from North Africa to the Balkans, endangering at the same time the 75,000-strong force in Crete. The Aegean thus emerged as a new frontline from the spring of 1943.

Other than Crete since its occupation in May 1941, there was no permanent German force garrisoned on any of the Aegean islands under Italian control. This would now change. In March 1943, an assault force *Sturmbrigade Rhodos* comprising units from the 22 Infantry Division Crete commanded by Colonel Freiherr von Lützow was deployed to Rhodes in order to bolster the Italian force. However, in May, the brigade was upgraded to divisional strength under a new commander, 51-year-old Lieutenant-General Ulrich Kleemann.[24]

Born in 1892 in Langensalza into a military family, Kleemann was a professional soldier who belonged to a generation of *Wehrmacht* officers whose careers after 1933 rode in tandem with the fortunes of the Third Reich.[25] He had joined the army in 1911 as a cadet, and saw action during the First World War, which saw him promoted to First Lieutenant in 1916. After the establishment of the Republic in 1919, his career appears to have stalled, probably due to the restrictions imposed on the army under the provisions of the Versailles Treaty. It took him ten years from 1923 to 1933 to advance from *Rittmeister* (captain in light armoured division) to major, in spite of glowing reports. In contrast, the five years following Hitler's coming to power saw rapid promotion. In 1936, he gained the rank of Lieutenant-Colonel, becoming full colonel two years later. In recommending Kleemann for promotion to full colonel, his commanding officer described him as a 'responsible personality, mentally fresh, agile, and versatile. Generous and very sympathetic (*"sehr wohlwollend"*). Possesses good natural military aptitude and tactical talent. Quick decision-making ability.'[26]

In November 1941, as commander of the 3rd Light Armoured Brigade fighting on the Eastern Front, Kleemann was promoted to Major-General, the rank his father had held. He also received the Iron Cross with Oak Leaves, one of the highest military honours for his service on the Eastern Front. The following January he was seconded to the Führer-Reserve (*Führerreserve*) in Berlin, where he remained until 10 April, from which date he took command of the 90th Light Africa Division serving under Field Marshal Rommel. However, the climate of the North African desert damaged the corneas in both eyes, and, in September 1942, he was granted sick leave before rejoining the *Führerreserve* in November to await a new command.[27] This came six months later. In May 1943, Hitler appointed Kleemann to the command of the new division in Rhodes, at the same time promoting him to Lieutenant-General.[28] Thus, with the personal endorsement of Hitler, Kleemann arrived in Rhodes as commanding officer of the newly created *Sturmdivision Rhodos* (Assault Division Rhodes). Accompanying him when he landed at Gaddura military airfield on 4 June was a small staff of seven officers, among whom his closest advisers were his adjutant, 31-year-old Captain (later Major) Klaus Goedeckemeyer, his chief of staff, Major (later Lieutenant-Colonel) Philipp Heinz, and military intelligence officer 1st Lieutenant Dr Wilhelm Brenner.[29]

The new division comprised the existing battalion augmented by an array of units drawn from elsewhere in the Mediterranean, each with varying battle experience and competence.[30] Grenadier Regiment 440, for example, was redeployed from the island of Lemnos and a company of the *Bewährungsbataillon* 999 (so-called Penal Battalion) en route to the Peloponnese was diverted to Rhodes.[31] Four battalions from 22nd Infantry

Division based in Crete, arrived in Rhodes that spring. This force would play a key role in seizing the major islands of the Dodecanese in the late autumn. In addition, there were two combat groups comprising the Grenadier Regiment (I-III), the largest force with 2,823 officers and men commanded by Colonel Hess, and a battalion of Fusiliers (formerly Stab ii./I.R. 16), commanded by Major Aschoff. This last force would be responsible for expelling the British from the island of Simi in October 1943.[32] A light armoured division under the joint command of Major Count von der Schulenberg, Major Count Wedel and Major von Oertzen made up the other key fighting force. An array of support units, including a company of sappers (*Pionierkompanie*) from 22nd Infantry Division, as well as other support units from *Bewährungsbataillon* 999 made up the rest of the initial force. At the beginning of 1944, Fortress Infantry Brigade 939 (one of whose two senior commanders Colonel Otto Wagener – from December 1944 Major-General – would succeed Kleemann as commander of the Dodecanese in September 1944) was deployed to the island in anticipation of an Allied attack.[33] By the end of August 1943, Kleemann's total force on Rhodes comprised little more than 6,645 men. The Italian garrison numbered almost 42,000. Thus, the *Sturmdivision Rhodos* was outnumbered by a ratio of 7:1.[34]

*

Until the German seizure of the Dodecanese, overall command lay with the supreme commander of Italian forces in the Dodecanese (*Superegeo*), a relationship that caused General Kleemann concern after Mussolini was deposed in the summer 1943 and a new commander of ground forces arrived from Rome.[35] Hitherto, relations between Germans and Italians had been good, according to Kleemann's reports. The two garrisons carried out joint manoeuvres, shared intelligence and generally complemented each other's military capabilities. There was also a high degree of social interaction, especially with games of soccer highly favoured by the two garrisons. The governor and supreme commander of the Dodecanese, Admiral Inigo Campioni, a highly respected veteran of the First World War and loyal to King Victor Emmanuel, was both a courteous officer and a consummate diplomat, ensuring cordial relations with the German command and with Kleemann in particular.[36]

This cordial atmosphere changed after the Marshall Badoglio-led coup against Mussolini on 25 July 1943. A two-hour briefing of Kleemann's staff officers and unit commanders at 10.00 am discussed the changed situation and the balance of forces in the Eastern Aegean. Kleemann emphasized to his officers the need to be prepared for possible attack by the Allies, noting that key targets would be the military airstrips and the harbour. For tactical reasons, Kleemann divided the island into four military zones in the event of an Allied attack. It is telling of the degree of Kleemann's scepticism about continued collaboration with the Italian garrison, that nowhere in this briefing were Italian regular forces mentioned as a *co-defendant* of the islands, although Italy was formally still part of the Axis. Instead, a brief discussion took place among the divisional staff officers on the 'pros and cons' of arming the Italian Fascist Blackshirts as a reserve, with Kleemann concluding that they were not an adequate operational force.[37]

On the evening of Mussolini's removal from power, the leader of the 1st Battalion of the Legion of Black Shirts quartered in the community of Alaerma (present-day Laerma), Consul (Colonel) Peretti, described as being 'clearly apprehensive and animated', met with Kleemann to 'put himself and his legion at [Kleemann's] disposal'. He was convinced that the change of regime in Rome spelt the end of fascism unless the Germans intervened militarily. Peretti, correctly as it transpired, was convinced that Badoglio (whom he erroneously considered a Jew and accused the Italian high command of being little more than a clique of traitors), would withdraw Italy from the war. It appears that Peretti was also worried that the two legions of Blackshirts would be disarmed by regular Italian army officers, and thus was looking to Kleemann for protection. Kleemann enquired if the Legion could be relied upon to side with the German garrison, to which the Fascist leader replied, 'it could be'. Kleemann stated that his task as German commander was to continue the fight against Britain and America, and, in the event that Badoglio sought an armistice, 'he would very much welcome if the Blackshirts put themselves under his command'. To this end, Kleemann encouraged Peretti to contact the 201 Battalion of the Legion quartered in Rhodes to see if its members were amenable to such an arrangement. In short order, its commander, Consul (Colonel) Enzo Celebrano, confirmed the Fascists' willingness to join the German force.[38]

The following day, Kleemann met with Admiral Campioni who read out the King's proclamation concerning the change of regime. Campioni also emphasized that the Axis stood firm and Italy's role in the war against the Allies remained unchanged. Kleemann then went to see the commander of the 14,000-strong 50th *Regina* Infantry Division, Major-General Michele Giacomo Scaroina, and informed him of Campioni's assurances. Scaroina said he had also heard the same from the governor. The report of this meeting recorded that 'A delicate matter was perhaps the position of the Blackshirts, who had been immediately informed that they would continue to be part of the command of *Regina* Division and that their position as active troops had not fundamentally changed.'[39] Immediately following Mussolini's removal from power, a special decree incorporated the Legion nationwide into the Italian army. As in Italy, there was considerable friction between Fascists and senior army officers in Rhodes.[40] Clearly, Peretti and Enzo Celebrano, the leaders of the Blackshirts, did not trust the Italian military commanders on Rhodes. To assuage any doubts Kleeman may have harboured, Scaroina expressed his hope that the Berlin-Rome axis would remain unaffected by events in Rome, and that the war against the Allies would be prosecuted even more vigorously. The German commander remained cautious despite Scaroina's assurances, noting that:

> These views seem to express the personal thoughts and feelings of General Scaroina, who, however, in his situation, could not otherwise express other thoughts and feelings. The newly altered situation is certainly a big surprise for him too. He acts as a soldier and emphasizes that as such he has to obey the orders of his superiors. Taking a political stance against a general who is appointed by the king is for him out of the question. Such a position among Italian generals depends entirely on the intentions of the new Badoglio government.[41]

Captain Bayer, the Division's translator who liaised with the Italians, reported how Captain Bogetti, an Italian officer, had assured him that Italy 'was so deeply entangled (*verstrickt*) in this war, as to make a rupture in the German alliance out of the question.'[42] However, there were hints of a very different stance among the officer corps and in the ranks too. In conversation with Lieutenant de Luca, a junior staff officer from *Regina* Division, Bayer also learned many Italian officers were highly critical of Mussolini and the Fascist leadership. Moreover, De Luca appeared to suggest that there was a degree of scepticism among regular army officers as to whether cooperation between the two garrisons could continue.[43] Indeed, in the subsequent battle for Rhodes in September and on some of the other islands, notably Kos and Leros, the fiercest resistance to Kleemann's forces came from units of this Division, together with the Italian artillery batteries and the air corps.

Despite expressions of loyalty and hitherto amicable relations, there was also widespread suspicion among officers of the German garrison that reflected Berlin's reservations vis-à-vis the Italians. In the weeks following Mussolini's removal, relations between the German and Italian garrisons in Greece deteriorated sharply as the attitude towards the Italians among German occupation forces changed for the worse.[44] This was evidently also the situation in Rhodes. There were repeated instances when German officers and ordinary soldiers failed to display respect towards their Italian counterparts by not greeting officers with the customary salute. By mid-August, Kleemann, prompted by continuing reports of poor behaviour, issued a directive to his officers to cease 'dismissive criticism' of the Italians.[45] Nevertheless, Kleemann too had his doubts.[46]

Earlier that month a new commander-in-chief of land forces *Superegeo* had arrived in the Dodecanese – Lieutenant-General Arnaldo Forgiero. In retrospect it is likely his mission was to strengthen the Italian strategic position ahead of an armistice with the Allies. In theory, the German force was under the Italian high command. Forgiero wanted to make this relationship clear to Kleemann. He had barely arrived on the island when he sent orders to Kleemann effectively subordinating the *Sturmdivision* to Italian tactical operations. Forgiero instructed that the German force should confine itself to a small area of difficult terrain in the north-central valley near Psito (Psinthos), effectively trapping it in the event of hostilities. Kleemann suspected that Forgiero's intention was to neutralize the division, originally conceived as a mobile attack force. He wrote to his superiors in Army Group E in Belgrade expressing the view that Forgiero's demand amounted to a negative shift in military relations on Rhodes. Clearly with their consent, Kleemann subsequently replied to Forgiero on 11 August, pointing out that concentrating the *Sturmdivision* in the manner demanded by Forgiero would amount to a tactical error in the event of an Allied attack. In such matters, Kleeman declared, he reserved the right to act independently.[47]

Suspicions about Italian intentions were heightened by the fact that German military intelligence reported that British and Allied forces were preparing an offensive against the Peloponnese with a diversionary attack against Rhodes.[48] At the beginning of August, therefore, German field commanders were ordered to prepare for *Operation Axis*.[49] Kleemann had already began briefing his officers and reorganizing them into smaller mobile tactical units (*Kampfgruppe*) and assigning each one to strategic areas of the island so as to be ready to strike.[50] By early September, British military intelligence reported heightened German activity and strengthening of troops in the Peloponnese, and on the islands of Scarpanto, Milos and Rhodes, as well as the mustering of various naval craft to supply the islands with food and war materiel.[51]

On Rhodes, the battle for control of the island was set in motion on 8 September with the first news in the early evening of the Italian acceptance of General Eisenhower's conditions for an armistice.[52] While there were reports of jubilation among the Italian troops that they were withdrawing from the war, there was also the suspicion that the Italian garrison on Rhodes would rally behind Badoglio, now considered a traitor to the Axis cause, and fight the Germans. Kleemann thus ordered his officers to prepare their units for battle and to act on their own initiative. Meanwhile, the Italian commander, General Forgiero, ostensibly to avert conflict between the erstwhile allies, asked Kleemann to confine his troops to barracks.[53] Kleemann was prepared to comply as long as the same condition applied to the Italian force. There were reports, however, that heavily armed reserve units of the *Regina* Division based at Campochiari (present-day Eleousa) were in fact mobilizing. Kleemann issued a general order to unit commanders to act as they saw fit and without recourse to further orders. The two garrisons thus readied themselves for the inevitable showdown.[54]

At 10.00 pm, Kleemann received the order from General Löhr to launch *Operation Axis*.[55] Kleemann had first to secure strategic targets, notably the airfields. The hitherto good relations with Italian military commanders had left open the possibility of negotiations without the need to resort to force. Thus, at 11.45 pm, Kleemann with a small retinue of staff officers went to Forgiero with a set of conditions that included shutting down the airfields and confining ships to port, as well as unhindered movement of German troops on the island. Forgiero was unable to give Kleemann the assurances he sought. In the early hours of the following morning, reports mounted that the Italians had set up roadblocks, hindering the movement of German troops. Meanwhile the Allies dropped leaflets in Italian and Greek containing the armistice conditions. At this point, Forgiero dispatched an invitation to Kleemann to accompany him to Admiral Campioni. However, Kleemann declined, responding 'he was busy', and instead ordered his battle units to seize strategic points on the island, notably the three airfields at Maritsa, Gaddura and Kattavia. Once his men were in their positions, Kleemann let Forgiero know that he was ready to meet the governor at his residence in the Knights' Castle.

At this meeting, Kleemann reiterated terms for an armistice between the two garrisons, and to the consternation of Campioni and his officers, reports began to arrive of the German capture of the airfields. In order not to derail negotiations, Kleemann proposed to withdraw his men to the periphery of each airfield. He was at pains to avert fighting – perhaps because he was unsure whether his division would be able to overcome the much larger and better-equipped Italian force. Returning to his headquarters, Kleemann saw for himself the mobilization of a heavily armed reserve battalion of the *Regina* division at Campochiaro (present-day Eleousa).[56] Nevertheless, by 7 am his troops were mobilized, and *Operation Axis* was fully underway. Light armoured units of III Grenadier Regiment were deployed to Campochiaro with the task of disarming the 50th Artillery Regiment of *Regina* Division. At Campochiaro Kleemann's adjutant, 30-year-old Captain Goedeckemeyer, instructed Scaroina to lay down weapons. Upon Scaroina's refusal to comply with this ultimatum, Goedeckemeyer took him and his staff prisoner. The 57-year-old Italian general, with a long and distinguished service career, had little stomach for a fight for he ordered the raising of a white flag in order to avert bloodshed. Similar bloodless actions occurred elsewhere that morning, but during the course of the afternoon, a sterner resolve to resist among units of the Italian force became noticeable, especially close to the airfields of Maritsa and Gaddura, where the Italians' superior artillery located on Mount Filermo and Mount Paradiso inflicted heavy losses on the German batteries.[57]

Nevertheless, the German offensive was both swift and decisive. By the evening of the 9th, German units of III Grenadier Regiment under the command of Lieutenant-Colonel Fink had secured strategic areas of the island, including the region of Psito, and thus cutting Italian lines of land communication. The operation was concluded the following day with the assistance of 200 men from company IV/999 Penal Battalion led by Major Winter. These men were not usually under arms; to prove themselves worthy of regaining military honour, they threw themselves into battle with gusto, as Winter later testified.[58] Elsewhere, there were still pockets of heavy resistance, but also increasing signs of fatigue among Italian troops. By 3 am the following morning, the Italian artillery on Mount Filermo and Mount Paradiso had been neutralized. By mid-afternoon on the following day, Scaroina issued the order to his commanders to lay down their arms. The path to Rhodes was now open. Later that evening, Kleemann sent a message to Army Group E stating that the Italians were prepared to surrender and therefore he was seeking permission to put conditions to Campioni for the capitulation.

During late morning on 11 September, Captain Goedeckemeyer accompanied by the Division's translator Captain Bayer went with General Scaroina to Admiral Campioni carrying Kleemann's conditions for the Italian surrender. The governor had just 30 minutes to decide whether to accept or to reject these terms. By 12.25, he had accepted them. At 3 pm in the village of Afando, in the presence of Kleemann and his staff officers, Campioni signed the Italian capitulation.[59] By late evening, the entire island was under German control. The swift securing of Rhodes by Kleemann's forces thwarted British plans to relieve Campioni's garrison. Despite a British brigade having been made ready to embark for Rhodes, Churchill's envoy, Lord Jellicoe was unable to reassure Campioni that troops would arrive within the week, nor could he guarantee their fighting quality vis-à-vis the German forces.[60] Thus, as military historian Jürgen Rohwer concluded: 'the Brit[ish] occupation of the island became impossible.'[61]

Nevertheless, Churchill was adamant that the Allies could still seize the Dodecanese islands *in toto* from the Germans, now that Italy was out of the Axis. He therefore ordered a task force to be assembled. Codenamed *Operation Accolade*, the intervention reconnected to London's earlier endeavours in the Aegean.[62] Its success was vital to reasserting British hegemony in the Eastern Mediterranean, and this meant regaining control of Rhodes, Kos and Leros. Despite Kleemann's success, the German war effort was faltering elsewhere, and Churchill was determined to seize the opportunity, apparently telling his most senior officer in Egypt, Field Marshal Henry Wilson, 'It is time to play for high stakes. You must improvise and dare.'[63] A military success in the Aegean would leverage Ankara into abandoning its neutrality to join the Allies, further isolating the German force on Crete, and cutting off the escape route for the remainder of the Afrika Korps.[64]

However, Churchill's so-called 'folly' in the Aegean found itself in competition with theatres of war elsewhere (Sicily and the Far East, as well as preparations for the Normandy landing). Without aid from the Americans, British military leaders were sceptical about the viability of *Accolade*. Moreover, as in 1941, British policy was plagued by conflicting opinions between Whitehall departments, leading to equivocation on the best way forward. Consequently, Churchill found himself at odds, not just with General Dwight Eisenhower, the supreme Allied commander in the Middle East, but also with his own military commanders. Air Chief Marshall Lord Arthur Tedder, one of the joint chiefs of staff Middle East and Eisenhower's deputy, for example, poured cold water on the scheme.[65]

Nevertheless, Field Marshal Wilson, like Churchill, was bullish about success and summoned the Major, Lord Jellicoe of the Special Boat Service to a meeting in Cairo, at which the British chiefs of staff Middle East instructed Jellicoe to parachute into Rhodes and persuade Campioni to hold out against the Germans until British reinforcements arrived.[66] Accompanying Jellicoe were a radio operator and 'Major Julian Dolbey', acting as interpreter.[67] Their mission took on semi-comedic aspects. Dolbey badly broke his leg in the jump, and whilst Jellicoe made his way to the governor's palace, his presence in the Castle on the 9th coincided with the arrival of Kleemann and his retinue. While Kleemann went into negotiations with Campioni, Jellicoe was hidden in the vaults of the governor's palace.[68]

Before Kleemann's arrival, Jellicoe had tried to reassure Campioni that British troops were en route for Rhodes, but the governor, remembered by Jellicoe as 'a perfectly honourable gentleman', remained hesitant, not least because he learned from Jellicoe that it would be at least a week before reinforcements arrived. The Italian forces, said to be wholly inexperienced in warfare, were too demoralized to offer sustained resistance to the Germans.[69] Kleemann's forces had already seized the airfields, but the port was still under

Italian control and Jellicoe could thus be spirited by boat to Castellorizo and from there to Cairo. Meanwhile Dolbey was evacuated to Cyprus, but the radio operator remained hidden on the island. The mission was not without some dividend to the British: the Italians handed to Jellicoe the maps of the Italian minefields in the Aegean Sea.[70]

Despite the resistance from his chiefs of staff and Eisenhower, Churchill gave the order for *Accolade* on 25 September.[71] Originally, the plan was for Force 292 to attack Rhodes. However, just two days later, it became clear that the Americans were not going to provide air cover and a last-minute alteration took place.[72] Churchill did not give up hope of contesting Rhodes, even though *Accolade* had come too late for it; his attention turned to the islands of Kos and Leros as strategic targets in the Aegean.[73] In early October, at least 3,000 men and munitions were transported to the Eastern Mediterranean – in all about two brigades, but as Jellicoe recalled, this was too little and too late to wrest control of the Dodecanese from the Germans. British forces on both islands suffered heavy losses before surrendering. Poor planning had plagued the operation, indecisive leadership, and poor-quality troops proved no match to the smaller and resolute 'battle groups' – *Kampfgruppen* – of German troops.[74]

Not capturing Rhodes in the first place meant that the campaign to achieve mastery over the Eastern Aegean would be frustrated, even had the British scored success in Kos and Leros. Reflecting on the events for the battle for Rhodes and the struggle for the Aegean a month after its ending, Rear-Admiral Sir Algernon U. Willis noted:

> Apart from Rhodes, the Italians' attitude was co-operative in the islands visited by us, though the fighting value was low. It was considered that even if Leros were reinforced by such British troops as were available and Kos airfields developed and defended adequately, we should not be in a secure position to continue operations in the Aegean until Rhodes was in our possession.[75]

The quality of Italian troops throughout the Dodecanese was variable, as noted by Jellicoe. Undoubtedly, Italian soldiers had had enough of the war by 1943 and simply wished to go home.

Ironically, neither Field Marshall Maximillian von Weichs, the supreme commander of German forces in the Balkans, nor Admiral Dönitz was convinced that they could hold out against British firepower in the Aegean when they met Hitler at a special conference on 24 September.[76] Nevertheless, Berlin understood the threat of a German rout in the Eastern Aegean raised the possibility of Turkey entering the war. Therefore, Rhodes was to be held at all costs.[77] Weichs and Dönitz worried needlessly for there were serious shortcomings on the Allied side. Without the Americans, the British could not provide superior air cover needed to support naval operations. There were shortages of vessels, fuel and men because of the focus on southern Italy (Eisenhower was not prepared to allocate these to what he saw as a 'sideshow'). Finally, strategy and operations suffered because of the lack of a clear chain of command. Indeed, there existed three commands: in Cyprus (air), in Cairo (land) and in Alexandria (sea). Coordination of the three branches via Allied Forces Headquarters of Supreme Allied Command in the Mediterranean in Cairo was not smooth.[78] The lack of military logistical and troop support meant that British command Levant was pursuing a tactic of 'smoke and mirrors', whereby 'It was hoped by a display of activity to induce the enemy to believe we were capable of exerting greater naval strength in the area than was actually the case.'[79]

It is tempting with hindsight to argue that had Campioni and his senior staff faced down Kleemann's forces, and had British planning been more efficient, then the tragic fate of the Aegean Jews might have been averted. At the time, no one could have anticipated what would happen ten months later. Many years later, in the early 1990s, Jellicoe stressed that Campioni, mindful of his men's poor morale, made the right decision not to engage further with Kleemann's division, thereby avoiding unnecessary loss of life. Moreover, not only was there indecision in Whitehall, but British operational planning in the Mediterranean was also poor and resources were lacking, as Jellicoe attested. In a surprise meeting with Churchill in Cairo, Jellicoe recalled how when asked by 'the Great Man' 'why things had gone so wrong', he had made it clear that it had been a 'folly to embark on the Aegean Campaign' without any clear plan or prospect of capturing the airfields on Rhodes.[80] Indeed, the improvised nature of the operation has led one historian to describe London's approach as a 'shoestring strategy'.[81] Seen from this perspective, securing the safety of nearly 2,000 Jews from deportation was simply never a strategic consideration. It is probably the case too that no one among the Allies imagined that Berlin would divert scarce vital resources to such a task. Deporting the island's Jews was also least among Kleemann's considerations. His task was to hold a difficult defensive position in the Dodecanese. For the British, the imperative was to defeat Germany. The fate of a small Jewish community in the Eastern Aegean was not at the centre of either Kleemann's or Allied concerns.

*

The battle for Rhodes was short, barely 48 hours. Casualties among the Germans were light compared to those inflicted on the Italians. The *Sturmdivision* reported 91 fatalities and 212 wounded, and two missing in action. Flak Battery 806 suffered the heaviest losses, including the death of its commanding officer Lieutenant-Colonel Enge, as well as four other officers; the Grenadier Regiment also bore heavy casualties.[82] Meanwhile, figures for Italian casualties are difficult to gauge with accuracy. Some sources indicate 447 Italians were killed during the fighting, and 300 wounded, while other sources estimate a much lower figure of those killed during the battle but include subsequent casualties and their causes. According to historian Aldo Levi, eight officers and 117 NCOs and men were killed during the actual fighting, but they incurred 300 wounded, with added casualties after the ceasefire.[83]

The decision by Marshal Badoglio to withdraw Italy from the war elicited a vengeful response from Hitler, who saw this as betrayal.[84] In response, on 13 September, Hitler ordered the summary execution of Italian troops who had resisted German forces. The most notorious example of carrying out this directive was the execution of over 5,000 officers and men of the 33rd Infantry Division *Acqui* after they had surrendered, including the commanding officer, General Antonio Gandin, on the island of Cephalonia, and immortalized by Louis de Bernières in the novel, *Captain Corelli's Mandolin*. Similarly, on the island of Corfu, 280 Italian officers of the 18th Infantry Division *Acqui* were summarily shot after capitulation.[85] General Wilhelm Müller, who commanded the 22nd Infantry Division, after securing Kos, ordered the summary execution of over eighty Italian officers from 10th Regiment *Regina* Division.[86]

While there is no firm evidence that Kleemann condoned similar acts of retribution, and in his interrogation in Nuremberg in 1946 he denied he had ordered such acts, according to Italian – albeit unverified – sources, after the battle for Rhodes, forty members of the *Regina* Division were summarily shot without due process, and fifty Italian soldiers were subsequently tried by a German military court and executed.[87] Levi also estimates that until the end of the war there were a further 232 deaths in captivity either inflicted or from natural causes. These figures exclude 6,500 Italian military internees missing at sea, and presumed drowned.[88] More than 4,000 of these fatalities are accounted for by the sinking of the old steamer, the *SS Oria* which had left Rhodes for Piraeus in early February 1944, but which ran aground in stormy seas on the islet of Patroklos in the Saroni Gulf, 3 kilometres off Cape Sounion. There were only twenty-eight survivors, among them twenty-one Italians (out of 4,190 prisoners), six German guards and a sole Greek from the ninety-strong crew.[89]

The tragedy of the *Oria* has some bearing on the story of the deportation. The question of dealing with Italian military internees became a source of tension between Kleemann on the one hand, and *Admiral Ägäis*, Vice Admiral Werner Lange and the supreme naval commander *Südost* Admiral Kurt Fricke, on the other hand. Immediately after the battle (15 September), General Löhr had visited the island to praise Kleemann and his men, and also to emphasize the removal of the Italian prisoners, considered a potential threat to the security of the Dodecanese. However, the removal of more than 37,000 Italians before a deadline of mid-February proved logistically difficult because of inadequate air and naval transportation and the lack of fuel.[90] Lange and Fricke, like Hitler, considered the Italians as traitors and were resolute in their intention to deport them to prisoner-of-war camps in Germany or to labour camps further east by any means.[91]

Given the lack of adequate transport, this would have meant utilizing any shipping available and cramming the prisoners into the holds. Kleemann was not prepared to condone this, even if it meant drawing Löhr's ire.[92] The tension over removing Italian internees from the islands casts some light on Kleemann's character. There was simply not enough space on available ships for the numbers involved. Fricke and Lange nonetheless insisted that the ships be crammed to overcapacity, to which Kleemann responded that there had to be lifejackets and lifeboats proportionate to the number of internees.[93] Kleemann, as we saw above, was cast in a traditional military mould that had shaped him long before the coming of the Third Reich. The general was thus prepared to resist the intense pressure from his superiors to follow

Hitler's *Führerbefehl* if this led to a breach in the Geneva Convention through inhumane treatment of prisoners.[94]

Meanwhile, Lange had demanded the execution of governor Admiral Campioni, who, in his own words to Kleemann, was 'virtually under house arrest' in his quarters in the Knights' Castle since signing the capitulation.[95] The governor requested his duties be transferred to Iginio Faralli, an 'extremely experienced civil administrator' who as vice-governor 'in fact had been the real trustee of the Italian administration for the previous two years'.[96] Lange's bloodlust was eventually fulfilled, but not by Kleemann. Campioni was sent to a German-run prisoner-of-war camp in Poland and later transferred to Verona in the Republic of Salò. Here, along with other senior military figures and the son-in-law of Mussolini, Count Galeazzo Ciano (who had been a co-signatory toppling Mussolini in July 1943), Campioni was tried by a Fascist military tribunal, sentenced to death and executed.[97]

Apart from the three days of fighting after the Italian armistice, the German garrison in Rhodes experienced the rest of the war as a 'quiet front', which had few of the jagged edges of the Nazi occupation elsewhere in Greece and in the Balkans. This was despite the continuous harassment by British and Greek commandos.[98] By the end of September, a military administration led by Hans Helmut zur Nedden, a career administrator who arrived on Rhodes soon after the end of the battle, was established and quartered in the Castello.[99] The garrison was reorganized, and smaller garrisons established through the islands. Arrangements to remove the substantial numbers of Italian military internees continued, although logistical bottlenecks hampered their removal from Rhodes into the summer of 1944.

Ordinance Nr 8 retained the Italian administration but in a civilian capacity.[100] In keeping with Oberkommando des Heeres (German High Command – OKH) orders, Kleemann initiated the recruitment of Italian military and *Carabinieri* willing to take an oath of allegiance to Hitler. While most Italian soldiers preferred to end their part in the war in the hope that they might return home, a sizeable minority, especially among mid-to-higher-ranking officers, chose to cross over to the German side. Thus, Colonel Enzo Manna who commanded the 331 Infantry Regiment in the Calitea region, a few days after the Italian capitulation, declared himself ('with some conditions') for the Germans.[101] Manna was joined by Lieutenant-Colonel Fanizza, the chief of staff, and Lieutenant-Colonel Angiolini, while Lieutenant-Colonel Masini put his entire battalion at Kleemann's disposal. From the *Carabinieri*, Colonel Mittino declared his fealty to the Fascist cause.[102] At least sixty-one *Carabinieri* officers and NCOs crossed over to the German side, and it is likely that the remaining 520 *Carabinieri* could be relied on. Additionally, 1,891 so-called 'independents' (including members of the Fascist Blackshirts) expressed their allegiance to Hitler's war in the Dodecanese.[103]

By the end of October, a further ten Italian officers and 180 NCOs and ordinary ranks had sworn allegiance to Hitler as armed auxiliaries, known as KAWIs, while forty-five officers and 1,859 NCOs and ordinary ranks had signed on as unarmed auxiliaries (so-called HIWIs), but only 20 per cent of these took the oath. The first group was assigned to coastal guard and the latter to constructing roads and fortifications. The numbers of both groups soon swelled, clearly a testimony to the efforts of Major Migliavacca who recruited from the military internees. By the end of the year, at least sixty officers and another 1,265 NCOs and men had taken the oath as KAWIs, whereas the corresponding numbers for HIWIs had declined to eight officers and 1,686 NCOs and men.[104] In Kos by June 1944, there were around 230 Italians serving the Germans, mostly in the Flak (KAWI), but also as helpers (HIWIs).[105] From the Italians' perspective, the motivation either was ideological and/or material conditions (KAWI), or just better food and clothing (HIWI). However, improved rations came at a price for treatment by the Germans was harsh, and, by 1944, desertion (with deadly consequences if caught) was frequent.[106]

Meanwhile, around a dozen officers from the Fascist Blackshirts from 201 Legion in Rhodes town joined their leader Enzo Celebrano, and declared themselves for Nazi Germany.[107] Altogether, around 270 of an estimated 1,605 Legion members volunteered to side with Kleemann's forces. The reliability of the rest of the 201 Legion was less certain, and of those individuals who initially sided with the Germans, a large number showed a change of heart within a few days. Celebrano, in a subsequent note to Kleemann, recommended weeding out the unreliable elements and reorganizing the two legions into a single Aegean battalion.[108]

By the end of 1943, military garrisons had been established throughout the Dodecanese, their strength reflecting each island's strategic importance (Table 4.1). Kleemann had sought to integrate the Italian collaborators

Table 4.1 German and Italian forces in the Dodecanese (July 1944)

Island	Army	Luftwaffe	Navy	Italian	Total
Rhodes	9,754	877	178	4,827	15,636
Kos	2,238	159	40	678	3,115
Leros	1,769	73	1,460	691	3,993
Samos	764	–	113	1,280	2,157
Scarpanto	981	26	13	126	1,146
Stampalia	124	–	126	27	277
Calino	156	–	29	39	224
Simi	145	–	8	31	184
Piscopi	103	–	–	50	153
Nisiro	70	–	–	25	95
Levita	41	–	7	11	59
Alimnia	59	–	–		59
Total	**16,204**	**1,135**	**1,974**	**7,785**	**27,098**

Source: BA-MA RH26/1007/14, Bl. 316: Kommandant Ost-Ägäis, 1a, Br.B.Nr 5546/44 geh. (KTB 76).

and thus they too were integrated into various units of the garrisons.[109] On Rhodes, they constituted about a third of the total force, many of them were mere auxiliaries without weapons, and the fighting quality of those under arms became increasingly questionable. After the Allied landings in Italy and their retaking of Rome, several Italian officers in conversations with German officers reiterated the view that Italy was committed to Mussolini and Hitler. It was reported that for these officers the fact 'that their homeland has fallen into the hands of the Allies, had the effect that they now stand more firmly by our side than before'.[110] Nevertheless, it soon became clear that Italian collaborators were unreliable.[111] When the British attacked the island of Simi in 1944, the Italian garrison, contrary to its orders, capitulated, to Kleemann's fury.[112]

By the summer of 1944, Italian soldiers and Fascists were (once again) considered 'lacking' (*mangelhaft*) in their commitment to maintaining Germany's position in the Eastern Aegean. There were reports that Italian military internees who had opted to work as HIWIs were becoming increasingly 'civilianized' ('*zivilisiert*'). 'He wears civilian trousers, a civilian shirt, goes about without a cap, he does not wear his armband, or he has it rolled up in his sleeve.'[113] There was talk of a 'disintegration' (*zerfall*) among the

Italian collaborators generally, also among the Celebrno's Fascist League, which had never developed into the effective fighting force Kleemann had hoped it might become.[114] Eventually, he ordered its disbandment. The majority of Blackshirts (84.5 per cent) was dispersed among various German army units, while the remainder were re-categorized as military internees.[115]

Notwithstanding some fluctuation, the German force on Rhodes by the summer of 1944 stood at 10,435 men, including 208 officers, 1,711 NCOs and 7,011 ordinary ranks. Thus, the strength of the entire force in the Dodecanese was barely that of a full division, with discipline among the troops deteriorating, as too were material conditions generally.[116]

The battle for Rhodes and the subsequent military occupation of the Dodecanese according to historian Gerhard Schreiber would be Germany's last triumph of the war.[117] However, it was in effect a pyrrhic victory. While *Sturmdivision Rhodos* controlled the islands and the *Luftwaffe* provided relative air superiority during daylight hours from the summer of 1944, the German fleet in the Aegean commanded by Admiral Werner Lange, who took command of *Admiral Ägäis* in February 1943, did not dominate the waves.[118] Shipping – and therefore supplies – was at a constant risk from attack by the Allied navy, and coastal defences were designed to repel large-scale attack, but not British commandos who stepped up harassment of the Germans.

By the summer of 1944, the Germans in the Dodecanese were increasingly isolated and under strain. Kleemann was short of nearly a thousand men and both the amount and maintenance of military equipment and the continued provisioning of the garrison was far from satisfactory with Allied naval operations adversely disrupting supply lines.[119] Kleemann's position in the Eastern Aegean was dependent upon several factors beyond his control. Allied air strikes intensified from early spring of 1944, once the worst of the winter weather was over. Until the end of June, when a squadron of German fighter planes was deployed to Rhodes, the Royal Air Force continued its onslaught against Rhodes, Kos and Leros, striking their ports and airfields repeatedly.[120]

*

The three-day battle between Italian and German forces does not appear to have impinged directly on the population of Rhodes.

Even after the Germans established their control over the islands, Jews remained unaffected, despite a panoply of new restrictions on the civilian population that were put in place. An Ordinance (*Verordnung*) of 13 September decreed, among other things: the reporting within 24 hours of radio sets and of carrier pigeons; it forbade listening to foreign broadcasts (usually, this meant the BBC); it imposed a 7 pm curfew with exceptions only for those on air raid duties, essential workers and medical professionals, as long as these were carrying exemption documents. Military courts were established with jurisdiction over civilians, with severe penalties (including death) for any transgressions that might be construed as acts of resistance or sabotage.[121] Restrictions also were imposed on fishermen who were no longer able to fish beyond a 500-metre zone off the coast, and then only in daylight, in Ordinance Nr 3 in 17 September.[122] Finally, new identity cards were introduced and arbitrary street checks by the German Field Police and the *Carabinieri* were enforced.[123] These checks would eventually lead to a separate list of Jews being compiled by the Italian authorities that would facilitate their deportation.

Alice Tarica, who was in her early teens in 1943, stressed 'surprisingly, *Wehrmacht* soldiers behave[d] impeccably'.[124] Before the military situation worsened from the spring 1944, the German garrison had learned to accommodate itself to life under the Aegean sun. In the period from the battle until the deportation, members of the garrison clearly fraternized with the island's inhabitants, including its Jews. While most of the garrison dispersed to various parts of the island, and lived under canvas, or had taken over former Italian encampments and barracks, a sizeable number were billeted in Rhodes town and in the larger villages of Trianda (present-day Ialyssos) and Kremasto. This meant that Germans and islanders lived in proximity to one another, making social contact unavoidable.[125]

As well as the temple of ancient Ialyssos on Monte Smith, or the ruins of ancient Kamiros, or exploring the narrow streets of Lindos and its acropolis, the old town of Rhodes encompassing both Turkish and Jewish shops proved a favourite haunt for off-duty soldiers (Illustration 4.1).[126] After the dust of the battle for Rhodes had settled, soldiers became tourists, as Stella Levi recalled in one of her conversations with American author Michael Frank.

Piazza Carlo III, also known as Piazza del Fuoco after fire
1872, Rhodes Old Town (Turkish/Jewish Quarter).
Photograph taken by Feldwebel Otto Stenker, after May
1943 – before July 1944

Illustration 4.1 Piazza Carlo III in the *Juderia* (popularly referred to as Piazza del Fuoco after the fire 1872), taken by Feldwebel Otto Stenker, *Sturmdivision* Rhodos
Source: Unknown ownership (author's copy)

In the moment, though, the first few days we were absolutely terrified, we locked ourselves up in our houses as soon as curfew was called, around six o'clock when the shops were ordered closed. No one went out. Once, we heard the distinctive steps of a German soldier walking by – my mother said we should consider escaping by way of the terrace upstairs. He had come to the *Juderia* to sightsee, it turned out.[127]

The garrison also settled down to a mundane life that offered a social calendar for officers. Stella also recalled parties she attended at the house of friends in plush Via Victor Emmanuel III, at which upper-class Italians and German *Wehrmacht* officers were present. On at least one occasion, that of a birthday party of a close girlfriend, she was convinced she glimpsed General Kleemann, who, together with other officers, observed from the balcony of the neighbouring house the young women singing; and that he good-humouredly requested they sing a popular song for him in French.[128] This encounter (which appeared to have occurred before the battle for Rhodes) later emboldened her and her friends to visit what she believed to be Kleemann's office in the Castello sometime in early 1944, in order to spare the Italian soldier-husband of one of the young women from imminent deportation to Germany.[129]

Campioni's accommodating approach towards Jews remained unchanged under the German occupation. Jewish observance and practices continued unmolested by the German military administration under zur Nedden. As mentioned already, some normalcy to Jewish life had returned under Campioni and this remained the case after the demission of his governorship, albeit life in the *Juderia* was 'now muted and on uneasy alert'.[130]. The B'nai B'rith continued to organize charity balls and lotteries to raise alms for the poorer families of the *Juderia*. Thus, the life of the community continued more or less as before, routine wartime restrictions notwithstanding. Licences to trade or to carry out other commercial activities continued to be issued to Jews of 'good conduct', but scrutinized by Mittino and his men. Similarly, the authorities continued to grant permits to travel to and from the other islands to either visit family, or conduct business, albeit dependent upon prevailing conditions. The Germans, although ultimately in control, left such matters to the *Carabinieri* to administer.

The long ten months between seizing the islands and the destruction of the Jewish community were not characterized by Nazi repression. On the contrary, Jews enjoyed the same rights as other islanders, albeit within the limits arising from wartime conditions. Indeed, Kleemann pursued cordial relations with the islands' Jews, saving his distrust for anglophile Greeks.[131] If the Jews of Rhodes and Kos shared the 'illusion of safety' that Salonica survivor and historian Michael Matsas described in his account of the catastrophe on mainland Greece, it is because there was no hint of the violence that was about to befall them.[132] Only in retrospect could survivors believe that once the Germans had defeated their erstwhile Italian ally and routed the British forces their fate became inevitable. Lucia Garzolini, the daughter of the merchant Hizkia Franco from Kos, reflecting many years later on the deportation from Kos, believed preparations were set in motion once the Germans seized the islands.

It was only nine months before our eventual deportation that at some point in time the Germans, after seeing what the Italians did [the armistice with the allies], sent more troops to the islands. But the local population was not aware of anything, and even the Germans that were on the island were acting very normal and polite with all the population. We did not know, but in the meantime, they had taken all the information on Jewish families.

They took all the addresses and knew who was living where and they already
had all the information on Jews. They were not showing anything, but they
had already started.[133]

Yet, until their deportation, Jews did not feature in the garrison's monthly
situation reports. Two soldiers, who recorded their stay on Rhodes, also do
not appear to have mentioned Jews at all. Both of them entered the *Juderia*
on more than one occasion, and at least one of them, Otto Stenker, captured
with his Leica camera everyday life in the heart of the old town with its myriad
Jewish-owned businesses.[134] Erhart Kästner, an avid explorer of the islands,
was effusive about Rhodes' old quarter and its 'orientalism'. Kästner had
arrived on the island long *before* the deportation and as we know from his
journals, he explored the streets and alleys of the Turkish and Jewish quarters,
but Jews as individuals or collectively are simply absent from the landscape he
describes.[135]

Why this invisibility? After all, nearly 2,000 Jews concentrated in a relatively
small geographically defined area by its bazaar pulsating with life and
frequented by soldiers looking for souvenirs or items to barter, could hardly
go unnoticed. We know from anecdotal evidence, ordinary soldiers and the
military administration had regular contact with Jews. The Jewish-owned
large warehouses of household and industrial goods (including olive oil, soap,
building materials), could hardly be ignored by the military administration set
up at the end of September 1943, nor by the army quartermaster and ordnance
officer whose task was to provision the garrison.[136]

The answer to these questions is possibly threefold. First, the military
administration on Rhodes had only a material interest in Jews insofar as they
acted as brokers or providers of essential goods, especially foodstuffs. Second,
for many ordinary soldiers of the garrison Nazi ideology appears to have carried
little weight and thus the Aegean lacked most of the features of the barbarized
racial war found on the Eastern Front.[137] When staff sergeant (*Oberfeldwebel*)
Otto Stenker, one of the soldiers mentioned above, visited the *Juderia* with his
camera, he focused on the 'orientalism' of its bazaar and its alleyways leading
off from the *Juderia*'s commercial heart. His photographs do not present Jews
as 'a people apart', to borrow historian David Vital's phrase. This could be for
a third reason. The outward appearance of Jews across the generations was

often indistinguishable from their Turkish or Greek neighbours; nor were they marked as Jews, as in Salonica. Indeed, the Jews were for many German soldiers an innocuous presence in the townscape, as former First Lieutenant Hermann Neeff told war crimes investigators after the war:

> There was also a Jewish quarter through whose streets I once went. I did not get the impression that this quarter was more thickly populated than usual. Also under no circumstances did I get the impression that the Jewish quarter was subject to any special or even loose surveillance. [...] The streets of Rhodes appeared entirely peaceful.[138]

Neeff was responding to the question whether the German force treated Jews differently to other population groups, and his testimony corroborates that of other former soldiers about the garrison's largely benign attitude towards Jews.

Much of the anecdotal evidence provided by survivors of the deportation in post-war testimonies suggests a largely cordial relationship between Germans and Jews. Lucia Garzolini, whom we cited above, remembered how on Kos 'The relation [*sic*] with the Germans was very good, I mean – normal. And there was nothing against us on behalf [*sic*] of the Germans.'[139] Indeed, many soldiers frequented her father's store to 'buy merchandise, pay and [were] well-behaved. They were not aggressive to us.'[140]

On Rhodes, Kleemann possibly led by example. Although the general was a self-declared National Socialist, and through his oath to Hitler taken in October 1934, loyal to the commander-in-chief, he does not appear to have adhered too closely to the antisemitic ideas of his *Führer*.[141]

In 1940, *c.* 515 refugees arrived from Central Europe after the river steamer *Pentcho* in which they had escaped the continent had foundered in rough seas near the rocky islet of Kamilonisi, about 100 nautical miles from Rhodes.[142] Eventually, with Italy's entry into the war, and in increasingly difficult conditions on the island, the greater majority of these refugees were transferred to the prisoner-cum-refugee camp of Ferramonti in Sicily. Among the refugees rescued from the *Pentcho* was 30-year-old Sidney Fahn, a Slovak from Brezova. He recounted in testimony in the mid-1960s, how two years later governor Campioni granted him and his wife, and his brother Rudolf, leave to remain on the island instead of being transferred to Ferramonti. The brothers were skilled furriers and tanners, and were thus given the licence to manage Fratelli Victoria, a leather factory. Their skilled handiwork soon proved popular with Italian officers and administrators.[143]

In John Bierman's account of the fate of the *Pentcho* refugees, the brothers were subsequently engaged by General Kleemann to make new riding boots.[144] Other staff officers in need of leather coats and boots also employed the services of the Fahns. Under the occupation throughout Europe, utilizing skilled Jewish labour was of itself not unusual among German staff officers. However, Sidney saw nothing exploitative in the contracts. As well as receiving payment from their German clients, the Fahns retained the privileges granted by Campioni that many other islanders whether Jews or gentiles were denied.[145]

While most contacts between Germans and Jews were transactional, there were social encounters that took place outside this nexus. That is to say, friendships formed between soldiers and Jews. Lucia Amato remembered how 'when the Germans arrived ... they were not bad, you know'. Moreover, when her family moved out to the safety of the village of Trianda during the aerial bombardment of Rhodes town in the early spring 1944, she recalled, 'the Germans were there and they said "oh, the Jews are here, they are lovely." Yes, they wanted to dance with the Jewish [girls] and the girls didn't want to.'[146] Nevertheless, some young Jewish women struck up close friendships with German soldiers. Indeed, for a brief period at least, a member of the secret military police – *Geheime Feldpolizei* – even dated Becky Hazan.[147] Stella Levi recalled how she knew a number of Kleemann's staff officers. Over the course of the German occupation, she became friendly with a junior staff officer from Vienna while frequenting the Rotunda (today Elli beach). She had found him interesting from his appearance, and they struck up a conversation, chatting in French. The young man displayed no outward sign of discrimination towards her.[148] In much the same way that young Italian soldiers had courted the young women of the *Juderia*, so too, did young German soldiers, who frequently went into the Jewish quarter to flirt with them.[149] Nevertheless, for most, liaisons remained transactional. Certainly, we know from a few *Carabinieri* reports that the Turkish and Jewish prostitutes located in the old town were popular with soldiers from both garrisons.[150]

The youthfulness of the staff officer at the beach (Stella recalled he was around the same age as her) was typical of the junior officers of Kleemann's division. Erhart Kästner, who had his fortieth birthday in March 1944, mentions sharing a tent with a 'young officer' on Mount Filermo shortly after arriving on Rhodes.[151] Indeed, junior officers who had not come up through the ranks were usually in their early twenties, such as 22-year-old Hermann Neeff, the lieutenant quoted above, or first ensign Karl Wurmseher (born in 1920). Also among the ordinary ranks by this point in the war, the age range could be even younger. The historian Andreas Kunz has shown that well over half a million mid-teenage youths (born between 1926 and 1928) were called up for military service from 1943.[152] Kästner's personal account of the prisoner-of-war camp in Egypt, where from summer 1945 he and his comrades from Rhodes and Kos were confined together with fellow soldiers captured on Crete, mentions the presence of 1,200 boy soldiers.[153] Just how many of these youths were among the troops sent to Rhodes? There is little direct information to allow a firm answer to this question, although anecdotal evidence, not least about their leisure time activities, or their reading habits, for example, points to their presence.[154]

Before the moment of deportation in the summer of 1944, there is little evidence pointing to racial hostility towards Jews on the part of the German occupying force. No doubt, there were those who held antisemitic beliefs across all ranks, from officers to ordinary soldiers. The *Stadtkommandant* Colonel Wröndel, described as a fanatical Nazi by Kleemann's adjutant in post-war testimony, for example, attempted to impose Nuremberg Law-style measures against the island's Jews. Shortly after arriving on the island, he ordered the erection of notices forbidding Jews to use the municipal beaches. However, Kleemann intervened to issue a counter-order removing the signs. This intervention led Wröndel to refer to Kleemann as the 'Jew General' during a drinking bout with fellow officers and subsequently this led to a disciplinary reprimand and Wröndel's removal from the island.[155]

The garrison had its fair share of Nazis like Wröndel, such as the 30-year-old medical Staff Officer for Battalion 999, Dr Christian Koskewitz, described in post-war investigations as 'cold blooded' and 'a typical Nazi'; or First Lieutenant Walter Mai, who was described in British military sources as 'dark, squat, and of brutal appearance' and 'devoid of moral sense'. There was also First Lieutenant, later Captain, Dr Helmut Meeske, a 30-year-old judge, who arrived in April 1944, and who was described by his British captors as a 'brutal arrogant type spurned on by ambition and completely unscrupulous'. The

Division also had its share of Party Cadres tasked with political indoctrination. Among them, Lieutenant Karl Bohme, or Lieutenant Dr Brenner, who in civilian life had been a senior state prosecutor (*erster Staatsanwalt*) in Berlin, and Professor Rolf Wagenführ, a 'doctrinaire Nazi', who was 'highly intelligent', but nevertheless 'had a great need to prove himself'. Wagenführ, according to British intelligence officers, 'possess[es] much knowledge but lacked insight', and they concluded he was 'obsequious' and an 'opportunist'.[156] However, despite the roles of these officers, there is no evidence of anti-Jewish propaganda in the programmes they organized for the garrison. Furthermore, none of the above was involved in the deportation.

We cannot say the same for the secret field police (*Geheime Feldpolizei* – GFP) or the regular military police. The GFP in Greece stood under the overall command of *Oberfeldpolizeidirektor* (the equivalent of an SS-Lieutenant-Colonel) Dr Roman Loos, based in Belgrade, and thus did not come under the direct jurisdiction of field commanders, such as Kleemann, although there was cooperation.[157] The unit on Rhodes comprised fewer than a dozen officers at the time of the deportation. Officially known as Sekretariat VI (Rhodes), it had been originally a sub-unit of GFP 510 based in Crete, and one of five secret military police units operating in Greece. We know little about this Rhodes office, not least because of efforts to disguise records of its existence, shortly before the Germans withdrew from Greece.[158] Nevertheless, it is possible to put together a rough sketch of the unit from existing sources.

Before its deployment to Rhodes, as GFP 510, its members had seen service in Salonica and Athens, although not necessarily the same men each time. There were further changes in personnel after 1 April 1944 when the unit came under the command of Athens, becoming GFP Branch 611.[159] By the time of the deportation, it comprised thirteen men led by *Kriminalkommissar* Adolf Manshausen, assisted by a sergeant-major (*Oberfeldwebel*), a sergeant, six lance corporals, a corporal and a private.[160] Although its principal role was to combat subversion, the GFP was deeply involved in the deportation, and hence murder, of Jews.[161] Working closely with the Commander of the Security Police and the Security Service (*Befehlshaber der Sicherheitspolizei und des Sicherheitsdienstes*), *Standartenführer* Walter Blume in Athens, GFP units were involved in the deportations from Salonica in 1943, and the deportations from Jannina, Athens, Corfu, Crete and, finally, Rhodes and Kos in 1944.[162]

There was little love lost between the GFP and the local population or, indeed, in parts of the garrison. Soon after the deportation, unknown assailants bombed their office in Via Francesco Crispi (located in the Neocori, today Odos Amerikis). We cannot today say if there was a connection between the two events. Nevertheless, at the time, there was widespread consternation not only among Italian collaborators but also within the German garrison at the news of the pending deportation. The extent of dismay was serious enough to cause Kleemann to issue a directive on 16 July to his unit commanders forbidding all discussion of the fate of the Jews.[163]

This is the only time – apart from his order to remove anti-Jewish signs – that we see any reference to Jews in any of Kleemann's orders. In issuing this directive, Kleemann asserted that only he as commanding officer and a National Socialist had the authority in the Dodecanese to decide on matters of Reich policy as far as these concerned the Dodecanese and its Jews.[164] This order is extraordinary not for what it proclaims, but for the fact that Kleemann had to issue it in the first place. Unlike his counterpart on Crete, the notorious General Bräuer, Kleemann did not harbour a murderous antisemitism.[165] It clearly indicates how the deportation provoked intense disquiet among many ordinary soldiers, thus further threatening military discipline.[166]

*

Kleemann's victory in the Eastern Aegean at the very moment that Germany was facing impending defeat had the effect of repositioning the Aegean islands of Rhodes, Leros and Kos, as well as the Ionian Island of Corfu in German military strategy. These islands took on greater military significance, becoming strategic fortress redoubts in a precarious frontline.[167] It was at this point too, that they were propelled to the frontline of the Nazi racial war against the Jews. Eichmann's office in Berlin's Kurfürstenstraße (at Nr 115/166) in collaboration with Walter Blume as chief of the SS and Security Police in Athens, and with the explicit approval of General Löhr as head of German High Command Army Group E in Belgrade, now put into action the final act against the remaining Jews on the Greek mainland and in the islands.[168]

5

Deportation

It is difficult for you to understand ... because we were innocent people. We hadn't committed any crime. Our crime was only that of having been born Jewish.[1]

Preparations for the deportation of Jews in areas of Greece under German control started in earnest in early 1943.[2] On 13 February, Dr Max Merten, head of the military administration in Salonica, issued a number of edicts, among them one ordering Jews in Salonica to sew a 10 cm by 10 cm yellow star over their heart and on the right shoulder. They were also ordered to register their property and, on 25 February, a curfew was imposed. Eventually the Germans began concentrating Jews in the Baron Hirsch ghetto close to Salonica's main railway station. Between March and August 1943, Eichmann's agent in Greece, 32-year-old SS-Captain (*Hauptsturmführer*) Dieter Wisliceny, organized nineteen transports from the city to Auschwitz or to Treblinka, comprising approximately 50,000 Salonican Jews.[3]

These deportations did not include the circa 13,000 Jews living in the Italian-occupied zone of Greece.[4] The Italians had proven to be reluctant partners in the unfolding genocide. Hitherto there had been numerous complaints by the German authorities that the Italians were thwarting anti-Jewish policy by responding sluggishly to requests for cooperation, or by providing refuge to Jews who had sought safe haven in the Italian zone. Indeed, at one stage in early summer 1943, allegedly Italian authorities threatened to arrest Wisliceny if he again ventured into the Italian occupation zone in his hunt for Jews who had escaped the Germans.[5] Nor were the Jews in the Dodecanese islands affected by Wisliceny's efforts to remove Jews from Greece or the islands.

This situation changed radically after Italy's armistice with the Allies and its subsequent occupation by the Germans. From the autumn of 1943 until the summer of 1944, successive waves of deportations took place from the former Italian spheres of influence, commencing in German-occupied Italy itself in mid-October 1943. The Irish minister to the Vatican City a few months later reported to his superior in Dublin at the beginning of December of 'a severe new anti-Jewish ordinance in Italy' which rendered Jews enemies of the German-installed fascist Salò Republic.[6] Thomas J. Kiernan exhorted his government to 'plead for justice, goodwill and clemency' for Italy's Jews.[7] To no avail. Among those arrested by the *Carabinieri* in Genoa on 3 November, taken to Milan and from there deported to Auschwitz on 6 December 1943, was Genoa's chief rabbi, 39-year-old Riccardo Pacifici, the former director of the rabbinical college in Rhodes.[8] His wife, Wanda Abenaim, also was arrested on 26 November in Florence, transferred to Verona and from there deported on 6 December to Auschwitz, arriving five days later. She, like her husband, did not survive.[9] They are the first known deaths of Jews closely associated with Rhodes and Kos. Historian Liliana Picciotto has estimated that 8,564 Jews were deported from mainland Italy. When we add those formerly under Italian control from Crete, Corfu, Rhodes and Kos from this period until the summer of 1944 who were sent to Auschwitz or Treblinka the figure is 11,126 (see Table 1.1 in Chapter 1).[10]

This phase of the Holocaust resulted from planning dating back to the Wannsee Conference, if not earlier.[11] By the time of the meeting in Berlin, convened and presided over by Reinhard Heydrich as head of the *Reichssicherheitshauptamt* (conventionally translated as Reich Security Main Office or RSHA),[12] the decision had been taken to comb Europe under German control and to implement a 'total solution' (*Gesamtlösung*) to the Nazis' 'Jewish Question'. Henceforward, administrative coordination would facilitate ideological imperative. For Hitler and his paladins, it was a question of timing – in 1941/42, with Germany at the height of its continental power, the opportunity to make Europe 'Jew free' (*Judenrein*) had availed itself, but this would not last indefinitely. Indeed, by 1943/44, that window was rapidly closing. By 1943, the RSHA was running against the clock, as Germany conceded military advantage. In this regard, when viewed through a Nazi lens, the ideological imperative became even more pressing to complete the destruction of European Jewry, thus sealing the fate of the Aegean Jews. In what follows, we first examine the organization and implementation of genocide in the Aegean, before going on to chart the experiences of the victims during the tragedy of the deportation to Auschwitz.

*

The justification by the RSHA for the deportations from Greece and the Aegean islands was that of military security. In a memorandum on preparations for the 'Final Solution' in Europe of 11 July 1942 to the German Foreign Ministry, SS-Lieutenant-Colonel (*Obersturmbannführer*) Friedrich Suhr referred to Jewish exiles in Greece as a dangerous fifth column, poor Greek Jews as the breeding ground for communism, and wealthy Jews as manipulators of the black market thus endangering the 'inner front'.[13]

Horst Wagner from the German Foreign Ministry's Inland Group II with responsibility for 'Jewish affairs' agreed with him. At the start of the preparations for deportations from Salonica in February 1943, Wagner referred to Jews in Greece (and by extension in the islands) as a 'security risk' in correspondence with his colleague Eberhard von Thadden,[14] and added another dimension to the murderous intent of the Nazis while the deportations from Salonica were still ongoing. The desk perpetrators in the German Foreign Office now cast their eyes beyond the German occupation zone to the Italians, concluding: 'A postponement due to the difficulty of registration or for transport reasons does not appear justifiable both in terms of defence, and in the interest of Germany's reputation in Greece.'[15]

Thus, a combination of ideological racial zealotry, reputational arrogance and a bureaucratic mind-set sealed the fate of the Jews.[16] With dogged relentlessness, the SS strove to achieve Nazi racial goals in its 'war against the Jews' where Germany was in military control. Wisliceny suggested as much in his post-war interrogation when he elucidated Nazi thinking at this juncture of the war. 'As the war progressed', he stated, 'and as it became clearer that German victory was out of the question, Eichmann insisted on the complete implementation of deportation and the annihilation [of the Jews].'[17]

The deportations from the Eastern Aegean were part of the 'final wave' of removing Jews from Greece following Italy's capitulation.[18] With the full occupation of Greece and the islands from September 1943, the scene was set for the deportation of Jews.[19] It was only the following spring, however, that planning turned into action on the mainland and on the islands. It began with 'night and fog'-type actions between 23 and 25 March 1944 against Jews in Athens, on the peninsula of Eubioa (Northern Aegean), and in Ioannina in the Epirus, which, after Kavala, was the largest of the smaller Romaniote communities; similar actions followed against the Jewish communities of Preveza and Arta.[20] Close on the heels of these mainland actions, SS officers turned their attention to the island communities of Corfu, Crete, Rhodes and Kos in June and July 1944.[21] In total, nearly 7,000 Jews were deported during these actions from March to July, with the majority killed in either Auschwitz or in the Nazi labour camps. Given the timing of the deportations, in the final months of the German occupation of Greece, it is difficult to agree with Götz Aly's interpretation that the implementation of Nazi racial policy was part and parcel of German military aims.[22] Indeed, as we shall see, it ran counter to military needs on the ground.

The failure of the British to seize the Dodecanese islands from the Germans sealed the fate of the Aegean Jews, according to some scholars.[23] Moreover, it is claimed that the deportation from the island occurred in full view of British warships, which is unlikely; or that en route to Auschwitz there had been an opportunity to bomb the railtrack.[24] Even so, this view assumes that the Allies had full or even reliable knowledge of what was transpiring in the Aegean as far as Jews were concerned. However, this was not the case. An example of poor knowledge partly explains the sinking a month earlier of the Greek steamship *Tánais* by a British submarine in Aegean waters. The submarine's commander had mistaken the ship for a military vessel, not knowing that on board were approximately 300 Jews from Crete on the first leg of their transportation to Auschwitz.[25] The fact remains that even at this late stage in the war, there was little-to-no information intercepted by the Allies indicating the Germans were planning the deportations.[26]

The deportation from Crete, as with Corfu and later Rhodes and Kos, took time to organize, as had been the case with the scattered Jewish communities on the Greek mainland. Nevertheless, arrangements were in place by the early spring. The deportations were to be swift and without warning, with emphasis on surprise. Indeed, intelligence officers of Army Group E when referring to the removal of Jews from Corfu used the analogy of a 'thunderbolt'.[27] After the war, Kleemann's former adjutant, Klaus Goedeckemeyer, recalled how the action in Rhodes too was 'surprisingly quick'.[28]

Responsibility for the deportation of Jews from these small mainland communities was initially in the hands of SS-Captain Paul Alfons von Manowsky, a career police officer with the civilian rank of detective superintendent (*Kriminalkommissar*). Manowsky led the eleven-man team of SS officers based in Ioannina, but by June responsibility for the remaining deportations had shifted to Wisliceny's successor in Greece, Anton Burger.[29] Originally deployed to the counter-espionage unit in Athens, Burger was reassigned to organize the deportation of the remaining Jews on the mainland and in the islands.[30] Burger's aptitude for the job was undisputed. Personally loyal to Eichmann, he was a cruel antisemitic thug, described by Wisliceny in post-war testimony as one of Eichmann's 'blind obedient' and 'primitive' underlings.[31]

Burger was an Austrian Nazi with a chequered past. He was born in Neunkirchen, Lower Danube, in 1911, and had left school at 14 to train as a commercial employee (*kaufmännischer Angestellter*), before volunteering for the Austrian army in April 1930. Three years later at the end of July, he was dishonourably discharged, ostensibly because of his membership of the Austrian branch of the Nazi Party's *Sturmabteilung* (SA). Unemployed, he drifted to Germany, serving the Nazi Party in various but mostly marginal roles, and of no fixed abode, frequently sleeping in SA-Heime (hostels).[32] He remained in the SA until 1938, when, at the end of July, he joined the SS in Vienna, obtaining a position in Eichmann's euphemistically titled 'Central Office for Jewish Emigration' in 1938. Henceforth, Burger's career took off, and within four years he had attained the SS rank of *Obersturmführer* equivalent to a lieutenant in the *Wehrmacht*. Burger's work in the Central Office impressed Eichmann, for after the annexation of Czechoslovakia, he was reassigned to its equivalent office in Prague, and subsequently took charge of its branch in Brno. In July 1943, Burger succeeded Siegried Seidl as commander of the ghetto-camp of Theresienstadt (Térézin), remaining there until his secondment to Department IV B4 in Athens in January 1944.[33] A year later, Burger returned to the Brno office as chief of staff until the end of the war, and from where he sought to hide his tracks.[34]

Burger's ruthlessness in persecuting Jews and his administrative efficiency had earned him promotion. His virulent antisemitism and his close association to Eichmann cast him as the ideal replacement for Wisliceny, even though he did not have a police background, unlike many of his colleagues at the so-called Eichmann Referat IV B 4. The section leader was SS-*Hauptsturmführer* Johannes Böhm, a *Kriminalkommissar* (detective superintendent) who had previously served in the murderous Einstazgruppe B in Bialystok.[35] In spite of the chain of command, Burger appears to have conducted himself independently, consulting directly with Eichmann's office in the Kurfürstenstrasse in Berlin. In the 1960s and 1970s, war-crimes investigators put together a description of Burger (only one photograph survives in his SS personal file). 'Notable [features] of this 180-centimeter tall man', who, like Wisliceny, was in his early thirties, 'were his big ears, his brown eyes and his uniquely, distinctive, small hands. He had a muscular figure and a hard Austrian accent.'[36]

Burger's assistant was 40-year-old detective (*Kriminalsekretär*) Friedrich Linnemann, an experienced Gestapo officer, who, since 1942, held the SS rank of *Untersturmscharführer*. Linnemann was one of three clerical employees (*Sachberarbeiter*) attached to the Athens office of IV B 4, the unit responsible for organizing the persecution of Jews. He was experienced in conducting anti-Jewish measures, having manned the Gestapo's 'Jewish desk' in his home city of Bremen, as well as having served in a similar capacity in Krakow, Poland.[37] Linnemann was initially assigned to the Abwehr desk in Athens, and like Burger, given his background, was transferred to IV B 4. He was already in Athens when Burger arrived in early March. The pair must have made an incongruous appearance: Linnemann was heavy-set and shorter than Burger by about ten centimetres, whereas Burger was tall and wiry in physical appearance.

According to his own testimony during post-war investigations into his role in persecuting Jews, Linnemann admitted his 'specialism' was the creation and maintenance of the *Kartei*, the card index of Jews. Even though he attempted to downplay his own part in the deportations of 1944 by stating he did not approve of actions against Jews, Linnemann indeed played a key role for the *Kartei* was an integral part of the deportation process. Survivors of the deportation recall two SS officers and their translator. But in fact, Linnemann was assisted by Hans Selle, another detective with the SS rank of Sergeant (*Oberscharführer*).

Their translator, Constantinos Recanati, a German-speaking Greek from Salonica and fluent in Ladino, conveyed Burger's instructions. This role meant that many of the survivors remembered Recanati more than they did the other three men when they arrived in Rhodes in July 1944.[38]

No sooner had he arrived in Greece than Burger got to work. After liquidating the mainland communities, Burger's team travelled first to Corfu and then to Rhodes to lay the groundwork for the deportations.[39] It appears Burger and his team arrived on Rhodes by special flight (*Sonderflug*) during the night of 12/13 July, without having informed Kleemann beforehand. Indeed, Burger appears to have by-passed the military leadership on Rhodes, making contact instead with the head of Branch 611 of the Secret Military Police (*Geheime Feldpolizei*), *Kriminalkommissar* Adolf Manshausen.[40] It is a matter of speculation as to why Burger chose not to contact Kleemann's office directly. Perhaps Manowsky's experience with an uncooperative commanding officer in Corfu had shown Burger it was better to circumvent the regular military.[41] In the event, Burger presented Kleemann with a *fait accompli*.

The precise sequence of Burger's movements after arriving at the military airbase at Gaddura is unclear. He eventually appeared at Kleemann's headquarters in Pervegna in the early hours of 13 July. The reception was frosty and the meeting ended badly, with a clearly irritated Kleemann refusing to cooperate with Burger. This stance provoked the SS officer to make threats to kill the general (albeit not directly!) according to eyewitnesses.[42] Unable to use either telegram or telephone at Pervegna, Burger went to the port of Rhodes, where he sought and received the assistance of the port commander Fritz Gädecke.[43] From there he was able to contact either the head of the security police or *Sipo* (*Sicherheitspolizei*) in Greece, 38-year-old SS-Colonel (*Standartenführer*) Dr Walter Blume in Athens, or possibly Eichmann's office in Berlin, in order to secure Kleemann's cooperation.[44] Eventually, at around 7.00 am, Burger received a call to his billet in Hotel Therme from Kleemann's headquarters to say that the military would now cooperate.[45]

Later that day Kleemann issued Order No. 30, which stipulated the registration of *all* inhabitants from Rhodes town who, as we saw in Chapter 4, had dispersed to the villages because of the aerial bombardments. However, village mayors also had to register Jewish households separately in a 'special' list. In addition to this registration, Jews were to be confined to Rhodes town from midday 17 July and to the villages of Kremasto, Trianda (today Ialyssos), and Villanova (today, Paradiso), to where they had fled following the aerial bombardments of the *Juderia*. If they failed to follow this order, they faced the prospect of a fine or imprisonment.[46] Meanwhile, Kleemann assigned members of the regular *Feldgendarmerie* (military police) from Penal Battalion 999, commanded by *Oberleutnant* Karl Sommer to ensure embarkation was carried out 'humanely', in the words of Kleemann's adjutant.[47] Burger and Kleemann never met again.

Securing military cooperation was necessary to facilitate the actual deportation. Kleemann had little room for manoeuvre once he received the instruction from his superiors in Army Group E to cooperate with Burger.[48] Thus, Kleemann's role during the deportation, ascribing to him sole responsibility, is misplaced.[49] In separate testimonies, two of his former staff officers spoke of Kleemann's 'absolute anger' at the action in Rhodes and Kos, not least because he believed it would stir up partisan activity. Accounts of the general's response are corroborated by Recanati's testimony to prosecutors. However, there were also Kleemann's own personal misgivings at play. His chief staff officer (1a) Major Kronbein, who arrived on the island after the deportation, stated to war-crimes investigators that Kleemann 'had repeatedly told me and continuously expressed how much he detested the actions of the SD (*Sicherheitsdienst* – Security Service)'.[50] However deep his own fealty to Hitler, Kleemann clearly did not share his murderous intent towards Jews.[51] When Captain Johannes Matthes arrived in Rhodes nearly two months later, he heard about the deportation from fellow officers, and told post-war investigators 'the entire divisional staff had been extremely angered by the action'.[52]

Recently discovered documents appear to corroborate this testimony. These reveal that the German Secret Military Police (*Geheime Feldpolizei* – GFP) had been preparing the ground for the deportation of the communities in Rhodes and Kos as early as mid-April and *without* Kleemann's knowledge. A note dated 17 April from *Carabinieri* Colonel Mittino to the municipal administration of Rhodes, requested the compilation of a separate list of Jews in duplicate during the weekly control of the population's identity cards. The municipal office responded on 11 May. In early July, a few days before Burger and his men arrived on the island, according to Rino Merolle (whom we encountered in

Chapters 2 and 3) in testimony to the British in 1945, mentioned how officers from the GFP went to the municipal offices and demanded a copy of the 1940 household census. This census was vital for it would allow Linnemann to cross-check the names of those on the *Carabinieri* list.[53] Finally, a handwritten note from 21 July indicates the existence of two deportation lists compiled by the Italian authorities, one for their retention, and the other presumably intended for the *Geheime Feldpolizei* at their office in Via Francesco Crispi (today Odos Amerikis).[54] We can assume that probably for this reason Manshausen, as head of the *Geheime Feldpolizei* in Rhodes, was notified of Burger's pending arrival, whereas Kleemann was not informed. Indeed, the suspicion looms large that Kleemann was ignorant of the preparations underway for the deportation until the moment Burger appeared. The GFP was not in his chain of command, but came under the authority of Roman Loos as overall head of the GFP in Greece, and Walter Blume as chief of the Security Police and Security Service in Athens (*Befehlshaber der Sicherheitspolizei und des SD*).[55] The same was the case for the *Carabinieri* – which, since September 1943, had been subordinated to the *Höhere SS- und Polizeiführer* (HSSPF) in Italy.[56] This would in part explain Kleemann's anger at Burger's unannounced arrival, not least because by-passing him undermined his authority as commanding officer of the Dodecanese.

Thus, in order to carry out the deportations as efficiently as possible, the cooperation of the civilian administration was paramount, as revealed by Kleemann's adjutant Klaus Goedeckemeyer in his post-war testimony.[57] As we saw, the order of 13 July compelled local mayors to compile a separate list of Jewish families. At the higher echelons of the *Governatore* led by Vice-Governor Iginio Ugo Faralli and of the *Carabinieri*, were members of the Italian fascist party who had thrown in their lot with the Germans, not least among them Colonel Ferdinando Mittino. The *Carabinieri* drew up the deportation list, probably based on the separate register of Jewish identity cards. It is not certain if the mayor of Rhodes, Antonio Machi, was personally aware of the preparations to deport the Jews. However, as we noted, in order to verify the *Carabinieri* list, Burger's associate Friedrich Linnemann had to use the 1940 household census, and in order to do this, he required the cooperation of the mayor's office. Without this cooperation, Linnemann's work of checking and cross-referencing Jews assembled at the *Aeronautica*, which at the time served as the city military office (*Stadtkommandatur*), would have been difficult – now all he had to do was to tick off the 1,661 names on the final copy presented to him by the Italians.[58]

The deportation from Rhodes followed a familiar pattern of SS officers meeting the army commander, the local police and civilian administration to agree the timetable for registration, concentration and deportation. Jewish community leaders were co-opted to convey the order for the Jews to assemble on a given day, at a given time, at a given place. The military police, assisted by local gendarmes and army units, tackled the second and third stages of concentration and deportation. The leaders of the Rhodes community too, were drawn into this stage of the planning. Hizkia Franco in his account mentions a meeting during the evening of 18 July, between a German officer and community leaders Giacobbe Franco and Rahamin Coen.[59] They were instructed to ensure that all adult males report with their identity papers and work permits the following day to the German *Kommandatur* in the *Aeronautica*. Gathered at the building, the acting president of the community Giacobbe Franco is remembered as acting as the go-between, stepping outside the building to tell the women gathered there that they too were to return the following day with enough belongings for a ten-day journey.[60] In Rachel Hanan's recollection, as in that of Lucia Sciarcon Amato, the Community leaders informed the families in the villages that they had to report to the *Aeronautica*. Survivor accounts of this vary slightly, but it is likely that the regular *Feldgendarmerie* already based in some of the villages, together with the *Carabinieri* and Jewish 'volunteers' toured the three villages of Trianda, Kremasto and Villanova with loudspeakers, as stated by Recanati when questioned after the war.[61]

Once inside the building, Burger and Linnemann ensured the valuables that had been brought to the *Aeronautica* were collected. Laura Varon remembered this aspect of the deportation vividly.

So I went to the building and was a lot of confusion and beating up and I saw one young man all bleeding and cut everything. And while I was entering I saw these two Nazis, one was short and heavy and bald. He looked to me like … I had the impression that he was like a pig, you know, a pig. And the other one was handsome. I saw only his back. He was handsome. They were all like a pirate after the pillage. They were satisfied, you know, like that,

looking at the bags of gold, another bag of silver, another bag of money, a lot
of gold, and they were very satisfied. And then I went inside and three days
later they took us to the port and with three small ships, commercial ships,
we left Rhodes.[62]

On Kos, the process of rounding up had been similar, although the community
was taken at the same time and there were no reports of looting valuables. The
ninety or so Jews on the island were brought to the town's administrative building
and held there until the arrival of ships from Rhodes. Lucia Garzolini remembered,

> When they rounded us up on July 21, 1944, they lined us up in the courtyard
> of the governor's palace, and we stayed there for 24 hours without food or
> water. And we thought we were going to be kept somewhere on the island, as
> a kind of prisoner camp of some kind. We had no idea what was happening.
> It was a Sunday. Germans came unexpectedly and circled our place, said all
> of us would have to leave. We prepared our suitcases; the Germans told us to
> bring not too many things.[63]

The concentration, registration and finally the deportation lay in the hands
of Burger, assisted by Manshausen's Secret Field Police, the *Carabinieri* and
units of the Military Police from Penal Battalion 999 (mot.) whose task was to
'ascertain and gather' the Jews.[64]

Compiling registers of people and property was the first stage in the system
of annihilation. This required the cooperation of willing helpers, particularly
among the civilian administration and the *Carabinieri*. The household census
of 1940 was instrumental in this respect. Preparation too, relied on willing
helpers. Again officers from the *Carabinieri* played a role in this; but the key
players were Manshausen and his men in the GFP. It is a telling omission
that after the war, sergeant Ruschmeyer who testified to British intelligence
officers against Kleemann's successor, General Wagener, kept silent on his own
role in the GFP. Before the war, Ruschmeyer had served in the uniformed
police force (*Schutzpolizei*) of his home town of Dortmund. Because of his
policing experience, Kleemann approved his transfer from his regular army
unit to the GFP.[65]

As well as willing collaborators, or those under orders, there were unwilling
helpers who had little choice in the matter. From the very beginning of the
Third Reich, the Nazis co-opted Jewish leaders and organizations in their

self-destruction. Thus, the leaders of the Jewish community on Rhodes (and presumably on Kos) too, were pressed into facilitating an orderly organization of the deportation. However, Jewish elders did not remain passive 'lambs to the slaughter'; instead, they appealed to the Italian mayor for protection. By this stage, however, it appears the mayor had become a passive onlooker in the process of deportation. As Merolle told the British after liberation of the island: 'Messr. Bohor Alhadeff, Jack Alhadeff, Mois[e] Soriano, Haim Tarica, Iacof [Giacobbe] Franco, expressed their wish that the Italian Authorities inform themselves of what was happening [to the Jews] and do everything possible to place them under their command and to protect all their interests.' However, such an intervention by the Italians on behalf of the hapless Jews cut no ice with Burger. Merolle continued: 'Dr Antonio Macchi was the first to present himself in his official capacity as mayor of Rhodes and ventured to make contact with the imprisoned Jews. He was threatened and almost attacked by the SS officer from Berlin [i.e. Burger].'[66]

The *Aeronautica* was located along Via Dante Alghieri (present-day Odos Dimokratias) opposite the western wall of the old town. Having summoned all males from the age of 15 years to assemble in the large area to the front of the Hotel *Therme* close to the *Aeronautica*, Burger's team methodically checked Jews against the list compiled by the Italians. Stella Levi who accompanied her blind father to the *Aeronautica* carrying his passport and identity card, recalled how the Germans called out the names of the men from a list. Using the population census of 1940 and the deportation list prepared by the *Carabinieri*, Linnemann was able to expedite the process relatively easily. Once completed, the men were taken to the barracks of the Division *Regina* adjacent to the *Aeronautica*. Their womenfolk, parents, grandparents and children were ordered to attend the next day.[67]

In order to extend the process to the rest of the community scattered across the island, Burger's translator Recanati later claimed Linnemann selected twenty 'volunteers' from the young men gathered there to act as stewards, providing them with white armbands. These young men might have been the messengers Rino Merolle mentions in his post-war statement, who were sent to the villages to tell the women that they and their children should report to the *Aeronautica* the next day, bringing with them money and valuables, as well as a small suitcase and provisions for a ten-day journey.[68] While there was undoubtedly confusion or apprehension among some of the victims as to what was happening, at this initial stage the process was devoid of physical violence, the families were together, and the co-optation of the community leaders lent an air of reassurance.

Testimonies of the deportation vary. Survivors could not know the intricate detail of what was happening to them: they were not privy to the plans to deport and eventually kill them. Moreover, many of them were youngsters at the time. We cannot say the same for the garrison. By this stage of the war, knowledge among soldiers (and the German civilian population) of the destruction of Europe's Jews was widespread. Post-war claims of non-knowledge, especially among members of the military police units as to what was occurring and would occur to Jews once they reached their destination, stretches the credulity of even the casual observer. Indeed, as one former soldier put it many years later, the deportation of the Jews from Rhodes was 'openly discussed' in the garrison, and Brenner's own reports mention widespread unease in some quarters of the garrison about what would befall the Jews once they left the island.[69] It was this disquiet that led Kleemann to issue, on 16 July, his directive to unit commanders to suppress discussion of the deportation.[70]

The three-day sojourn in the barracks was not planned (the deportation was planned originally for 18 July), but due to the shortage of fuel for the journey to Piraeus and the need to commandeer ships. The deportation plans faced another obstacle: namely the young Turkish consul Selahattin Ülkümen. A career diplomat, Ülkümen was 30 years old at the time of the deportation and had arrived in Rhodes in January 1943, as neutral Turkey's representative in the Dodecanese. He was to play a key role in helping some of the Jews and their families evade deportation; in all, fifty-five persons.[71] Either they were spared the indignity of reporting to the *Aeronautica* or, if already incarcerated in the building, they were soon released because Ülkümen was able to secure their exemption from the action. The former president Hizkia Franco had already left the island for Turkey as a consequence of the Race Laws, leaving behind his son Giacobbe in Rhodes and his daughter Elisa in Kos.

During investigations into Anton Burger, the Austrian SS-Captain who executed the deportation of the Rhodes and Kos Jews as well those from Corfu and Crete, his translator Costantinos Recanati was interrogated several times. During these interrogations, Recanati told investigators how Jacques

(Giacomo) Alhadeff and others while being held in the *Aeronautica*, bribed the Germans to allow Ülkümen to furnish Turkish papers, thus exempting them from deportation. From the safety of his new home in Mannheim Germany, Recanati spoke on the aspect of buying safety.[72]

> As I was leaving the property [i.e. *Aeronautica*] again, one of the Jews, Jacques Achadef [*sic*] – he is today, the owner of the textile factory 'Bretagne' in Athens – stopped me and said that I was Greek after all, I should help him. Linnemann noticed this conversation. He asked me what was going on. I told him the truth. Linnemann said that was only possible if the Jew in question could prove that he was a Turkish citizen. I then spoke to Alchadef [*sic*] again. He said it could be done, because at least the wives had never lost their Turkish nationality, he was only an involuntary Italian (*Zwangsitaliener*), i.e. Italian citizenship had been forced on him. Alchadef now drew up a list of alleged Turkish Jews. He gave it to me and I told him he had done it clumsily. He had written down the richest Jews and that was bound to attract attention.[73]

Recanati was by and large an unreliable and self-serving witness. Yet the core of his account is corroborated by another source, namely by Bension Menascé in an affidavit made in February 1945, after he and his wife arrived in Marmaris.

In Menascé's account it becomes clear that saving Jewish life was possible, but this came with a price tag.[74] Indeed, Bension Menascé and Jack Alhadeff were able to secure their and their families' safety by procuring from the Turkish Consul, papers, even though they were not officially Turkish. Of the fifty-five persons saved by the Consul, only thirteen were actually Turkish citizens and a further five were spouses. The majority only had tenuous connections to Turkey. The saved included those spouses who did not hold Turkish citizenship, like Daniel Turiel, the husband of Mathilde; she was a Turkish national. It was claimed that Giacomo (Jack) Alhadeff's wife Batami had a relative who was a senior military officer in the Turkish army (she was actually born in Beirut, Lebanon when it was still part of the Ottoman Empire, and her stepfather had been the British Consul on Rhodes before the war). Moreover, the pair and their son, 9-year-old Izzy (Isaaco), were Catholics and held Italian passports. Indeed, the majority of those saved by Ülkümen were prominent Jews in possession of Italian passports. Others holding Italian passports included the merchant and rabbi 66-year-old Giacobbe Maio and his 60-year-old wife Marie, or the Community notable Haim Tarica and his wife Amelie, or 60-year-old Bension Menascé and his wife Caden. Menascé was a banker and director of the Alhadeff company. After arriving in Marmaris in February 1945, he recounted how he had sought to persuade Ülkümen to secure papers for their release.

> Among this number (held in the *Aeronautica*), there were about 20 Jews who were Turkish subjects or who were related to these subjects. The Consul immediately visited the camp and put aside about 30 people. When I saw that the Consul had separated these 30, I tried to approach him but was prevented from doing so by a German officer who struck me and sent me reeling to the ground. A little later, I was able to take advantage of a moment's absence of the officer, and I spoke to the Consul who was already informed of the fact that I had been the professor of his Ambassador in Rome, Mr Baghib Bey, his superior; besides that, the Consul knew that I had a thorough knowledge of the Turkish language, and I explained to him that all our relatives, beginning with my wife, are of Turkish origin, in spite of the Italian passports that were in our possession.
>
> [...]
>
> In this way we left the camp and immediately I drew up documents myself for the others, acceptable to the Community, but not by the Germans. The Turkish Consul lived in Mixi, near Trianda, his embassy in the city having been destroyed by bombs. I had to make this long trip 5–6 times a day to try to persuade him to come to the camp. But the Germens had intimidated the Consul by making him believe that he was assuming a great responsibility by liberating the rich and leaving the poor; in other words, the Consul was afraid to make new demands though I had promised to give him 300,000 lirettes for any Turkish charitable organization.[75]

Menascé's account presents a different image to that later recalled by survivors. It is not just because he recounts the process by which the round-up and concentration of 1,661 Jews in the *Aeronautica* (which he says had previously been prepared for this purpose), but for what it tells us, factually, about the role of Ülkümen, who interceded once he heard that Turkish Jews were among those incarcerated. We learn that the 30-year-old consul had been sufficiently intimidated by Burger as to be reluctant to act beyond his initial intervention. Moreover, it is Menascé's own actions to save his circle of friends and family – some of whom had only tenuous claim to Turkish protection – that is of interest. We can see from his account that Jewish freedom could be bought (as we know from elsewhere was the case). While the Consul may have not been swayed by 300,000 lirettes, Burger and his henchmen could be.

Similarly, the influential Soriano family, including Maurice, who would become the post-war president of the Community, were able to avail themselves of the protection of the Turkish Consul, in spite of Italian citizenship. An examination of those saved by Ülkümen show that they mostly hailed from the elite stratum of Jews, among them, Lina Kantor's parents, Alberto and Renate Amato, exempted because of the Turkish grandmother Rachel, and the fact that Renate née Cori had been born in Smyrna. Alberto had abandoned Judaism when they married, becoming a Catholic, like his wife. Not part of this elite group was the small number of partners or wives of Italians who had converted to the Catholic faith, such as Vittoria Sidis-Litrici and Bulissa Cugno with her two children.[76]

There were many among those who would be deported who could have claimed Turkish protection – among them Salomon Varon and his family (in spite of his stateless condition), or the Alcana families, given their close familial ties to Antalya. No doubt, it would have been an impossible task for Ülkümen to have attempted to save the dozens of families whose members had come from Milas, Smyrna/Izmir or Antalya. Lina Kantor (who had been put into the care of a non-Jewish family) recalled what her father Alberto Amato later told her, when he, her Turkish grandmother Sara Cori, and her mother Renata Cori left the *Aeronautica*. Those who remained 'you know, crying, saying what about us, what about us, we also have Turkish connections, can't you help us'.[77] These families were not in a position to influence the Turkish consul; nor did they readily have the necessary financial means to purchase the papers needed for their freedom. Although we should treat Recanati's post-war testimony with some caution, at one point he appears to throw some light on Ülkümen's frustration with the actions of the Jewish elite. According to Recanati, Ülkümen furnished the Germans with a list of 125 Jews with a claim to Turkish documents, over half of whom were rejected, among them the Community's doctor, David Gaon and his wife and children.

*

The timetable for deportation from the Dodecanese was to be brief, a 'thunderbolt' of merely a few days. Originally expected to be completed by 18 July, the arrangements for deportation lasted nearly ten days.[78] What Burger had not bargained for was the mass exodus to the villages because of the heavy aerial bombardment of Rhodes. The dispersal necessitated Kleemann's order of the 13th. In addition, there was a problem mustering adequate shipping and finding diesel (in short supply). As a result, the Jews of Rhodes remained incarcerated in the barracks adjacent to the *Aeronautica* for three days. By Sunday morning of the 23rd, three supply motor ships that had arrived the day before from Leros with adequate diesel had been secured. The community was escorted on foot by members of the *Geheime Feldpolizei*, assisted by the military police of the Armoured Grenadier regiment commanded by Lieutenant Siebold, via the Mandraki and then along the town walls to the dock where the ships were anchored.[79]

Today it is possible to reach the port from the *Aeronautica* in not much more than half an hour. It is not a great distance, but in the context of uncertainty and in the rising July heat, it took on the inverse appearance of Abraham leading the Jews to the Promised Land. For Laura Varon, the trek took on the semblance of 10 miles, rather than a few kilometres. Half a century later, survivors described how the column, led by their president Giacobbe Franco, marched in rows of five with heads bowed. With hindsight, Stella Levi described the column as a 'funeral procession', 'with Jacov Shalem Franco as its leader, perhaps I feel for him most, as he must have been suffering deeply leading his community to death'.[80] They marched in their family groups. Sara Jerusalmi (née Notrica) walked with her maternal uncle Behor, her aunt Rosa, and her cousins Lucia and Davide.[81] Forty-five-year-old Salomon Varon walked together with his wife, Regine Coen and their four teenage children, Lora (Laura), Giuseppe, Ascer and 14-year-old Stella. In the column were the families of Samuele Angel, Ruben Hasson and Celebi Alcana. Celebi led his adult children and grandchildren, over thirty persons in all. His niece, Miru Alcana, walked alongside her parents and brothers. Merolle's wife, Matilde Alhadeff, was not among the deportees. He had managed to hide her and their baby son in one of the nearby villages (possibly Koskinou or Asguro).

However, at least thirty-two members of her extended family together with her sister and widowed mother were on the transport.[82]

At the harbour, the community stood in the midday heat, facing the ancient walls until embarkation in mid-afternoon. According to one testimony made in 1947 by Erwin Lenz who had been attached to Penal Battalion 999, the guards beat the Jews if they dared to turn around. But Lenz's testimony was later called into doubt, and none of the survivors mentioned beatings until they arrived in Piraeus. Once boarded, there was further waiting, because the departure took place under the cover of darkness – at 9.00 pm, to be precise, when the ships left for either Kos or Leros via Piscopi.[83]

At this stage, many in the Community believed they were being sent elsewhere on the island. Stella Levi recalled there were rumours that they were being sent to a work camp, but it was not clear to her where this was. As Lucia Capelluto remembered: 'rumour had it that the Jews had to be relocated in the villages of the island, but alas this was not the case.'[84] Her account is echoed by Lucia Franco Garzolini, who 'thought we were going to be kept somewhere on the island, at a kind of prisoner camp of some kind. We had no idea what was happening.'[85] After the war, Maurizio Soriano recalled how during their incarceration at the *Aeronautica*, 'we were told that we would be transferred to a neighbouring island where we would stay until the end of hostilities'.[86] The community was thus reassured after they were informed by the SS officers through the translator Recanati that they would be taken off the island to another island for the duration of the war. The subterfuge continued. Upon arriving in Piraeus, they were told they were being sent to Germany to work, as Laura Varon, who had just turned 17 the previous month, recalled.[87] As elsewhere in Europe, the SS maintained the fiction of 'resettlement' or 'going to work in Germany' as a means to maintain compliance, when in fact they were being sent to their deaths.[88]

The Germans cloaked the process of concentration, confinement and deportation in lies. At each stage, the victims were assured the measure was temporary. As Alberto Israel angrily told Marcello Pezzetti in *The Longest Journey*, 'It all began with a lie. They took us all the way to Piraeus, entirely through lies.'[89] But even if there was an inkling of doubt about the ultimate aims of the Nazis, at the moment of entrapment and disorientation, the result was disbelief among the captives that worse could yet befall them, as captured by Laura Varon's answer when asked about the community's response: 'we didn't believe … we didn't want to believe.'[90]

Three supply ships that had arrived on 22 July from Leros, after unloading were refuelled and made ready to depart for Piraeus at 9.00 pm the following day, but now with human cargo.[91] Because of intensified Allied operations in the Aegean, progress was slow, with the convoy having to anchor by day and travel under cover of dark to avoid aerial attacks; hence they anchored at the small island of Pitscopi (present-day Tinos) soon after leaving Rhodes.[92] Meanwhile, in a similar *blitz* action, the ninety or so Jews of Kos were ordered to present themselves on 23 July at the local stadium. Elisa Franco Hasson, the daughter of the former president of the Community in Rhodes Hizkia Franco, remembered how,

> One day at the end of July 1944, an official communiqué was published by the Germans, stating that all the Jews in Cos were to gather at the stadium and take with them a minimum amount of luggage for travelling. … The whole community was there, there was no way of escaping. We waited for several hours, then we were put on a small cargo ship to Greece. It was a long journey. Off the coast, we saw three other cargo ships carrying all the Jews from Rhodes who had suffered the same fate as us, and they were sailing to the same destination.[93]

In actual fact, the two parties were joined at either Samos or Leros where they also took on provisions. According to a number of accounts, this was because the German captain of the convoy refused to lift anchor until the deportees had been adequately supplied. Laura Varon remembered this act of kindness from the merchant navy officer, who addressed her people she later remembered 'as if friends', and whom she described as 'blond, nice, a little short', nonetheless 'in normal times you could fall in love with him'.[94]

The journey on these crammed ships was gruelling, for the Aegean Sea was 'cruel' according to Violetta Fintz (née Maio). 'The people were vomiting', she recalled, 'the children crying, the pregnant mother in pain … it was terrible to see and to hear […] they couldn't do nothing.'[95] It was late July and the Mediterranean heat in particular was unbearable, as Lucia Capelluto remembered. 'The heat was stifling. Even the sun had no pity on us and its rays bored into us unmercifully. By mid-day we felt we could stand it no more. Our thirst was overwhelming.'[96] In spite of the provisioning of the ships, Vittorio Hasson, 16 years old at the time, recalled hunger and thirst, and the absence of proper toilets. There was also the uncertainty of where their destination lay. 'We were sad and anxious. Where were we being led [to]? There were few soldiers, and they were not aggressive. We could easily have run away. But where to go? All the islands were in German hands. We asked ourselves a thousand and one questions.'[97] Some guards tried to alleviate the conditions; at least this was the case on Rachel Hanan's ship. There was a detail of three or four soldiers guarding the prisoners on each ship, 'not SS, but conscripts … they were very good to us'. Thus, she told how the deportees were allowed to take turns to prepare food in the ship's cramped galley. Because the ships laid anchor during the glaring heat of the day, some of the prisoners were even allowed to bathe in the sea.[98] Stella Levi recalls something similar. When they stopped at Samos, according to her testimony, they were already dirty from the heat and asked if they might bathe. The captain acceded to this request and so Stella and her friend Clara took a swim.[99] Nevertheless, there were fatalities among the old and sick.

The largely benign treatment during this stage of the transport in all likelihood nurtured the belief that indeed they were being relocated. Certainly, no one guessed that this was a transport to death. In later recollections, survivors mention this false sense of security, but they also emphasize that they would never have abandoned their families, such was the deep bond of the family unit.[100] Neither Rachel Hanan, nor Stella Levi nor the latter's friend Clara Gabriele, thought to escape once they received permission from the ship's captain to bathe in the Aegean waters.[101] 'We would *never* have left our parents there', was Stella's emphatic answer to the question why she did not attempt to get away. There was thus no attempt to escape, although this would have been possible.[102] And, as we saw with Vittorio Hasson's recollection, where would they escape to?

Finally, after eight days at sea, the convoy arrived at Piraeus where it was met by Burger. It was only here that the brutal treatment began as guards beat and cajoled the elderly, sick and young in equal measure as they loaded them onto waiting trucks bound for the SS-run prison of Haidari. Stella Levi remembered how she had to fend for her blind father who was mercilessly beaten by the waiting guards because he was too slow; 'I kind of pushed him into the trucks with my uncle.'[103] Sara Jerusalmi witnessed the scene preceding the panic to get Stella's father onto the truck.

> I had in my memory something very tragic [...] a man who didn't had a wife, he had a daughter Joanna, it was a blind man and the Joanna it was [...] no the mother was deaf, sorry ... it [she] was helping the mother and this man he was standing out of the boat a German came and he pushed him, he throw him in the floor [...] he never came out [of the boat] because it was [...] it was the end of this man, and many things like that, that is what I saw with my eyes, many things like that [...].[104]

At the disembarkation in Piraeus 'we started witnessing the horror and the violence' Rachel Hanan recalled.[105] Laura Varon remembered how 'When we arrived in Piraeus there was a lot of confusion ... dogs and Nazis shouting.' Varon told her interlocutor how it was a windy day 'and I saw papers flying all over'.[106] She was convinced that some elderly rabbis, unable to get up and mount the trucks, were shot 'execution style', although this is not corroborated by the testimonies of her brothers, Ascer and Josef, who were also with her and their parents. Violetta Fintz remembered seeing ten people, including the wife of one of the rabbis, left on the quayside face down.[107] Stella de Leon (née Hasson) also remembered the beatings.[108] There were plenty of instances of cruelty on the part of the guards meeting the ships, especially against those too slow to disembark from the ships and who had difficulty mounting the waiting trucks, as we saw in the case of Stella Levi's blind father. A month before, during the deportation from Corfu, the transport of Jews stopped-over on the island of Lefkadia, but when a rabbi accepted a parcel of food from an Orthodox priest, he was shot by Burger, thus lending credence to the murderous scene referred to independently of each other by Varon and Fintz.[109]

The brutality intensified on arrival at Haidari. Here, kept apart from other prisoners, and the men separated from the women and children, the Aegean Jews suffered harsh conditions, without adequate sanitation, water or food. Moreover, they were subjected to wanton sadistic behaviour by the camp guards. Stella Levi like many of her contemporaries found it hard to recount the horrors of Haidari to a younger generation, becoming visibly upset in the process of her interview. During her interview in 1995, Flora Fils (née Hasson) recollected how an elderly rabbi was given a fatal beating at the camp and she was aware of a number of other deaths, although she could not recall the exact number.[110] The deportees were easy prey. 'They took from us all our clothing, the tins of meat and other provisions', Capelluto recalled.[111] It was probably here when Violetta Maio Fintz's loop earrings were torn from her ears, scarring her in the process. Here also, for the first time, some children witnessed death. Fourteen-year-old Alice Tarica and her cousin, Marie, 'noticed a woman we knew lying on the ground in a very bad way. We found some water and put a few drops on her lips. She took our hand and, before our eyes, breathed her last. This scene – my first direct contact with death – shook me to the core.'[112] Individual accounts of the three-day internment at Haidari differ in detail as one might expect, but agree on the dehumanizing treatment. Women and girls were humiliated and subjected to sexualized violence when male guards subjected them to intimate body searches for jewels, coins and other precious items.[113] The men were also badly beaten; and their shoes and belts taken from them. The beatings were arbitrary.

A few months before their arrival at the camp, the International Red Cross had compiled a report expressing concern about the treatment of prisoners in Greece, and made particular mention of conditions in Haidari, one of the many camps that thrived on a climate of 'anguish' and where guards kept prisoners 'in [a] lamentable moral and physical state'.[114] After the war a Greek witness who had been incarcerated in Haidari at the same time as the Jews from Rhodes and Kos, told war-crime investigators how the camp guards had gratuitously insulted and tormented the Jews from Corfu a month before, and now meted out the same treatment to those from Rhodes and Kos.[115]

A group of young Jewish women survivors interviewed by Massimo Vitale in Rome in June 1945, told him: 'We were taken from Piraeus to Haidari and the men separated from the women, these last were completely and brutally stripped in order to be searched by SS soldiers for hidden gold and jewels. Whoever showed the slightest modesty was slapped and whipped in the face.'[116]

Lucia Capelluto recorded how before leaving the camp, 'we were stripped again for a final check and the slightest thing of any value was taken from us. This time the guards made the parents undress in front of their children.'[117] This final indignation was too much for Michael Menascé, according to his brother Jacques (Giacomo) in a letter to Avraham Galante in 1946. 'Outraged by this indecency, [Michael] had the courage to protest with vehemence; he was religious, and this exhibition seemed a monstrosity [to him]. The Germans furious at his attitude, cruelly beat him until death ensued.'[118] In fact, the conservative and deeply religious Menascé, who at the time was in his early seventies, survived the beating. However, his physical condition deteriorated during the journey to Auschwitz, no doubt exacerbated by his diabetes, and he subsequently died en route. His wife, Regina (née Jerusalmi), seventeen years his junior, was gassed on arrival at Auschwitz.[119]

Who were these SS guards in Haidari who demonstrated such gratuitous brutality towards their captives? Why did they act in such a brutal and sadistic manner towards their helpless victims? The surviving sources, as with so much to do with perpetrators of the Shoah at the lower echelons of the Nazi apparatus in Greece and the islands, are patchy. Nonetheless, enough documentation has survived making it possible to piece together part of a picture. What emerges from these sources is that of the roughly two dozen guards who are identifiable as present in the camp in July 1944, the majority were mostly ethnic Germans (*Volksdeutsche*) from poor rural communities in Hungary and Romania.[120] Aside from this geographical/ethnic characteristic, they bear some fleeting resemblance to the so-called 'ordinary' men-turned-perpetrator studied by historian Christopher Browning and social psychologist Harald Welzer.[121] The majority were between 30 and 40 years old; they were 'family men' with wives and children. By joining the Waffen-SS, they found employment to help overcome poverty, coming as they did from structurally economically backward areas. Possibly, they also could avoid a precarious frontline alongside their compatriots.[122] Thus war and the devastation of the Jewish families of the Aegean, as well as other victims, provided these men with material opportunities, no matter how apparently trivial the trophy.

The camp at Haidari had opened as a military barracks-cum-prison in the mid-1930s under the Metaxas regime. By the beginning of the 1940s, it served as a prison for political dissidents, including several Greek army officers. After Greece's capitulation in April 1941, it came under the jurisdiction of the German security police. Thus, from October, the camp was run by the SS as a prison for Greek political prisoners and hostages, and eventually as a transit camp for Jews 'swept up' in raids preparatory to deportation. The estimated 1,700 Jews arrested by Burger and Linnemann in Athens on 24 March, the circa 1,800 Jews deported from Corfu in June, and eventually the Jews from

Rhodes and Kos, were all incarcerated in Haidari for mostly short periods before being sent to Auschwitz on the next available transport.[123]

Scholarly accounts of Haidari tend to focus on its first commandant, the notorious and sadistic *Sturmbannführer* Paul Radomski, who was assigned to Haidari in November 1943.[124] Under Radomski's regime conditions were gratuitously brutal, with former inmates describing it as 'the heart of hell'.[125] Radomski's criminal character and behaviour knew no bounds and after threatening to kill a fellow SS officer, he was disciplined, demoted, removed from Haidari and eventually reassigned by Eichmann to Riga at the end of 1944.[126] Thus by the time the Jews of Rhodes arrived in Haidari, Radomski had been replaced by *Untersturmführer* Karl Fischer, an Austrian detective (*Kriminalangestellter*). Fischer's deputy, Hans Löfler, was also a detective with the SS rank of *Sturmscharführer*, and two other police officers, one of whom, Alfred Pick, acted as Fischer's driver.[127]

However, the change in camp commandant altered little in terms of the murderous conditions prevailing in Haidari. Witnesses described Fischer, whose own reign of terror extended from April to September 1944, as 'big, cross-eyed, with coarse features'. His immediate associates appear to have emerged from some hideous circus of the grotesque. Emmerich Kowatsch, identified by a Greek former inmate as one of the camp's principal torturers, was 'small, thin, [and] bald with a furrowed face and two amputated fingers'. Another, Georg Schmitzer, was said to be blind in one eye. Unlike Fischer and his deputy Löfler, who were Austrians, both Kowatsch and Schmitzer were ethnic Germans from Hungary.[128] Surviving documentation provides some information on their ages and social status. When, in April 1944, the guards complained their poor wages were not enough to support their families in Hungary and Romania because of inflation, Fischer compiled a list of these men with personal details on marital and family status, and the level of supplement they should receive. We also learn in some cases when they joined the SS.[129]

Schmitzer, for instance, was a 31-year-old married man with two children from the town of Baczentivan and received an extra 150 Hungarian pengös as family support. He had joined the Waffen-SS at the beginning of October 1943, despite his disability (the glass eye), which might account for why he had not seen service on the front and had no military or other distinctions.

Schmitzer's vita is not dissimilar to that of several other men, such as Andreas Schön or Johann Ottenthal. They were the same age, give or take a year, and had joined the Waffen-SS at the same time as Schmitzer. Both men had only one child each and came from the same town (Scatalje), and each received an extra 130 pengös to support their families. After the war, these two men were interviewed as witnesses (and not as perpetrators) in the case against Linnemann for war crimes, and we learn from their testimony that both were unskilled labourers.[130] Kowatsch, identified by a Greek former inmate as one of the principal torturers, was one of the younger men at the camp; he was barely 21 years old and single when the Jews from Corfu and later from Rhodes and Kos arrived and suffered at his hands. Like many of his fellow guards in Haidari at the time, he too had joined in October 1943 and was deployed to Haidari the following November.

Indeed, all the guards at the camp during the period of the deportation had arrived shortly after the Germans had overrun the entire country and the islands formerly under Italian control. These were men of a coarse social disposition, and themselves lived in penury and brutalized conditions. Deployment to the camps also freed them from the likelihood of being sent to the front. Their background offers only a limited explanation for the cruelty and dehumanizing treatment to which they subjected the inmates of Haidari. In the final analysis, the Holocaust was a form of naked Hobbesian violence, enabling those frequently on the receiving end of state-sanctioned violence to exercise this brutal power themselves and with impunity. Such guards were a vital auxiliary force for Himmler's SS. These ethnic Germans (*Volksdeutsche*) numbered around 140,000 in Central, Eastern and Southeastern Europe. They hunted and murdered Jews in the forests of Eastern Europe, in the villages of the Carpathians, the Balkans and the Baltic; they guarded the concentration camps of the SS archipelago; and in the final phase of the war provided an additional if unreliable fighting force.[131]

*

The families were re-united only when embarking for Auschwitz (Oswiecim) in the so-called Generalgournement of Poland. After three days in Haidari, during which time there had been further fatalities at the hands of the guards, the Jews of Rhodes and Kos were brought to nearby Roufa station where freight trains waited to embark on the final leg of the journey to Auschwitz.[132] This transport with the designation Convoy 44R comprised more than thirty freight wagons each crammed with up to seventy persons.[133] Jack Hasson remembered how:

> 65 people were packed into each cattle truck and we were kept as family units as much as possible. Packed up like sardines, with no place to sit. Sanitary conditions were of no importance to our captors. Almost no food was supplied on our journey, which lasted two weeks, but there was [*sic*] two large barrels of water per truck which was rationed and controlled by one of our own.[134]

His grandmother Behora, was among those whose corpses were left on the side of the tracks.[135]

In addition to the Jews from Rhodes and Kos, were approximately a further 600 deportees, among them 20-year-old Rachel Perahia Margosh, an assimilated Sephardi Jew from Drama in northern Greece, who with her family had been in hiding in Athens until denounced by a family 'friend'. Rachel remembered the Jews from Rhodes and Kos in her testimony many years later.[136] For many of the deportees, especially for children such as Sami Modiano, this was the first time they had seen a train in real life, and for too many, it would be the only journey by such means. The boyish excitement of seeing a locomotive for the first time was suppressed by the nature of the experience. Eliezer Surmani, for example, could not bear to travel on a train for the rest of his life because the sound of the locomotive brought back the 'bad memory' of that final journey with his family.[137]

Provisions for the journey consisted of melons or cucumbers, onions and three barrels of barely drinkable water. A separate barrel was provided for toilet functions. Small vents near the top of the wagons provided the only air in the sweltering heat. Violetta Fintz described fifty years later what awaited her family, neighbours and friends as they climbed into the freight cars:

> We entered the truck and we saw [on] one side a little heap of dry onions, the other side a little heap of mouldy bread, one barrel of water and one barrel for the necessity […] Now this was it […] was our food for the journey […] with […] In this heat […] weather […] we ate onion […] and 70 people

in … in one day the barrels was empty […] already when [we] use to do the necessity, the barrel was over-flooded [Violetta raises her voice and gestures with her hands]. We used to sit there on top, there was not other alternative, only after two or three, four days they used to open the door take the dea[d] off the truck and empty, send some of the girls or boys to empty the barrel and to fill the water again.[138]

Today, a train journey from Athens to Oswiecim takes a bit more than one and a half days. In the stifling summer heat of 1944, the 1,389-km distance took thirteen days. There was no direct line to Auschwitz in 1944.[139]

The transport left Athens for Larissa on 3 August; and from there journeyed to the freight station of Salonica, before snaking through the Balkans. It travelled via Skopje (Macedonia), Niš and Belgrade (Serbia). It stopped at Budapest central station (Hungary), and then halted in Austria at Vienna's Nordbahnhof, having come via Bratislava (Slovakia). From Vienna, it took secondary rail-lines travelling through Břeclav, Prerov and Novy Bahumin (all in present-day Czechia) to Auschwitz (Map 5.1).[140]

Each time the transport crossed national borders, drivers and crew were replaced accordingly, and military guards were changed. All of this involved detailed administrative planning and coordination.[141] Meanwhile, during this arduous trek across Central Europe, further prisoners were added by the SS, so that at the end of its journey, the transport was carrying approximately 2,500 people destined either for the gas chambers or to become slave workers in Auschwitz and beyond.

There were a number of stops as the convoy snaked its way through central Europe. Steam technology dictated regular stops to haul water, during which a small number of the deportees from each wagon dismounted to refill the barrels and at which stage the dead were removed from the wagons.[142] One of the minor halts was near the southern Moravian town of Březová, and it held out the prospect according to the testimony of Sidney Fahn, the Slovakian Jew we encountered earlier in Chapter 4, to show off to his father the newly born grandson through the opening of the truck.[143] Some of the stops were by arrangement with the International Red Cross which monitored the transport (but could not intervene) and provided bread, for example at Budapest.[144] At some of these halts, sometimes locals would try to throw food to the victims, as in the above-mentioned stop at Březová. However, according to Lucia

Map 5.1 Route of deportation to Auschwitz; © Peter Palm

Capelluto's testimony, 'The Germans seized this heavenly food for themselves and at that moment they told us they would not be giving us anything further.'[145] At other times, the deportees were allowed to descend the train for toilet purposes, usually when the dead were off-loaded and their corpses either left or burned at the side of the rails.[146]

In the letter we cited above from Jacques Menascé to Avraham Galante, Menascé claimed how at these stops a small number of the younger members of the community managed to escape.[147] However, these attempts would have been both rare and difficult. Certainly, the guards were vigilant, as Rachel Hanan recalled many years later. A guard had beaten her after straying too far from the rails in her quest for more privacy to relieve herself.[148] For the most part, the victims travelled in silence, cowed by the violence of the journey. Victor Hasson recalled to his daughter Stella,

> I know that we passed through Hungary and Czechoslovakia. For the rest …
> We had no contact with the population. And there were at least fifty guards.
> Nobody tried to escape. I stayed close to my mother. She held us in her arms.
> She didn't say anything, probably so as not to frighten us. My grandmother
> was also silent. She was strong, the 'nana' Bulissa. In the carriage, moreover,
> it seems to me that there was complete silence. I didn't pay any attention to
> what was going on there.[149]

Deprived of adequate food and water for most of the journey, 'during the final three or four days everyone felt finished', Lucia Capelluto recalled. 'We lay on the floor on top of one another. The heat, the filth, the stench was unbearable. The children hadn't even the strength to cry'.[150] Violetta Fintz also provides a stark account of these conditions.

> It was something which you can die, everybody was with one little … a …
> little petticoat, nothing else. I remember I had next to me a mother with one
> year old girl … and she used to lick her mother … what you say, transpiration
> [i.e. perspiration] because she was so thirsty … You didn't know … what to
> do.[151]

Laura Varon later testified how her little niece and nephew Mattie and Jaco 'were thirsty … they were hungry and they probably were screaming and crying'.[152] However, such was the trauma of the journey that Laura blanked out the experience. 'I really don't remember [...]. What happened in the cattle cars is like a blank in my mind … you know, in my subconscious.'[153]

The trauma of the train journey had a lasting impact on survivors.[154] Stella Levi, like Varon an articulate witness, found the experience humiliating and 'so horrible I think I blocked out all this … the journey'.[155] Meanwhile, Laura Varon's brother Ascer remembered 'a lot of things' but only vaguely and mostly in fragments. For instance, Ascer told his interviewer in early 1998, that although he could not recall exactly, he thought the journey lasted three or four days, when as we know, it lasted nearly two weeks.[156] Violetta Fintz's description of the degradation of the toilet barrel speaks to the lasting affront especially to such a religious-conservative and dignified people, as does Lucia

Capelluto's reference to the humiliation of forcing parents to undress in front of their children prior to their departure from Haidari.

For some survivors, the solidarity of the close-knit community was in evidence as meagre rations were shared. However, such accounts are also tempered by recollections of regret. The train journey was an emotional trial for all.[157] Laura Varon recalled her father lamenting how 'we could have been in Palestine by now' (referring to their earlier attempt to get there in 1939 after the expulsion order).[158] The same thought may have crossed the mind of 36-year-old Nissim Sabetai as he sat with his wife Sarina, three years his junior, and their two small sons, Salomon and David. Sabetai, a travelling salesperson of fabrics employed by Nissim Capelluto, was originally from Smyrna and had settled in Rhodes in 1924. Like the Varons, the Sabetai family too had been expelled and was bound for Palestine via Italy, but after spending two months in Italy, the outbreak of war prevented the family from travelling further and they subsequently returned to Rhodes.[159]

Alice Tarica remembered how her parents were 'as sad as they were frightened' as to what lay in store for them. However, there was also bickering and recrimination as it became clear to adult family members that something more terrible lay ahead. Indeed, Alice remembered her father was angry with members of his family for abandoning them.

> My aunt who had gone off to the Belgian Congo without us, for example, was rich enough to have taken us out of Rhodes. He had asked her for a favour … we would never have been a burden to her. She was my grandfather's own daughter. When he (her father) looked at him, suffering so, he asked himself why they hadn't done more to save us.[160]

At times just heavy silence hung over the occupants of the wagons.

In spite of the palpable sense of foreboding on the journey to Auschwitz, there was still some hope that no further harm would come to the community, reinforced by the continuing deceit when they arrived at Auschwitz. Many years later, this deceit still rankled with Miru Alcana as it did with Alberto Israel. For Alberto, telling his story to Marcello Pezzetti nearly seventy years later, the murder of his family in Auschwitz that had begun with the round-up in Rhodes, had been cloaked in lies and deceit from the outset. 'What breaks me up', Alberto told historian Marcello Pezzetti, 'is all the suffering my father and mother endured to end up in a gas chamber.'[161] Whereas Alberto understandably remained angry at the senselessness of his parents' deaths, others sought to reconcile themselves to this fate. As far as Eliezer Surmani was concerned, referring to the deaths of his father and his two sisters, Rachele, four years his senior, and 10-year-old Maria (in Maria's case, he never gave up hope that she might have survived), fate had played its hand and there was little one could do against such a powerful force.

This reference to 'fate' or 'destiny' expresses the sense of powerlessness of victims at such overwhelming odds. Nor could Eliezer like so many of his compatriots from the community, from the president Giacobbe Franco to teenagers like himself, imagine the intentions of Germany. 'I never expected a country from so many miles away to come to an island and annihilate the whole community ... you know?'[162] As Alberto Israel put it, 'Even the smartest most intelligent among us could not have imagined such a thing.'[163] The older Sami Modiano, sitting on a rock outside the old walls and facing the sea, reflected: 'It is difficult for you to understand ... because we were innocent people. We hadn't committed any crime. Our crime was only that of having been born Jewish.'[164] Certainly, for many of the Jewish inhabitants of Rhodes and Kos, their cordial relations with the German occupiers had left them complacent about the nature of Hitler's war – thus no one had expected the action of July. For those who had survived the gruelling journey from the Aegean to Auschwitz, the terror of that journey would be overshadowed by the shock of their arrival at a place they could never have imagined existed.

6

Auschwitz and Other Camps

We felt the awful evil of that place around us as we stood there, and then
we came silently away back to where the remnant of the people were now
coming back to life upon an earth in which most had no home left, many
no country and few any chance of ever finding content or peace again.[1]

Many of the community's elderly, weak and sick died during the three weeks it
took to travel from the Aegean to the newly constructed ramp of Auschwitz-
Birkenau.[2] According to Hizkia Franco's account written two years after the
end of the war, there were a total of forty deaths, including five persons who
died at sea en route to Piraeus, 'about a dozen' who succumbed in Haidari,
and twenty-two who died during the thirteen-day journey to Auschwitz.[3]
Thus, just over 1,700 deportees from Rhodes and Kos arrived at the camp on
16 August, a Wednesday. They constituted the majority of the circa 2,500 Jews
on this last transport from Greece. Of this number 346 men and 254 women
were admitted to the camp.[4]

The violence of the deportation from Rhodes, the short sojourn in Haidari
and the transport to Auschwitz traumatized the community and became
deeply embedded in survivors' emotional memories. Decades later, Giacomo
[Jack] Hasson, simply refused to recall the horror of the train and its arrival at
Auschwitz; perhaps because his grandmother Behora died on this journey, and
at the end of it, the gas chamber awaited his father.[5] For some, there was a sense
of foreboding. For many there was utter incomprehension as to where they
had arrived or what was happening. Giuseppe Coné remarked many years
later, the people who shared his wagon 'didn't have any idea what was going
to happen. They weren't scared for that because they didn't know it was going
to happen.'[6] Violetta Fintz recalled how her mother, Rachele Maio, on seeing

the inmates who met them at the ramp with 'shaven heads and ill-fitting pyjama-like uniforms […], believed they had been brought to an "asylum of mad people".[7] The Aegean Jews were not alone in this impression. In his classic account of his incarceration in Auschwitz, Primo Levi describes the scene that met him and his fellow deportees when they arrived a few months earlier:

> two groups of strange individuals emerged into the light of the lamps. They walked in squads, in rows of three, with an odd, embarrassed step, head dangling in front, arms rigid. On their heads they wore comic berets and were all dressed in long striped overcoats, which even by night and from a distance looked filthy and in rags. They walked in a large circle around us, never drawing near, and in silence began to busy themselves with our luggage and to climb in and out of the empty wagons.[8]

There would have been little difference to this spectacle in mid-August, when the last transport from Greece arrived. In the literature, the arrival of this last transport from Greece has been overshadowed by the fate of nearly half a million Jews from Hungary two months earlier, and that of the 67,000 Jews from the Lødz ghetto shortly after. On reaching Auschwitz, suffering fatigue and in distress, there was for some a sense of relief that the gruelling journey was finally over. Thus Eliezer Surmani, who was 16 at the time, was 'glad when the [train] journey ended'.[9] And while some of the captives might have 'expect[ed] the worst', the lack of knowledge of the true purpose of the place they had been brought to meant that even the most apprehensive among them was unlikely to have expected 'the unthinkable', to paraphrase French survivor Charlotte Delbo.[10]

Indeed, for those who arrived exhausted, there was little time to think. Violetta Fintz remembered the strange language barked at them: '*Schnell, schnell*' and '*raus*'.

> We come … *schnell* and *schnell*; we don't know what *schnell, schnell* … quick, quick [means] and hitting us and again with all the cruelty we come down of [*sic*] the train […] I come down my sister Miriam and my mother the one side … me and Miriam. The German come and he pulled my mother from the hair and he gave me one [blow] on my head because I said 'ciao mama'. That was the last time I saw my mother. I didn't see my father, I didn't see anybody else.[11]

Among those disembarking from the transport was Allegra Alcana, whose 42nd birthday would have occurred on the 19th. She was the widow of Avner Hanan (who had committed suicide a month earlier), and led her four children. They arrived together with Avner's brother Ezra, his wife, Maria Ventura and their six children, including 4-year-old Giacobbe and their 2-month-old baby Salva (Illustration 6.1).[12] The mothers with their younger children and the three grandparents were motioned to the growing line of those deemed unfit for work. Four of the Hanan children, Lea, Ascer and Alberto with their 16-year-old cousin Sara, were motioned to the right where they awaited a further inspection by the camp doctors to ascertain if they were fit to work. Alberto was only 8 years old at the time, so his inclusion in this group remains a mystery. All four would survive the Holocaust.[13]

Similarly, the extensive family and kin of Miru Alcana disembarked from the freight cars onto the ramp, as too did the family of Matilde Alhadeff, who as we saw remained on Rhodes hidden by her Italian lover, Merolle.

Illustration 6.1 Ezra Hanan and Maria Ventura family, May 1939: Amalia, Sara (standing behind her father), Violetta and Bulissa (held by her mother)

Source: Courtesy Genika Archeia tou Kratous/Archeia Dodekanisou GAKR Carabinieri 6.PS.110

Her elderly aunts and uncles and the four youngest children of her cousins were sent to the left. The entirety of Matilde's family did not survive the war, according to her own testimony.[14] The family of Achille Da Fano and Gioia Arditti suffered a similar fate of forced separation and destruction (see Illustration 2.3, Chapter 2). The Italian barber, who was 38 years old and his oldest daughter, Giuseppina, who had turned 16 that May, went to the right at the ramp, but Gioia and the three younger girls, Maria, Elsa and Annetta, were sent to the left. Also among the deportees who disembarked onto the notorious ramp at Auschwitz on 16 August was Elia Levi, the 33-year-old telegraph employee we encountered in earlier chapters. Accompanying him was his 30-year-old wife Rachele Galante Levi and their 4-year-old son Isaaco, named after Elia's father, as was the custom. The couple had married in February 1937 and had made their home in the Via Sotto I Fichi. Rachele was heavily pregnant when they were deported from Rhodes three weeks earlier, and gave birth during the transport.[15] This baby girl, named in the CDEC records simply as 'Neonata' ('newly born'), was probably the youngest victim, 90 years junior to Fassana Menascé. Born in the middle decade of the previous century, Fassana was among the oldest cohort of the deportees to arrive at Auschwitz, that is, if she had not already succumbed to the ardour of the journey.[16] The fate of the young and the old cohorts was sealed at the gates of Auschwitz (Table 6.1).

In spite of their bewilderment, the deportees were quickly organized at the ramp in Auschwitz into 'useful' and 'useless' bodies in relation to the needs of the Nazi war economy.[17] In a deposition made in 1945, Rachel Hugno Hanan told her interlocutor how

> she had been separated together with the other young people from the elders, who were gathered for an unknown destination; together with the elders were gathered the children and those women, even if they were young, who had a child in their arms. Among them was also an unmarried sister of hers who was holding a small nephew in her arms, he was separated from the group and shot.
>
> An infant child, on the other hand, was wrenched from its sturdy mother's arms and slammed by a German against the wall with such force that its bloodied brains plastered it: the screaming mother was forcibly thrown back into the group of youths.[18]

However, the process of disembarking more than 2,000 deportees and sorting them into crude categories of 'useful' and 'non-useful', had to be expedited with the minimum of fuss. For this reason, the use of direct physical violence was kept to a minimum, if employed at all. Thus, it is questionable if at disembarkation small children were shot or babies were torn from their mothers' arms and thrown against the tracks, as reported by some Aegean survivors.[19] Paradoxical as it may seem, individual or arbitrary acts of violence at the ramp were not permitted for fear of disrupting the process of selection.

The reception of the newly arrived deportees at Auschwitz had to be expedited with as little fuss as possible so as to avoid panic from spreading among them. First, two columns based on gender were formed and proceeded to approach what Miklôs Nyiszli, a Hungarian doctor who arrived in May 1944, without irony referred to as 'the selection committee' comprising doctors and guards. At this point, two further columns were created, one on the left and one on the right. The sick, the elderly, children under 14 and babies with their mothers were sent to the left. The sturdy-looking young and tough-appearing adults, or those with particular skills or training required for the administration of the camp, were motioned to the right.[20]

The initial selection of individuals to live or to die was as swift as it was arbitrary. There was little 'science' involved. The doctors conducting the selection sometimes acted capriciously, sometimes subjectively, and mostly by cursory impression. Nyiszli, recorded how 'In single file, men, women, children, the aged, had to pass before the selection committee.'[21] Its members were interested only in whether the right column could be filled with those thought capable of being put to work. Writing a decade after arriving at Auschwitz, Primo Levi recorded of the roughly 600 people on his transport, 'the night swallowed them up, purely and simply. Today, however, we know that in that rapid and summary choice each one of us had been judged capable or not of working usefully for the Reich.'[22] On Schlomo Venezia's transport from Athens that arrived in Auschwitz on 11 April 1944, 648 women, men and youth were motioned to the right; the remaining 1,200 deemed unfit to work were sent to the gas chambers.[23] This was a relatively large proportion to be admitted (*c.* 35 per cent) and much higher than those admitted to the camp in the case of the Aegean arrivals: barely a quarter of the transport was admitted to the camp.[24] The distinction between 'left' and 'right' cut through entire families, as we saw above. Thus Violette Fintz, who would turn 33 years old a month after arriving, went to the right and was admitted to the camp, while her mother was sent to the left and gassed.[25]

But one should not overstate 'German efficiency'. There were loopholes in the system through which one could escape and survive, at least for a period.[26] Among the Athens group in April was Erikos Sevillias and his 12-year-old nephew Joseph Raïs. Sevillias' memoir was written soon after liberation, but only discovered and published after his death in 1974. It recounts his deportation from Athens at the hands of Burger and Linnemann, his subsequent incarceration in Nazi camps, and his liberation. His arrival at Auschwitz is cited here at length.

> When we got down from the cars they told us that we were at Auschwitz in Poland. They let us take nothing from the cars except the clothes we were wearing. [...]
>
> When all of us had gotten down, they collected us in one part of the station in a big open area. An officer arrived and when he had looked us all over well he ordered the women to separate from the men. Later on we learned that he was a doctor who made the selection. He went first to the women and began to separate the old women and the mothers with small children on one side and the young women on the other. We who were looking on couldn't understand why this was happening. [...]
>
> When the officer was finished he came over to us and asked first of all if there were any twins among us; if so they should move to one side. [...]
>
> As with the women, he then started to separate us: old men, children, the sick people on one side and the young men and those who were strong on the other. I was a real mess. I looked like a tubercular; jaundiced, unshaven, and emaciated after the trip and even though I was only 43 years old I looked like an old man. That's how, when he had examined me, he made a sign to go with the old men, along with my little nephew. On the other side were my brothers-in-law and my older nephew. Since we didn't know where either group was going, my brother-in-law shouted to me to jump unseen over to their side so that we would not be separated and thus stay together, because they might take the old men and boys somewhere else. I asked someone I knew to look after the little boy who wanted to stay with the other children,

hoping that I would be able to get him later. When the Germans weren't looking I took a jump and made it to the other group. As I jumped, so did others from one side to the other in order to be with their relatives.[27]

In Sevillias' account we see three factors at play that are important to our understanding of the process facing the Jews of Rhodes and Kos when they arrived that summer. First, there was a person's age and appearance. Second, the importance of family networks and keeping together where possible. Third, the somewhat chaotic situation in which the deportees found themselves where the difference between death and life was not simply whether or not Dr Josef Mengele or one of the camp's other doctors signalled to the left or to the right, but where there was still some space for choice determined by random luck.[28] In this chapter, we turn to each of these factors as they relate to the Aegean Jews.

*

Many accounts of the Holocaust portray the Jews as unsuspecting victims, passive and hapless objects of Nazi aggression. We find this image in some of the diaspora accounts of the Jews of Rhodes and Kos. Thus, Joseph Alhadeff asks: 'But what else could they do, these poor people, considering that the great majority of the Jewish population [of Rhodes] consisted of women, children and men of mature years? There were very few young people; most of them had left the island before the war.'[29] Such portrayals are common in many accounts of the Holocaust where the presence of the elderly and children is emphasized to explain passivity.

On closer examination, however, we must correct Alhadeff's description of the demographic profile of the deportees. The Jews from the Aegean comprised several generational cohorts (Table 6.1). Our analysis reveals that the largest cohorts among the Jews of Rhodes and Kos whose details are known were both mature adults born in the two decades from 1900 (numbering 438) and young people born in the decade from 1920 (464). Together these two cohorts not only represented more than 50 per cent of the transport, but they also had the highest proportion of survivors: 12.3 per cent and 23.9 per cent respectively (those entering Auschwitz after the 'selection' on 16 August comprised mostly

Table 6.1 Age cohorts of deportees from Rhodes and Kos[30]

Age cohort	Deported	Died	= %	Survived	= %
1850–59	8	8	100	–	–
1860–69	56	56	100	–	–
1870–79	44	44	100	–	–
1880–89	93	92	98.9	1	1.0
1890–99	156	154	98.7	2	1.2
1900–09 } 1910–19 }	438	384	87.0	54	12.3
1920–29	464	353	76.0	111	23.9
1930–39	254	247	97.2	7	2.75
1940–44	103	103	100	–	–
Totals	1616	1441	89.1	175	10.8
	[1651]	[1447]	[87.6]	[204]	[12.3]

Source: Based on data from Centro di Documentazione Ebraica Contemporanea (CDEC). My calculation. The figures in parenthesis are based on the *Carabinieri* list of deportees and post-war data reported by the World Jewish Congress.

the latter cohort). Jews aged 65 and above numbered 109, or less than 6 per cent of those deported from the Aegean. Meanwhile children, at the time defined by the ICRC as under the age of 14 years, numbered 357 (including infants), a large cohort comprising about a fifth of those deported; but not, as we can see, the largest. Of the two youngest cohorts, only a handful of male teenagers, including those whose testimonies appear in this book, survived the deportation to Auschwitz and the subsequent camps.[31] A small number of girls, including 13-year-old Alice Tarica and Stella Benun, whose 13th birthday took place two days before arriving in Auschwitz, or 15-year-old Sara Hanan, the daughter of Ezra Hanan, were admitted to the camp and also among the teenage survivors from the transport.[32]

The age structure of the deportees from Rhodes and Kos alone cannot explain the reason for 'passivity'. Rather, this assumed passivity of the Jews from Rhodes and Kos can only be understood when one considers the exhaustion of the journey, their bewilderment upon arrival at a strange and yet undetermined destination whose real purpose fully eluded the victims, as we read in the quote from Sevillias. Even if naked violence was absent, conditions upon arrival harboured threat and intimidation, themselves violent characteristics of the camp. Finally, as we noted earlier in this study, Sephardi culture was built around close-knit family structures which presupposed familial loyalty and obedience. Among the 346 males from the transport selected for work was young Alberto Israel, whose 17th birthday occurred four days after arriving at Auschwitz.[33]

> Once in Auschwitz, we came to the selection. My mother went to the right with my sister and I went with my father and my brothers Elia and Aronne. My brothers were sent to the right to work. I wanted to go with my father. Who could protect me better than him? He said: 'Go with your brothers!' – In Rhodes we were good at one thing. We were obedient. 'Go with your brothers!' The SS [man] made this gesture [nod of the head]. I don't know why. He [father] gave me a hug and went off to the left and I went with my brothers.[34]

Alberto's experience with the SS guard was not universal, but it also was not unique. Alice Tarica who was only 13½ years old, was similarly saved by the arbitrary action of a guard and possibly because he took her to be older. According to her cousin, Elisa Franco Hasson, Alice was developed for her age and easily mistaken for older.[35] Meanwhile, Alice's mother had no idea as to the purpose of the processing at the ramp, as Alice recalled in the late 1990s.

> The selection began on the platform, without delay. Once again, we were separated: on one side, the men – I saw father and grandfather join their column, on the other side, the women, either old or with children. My two sisters were directed to a third line, where the young and apparently healthy women were. Barely thirteen years old, I stayed with my mother, Maurice, and Esther. It was then that an SS man – a big man with small round glasses masking a cruel look, obviously an important person – grabbed me and pushed me towards the line where my sisters were: 'You, over there!' My mother begged him: 'No! Please, she is too young.' Of course, she had no idea of the fate that awaited her and thought to protect me. One of the Greek prisoners stopped her at once: 'Don't say anything, let her go. You will find her later.' And he sent me to join Sol and Ketty.[36]

Her mother, twin brother Maurice and younger sister Esther, together with those men, women and children who failed this initial selection at the ramp were ushered to the sidings along the barbed-wire fencing from where they

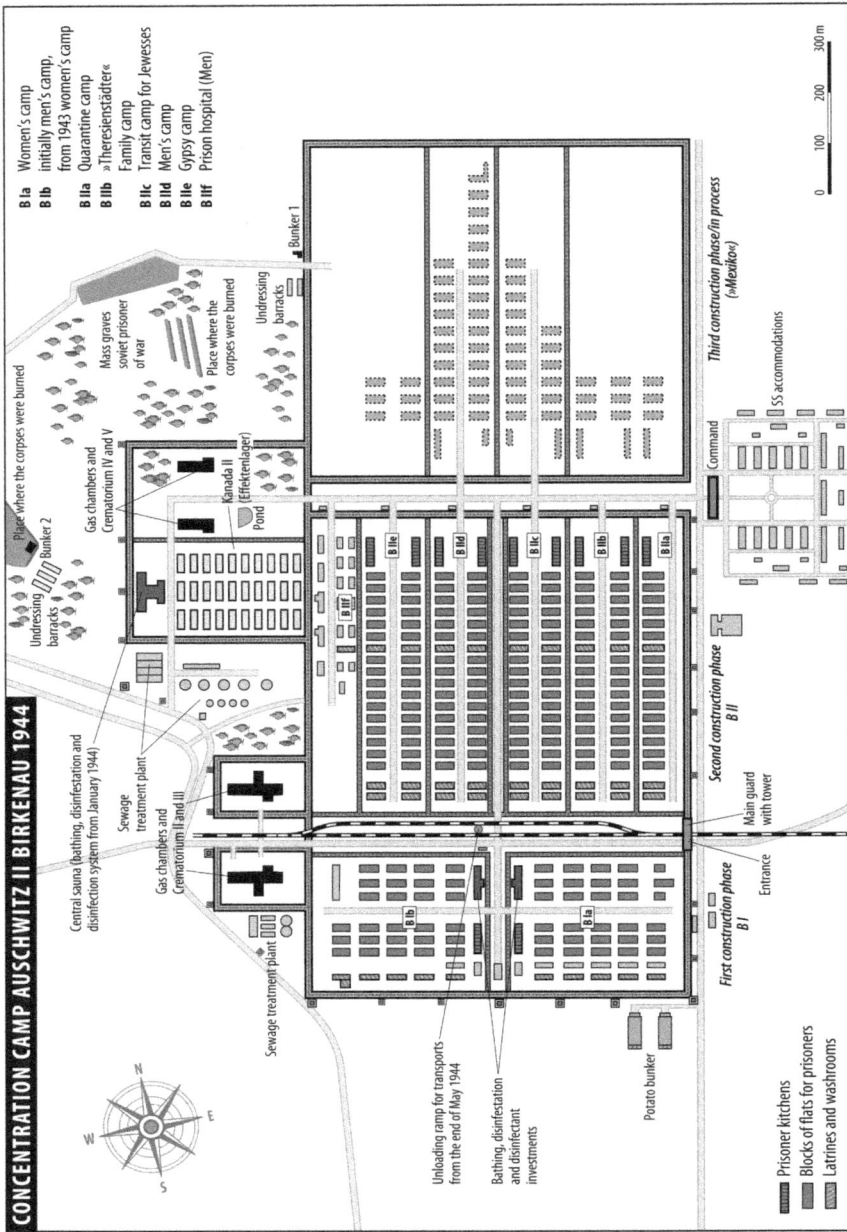

CONCENTRATION CAMP AUSCHWITZ II BIRKENAU 1944

B Ia — Women's camp
B Ib — initially men's camp, from 1943 women's camp
B IIa — Quarantine camp
B IIb — »Theresienstädter«
B IIc — Family camp
B IId — Transit camp for Jewesses
B IIe — Men's camp
B IIf — Gypsy camp
B IIf — Prison hospital (Men)

0   100   200   300 m

Place where the corpses were burned

Bunker 2

Undressing barracks

Mass graves soviet prisoner of war

Place where the corpses were burned

Undressing barracks

Bunker 1

Gas chambers and Crematorium IV and V

Kanada II (Effektenlager)

Pond

Central sauna (bathing, disinfestation and disinfection system from January 1944)

Sewage treatment plant

Gas chambers and Crematorium II and III

Sewage treatment plant

Third construction phase/in process (»Mexiko«)

SS accommodations

Command

Second construction phase B II

Main guard with tower

B IIf

B IIe

B IId

B IIc

B IIb

B IIa

First construction phase B I

Entrance

B Ib

B Ia

Unloading ramp for transports from the end of May 1944

Bathing, disinfestation and disinfectant investments

Potato bunker

Prisoner kitchens

Blocks of flats for prisoners

Latrines and washrooms

Map 6.1 Auschwitz-Birkenau, 1944; © Peter Palm

made the final stage of the deportation on foot to a clearing in the copse of trees close to the gas chambers.

Today we know a great deal about the selection process at the ramp in Auschwitz-Birkenau. Not only did members of the camp's resistance record the horrors of Auschwitz, and many survivor-victims too have described their experiences at the ramp subsequently in numerous interviews and memoirs.[37] The perpetrators themselves also documented the process in the minutiae of the camp books. In the case of over 400,000 Hungarian Jews who arrived in several transports in the late spring and summer of 1944, the camp photographers Bernhard Walter and Ernst Hoffmann photographed their arrival and selection. These images survived the war, and depict the route from arrival to the descent into the gas chambers.[38]

Whilst the entire process may have been standardized, the experiences of the victims were far from uniform, as Nyiszli, the doctor we cited above, observed. 'In the moments that followed [disembarkation from the freight wagons] we experienced certain phases of what, at Auschwitz, was called "selection". As for the subsequent phases, everyone lived through them according to [their] particular fate.'[39] These experiences were subordinated to the procedure common to all those arriving: the disembarkation from the trains had to be quick; the sexes segregated; the physically weak segregated from the able-bodied, and so on, and as we have noted, with the minimum of fuss.

Facing the 'selection committee' at arrival and subsequent experience in the camps was also determined to a large degree on the mental resolve of an individual. Sevillias and his brothers-in-law were 'up' for any challenge, as they had been in civilian life. The former army officer and doctor Nyiszli was assertive and carried himself with a confidence that awed the lesser-educated guards. He, like Sevillias, was prepared to take risks. Schlomo Venezia from Salonica was 'street-wise' and quickly grasped the purpose of the inspection, passing himself off as a worker, as too did the student, Max Mannheimer from Czechoslovakia. The Salonican Jew, Salvator Kounio, like Nyiszli, was an educated man who radiated natural authority. He was prepared to bluff about his two children's ages, thus saving them upon arrival in March 1943.[40] It is possible that the fathers of Sami Modiano and Moise Cohen also apprised what was taking place, and lied about their sons' ages. Or, as in the case of Alice, the guards stewarding the deportees as they disembarked took them for older. Both boys were considered 'big' for their age and appeared strong. Such reactions provided some on arrival an initial step on the path to survival, though it by no means guaranteed survival subsequently.[41]

For those too numbed by the journey, and absorbed with the hurried confusion at disembarkation, a different experience awaited. Stella de Leon, who was 18 years old at the time, arrived with her family, including her nine months pregnant sister Rachele, who was married to Miru Alcana's brother Nissim. Stella remembered climbing down from the wagon holding the hand of her niece, Yohevet, while her sister demanded the return of the child to her. The sisters were arguing over who should take the child, until a guard took the child and handed it back to its mother. This was the last time Stella saw her sister or her young niece. She too explained how everything took place very quickly with only the order '*Schnell! Schnell!*' fixed indelibly in her memory of that moment. Of her eight siblings and parents, only she and her sisters Flora (Fils), who had turned 15 years old on 22 July, and 13-year-old Gianette (who would die from typhus in Bergen-Belsen) were motioned to the column that would enter the camp as slave labour.[42]

Flora Fils, like Laura Varon, had difficulty remembering much about the journey to Auschwitz, but recalled how she stayed close to her mother throughout the thirteen days in the freight wagon. When they finally arrived at Auschwitz 'It happened so fast we didn't even know … And we never get to say goodbye to them.'[43] The speed and confusion experienced by the newly arrived at Auschwitz – who had no idea where they had come to – after the strain of the thirteen-day voyage in crowded and airless freight cars, is captured by Sara Jerusalmi: 'All of a sudden', she recalled, 'where is papa – all of a sudden … mother is gone.' Clara Soriano's parents similarly 'disappeared' in the commotion of arrival, as too did Sara's younger brother, 16-year-old Salvo.[44]

There were some who could remember details relating to the indignities of the journey, but who, like Jack Hasson, blanked out the arrival and the selection on the ramp where families and loved ones were separated from each other. Like Sevillias, Jack's father's beard made him look older (he had 'celebrated' his 47th birthday six days earlier en route to Auschwitz) and this together with his dishevelled appearance after thirteen days of suffering in the freight wagon, sealed his fate.[45] In her recollection of the transport's arrival at Auschwitz, Anna Almeleh effaced that moment completely from her account, jumping instead to the experience of the showers, shaving of body hair and the process of tattooing.[46]

Fifty years later, the ordeal of the arrival at Auschwitz was still vivid in Lucia Amato's mind. She remembered the overcrowded platform, the confusion and the separation from loved ones, but most of all, she recalled her incomprehension as to what was going on.[47] Eliezer Surmani who arrived with his widowed father, siblings and grandparents, recalled how he became separated from the latter and his two youngest sisters, whereas he with his father and two other sisters joined a different (i.e. right) column at the ramp. He had no idea as to the meaning of the separation or the purpose of the camp, but was simply overwhelmed by what confronted him. His lasting recollection was not the moment of separation but of the countless barracks of Auschwitz.[48] Similarly, the arrival at Auschwitz was engraved indelibly in Matilde Arbib's memory, as we can see from her testimony to the Israeli police in 1964.[49] She was in her mid-teens when she arrived at Auschwitz with her parents, Giuseppe and Ester Sciarhon, and four siblings. The family had lived in the heart of the *Juderia*. Whereas her parents and younger brother Mosé, who was 13 years old, were sent to the left and gassed, Matilde was admitted to the camp with her older brother and sisters. She would be the sole survivor from this family.[50]

As recounted by Sevillias, and as we saw with Nathan Hasson, a dishevelled appearance could determine the fate of a new arrival. Eliezer Surmani remembered how his father tried to make himself appear 'young' as they approached the doctors. However, he was unsuccessful. Eliezer never saw his father again after the initial selection. And yet, some older men, such as Ruben Alhadeff, the 61-year-old itinerant trader we briefly encountered in Chapter 2, were admitted to the camp because they appeared strong in spite of their age. Here, the decision to motion to the right or left seemed arbitrary. Many of the early and mid-teenagers were put in the column with their mothers and babies, or if they were holding hands of smaller children, or helping their grandparents. However, Moise Cohen and Sami Modiano, both just 14 years old but considered 'tall' for their age, joined the column for work. Sami's widowed father was also motioned to the right, but his sister Lucia three years older than him was sent to the left. Sami's uncle Moses and aunt Grazia were gassed on arrival, but his older cousins Samuele, Elisa and Lucia were admitted to the camp, although only Lucia, like Sami, would survive.[51]

Death, and its constant threat, became a defining characteristic of the deportees' experience of the camps from their arrival to the liberation of the few who survived ten months later. The large and young family of Boa[z]s Berro, who until the deportation had navigated the villages of Rhodes selling his wares, experienced the same arbitrary fate. Boaz was married to Giamila Alhadeff, the second oldest child of Ruben Alhadeff, mentioned above.[52] The couple had six children, all close in age. The eldest was 11-year-old Uriel, named after his paternal grandfather; then came Rebecca who was born in 1935; she was followed by Ruben, born in 1937 and named after his grandfather; Estrella (Stella) was born in 1939, and named after her maternal grandmother; David was born in 1941, and finally there was Fani [Fany], just 18 months old. On arrival at Auschwitz, this young family like other families was torn apart. Giamila together with her six children, her mother Estrella and Giamila's 65-year-old mother-in-law, Fassana Pelosoff Berro, her two sisters Matilde and Zimbal, and Zimbal's 8-year-old son Jeshua, were sent to the column that snaked its way to the wooded clearing close to the gas chambers to await the 'showers'. Meanwhile, her father, her sisters Caden and Reina (Regina), and her brothers Samuele, who had been a fruit-seller in Rhodes, and Saul, together with Boaz and his brothers Nissim and Salvatore, Matilde's husband, Nissim Hasson and his brothers Aronne and Salomon, were admitted to the camp.

One by one the members of this large, extended family perished, either as a consequence of the selections in Auschwitz in September and October, or from disease and exhaustion in Mauthausen and Dachau, to where some were later transferred (see below). Nissim Hasson was the first to die on 12 September at the first selection; Boaz's brother Salvatore Berro died on 18 September at the second selection; his other brother Nissim Berro died nine days later; Boaz died in mid-October after a further selection. Ruben Alhadeff's 23-year-old daughter Reina was probably selected for gassing on 27 October, just before many of the Jews from Rhodes and Kos were dispersed to other camps. Her brother Saul died in Mauthausen on 23 April.[53] Their father Ruben Alhadeff, who had turned 61 on 21 July, and was thus among the oldest of the Aegean deportees to be admitted to Auschwitz, did not survive. He too succumbed, apparently in Bergen-Belsen.[54] Only 30-year-old Caden, Ruben's third oldest child survived the Holocaust.[55]

While all the Varon children, together with their father and uncle Rahamin, were admitted to the camp, their mother and Aunt Diana and her young children, Giacomo and Matilde, were gassed together with the grandmother and other aunts upon arrival. Within a fortnight, her father Salomon too was sent to the gas chambers after being confined to the infirmary, possibly heartbroken and depressed (Varon recalled he 'was crying all the time' because 'he missed mother').[56] Like Salomon Varon, Stella de Leon's aunt fell sick from grief after two weeks and was similarly sent to the infirmary and from there to the gas chamber.[57] Stella Hasson remembered how in the first few weeks of arriving, the attrition rate among those admitted to the camp was high.[58] For some, the shock of the camp was simply too much. According to Stella Levi, thirty young women died within the first weeks, having given up the will to live. Laura Varon recounted the story of her friend Matilde Israel who got up from her bunk in the early hours of their first night in Block 20 in the women's camp where they were quarantined, screaming, and turning in frenzied circles before collapsing to the floor dead.[59] Miru Alcana also spoke of many girls from Rhodes who became numbed with shock and fell into a depression and then 'gave up and died'.[60] Despair, as well as trauma and loss of loved ones, drove some to commit suicide. Thus Eliezer Surmani's sister electrocuted herself on the wire dividing the women's and the men's camps.[61] The camp was, as Miru recalled, a 'tomb of the living'.[62]

The camp medical doctors and orderlies carried out frequent 'selections' in order to remove those considered too ill or unfit for transfer to a labour camp. Alberto Hanan survived four such selections but 'several of my compatriots were on [these] occasions eliminated'.[63] It was during one of these roll-calls that Jack Hasson's best friend, Joshua Fintz, was selected. Jack's uncle Jacob had been selected a 'few days' after arrival (possibly at the end of the so-called quarantine period).[64] Meanwhile, 16-year-old Renée (Renata) Avzaradel, the younger sister of Clara Soriano, was sent to the gas chamber at the selection in late October, prior to the transfer of prisoners to Dachau. Similarly, Rachel Hanan's younger sister Fortunate, who was of the same generation as Alessandro Angel, Jack Hasson, Eliezer Surmani and Alberto Israel, was condemned to the gas chambers after being sent to the camp infirmary, whereas her older sister Diamante, also in the infirmary, survived the selection by the doctors.[65] Violette Fintz recalled how they lived in fear of these selections when they had to stand naked with their camp dresses over their arms. At one of these selections, prior to being sent to Dachau, Violette's younger sister Miriam (she was 19 years old) was sent to the gas chamber.[66]

Alberto Israel's brothers also would not survive the camps; Elia was gassed in Auschwitz a week after Yom Kippur at the beginning of October after a selection (one of the last), and 19-year-old Aronne died in Mauthausen on 18 April 1945. Alberto would be liberated from Mauthausen-Ebensee a few weeks later, and his sister Giovanna would be among those liberated from Bergen-Belsen.[67] Alberto's contemporary, 18-year-old Alessandro Angel, arrived on the transport together with his siblings and mother Rebecca Alhadeff and father Samuele, the perambulatory sweet-maker we encountered in earlier chapters. While Alessandro was admitted to the camp, his parents and his younger sisters, 13-year-old Maria and 8-year-old Bella, were almost certainly sent to the gas chamber; it is likely that his father, 64 years old, frail and deaf would have been gassed on the day of arrival. We do not know what happened to his younger brother Haïm, who left Haidari for Auschwitz on his 15th birthday, or to his older half-sister, Gioia. Beyond the deportation list, there is no further record for either. In Alessandro's case, respite from death was temporary, for like so many of his compatriots transferred to Mauthausen in late January, he too would die a few weeks before the camp's liberation.[68]

*

The process of admission to the camp was bureaucratically protracted and wearying as prisoners passed through various stages of admission. Having satisfied the inspection at the ramp that one was fit to work, the victims were taken to another barrack to be registered; next their head and body hair was shaved; finally they were made to shower after which they were disinfected with Lysol; at this stage in the admission process, the prisoner's own clothing was replaced by ill-fitting camp garb. Throughout the process, they were beaten and abused.[69] What one received to wear 'was a matter of luck' according to Sylvia Berro. The new female inmates only arrived at their barrack – in this case Block 20 – in the very early hours of the morning and had barely slept (if at all) before being woken at dawn for the first roll-call. Stella de Leon remembered it was 3 am when she and her sisters arrived at the barrack, but were then wakened an hour later for the roll-call. Sara Jerusalmi recalled, 'we were so tired, so finished, destroyed and we just want[ed] to put our heads somewhere'.[70] This first roll-call is also imprinted in Laura Varon's memory. Her 13-year-old sister, Stella, had been so distressed by the whole process by the time they got to their bunk, that Laura had to impress upon her that this was 'no time for crying' and that one had to 'stay strong'.[71] It was only after the first roll-call, where the young women stood a metre apart in rows of five, and in the days that followed, that the tattooing of a camp serial number on the left forearm took place. The women of Rhodes and Kos received the numbers A24215 to A24468, while the men were numbered B7159 to B7504 following the alphabetical sequence of their family names.[72]

Tattooing prisoners was primitive and carried out with varying degrees of competence by so-called *kapos* – inmates who had been assigned this function – and pain was invariably inflicted; there was also a serious risk of infection. Eliezer Surmani, who would have been to the rear of the line, remembered that the *kapo* who tattooed the number B7488 into his arm, used a piece of wood and what he described as a 'nail' (needle) dipped in ink. 'It hurts a little kid … ' he recalled in an interview, making a sound of 'tic, tic' to mimic the tapping of the wood on the nail.[73] Stella de Leon's arm bled as she received the number A24348 emblazoned on the inside of her left forearm; her sisters Flora and Gianette, received the sequential numbers immediately before and after.[74] Tattooing left an ugly scar that was both physical and emotional. As Sara Jerusalmi, who was tattooed with the number A24430, recalled 'it was not painful but it [was] humiliating'.[75] After the war, Stella Levi and her sister Renée had the numbers removed from their forearms at the earliest opportunity.[76]

For the young women of Rhodes, one part of the process of registration brought what they later remembered as a comedic aspect to the tragedy. Many of the women interviewed in the 1990s recalled how once shorn of their hair they looked at each other, nervously giggling and crying at the same time, exclaiming, 'you look like your brother!' and 'you look like your father!' But there was little else to laugh about and nor did shaving mitigate the sexual violence implicit in the process. The conditions were brutal from the outset, with frequent beatings so that in the case of 22-year-old Rebecca Hazan her compatriots referred to her as 'Becky blue' because of the extensive bruising.[77] These beatings were often meted out not by regular guards but the *kapos*

– those prisoners put in charge of a barrack. Stella Levi recalled how the *Blockova* – the woman prisoner in charge of her block, would beat the girls, as happened to her sister, Renée. Stella, however, retaliated on occasion, to protect the younger women. Some of the women gave accounts of how Miru Alcana on one occasion interceded physically to protect one of the younger women from a female *kapo*, and herself received a severe beating that knocked out her front teeth.[78]

There were other aspects to camp life that were negative – indeed, that ranged from sheer unpleasantness to life-endangering for the new inmates. Laura Varon remembered being given some mashed rice to eat that had the flavour of Clorox bleach (Anna Almeleh thought it could have been bromide), probably to halt menstruation, which made her sick. The lingua franca was predominantly German (guards and administration), and Polish and Yiddish among Jewish prisoners. Sometimes French might be spoken and so communication eased a little, as Stella Levi eventually found. But language remained the greatest obstacle for the Jews of the Aegean. 'We were in such awful condition after the trip, and we understood so little because very few people [in the camp] spoke Ladino', Stella Levi recalled in an interview with the *Jerusalem Post*. Moreover, as she pointed out, 'Many of the Ashkenazim did not accept us. To them, if you didn't speak Yiddish, then you weren't Jewish. They didn't think the Jewish world existed outside of their shtetl.'[79] In such conditions, for the Jews from Rhodes and Kos kinship and close friendships became vital for their chances of survival.

As suggested by the evidence, many of the Jews from the Aegean who entered Auschwitz were quite young and thus fairly innocent of the cynical if not deviant modes required to survive. As Clara Soriano, who entered the camp with her 16-year-old sister Renée Avzaradel (two years' younger than Clara) noted, 'we were very young.'[80] As a result, many were easy prey to more hardened inmates. Theft among prisoners, usually during the night, was common. The most prized item was bread, given its currency value. Gella Hanan was 'saving' four slices of black bread in order to exchange these for a knitted garment for her younger sister, Daisy. She had managed to save three, at which point a fellow-prisoner stole these and she had to start over.[81] Frequently, a utensil, the tin bowl or spoon, without which one could neither eat nor drink, was also taken. Thus night hours afforded little opportunity for rest, but instead were experienced as a 'nightmare' when fights broke out.[82] Bread was not just for sustenance, it was also used as currency among the prisoners and was thus guarded jealously; its possession was empowering, and its loss reduced the chances of survival. This was the reason why Sara Rachmani was tormented and driven to despair when her precious piece of bread was stolen.[83] It was not uncommon for a prisoner who complained to the *kapo* in charge of the block that bread had been taken, to find themselves targeted for punishment, which is what happened to the older brother of David Galante.[84]

Name-calling among the prisoners was common, with Polish inmates referring to the Rhodes women as 'spaghetti' and 'stupid Greeks'.[85] Alica Tarica recalled, 'Generally speaking, the Rhodes girls didn't fight back. Our friends from the East were much more recalcitrant. They were also tougher, even towards the women in our community: they didn't hesitate to hit us and push us to the ground.'[86] The young people from Rhodes and Kos were tormented in another way too – that also could result in giving up their will to survive. As we have seen, Sephardi families were close-knit, with emotional bonds deeply ingrained in the culture of the young. Miru Alcana remembered how 'In Auschwitz, [we were] separated from our parents. They told us we would see [them] every night but you young people, you will go to work. Then every night, you will meet your parents.'[87] Many of the young women who survived recalled the deep sense of loss of being separated from their mothers. And they recounted how – ironically because they did not understand that their parents had been murdered – in the first weeks they sang songs like *Mama sono tanto felice* ('Mother, I'm so happy') in the hope that their mothers would hear this, until Polish prisoners pointed to the chimneys.[88] The popular songs of the *Juderia* in particular became a means by which the young women of Rhodes could communicate and raise morale among themselves. Sometimes, singing might help to improve, relatively speaking, one's condition. On one occasion when Anna Almeleh found herself cleaning the kitchen in Auschwitz, she was asked to sing *Santa Lucia* and in return received a few more potatoes.[89] According to Violetta Fintz, one young woman from Rhodes was made to dance the bolero by a lesbian female *kapo* who allegedly made the young woman her concubine.[90]

The Aegean Jews thus had to learn the techniques and strategies for survival quickly if they wished to survive the unremittingly harsh world of Auschwitz.

They had to learn how to make themselves useful by working, whether it was carrying bricks or being assigned to a relatively lighter task, such as fetching water or kitchen duty. They avoided drinking water and they quickly learned not to report ailments for fear of being sent to the infirmary, which in fact acted as the ante-room to the gas chamber. They learned how to forage the bins near the kitchen for scraps, such as raw potato peel and waste cabbage, a practice that also helped them to survive later camps, despite the danger of diarrhoea that could be life-threatening.[91] In vocabulary common to the inmates, this was known by the German term *'organisieren'* – or 'to organize'. Adjusting to the 'jungle law' of the camp came at a personal cost. Elisa Franco Hasson recalled:

> The most terrible thing was that we could not build up any reserves (of food) because we did not have any privacy. Every time one of us put a small piece of bread aside, to eat later in the day when hunger would become piercing, her hiding place would be cleared out. None of us resisted the temptation to steal from our neighbour, absolutely none. Horrible battles would ensue. And for what? For a ridiculous piece of bread. Among men, it was similar. That we were driven to react like animals, having lost all dignity, is what hurts me the most in retrospect.[92]

Not surprisingly, some of the deportees retreated into an inner world to escape the horror of the 'outside' world of the camp. In order to avoid thinking about her predicament, Rachel Hanan cast her mind back to the happier moments of her life on Rhodes, and these memories helped her to face the horror and brutality of the camp.[93] Stella Levi belonged to the slightly older cohort of young women and, like Miru Alcana, was resolute in her will to resist the cruelty, whether inflicted by the camp's regime or deployed by the *kapos*. 'You don't want to absorb that kind of terror because if you let the terror come and the horror get into you, you know you are going to die.'[94]

Staying together with siblings and friends was important for survival because it provided solidarity and mutual support. When the Athenian Errikos Sevillias 'jumped' from one column to another, he did so because he wanted to face whatever was to come together with his brothers-in-law who were of the same age. Similarly, for the Jews of Rhodes and Kos, the value of staying together in the face of adversity was paramount. Many years later, the women of the *Juderia* remembered how being together with siblings, cousins and friends was an essential ingredient for survival, albeit no absolute guarantee.[95] Flora Fils, the sister of Stella and Gianette Hasson, went scavenging together with Stella Surmani and Clara Soriano, finding scraps for the entire group of six girls who had managed to remain together in Auschwitz and again in Bergen-Belsen. This helped them survive together until liberation, making the death of young Gianette three days before the liberation of the camp by British soldiers all the more poignant.[96] Sara Jerusalmi managed to stay with her cousins or close friends throughout, moving together with them from camp to camp until liberation at Dachau at the end of April 1945, when she was freed together with her cousin Stella Levi.[97]

Solidarity networks existed among the men too, with older siblings, relatives or sometimes even strangers doing their best to look out for the boys.[98] The timing of the transport's arrival in Auschwitz in mid-August coincided with an increasing demand for labour, especially with the opening of a satellite camp at Rydułtowy in September.[99] This was the *Charlottengrube*, a coal mine (*Steinkohle*) that was part of the Reichswerke Hermann Goering.[100] By November over 900 Jews, mostly Hungarian, carried out forced labour under inhumane conditions. One former Polish prisoner recalled, 'After a certain period at work in the mine, prisoners died off from exhaustion and starvation. The ones who were finished off the fastest were Jews from Greece, who were unaccustomed to the winter climate.' These victims were in fact, the 'dozen or more Greek Jews from Rhodes'.[101] The prisoners suffered violence, mostly at the hands of the *kapos* rather than from the older guards.[102] However, not all *kapos* were brutal towards the boys from Rhodes and Kos. An individual's situation depended on the disposition of the *kapo*. Their behaviour towards the boys could make all the difference to survival, as both Eliezer Surmani and Jack Hasson found when they were sent to the *Charlottengrube* in mid-September. In fact, Jack's *kapo* was a fellow Rhodian, Alberto Hanan (who we will again encounter in Chapter 8).[103] However, not everyone had that sort of luck. For example, Ascer Varon later testified how he suffered a severe beating at the hands of 'the *kapo* with the broken nose'.[104]

Violence in the camps existed at every level, and it is well-nigh impossible for us today to properly comprehend its multifaceted character or to gauge its long-term impact on the psyche of survivors traumatized by the experience.[105] Certain aspects of camp life remained unspoken or merely hinted at by survivors. For instance, when many years later during an interview, Laura Varon spoke about overcoming starvation in Bergen-Belsen, her listener is forced to speculate that she was in fact talking about cannibalism in the camp, a phenomenon corroborated by a British army medical officer at the time of liberation and reported in the *Manchester Guardian*. 'The prison doctors tell me that cannibalism is going on', the medical officer said. 'There was no flesh on the bodies; the liver, kidneys, and heart were knifed out. There were five to seven births daily, but there was no water.'[106] Harold Le Druillenec, another liberated prisoner, recalled how 'Jungle law reigned among the prisoners; at night you killed or were killed; by day cannibalism was rampant.'[107]

The occurrence of births mentioned by the medical officer should not surprise us. Several survivors in later life also hinted at sexual predation in the camp, perpetrated by both sexes and if not by camp guards, then usually by the all-powerful *kapos*.[108] Iakovos Kambanellis, who as a Greek student was incarcerated in Mauthausen at the same time as the Aegean Jews and who after the war would write the song cycle *Mauthausen*, recalled how that camp had a brothel not only serving camp guards but also the hated *kapos*.[109] Its purpose was to divert males from homosexual practices, with entry costing 2 Marks 50 pfennig.[110] The victims of sexual predatory advances were invariably the young of both sexes. The Aegean women refer to young female prisoners who were 'requisitioned' by female *kapos*. But there were also instances of friendships, usually involving older prisoners adopting a younger inmate. Although her published memoir is not explicit in this regard, Alice Tarica, who was 13½ when she arrived in Auschwitz, mentions that the older women, especially the feared *kapo* Magda – a veritable monster – in Block 20, both tormented Alice and took pity on her because of her young age.[111]

References to sexual abuse made many years later, often remained oblique. As Beverley Chalmers noted, 'Survivors didn't talk about anything having to do with sex because they didn't want their children and grandchildren to know what had happened to them.'[112] Entirely omitted from survivor testimonies (and until very recently largely absent in the literature) is any reference to men and in particular to boys being subjected to sexual abuse, even though this commonly occurred in the camps.[113] The 'trope of sexual violence', to paraphrase literary scholar Kerstin Steitz, in remembering experiences of the Holocaust, thus either remained conventionally gendered or was entirely absent in the recollections of the Aegean Jews.[114] While survivors could talk about deportation, disease and death, cannibalism and sexual abuse in the camps remained taboo subjects.[115]

In the early 1950s in Paris, Salomon Galante told Miriam Novitch, 'around forty young' men had already died by the time of the transfers from Auschwitz to other camps in September and October. Deaths within the camp at Auschwitz occurred mostly because of the selections. It was only when the deportees were transferred to other camps that mortality rates among males began to soar. The explanation for the high death rate among men and boys is provided by the exacting regime they had to endure. Conditions at *Charlottengrube* were particularly harsh, with long shifts of up to 17 hours and sometimes with as little as four hours sleep.[116] The hygiene conditions at *Charlottengrube* were poor and death from typhus was a constant threat. This is how Rachel Hanan's father Isaac Hugno, the renowned tailor of Rhodes, died.[117] Others, such as Sara Jerusalmi's brother, Salvo, driven mad by hunger, began to eat coal they hewed from the mine, and this allegedly killed them. Suicides were not uncommon.[118]

*

Many of the Aegean deportees clung to the belief that they had been brought to a place of work, or were yet still to be 'resettled' (this term was in fact a Nazi euphemism for murder), and, once the war was over, they would be allowed to return home.[119] In actual fact, there was very little work for them in Auschwitz at this stage of the war, in particular for the women.[120] For this reason they were sent to other camps where demand for labour was more pressing, barely ten weeks after arriving.

Thus, on 27 October, 497 female Jews, among them many of those from Rhodes and Kos, were assembled in Auschwitz II in preparation to being dispersed to other labour camps.[121] This transport was to be the first of many for the women of Rhodes and Kos until liberation in the late spring. Miru Alcana, for example, after working outdoors carrying blocks of cement in Auschwitz, eventually found herself among 301 women of different nationalities working in a munitions factory in Wilischthal, a sub-camp of KL Flossenbürg for women prisoners.[122] Miru was among a group of thirty-nine Italian Jews (mostly from the Aegean) that included Lucia Sciarcon (Amato), Diana Galante and her two sisters Felicia and Gianette (Gianette would not survive the camps), Allegra Franco, Allegra Leon and Elisa Franco, the daughter of Hizkia Franco, the community's former president who had left for Turkey before the deportation. Lucia remembered there were 'about fourteen of us together; we were lucky'.[123] This gave both strength and comfort.[124] At Wilischthal they worked as slave labour for the Draht- und Nagelwerk Wilischthal and the Deutsche Kühl- und Kraftmaschinen GmbH, assembling component parts of submachine guns, or were deployed at the smelting furnaces, working alternate day and night shifts that lasted twelve hours under the supervision of civilian workers.[125] The factory appeared not to have operated on Sundays, as Miru Alcana recalled, because the German civilian workers went to church and rested on that day. The women, however, did not rest. They were sent to clean the streets of the town and the toilets in the train station.[126]

Conditions here for the Jewish women at the hands of Helene Klofik, the head of the fifteen female camp guards, while harsh, were nonetheless marginally better than elsewhere. The guards were predominantly young, some of them previously employed by a daughter company of Dynamit Nobel. Klofik, who hailed from Magdeburg, was slightly older and had worked at the Osram factory in Berlin before retraining as a camp guard.[127] Lucia remembered how on each Sunday they received potatoes with curd cheese, and how there was the occasional sign of humanity shown by individuals from the regular workforce, even though conversing with Germans was forbidden.[128] Together with around thirty other women, Lucia and Miru and their friends were transferred in a group of 295 women to Theresienstadt in mid-April when Wilischthal was abandoned.

Women frequently faced physical violence similar to that meted out to men.[129] We saw above how Becky Hazan was frequently beaten by one of the Polish female *kapos* and how Miru Alcana had her teeth knocked out and her eyesight impaired at the hands of her Polish *kapo*. Another female *kapo* in Auschwitz made Sara Jerusalmi kneel outdoors with outstretched arms holding two concrete bricks as a punishment for 'stealing' (*organisieren*) clothes for her sick brother Salvo (who later died in Mauthausen).[130] She was eventually transferred to Dachau.[131] Violette Fintz later recalled the unremitting cruelty of the *kapos*. She too had had to move blocks of cement while in Auschwitz before her transfer initially to Dachau (among eighty-four women from Rhodes and Kos, a number of them sick with dysentery), where she worked as a cleaner in the relative comfort of the kitchen. Eventually she too was sent to Wilischthal. Here she had to haul wagons loaded with munition parts.[132] Kitchen work could be a lifesaver, not least because of access to scraps of food. Access to extra scraps of food enabled Sara Jerusalmi and her five cousins, including Stella Levi, to survive Dachau and its sub-camp Kaufering II.[133] Stella too had to work for the SS in as many as three sub-camps of Dachau, including Landsberg; in one of these, Türkheim, she unloaded heavy slabs of concrete. Eventually, Stella was transferred to the smaller women's camp-section of the SS-run camp at Allach, from where she was liberated by soldiers from 42nd Division of the US Seventh Army on 30 April.[134]

The brutal camp conditions, the exhausting work shifts, the inadequate sustenance, and the buffeting from labour camp to labour camp as looming defeat forced the Germans to retreat towards their own borders, all counted against chances for survival.[135] The unremitting cruelty of these so-called 'death marches' back towards the Reich is extensively documented.[136] The Third Reich was finished; nonetheless, its irrational logic persisted and continued to take its toll. Frequently in a weakened state by the time they arrived at a new camp, prisoners easily succumbed to exhaustion. In such cases, the camp administration 'selected' those they considered too weak to be of any use, dispatching them without mercy.

A number of the men and boys from Rhodes and Kos were transferred to the *Charlottengrube* around the time of Yom Kippur in September. The work shifts at the mine were long: up to seventeen hours in some cases. Nevertheless, for Ascer Varon, the mine was an improvement on Auschwitz even though 'it was horrible' because the food was better.[137] However, with the Soviet army advancing by December, the mine's days were numbered. On 18 January around 120 men and boys from Rhodes and Kos were transferred under chaotic conditions, together with other prisoners from *Charlottengrube*, to Mauthausen.[138] Unlike the women who had travelled by train or truck, the men marched by foot for the 200 or so kilometres of the 495-km distance and then by train, taking several days to reach the camp via the town of Ratibor. The small number of male survivors from Rhodes who were interviewed many years later only vaguely recalled aspects of this gruelling journey. Eliezer Surmani thought the journey had taken just three or four days, whereas his Salonican compatriot Heinz Kounio apparently also in this transfer, the 17-year-old son of Salvator we met earlier, thought it took a week.[139] The Hungarian doctor Nyiszli, who in fact was among a different group transferred to Mauthausen that January, recorded that the journey took closer to three weeks. By the time Nysizli's group reached the town of Ratibor on foot, nearly 1,000 prisoners had died from exhaustion or an SS bullet, according to the doctor's account. Of the original 3,000 who had left Auschwitz-Birkenau and the blazing fires lit by retreating SS guards, only half arrived at the gates of Mauthausen on 25 January.[140] Nysizli later wrote how, 'Our strength all but gone, we at last entered the gates of the KZ and lined up, in the gathering dusk, on the Appelplatz.'[141] Whether on this 'death march' or among a different group, for the circa 120 teenagers and men from Rhodes and Kos, this was to be their final and most extreme test of endurance, which many would not survive.

In a rare account by a Rhodes survivor made just four years later, Alberto Hanan described how the prisoners were forced to march on foot in temperatures of minus 26° Celsius for the first 24 hours before reaching a train station. There, they were herded onto open freight wagons, 100 men to a wagon, and journeyed for six days and six nights without bread or water. According to Hanan's recollection, about one-third of the convoy perished in these conditions. They eventually arrived at

> Mauthausen in a most lamentable state, we would have been taken for shadows; we were left without any shelter in the snow for 40 hours [waiting] to go to disinfection. I was kept in Mauthausen until the beginning of February and then transferred to Gusen I, 7 km away, where I worked in the 'Messerschmidt' factory, hidden in the bowels of the mountain. On the other hand, my three brothers were taken to Eben-Zee [*sic*] and Dachau where they met a horrible death.[142]

Conditions in Mauthausen were worse than anything the deportees had experienced to date.

Together with its ancillary camp (*Nebenlager*) Gusen and an assortment of satellite camps, Mauthausen was established in 1938 near Linz in Austria (renamed Ostmark), mostly for political opponents and criminals. Throughout the war the largest category of prisoner was that of 'protective custody prisoner' (*Schutzhaftling*), of whom Poles figured prominently. There was also a large number of Soviet prisoners, but almost every country was represented among its inmates (including captured Allied military).[143] Until 1943/44, Jews had not figured prominently among the 'fixed' incarcerated population (the arrival of young Dutch Jews in 1941/42 was temporary, for they were soon murdered). This predominantly gentile profile changed in the latter stages of the war, notably with the arrival of Hungarian Jews, and with the progressive transfers of Jewish prisoners from elsewhere, notably Auschwitz. Thus whereas there had been only twenty-two Jews at the camp in March 1944, by August they numbered 10,637 out of a total camp population of 59,269 (i.e. nearly 18 per cent of the total). The respective numbers had grown again by the beginning of 1945, when there were 24,097 Jews, including the Aegean Jews, out of a camp population of 78,6881 (or 30.6 per cent of the total). However, death and transfers to other camps had reduced the Jewish population by 10,000 by the end of February.[144]

By the later stages of the war, if not already before, under its commander Franz Ziereis, Mauthausen had gained notoriety as one of the most violent sites in the SS-camp system.[145] Scholars have estimated that during the seven years it functioned, in the region of 90,000 of the circa 190,000 prisoners incarcerated there at one time or another died. The death rate was increasing sharply, mostly due to overcrowding and the camp's murderous response to this. When the Jews of Rhodes and Kos arrived on 25 January, Mauthausen had become something akin to a clearing house for prisoners. In mid-January it had a population of nearly 11,000 (Gusen had at least 24,000 by this time), and together with its other satellite camps, the total prison population numbered 73,380. By the end of the first week of March, it had reached its peak with 84,472 male and 1,043 female prisoners.[146] This posed logistical problems for the camp administration, and apart from transferring prisoners elsewhere, for instance to Bergen-Belsen, the camp guards resorted to the systematic killing of prisoners unable to work in order to make room for new arrivals.[147]

Following the obligatory roll-call upon their arrival, the deportees were quarantined for a number of days. At the end of this period, a selection took place which some of the Aegean Jews failed to pass. Thus, the lives of Isacco Alcana, 17-year-old Viktor Alcana, 22-year-old Sadok Alhadeff and 31-year-old Vittorio Hasson, the brother of Sylvia (Berro), were ended at this roll-call, just six days after arriving at the camp.[148] They had survived arrival at Auschwitz, the brutality of *Charlottengrube*, and the gruelling experience of the march, only then to be 'selected' as unfit to work. And even after passing the selection at the end of the quarantine period on 31 January, the Aegean Jews faced annihilation through extreme labour conditions, either in the notorious '*Wiener Grube*' – the stone quarry, where the winter shift was at least nine hours in extreme weather but otherwise longer – or the factories of Ebensee.[149] The prisoners of Mauthausen faced starvation and unremitting violence as they hewed granite blocks from the cliff and broke these into smaller sizes with hammers, which then had to be carried on the prisoners' backs up the 186 steps of the 'stairs of death' leading from the quarry. Utterly exhausted by this, and receiving constant beatings from the guards and *kapos*, many of the prisoners failed to reach the top. It was, as Ascer Varon stated without irony, 'dangerous work'.[150] Ascer contracted scarlet fever and was confined to the camp infirmary. In spite of its deadly notoriety, this gave him some respite from the excesses of slave labour, and he survived.

The majority of the men and boys from Rhodes and Kos were transferred to Mauthausen's sub-camp at Ebensee. The camp was established about 80 km from Mauthausen in late 1943 and by the time of its liberation on 6 May 1945 had housed over 27,000 prisoners from every part of Europe. The largest contingents, however, were made up of Soviet prisoners, Poles and Jews. By early 1945, there were over 18,000 prisoners used as slave labour in a network of tunnels. Originally intended as a site for the development of Nazi Germany's intercontinental rocket system, it was by the time the Aegean Jews arrived almost exclusively given over to the production of parts for tanks and lorries of the Steyr-Daimler-Puch Werke and the Nibelungen Werke (located in tunnel B). The production of fuel from crude oil started within the framework of the *Geilenberg* programme in February (located in tunnel A).[151]

The Aegean Jews worked alongside other prisoners in eight- to eleven-hour shifts mostly in the fuel production in the section of the camp codenamed

'Solvay'; a number of them worked in the limestone quarries, and a smaller number were assigned to 'Zement', where in fact they worked in armaments production.[152] The camp commander, Anton Ganz, described as 'brutal, dictatorial and crude' was driven by production targets, with human life the least of his concerns.[153] Moreover, Jews not only suffered at the hands of their captors, but also faced discrimination from fellow inmates, as remembered by Solomon J. Salat, a Jew who arrived in the camp in February 1945.[154] The conditions in Ebensee were thus as brutal as in the main camp, and the work in underground tunnels was hazardous and exhausting and soon took its toll on the prisoners. Starvation and disease was rife. The prisoners' diet consisted of a 'coffee' (substitute) in the morning, boiled potatoes and cabbage at midday and a piece of bread and water in the evening. Sanitation was rudimentary with a general lack of water for washing; thus maintaining hygiene was impossible, and lice infestation common. Clothing was also inadequate for the bitter, inclement weather.

In the one and a half years of its existence, around 8,200 prisoners died in Ebensee, of which 38 per cent were Jews (followed closely by political detainees: 32 per cent and Soviet prisoners: 14 per cent).[155] Florin Freund in his study of Ebensee, has shown that Jews suffered the highest rate of death (39.18 per cent). He estimates that 95 per cent of the 1,503 Jews in the camp infirmary in early 1945 died. The prevailing conditions in the winter months of 1944 and in the early spring 1945 meant that for new arrivals the prospect of surviving in the camp was bleak. Indeed, Freund has shown that 82.3 per cent of all deaths in the camp from November 1943 when it became operational until its closure occurred in the three months from February 1945 and the camp's liberation on 6 May, with March and April being the worst months.[156] Over this same period, of the 120 Aegean Jews known to have been registered in Ebensee, 76 died – or 63.3 per cent.[157]

As historian Marc Buggeln noted for the camp at Neuengamme near Hamburg, with greatly weakened immune systems through malnutrition, plagued by illness, and suffering fatigue, even the slightest exertion took its deadly toll.[158] Following their arrival and deployment into work colonies, the Aegean prisoners' death toll mounted at an alarming rate on a daily basis.[159] Too sick or enfeebled to continue working, Jewish prisoners were sent back to Mauthausen main camp infirmary in Block 6, where, if they did not die unaided, they were killed by the orderlies who injected either gasoline or benzene or phenol into their severely weakened bodies.[160] After arriving in Mauthausen, 18-year-old Alessandro Angel together with some of the other boys, was admitted to the camp's 'Jewish hospital' in Block 6, suffering from oedema. There he was attended by Dr Zoltan Klar's staff. Unlike Ascer Varon, who also was admitted to Block 6 and who would survive, Alessandro died shortly later.[161] The early spring took a heavy toll. On 6 March, 22-year-old Rafaele Turiel succumbed to the brutal camp system; 23-year-old Chaim Cunio (Haim Hugno) died on 24 March; 38-year-old Giuseppe Menascé died on 22 April, after six weeks' toil. Three or four days later, 19-year-old Isacco Israel was killed; he was possibly among the 269 Jews condemned to die after a 'selection' on the 25th.[162]

Medical Block 6 was frequently the final stage in a victim's life. After facing a selection by a doctor who 'judged the general condition of each one with a superficial glance, instantly deciding their fate',[163] prisoners, who in the eyes of the doctor were deemed too sick or unfit to work, were entered on a separate transfer list. On arrival in the so-called infirmary, a further examination awaited the sick; if deemed incurable, death was inevitable. As Primo Levi and Leonardo De Benedetti noted in their 1945 report on the process in Auschwitz, 'at all events, it was only a lucky few who were removed from the list and readmitted to hospital ... the majority were condemned to death.'[164]

Mauthausen's doctors oversaw the killing of prisoners. In August 1944 the camp's medical unit received a new chief, Dr Waldemar Wolter (1908–47), with fellow SS doctors such as Dr Enno Lolling, originally from Berlin, Friedrich Entress (1914–47) and Helmuth Vetter. These young doctors (all in their early thirties) oversaw selections, and either personally delivered or supervised lethal injections, and ordered the transfer of prisoners to the so-called sanatorium (*Heil- und Pflegeanstalt*) at Ybbs on the Donau, where they received lethal injections, usually to the heart. One witness giving evidence after the camp's liberation stated how this type of action occurred more frequently in the latter phase of the war when 'from the infirmary of the concentration camp Mauthausen, all weak prisoners were taken away in buses in one go, between 40 and 80 of them'.[165]

However, prisoners were also murdered in the camp's own infirmary located in the notorious 'sanatorium' complex (*Genesungslager*) where a special unit was created under the direction of the SS sergeants Josef Leeb, Eduard Klerner, and possibly Stefan Mallschitts. The death lists on particular days make grim reading, with hundreds of prisoners murdered. According to another prisoner who worked in the camp's administration and who was privy to the method of documentation, the method of killing prisoners was by lethal injection but frequently disguised by inserting a 'natural cause', such as exhaustion, circulatory collapse, heart failure, pneumonia or typhus (all of these were present in the camp system of Mauthausen).[166] Thus a hand-scribbled note tells us that Regina Capelluto's son Raimondo Capelluto died on 15 April of pneumonia, just eight days after his 25th birthday (Illustration 6.2). In some cases, the death certificate did not even enter a cause of death, as happened with 22-year-old Sadok Alhadeff, whose life was terminated at the end of the quarantine period on 31 January.[167]

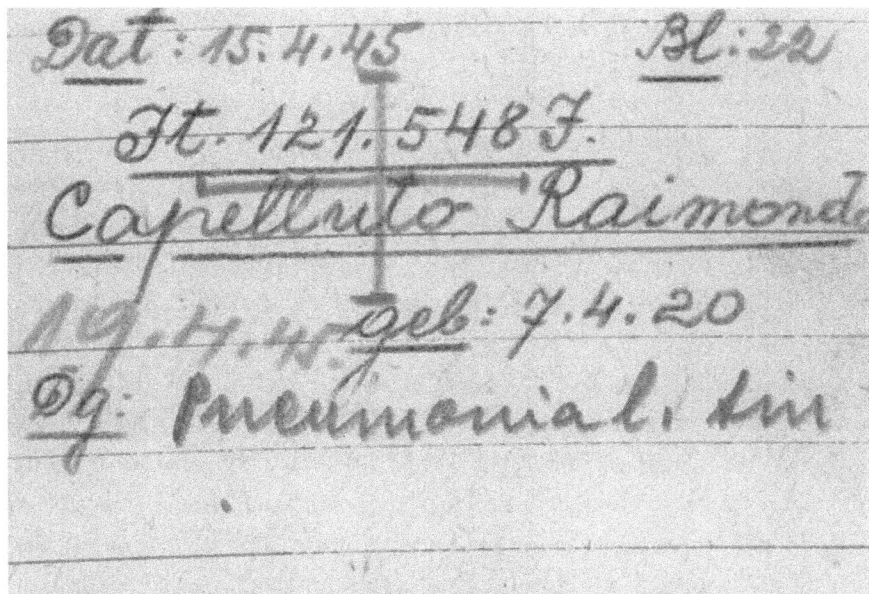

Illustration 6.2 Mauthausen death notice of Raimondo Capelluto[168]
Source: Courtesy Yad Vashem Archives

By the time of the camp's liberation in the early afternoon of 5 May 1945, between 82 and 86 boys and men from Rhodes and Kos had perished; that is, almost 80 per cent of those transferred from the *Charlottengrube* to Mauthausen. The camp's death registers also reveal how the younger cohorts were extremely vulnerable to the camp's brutal conditions and its murderous policy, especially towards Jews and Russians.[169]

The largest number of fatalities were in their early twenties, including Raimondo's younger brothers Giacomo and Ascer, who perished shortly after their older brother. Haim Hugno (Cugno) who would have 'celebrated' his 21st birthday on the day the camp was liberated, died on 3 March. Altogether, this age group constituted about 40 per cent of the dead whose names we can ascertain. Alessandro Angel's cohort of teenagers (born between 1926 and 1928) made up 20 per cent of the Mauthausen-Ebensee dead. This was the same proportion as those in their thirties, such as Giuseppe Amato, who died 21 April on what should have been his 30th birthday. Nissim Hasson's brother, Salomon, who, like his brother-in-law Samuele Alhadeff, had been a fruit-seller in Rhodes, died at the end of the first week of March 1945 in Mauthausen. His other brother-in-law, Saul Alhadeff, died on 23 April 1945.[170]

There were just four older men among the Aegean prisoners (in their early forties), who succumbed to the brutal conditions in Mauthausen: Alberto Benveniste who died 13 February, Marco Menascé who died two weeks later on the 26th – two days before his 42nd birthday, Giacomo Hugno who died on 27 March and Giuseppe Coen, who died three weeks later on 19 April. Alberto was 42 years old, Giuseppe was 44 years old and Giacomo was 45 years old. Of the circa 120 Rhodes men and teenagers who arrived at Mauthausen in January, only twenty-eight were recorded by the summer of 1945 as having survived.[171] For those who clung to life, the threads were thin. At the time of their arrival on 25 January, Mauthausen with its ancillary camps had a total of 78,681 prisoners, of whom 24,097 were Jews.[172] Teenagers and men between 20 and 40 years old predominated among the Jewish prisoners, as they did in the camp's population at large. The youngest cohort were the most vulnerable, as we can see from Table 6.2. Indeed, the distribution of deaths among the different age cohorts of Mauthausen and its sub-camps is striking.

Table 6.2 Jewish prisoner deaths at Mauthausen and its satellite camps by age cohort, January–March 1945, as a percentage of all prisoner deaths

	<20	20–30	30–40	40–50	50–60	60–70	70–80
Age cohorts							
Month: January							
Jewish prisoner deaths	1,257	189	244	365	319	112	22	6
% of Jewish prisoners in each age cohort who died in the month	100	15.0	19.4	29.0	25.3	8.9	1.75	0.47
Total of all prisoner deaths	4,043	405	954	1,246	974	371	75	17
Cohort %							
%	100	10.0	23.5	30.8	24.1	9.1	1.8	0.42
Jewish % of total	31.06	**46.6**	25.5	29.3	32.7	30.1	29.3	35.3
Month: February							
Jewish prisoner deaths	1,721	232	426	466	414	162	21	0
% of Jewish prisoners in each age cohort who died in the month	100	13.5	24.7	27.07	24.0	9.41	1.2	–
Total of all prisoner deaths	4,604	448	1,261	1,417	1,015	415	45	3
Cohort %							
%	100	9.7	27.4	30.77	22.04	9.0	0.97	0.06
Jewish % of total	37.38	**51.78**	33.78	32.88	**40.78**	39.0	26.6	–
Month: March							
Jewish prisoner deaths	2,549	182	578	786	797	182	24	–
% of Jewish prisoners in each age cohort who died in the month	100	7.1	22.6	30.8	31.2	7.1	0.9	–
Total of all prisoner deaths	7,375	471	2,066	2,391	1,810	564	71	2
Cohort %							
%	100	6.3	28.0	32.4	24.5	7.6	0.9	0.02
Jewish % of total	34.5	**38.6**	27.9	32.8	**44.0**	**32.2**	**33.8**	–

Source: ITS Digital Archive, Arolsen Archives: 1.1.26.0 Zu- und Abgänge im KL Mauthausen März 1943–Mai 1945. Data after March is not comparable for the previous three months and is therefore omitted.

The overall death statistics are compelling and show that the rate of attrition among Jewish prisoners was higher than that for the camp per se.[173] And as we can also see from the data, as the weeks progressed the chances of survival for particular age cohorts narrowed. Mauthausen's satellite camp (*Nebenlager*) Gusen demonstrated extreme conditions of brutality. According to some sources, the death toll in the final four months of that camp's existence exceeded the combined total of the preceding years.[174] In this regard Gusen's death toll matched that of the sub-camp Ebensee, 80 km distant from the main camp where most of the Aegean Jews were located. In this latter camp, 82.3 per cent of the circa 8,200 deaths in the camp's brief existence took place in the last four months before liberation on 6 May.[175]

Between February and April, the young men and teenagers from Rhodes and Kos whose names are known died on almost a daily basis in Ebensee. In this respect, Eliezer Surmani, like Salomon Galante, was lucky to survive the camp until liberation. At the time, Surmani had no idea where he was or for how long he had been in this camp. His experience of deportation and his young life shunted from camp to camp remained shrouded in a haze, as he later recalled 'I didn't even know how old I was.'[176] He was in fact just 17 years old. Alberto Israël probably spoke for many of the Aegean youths when he wrote, 'the most beautiful years of my adolescence were swallowed up by the anguish of nothingness'.[177] In the final period of the camp's existence, the total number of Jews among the prisoners declined radically.

As we saw above, by the time the Aegean Jews arrived in Mauthausen on 25 January, there were over 24,000 Jews there and in its satellite camps. By the end of February there were 14,171, while the total prison camp population had by then increased to 83,399. Despite the fact Jews accounted for just under 17 per cent of the camp population, they were overrepresented among the dead: the proportion rising from 31.09 per cent in January to 37.36 per cent by the end of March (Table 6.2). As in the case of Salomon Galante's brother, Davide, many died in the final weeks and days before liberation. April may have been the deadliest month as the camp entered into its final phase, with wholesale killings of the weak and sick, among others, taking place. In Gusen, for example, over the three days of 22–24 April, 1,606 prisoners were either gassed or bludgeoned to death with staves and axes. Overall, 10,791 men and 32 women were killed during that month.[178]

Deaths continued during liberation and in its aftermath, as the camp's brutal regime continued to take its toll on the inmates. Sara Jerusalmi's younger brother, 16-year-old Salvo, died on 5 February, six months before his birthday in July.[179] Nor did Stella Benun's brother, Elia, live to celebrate his 17th birthday on 26 June, for he died the month before, on 15 May.[180] Similarly, Baruch Benatar, the son of the popular trousseaux maker, Giuseppe Benatar from the Piazza Principe, died on 2 June 1945. He would have turned 20 that month and had aspired to be a dancer and teacher. Four days later, Giuseppe Levi from Kos passed away. He would have turned 34 years old a month later on 8 July.[181] The poignant timing of these deaths was replicated in other camps. Jack Hasson's sisters, 20-year-old Laura and 15-year-old Gianetta, both died, either in Dachau or in Bergen-Belsen shortly after liberation as a result of their appalling physical condition.[182]

Terrible as the experience was for those who would emerge from this situation, one factor we have not yet mentioned influenced the chance of surviving the camps. This was timing. The relative lateness of the deportation, at a point in the war when Hitler's 'thousand-year Reich' was in fact crumbling, meant a small but significant advantage in the struggle for survival. Primo Levi was one of the first survivors to articulate the importance of this sometimes-overlooked fact. 'It was my good fortune to be deported to Auschwitz only in 1944, that is, after the German Government had decided, owing to the growing scarcity of labour, to lengthen the average lifespan of the prisoners destined for elimination; it conceded noticeable improvements in the camp routine and temporarily suspended the killings at the whim of individuals.'[183] The organization and routine of Auschwitz meant that those admitted to the camp on 16 August spent the first two weeks in quarantine. The Nazis were paranoid about the spread of disease – and their own propaganda associated Jews and disease, hence the shearing of body hair, the use of disinfection and so on, before being quarantined in Block 20 in the case of the women and girls, and Block 17, for the men and boys.[184] After a fortnight they were moved to other barracks and assigned work with no immediate purpose other than to keep prisoners occupied.

In a posterity letter to her children dated 1952, Gella Hanan (now married as Gella Halfon) wrote: 'We were forced to work hard in minus 26-degree Celsius temperature [...]. Some worked in the kitchen, others in the foundry, others breaking stones, or pulling carts like donkeys. Others clearing the snow, and others carrying coal.'[185] In other camps, the prisoners were put to work for the Nazi war economy.

The transfers to other camps determined to some degree if the chance for survival was increased or decreased. Around 1,500 women were transferred to Dachau at the end of October, among them were most of the women and girls from Rhodes and Kos who survived the earlier selection. The fact that they were transferred to Dachau, even though it too had become a charnel house by spring 1945, rather than to Bergen-Belsen, possibly improved their prospects for survival, especially if they were able to stay together as siblings or in close friendship groups. Most of the women of Rhodes and Kos who left Auschwitz at the end of October were buffeted from camp to camp, sometimes walking or travelling by freight trains or in open trucks. For strong women like Miru Alcana, the odyssey through the labour camps before ending up in Theresienstadt in the spring of 1945 together with forty-five other young women from Rhodes and Kos, fortitude and sheer determination to fight against her situation, kept her going until the end. She, like her female compatriots, was never long in one place, and this helped too.

Thus the actual period incarcerated in Auschwitz was relatively speaking a brief one for the Aegean Jews. Alberto Hanan and his brothers spent just over a month in the camp before they were transferred to *Charlottengrube*. Each sojourn in the various camps was equally brief albeit this did not alleviate the brutality at each stop. Salomon Galante in an interview conducted by Miriam Novitch in Rome in early 1952 provides an impression of his odyssey from camp to camp. 'After the hell of Auschwitz-Birkenau came that of Mauthausen, then the walk to death lasting three days from the camp at Mauthausen to the mines at Ridehaut (i.e. Rydułtowy) and there, blows, famine, exhausting forced labour. And there was the hell of Ebensee where my brother died, the last member of my numerous family.' Luckily, shortly after arriving at Ebensee, American troops liberated the camp and Salomon was once again a free man.[186]

Map 6.2 Transfers from Auschwitz to other camps, December 1944–January 1945; © Peter Palm

*

The Nazi concentration camps were liberated one after the other, as Soviet, American and British troops pushed the Germans out of occupied Europe and deeper into their own territory in the spring of 1945. With their advance, they made horrific discoveries as they breached the perimeter fences of the SS concentration camps.

When Soviet troops arrived at the gates of Auschwitz on 27 January, there was a mere handful of Jews from Rhodes and Kos. Those who remained behind were mostly sick, like 24-year-old Ruben Alhadeff.[187] Among the children and youths liberated from Auschwitz was Sami Modiano. He was one of the 234 youths in their mid-teens rescued by Soviet troops.[188] By the time Auschwitz was liberated, the majority of men and boys from Rhodes and Kos had arrived at Mauthausen before being moved to the sub-camp Ebensee, among them 35-year-old Giuseppe Coné, whose wife Maria Cugno (Hugno) and three children perished on arrival at Auschwitz, and Alberto Hanan, whose entire family was also murdered.[189] A small number of men were in Gusen, whilst 14-year-old Moise Coen was the sole Jewish prisoner liberated from Wels, a sub-camp of Mauthausen.[190] Altogether, the Mauthausen survivors appear not to have numbered more than forty-four men and boys, among them Alberto Israel, Eliezer Surmani and Giacomo (Jack) Hasson.[191]

At the time of liberation, many women and girls were in Dachau, a few kilometres north-west of Munich or in one of its satellite camps, notably Allach and Kaufering (Türkheim).[192] Among the youngest of these female prisoners was Alice Tarica who had turned 14 years old in February 1945.[193] The youngest, however, must have been Stella Benun, who was still 13 when liberated from Bergen-Belsen.[194] At least forty-six women, including Miru Alcana and Elisa Franco, were in the ghetto-cum-camp of Theresienstadt (Terezín), having recently arrived from Wilischthal, a sub-camp of Flossenbürg together with thirty of their Aegean compatriots.[195] A small number of young women were in Bergen-Belsen in Lower Saxony, among them 18-year-old Regina Menascé and Mathilde Capelluto, and a smaller number still were in Buchenwald, such as Ascer Hanan, who was confined to the so-called children's block, *Kinderblock* 66.[196]

The Nazis abandoned the camps in haste as the Allied and Soviet armies closed in on them, taking their prisoners with them on a final forced march. Those prisoners too sick to move were either murdered or simply left behind in the most appalling conditions.[197] In Bergen-Belsen, as elsewhere, disease was rife: in particular, typhus, diphtheria, scarlet fever, chickenpox, measles, erysipelas, scabies, impetigo and other skin diseases were common.[198] This camp was the third major camp to be liberated after Majdanek and Auschwitz. The British and Canadian soldiers who entered the complex on 15 April were unprepared for what they encountered.[199] The camp was a charnel house filled with emaciated sick prisoners, and rotting corpses piled in heaps, almost everywhere they looked. The prisoners who clung to life, like Mathilde Capelluto and Laura Varon, were barely distinguishable from the dead. Many years later Dick Williams recalled the moment he and his unit entered Bergen-Belsen:

we went further on into the camp, and seen these corpses lying everywhere. You didn't know whether they were living or dead. Most of them were dead. Some were trying to walk, some were stumbling, some on hands and knees, […]. The stench […] was fearsome. They were lying in the doorways – tried to get down the stairs and fallen and just died on the spot. And it was just everywhere. Going into, more deeper, into the camp the stench got worse and the numbers of dead – they were just impossible to know how many there were […] Inside the camp itself, it was just unbelievable. You just couldn't believe the numbers involved […] This was one of the things which struck me when I first went in, that the whole camp was so quiet and yet there were so many people there. You couldn't hear anything, there was just no sound at all and yet there was some movement – those people who could walk or move – but just so quiet. You just couldn't understand that all those people could be there and yet everything was so quiet […]. It was just this oppressive haze over the camp, the smell, the starkness of the barbed wire fences, the dullness of the bare earth, the scattered bodies […], striped grey uniforms […]. The sun, yes the sun was shining, […]. Everything seemed to be dead. The slowness of the movement of the people who could walk. Everything was just ghost-like and it was just unbelievable that there were literally people living still there. There's so much death apparent that the living, certainly, were in the minority.[200]

Williams stated how on the first night of the liberation, 500 camp inmates died from malnutrition, thirst and disease.

He recalled that as a staff captain in Supply and Transport,

> My job was to see whether there was food and water. When I went to the cookhouse, all I found was 50 kg of rotting turnips. The prisoners were emaciated, absolutely shrunken. And yet it took just a day for [British] engineers to restore the water supply. This wasn't a death camp, but a camp of death. It was wilful deprivation of food and water.[201]

It was in such conditions that Giuseppina Da Fano, the 16-year-old daughter of Achille Da Fano and Gioia Arditti, perished.[202] She had been transferred to Bergen-Belsen from Kaufering labour camp in mid-December, after which we lose sight of her.[203] Thus, we do not know if she died before or after liberation, unlike 21-year-old Sara Capelluto who died in Belsen on 27 April, just twelve days after its liberation.[204] As Miru Alcana reflected many years later, 'how we survived, I don't know, don't ask me'. In her case, as she also testified, it was the will to live and not to give up, that drove her to overcome such adversity.[205] Conditions were treacherous in all the camps by the time of liberation, and sometimes willpower alone was not enough given the conditions that prevailed in the camps. Within weeks of arriving in Stutthof, 27-year-old Leon Israel, formerly an office clerk originally from Rhodes, who had in fact been arrested in Brussels on 19 May and deported to Auschwitz in October and subsequently transferred to Stutthof, died from 'exhaustion' at 7.30 am on 6 December 1944.[206] Starvation was acute and disease rife across the camp system, and their impact felt beyond liberation. In Ebensee the overall death toll among prisoners in the days immediately following liberation rose to 735, with more than a thousand confined to the hospital, suffering acutely from malnutrition, disease and sheer exhaustion.[207]

Because of the fear of typhus spreading uncontrollably, Allied forces quarantined former prisoners until the danger of infection had passed.[208] Thus, given such conditions, liberation did not mean freedom to leave the camps and commence their journeys home. Alberto Hanan, after his liberation from the Mauthausen complex, remained in an American Red Cross hospital for about a month until he was fit enough to make the journey to Bolzano in the South Tyrol that August.[209] Stella Levi and Lucia Franco remained with their close friends at the Dachau sub-camp Allach for a period after their liberation. In some regard, they had been lucky to have been placed under the supervision of civilian workers from the Organization Todt, some of whom (though not all) occasionally displayed a common humanity and thus sought to alleviate the prisoners' condition. Lucia had also been fortunate in that she was able to work in the kitchen, the consequence of an intervention by an SS doctor who appears to have been kindly disposed towards her. Food from the kitchen, shared among her close group in the camp, ensured survival. It also hastened their recovery after liberation, as Lucia put it: 'we were not sick, just miserable and skinny.'[210] Certainly, by the time Lucia, Stella Levi, her sister Renée, Susana Levy, Rebecca Capelluto and Alice Tarica, had their photograph taken in Bologna in June together with a group of young soldiers from the Jewish Brigade, they looked nourished.[211]

Exhausting labour in winter conditions, poor hygiene in the overcrowded camps, the lack of food and the final brutal transfers between camps, took their toll on the health of survivors. Having barely survived on a daily ration of thin 'wash' (soup) and 125 grams of bread, Sami Modiano recalled that he weighed barely 23 or 24 kilos at the time of his liberation. In the final hours of Auschwitz, the guards attempted to force-march the remaining prisoners but got little further than 3 km before they abandoned them. Sami had already collapsed.

> And when the Russians came, I can't remember a thing. I remember when I opened my eyes and saw a woman from the Russian military. A woman from the Russian military trying to … [Sami rubs his face when saying this]. She covered me with a blanket and I thought I was having a dream. I was losing myself and coming back, I would open my eyes and saw me walking to death, anguish for death, struggle for life [Sami repeats: anguish for death, struggle for life]. And in the end, it must have been several days later, I realized she hugged me tight, being happy, laughing. And I said to myself, why is this woman laughing? Am I dead and gone to heaven already, I thought. But it was real. She was a Russian woman, and I realized it was a victory for her. She was a doctor that had win [sic], she had beat something that, as a doctor she had saved the life of a person who was near death. Because I was not the only one this doctor was attending. There were others, the lives of whom, unfortunately, she didn't manage to save. And when she saw that a 14-year-old child had pulled through, that was a victory for her.[212]

Sami soon recovered from his delirium, and remained confined to a hospital bed until he had recovered sufficiently to undertake the journey to Italy.[213]

Among the living when Williams entered Bergen-Belsen, but unknown to him, was another teenager from Rhodes, 17-year-old Laura Varon who had arrived from Dachau the previous month.[214] She later recounted the moment of liberation in her memoir. 'And almost before I knew what was happening', she wrote,

> I was in the arms of my liberator. He carried me, like a limp, light little doll, from where I had prepared to die to the back of a truck just outside the barrack. [...] Ever so gently, they lifted a few more of us into the truck. Moments later, a soldier carefully lifted the [tail] gate, ever so quickly latching it in place.

Suffering from typhus and dysentery, Laura and her fellow sick prisoners were brought to the camp infirmary where nurses and medical personnel took care of them. Laura continues,

> I found myself lying in a little bed in the middle of a huge room full of little beds, and full of women like me. It was noisy compared to the whispers of the barrack, but I welcomed the sounds of life [...]. At some point after the truck had arrived, they had cleaned me, shaved my hair, and dressed me in a white linen hospital gown. I lay there quietly now, watching and looking and revelling in the absence of fear and the stench of death.[215]

Eventually, on 27 July, Laura was transferred to Ystd in southern Sweden where 'her' carer Ingrid, nursed her back to health over the following months.[216] She was one of the fifty or so minors among the 6,500 former Belsen prisoners sent to Sweden that summer under the auspices of United Nations Relief and Rehabilitation Administration (UNRRA), to recuperate.[217] By autumn, Laura was well enough to be sent to Italy, and made her way to Rome.[218] Laura was lucky. Both of Eliezer Surmani's sisters, Sara and Oretta, died during recuperation, as too did Miriam Maio.[219]

Violette [Maio] Fintz was lucky to survive liberation, unlike her sister Miriam. The three sisters (Violette, Miriam and Sara) had been transferred from Dachau to Bergen-Belsen in January, where they appear to have been among a small group of nine young women from Rhodes. All three survived the cruelty of this notorious camp to experience liberation, but they were very sick, Sara and Miriam in particular. 'Everywhere you used to see [...] dead people', recalled Violette in 1992.

> And this situation, it couldn't get better. [...] In fact, I left Sara and Miriam to be transported by ambulance. And the night passed. They never came to the hospital because I was checking every day if it was their name in the hospital. And the month after, on the 14th of May, they brought Sara to me in a bicycle, and Sara told me Miri died. Miriam died on the bath which they had done out in the cold and she caught pleurisy or pneumonia and she died. For me, probably – I was accepting the death of my father and mother. I didn't know about Leon, I didn't know ... but this death of this young girl of 21, a beautiful girl which was looking forward to live, and to lose her like that, it was for me the end. I became very, very depressed, and when Sara came, I saw Sara: she was also very bad, and I had a fear to lose her too.[220]

Weakness from disease and malnutrition meant that former prisoners were unable to endure simple acts of hygiene and kindness, such as bathing or being fed, if not medically supervised. Jack Hasson's older sister Laura, for example, having survived the cruelties of the camps, died soon after liberation – her weakened body unable to stand the shock of food. Similarly, Regina Capuia's younger half-sister by 28 years, Rachele Menascé, also survived the trek through the Nazi camps only to succumb in Bergen-Belsen's infirmary barely a month after the ending of the war. She was 25 years old at the time of her death.[221] This camp, even after its liberation, remained a 'hell' for survivors, as Clara Soriano (née Avzaradel) recalled.[222] Sara Surmani (the daughter of Abramo Surmani and no relation to Eliezer) also was sent to Sweden to recover from her incarceration in Bergen-Belsen, but her condition was such that she died on 12 October, barely a month after her 16th birthday. Her older sister, Oretta (b. 1923) had already died in Bergen-Belsen shortly after liberation. No one from this family survived.[223]

Not all survivors from Rhodes and Kos recalled with the clarity of Laura or Violette their condition upon liberation. Severely weakened through disease, brutalized by the camp regime, and suffering malnutrition, for some the memory of liberation remained shrouded in a haze. Jack Hasson could not add much more to the account of his liberation from Ebensee camp at the hands of American soldiers in early May, other than that he weighed barely

27 kg – half the weight expected of a healthy 17-year-old man, and he had no clue as to where he was.[224] Indeed, it was common to efface traumatic events from memory, if only to remember them differently in later years.[225] Nevertheless, survivors' experiences, as later recalled, restore a grainy texture to the post-war landscape.

In Violette Fintz's recollections, there is a sense that liberators simply 'muddled through' the unprecedented conditions that confronted them. There was nothing in living memory to prepare those who traversed the camp landscape after liberation for what they found. Rabbi Abraham Klausner, who at the time was a 30-year-old US military chaplain, recalled his bewilderment and sense of powerlessness at his first sight of survivors in Dachau when he went there following the camp's liberation three weeks earlier on 29 April. He later described what he found when he entered the camp on the morning following his arrival.

> Well, I came into Dachau at night, and I saw nothing except the main square coming through the big gates. And of course, I waited for the morning quite anxiously and when morning came, I walked through the barbed-wire gates into the barracks area, and selected one of the barracks. I entered it and there met the first of the survivors. It was a difficult experience for me because I was not confident that I could serve a purpose. I had nothing to offer. I had nothing to give. People needed amenities, needed attention of various kinds, and I had nothing. But nevertheless, there I was in Dachau and I felt I had to do something, and so I entered the barracks and stood there, terribly disturbed. Here we were in a period of liberation and the people were still in barracks, stretched out on shelves. There were three rows of shelves, nothing other than the shelves. There wasn't a … a piece of linen of any kind. There wasn't a bar of soap. There wasn't a chair, place to sit down. It was just a, a dirty situation and here were the people either stretched out on the shelves or moving about listlessly. Paid no attention to me as if I didn't exist. No one came towards me to say, 'Welcome', or, 'What is it you want.' They just, uh … I was just an apparition.[226]

Sami Modiano's 22-year-old cousin Lucia, the daughter of Grazia and Moses, was among those listless figures described by Klausner. Their condition provoked his fellow soldiers into unlawful violence against captured camp guards. Klausner recalled how GIs, outraged by what they found, wounded the

German guards before handing them over to prisoners who took retribution, and in at least one case, beheaded one of their former tormentors with an American bayonet. This may have been what Gary Barker, a driver with the US 685th Ordnance Ammunition Company observed when he arrived at Dachau shortly after its liberation. Barker recalled, 'My colonel and I […] paid a visit to Dachau a couple of days after liberation. We did find one storm trooper with his head cut off. One of the prisoners had been able to get a knife and relieve him of his head.'[227]

Nor were *kapos* who had brutalized their fellow-prisoners spared retribution.[228] Lucia Franco relayed the story of a Hungarian female *kapo* called Magda who allegedly was killed by fellow-prisoners in Dachau.[229] Heinz Kounio, a Greek Jew from Salonica who was the same age as Jack Hasson, remembered how in Mauthausen, Russian and Jewish prisoners rounded upon one of the *kapos* and meted out to him the same violent death that their compatriots had suffered, namely by throwing him alive into one of the ovens.[230] Meanwhile, in Ebensee it was reported that liberated prisoners killed fifty-two *kapos* and camp functionaries.[231] Nonetheless, in their testimonies made many years later, Aegean survivors made few references to retribution, and when they did, these were often based on hearsay, rather than direct witnessing (or even participation).

*

Of the 2,500 deportees who arrived at Auschwitz on the morning of 16 August 1944, roughly a third comprising 345 males and 243 females were admitted as slave labour to the camp, and the rest gassed that same day.[232] As we have seen in this chapter, the chances of surviving the Nazi archipelago of death became increasingly slim for many of those belonging to the former cohort; perhaps little more than a third to 40 percent survived. One of the earliest survivor lists compiled by the Rhodes Survivors Aid Committee based in Via Condotti in Rome, shows that 204 Jews from Rhodes and Kos emerged from the camps, the majority of them female. Of the circa 195 survivors who were in Rome in early 1946, just thirty-six were male. This figure represents just 10.4 per cent of the original number of boys and men admitted to Auschwitz on the 16 August. The survival rate for the young women was by comparison much better at 74 per cent of those admitted to Auschwitz, conforming to the general pattern of gender-specific survival in the camps.[233] Not just solidarity networks but also work conditions played a part in this. The majority of men and boys had to carry out heavy labour under extreme conditions and in an atmosphere of deadly attrition in the final phase of the war. It is not surprising therefore, that in terms of the gender ratio of survivors in Italy in 1946, the proportions were respectively 18.5 and 81.5 per cent male to female.[234] For these survivors, life beyond the barbed-wire fences now beckoned.

The Spoils of Deportation

Everybody said they had been killed [...] I lived there, and the Germans had closed the Jewish homes up [sic] and placed the seals on them. But after they left, a month or two later, we opened the doors and took over their homes, whoever got there first. We took even the food that was left.[1]

Some years after the war, Lawrence Durrell, who served as information officer with the British Military Administration on Rhodes between 1945 and 1947, recalled his encounter with a Greek peasant who acted as a guide to visitors climbing Mount Filermo. Durrell was surprised to see Peter's humble mountain cottage furnished with fine furniture, various valuable objects and a painted piano. 'In order to reach the privy at the back of the house one had to pass through a ground-floor room whose furniture would have delighted a surrealist', wrote Durrell. He continued:

There, standing upon the earthen floor, without any attempt at premeditated arrangement, I saw a sewing-machine, several Louis Quinze pieces, a Sheraton sideboard desk, a typewriter, and a very handsome grand piano. The piano had been whitewashed. The reason for this accumulation of treasures is a simple one; during the period of acute starvation in Rhodes the peasants refused to trade their vegetables for money because they were afraid of fluctuations in value, or even of the Italian liretta being recalled in exchange for some valueless occupation currency. They would accept articles of value, however, in exchange for vegetables; so it was that one saw caravans of carts setting off from the town every morning for the interior loaded with furniture, pictures, typewriters, plate, linen etc. In remote villages these objects were freely exchanged, and now the peasant houses are crammed with them. And the whitewashed piano? Peter's explanation has a certain nobility about it. 'Of course we whitewashed it', he said, 'You know as well as I do that black is the colour of mourning. We did not wish to attract a death to the house. So we painted the piano white.'[2]

Durrell's anecdote casts a thin beam of light onto the wartime barter economy in Rhodes. The list of items not only tells us about what was being traded for food, but also what may have happened to Jewish property after the owner's deportation.

Research into the sequestration of Jewish-owned property in Greece or the Aegean islands during the occupation and after the deportations of its owners, and its transfer to non-Jewish ownership, is still in its infancy.[3] What happened to Jewish homes in the wake of the deportation? What became of their contents? What happened to the personal belongings of families? The Jews of Rhodes and Kos left behind an extensive range of assets, ranging from domestic and commercial properties to general supplies in their warehouses, to small-item goods in their shops, to the household contents of their homes, even the food in cupboards, and finally, their intimate possessions.

From the description provided by Durrell, some of the contents of Peter's house are suggestive of property taken from Jewish homes. Certain items, the Singer sewing machine, for example, might well have come from one of the many tailors of the *Juderia*, such as 40-year-old Nissim Levi, who until the deportation lived in Via San Giovanni (Odos Agios Ioanni). Nissim's own Singer sewing machine was among the many Jewish possessions later distributed among the local population.[4] Meanwhile there were few households on the island comparable to the Alhadeffs, Notricas and Menascés, who were wealthy enough to possibly own eighteenth-century Louis XV furniture (whether original or replica) or a Sheraton sideboard desk from the same period, or, indeed, a grand piano.[5]

After the deportation of the islands' Jews, their homes and furniture, comprising beds, tables, chairs, heavy chests and decorated wardrobes, their kitchenware and household items such as fine cotton or linen tablecloths, pillows, duvets and bed linen, and personal clothing, especially embroidered festive costumes, were left for the Italian administration to distribute among the population at large. Such items were of no interest to Burger and his men, who instead made off with the jewellery and silverware they forced Jews to relinquish in the *Aeronautica*. According to eyewitness accounts, Burger and his accomplices transported ten sacks stuffed with jewellery and coins collected from the victims at the *Aeronautica* when they left the island by air.[6] Among the personal possessions that many women brought with them to the *Aeronautica* were personal heirlooms, perhaps of slight monetary worth but of immense sentimental value, especially where these had passed from mother to daughter over generations. Rather than surrender these to Burger and his men, some of the women threw coins and their jewellery, even silver cutlery, into the toilets. Diamante Hugno's family had entrusted their precious items with a friendly Greek neighbour for safekeeping, but when instructed to bring such things with them to the *Aeronautica*, her mother complied. The neighbour protested, saying it was a trick by the Germans and to take half of her goods. Diamante recalled her mother saying:

> 'listen, my husband [...] what we have got and I have to bring everything.' So she gave it to us all back [*sic*]. And when we went inside, the first day we were all reunited with the men. They (the Germans) started to tell us what we have got and what we have to give. Otherwise if they keep a piece of something for the family then they are going to kill 7 people of the family. Who was going to keep a bracelet, or a bag or a ring in the bag when we have got this fear? And we gave everything, everything, everything.[7]

Burger's translator Recanati, when interviewed by a war-crimes investigator on 20 July 1964, twenty years almost to the day when the Jews were trapped in the *Aeronautica*, testified that the SS-men in fact loaded nine suitcases of confiscated jewellery, watches and silverware onto their aeroplane when they left for Athens.[8] Some families buried or hid precious items in their homes, in the expectation that these would be retrieved once they returned.[9] 'One thing that sticks in my memory', recalled Alice Tarica, 'is how my mother and aunts decided to bring only a little gold hidden in their belts. The rest of it they decided to bury. That night in the light of the full moon, they were outside burying sacks of gold in the ground under the chicken coop ... I remember it very well.'[10]

Meanwhile, the Italians scrupulously recorded the contents of the commercial warehouses preparatory to their distribution. It was a different matter with the German occupation troops. Lina Kantor, who was 8 years old in 1944, recounted four decades later what happened to prized possessions.

Her mother, Renate Cori, hailed from an Italian banking family, and was related through marriage to the Alhadeff banking family. Renate had trained as a classical pianist at the music conservatoire in Bologna before marrying Alberto Amato, a wealthy entrepreneur from Rhodes, and a director of Salomon Alhadeff & Sons. The family resided in Via delle Girandole in the smart suburb of Neocori in an apartment 'furnished in the Italian style'. They also owned two pianos: an upright and a Steinway grand until one day 'German soldiers came' to seize them. However, the soldiers only managed to remove the upright. The grand remained in the home with its legs removed, the body boxed-in and a mattress laid over it. Because they could produce documentation entitling them to the protection of the Turkish consul, Lina's family was not deported. However, she and her parents were among that small number of Jews holding Turkish documents later repatriated to Turkey as part of a mass population transfer between November 1944 and January 1945.[11] After their departure, soldiers and civilians looted their home, looking for any item of value to trade on the black market. Nevertheless, when they returned to Rhodes after the war, Lina's family was eventually reunited with both pianos. Whether by this time their Steinway had been painted white is a matter for speculation.[12]

As we noted in Chapter 3, Mussolini's so-called Salò Republic had declared Italian Jews 'national enemies' in late 1943, laying the ground for the expropriation of their property. Five years earlier, provisions under Article 10 of the Italian Racial Laws forbade Jews from owning businesses of national importance, urban property or land above a certain threshold. Some among the Jewish elite were able to circumvent this stipulation either by transferring ownership or moving these assets abroad (as in the case of the Alhadeffs), or because the law was not rigorously enforced.[13] In general, personal fixed and movable property on Rhodes and Kos remained largely unaffected by the Racial Laws and was to provide 'rich' pickings for erstwhile neighbours and others during and after the deportation.

As elsewhere in Europe, in Rhodes and Kos the asset-stripping of victims went hand-in-hand with their deportation. Despite incidents of localized looting of Jewish property in the wake of the deportation, both Italian civilian and German military administrations were at pains to instigate an orderly transfer of ownership. In general, however, the spoliation of Jewish property was left in the hands of the Italians. To this end and in preparation for dispersal among the population, the *Governatore* sealed homes and warehouses and compiled inventories of Jewish property. In just four instances were German military officers involved in inventorizing and sealing Jewish homes. This concerned the families of Haim Alhadeff and Moses Levi in the village of Monolithos, and Giacobbe Halfon and Leone Capelluto in nearby Siana. They had left their homes on 17 July for Rhodes as instructed by Kleemann's order of 13 July, and the day after their deportation their homes were sealed.[14]

Not only did the Italian administration in the Dodecanese (and the German military) reap the benefit of sequestered Jewish property; neighbours and other residents of Rhodes also became *post facto* accomplices to and beneficiaries of the spoliation of the Aegean's Jews. As we shall see in this chapter, they also actively took part in spoliation of Jews through theft and looting.[15]

*

On Rhodes, arrangements for the disposal of Jewish property began before the community had embarked on its forced journey to Auschwitz.[16] As we saw in Chapter 5, according to Rino Merolle the mayor of Rhodes, Antonio Macchi, had sought to intercede on behalf of the Jews incarcerated in the *Aeronautica*. In his statement to the British, Merolle reported, 'Subsequently, the same mayor together with his Excellency Vice-Governor Faralli, contacted the German military administration from whom they learned that according to the agreements between Berlin and the Fascist Republican Government of Rome, all Jewish assets passed under the protection of the Italian Government.'[17] Already in 1942, Hitler had declared Jews as 'instigators of the war' and therefore their property was to be forfeited, a sentiment echoed by Mussolini in November 1943.[18]

The 'protection' that Merolle spoke of amounted to little more than the *Governatore* asserting proprietorial rights over Jewish assets. Indeed, no time was lost. On the Friday the Jews of Rhodes were incarcerated in the *Aeronautica* (21 July), a 'Commission for the Seizure of Jewish Property' was created by decree to manage the sequestration of Jewish property. This commission was nominally under the aegis of the vice-governor, Iginio Ugo Faralli.[19] Meanwhile, another decree (*decreto* No. 94), issued the same day, forbade the transfer or mortgaging of Jewish property, making null and void any such agreements made after 15 July. This will have affected property left in the care of neighbours or friends.[20] A further decree on 27 July (*decreto* No. 98) underwrote outstanding loans of Jewish debtors to creditors, but with upper limits determined on a case-by-case basis. Meanwhile the decree of 3 August (*decreto* No. 102) created several sub-committees (*sottocommissioni*) to administer different types of assets, namely fixed and movable property, rents, bank accounts, insurance policies, debts, and claims for repair work and maintenance to Jewish property damaged during the aerial bombardments earlier that spring.[21]

It appears that only the records of *sottocommissioni* III, V and VI have survived, albeit only partially. The fifth and sixth sub-committees had the task of locating and creating inventories of household property left with neighbours. Although these records are incomplete, they are nonetheless extensive. Meanwhile records from the first, second and fourth sub-committees are patchy, comprising scattered receipts for rents, invoices for repairs and a few insurance policies. Taken together they provide some insight into Jewish assets and their spoliation. The proceedings of *sottocommissione* III chaired by the architect Rodolfo Petracco, a member of the PNF, with Arturo Morreale as deputy chair, provide an exception to the unevenness of the records.[22] The sole purpose of this sub-committee was the evaluation of the extensive stocks in the warehouses of the Alhadeff family businesses. Michele Tura, also a member of the PNF and the *Governatore*'s chief accountant, oversaw the actual work, completing the audit in November. We shall return to the work of this sub-committee below.

The date of Faralli's decree of 21 July, when the Jews were still on the island, indicates the administration's complicity in their fate, despite Merolle's benign account of events to the post-war British military authorities. The deportation of the Jews and their subsequent fate at the hands of the Nazis cannot have left any doubt among Italian administrators that the rightful owners would not be returning. Consequently, the deportation of the Jews of Rhodes entailed a material dividend to the local population, as it had done after the transportation of Jews from Corfu earlier that summer.[23] However, the process was more complex than simple expropriation and re-allocation of Jewish-owned property to gentiles, as occurred elsewhere in Greece or in Germany with so-called 'popular auctions' of Jewish goods.[24] The records of *sottocommissione* VI, co-chaired by Vito Zicherelli, show that many household and personal items had been entrusted to friends and neighbours by the deportees, either as they vacated their homes during the bombardment of the *Juderia*, or when they received the order to report to the *Aeronautica*. The records also show that there was looting by neighbours and soldiers. The lists compiled by the authorities, which meticulously recorded household and personal items, and the accompanying reports, offer a rare insight into the administrative process of spoliation at source.[25] The records pertaining to payment of rents throw a light on beneficiaries of vacated Jewish homes. Meanwhile, the records of *sottocommissione* III provide both an inventory of the Alhadeff stocks and show how the German administration took an interest in certain supplies.

Jewish-owned fixed property (buildings) in Rhodes was extensive, and as one might expect, concentrated mostly in the old city. Their aggregate value at the time of deportation is difficult to assess because there is no known contemporary evaluation.[26] However, an eight-page dossier, compiled in 1962 by the Board of Jewish Deputies of Greece of properties once owned by the deportees from Rhodes, lists 385 private dwellings, as well as a few commercial and industrial buildings. Together their total worth came to I£7,138,500.00, which converted to approximately US$11,421 at that date. In contemporary values, this would amount to around US$169,000, but in 1944, in a small island community in the Eastern Aegean, this constituted considerable capital.[27] This dossier also confirms the spectrum of property wealth, underpinning what we saw in Chapter 2 regarding material differences within the Jewish community.

All Jewish-owned property now passed to the *Governatore*, with some of it, notably Jewish homes located in the Neocori, allocated to German officers as billets.[28] The palatial home of the banker Isaac Alhadeff was set in a large park abutting the Foro Italico that joined the Mandraki and sea front. The family had purchased it from a wealthy Turkish widow in 1923. His younger son Nissim recalled how his father enjoyed working in the vast garden, aided by a gardener. Lina Kantor, who was related by marriage to Nissim through her mother's family, remembered, 'They had this most beautiful villa and a lovely garden, right under Mandraki.'[29] Isaac and his wife Rebecca Cori (the sister of Lina's mother) moved to Alexandria where the family owned property and business interests; but Nissim's older brother Jack (Giacobbe) remained in Rhodes to take care of the business.[30] According to Nissim, the German

Kommandantur was quick to move in on the Alhadeff home, sequestering it for its own use after Jack, his wife Batami and their 9-year-old son Izzy (Isacco) were expelled to the island of Symi at the beginning of 1945.[31] The German occupiers thus reaped some material benefit from the deportation of the Jews of Rhodes. As we shall see below, the German military acquired various items from the Alhadeff warehouses, once these had been inventorized by Tura's sub-committee. Not only were Jewish homes allocated to the garrison for use as billets, seized furniture from Jewish houses found its way into officers' accommodation located in former Italian barracks. And as suggested in Durrell's observation, personal items left behind by the families were traded on the wartime black market.

The German garrison was neither the sole beneficiary, nor the main one. The beneficiaries of spoliation of Jewish property ranged across a broad social, economic and political spectrum on the island: from private individuals to local businesses, to larger Italian corporations, such as the flour refinery Agostini, to members of the PNF and the Italian administration. Indeed, the Italian administration was the primary beneficiary of sequestered Jewish property. As the *Governatore* took possession of properties, it re-allocated the tenancies. For example, between July 1944 and March 1945, the Italian administration collected at least I£50,000 in rents (the equivalent of US$6,143.75 at the time of writing[32]) – for private and commercial properties now let to non-Jews. The income from these properties was processed through the Bank of Sicily, the official bank of the Dodecanese Administration and which also profited from the divestment of Jews.[33]

Thus, Irene M. moved into a modest house in the *Juderia*'s Via Elia de Bosco (today Odos Kisthiniou) for a monthly rent of I£157.50 paid to the Italian administration. The municipal treasury collected I£695 from Angelo M. for the period from 24 August to the end of January 1945 for what had been Nissim Hanan's home also in Via Elia de Bosco, after Hanan and his wife and four of their five children were deported.[34] Matteo E., a 45-year-old Levantine Italian (born in the village of Trianda) and employee of the Bank of Sicily, paid the *Governatore* a monthly rent of I£230 between August and November for the tenancy of a modest dwelling he acquired after the previous inhabitants had been deported.[35] Matteo E. had also received household items from other victims in a dubious manner, as we shall see below. For five months, after the deportation, from mid-August 1944 until mid-January 1945, the lawyer of Jack and Batami Alhadeff, Dr Franco A., transferred a total of I£3,650 in rent to the *Governatore*. After the Alhadeffs' departure, one of their properties was allocated to Policarpo A., whose family had been made homeless after the aerial attack of 28 June that had caused considerable damage in the smarter suburbs. The new tenants paid the monthly rent of I£730, suggesting the house was substantial.[36] The property, in Via 4th Maggio (today Odos Irðon Polytechnieon), had once been inhabited by 62-year-old Moise Ferrera, who was among the deportees together with his 60-year-old wife Rosa Hasson and her 79-year-old mother Gioia. Meanwhile, *Carabinieri* Captain M. paid a monthly rent of I£345 for another property in Via 4th Maggio. It appears that a number of these properties, including some of those in Via 4th Maggio, had been owned by the Alhadeff company with a rental income of between I£6,516 and I£7,979. These sums now transferred to the coffers of the *Governatore*.[37]

Another property that yielded a large sum of money to the Italian administration was that belonging to the president of the Jewish Community at the time of the deportation, Giacobbe Franco, in Via Francesco Crispi (today Odos Amerikis) located in the Saint John (Aγios. Ιωαννησ) neighbourhood of the Neocori. After the deportation and murder in Auschwitz of Franco, together with his wife Rosa and their two adult children, Rachele (1916) and Aronne (1921), the Rhodes treasury collected I£1,875 in rent for the four months from 11 August to 15 December from an Italian tenant, Orazio B.[38] Similarly, the Italian Military Association (*Unione Militaire*), a veterans club, was among the twenty-three beneficiaries who together paid a total of I£7,070.30 in rent to the authorities in October for formerly Jewish premises.[39] All payments of rents were made through the Bank of Sicily, which enjoyed a brisk business from the spoliation. The foregoing sequestrations were of mostly large properties. Nevertheless, no asset was too small for the sub-committees dealing with assessing Jewish property, as we shall see.

Meanwhile, the biggest prize for the *Governatore* was the commercial empire of Salomon Alhadeff & Sons. The Alhadeff enterprise was extensive and more complex to audit than most of the Jewish businesses that fell into Italian hands. The audit of the company's warehouses, overseen by Michele Tura, took months to complete, causing some irritation to an impatient German military administration.[40] The result of Tura's stocktaking is two meticulous inventories listing every single object in the business's warehouses with an aggregate value of I£700,000, or approximately US$86,150.24 in current values.[41]

The Alhadeff commercial dynasty had its origins in the trade in spices and tobacco begun by Hadji Bohor in the early nineteenth century. By the time he was 50, Hadji Bohor had become one of the island's most prosperous residents.[42] After Hadji's sons entered the business, his older son, Salomon, established the Alhadeff bank in a disused mosque on the main square of the old quarter, which was still operating at the time of the deportation. Hadji's three grandsons, Isaac, Ascer and Joseph, expanded the business of what was now Salomon Alhadeff & Sons so that by the beginning of the twentieth century the family is reputed to have controlled 90 per cent of the island's economy.[43] As we saw in Chapter 2, Isaac parted company from his two cousins after a boardroom dispute concerning Isaac's son Jack.[44] As already mentioned above, when Isaac and his wife moved to Alexandria in 1938, his son Jack remained in Rhodes to oversee the business, remaining on Rhodes until January 1945.[45]

Salomon Alhadeff & Son had been able to continue its business of importing goods *en gros* and supplying these to local businesses until the summer of 1944, apparently with little disruption.[46] Its warehouses were thus well-stocked when Tura officiating for Morreale's sub-committee, compiled seventy-three reports between August and November. Each of these reports, like those of the sixth sub-committee, pedantically listed every item of the company's stocks, as well as the administrative process involved in establishing the inventories. For example, it recorded which members of the sub-committee took part in inspections, when they arrived at the warehouse, who else was present, what they viewed, what was transferred to the administration's own depository under guard (even the names of the guards are provided), to whom items were allocated, and at what hour the sub-committee ended its inspection. A four-man delegation from Morreale's sub-committee commenced its work at 8.30 am on the day it was created and conducted a preliminary viewing of the Alhadeff warehouses, accompanied by six employees of the company and, on later occasions with director Bension Menascé present, who, as we previously saw, had been spared deportation. A second meeting occurred on 7 August, again at 8.30 am, that assessed the contents of the company's warehouse office, scrupulously listing every item. Further visits took place over the following days and weeks, frequently in the presence of officers from the German military administration or the Division's procurement desk.

It was common for members of the German military administration to be present at the opening of the Alhadeff storerooms, usually to determine how they might satisfy their own requirements. Thus, German officers from the military administration (*Militärverwaltung*) were present at the second inspection on 7 August when storeroom No. 9 containing glassware, haberdashery and household goods was opened; they came away with drinking glasses and wrapping paper. Four days later, on 11 August, when Tura inspected the Alhadeff warehouse for the seventh time, the Germans took a small number of textile items from storeroom No. 8. The next day, they returned and removed some more hardware items with a value of I£301. These were modest items, but in a context of severe shortages as supplying the islands became more precarious, any item, small or mundane, was coveted.

For instance, in the sub-committee's third and fourth reports of 8 and 9 August, relating to the store containing glassware and household items, Tura reported tableware valued at I£10,561.00 was transferred to the German administration (possibly for the officers' mess). The following afternoon, at the invitation of the president of the government commission, Dr Toni Piero, Michele Tura, and Carlo Giornetti from *sottocommissione* III, together with five other senior Italian officials, met with a delegation from the German military administration accompanied by a guide who also acted as translator (the engineer Giulio Tomassi). This meeting lasted an hour and a quarter with the group agreeing to reconvene the following day to view the remaining rooms.[47] At this second meeting, they again inspected storeroom No. 8 containing textiles, household goods and glassware, and discussed contracts for purchasing some of the items from the Italian administration.[48] These were neither the first nor the last items acquired by the Germans to satisfy everyday routine needs. As we saw above, four days earlier the *Kreiskommandantur* had taken possession of several hardware items as well as the abovementioned tableware, and 3 kg of wrapping paper.[49]

*

The files of the Commission for the Seizure of Jewish Property open a window on the material inner life of many households in the *Juderia*. Unlike in the case of the Alhadeff business, the auditors did not place a valuation next to the mundane possessions left behind by the families of the *Juderia*.[50] The lists themselves are rough and ready, frequently scribbled in blue or lead pencil on scraps of paper. On occasion, there are completed typed lists. In a number of cases, they tell a story of household poverty; in other cases, we see a degree of affluence and comfort. Nevertheless, however comfortable or poor some Jewish families were, their belongings and their homes provided 'rich pickings' for their immediate neighbours and other citizens. In a context of wartime deprivation, everyone hoped to gain something from Jewish spoliation.

However, before Jewish goods could be distributed among the local population, the Italian administration had first to ascertain the extent of the property left behind. To this end, the *Governatore* established the various *sottocommissioni* to compile inventories. The sixth sub-committee chaired by Vito Zicherelli was tasked with compiling the household inventories and collating these, reporting in the late autumn to Farralli's commission. The decree of 21 July stipulated that citizens had to report all Jewish property left in their care. The level of compliance among the population with the decree ordering the registration of Jewish property held by neighbours or friends was quite high. This might well be because a stiff penalty of between three months' to five years' imprisonment was threatened for non-compliance.[51] Thus, four days after the deportation, Michele M. reported to the sixth sub-committee the possessions of Giuseppe C[H]asson who, during the aerial bombardments, had rented a house from M., in the small Turkish-inhabited village of Asguro, on the southern outskirts of Rhodes. The scale of the task of inventorizing and securing Jewish properties must have been overwhelming because M. wrote again in September stating that after an initial visit by its officials, no one from the sub-committee had returned to remove the items. Meanwhile, the house had been broken into and some of Hasson's property stolen.[52]

Similarly, it took the sixth sub-committee nearly three and a half months after the deportation, to finally take possession of the household property of 37-year-old Nissim Capelluto and his wife, 30-year-old Esther Codron. They had married in 1934 and lived in Via Generale Ameglio 26 (today Ethnarxou [archbishop] Makariou). After the bombardment of the lower end of the *Juderia* adjacent to the harbour, the Capellutos had rented two rooms from an Italian woman, 51-year-old Signora P., originally from Reggio Emilia and now residing at No. 7, Via 4th Maggio. Responding to the decree, P. made a declaration a few days after the deportation, in which she listed the items left behind by the family, including the couple's matrimonial bed and the beds of their two young children, 9-year-old Roberto (Reuben) and his younger sister Estrella, as well as five chairs and a marble top sideboard.[53]

The reports of this sub-committee are revealing for what they tell us about Jew-Gentile relations during a period of crisis. The aerial bombardment of the *Juderia* from early 1944 until the summer had forced many Jewish families to seek refuge beyond the *Juderia*. In doing so, they entrusted their personal property with friends and neighbours for safekeeping. They showed the same degree of trust in their Christian and Muslim acquaintances to look after their goods when the order came to report to the *Aeronautica*. Thus 25-year-old Clara Halfon, a seamstress, lived with her mother and 21-year-old brother Giacobbe and 31-year-old sister Rica at Via Armando Diaz 26 at the time of the deportation.[54] The family had left their possessions comprising two chests of worn clothing, one gramophone and records, her sewing machine and two mattresses, with their neighbour Maria B., who lived a few doors away in the same street. They also left behind a chest with four quilts and two pillows. While her mother and siblings did not survive, Clara was admitted to Auschwitz and later transferred to Dachau on 27 October, from where she was liberated in May 1945.[55] The neighbour duly reported the contents of the Halfon household in her care to the authorities, which duly arranged for their deposit in the municipal-run warehouse.[56]

Meanwhile, Signora Despina C., who lived in Via Filippo Corridoni (today Odos Mitropoleos), wrote to the authorities on the day the decree was promulgated regarding the belongings of Rosa Ventura and her husband, Isaaco. Despina C. had been born in Smyrna [Izmir] in 1909, just like Rosa and Isaaco, who were nearly twenty-five years her senior. As with so many residents of the *Juderia*, Ventura had entrusted Despina C. with her clothes and a few household objects gathered in a single chest. Among the items were two cotton duvets, three feather pillows, and assorted bed sheets, one cushion for a couch, coffee pots, two plates, and one round table. There were also three pairs of men's trousers; four men's jackets and one lady's jacket; four women's outfits; four pairs of socks; one man's and one lady's outer jacket (*paleto*); two men's and two women's umbrellas; and underwear.[57]

Typical of household contents belonging to the poor of the Jewish community was that of the Scemaria's family, a household consisting of eight persons, according to a deposition by Mario Lanari: Marco, his wife Mazaltov, their three daughters Dora, Esther, Giovanna and their son Giacomo and Marco's father, 89-year-old Giacobbe.[58] Marco Scemaria was a tinsmith whose fortunes had waned during the war, and whose daughter Esther worked for the Italian construction company Alfredo Lanari. During the bombardment of the *Juderia*, the Scemaria family, like many families, left their home in Via Francesco Flotta No. 9 (Porta a Mare 27) to seek refuge in the hilltop village of Koskinou, some 7 kilometres from the town. Before leaving for the village, they divided and left their possessions for safekeeping with two neighbours, the workman Elefterio M., and Flacca (Vlacha) G., a housewife. After the deportation, Esther's employer, Mario Lanari collected their possessions and presented these to the *Carabinieri*.[59] The inventory of 5 August listed among their possessions five metal beds and mattresses, nine dresses, three pairs of men's trousers and other used clothes, a small wardrobe, a mirror, a shoe cupboard and 'steps' (i.e. ladder) (see Illustration 7.1).[60] The house was sequestered under Decree 93 of 21 July, and their belongings distributed. The family Singer sewing machine and armchairs 'in the Viennese style' soon found new owners.[61]

The surviving records allow us to identify in several cases the beneficiaries of the sequestration of Jewish homes and personal property. In many of these cases, the recipients were neighbours or welfare-needy families, including some who had lost their homes and possessions during the aerial bombardment of Rhodes earlier that spring. One must assume that the authorities now saw a means to alleviate their distress through the distribution of Jewish property. Thus, Dante Zarli, the director of postal services in Rhodes who chaired *sottocommissione* V, instructed a trustee of the Rhode's branch of the *feminile fascisti* (FFRR) to donate items taken from Jewish homes to a certain Maria B. This beneficiary is described in the files as a 'victim', and judging from the items she received, possibly a mother fending for herself during the war years.

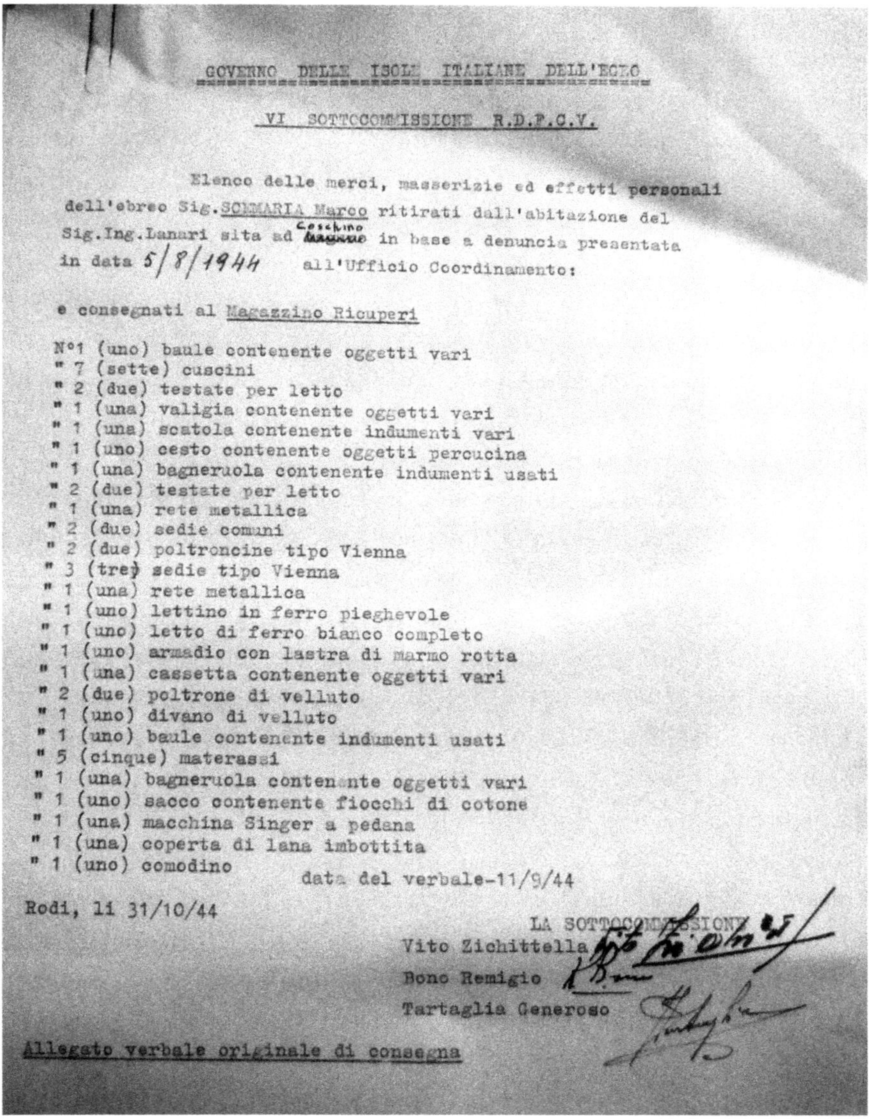

GOVERNO DELLE ISOLE ITALIANE DELL'EGEO

VI SOTTOCOMMISSIONE R.D.P.C.V.

Elenco delle merci, masserizie ed effetti personali
dell'ebreo Sig. SCEMARIA Marco ritirati dall'abitazione del
Sig.Ing.Lanari sita ad *Coschino* in base a denuncia presentata
in data 5/8/1944 all'Ufficio Coordinamento:

e consegnati al Magazzino Ricuperi

```
N°1 (uno) baule contenente oggetti vari
"  7 (sette) cuscini
"  2 (due) testate per letto
"  1 (una) valigia contenente oggetti vari
"  1 (una) scatola contenente indumenti vari
"  1 (uno) cesto contenente oggetti percucina
"  1 (una) bagneruola contenente indumenti usati
"  2 (due) testate per letto
"  1 (una) rete metallica
"  2 (due) sedie comuni
"  2 (due) poltroncine tipo Vienna
"  3 (tre) sedie tipo Vienna
"  1 (una) rete metallica
"  1 (uno) lettino in ferro pieghevole
"  1 (uno) letto di ferro bianco completo
"  1 (uno) armadio con lastra di marmo rotta
"  1 (una) cassetta contenente oggetti vari
"  2 (due) poltrone di velluto
"  1 (uno) divano di velluto
"  1 (uno) baule contenente indumenti usati
"  5 (cinque) materassi
"  1 (una) bagneruola contenente oggetti vari
"  1 (uno) sacco contenente fiocchi di cotone
"  1 (una) macchina Singer a pedana
"  1 (una) coperta di lana imbottita
"  1 (uno) comodino
```
data del verbale-11/9/44

Rodi, lì 31/10/44

LA SOTTOCOMMISSIONE
Vito Zichittella
Bono Remigio
Tartaglia Generoso

Allegato verbale originale di consegna

Illustration 7.1 Scemaria household possessions

Source: Genika Archeia tou Kratous/Archeia Dodekanisou Ι.Δ.Δ. ΕΤΟΣ 1944, ΦΑΚ 53 and GAKR
Ι.Δ.Δ. ΕΤΟΣ 1944, ΦΑΚ 195

She received '1 old armoire, 1 old table, 1 broken baby carriage, 2 old beds, various books and other valuables', all collected from different Jewish homes in the *Juderia*, as well as 'from a house whose address [the trustee] cannot specify: 4 chairs, 1 bed, 1 sofa [and] 1 table'.[62]

Similarly, 46-year-old Regina Capelluto, a widow who lived with her three adult sons in Via Ammiraglio Legnani 20, had entrusted the family belongings to a neighbour during the aerial bombardment of the *Juderia*.[63] This person duly wrote to the authorities 'The widow Mrs Regina Capelluto on the 19th of the present month [i.e. July] following the order of the German Command left her house in Via Ammiraglo Legnani 20 and placed the following items in my care.'[64] The family's personal possessions were quite extensive, filling five suitcases and four sacks in addition to ten 'Vienna' chairs and four wicker chairs. The sub-committee compiled at least five lists between 14 and 24 August. However, the process of inventorizing Capelluto's property also suggests that some of it had been taken by locals. Six days after their arrival at Auschwitz, where Regina was gassed while her three sons Raimondo, Giacomo and Ascer were admitted (they subsequently died in Mauthausen, see Chapter 6), some of the worldly possessions of this family were retrieved from a Bank of Sicily employee Matteo E., in Via Lungomare Duca di Genova along the seafront of the Neocori district (today Akti Kanari). Further items were retrieved by the authorities from three other locals: Stamatia S., Vassili G. and Carmelo C. The items were removed by the *Carabinieri* and stored in the municipal warehouse.[65] While it is possible that Capelluto might have entrusted her possessions to these people too, they were not close neighbours, and it seems unlikely that she would have dispersed her property so widely.

As with most of the inventories, the possessions of Rosa Alhadeff and her husband (Marco) Hasson were initially scribbled in coloured or lead pencil on a few scraps of paper before being typed and added to a final report (it is not clear if this was completed in October or November). Rosa was born in 1887, the younger daughter of Gioia Menascé and Giacobbe Alhadeff (she had a sister Allegra, who was a year older). Allegra lived at Via della Tramontana 10, where their father Giacobbe (b. 1861) had owned a haberdashery business until his death in 1942. Rosa had married Marco (b. 1883) on 24 December 1914.[66] Although the couple appeared to reside at the same address as Allegra, Rosa and her husband also owned a property at Via Sigismondo Malatesta

3005, where their relative Salomon Piha lived on the ground floor, and who also acted as caretaker.

The paperwork dealing with the disposal of their property reveals Rosa and Marco had been comfortably off. A locked safe containing passports and some cash was handed over to the municipality. They had left their possessions in the care of Michele M., a night watchman (*Carabinieri*). A case of surgical instruments found at the Alhadeff-Hasson property was handed to the Italian medical depository, while the couple's rugs were coveted by Antonio Macchi, the town's mayor, and deputy to Vice-Governor Faralli. The Mother Superior of the Catholic nursery *Piccolinia* also received an oriental rug from the couple's inventory on 28 September and a further four oriental rugs in November from the home of Matilde Rahamin.[67] Michele M. had also safeguarded the property of Hizkia Franco's stationery shop, located at the same address, as well as items that had belonged to Salomon Piha. And these too were duly sequestered.

For some beneficiaries, such as Matteo E., a member of the PNF, who had clandestinely sequestered Jewish property, spoliation might have provided a means to offset expenses, in his case arising from investigations into his allegedly adulterous wife, Giorgetta.[68] Others, like the *Carabinieri* officers, may simply have been rewarded for their loyal service to the Italian state. A smaller number, like the mayor Antonio Macchi or the Mother Superior of *Piccolinia*, probably benefited because of their positions in the hierarchy of local power. The latter also received from the authorities several oriental rugs that had once belonged to Matilde Rahamin.[69] Such favouritism among those connected to the nexus of power stirred up resentment in some quarters of the local population, where there was a growing sentiment that they were being excluded from the windfall.[70] However, for the majority of those who acquired Jewish property, in nearly all the cases of spoliation, gains were modest (if that is the right terminology) given the predominant impoverishment of the *Juderia*'s inhabitants. Nevertheless, in the context of wartime shortages even the smallest item, much used and broken, assumed a material premium.

In a small number of cases, non-Jews appealed to the authorities for Jewish property in lieu of repayment of an outstanding loan or claimed back an item that had been bought on hire purchase without having completed the payments, or requested the return of a particular household item or piece of furniture left with a Jewish acquaintance during the bombardment. In such cases, the chair of *sottocommissione* V dealing with claims against Jews asked Mittino's office to investigate the veracity of such claims, which it did with painstaking efficiency.[71]

*

The role of the 'Commission for the Seizure of Jewish Property' headed by senior Italian administrators brought to the spoliation of Jewish property a semblance of legality. As previously mentioned, there are only four known cases, those in the villages of Monolithos and Siana, where the process of documenting and securing property took place in the presence of Herbert Frick (described by *Carabinieri* Antonio Salvate as a *Maresciallo*, akin to staff sergeant) from the *Geheime Feldpolizei* stationed in the town of Apollachia. Frick's men removed the families' household and personal items from the houses in February 1945.[72] One cannot help but note the irony of framing theft in a cloak of legality given the murderous context in which spoliation was taking place. However, this 'orderly' method to the disposal of Jewish property came under pressure from two directions. First, from the German military administration, which quickly became exasperated at what it perceived to be foot-dragging, corruption and incompetence on the part of the Italian administration. Second, the resort to looting by neighbours, Italian officials and German soldiers posed a challenge to public order and exposed the rapacious character of spoliation. A legal framework (decrees) and an orderly administration of sequestration via the *sottocommissioni* therefore disguised the role of the *Governatore* in this ugly episode. Acts of looting by locals threatened this self-deception by revealing the Hobbesian nature of spoliation.

The inability of the authorities to stem a worsening food situation, and to ensure the provision of everyday items, led to popular 'requisitioning' by locals of their erstwhile Jewish neighbours. Over time, as the Allied blockade of the islands bit deeper into the fractured wartime economy, any item considered of value and therefore tradeable was taken. Even though the *Carabinieri* had sealed the homes of the deported Jewish families, this did not deter looters. Mittino reported at the end of August,

In the circumstances, it becomes clear that in placing the seals on the doors of the houses and warehouses of the interned Jews, no securing was made of the internal doors as well. Furthermore, at first the greater number of seals were applied at a height of 1 to 1.50 meters from the ground, thus easily removable even by street urchins. The same seals then consisted of a simple tab of cloth or a piece of string that joined with two sealing wax stamps the two panels of the door, which was not always locked or barred.[73]

Mittino's observation reveals probably a degree of incompetence on the part of the authorities, rather than connivance at looting. Standing in a doorway in the old quarter of Rhodes in 2013, and questioned by Marcello Pezzetti about what had happened to Jewish homes in the aftermath of the deportation, Charalambos Anamourlis, who would have been about 12 years old in 1944, responded,

> Everybody said they had been killed [...] I lived there [pointing further down the alley] and the Germans had closed the Jewish homes up [*sic*] and placed the seals on them. But after they left, a month or two later, we opened the doors and took over their homes, whoever got there first. We took even the food that was left [...] I'm not ashamed to say so. There was so much hunger [...] because if we didn't do it, we all would have starved to death.[74]

Looters, however, looked not only for food.

Compared to Michail Zaraftis's poor family, even poor Jews were considered prosperous by their neighbours. Zaraftis was about 15 years old at the time of the deportation and had joined in the looting of Jewish homes, taking 'anything they wanted, from clothes to utensils to furniture'.[75] In a small island with predominantly poor Greek inhabitants, rumours about Jewish riches gained ground quickly. Michail Panagos, who was also a boy at the time, remembered, 'Before the Jews left, rumour has it that they buried a lot of gold. When they were gone, the locals dug it out and kept it. A lot of people became rich suddenly.'[76] This recollection of 'rags to riches' by someone who was 10 years old at the time is revealing for what it tells us about contemporaries' perceptions of Jews. We know from survivor testimonies that some families did indeed hide silver or jewellery in their houses, but these were mostly small heirlooms and probably of limited monetary value. Nevertheless, as we heard from Michail P., rumours soon spread among locals of Jewish 'buried treasure'.

In fact, locals removed from the homes of the deportees whatever they found useful or potentially remunerative as 'hard currency' in lieu of an increasingly worthless Italian lira.

During the aerial bombardment of Rhodes, Haim Benun and his family moved to the village of Asgura, a few kilometres south of the old city. At the time of the deportation, they entrusted their possessions to Mehmet R., and following the decree, the latter submitted these to the authorities.[77] Meanwhile, their former home in Via San Giovanni (today Αγιος Ιοαννη – St John), a long street stretching south from behind the *Aeronautica* and barracks to the mainly Greek quarter of St John, which had been sealed by the *Carabinieri*, was broken into and many household items taken. The *Carabinieri* began their inquiries at the property of Benun's 45-year-old Turkish neighbour, C. The investigating officers reported how 'in the searches carried out, a metal-plated cup was found buried in the garden adjacent to C's house.' In addition to this find, the officers also discovered:

> 2 cheese bowls, 13 pieces of soap, 1 white metal towel holder with lid; 2 metal fruit bowls; a cigarette case; a ceramic 'Iraco' water set; a teapot; a jug, 2 sugar bowls with their lids; 24 saucers, 10 teacups and 6 coffee cups; 12 fruit bowls; 2 briquettes and two car batteries, one consisting of six batteries and the other, of a single large one.[78]

When they searched the home of C's accomplice, the officers found a dress that had been purchased by the Benun family a few days before their deportation. All the items from both houses were confiscated by the local *Carabinieri*.

Nissim Sciami's home was also looted by a close neighbour, 37-year-old Fatma I. She made off with his Singer sewing machine, an oriental rug, a coffee table, an iron, 5 terracotta plates, 5 water glasses and a bread bin, the prized possessions of this family of five.[79] In another case of larceny, Cadir O., a 43-year-old Turkish prostitute popular with German soldiers billeted in the Via San Giovanni, where she also lived, helped herself together with a female friend to two chests containing various items and clothing from the home of Haco (Isaaco) Capelluto.[80]

To escape bombardment of the old town, widower Ha[e]zkia Al[c]hana moved with his eight children aged between 8 and 23 years old, as well as his son-in-law and two grandchildren, from their home in Via Malatesta

Sigismondi to a rented property in Via San Stefano.[81] Alcana turned 55 years old during the transport to Auschwitz, and the entire family perished there. The family had left behind their possessions gathered in four chests 'in very poor condition', four sacks of used clothing, two sacks of quality cotton [cloth], two packages containing quilts and pillows, and three lamps (*portoloumi*). His landlord, Ali Sala C., wrote to the *Governatore* at the beginning of October explaining that Alcana had quickly fallen into arrears, and the rent had remained unpaid since the deportation. Keen to gain new tenants, Ali Sala C. requested that the authorities come and remove Alcana's property from the sealed house so he could carry out necessary repairs, to be able to rent it again. However, when a member of *sottocommissione* V returned to the house, he found it had been broken into and only a few sacks in poor condition were left behind. The culprit (or culprits) was never found.[82]

In what appears to be a similar case of mysterious disappearance of Jewish belongings, Zarli noted in his 83rd report of 25 August 1944, how Anna M. had occupied a house in Via Bonifacio Scarampi (present-day Οδος Τληπολεμον).

> It is noted that the house No. 13/15 Via Bonifacio Scarampi [visited only by officers from this commission] belonging to Donna Hasson, has been arbitrarily occupied by Anna M., who says she only found an open trunk containing old linen, a table and a wooden canapé. M. added that another chest containing valuable possessions was taken by Hasson herself to the S/S Pomezia cook's house in Via [San] Giovanni.[83]

There is no mention in the file as to the subsequent location of the 'valuable possessions.' In his extended report of 28 August, based on information he received from *sottocommissione* V, Mittino observed,

> From the investigations carried out by this office, regarding the removal of all or almost all of the contents of the houses in the walled city formerly owned by the interned Jews, it was possible to establish the following:

> From the house numbered 52 of Piazza Principe formerly owned by Masliah, Rosa, widow of Isaac Hanan, only two mirrored doors of a bookcase cabinet have been removed. No other furniture was noted missing. From the houses marked with numbers 37- 39- in the same square, formerly belonging to the Jewess Hanan, Sarina, only a medium-sized free-standing wardrobe was removed.[84]

The thefts from these properties were at the modest end of the spectrum of thefts from properties 'of the interned Jews' reported by Mittino.

The Italian authorities were assiduous in pursuing cases of looting. However, it is impossible to ascertain the extent of theft, although the surviving reports of *Carabinieri* investigations into individual cases document what was taken, and shed some light on who the perpetrators were. The looters included Greeks, Turks and Italians, and involved neighbours as well as strangers and soldiers, who took whatever they could carry off in their arms or in handcarts. The physical geography of the *Juderia* comprising narrow alleys and the architectural layout of the houses provided concealment for thieves and rendered detection difficult. As Mittino observed, 'As is known, many houses in the Jewish quarter are linked with each other via courtyards and therefore surveillance from the outside is difficult.' Theft took place behind the security of the walled courtyards.[85]

Detection often failed to discover thieves, but chance might play a role in apprehending looters. Mittino noted how 'military personnel on several occasions surprised and arrested about fifteen people in the act of committing thefts in the various homes and warehouses of the interned Jews'.[86] For example, in mid-August, *Carabinieri* investigated the theft of four velvet rugs embroidered with gold, six altar rugs and an altar covering also embroidered with gold, which had been taken from the Kahal Shalom Synagogue.[87] The thieves were a 28-year-old housewife Ambella C., and a 13-year-old girl, Maria C., who lived in the same street as the synagogue and who had entered the building through a side door. The older woman was typical of looters – an otherwise law-abiding citizen who saw an opportunity in the deportation to acquire items they could either use themselves or barter on the flourishing black market. In this case, the older woman wished to use the material to sew clothing.

A month after perambulatory trader Boaz Berro and his family had been deported to Auschwitz, thieves broke the seal of their home in Via Ammiraglio Bonaldi and entered it, removing many items.[88] Because Professor Giuseppe Scandol of the sub-committee had compiled a meticulous inventory of the Berro household, the authorities were able to determine what thieves had taken. The Berro family was not among the poorest of the *Juderia*, but neither was it a particularly well-off household. The items taken from their home reflect this.

Aside from a box of dried beans, the thieves made off with a number of pillows and linen pillowcases, as well as a pair of old linen duvets, baby clothes, strips of canvas cloth and various laundry, a mosquito net, a bucket and dishes, and what may have been an heirloom: a grandfather clock. The authorities quickly identified the culprits as residents from the Scialacca neighbourhood in the Turkish quarter, including a 15-year-old Turkish girl, Hagi C. H.[89]

Looters removed not just movable household or personal items; they also took fixtures from the houses. On occasion, the dismantling must have been quite extensive, because the authorities struggled to distinguish between damage to Jewish property caused by the earlier aerial bombardments and plundering.[90] In one case, German and Italian soldiers ransacked Capelluto's house in Via Generale Ameglio in April 1945: just weeks before the capitulation, apparently aided by individuals from the municipal technical office. They made off with wooden fixtures and floor tiles.[91] In another case, a 17-year-old Greek youth Elefterio Z., who lived in the Piazza Principe, removed around seventy tiles over a period of two months from the roof of an unidentified house once inhabited by a Jewish family. He had stored the tiles in order to sell each at I£16. Usually, the authorities took a dim view of looting Jewish property, but in Elefterio Z's. case they were lenient in view of his previous good conduct and having expressed regret at his behaviour. The confiscated tiles were put at the disposal of the Office for Public Works.[92] The example of Elefterio Z. is instructive in another sense. As one might expect, adults feature heavily in the looting of Jewish houses and businesses, but children and youth were frequently present, and sometimes acted without knowledge of their parents, as we see in the foregoing examples.

The poor of the *Juderia* were easy targets, not least because the securing of their properties was rudimentary, as we saw from Mittino's report, and due to the physical layout of the area that allowed thieves to slip away. The property of Rhodes' wealthier Jews in the *Neocori* posed more difficulty for the opportunist burglar-cum-thief, but for some looters there were few obstacles.

As we saw in the examples of Lina Kantor's family grand piano and in Capelluto's property in Via Generale Ameglio, it was not unknown for Italian and German soldiers to loot Jewish property, especially given the prevailing shortages on the islands. The head of *sottocommissione* VI, Dr Pietro Raffaelli[93] reported what he and his colleagues found when they arrived at the shop of the jeweller Isacco Benveniste in the Via Generale Bastico on 11 August.

> The commission [...] went this morning to open the house of Benveniste [...] to proceed with the requisition of the property contained therein. The door and the windows were closed. No external signs led one to believe that unknown persons had entered to ransack the house. Not being able to obtain the key to the door, the members of the commission had to force entry through a window. The doors of the rooms were found forced open; wardrobes [and] trunks had been rummaged through with evident signs of removed objects. In one room, many open cases for gold or precious objects were found [emptied] on the table; not a single gold item has been traced.
>
> When questioned, the neighbour De Luca, who is the owner of the restaurant of the same name, testified that on the day after the arrest of the Jews, German soldiers entered the house. De Luca telephoned the *Carabinieri*. Shortly afterwards, other German soldiers arrived (apparently from the German police), who entered the house and after a while they all left carrying bundles.[94]

Benveniste and his wife Matilde originally hailed from Smyrna (Izmir). The 67-year-old was considered 'a jeweller of great importance', who had also served on the Council of the Jewish Community.[95] The *Carabinieri* who investigated the theft established that the soldiers removed 'extremely precious items' from the shop, albeit without specifying exactly what was taken.[96] The Italian legal authorities had no jurisdiction over German soldiers, and so the case was transferred to the German Secret Field Police (*Geheime Feldpolizei*) – not surprisingly, given the role the GFP had played in the deportation, the trail went cold.

The *Carabinieri* nevertheless investigated diligently those cases that fell under its purview. When thieves targeted the guarded Alhadeff bank in early 1945 and attempted to make off with one of the strongboxes, *Carabinieri* officers left few stones unturned in their effort to apprehend the culprits – who happened to be former Italian soldiers. Either the soldiers were after its contents (unbeknown to them it was empty) or they were after the metal to trade.[97]

Increasingly objects that had value were sought out as the following case illustrates. The home of a prominent member of the Jewish Community

Council, Mosé Soriano, was also broken into that summer.[98] Soriano's home was in Via Parpaglia Giovanni located in the *Neocori* suburb, the chairman of the 5th sub-committee found that,

> despite having intact seals, the house was burgled by unknown persons who had entered from the terrace. A gramophone, a chandelier and a trunk containing linen have been removed from [the purview of] this commission. [Remaining] were four wooden canapés, an upholstered sofa, two wardrobes, a mirror, a table, a pantry, a cabinet with three mirrors, one of which is broken.[99]

The items taken from Soriano's house were not only easily transportable; they also commanded a higher exchange value on the island's black market.

By the spring of 1945, conditions in Rhodes had deteriorated badly and despair drove many civilians and soldiers to theft, taking whatever they could lay their hands on in order to barter on the black market, for either food or profit. Thus, looting of Jewish homes and warehouses on Rhodes continued into the final days of the war, whenever and wherever the opportunity arose to turn a Jewish family's misfortune into a profit.

*

We saw in Durrell's account at the beginning of this chapter that there was a lively black market on Rhodes, undoubtedly encouraged by worsening material conditions in the Eastern Aegean. The spoliation of Jewish property thus also spawned a cottage industry of barter, but it also literally put food into the mouths of neighbours.

The reference to hunger in the testimony of Charalambos Anamourlis cited earlier is relevant to the discussion of 'popular' sequestrations of Jewish property. The lack of food had become a preoccupation for the inhabitants of wartime Rhodes and it left its mark on youngsters especially, as mentioned previously in Chapter 3. By the time 13-year-old Maria C., or 15-year-old Hagi C. H., or young Charalambos broke into the homes of their deported Jewish neighbours, hunger had become an acute daily concern on the island. Neither Rhodes nor fertile Kos suffered famine to the extent of other islands of the Aegean or, indeed, of mainland Greece, although by the early spring of 1945 there was acute hunger.[100] Nevertheless, the island faced food shortages from late autumn 1943, and especially after the Allies intensified their policy of sea-borne harassment and blockade from early spring 1944. Thus, despite fertile conditions – especially in the northern part of the island, provisioning in Rhodes deteriorated rapidly. There is adequate evidence (notably from the German garrisons) to show that conditions were sufficiently bad even before the deportation, spurring both the local population and Italian and German soldiers to resort to theft (of mostly animals) to stave off hunger.[101]

Before the summer of 1944, the Allied naval blockade of Rhodes created a lively black market in food and small livestock that in turn created artificial shortages. Three groups had some advantage in this situation: peasant producers, traders and soldiers.[102] Possibly, this also partly explains Kleemann's positive disposition towards the Jews because through their trading networks, Jewish merchants had managed to keep their stores supplied despite the naval blockade of Rhodes and Kos. Some historians, using a limited range of sources, see the Germans' nervousness over the supply of food as a reason to engage in genocide. For instance, German military intelligence sources claimed the Greek mayor and residents of Corfu had welcomed the deportation of their Jewish neighbours as an opportunity to refill empty cupboards with the food and household items they left behind. In the case of Rhodes, the Berlin historian Götz Aly has argued the primary motivation for the destruction of the Aegean Jews was material. Aly emphasizes food shortages as the principal reason for deporting the island's Jews, citing German officers allegedly overheard saying there were now a 'thousand persons fewer to feed'.[103] Whilst the deportation from Rhodes and Kos possibly provided some short-term material relief, it did not provide the key motive as argued by Aly. Instead, the chief motor driving the destruction of the Aegean Jews was ideology; food from Jewish cupboards was merely a small windfall in the struggle against wartime hunger.

Nevertheless, the Germans on Rhodes probably hoped to capitalize on the distribution of food and household items, and thus to maintain or gain the loyalty of the local population.[104] In his monthly report compiled a few weeks after the deportation, Dr Brenner, Kleemann's intelligence officer, noted a slow shift in attitude among the public to the deportation (which had been hostile to the action):

> In the meantime, a certain turnaround in public opinion is emerging. The Commission, formed by the Italian Government for the registration and appropriation of Jewish possessions, unexpectedly found considerable quantities of everyday goods and objects that had long since disappeared from the market in the warehouses and private homes on Rhodes of deported Jews.[105]

Brenner was primarily referring to the extensive stock of the Alhadeffs' warehouses and to the storehouses of the substantial merchants, rather than the cupboards of the poor. Perhaps he saw the (albeit limited) propagandistic value in the opening of the warehouses, and how this might counteract the consternation at the deportation among the garrison and the general abhorrence of the Germans the action produced in the public more generally. However, Brenner also had to concede, 'That since there has never been a "Jewish question" in the Aegean region in the German sense, it cannot be assumed that a decisive departure from the previous outlook will occur.'[106]

*

The inventorization of Jewish property was largely completed by the end of the year. Everyone on both Rhodes and Kos stood to gain with impunity in some large or small way from the persecution and spoliation of Jews. There was little expectation that they would return. Nevertheless, after the liberation from the camps, a few survivors of these families did return to the islands to retrieve what once was theirs. Among those who returned to Rhodes were the banker Jack Alhadeff and Maurice Soriano. They recovered their assets and remained on the island, accommodating themselves to the new circumstances of Greek sovereignty. There were others who returned and who also remained, like Robert Hasson, Mosé Sulam and Lucia Modiano. However, for most returnees whose homes and familial belongings had all but disappeared behind the closed doors of former neighbours and new arrivals to the island, little was retrieved. For these young men and women survivors, who as Aegean Jews had grown up in close affinity with Italy, *enosis* with Greece, based on ethno-exclusionary nationalism, meant they could no longer remain unless they took Greek nationality. They left the island empty-handed.[107]

8

Return to Life

At least for some of us there was a return journey.[1]

If the road to Auschwitz was 'twisted', to paraphrase historian Karl Schleunes, then the journey back to life for the community's survivors also was characterized by its own twists and turns.[2] As we saw in Chapter 6, the circumstances of liberation for Jews were largely chaotic as the camp system collapsed, and the fate of survivors remained uncertain due to their severely weakened conditions. Neither did the end of war bring clarity. For nearly a year after the camps were opened, mystery continued to shroud the fate of the Aegean Jews, as we can see in the following quote from a secret report of the Ha'mosad LeAliya Beit.

> During German rule, about a year and a half ago, approximately 2000 Jews were exiled in five ships to an unknown destination. According to rumours, two or three of them have drowned. There was another rumour that the Jews of Rhodes are in Romania and afterward there was a rumour that they were sent to Greece and from Greece to the detention camps in Germany, but we still don't have a reliable source about what happened to them. The last information has arrived by telegram from relatives of the Menashe [*sic*] family from Alexandria to their relatives in Rhodes, which says that 1000 Rhodes's Jews are in a detention camp in Germany and that they are planning to return to Rhodes. Even this information is informal, as we don't know what the original source is.[3]

Alas, not 1,000 survivors, but a mere remnant of the Aegean community made its way back from the camps. The number of survivors varies depending on from when the figures date. Small lists of survivors started to appear over the course of the summer, but it was only in November 1945 that a more

comprehensive list of 204 survivors in Italy was circulating. If we add the
62 persons who were repatriated to Turkey in January and February of that
year, a total of 266 survivors is arrived at, or 14 per cent of the circa 1,800 pre-
deportation population.[4] It is highly likely the small group of Jewish escapees
from Kos located on Cypress in 1944/45 were not included among the Italy
survivors, so that an even higher number survived persecution.

As we saw in Chapter 6, for some, liberation did not bring deliverance
from death. In the weeks following the opening of the camps, several Aegean
deportees who had survived the brutality behind barbed wire perished, their
bodies too fragile to recover.[5] For others, an extended period of recuperation
awaited them. Once nurtured back to health, they began a journey that took
them down many paths. For these lucky few, the post-liberation return to life
would last longer than their ten months of captivity. It was a period bringing
euphoria and relief as their ordeal ended. This emotion could not erase the
pain of loss. Nevertheless, some survivors found love anew. For some, it was a
period of adventure, while for others, it was a time of frustration and thwarted
ambition. For most of the survivors, the quest for a new and happier life began
almost immediately following liberation.[6]

Nonetheless, this was also a period of uncertainty until a destination had
been determined. Survivors found this journey to a new life was itself beset
with administrative hurdles or cultural and sometimes, personal, clashes.
Moreover, when they finally arrived at the end of this journey, adjusting to a
new beginning could prove difficult and protracted. This chapter accompanies
the survivors on their journey from liberation to the threshold of a new life.

*

The survival and return to life of the Aegean Jews was initially obscured by
rumour and a basic lack of information. Long after the extent of the Nazi
genocide of Europe's Jews had become known, the fate of the Jews from
Rhodes and Kos remained clouded. Reliable information had been difficult to
obtain in the context of war, and in the confusion of the liberation period this
situation did not improve. There had been snippets of information smuggled
out of the islands by agents of the British Special Operations Executive (SOE).
The wartime BBC Athens bureau – broadcasting from Cairo – had reported

on the transport to mainland Greece of the Rhodes and Kos Jews at the end of July, barely a week after it happened. There was, however, no clarity as to where they were being taken, with some believing they were being detained in the Piraeus region, and others believing they had been transported further afield: either to Germany or to Czechoslovakia.[7]

While the reports were erratic, the news of the transport nonetheless reached the community of the Belgian Congo, which sought information through Belgian diplomatic channels, as well as their own diaspora networks. Already on 22 August, the leaders of the New Zionist Organization in Elisabethville wrote to their contact Eliyahu Rozio in Haifa asking him if he had news.[8] A month later, in September, the Jewish Congregation sent a telegram to the Chief Rabbi of England, asking if news had reached England of the whereabouts of their Aegean relatives. They asked Rabbi Schonfeld if the deportees could receive British protection if they were in Czechoslovakia.[9] Only after these initial approaches did news of the deportation begin to circulate more widely. Nevertheless, hard information was still lacking, as evidenced by the Foreign Office (FO) response in early October to Vicomte de Lantsheere from the Belgian Embassy. Paul Mason from the FO's refugee desk was apologetic for the lack of information but remained upbeat. He was convinced that the deportees had not been moved out of the Piraeus region because of transport shortages (the Germans were in the process of evacuating Greek mainland and needed every available means for this), 'it seems possible, therefore, that when the Piraeus is liberated the Jews from Rhodes may still be found there: but of course, one cannot be sure of this'.[10] Unfortunately, Mason was correct to introduce this caveat, for as we know, at the time of writing his memo, most of the Aegean Jews had already been murdered.

As the war neared its end, there were rumours circulating about the camps that fuelled apprehension among the Rhodes diasporas. The fate of the Aegean Jews was, however, still shrouded in mystery so long as there was no official confirmation of what had happened to them or where they might be. In correspondence with Donald Hurwitz from the American Jewish Joint Distribution Committee (AJDC or JDC, commonly known as the 'Joint') in New York three weeks before the liberation of Auschwitz, Leo Gallin, the chief executive of the United Jewish Welfare Fund based in Los Angeles, noted there were approximately 300 families in Los Angeles, and thus constituting the second largest Sephardi community in the United States, who 'have relatives on this island [Rhodes], and they are very much disturbed over unspecified radio broadcasts indicating that the Jewish colony on that island has met with a disaster at the hands of the Nazis'.[11]

Reports of the deportation of the Jews of Rhodes and Kos had circulated in London already in July and August 1944, although firm information on their subsequent fate was lacking. After Auschwitz was liberated and news of its grim conditions spread across the world, concern for the whereabouts and safety of the Aegean Jews magnified. As further camps were liberated one after the other over the course of the spring, evidence about their horror mounted, but there was still little specific information relating to Rhodes or Kos, leading to a wave of urgent requests for news. The Rhodesli community in the Congo, for example, through the Belgian embassy in London, contacted Clementine Churchill in London seeking information. As the Prime Minister's wife, Mrs Churchill had access to a vast Whitehall apparatus. She was in fact the Chairperson of the British Red Cross Friends of Russia and as it happened, the Rhodesli in Elisabethville were prominent donors to its chapter there. Nevertheless, despite various Whitehall departments making enquiries on her behalf, Viscount de Lantzheere from the Belgian embassy in Congo was unable to furnish satisfactory information.[12] The community in the Congo, as in Salisbury (Rhodesia), and elsewhere, remained in the dark.[13]

Not only were concerned community leaders in the diaspora enquiring into the fate of their co-religionists, but individual relatives were too. In early 1945, Harold Trobe from the Paris office of the Joint found himself busy fielding enquiries from relatives about family members. In a communiqué to Arthur Fishsohn at the American Consulate in Istanbul, Trobe added: 'May we advise you at this time that through our Rome office we are receiving quite a number of inquiries concerning people in Rhodes.'[14]

Among those enquiring was dental surgeon Dr Morris Capouya (*sic*) in Montgomery, Alabama. He wrote to Trobe's office in April enquiring about the whereabouts of his parents Nissim and Esther Capuia and his sister Dora.[15] Capouya had heard about the liberation (of Auschwitz) by the Russians. As news of Jewish camp survivors filtered through, he also heard there was a list of Aegean survivors. Trobe's colleague, Jeannette Robbins, however, had not heard of such a list, but offered to make enquiries. Eventually, in July, she could only write to confirm they had been deported, but their subsequent fate remained unknown. In time, Dr Capouya would learn of the murder of his parents in Auschwitz, but he would be reunited with his 30-year-old sister.[16] Meanwhile, Norman Fresco in Los Angeles also wrote to the Joint that late spring in the hope of getting some knowledge of his sister Naile, his brother-in-law Dr David Gaon and their daughter Gilda (whose name appears as Zelda in the letter). 'Not having heard from them during the war, I am naturally anxious to learn of their whereabouts', Fresco wrote.[17] Although Dr Gaon, one of the Community's prominent notables, and his wife originated from Smyrna, they were not among the few to obtain Turkish documents and thus be spared deportation. The family did not survive Auschwitz.[18]

Similarly, the young doctor Alessandro (Alexander) Benatar contacted Trobe's office in February 1945 in the hope of obtaining news of the whereabouts of his family – unaware that his parents were among those killed in Auschwitz.[19] Around the same time, Private Salvatore Elkana of the 1st Battalion Palestine Regiment, now in liberated Italy, contacted Trobe. The 'last news Pte Elkana has had from his family were [*sic*] in 1943.'[20] Elkana was in fact Miru Alcana's first cousin Salvatore Alcana, a younger son of Celebi Alcana, who had immigrated to Palestine in 1938. As we saw in Chapter 6, his extended family, barring Miru, was destroyed in the camps. Only his younger brother Giuseppe, who escaped from Rhodes in September 1943 and made his way to Palestine, remained of this large extended family.[21] Meanwhile, Mazaltov Hasson's daughter 'has not heard from her [mother in] a very long time' and was now searching for news of her.[22]

Another request at the beginning of August for news of family members came via UNRRA's Cairo office to UNRRA in London. It concerned the families of Samuele Mizrahi and Behor Alhadeff. The families were related by marriage, for Samuele's sister Mazaltov was married to Behor (Illustration 8.1).[23] The request for information was made on behalf of Behor's eldest daughter Rebecca Alhadeff who had immigrated to the Congo in 1939.[24] However, none of Rebecca's family comprising the 87-year-old grandmother, the four parents, three adult children and three teenage children survived the deportation and camps.[25]

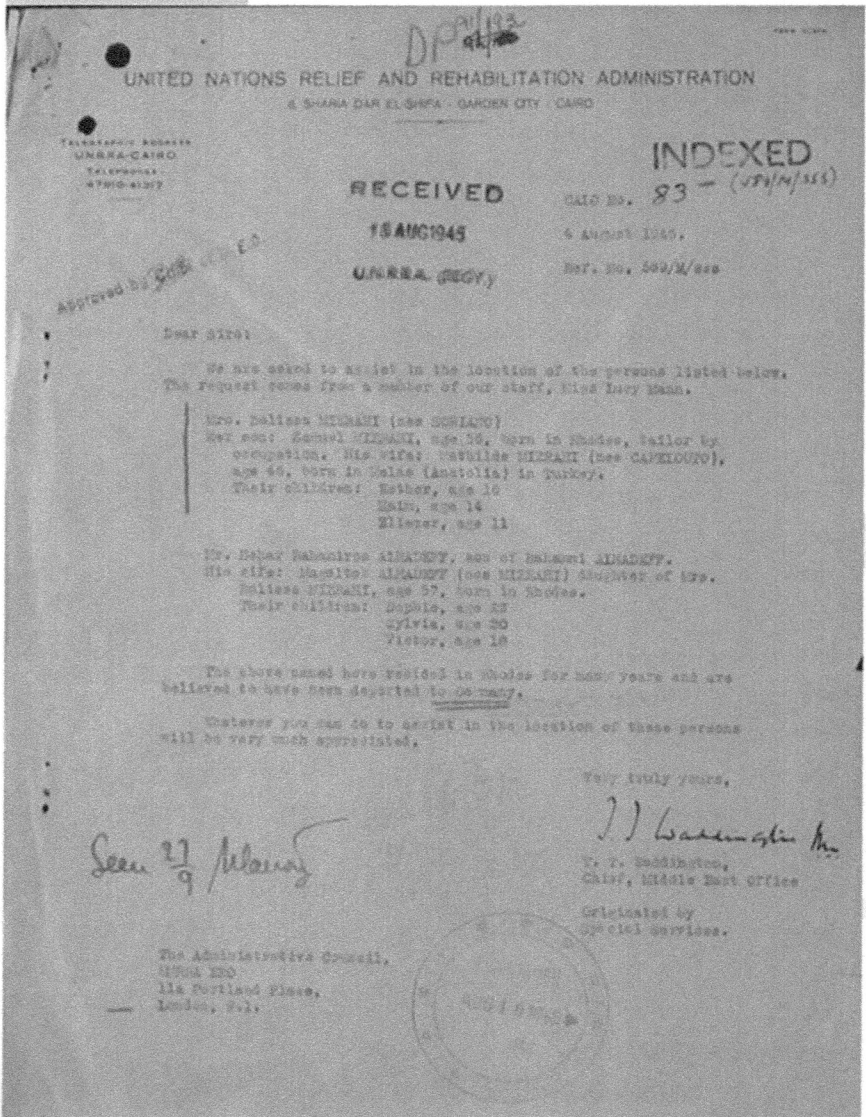

Illustration 8.1 Searching for relatives[26]

Source: Courtesy ITS Digital Archive, Arolsen Archives

Enquiries into the whereabouts of loved ones continued unabated, and included searches for family members by survivors as they arrived in Italy over the summer of 1945.[27] These enquiries continued into 1946. Viewed together, they form a mosaic of knowledge of the violence perpetrated against Jews; taken individually, they also suggest how relatives clung to the hope that their loved ones had somehow survived the deportation and camps. For what the head reasoned, the heart countered with hope. This is evident even among survivors. For decades after the Holocaust, Eliezer Surmani clung to the idea that somehow his younger sister Maria, 11 years old at the time of the deportation, had survived against all the odds stacked against younger children arriving at Auschwitz.[28]

In 1945, concrete information about loved ones was, nevertheless, thin. For survivors, word of mouth and lists posted at Red Cross and Jewish information centres, such as the weekly bulletins published by the *Comitato richerche deportati ebrei* in Rome listing survivors as they returned, were the only channels for obtaining news.[29] As the Aegean Jews made their way to Italy, their names appeared on such lists, and in this manner, they soon were able to reconstitute themselves as temporary communities in safe houses.

*

One of the first questions asked by survivors from Rhodes and Kos once they had recuperated, was 'where to?' Four decades after liberation, Miru Alcana spoke for many of the Aegean survivors, when she recalled the question facing them, 'Where to go, what to do?'[30] By the time of their liberation, the survivors knew that their community had been 'turned into ashes' in the furnaces of Auschwitz, as Alberto Israel angrily recalled.[31] There were also other factors to consider. As Alberto told Marcello Pezzetti in 2013,

> When the war ended the British and Americans said to us 'Rhodes has been occupied by the Greeks. You can go back to Greece.' But we're not Greeks. We're Italians and we go back to Italy. Nobody said: 'I'm going back to Rhodes.' Not a single Jew went back to Rhodes. Not one! They all went back to Italy.[32]

Alberto's recollection notwithstanding, we shall see that some survivors of
the camps did return to Rhodes and Kos, albeit for a short period. There was
a complex administrative and legal process involved in determining where
a survivor ended up. In this context, survivors were not free agents to go or do
as they pleased. Indeed, Alberto's recollection suggests a tension between the
bureaucratic cultures of the international agencies dealing with refugees and
the desires of individual survivors.

The end of the war and the liberation of the camps brought with it a refugee
crisis. Reportedly, millions of men, women and children were on the move
in post-liberation Europe.[33] They included not only victims displaced by the
ravages inflicted by Germany's war-machine: former prisoners of war, slave and
forced labour of all nationalities, and those subjected to Nazi racial persecution,
but also those who had been part of that machinery of conquest and terror.[34]
They were now escaping justice or fleeing the Soviet Army. In the period
immediately following liberation, military administrators had to determine the
identity of a displaced person, filtering out war criminals and other 'unworthy
types' hiding among refugees.[35] This was a formidable task given the numbers
involved and the chaotic conditions in the wake of war and occupation.

With hindsight, determining the claims of former inmates of the camps
might seem straightforward, but it was not. Many of those on the move were
without identity papers, making the process of registering them as Displaced
Persons (DPs) cumbersome. The task of handling the problem of displacement
fell to the United Nations Relief and Rehabilitation Administration (UNRRA,
1943–47). In early 1945, that is before the war had ended, UNRRA estimated
there were 10,829,565 displaced persons belonging to Allied countries in
Europe, most of them located in Germany.[36] After May 1945, the numbers
doubled.[37] In this context, administrative expediency on the part of UNRRA
and from 1947, its successor, the International Refugee Organization (IRO),
led frequently to situations where a victim-survivor's desire to determine their
own fate was sacrificed at the altar of administrative expediency or because a
victim-survivor's narrative did not conform to a field officer's understanding
of what a refugee profile should look like.[38]

Ascertaining an accurate number of liberated Jews among the displaced
population is fraught with difficulty. The estimates of Jewish survivors range
considerably, from 90,000 to nearly a quarter of a million for the period

between 1945 and 1952.[39] Thus, when seen against this larger landscape, the surviving Jews from Rhodes and Kos, numbering 204, represented only a tiny fraction of this human tide. Nevertheless, their experiences of the journey from the camps back to life shared the same characteristics of many Jews who left the camps in the summer of 1945.[40]

The Aegean survivors were principally in six locations at liberation and consequently they were dependent on the corresponding military authorities that now administered the camps: namely, the Soviet Union (Auschwitz, Theresienstadt), the United States (Buchenwald, Dachau, Mauthausen) and Britain (Bergen-Belsen). In addition to the military, there were also civilian authorities, international organizations and voluntary agencies tasked with providing relief, repatriation or resettlement, foremost among them UNRRA and later IRO.[41] In addition to the Joint, there were other Jewish agencies, such as the World Jewish Congress (WJC), the American-based Federated Jewish Fund, as well as the International Committee of the Red Cross (ICRC) providing assistance to Jewish DPs. For example, in the American occupation zone of Germany the Central Committee of Liberated Jews (*Sh'erit ha-Pletah*) emerged to represent Jewish survivors. In Italy, the *Unione delle Comunita Israelitiche*, the official representative body of Jews, appeared to be less effective than the *Sh'erit ha-Pletah* in leveraging on behalf of Jewish DPs, mostly due to lack of funds. More effective, but also working within financial constraints, were the Jewish relief and resistance organization DELASEM (*Delegazione per l'assistenza degli emigranti ebrei*).[42] These latter organizations provided aid and negotiated with the various international agencies. Aside from these supra-organizations, individual survivors formed their own self-help groups, mostly in urban centres. Survivors thus had to negotiate with the various agencies that had responsibility for determining a survivor's legal status, and later, destination. As we shall see in this chapter, the relationship between the Aegean survivors and transnational agencies was frequently a fraught one.

*

In the confusion that characterized the aftermath of war in Europe, many Jewish survivors fended for themselves rather than waiting for their liberators to determine their return to life. During this early post-liberation period, the Standing Committee on Displaced Persons was airing concern that 'Recent reports indicate that considerable numbers of Italians who have been externally displaced are trekking homeward and are pouring into Northern Italy and wandering south.'[43] Indeed, between 1 June and the end of August 1945, somewhere in the region of 13,000 DPs arrived in Italy. Most of the Aegean Jews arrived courtesy of the Allied military, either by hitching lifts in army trucks or having received train vouchers and other material support, such as clothing, food and cash for the journey, usually from the Joint. Their journeys, in a war-ravaged continent where communications and transport networks had been severely disrupted, were circuitous (Map 8.1).

Miru Alcana's and Sylvia Berro's accounts of the journey from Theresienstadt were typical of the experience of the women liberated with them. After remaining for a short period in the ghetto-camp, where they cooked and cleaned for their Soviet liberators in return for food, they travelled first to Prague and then to Innsbruck in Austria, before moving on to Bologna in the summer of 1945.[44] In Prague, they received a small subsidy 'and we can go shopping or to (sight) see', Miru remembered. 'We didn't pay the carfare (bus) because when we showed the number of our arm, they didn't say nothing. We used to run from one bus to the other, free, free rides we had.'[45] In Bologna they were helped by the Jewish community. When they arrived at the end of August, the building in Via de'Gombrutti bore the scars of war, for it lacked windows and doors, and the survivors of both sexes slept in the hallways.

Similarly, 19-year-old Clara Avzaradel had been among the same group of women liberated by the Russians from Theresienstadt. She was the daughter of Baruch Avzaradel, the butcher we met in Chapter 3. Clara recounted how her journey took her first to Linz then to Sopron (Hungary) and from there to Bologna, where she would remain for fourteen months.[46] Gella Hanan was lucky in that after her liberation from Dachau and sojourn in a hospital in Munich, where she recovered from typhus, she travelled to Milan, still weighing only 39 kg. There she worked for a period as an interpreter for the Jewish Brigade under the command of Major Aranoff, before moving to Rome where she joined the other Aegean survivors.[47] Her brothers in the Belgian Congo soon arranged for her emigration to Bukavu near Lake Kivu.[48]

Meanwhile Lucia Franco, the daughter of the haberdashery merchant Hizkia [Haim] from Kos was taken in an army truck to Munich and from

Map 8.1 From the camps to Italy, summer 1945; © Peter Palm

there she travelled south to Bolzano in the Tyrol. Although Lucia did not say in a later interview what transpired in Bolzano, it is probable (as we know from other cases) that she was officially registered and processed as a DP, before arrangements were made for her further travel southwards. Her next stop was the town of Modena, where local representatives from the Jewish community looked after her. Eventually she arrived in Bologna where she was surprised to learn that her older brother who had immigrated to Palestine in 1938, and who subsequently had joined the Jewish Brigade of the British Army, was in the vicinity with his unit. Lucia stayed a month in Bologna before moving to Florence and, eventually, she travelled home to Kos. However, like many survivors, when Lucia found nothing remained of her community to keep her there, she returned to Florence where she met her future husband, Nino Garzolini, a former Italian soldier she had known in Kos, and who also had been incarcerated in Auschwitz.[49]

Between July and November 1945, the 204 Aegean survivors arrived in Italy either individually or in small groups. Maurizio Sciarcon, after a short stay in a hospital in Salzburg, (where, incidentally, he was together with Achille Da Fano), entered Italy via the Brenner Pass under the auspices of the ICRC. Maurizio spent his first days in Rome in July 1945 at the main DP camp based in Cinecittà (the former film studios) before being moved to Ostia where a number of the Rhodesli teenagers were housed. Here also, they were interviewed by representatives of both DELASEM and the Comitato Ricerche Deportati Ebrei (CRDE), and received training in practical trades, most likely in preparation for Palestine. However, when he heard his sisters Julia (Gioia), Caden and Lucia (Amato) were in San Polo Sabino, about 60 km from Rome, Maurizio left Ostia to join them. He remained there for two years, met and fell in love with Lina (Quintilina) Picchi and married her in 1947. The couple remained in San Polo until the summer of 1948, aided by UNRRA/IRO, before joining his older brothers Matteo and Isaaco (both of whom had escaped Rhodes prior to the deportation) in Tel Aviv.[50]

Among Maurizio's friends staying in Ostia were Giuseppe Varon, Jack Hasson, Giuseppe Cugno (Hugno) and Eliezer Surmani, and Sami Modiano, four years his junior.

Sami was 15 at liberation, one of the 234 youth of both sexes between 14 and 17 years old in Auschwitz in January 1945.[51] His account of returning to life has the appearance of an adventure.[52] His initial intention had been to return to Rhodes, but circumstances led him elsewhere. Initially, Sami was transferred from Auschwitz to a Soviet-run camp where he found himself among a group of around a thousand captured Italian soldiers who had fought with the Germans on the Eastern Front. Here, he also met a fellow survivor from Auschwitz, Settimio Limentani.[53] The pair, fearing they would be sent to Siberia (according to Sami's memoir), decided it was better to escape the Russians. They fled the camp at the end of August, arriving in Austria at the beginning of October, and eventually crossed into the Italian Tyrol via the Brenner Pass. Looking back, Sami recalled, 'When I think of the difficulties of that journey, the fact that we could only move in the dark, the injury of Settimio and all the detours we made to get around cities and checkpoints, it amazes me that we managed to do it in such a short time.'[54] Arriving at an American military base, they were first deloused and afterwards, fed.

> The soldiers, keeping us at a safe distance, forced us to undress and disinfected us. They threw away our clothes and burned them, then put us in a shower. Only after giving us new clothes did they listen to our story. We explained that we were Italian Jews, who had escaped the Nazi camps and that we just wanted to return to Italy.[55]

After this adventure on foot, they made their way by train to Rome from where Sami hoped to continue his journey to Rhodes, but instead he was to remain in lodgings in the seaside resort of Ostia (close to Rome) for the next two years. Affiliated to the Rhodes Survivors Group in Via Condotti, he learned a trade under the *Hachsharoth* scheme. Judging from his account, it must have been the middle or end of October when he and Settimio arrived in Rome, a full nine to ten months since the liberation of Auschwitz.

However, the greater majority of those finding their way to Italy were not Italians, nor were they all Jewish. Many were from the Baltic States and Central and Eastern Europe, who were escaping the Russians.[56] They were overwhelmingly concentrated in the various DP camps spread throughout Italy (some of which, like the Fossoli camp in the south, had previously held Jewish internees). There were at least a dozen major camps in post-war Italy catering largely for displaced Jews. The principal one coordinating the administration and liaising with the AJDC and the Central Committee of Liberated Jews was located in the film studios of Cinecittà in Rome.[57] Conditions in these camps were far from ideal because of overcrowding and lack of basic facilities; there were also intermittent violent clashes between different ethnic groups, or indeed, between Jewish activists of different political persuasion, and in too many cases, there was evidence of rampant antisemitism.[58] Nor was it unknown for camp guards to act violently vis-à-vis DPs.[59] The Aegean survivors were unwilling to enter these transnational camps, preferring to remain instead in so-called out-of-camp shelters.

It is likely that mostly Italian Jewish DPs comprised the circa 600 out-of-camp survivors in Rome, who had loosely aligned themselves with the Organization of Jewish Refugees.[60] Following an enquiry by Rhodes diaspora in the Belgian Congo in 1945 into the whereabouts of possible survivors, British civil servants in London and administrators at the Jewish Relief Organization soon learned that survivors from Rhodes and Kos were among the residents of these out-of-camp shelters.

In the summer and autumn of 1945, the out-of-camp shelters acted as magnets for the survivors. Individually and in small groups, survivors made their way to any one of these as they received news that a brother or sister or close friend had arrived. After their liberation from Auschwitz, Diamante and Rachel (Hugno, the daughters of the 'renowned tailor') decided to make their way back to Rhodes. However, when they reached the port town of Brindisi, they learned that their Aegean compatriots were in Bologna. They changed direction and headed back north.[61] In Bologna the sisters were reunited with their close friends from Rhodes, among them Stella Levi. Diamante remained in Bologna for one and a half years. Stella was liberated from Allach, a sub-camp of Dachau, and she too made her way to Italy, first to Bolzano in the Italian Tyrol, and then to Modena, before eventually arriving in Bologna. She spent a mere 48 hours in Modena, where the small Jewish community provided food, shelter and civilian clothes (she previously received US army fatigues to wear).[62] In Bologna, Stella met members of the British Army's Jewish Brigade who urged her to go to Palestine, but she chose instead to travel further south to Florence and then on to Rome.[63]

The shelters had ad hoc committees that liaised with governments and non-governmental agencies on behalf of survivors. They provided temporary and medium-term accommodation for many of the survivors until such time when their legal status could be determined by the authorities. The shelters also acted as information bureaux by posting lists of the missing for survivors seeking each other. This is how Lucia Franco was found by Nino Garzolini, who had scoured the list posted in San Polo. Importantly, as we shall see in the case of the Aegean Jews, the shelter provided tangible help in negotiating the path to emigration.[64]

The principal out-of-camp shelter for the Aegean Jews in Italy was located in a large town house at 5 Via Condotti in Rome. The Via Condotti was (and still is) a fashionable street that stretched from the Spanish Steps to the bifurcation of Via della Fontenella and Via del Corso (ending on the one hand at the Ponte Umberto I and Ponte Cavour, two of the thirteen bridges that spanned the River Tiber).[65] The expansive town villa was home to sisters Vittoria and Teresa Buciuk, who originally had resided with their divorced mother Sipura Coen in the *Juderia*'s Via Sigismondo Malatesta until 1939.[66] Teresa had married Giovanni Cavalli, an Italian citizen, in 1935, and converted to Catholicism. Teresa thus escaped the deportation, for we find her among those five converted Jews transferred from Rhodes to Turkey on 13 January 1945, possibly accompanied by her mother.[67] It is not clear when Vittoria left Rhodes, or when she arrived in Rome, nor why she should have gone there in the first place. It is possible that she too had married an Italian (she is once mentioned as 'Mrs. Castrucci' in the documentation).[68] Nonetheless, from fragmentary testimony, after the Germans took control of Rome in September 1943, she went into hiding, only re-emerging after that city's liberation by the US Fifth Army in June 1944. Vittoria, formerly a dressmaker on Rhodes, now became a 'tireless advocate' of the Aegean Jews according to one official of the WJC, and thus the key figure in organizing aid for survivors from Rhodes and Kos until she and her sister and mother emigrated to the US in 1950.[69]

Until their own departure from Rome in 1950, the Buciuks were the driving force in representing and defending the interests and rights of the Aegean survivors, especially by strengthening the support network with the diaspora. It is not clear from the evidence if the house in Via Condotti was the property of the Castrucci or Cavalli family. Many of the survivors fondly remembered the refuge in the Via Condotti and its organizer 'Madame Vittoria'. Even though he had lodgings at the orphans refuge in Ostia (together with Jack Hasson), Sami Modiano recalled in his memoir,

> I had heard of a place in Rome, an apartment at Number 5 in Via Condotti, which was a kind of support point for my fellow islanders. There a certain woman provided hospitality to some of the one hundred and twenty

Rhodesian girls who survived the extermination camps. She called herself Madame Vittoria, she was about fifty and she was herself a Jewess from Rhodes.[70]

Vittoria was actually ten years younger than in Sami's recollection. Others who stayed with the Buciuks could not praise the sisters enough.

The Via Condotti and its sister refuges (see Illustration 8.2) not only provided material and practical support, but also filled a space where the *Juderia* had been in the psyche of the survivors. They became, in a sense, an ersatz *Juderia* cementing the bond of survival learned in the camps. Thus, the Buciuks' most important work was not only that of easing the material side of the return to life, but in restoring the emotional foundations for a new lease of life.

We know too little about the organization of the refuge in the Via Condotti, or indeed, of any of the out-of-camp shelters.[71] The Buciuks, and Victoria in particular, managed the Rome refuge with the assistance of 30-year-old Alexander Benatar, the young doctor we encountered earlier. He had qualified at the University of Padua in 1939, obtaining his qualification to practise from the University of Pisa. Prevented from returning to Rhodes after Italy's armistice in 1943, Alexander remained in Italy but was eventually arrested and interned for oppositional activities. Luckily, unlike that of his contemporary Primo Levi, his Jewish identity remained undetected and he was not deported, but imprisoned in Italy.[72] In the aftermath of war, he remained in Rome becoming a key figure among the group of survivors, probably until the early autumn of 1946 when he acquired an affidavit in preparation for obtaining a visa and resettlement to the United States.[73]

Until 1950, the survivors, led by the Buciuks at 5 Via Condotti, remained closely affiliated to the Rhodes Survivors Aid Committee with a branch each in New York and in Seattle.[74] Under the Buciuks, the Rome Committee's main activities included securing material and financial support from relatives in the Rhodesli diaspora, as well as advocating for them vis-à-vis the agencies dealing with the post-war refugee problem. Few of the survivors at that time expressed a desire to leave for Palestine. Instead, the majority preferred to resettle, either in the USA or in Rhodesia or in the Belgian Congo where they had family connections. Here, Vittoria's tenacity when dealing with the relevant authorities proved vital to achieving this goal (we return to this below).

1946 photo of mostly Rhodesli Holocaust survivors gathered for a photo at an excursion near Rome.

First row: the first two are Italian Jewish women, Bella Cohen Israel, Matilda Hanan, Angelo Castrucci, Zimbul Buchiuck, Victoria Buchiuck, Stella Levi, Sarah Hanan Gilmore, Clara Gabriel and Stella Surmani. **Back row:** Moshe Cohen, Clara Avzaradel, Anna Cohen, Italian friend, Rachel Cohen, Italian friend (in back), Vicki Cohen, Stella Hasson, Clara Halfon Codron and Regina Menashe. **3 people in front:** man with accordion unknown, Rachel Almeleh and Matilda Sharhon. **Tree:** woman behind the tree is Laura Varon. The man playfully on the tree is Moshe Galante.

Illustration 8.2 Rhodes Survivors Group in Italy (*c.* 1946)

Source: Courtesy Rhodes Jewish Historical Foundation Archives

In addition to the house in Via Condotti, there were a number of smaller refuges providing shelter and helping the Aegean Jews, notably that located in the synagogue and Jewish communal buildings at 9 Via de'Gombruti in Bologna, and which may have had some connection to Villa Emma near Modena, also run by DELASEM.[75] There was another small shelter in Florence at the Pensione Annalena located on the second floor of the famous medieval Palazzo at 34 Via Romano, where Carlo Levi wrote part of his celebrated memoir *Christ Stopped at Eboli*. The DELASEM also had a shelter in Florence's Via la Marmosa. In Milan there was a hostel at 10 Via Lodovica Settala, where some of the Aegean survivors stayed, and it seems there was also the possibility of lodging privately.[76] By the end of October 1945, some 116 Aegean survivors had reached Italy, located in Rome (48), Milan (46), Florence (22).[77] The survivor population in Italy was fluid as a consequence of new arrivals and departures. By late November, the Athens office of the Joint filed a report putting the number of survivors in Italy at 204.[78] By February this number had fallen to around 153, half of whom were in Rome and its environs; it fell again to 115 by September, as survivors either returned to Rhodes or left for new destinations.[79]

Although little is known about the everyday life in the refuges, the surviving sporadic documentation suggests regular communication between Rome, Bologna and Milan. As already noted, the Buciuks in the Via Condotti remained the focal point for all the survivors following liberation. As such, it was the point of contact for relatives in the USA, the Belgian Congo, and Rhodesia wishing to send financial support either directly or via one of the official Jewish channels.[80] The correspondence between Vittoria Buciuk and UNRRA, IRO and AJDC as well as the reports of their field officers, cast some light on conditions the Aegean Jews faced while in Italy.

*

For a number of years after the war had ended, Europe's national economies remained in desperate straits. Not only had the physical destruction of combat left many towns and cities in rubble, but whole economies too lay in ruin, bedevilled by high levels of unemployment and inflation. Recovery only got underway after the introduction of Marshall Aid at the end of the 1940s.

Italy, like much of continental Europe, was war-ravaged, its economy on its knees and its people suffering the afflictions attendant on a depredated nation. Vittorio de Sica's masterful and moving cinematic depictions of these post-war conditions in the 1946 film *Shoeshine* (*Sciuscià*) and *Bicycle Thieves* (*Ladri di biciclette*) made two years later in 1948, found their real-life counterparts in many reports compiled by UNRRA's field agents about DPs.[81]

In the mid-1940s, there were around 3,500 DPs in Italy's urban camps. Whether Italians or non-nationals, conditions were very difficult for them. To alleviate the distress of Jewish survivors, UNRRA, AJDC and DELASEM contributed a small monthly subsidy. The level of cash support varied from case to case, but in general, it amounted to no more than a few thousand lire per month. Thus, Lea Habib and Vittoria Coen each received I£2,000, but Stella Levi, Lucia Franco, Alice Tarica and Renate Capelluto had to make do with I£500.[82] However, rampant inflation soon negated this sum, and led some UNRRA officials to suspect that out-of-camp DPs were engaged in black-market and criminal activities. According to a report circulated to Martin Germandof, the director of UNRRA's VTC programme in Italy, 'It is obvious that everybody living in Italian communities must have some other income, as nobody could live on 1400 lire and a small food parcel or 3000 lire a month.'[83] Another officer observed how the situation in the towns and cities 'is very difficult. With the inflated prices of shelter and food they cannot manage to live on the subsidy they receive from UNRRA and it is almost impossible for them to obtain work. This leads to demoralisation such as fraudulent drawing of subsidy from UNRRA on several names and black-market operations.'[84] In order to alleviate the conditions giving rise to criminal activity among DPs outside the purview of official organizations, the writer recommended their transfer to UNRRA-run camps where they would be subject to supervision.

This recommendation, however, did not sit well with the Aegean survivors in spite of their straitened circumstances. The small monthly and financial support package from UNRRA and later from IRO was not enough to sustain them, especially given the constantly rising cost of living (exacerbated by inflation). In one of her appeals for financial support, Vittoria wrote: 'we must emphasise the fact that life in Italy is so expensive now that although these help is given [sic], the economic situation of these refugees is very difficult owing to the impossibility for them to find any kind of profitable and honest work.'[85]

Payments to individuals in the out-of-camp shelters, varied according to need. It appears that some of the Aegean survivors received only small amounts, as we saw above in the cases of Stella and Renate Levy, Suzanna Levy, Alice Tarica, Lucia Franco, Renate Capelluto and Ester Scialom. With inflation rampant in the early summer of 1945, I£500 would not have gone very far.

It is possible that this small amount was a cost of living 'top up' for training. Because most of the survivors were young and had been prevented from completing their education due to the imposition of the Italian Racial Laws, the Buciuks had managed to get Via Condotti recognized as a Voluntary Training Centre (VTC; also referred to as Vocational Training Centres or vocational training programmes), supported by UNRRA. VTC also functioned as *Hachsharoth*, preparing Jews for emigration to Palestine (*Aliyah*).[86] This system enabled youngsters such as Ascer Varon to receive training as a mechanic, or Stella Benun to learn tailoring. As a VTC, a small subsidy was added to the funds of the group towards training and preparation for resettlement. The scheme was important, given the survivors were youngsters or relatively young. By the end of 1946, of the 101 Aegean Jews remaining in Italy, 68 were on a *Hachsharoth* programme.[87] However, as we shall see, when the IRO overhauled its financial structure after replacing UNRRA in 1947, it withdrew the Condotti group's recognition as a VTC.[88]

The bleak financial picture notwithstanding, the Aegean survivors in Italy were lucky in that they could rely on material support from relatives in the USA, Argentina and the Belgian Congo. As Reuben Resnik from the Joint's office in Rome noted in correspondence with the US State Department, a 'group of former Rhodes residents now in New York [are] anxious to provide assistance for Rhodes survivors of concentration camps now in Italy'.[89] When in late November the Rhodes Survivors Aid Committee in New York tried to contact Matilde Capelluto in Bergen-Belsen, it asked the JDC to convey the message that 'if she will send a request card to [them], they will send a package to her'.[90] Clara Avzaradel also contacted the diaspora from her refuge in Bologna, making a similar appeal for support.[91]

Support from the diaspora was vital in supplementing UNRRA and Joint assistance, for without this support, survivors like Stella Sidis would have remained in a destitute condition, and in poor health.[92] In particular clothing and medicines were needed. Thus, in October 1945, the New York branch of the Rhodes Survivors Aid Committee purchased eight bales of second-hand winter clothing to the value of $809 from Isidore Freiberg's company on East Houston Street in New York to be sent to the survivors in Rome, Milan and Florence.[93] This material aid was important given the high rate of inflation in Italy at the time. Not only clothing, but also food packages and, vitally, medicines reached the group in Italy. Thus, aid to the tune of $2,000 was sent to Italy from Seattle for the provision of food, medicines and winter clothing in December for the Rhodes survivors to supplement their regular UNRRA relief.[94]

Financial aid from the Rhodes Survivors Aid Committee in the United States was usually channelled via the United Jewish Welfare Fund, the AJDC and other voluntary agencies. Financial support from the Rhodesli Jews in the Belgian Congo, however, appears to have been less coordinated and more sporadic. Moreover, despite efforts to manage the flow of financial support, there was little oversight as to how funds were being used by the group in Italy, which led to claims that this undermined the Joint's efforts to help the Aegean survivors. For example, Henrietta Buchman from the Joint reported with some exasperation how Rachele Alhadeff, the niece of Morris Alhadeff, who chaired the Rhodes Survivors Aid Committee in New York, not only refused to accept second-hand clothing which 'our representative states that other Rhodes refugees had received such clothing and found it perfectly adequate and satisfactory', but that she appeared to be staying in two refuges (Rome and Bologna) at the same time. She had received I£15,000 in support from the AJDC in Rome and her uncle was now expected to reimburse this sum.[95]

Tensions also existed between Rhodesli diasporic groups and the key agencies channelling funds to survivors in Italy. Some insight into the problem is gleaned from correspondence between Mrs Fred Pollock from the Los Angeles Women's Division of the Joint and Dr Kalman Stein of the WJC in New York. In one letter, Pollock summed up the problem: 'Seattle has sent several thousand dollars through the Joint, and though they are obviously dissatisfied because they have not heard directly as to what has been done with the money, I cannot tell you what their position from now will be.'[96] The Los Angeles community of Sephardim had expressed similar hesitancy to provide further aid. Meanwhile, David Mussafir, the uncle of Jack Isaac Lévy, as a leader of the Sephardi congregation in Montgomery, described as 'a small community of extraordinary wealth', accused the AJDC of 'graft' and refused to contribute further to the AJDC/United Jewish Appeal unless he was assured that all the funds went only to the survivors from Rhodes and Kos.[97] Already by October, donors were expressing concern as to how funds were being used on the ground. The Joint wrote to Maurice Soriano, the group's spokesman, in Milan asking for information regarding the exact numbers of survivors and precisely how he was distributing the recently sent $6,150 in funds.[98] As Pollock put it, the Sephardi Jews were 'good people ... but extremely difficult to work with'.[99] Nevertheless, relatives through their different associations continued to raise funds to support their relatives in Rome, Bologna, Milan and Florence.

Despite the important role played by out-of-camp shelters, UNRRA and its successor body, the IRO, eventually sought to close them down. Increasingly, the authorities wished to exert tighter supervisory control over DPs and to exercise direct control over the disbursement of aid. In the second half of 1947, when UNRRA was in the process of winding down its operations, and transferring its cases to the IRO, there was a hardening in policy vis-à-vis out-of-camp DPs, causing widespread concern and uncertainty among Jewish DPs about whether they would continue to receive assistance. The Organization of Jewish Refugees in Italy wrote in April to the Director General of UNRRA in Italy outlining the situation facing Jewish DPs, most of whom, unlike the Via Condotti group, wished to leave for Palestine or overseas.[100] A policy change in early 1947 had already indicated the trend, when eligibility for assistance was limited to the young (under 16) and those over 50 (females) and 55 (males) or those unable to find employment.[101] Given their demographic, the majority of Aegean Jews fell into the excluded category. Thus, in February and March 1947, 29 and 28 of their number were in receipt of assistance, but this was drastically cut to 4 the following month and to 5 in May.[102] As part of its reorganization of funding for DPs, the IRO Rome office contacted the Rhodes group in December 1947 to inform it that funding would soon stop 'unless [the members of the group] go to live in that organization[s] refugee camps'.[103]

Buciuk tried to reason with the IRO, stating that about twenty of their number were due to leave for North and South America and the Belgian

Congo. The remainder were waiting for affidavits from sponsoring relatives either in the USA or in the Congo, to enable them to obtain visas. In a similar vein, Kurt Grossman from the WJC wrote to the IRO Rome office at the end of the month, but he was unsuccessful in his advocacy of the group. The IRO remained unmoved by such appeals. Karl D. Feller, the IRO's Field DP supervising officer in Rome, wrote to Buciuk on 7 January 1948 warning her that aid would end from February. Feller curtly gave two reasons: '(i) [The] group did not constitute a V[oluntary]T[raining]C[enter] in accordance with IRO regulations and in agreement with AJDC', and '(ii) It appears also that the individual eligibility of some of the members of your group is doubtful.'[104] Facing the loss of status as a VTC and hence the financial subsidy that came with this, Vittoria Buciuk wrote again to Grossmann seeking his intercession with the IRO, and also with the Unione delle Comunita Israelitiche in Rome, which had hitherto been desultory in responding to Buciuk's requests for help.[105]

The group's difficulties were in part of its own making, as Pollock's letter indicates, but its behaviour was understandable. Once liberated from the Nazi camps, none of its members appeared prepared – it would seem – to subject themselves to a regulatory regimen in the DP camps. Moreover, conditions in nearly all the UNRRA/IRO camps were described in successive reports by its own inspectors as oppressive and squalid, whereas the out-of-camp shelters offered a modicum of comfort and safety.[106] Field officers repeatedly reported instances of violence in some of the UNRRA camps between Jews and gentiles, the latter mostly Central and Eastern Europeans who were openly antisemitic, as well as violent confrontations between different national groups.[107] Even where camps were designated for Jews, and Eastern European Jews predominated, the negative camp experiences of many Aegean Jews with Polish and Hungarian Jews was fresh. There was possibly a further reason for the group's reluctance to transfer to the official camps. As we saw above in the case of Matilde Alhadeff, the Aegean survivors travelled freely between the refuges in Rome, Bologna and Milan, especially when they heard news that one of their own had arrived or to visit their friends. Naturally, they were reluctant to give up this freedom. Nevertheless, their comings and goings between the refuges appear to have irritated officials.

*

For the vast majority of Europe's liberated Jews, there was little remaining of their former communities. The Nazis and their abetters had extinguished nearly all pre-war Jewish communal life wherever it had previously existed. This fact, coupled with widespread antisemitism, some of it violent, especially in parts of Eastern Europe and, in particular, in Poland, as well as resentment (or fear) that returning Jews would claim the property sequestered by local populations, led thousands of survivors to reconsider where they might start afresh.[108] Indeed, in 1947 over 50,000 Jewish DPs still under the administration of intergovernmental agencies expressed an unwillingness to return to their places of origin.[109] By this date, this number included most of the remaining Aegean survivors in Italy.

According to international agreement, DPs were to be either repatriated to their country of origin (once their nationality was determined) or to their last place of residence in 1938.[110] In order to determine their status, all DPs had to undergo a lengthy bureaucratic process to determine if they were to be repatriated to their country of origin, or if they qualified for resettlement in a country of their choice. In a number of UNRRA resolutions (Nos. 40, 57–58, 90, 92) governing the treatment of persecuted groups in matters of repatriation and resettlement that incorporated an earlier recommendation by the American lawyer Earl Harrison, Jews were to be categorized as *singularly* persecuted and hence exempted from the repatriation clause.[111] However, the Dodecanese had been an Italian possession, the Aegean survivors were initially considered Italian nationals which meant they were potentially excluded from resettlement, unless they could prove otherwise.[112] As we shall see, the onus fell on the Aegean survivors to plead their case for resettlement abroad rather than repatriation to the Dodecanese or to remain in Italy.

While some survivors could look forward to an early new start in life, others were less fortunate. By early 1947, there were ninety-two Jews from Rhodes and Kos still in Rome, and this number further declined by about a third over the ensuing months.[113] By 1950, only a handful remained either by choice or because they had become ensnared in the administrative apparatus of the various agencies dealing with them. The committee presiding over applications for resettlement often made decisions that appeared both to contradict the guidelines for dealing with Jewish refugees and certainly ran counter to the spirit of the UNRRA Resolutions. In a few cases, however, denial of resettlement was overturned upon appeal.

Their status lay in the balance for a long while, not least because of administrative 'red tape' surrounding clarification of their nationality. Their situation was complicated by the fact that Italy's former sovereignty over the Dodecanese meant they were in the first instance viewed as Italian citizens and therefore subject to repatriation. The onus was on the individual to prove to the interviewing field officer and the Preparatory Committee of the International Refugee Organization (PCIRO), in effect the body that took the final decision, that they had not previously possessed Italian nationality, and instead were stateless, and thus eligible for resettlement. While some did opt to remain in Italy, Buciuk argued that the majority had no real tangible connection to the country (other than language), whereas resettlement meant they could join relatives.[114] The choice of destination followed a pattern similar to earlier waves of migration. As in 1938/39, few of the Aegean survivors expressed a desire to go to Mandate Palestine, unless they already had close ties there. Instead, most of them preferred to resettle where they had relatives who could sponsor them, either in the Belgian Congo, Rhodesia or in the United States.

Sometimes, the choice was determined by forces outside an individual's control or simply through chance. Sara Notrica, for example, after recovering her strength in the camp hospital at Dachau, had to think about where to go. She had some command of English and therefore applied for a permit to go to the United States. However, because she was identified as Italian, she was deemed ineligible for resettlement and instead faced repatriation to Italy. She could not even return to Rhodes since Italian nationals were not eligible to enter the island, now under an interim Greek-British joint-military administration. A Belgian doctor, who befriended her, suggested that she return with him to Belgium, a proposal that surprised her cousins. However, this was not a bad idea, because her brother Rahamin was in Elisabethville in the Belgian Congo and she hoped to join him travelling via Brussels. Having arrived in Paris (en route to Brussels), Sara through a chance encounter was taken to a shop owned by a Jewish man originally from Rhodes where she learned of the presence in the city of another group of young women from Rhodes. Sara searched for them with the help of the police. The young women had left an unpaid taxi bill that had brought them to the attention of the Gendarmes. In this curious sequence of events, Sara was reunited with her cousin Laura Hasson and friends Sara Benatar, Anna Almeleh, Gianette Hasson and Gela Hanan. She eventually emigrated to the Congo where she joined her brother and met her future husband, Gabriel Jerusalmi.[115]

Applicants for resettlement had to be persistent in their quest, and on occasion, such persistence paid off. Giuseppe Mallel (b. 1908) after his release from Mauthausen made his way to Italy via Salzburg, probably in the company of Achille Da Fano (see Epilogue). Crossing into Italy, Giuseppe arrived in Rome via Modena and Bologna on an Allied army train in June 1945, and registered with the Rhodes Survivors group in Via Condotti; he stayed in the group's base in Via Lodovica Settala in Milan (where he was listed in October 1945). This was a period of forced idleness that did not suit the former wholesale trader. Mallel, therefore, was among those survivors who decided to return to Rhodes in 1946/47 to see what could be salvaged of their former lives. He travelled by ship via Naples and Alexandria to Rhodes in summer 1946, where he remained until July 1948. In Rhodes, as with so many other survivors of the camps, there was nothing left to retrieve of his business nor of his home in della Fasana. His wife Rebecca Hasson and their two children, Nissim (b. 1938) and Violetta (b. 1943) had been murdered in Auschwitz, as too were her and his parents and two of his sisters. Nevertheless, in Rhodes his personal circumstances changed for Giuseppe started a new family with Rosa Hanan, a 26-year-old survivor of the camps, whose widowed mother was killed in Auschwitz and whose brother Erzl aged 20 died shortly before the liberation of Mauthausen.[116] Giuseppe and Rosa married in 1947 and later that year they had a son, named Nissim (after his father and possibly in memory of his first child).

The family returned to Italy in July 1948, but with the intention of immigrating to Atlanta, Georgia, where his sister Perla and her husband lived. Perla and Isaac were prepared to sponsor Giuseppe and Rosa, and there was even the prospect of employment in the firm of Simon D. Horowitz. What should have been fairly straightforward became a long drawn-out process that stretched into the early 1950s. The issue was Mallel's status. Giuseppe was still technically an Italian subject in 1946 when he was issued an Italian passport for his journey to Rhodes – and this was to become the sticking point with the IRO over the next two years.

As part of the process for resettlement, Joseph, as he was now calling himself, was interviewed in early March 1949 by IRO field officer in Rome Irina Wassilchikoff who found him 'Very cooperative and full of details. Has concealed nothing according to my opinion. An educated man.'[117] Wassilchikoff's supervising officer, nevertheless, while conceding Mallel had suffered persecution, found he was technically no longer a DP nor a refugee, but an Italian citizen because of the passport and thus did not fall under the IRO mandate. This decision was in spite of Wassilchikoff's report stating 'Though [Mallel] has an Italian passport, he also has a Red Cross one and has more or less renounced Italian citizenship.'[118] Moreover, the family had no real connection to Italy, nor could they remain in Rhodes with its 'painful associations' and Mallel's 'fear of Greek communism'. The case was passed to a review officer at the IRO who found that Mallel's application should be supported. In their recommendation, the officer, S. E. Streeter, wrote

> [Mallel] obtained an Italian passport in 1946 before Rhodes island was ceded to Greece by the Peace Treaty when still he was an Italian subject, although not a citizen. Since the applicant is a refugee under para 1(a) and not 2, A1, the fact he is in possession of passport is in itself not sufficient to exclude him under any of the provisions of Section D.I. The applicant is not firmly established in Italy and did not opt for Greek or Italian citizenship according to the Peace Treaty.
>
> [...]
>
> His case is borderline.[119]

In Streeter's view, Mallel was eligible for resettlement under the IRO mandate and therefore recommended out-of-camp care and assistance pending resettlement. Despite this recommendation, Joseph's application for resettlement in the United States was declared inadmissible in a decision of 21 February 1950.

The Review Board had interviewed Mallel on 2 February in its Rome office in Via S. Nicola de Tolentino, and came to the conclusion that 'he is not considered to be a concern of IRO as an Italian citizen in his country of nationality'.[120] This conclusion was in spite of Streeter's differentiation between being a 'subject' and a 'citizen'. Joseph appealed to the board in a letter of 10

May 1950 in which he reiterated that he was not considered an Italian citizen by the Italian authorities themselves, and indeed, had been issued an alien refugee document by the Rome *Questura* (Alien's Office of the police). This appeal went before the PCIRO in Geneva, which committee upheld the decision of 21 February 1950.

Mallel did not give up for he appealed a third time.

Meanwhile, his sister (in all probability) in Atlanta had contacted the American authorities to press for his case, for in August that year, IRO Geneva headquarters wrote to its Rome office informing them that the United Services office for New Americans had been in contact with IRO in Geneva, apparently in support of Mallel. Rome was instructed to re-interview Joseph and to ascertain when exactly his passport had been issued, if it had been renewed and if he was or was not an Italian citizen. The contents of this letter suggest information either had not been passing between the various departments dealing with Mallel, or had been withheld. A number of attempts to contact Joseph directly and via the Condotti group failed. There is a gap in the sources from the end of 1950 when the eligibility office in Bagnoli forwarded Mallel's complete dossier to Geneva headquarters and a decision of the PCIRO of 25 May 1951, overturning the original refusal to grant Mallel recognition within the mandate.[121] What transpired in these five months to alter the PCIRO position? We simply do not have this information. However, the path now appeared cleared for the Mallels to resettle in Atlanta.

In a similarly contradictory, protracted case, 37-year-old Alberto Hanan after arriving in Bolzano moved on briefly to Modena where he stayed in a military-run camp for DPs. From there he journeyed to Milan, staying at another camp where he registered as a DP. At the beginning of October, six months after his liberation, he arrived at the Jewish shelter located on the upper floors of the synagogue in the Via de'Gombruti in Bologna.[122] This was to be his home for the next two years. On 30 September 1947, he moved to Via Condotti, by this date the sole refuge for the Aegean Jews, to await resettlement to the United States.

However, the decision on Alberto's future did not rest with him, but with desk officers at IRO. As in a number of other cases, there was not unanimity. Alberto initially was granted resettlement and was already at the processing centre in Bagnoli in southern Italy when this decision was overturned and he was deemed ineligible, though the reasons for this change are not apparent. In a letter challenging the decision to rescind his eligibility for emigration to the United States (more of which below), Alberto spoke of his 'unhappy memory' of the 'sad odyssey' from a life of misery in the death camps to his unsettled status in Rome.[123] In his letter of 9 January to the IRO Albert was unsparing of criticism.

> Four years have passed since my liberation, waiting and hoping to be reunited with two of my nephews who served in the American Army in the Pacific, and who are the only relatives I have left in the world. But, alas! after having obtained full eligibility for the United States by going through all the required formalities: medical examination, political inspection; American Consulate, Consular visa, and Commission for Embarkation on 25 November previous, what a surprise it was to receive the painful news of ineligibility while I was waiting to embark on 9 December 1949!

And concluded:

> I still can't believe that such a measure could have been taken at the last minute against a victim of Nazi fascism![124]

Vittoria Buciuk from her office in Via Condotti aired her concern. Not only had Albert been treated in an insensitive manner, Rachele Alhadeff, who having received her visa on 2 December, and was due to leave at the same time as Albert also found herself in the same situation. And there were at least another dozen survivors waiting to embark for the USA for whom the prospect of a last minute denial was looming. For Vittoria, Alberto's case touched a nerve, for he had sold everything, even his shoes, in order to make the journey to Bagnoli. Writing to Kurt Grosman in New York, Vittoria was emphatic as to the injustice of the IRO decision.

> In reading the enclosed report of Mr. Hanan, one cannot but recognize the right, the undisputed right, of Mr. Hanan to belong to category 'A' as persecuted and deported victim of Nazist [*sic*] brutality, for which reason he justly obtained eligibility to emigrate to the US; and on the other side the diposition to deprive him of all these rights beginning from December 14th, when he and the others had been called eligible just a day before, can only be called very unjust.[125]

She also corresponded with Dr Jiri Liban, an executive of the WJC in Geneva, seeking his intervention in the case.[126] Eventually, the Review Board of the IRO decided that Alberto was indeed, eligible, not necessarily because of his personal circumstances or that he was a victim of Nazism, but because a policy change in late January 1950:

> now makes it possible to accept Jews who submit 'compelling family reasons' because of what is believed to be the almost complete destruction by the Germans of the Jewish community on the Dodecanese [sic]. [Hanan], whose objections appear to be plausible, never acquired Italian citizenship and he is not excluded under Part II of the IRO Constitution. He is therefore considered WITHIN THE MANDATE OF THE ORGANIZATION.[127]

Returning to life was not a straightforward matter, as we have been witnessing. In some cases, the decisions of the PCIRO might have been driven by financial considerations; as with many agencies at the time, funds were tight.[128] Nevertheless, its decisions appeared callous, especially when following a narrow interpretation of the regulations by choosing to ignore in some instances, the recommendations of the interviewing field officer. When a person's experiences did not conform to conventional understandings of what constituted a refugee or displaced person, the outcome could be a negative one.[129]

The case of Vittoria Levi Balsamo provides a good example of this pernickety approach to regulations. Vittoria's biography, like so many from the war period, was complicated.[130] She was born in 1918, the daughter of Abramo Levi and Mazaltov Hasson and had been living at home with two older brothers and her parents in Via Teodoro di Saluzzo before the Racial Census.[131] It appears that Vittoria had been employed in the Rhodes library before her marriage to an Italian soldier called Balsamo. In February 1942, she bore his child, Marta (Mazaltov). Upon marriage, Vittoria appears to have converted to Catholicism (her IRO documents describe her as a Jew and not Catholic). Vittoria had evaded deportation in July 1944 by going into hiding with 2-year-old Marta. According to Vittoria's own account that December she was denounced by local Greeks to the Germans and taken into custody. On 13 January, classified as a 'Catholic Jew' Vittoria and her daughter were on the same fishing sloop *Mas* as Teresa Buciuk that took them to Marmaris in Turkey.[132] At this point, her biography becomes blurred.

In documents related to her case, Israel Levi, a carpenter five years her senior, was presented as her husband.[133] According to IRO documents, the couple had a son named Abramo (Vittoria's father's name), although Levi's paternity might have been assumed on the part of officials. Vittoria, in her application for assistance and resettlement, mentions how the Germans deported her husband in 1944, and she had not heard from him since. She does not specify if it is Balsamo or Levi she is referring to, but it is likely to have been the former, for her affidavit alludes to being together with Levi throughout the period leading to expulsion to Turkey. However, Levi is not recorded among the expellees to Turkey. His case file also presents them as a couple throughout this and a later period.[134] Their fortunes deteriorated further when little Abramo died en route to Marmaris. After a month in Marmaris, they were transferred to the island of Casos where they remained from February until July 1945. From there they returned to Rhodes, but discovering their families had perished and their property destroyed, they decided to go to Italy where they had heard others from the community were located. Repatriated to Italy in the autumn of 1946 together with other Italian nationals, they then moved south where Vittoria found work as a domestic servant to a family in Casteltrevano in the Sicilian province of Trapani, while Israel worked as a casual farm worker.

Israel suffered from acute rheumatism that incapacitated him. For this reason at the end of the 1940s, Vittoria travelled alone to Rome to register the couple's request to resettle in the United States where her uncle Nissim Hasson lived (in Brooklyn). Although the interviewing officer, Morini, was sympathetic in their description of Vittoria ('she seems very modest and simple') when they interviewed her in February, the couple were nevertheless classified as neither refugees nor as DPs but as Italian citizens, and thus not eligible within the terms of the IRO. This decision was problematic to say the least, given that Jews had been singularly recognized as victims by international agencies and therefore eligible for resettlement. Moreover, there was a degree of inconsistency among agency staff, whose subjective impressions about applicants had far-reaching consequences. When Vittoria presented again for interview in September 1950, the field officer, Irina Wassilchikoff, described her as 'A primitive person, with a rather confused story and little memory.' Nevertheless, Wassilchikoff qualified this judgement by adding Vittoria made a 'reliable impression'. Once again, the Eligibility Intake Officer, H. C. F. George, deemed her ineligible for resettlement. Vittoria's case was finally rejected by the PCIRO when it met her in Rome on 13 December 1950, declaring her case not within the IRO's mandate.[135] We have no idea what transpired after that date, whether Vittoria and Israel remained in Italy or if they managed somehow to leave for a better life overseas.

Cases such as that of Levi Balsamo, or Mallel and Hanan, open a window onto the tensions between survivors and the bureaucracies that sought to administer aid or determine their future well-being. On the one hand, one's story explained to a stranger who may not have experienced the trauma of war and who had power to decide one's fate, frequently met with scepticism. For example, the upheaval of war and occupation, the trauma of a dead child, the displacement of expulsion to Turkey, a subsequent life in camps, meant Vittoria could not provide a straightforward narrative to her recent biography. On the other hand, it is possible that in repeated form-filling and interviews, the storyline changed in response to particular questions or according to how the survivor perceived the desk officer. Survival meant adapting one's life story to fit the situation. There is a suggestion of this in Levi Balsamo's case – either the interviewing officers kept bad notes, or Vittoria was concealing something (for instance, the exact nature of the relationship with Israel Levi, for she could not have been married to him at the same time as with the Italian Balsamo). Meanwhile, the question of a respondent's credibility to the interviewing field officer of these organizations was partly influenced by the latter's perception of the completeness or accuracy of the details in the responses. Often there were errors of fact, or gaps in the narrative of the applicant. Field officers were trained administrators, and from entirely different worlds to that of many of the Aegean Jews they met in Italy. Sometimes, assessments were made on assumptions about the applicant's background or standing, as we can see in the different way Wassilchikoff commented on Mallel and Balsamo. Possibly, much got lost in both social as well as linguistic translation.

As we saw in Chapter 6, the camps had taught survivors, especially the younger ones, to become 'streetwise' if they were to survive in a situation where power lay in the other party's hands. A certain wariness can be discerned among some survivors when interacting with DP field officers. Ascer Hanan was 14 years old when he, his siblings, 16-year-old Lea (Lina), 12-year-old

Lora, 11-year-old Bulissa, and 8-year-old Alberto, together with their mother Allegra Alhadeff, the widow of Avner, arrived at Auschwitz.[136]

In some respects, Ascer's case bears similarities to that of Levi Balsamo's. Conflicting narratives, possibly arising from withholding information or poor memory, produced a confused and confusing storyline. Ascer explained to interviewing officers of the IRO how after his liberation from *Kinderblock* 66 in Buchenwald, and a month spent recuperating in hospital, he returned to Italy in July 1945, joining the Via Condotti group (although he does not appear on the early lists from that period). The period spanning his return to early 1947 forms an ellipsis in his narrative. From February 1947, he was in receipt of I£3,000 out-of-camp assistance from IRO and the Joint as part of the VTC. According to Ascer, in August that year the opportunity arose to take up employment in a furrier shop in Milan, working for an acquaintance from Auschwitz in return for board and lodging in Via Settembrini 45. Ascer told the IRO interviewer that he remained in Milan until September 1949, when he returned to Via Condotti in the hope of resettlement as a DP. The IRO forms show that at different times he considered repatriation to Rhodes or emigration to the newly established state of Israel. However, by the autumn of 1949, he sought emigration to the USA, probably to Los Angeles where his cousin Sara (Ezra's daughter) already had been resettled. He gave Vittoria Buciuk as a reference.

Recognition as a DP was vital to resettlement. In an interview on 23 September, Ascer outlined his life story, from elementary schooling between 1935 to 1940, being apprenticed at the age of 10 to a shoemaker until deportation to Auschwitz; the hard labour in various camps until his liberation. According to his account, he was the sole survivor since 'the whole family burnt alive – father, mother, two sisters and brother'. His IRO interviewing officer, J. E. Schoenack, expressed some sympathy for Ascer. 'Subject though very young', Schoenack noted on the form, 'has suffered very much, is still bearing on his left arm the number impressed in the Auswitz [*sic*] camp. He appears to be genuine in his sayings and willing to start a new life in USA.'[137] But as we have seen in other cases, a supportive comment was not always enough to convince a supervising officer at the IRO Eligibility Division. Thus it was in Ascer's case that the supervising officer at the Rome office, Karl Feller, rejected his application on the grounds that the 19-year-old was not a genuine refugee and therefore not within the IRO mandate. Why was Ascer considered not genuine?

There were inconsistencies in his narrative. In each interview, Ascer claimed never to have left Italy, producing his leave of stay permit issued by the Rome *Questura* (dated 16 February 1947) as evidence of his domicile status in Italy. As a stateless person, he was also in possession of a Red Cross passport, issued on 18 August 1948. In one interview, there is mention of a brief return to Rhodes in July 1945, the same time he claimed to have returned to Italy from Buchenwald. He told how he moved to Milan in August 1948, a year later than subsequently given (the difference in dates may simply be an error either by him or on the part of his interviewer). And then there is the question of his family. His father Avner did not die in Auschwitz, for as we know, he committed suicide in June 1944.[138] In all likelihood, his mother Allegra and probably 12-year-old Lora and 11-year-old Bulissa were gassed on arrival. But there is confusion regarding his older sister Lea (Lina in the IRO files) and his younger brother, Alberto (8 years old at the time of the deportation). They are referenced in his file as having been in receipt of out-of-camp assistance.[139] Moreover, according to IRO officers Alberto reported that Ascer was recruited by an unnamed Jewish organization and left for Israel (using his Red Cross passport) on 28 May 1948, two weeks after its founding, 'to do service'.[140] Ascer's sojourn in Israel, if he actually went there, lasted barely a year. Perhaps he had learned in the meantime that his cousin Sara had been resettled in Los Angeles. Whatever his reasons for leaving, serving Eretz Israel was no longer his preference, and he returned to Rome in 1949 with the intention of emigrating to the USA, information corroborated by Vittoria Buciuk.

The IRO went to some length to check his story and declared that he had indeed gone to Israel. As a returnee, according to the supervising officer, he was no longer considered a refugee within the mandate of the IRO and instructions were sent by the Rome office to the processing centre at Bagnoli in the south to discard his case. This decision was despite a recommendation made a year before by UNRRA that a persecuted person who had gone to Palestine (now Israel) but who had returned, should still be considered eligible for assistance.[141] Despite representations on his behalf by the Jewish

Organization of Refugees in Italy, his rejection was upheld at the beginning of December 1949, after which the files are silent on his subsequent whereabouts, as they are on his sister Lea and young Alberto.

However, the documentation itself contains anomalies. In the file, Lea is also referred to as Alhadeff, implying she had married. However, a Lea or Lina Alhadeff does not appear in related WJC and Joint files. And there is only one Alberto Hanan mentioned in any of the files. Ascer's case was being reviewed around the same time as that of Alberto Hanan and Rachele Alhadeff. Could it be that a clerical error was made? In a circular of 30 November, the head of the Eligibility Division in Rome, R. L. Gesner, wrote to the processing centre at Bagnoli mentioning the likelihood that Lea and Alberto might be trying to emigrate to the USA. Is it possible that the Alberto referred to in the reports who had reported Ascer had gone to Israel (or perhaps he had intended to go), was in fact Alberto Hanan, whom we discussed above? That Lina who was said to have gone missing (AWOL), was in fact Rachele Alhadeff, who had moved to Bagnoli at the time Ascer was being interviewed in preparation for her own resettlement? In no other records that are known to exist is there any indication that Lina or Alberto survived the Holocaust. Alberto was merely 8 years old when he arrived at the gates of Auschwitz and almost certainly went with his mother and sisters. Only their cousin Sara from Ezra's family is known to have survived, and she is the only one that Ascer mentions in his interviews as still living after the war. Nevertheless, the IRO administration clearly believed in its own inviolability. Any inconsistency must lie with the applicant.

The IRO officers appear bureaucratically pedantic in cases like that of Hanan or Levi Balsamo. The Aegean Jews had suffered terribly as a consequence of Nazi racial persecution and clearly had been displaced as a result of the deportation. There was by international agreement special provision to treat Jews de facto as a separate and special category of victims. And yet in some cases, field officers or their supervisors behaved contrary to this, adhering to a narrow interpretation of what constituted a refugee or DP. It should not surprise us when some Aegean survivors, for instance, Dora Scemaria and Matilde Sciarcon, decided against repatriation to Rhodes, and simply disappeared (they were supposed to have been on the steamer going there via Alexandria but went missing en route, rather like Lina Hanan).

As we saw in Chapter 6, the cohort of those born from 1930 constituted 15.7 per cent of the deportees, but only a handful of this cohort, or 2.75 per cent, survived; together with the cohort born from the mid-1920s, they now faced the world as orphans without the protection of parents or older siblings. Most of them had relatives in Katanga or Elisabethville in the Belgian Congo, or in Salisbury in Rhodesia, or in various cities of the United States, or in Buenos Aires in Argentina. However, for the first months of the liberation, they were subject to the supervision of the various agencies dealing with displaced orphans. Their experiences varied greatly. Orphaned child survivors, in particular, were entitled to protection according to UNRRA Resolutions 47, 57 and 58. However, in practice the treatment of Jewish survivors often contradicted the policy agreed at executive level, resulting in wide differences of practice.[142]

Like the cohort of older female survivors, teenage girls outnumbered their male counterparts. Their experiences of the return to life and a new start varied greatly. By June 14-year-old Alice Tarica, the only survivor from this middle-class family, was among the youth and child survivors looked after by volunteers at DELASEM-run shelters in Florence, Modena and Bologna and aided by the Joint. Interviewed in Brussels fifty years later, Alice reflected on the impact the experience of the camps had had on her.

> The JOINT organization started to work with me, as I was an orphan and a minor. They made papers for me. Through them, I was put in contact with a woman from an important Jewish-Italian family. She volunteered to take care of me. I was so badly off, that when they gave me some hand-me-downs from their own daughters, I started to cry. It was then that I realized how much my situation had been diminished – in all respects. ... I realized that I didn't have anything left in the world, and that I would have to live on aid from other people. ... I remember that this woman brought me to a Shabat at her house. She had property and a nurse for her children. She was very considerate – she let me sleep in the same room as her own daughter. There was never the least slight ... they were extraordinary people. But I cried. I cried a lot. ... Yes. I cried. I told myself, 'you're nobody now ... you have to live in the world of other people now'. I was unhappy. ... I had finally realized how far I had fallen – This degradation of a pampered, spoiled young child who never lacked for anything, until little by little, I became someone who was getting food, linens, and a pullover from strangers ... and that I couldn't understand.[143]

Alice stayed with the woman and her family for the weekend;

> I will always be very grateful to her. So then we went to Florence, where some of my friends in our group had acquaintances. We were very well received by the community. They put us up in a family pension. There were 5 of us, and they put us together in a big room. The Italians were fantastic. We had our days free and we ate well, and the community paid for it. We did some tourist activities.[144]

Meanwhile, 13-year-old Stella Benun was among the youngest, if not the youngest, of the survivors at liberation.[145] She was the daughter of Rachele Finz and Haim Benun and had three siblings – none of whom survived the deportation (her brother was Elia Benun who, as we saw in Chapter 6, died shortly before his 16th birthday after the liberation of Mauthausen).[146] Alone, and suffering from tuberculosis, she spent the six years following her liberation from Theresienstadt wending her way through the bureaucratic labyrinth of the aid agencies. Stella, like most of her compatriots, had experienced several transfers to a different camp, including Bergen-Belsen from where she was lucky to have been moved on. After a period of convalescence, she arrived in Milan on 8 September, was moved to Bologna before finally arriving in the Via Condotti at the beginning of 1946. Facing winter in Rome, her weakened constitution made her vulnerable to influenza that soon developed into pleurisy, and by 1948 had become pulmonary tuberculosis of both lungs. In August 1950, she was hospitalized at the Villa Giuseppina di Grotteferrata in Rome. Her incapacitation meant she was reclassified by the IRO in January 1951, as handicapped, rather than as a 'hard core' case, which impacted on whether she could receive further IRO assistance or indeed, if she might be eligible for resettlement. On appeal, later in May, her classification was changed back to 'hard core' with recommendation for a year of treatment in a sanatorium.[147] Stella's situation changed again within a month. In June the IRO agreed with the Joint that it would henceforth takeover responsibility of 'hard core' cases, including that of Stella.[148] Thus, Stella's teenage years were either spent in hospitals or being interviewed by caseworkers. Her case meandered through bureaucracy and misfortune for six years until we finally lose sight of her shortly before her 20th birthday.

Stella's undetermined fate, like that of Ascer Hanan, was not uncommon among teenage survivors from Rhodes and Kos. As we saw earlier, Sami Modiano had the good fortune to be in the company of someone older who, from Sami's description, was 'streetwise'. Others made no less adventurous journeys, but they were frequently alone and with little control over their situation. For 14-year-old Moise Coen (see Illustration 8.2), who had been the only Jew liberated from Wels, one of Mauthausen's sub-camps, the return to life included detention by *Carabinieri* and an unsympathetic IRO field administration. Repatriated to Italy in July 1945, we find Moise working on a farm in Oria near Brindisi two years later. How he came to be there is unclear from the records, but he clearly did not wish to remain there.[149] When he tried to return to Rhodes in October 1947, the *Carabinieri* detained him and placed him in the Fraschetta DP camp, before transferring him to the Cinecittà DP camp in Rome on 24 December at the request of the IRO field office. Moise remained in Cinecittà for five days pending a decision on his case.

Most of the boys were in their later teens at the time of liberation, but when Moise arrived in Italy in July 1945, he was still a young minor and poorly educated, having received barely four years elementary schooling. Primarily a Ladino-speaker, he spoke Italian and Greek only slightly and his writing and reading skills in all three languages were rudimentary. From an early age, he had helped in his father's grocery business until the deportation. Moise's parents, 68-year-old Isaaco and 55-year-old Allegra (née Fintz) together with his 9-year-old brother Aronne were murdered in Auschwitz, while his 17-year-old sister Sara did not survive the liberation of Bergen-Belsen. Now alone, it is likely IRO welfare officers handling orphan children placed Moise into the 'care' of the farmer in Oria, possibly under the *Hachsharoth* programme.[150] The sources are silent on his experiences with the farmer, other than that he sought to leave. His treatment by the IRO is no less telling of the administrative blindness to the plight of a youngster. Moise had an older brother, Giuseppe, who had immigrated to the Belgian Congo before the war, and now the boy wished to join him. For some inexplicable reason, and against UNRRA's own guidelines concerning the treatment of Jewish child victims, the officer reviewing Moise's application for resettlement turned down the request to join Giuseppe, deeming Moise eligible only for repatriation.[151]

*

The Jews of Rhodes and Kos were part of a large flow of displaced persons from the Dodecanese. Most of them were Greek exiles seeking to return to the islands. According to a contemporary source, by the beginning of 1946 the Aegean survivors were among around one million DPs, of which between 100,000 to 250,000 comprised Mediterranean (including Greek) nationals (mostly located in Nusereit – also spelt Nuseirat – a DP camp in Mandate Palestine) and those classified as stateless; and not all of them were Jewish.[152] There were also the Italians moving the other way (i.e. to Italy). They included the one thousand or so fascist party members and others formerly employed at various levels in the *Governatore* and the municipal administrations, or those who had been associated with quasi-state institutions, such as the Bank of Sicily, where the Levantine Matteo E. had been employed, or those who had been members of the *Carabinieri*, including Mittino. There were also wheeler-dealer characters like Rino Merolle with their affiliation to the PNF. For the sake of assuaging the Greeks, their repatriation to Italy became a desideratum for the British military authorities in 1946.[153] These circumstances were to have an impact on Jews returning to the islands in the aftermath of war.

Because of the dire material conditions that pervaded the Dodecanese islands in 1945, the administration in Rhodes was not able to manage a large and unregulated influx of returnees. The British Military Administration (BMA) that oversaw the Dodecanese carefully scrutinized applications. Its primary objectives were maintaining order by keeping out 'undesirables', and dealing with the health crisis resulting from famine. In the latter case, the ICRC was to hand. Meanwhile, UNRRA aided the BMA in managing the flow of population through its office in Rhodes, established on 14 August 1945.[154] Its remit was wide-ranging, but primarily it dealt with repatriation of Dodecanese citizens to the island, while aiding the BMA with the removal of 'enemy' aliens, that is, most of the abovementioned Italians, as well as assorted refugees and those deemed to be 'undesirables'.[155]

In the summer of 1945, the overwhelming majority of the 7,745 repatriated to the Dodecanese were Greeks, many of whom had been expelled by the Italians during the Italianization campaign before the war.[156] In 1945, returning to Rhodes and Kos was also an option for Jews. By the time UNRRA opened its Rhodes office in the late summer of 1945, eleven Jews and their families had returned to the island.[157] Their numbers soon grew. When Israel Jacobson from the WJC visited Rhodes in late November 1945, he reported the presence of thirty-four Jews and another eight who had returned to Kos. These were not survivors of the camps but those saved from deportation by the Turkish Consul, and later repatriated to Turkey. Nevertheless, Jacobson reported that thirty-seven survivors of the camps, gathered in Italy, were expected to follow.[158] From December 1945 until the following August, a further twenty-seven Jews in Italy expressed an interest in repatriation to Rhodes, and indeed returned.[159] On 15 February 1946, UNRRA Italian Mission had received a further twenty-two requests from survivors wishing to return to Rhodes and Kos. Of this number, fourteen arrived in Rhodes on 20 May, and a further seven on 3 June, and then another four on 4 July – totalling twenty-seven out of a prospective fifty-six.[160] Among the returnees were Amelie Menascé, Moreno Danon and Boaz Turiel, all from Kos.[161] As president of the Community, Elia Soriano actively interceded on behalf of those wishing to return. Writing to Major Miles Bailey from the BMA, in April 1946, in support of Rebecca Capelluto and Suzanna Levi, Soriano assured the Major, 'The ladies are respectable and well known to the undersigned.'[162] Eventually, by summer 1947, there were, according to Avraham Galante, sixty-one Jews on Rhodes, divided almost equally between camp survivors and those who had evaded deportation thanks to the intercession of the Turkish Consul, Selahattin Ülkümen.[163]

It appeared at this stage that despite the horror of the preceding 18 months, the community might be rekindled. What awaited the camp survivors?

The war had utterly transformed Rhodes. In early 1945, a delegation from the International Red Cross visited the Dodecanese in order to ascertain the level of aid required in the islands. Arriving on Rhodes in March, it found

> A visit to the city leaves an impression of indescribable sadness and misery. All the shops are closed, many houses are destroyed, most of the windows are without glass; the bombed streets could not be cleaned for a long time. From place to place, people without strength collapse onto the road. The hospital and the orphanage are full of seriously ill people whom the doctors let die for lack of medicine and food. They themselves and their nurses have little strength to carry out their duties.[164]

A tour of the rural villages elicited no better vista. The BMA together with UNRRA collaborated to alleviate the distress of the islands, with some positive results by the end of 1945.[165] Nevertheless, the ending of the Italian presence on Rhodes and Kos, as well as Leros, had negatively impacted the local economy. There was little opportunity to secure a modest material life and this, too, had a negative effect on the physical well-being of the population.[166] Nearly two years after the ending of the war in late 1947, Helen Nussbaum, a nurse working with the World Health Organization, visited the island and found 'the majority of the children still show signs of malnutrition and vitamin deficiency in the form of tuberculosis, adenitis, rickets, and ophthalmic diseases'.[167]

The Allied bombardment and sea-blockade of Rhodes and Kos in the final phase of the occupation had exacerbated the dire situation already developing in the summer 1944. With Jewish merchants gone, and whatever supplies they had stored in their homes and warehouses, sequestered by the authorities or plundered by neighbours and soldiers, famine set in, forcing the population to scavenge vegetation in the countryside, and to eating dogs, cats and rats.[168] Thus, the destruction caused by war, occupation and persecution, and the murder of their loved ones, cast the 'island of roses' in a different light, namely into an 'island of ghosts'. As Vittoria Balsamo stated in her failed attempt for resettlement, she did not wish to return to Rhodes because 'For us Rhodes means a cimitary [*sic*] and we cannot live there.'

When asked by Marcello Pezzetti why she had waited more than three decades before returning to Rhodes, Stella Levi explained she had not wished to return, 'Because I didn't want to see Rhodes again. I knew what awaited me there. In the *Juderia* I saw nothing but ghosts, though I recognised all of the houses with all those people who used to live in them and I saw these images, I saw them in my mind and they were like ghosts.'[169] Nevertheless, Stella's trepidation about returning was not universally held, as we can see from those who did return in the two years following liberation.

The elite families who had escaped deportation were the first to return, as we noted above. Well-connected and adaptable, they for the most part were also able to retrieve most if not all of their pre-deportation assets. They soon reconstituted the Jewish Council, electing Maurice (Moise) Soriano, the son of Elia Soriano, himself a former president, its new president.[170] The Jewish elite worked closely with the British military administration, in much the same way as it had adapted to the Italian occupation and, before that, to the Ottomans. In 1945, they were cooperating closely with the BMA on what to do with the prospective returnees, the majority of whom were young women.

> Plans for their reception and care are now being made by a Committee formed from the few Jews remaining in Rhodes, BMA and UNRRA. Present indications are that many can be employed by BMA in clerical work, in local factories and that work projects can be set up for those who cannot find normal employment.[171]

These plans were possibly well intentioned. How the survivors received them is not so easy to gauge, but the fact that most soon left the island seeking opportunity overseas is perhaps some indication.

Some, however, remained and they sought to re-establish a semblance of normal life, but this too was fraught with difficulty and in some cases, impossible. Sami Modiano's cousin Lucia Modiano received permission from UNRRA and the BMA in June 1946 to return to Rhodes. She was not part of the Rhodes Survivors' Group, but instead was in a shelter for Italian women in Sassari (Sardinia). The UNRRA repatriation officer in writing to her nevertheless recommended that she contact the Rhodes Group in Via Condotti, as well as apply to the Jewish refugee agency HIAS for assistance.[172] According to the information she provided in her application, she had a husband, Gavino Demontis, who was a Jewish native of Sassari, and who by trade was a cabinet polisher.[173] Unfortunately, his application, submitted a few months after Lucia's, to join her in Rhodes was rejected by the BMA.[174] In deciding individual cases, the BMA rarely gave the full reason for refusal, other than sometimes citing the lack of financial means, or internal security.[175] It is possible that the couple were in fact not married, although they appear to have been living together. Lucia having returned to Rhodes alone, eventually married 26-year-old Mosé Sulam. Sulam, together with some other young men, had escaped Rhodes by boat to Marmaris before the deportation, and subsequently joined the Greek Navy. After the German capitulation, Sulam had been among the first returnees to Rhodes. The couple, together with a handful of other Jews, now settled down to a long life on the island, becoming curators of the Kahal Shalom synagogue.[176]

The decision whether or not to return and then to remain on Rhodes and Kos depended on a number of factors, not least the socio-political climate on the islands. As we saw earlier in this study, there had been some instances of overt antisemitism in the islands under De Vecchi's regime, but even then it was largely confined to committed fascists such as the Spano family, and their supporters. Persecution at the hands of Italian fascists notwithstanding, Jews in the Dodecanese, especially the younger generation, who were now the majority of the survivors, had closely identified with Italian culture, and by 1947, with *enosis* looming, this appears to have fuelled resentment towards Jews *as Italians*. While there is little evidence to indicate systemic or widespread antisemitism towards returning Jews to either Rhodes or Kos, there were some recorded incidents of anti-Jewish behaviour among some sections of the Greek population.

Jacobsen's report of his visit to Rhodes in late November 1945 casts some light on the experiences of survivors who returned. He remarked on how the island's Jews were seen as close to the Italian occupiers, and how this elicited hostility among the Greeks towards them. Jacobsen then recounted an episode, without claiming this to be symptomatic of wider anti-Jewish sentiment. The BMA's British liaison officer, Captain Gregory had been working closely with Alberto Amato, who was a member of the newly reconstituted Jewish Council.

> That evening, when he, Capt. Gregory, went to get into his auto[mobile], he saw what he thought was a thick wire tied around his steering wheel. When switching on the lights he discovered a live, large rat tied by its tail to the steering wheel. [...] This is an indication of some problems that may develop between some of the Jews who have Italian names, and the Greek nationals, when the islands are returned to the Greeks.[177]

It is possible this was an isolated event. Greece had been one of the few countries in Europe without rampant antisemitism before the war.[178] The newly installed government in Athens was also one of the first in Europe to pass a law in 1945 for the restitution of Greek Jewish property seized by the Germans and collaborating Greek authorities.[179] However, this law only applied to those who had been living in Greece during the war. The Dodecanese islands had been part of Italy's colonial empire and, as such, were excluded from the law's application. Where claims were subsequently made, usually by heirs of the perished Aegean Jews, the path to restitution was strewn with bureaucratic difficulties.

Not just ghosts deterred the survivors from returning, for some of those who did return encountered a hostile environment. When Matilde Coen tried to visit her family home in Sigismondo Malatesta in 1961, the Greek inhabitants refused to let her inside to look for family heirlooms.[180] However, Matilde's experience while not isolated, does not appear to have been the predominant one; not everyone met with such blatant hostility from residents. Lucia Amato (now Sciarcon), for example, found Greeks welcoming when she returned to her old home in Via Ammiraglio Bonaldi years later. Alice Tarica too, found a positive reception from former neighbours when she returned in 1963 to Rhodes.[181] The reason for the difference, however, might lie in the fact that the *Juderia* in contrast to the Neocori was repopulated by propertyless Greeks displaced by war and repatriated to the island in 1946/47. Propertyless Greeks who moved into the 'abandoned' homes either felt a pang of guilt or were anxious that they might lose what they had recently acquired.

As suggested, not antisemitism per se was at the heart of hostility towards Jewish survivors who returned, but rather the perceived Italianism of the Jews (although, of course, this does not exclude a combination of both). Where a Jew happened also to be an Italian, remaining on the islands proved to be impossible. Achille Da Fano, a Jew originally from Venice, who had arrived as a young soldier in the early 1920s, and as we saw earlier in this study, had met and married Gioia Arditti, survived the depredations of the coalmine *Charlottengrube* in Rydułtowy and the notorious '*Wiener Grube*' of Mauthausen and the arduous labour in the tunnels of Ebensee.[182] After arriving in Rome via Salzburg, Achille returned to Rhodes together with another survivor, Fortunée Menascé.[183] Twenty-six-year-old Fortunée was a dressmaker who had been among the women transferred to Kaufering and Dachau, later joining the group of survivors in Via Condotti, where Achille also stayed. It is possible that they were among the first returnees to Rhodes, and already married when they embarked for the Dodecanese.[184] How long they remained on Rhodes is, however, a matter of speculation, because their subsequent whereabouts are obscured after sovereignty of the Dodecanese passed to Greece. On the one hand, Da Fano, as a former infantryman and an Italian national, might have faced expulsion together with other Italians in the period leading to the formal handover of the islands in March 1948. On the other hand, as an Italian he may have been loath to relinquish his Italian nationality. The couple were in Naples in 1948, when Fortunée gave birth to their son. Whether they remained there is not known. In either case, Fortunée, as his wife, would have accompanied him to wherever fate would now take them.[185]

In another case, Matilde Alhadeff stated that the Greek authorities arrested her husband, Rino Merolle. It is not clear when this might have happened – or indeed, if it was the Greeks who arrested him, for we know he made a statement to the British military authorities and probably while detained. Merolle was, as we saw earlier in this study, a former infantryman, as well as a member of the PNF. It is likely that Merolle was repatriated to Italy in 1946, together with other Italians, including fascists and members of the Italian administration in custody.[186] In any event, like Da Fano, he disappears from the historical record after providing the British with a statement about the deportation. As concerns Matilda's search for him, the records are silent as to whether they were ever reunited.

Unlike her parents and siblings, Sara Coen, who had worked in the accounts department of the Alhadeff department store, escaped deportation after her Italian partner (they lived together but were not married), 23-year-old Duilio Bartoccini, hid her in a Catholic monastery.[187] She gave birth to their son Mario in September 1944. Presumably, when they thought it safe to do so, they moved together but their life as a family was subsequently shattered when the Germans discovered her and her baby son. Sara and Mario were transported to Marmaris in early 1945. According to Sara's testimony in 1948, Bartoccini remained behind on the island, disappearing thereafter. After the German capitulation, she returned to Rhodes but remained just one day after hearing news that Jews from the island were in Rome. She soon discovered that her parents were dead. Sara also searched in vain for Bartoccini in his hometown of Orte (north of Rome).

Bureaucracy and misfortune dogged Sara's efforts to start anew. Coen joined the Rhodes group in Via Condotti, remaining there until 1949 or 1950. Meanwhile, she met another man she named as Alberto C., and by whom she had two children (a boy and a girl) in quick succession. He abandoned her when he left for the Congo within a year of Sara giving birth to their daughter, Regina. Thus, in 1948, she was alone in Rome (albeit with the Rome group) and receiving assistance from the IRO. Going back to Rhodes was no longer an option for her. Her immediate family, like that of Matilde and so many others, had perished in the Nazi camps and the family home in Via Sigismondo Malatesta had been destroyed during the aerial bombardments. There was nothing in Rhodes for her to return to. Thus, she first sought to emigrate to Buenos Aires in Argentina where her maternal aunt and cousins lived, and who were happy to sponsor her. Because of her circumstances, Sara was within the IRO mandate making her eligible for resettlement, but this is when misfortune struck again, for her baby daughter contracted TB making emigration impossible until the infant was cured. By the beginning of 1951, Sara had decided on Israel as a suitable destination.[188]

In some IRO affidavits, applicants expressed bitterness towards Greeks, as in the case of Matilde Alhadeff. In rare cases, malice lurked within the remnant of the Jewish community itself. As we shall see in the final chapter, some survivors and later generations viewed Jewish Rhodes through an Elysian lens. However, contemporary sources point to tensions left unresolved by the experience of deportation and suffering. The following case also opens a small window on the religious and generational tensions that we touched on in Chapter 2 and which, evidently, were still present after the war. As we have seen at various points, young women of the *Juderia* cohabited or married Italians. In the case of marriage, they sometimes converted to Catholicism, and for deeply religious Jews, this was tantamount to apostasy. Historically, conversions from Judaism to Christianity were commonplace, albeit for differing reasons.[189] However, as Alberto Israel mentions to Marcello Pezzetti in *The Longest Journey*, in Rhodes some among the older generation frowned upon marriages outside Judaism. Isacco Amato was one of those who could not accept a Jew relinquishing their religion and its customs. Bulissa Hugno (Cougno), whose Jewish family were Turkish nationals, had married an Italian soldier and converted to Catholicism upon doing so. Clearly with his aid, she and her two children also escaped deportation.[190] As with others removed to Turkey in early 1945, Bulissa sought to return to the island after the ending of the war. Now penniless, the 25-year-old mother contacted the Joint for financial aid in order to get home. Also writing to the relevant authorities, Amato articulated his objections to her returning to Rhodes, arguing she had failed to keep the 'traditional rites' of Judaism. It is doubtful that Amato's denunciation found a sympathetic ear among those in authority. Nevertheless, Bulissa did not join the other returnees to Rhodes, but instead left for Karpathos, after which we lose sight of her.[191]

We noted above how, from 1945, a small stream of Jews began to return to Rhodes and Kos and how, by May 1947, their numbers had grown to sixty-one. This was the high point of the original Rhodian Jews on the island after the war. Soon after, their numbers declined again, explained by the changed legal status of the Dodecanese which meant that they either had to adopt Greek nationality, or leave. The majority chose to leave. Moreover, as we saw in the previous chapter, remaining on the islands had been complicated by limiting to ethnic Greeks reclamation of so-called 'heirless property' formerly owned by Jews.[192] The survival of a Jewish presence in the Aegean now depended on an influx of displaced Greek Jews from mainland Greece, Egypt and Ethiopia. By the time of the 1951 census, the Rhodes Jewish community numbered just thirty-four, or little more than half its level of May 1947. This was a fraction of its pre-war peak of 4,310 (1931), and barely noticeable among the 6,325 Jews in Greece at that time.[193] Of those that remained in Rhodes, twenty-three had taken Greek nationality, while five held French passports. The nationality of the remaining six is unknown.[194] On Kos, there were no longer any Jews. Efforts by the Board of Deputies in Athens to restore Rhodes as a centre of Jewish Sephardi life in the Aegean thus faltered.

*

For nearly five years, the survivors in Via Condotti and its sister refuges in Bologna, Milan and Florence recreated the social solidarity of the *Juderia*. With the closure of these refuges, the surviving remnant of Jewish Rhodes and Kos dispersed to the different corners of the Sephardi Diaspora to start new lives. For those that returned to the Aegean, the houses, streets and alleys of the *Juderia* in Rhodes and their equivalent in Kos, appeared dead, a space filled by ghosts, as Stella Levi poignantly stated. However, the survivors not only took with them the story of what had befallen them and their families in 1944, they also took with them a memory of the *Juderia* frozen in time.

A 'Lost World' Remembered and Remade

Memory plays tricks, chooses, forgets, and enhances certain events and feelings.[1]

By the early 1950s, most of the survivors from Rhodes and Kos had settled into new worlds in South and Central Africa, the USA and South America. A few became pioneer settlers in the newly established state of Israel, and a few remained in Europe, including Italy.[2] With the passage of time, memories of the Jewish world in the Eastern Aegean receded, its contours becoming blurred.

This is not to say survivors forgot their murdered families and destroyed community. Nevertheless, the memory of people and place faded. In her later years, Laura Varon, for example, could no longer remember what her mother looked like.[3] As the past in Rhodes and Kos receded, it altered. The memory became nostalgic, frequently tinged with regret, and its brutal disruption recalled with anger. Alice Tarica, in spite of the joy a loving husband and beautiful children brought her in adult life, continued to be haunted by the memory of her scarred childhood with the murder in the camps of loving parents, and her twin Maurizio and older brother Sol (Salvatore).[4] The passing of time did not assuage Alberto Israel's anger at the Nazis for his stolen youth, or the little he could recall of it with clarity.[5] Nor did the 'dark space of the camp system inside' [the survivors] lighten with the passage of time.[6] Miru Alcana's bitterness at the Germans for what they did to her and her community did not lessen as she advanced in age. As American scholar Lawrence Langer has argued, the Holocaust never left a survivor's consciousness, rather, it resided in a parallel existence.[7] And as Mary Henderson, the Greek-born wife of the British diplomat, Sir Nicholas Henderson, who had been briefly incarcerated in Haidari at the same time as the

Aegean Jews, eloquently observed in her own memoir: 'then everyone is really two people, the person one knows and sees in the mirror and the other person that people think they know and see as one walks into the room.'[8]

However, positing a binary between memory and history about the life of the Jewish community before and since its destruction does not do full justice to the complexity of the past and how it is remembered. On the one hand, historians rely on factual evidence excavated from the archives. In our case, this archival evidence is scattered across the globe; generated by governments, official organizations and agencies. When pieced together, it sometimes challenges the narrative of the *Juderia* remembered as an Elysian-type world abruptly ended in July 1944. On the other hand, memories (or recollections) frequently offering their own discrete information can fill the silences that exist in documented evidence. An example of this is Elisa Franco Hasson's description of the increasing disorganization of camp life in Auschwitz in late 1944 and how this affected prisoners.[9]

As a historical lived place, the *Juderia* became a 'lost world', not least because in survivor testimonies there are many missing parts. Recalling events from her own life, Mary Henderson likened her memories of her past life to a pile of unordered photographs: 'some of the pictures as I look through them are blurred, foggy and faded but others are sharp and clear – they reveal every detail. Some are missing.'[10] Recollections were not only blurred, but also selective, and often hearsay or rumour is substituted for personal memory, such as in the account of local Fascists humiliating the president of the community, John Menascé, by forcing him to drink castor oil and making him run around the sports stadium.[11] Nor is Stella Levi's account in the film, *The Longest Journey*, of the trek from the *Aeronautica* to the three waiting supply ships in the port, a memory in the strict sense; rather, it is a reflection on it made in the light of subsequent events. Thus, only in retrospection could it be a 'funeral procession, with Jacov Shalom Franco as its leader, perhaps I feel for him most, as he must have been suffering deeply leading his community to death'.[12] But as most survivors, Stella included, acknowledge, no one knew what was in store for them.

Over the years, a repertoire of events or personalities has emerged providing a familiar and sequential meta-narrative.[13] In some accounts literary embellishment to satisfy an audience's expectation of how Nazis appeared, is common. In the *Aeronautica*, in spite of the fact that neither Burger nor Linnemann appeared in uniform, the perpetrators included an SS-Major in 'black uniform and the death's head badge'.[14] In later years, like Laura Varon, Miru Alcana was convinced that Kurt Waldheim, the former president of Austria, was the SS officer whom she saw in the *Aeronautica*, confusing him for Anton Burger.[15] On arriving at Auschwitz bedraggled and confused after the arduous thirteen-day train journey, some survivors spoke of meeting the notorious Dr Josef Mengele, even though at the time they could not have known who any of the senior camp personnel were.[16] In a similar vein of merging *post facto* knowledge with personal experience, Laura gave a description of Irma Grese, the notorious camp guard in Auschwitz and Bergen-Belsen, and discussed the possibility that a young girl she encountered in both camps might have been Anne Frank.[17]

In survivor recollections of pre-war Rhodes, Mario Lago was the 'good Italian', while De Vecchi was not. Governor Campioni became a 'martyr' with the occupation of the islands by the *Wehrmacht* in September 1943, while Kleemann's role in the ensuing Jewish tragedy remained misunderstood.[18] Similarly, the horror of the Nazi camps was populated by a cast of characters that helped to shape survivors' stories of what they had experienced.[19] It goes without saying that Jewish life was cruelly shattered by the violence of Nazi genocidal politics. This minted on the one hand, a nostalgia for a 'lost world', and on the other hand, the trauma of its destruction; nostalgia for the *Juderia* and the trauma of the last transport becoming two sides of the same coin that has persisted over generations.[20]

How was this 'lost world' of Jewish Rhodes and the moment of its destruction retrieved during the years and decades in the afterlife of deportation, camps and liberation? How were its fragmented, broken parts put back together? Indeed, what parts of the *Juderia* were remembered, and what was forgotten or lost? What role did memory play in this and how does it distinguish itself from lived experience? Finally, how have later generations re-imagined this 'lost world'? To try to answer these questions, this concluding chapter examines the memory and the *re*-making of Jewish Rhodes in the testimonies, memoirs and family narratives of the Aegean Jews.[21]

*

Immediately after the war the Aegean survivors newly arrived in Rome were interviewed by a Jewish agency to document the Nazi crime against them. The resulting testimonies compiled by Adolfo Vitalis, a Jewish former officer of the Italian Army, while not on a par with the recordings of Holocaust survivors carried out by psychologist David Boder in 1946, nevertheless provide an early snapshot of Rhodesli voices as they returned from the camps.[22] The affidavits are thin on detail, usually just a sparse factual account amounting to a few sentences, with only a few statements providing an in-depth 'subjective' narrative of events. They rarely provide life stories from before the deportation.

For survivors remembering was double-edged. On the one hand, the trauma of deportation and the horrible depredation of the camps were things that few deportees from the Aegean wished to remember. Certainly, this is what state prosecutor Dr Zeug from the newly established Central Office of the State Justice Administrations for the Investigation of National Socialist Crimes (*Zentrale Stelle der Landesjustizverwaltungen zur Aufklärung nationalsozialistischer Verbrechen*[23]) found in the early 1960s, during investigations into the deportations from the Ionian and Aegean islands and the part played by Adolf Eichmann and his office.[24] This was twenty years after the last transport from the Greek mainland.

Much of the literature assumes little interest was shown in the persecution of Jews until the Eichmann trial. This is not the case. To be sure, the roles in Greece and in the Balkans of the higher echelons of Army Group E, the SS-Captain Dieter Wisliceny (who organized the deportations from Salonica and elsewhere in the Balkans) or of Max Merten (the head of the military administration in Greece who signed off on the decrees against Jews) were the focus of investigations into and subsequent trials for German atrocities in Greek and Yugoslav courts.[25] However, there was in some quarters interest in the persecution of Jews too. Thus, it was that in June 1947 Ulrich Kleemann found himself in Nuremberg facing the tough and uncompromising questioning of a doughty American war crimes prosecutor, Walter Rapp, who was attached to Military War Crimes Case No. 7. Rapp was at pains to establish Kleemann's responsibility for the community's destruction.[26] However, Rapp relied on testimonies made by former members of the garrison on Rhodes.

The affidavits collected in Rome and elsewhere were never used as witness statements in these early war crimes trials. Nor were they used in the earliest legal proceedings against Germans facing Italian war crimes tribunals. Indeed, until the 1960s, apart from Rapp's terse confrontation with Kleemann, little attention was paid to the Jews of Corfu, Rhodes and Kos – even though their tragedy was known to national and international agencies, as we saw in the previous chapter.[27]

In the following two decades, war crimes investigators focused on those responsible for the deportation from the islands. As witnesses to the crime of genocide rather than as its victims, the survivors from Rhodes and Kos were called upon to respond to specific questions regarding the perpetrators. But most of them were unable to answer these questions. They simply did not know. Moreover, there was for some a reluctance to bear witness, to relive the trauma of the deportation and the camps. This is what the German prosecutor investigating the deportation found.[28] In the hope that the World Jewish Congress might have a better response from the survivors, Dr Zeug sought the help of its Geneva office, and Oscar Karbach, the newly appointed director at the Institute of Jewish Affairs in New York, to gather affidavits from survivors.[29] Even two decades after their deportation, it is possible that the trauma and the violence of the camps stifled the retrieval of the past, placing the experience beyond mere words.[30] However, it is also possible that the difficulties survivors had encountered with post-liberation relief and refugee organizations (as touched on in Chapter 8) made them wary of (in this case, German) officialdom.

There were involuntary and voluntary omissions of memory. Laura and Ascer Varon for example, had voids in their recollections of the deportation and camps, as too did Jack (Giacomo) Hasson. Laura for example, when asked about the train journey responded: 'I really don't remember [...] What happened in the cattle cars is like a blank in my mind, you know, in my subconscious.' Questioned further, Laura fell silent.[31] Stella De Leon, too, suppressed the memory of the deportation, first to Piraeus, the brief internment in Haidari, and then the train to Auschwitz.[32] Meanwhile, halfway through her short interview (50 minutes), Stella Hasson was more blunt, telling her interlocutor, Yitzhak Kerem, when asked about her experience in the camp: 'I don't remember and to tell you the truth, I don't want to remember.'[33]

Watching their testimony four decades after the deportation, one clearly sees the continuing impact of their trauma.

Meanwhile, both Susanne (Sultana) Levi and Becky (Rebecca) Franco née Hazan in interviews during the mid-1990s recalled the traumatic experience of arrival at Auschwitz, the separation from their parents (and their mothers in particular), and they recollect in general the brutality of the camps. But details of everyday conditions and fear of the selections that defined so many of the experiences of the victims in Auschwitz, or the subsequent transfer to labour camps in the Greater Reich, are simply missing from their narrative. It is not that either of the two was too young to remember – unlike for example, Jack Hasson – they were both around the same age, Becky was 23 and Susanne was 21; or that they were unable to comprehend what had happened to them. Rather, many decades later, they chose to withhold details, sometimes making brief cryptic allusions to rape and cannibalism, as we saw in Chapter 6 in Sylvia Hasson Berro's and Laura Varon's interviews.

In her interview, Clara Soriano (née Avzaradel) talked of the rapidity of the sequence of events as the deportees were processed upon disembarking from the train at Auschwitz. She was 18 years old at the time, and the violent separation from her parents without even time to say 'goodbyes' is clearly a moment of trauma that defies language. Indeed, instead of using words, Clara makes a motion with her eyes to denote that it all happened within a blink of an eye. According to scholar Lawrence Langer in his ground-breaking work on Holocaust survivors' testimonies, a victim's deep memory belongs to their emotional experience and is not easily transmitted to third parties. As we saw in Chapter 6, Clara's mother and father 'simply disappeared'. Their disappearance for Clara became a memory 'measured in terms of emotional intensity rather than by [chronological] time'.[34] Indeed, Clara tells her story in the present tense.[35]

The emotional intensity of the experience accounts for the non-linearity of survivor memory, especially where it is unmediated by subsequent knowledge of the Holocaust. What appears as confusion or 'jumbled up' to an interviewer or to the listener does so because of cultural conditioning that stipulates the past has a beginning and an end and therefore must appear in a rationally ordered sequence. For Clara, five decades after the deportation, there is no sequential distinction between arriving at Auschwitz and arriving at Bergen-Belsen – they share the same horror for her and therefore co-exist in the same moment, even though at least two and a half months separate each place. Her subsequent transfer to a camp near the town of Dessau in Thuringia and from there to Theresienstadt, from where she would be liberated shortly later in April, plays a subordinate role in her narrative. As historian Diana Greenway puts it,

> personal memory does not always handle interval very well in the process of encoding and storing data, the files of memory are rarely dated. Really strong or traumatic experiences – grief, shock, danger, injury, love – are remembered as if it were yesterday, however long, or short the interval the memory is just as clear. These kinds of memories are measured in terms of emotional intensity rather than by time.[36]

Indeed, events and time itself become compressed in survivors' memories. Varon recalled the march from the *Aeronautica* to the port as a 10-mile trek, when in fact it is a lot shorter, even when processing along the citadel's walls via the Mandraki, as the deportees did.[37]

Survivors in their later interviews (but rarely if at all, in the early post-war affidavits) do recount specific episodes from the horror of the camps and they remember certain persons, such as the hated 'blockova' Magda from the women's barrack in Auschwitz (who was believed to have been killed by fellow prisoners at liberation). But they recalled such events and persons in matter-of-fact terms, contrasting these dark moments by recounting stories of parents and grandparents, youthful pleasures of friendship, of solidarity and liberation. Until the wave of interviews from the late 1980s and early 1990s, their stories were simply 'put aside', surfacing for the main part only within their families and intimate circles, and even then, as we have seen, telling the story was not an easy matter.[38] Their experiences only slowly entered the public domain from that point, as interest in the 'ordinary' victims of the Holocaust gathered pace, partly facilitated by the growing popularity of oral history.[39]

The Hungarian writer and Auschwitz survivor, Imre Kertész, described how the experience of persecution and the camps remained as inextinguishable moments of pain in what he called the 'recesses of nameless, obscure places' of the psyche.[40] This was no less true for the Aegean survivors. Rebecca Capelluto Franco summed up this problem in an interview in 1987, when recollecting the deportation, the violence in Haidari and the train journey to Auschwitz: 'Really, after forty years it's hard [...] Every day, Haidari, the old man (beaten by the guards, AMc), is present, the moment of departure with the trains.'[41] Clara Soriano during her interview in Cape Town fifty years after liberation, at one point breaks down in tears and exclaims, 'What, do you want to know more? Suffering, humiliation, frustration (she sighs). What more? Tell me, what more?' And finally, when asked what memories or feelings she still harboured about the camps, responded, 'What remains? The atrocities I saw, they can't go any more (she pauses). Our misery, our misery. To be humiliated like that for nothing.'[42] Another candid account of this enduring pain can be found in Elisa Franco Hasson's short memoir, *Il Était Une Fois l'Île Des Roses* where she reflects on the murdered children of the *Juderia*.

> Children that I saw being born and growing up, as cute as a button, as sprightly as a button, as beautiful as a button. But they no longer exist, they never grew up. I often see them again, very much alive in my memory, and I suffer deeply. I'll never be able to forget that.[43]

Again drawing on Lawrence Langer's pioneering work on Holocaust memory, remembering the Holocaust was in fact not so much about something past, but a visceral experience with a constant heartbeat. The specific experience of Holocaust constitutes, in Langer's phrase, durational time.[44] As such it is better to think of survivors' encounters with the past not in terms of neatly boxed periods, but as simultaneity of the dis-simultaneous, to reverse the German-Jewish philosopher Ernst Bloch's concept of dis/synchronous time.[45] Thus, the emotional experience of the Holocaust transcends linear time.

Unless organized around a rubric of questions, survivors' memories when narrating events from an earlier life can appear fragmented and sometimes jumbled, rather like the analogy of the unordered photographs Henderson employs when talking about her own memories. Unlike recalling events in response to an interviewer's questioning, unprompted memories lack a coherent narrative. For the fragments of the past do not tell a linear or coherent story that is immediately comprehensible. As such, memory can be mercurial and shifting as the 'photographs' of the past are rearranged to offer a different perspective on the same life. Indeed, a memory, or the recollection of a particular event or experience from the past, is the result of a process in which there is in fact 'audience participation', whether in the guise of interviewer or as listener. Thus, when Lucia Sciarcon Amato at the start of her interview is asked to talk about her life on Rhodes, she goes straight to the deportation only to be called back by her interviewer Rebecca Ziman (the daughter of another Rhodes survivor Giuseppe Coné) to a linear or sequential narrative in which there is a beginning, middle and conclusion.[46] Something similar occurs in *The Longest Journey* when the floodgates of Alberto Israel's memory appear to open and a recollection that has entered his mind, but which is not part of the film's script, threatens to tumble out (like Henderson's 'photographs'). At which point Pezzetti with almost an imperceptible deft movement of his hand on Alberto's elbow turns the pair around and brings the conversation back to the script.[47]

Few survivors interviewed in the 1980s and 1990s refer to daily petty conflicts (other than the expected reference to Orthodox Christians hurling stones at Jewish children during Easter), or indeed, to crimes committed by Jews, even though as we have noted elsewhere in this study, these existed. Instead, survivors were asked by interviewers to 'tell us about life on Rhodes', thus inviting reminiscence rather than factual accuracy. The absence of references to a less comfortable past is as much a function of the interviewee to (naturally) paint their home life in the best of hues, as of the interviewer's wish to create a binary between 'good' and 'evil', thus delineating between before and after July 1944.

But not only is the participation of the interviewer or interlocutor a factor shaping memory. For the way the past is conjured up is also conditioned by lived experiences at the moment of recollection. As historian Zoë Waxman has observed, survivors narrate their experiences in terms of their own categories of comprehension, to which is added the experiences drawn from their subsequent lives.[48] Some survivors like Lucia Sciarcon Amato or Jack Hasson, who post-liberation found happiness in family life, when asked in their interviews about their feelings towards Germans, showed no or little residual anger in their responses. Instead, they sought out the positive aspects of their experiences in the camps, emphasizing solidarity and friendship.

For other survivors, the difficulty of cultural adjustment, unemployment, recurring poor health, and later struggles with obdurate bureaucracies over pensions and justice, all contributed to negatively shaping the lens of the past.

In 1992, nearly five decades after liberation from Theresienstadt, 77-year-old Miru Alcana was unable to find positive words for almost anyone, including her liberators, and her aunt in America who had sponsored her and with whom she quickly fell out. 'I had hard time because I didn't know the language and I couldn't find job. I had hard, very hard time. Beside my family I was not so happy. They didn't – we came – I didn't get along with them because their mentality was different of mine.'[49]

Least of all, and understandably, could Miru reconcile with her German persecutors: when en route to the United States in the summer of 1950, Miru was brought to Bremen to wait for her passage on a troop ship to New York. 'I was in Germany again for three weeks to see those lousy face of Germans. But I never came out from there, from my room. I never going to eat out because I don't want to hear the steps of the Germans and I don't want to hear their voice[s].'[50] Miru's life in the following decades was unsettled and marked by increasingly poor health, lack of money and disappointments with the world around her. This experience distinguished her memories of her earlier life on Rhodes before the dark shadow cast by the deportation and from the troubled path that ensued. As such, life in the *Juderia* could not be anything other than 'beautiful, beautiful.'[51]

*

The physical destruction of the families of the *Juderia* (and its smaller kin community on Kos) created a space for its resurrection within a memory landscape that over time grew estranged from its historically lived experience. The trauma of that destruction was counteracted by a desire to remember the 'good times' of the *Juderia* before the bad times of the deportation, the camps and death. This memory landscape was itself shaped and reshaped by the passage of time and by successive generations as the family story was told and retold. Whereas talking about the experience of the camps was frequently strained because it was difficult to both articulate (frequently those interviewed struggled to find words in English, which was not their mother tongue) and to comprehend, recalling a happier time in the *Juderia* was easier to envisage, and a more pleasant subject to dwell on.[52] When Lucia Franco Garzolini first went to the Congo, and was asked by her family and acquaintances about her experiences in the camps, she 'saw that I was telling some of the story and some people were hardly even listening, or believing in it. [...] Because they were living in a surrounding that was very comfortable and very easy and a lot of them had not seen that [deportation and camps].'[53]

In the decade following liberation, there was still little wider public comprehension of what had taken place against Jews during the war. For example, Alice Tarica as a teenager in Paris in the late 1940s was asked to explain to fellow school pupils the meaning of the number tattooed on her arm. She recalled, 'When my classmates asked me about the number tattooed on my arm, they didn't believe any of my stories. I was seen as a liar, trying to get attention by telling stories. So I decided not to talk about it anymore.'[54] In the two decades after liberation there was also a tangible hostile climate towards Jews that conspired to lower a veil of silence over the recent past. For this reason, Alice was asked by her cousin Huguette to cover up her arm because 'We don't want anyone to know we are Jewish.'[55]

Indeed, the stigma of the tattoo and the incomprehension it elicited partly explains why Stella Levi and her sister Renée cosmetically removed their Auschwitz numbers in 1946, around the time they settled in the United States.[56] Stella in her conversations with the author Michael Frank, later added that she did not wish to be identified as a victim.[57] Nevertheless, when Lucia Sciarcon Amato wanted to remove her tattoo before leaving Italy for Rhodesia (Zimbabwe), 'a doctor in Milan said no, I must leave it on because I must be proud to be alive'.[58] The experience of the camps remained mostly internal to survivors. The embarkation upon a new life meant not so much that their past was hidden or silenced, as merely 'put aside' as survivors coped with adjustment and building new lives for themselves.[59]

Gradually over time, for some survivors this 'putting aside' of the trauma of the deportation and camps passed as life circumstances altered. Virginia Gattegno (b. 1921), the daughter of the headmaster of the Jewish School (see Chapter 3), who with her sister Lea survived the camps, settled after the war in Venice with her husband Ugo Cipolato, a former soldier whom she had known in Rhodes. For four decades she remained silent about her family's deportation and murder in Auschwitz and Mauthausen.[60] She did not even raise it with her sister, 'Because she lived it as well. What was there to say?' But this 'putting aside' was due to another reason. Until the 1980s, she found that 'Many of the generation afterwards preferred not to know'. After being widowed in the mid-1960s, Virginia trained as a teacher and, later still, in the 1980s, she renewed her connection to her own past as age advanced to bear witness. 'Because if the survivors did not speak now, there was a risk of forgetting, of saying it never happened.'[61]

However, the shaping of memory through the acquisition of general knowledge is in evidence in many later testimonies. As we saw above in the examples of Lucia and Alberto, survivors, when asked about their families and early life, were 'helped' by their interlocutors in providing a 'coherent' narrative. The scholar Laura Jockusch, who has examined this phenomenon of memory incursion, refers to this as 'tempering' the survivor's experience with contemporary influences and post-Holocaust knowledge.[62]

Interviews of survivors conducted many years later contributed to creating a quasi-mythical 'lost world' of Jewish Rhodes in a pre-Holocaust past. In the light of their subsequent experiences, and post-Holocaust knowledge, the German occupiers could not be anything other than stereotypical 'Nazis', even though as we have seen, in Rhodes and Kos at least, there had often been cordial and sometimes more intimate relationships between individual German soldiers and Jews. In an interview conducted forty years after the deportation, Clara Menascé (née Gabriel), declared: 'First of all, all the Jews were afraid of the Germans because they had already known about their racism, but we didn't even know about the concentration camps [...] we had a terrible distrust.'[63] Elisa Franco Hasson went further to provide a description of a German officer billeted in her house on Kos that fits a popular crude stereotype of the drunken 'Nazi as sadist'.[64] Casting his mind back to 1943/44, Eliezer Surmani remembered the Germans 'looked vulgar'.[65]

In this regard, there is a big difference between the early factual responses by survivors to questions relating to what happened to them in July 1944, and later interviews where the question 'tell us a little about your life [on Rhodes before the deportation]' invites the survivor to reminisce. In the first decade or so after the war's end, the intention was to gather evidence in order to bring perpetrators to justice. By the 1990s, interviews had shifted the focus from perpetrator to victims' voices.

Over time, and in the absence of archival evidence, an imagined 'island of roses' grew up that presented the good times in Rhodes and Kos before the bad times.[66] In this myth, the 'lost world' of the *Juderia* seen through the lens of nostalgia, is an understandable reflex given the traumatic experience of the deportation and camps. It is a myth that has relied almost exclusively on memories garnered from various interviews or cultivated in memoirs and family biographies since the 1990s. Many of these memories are in fact an admixture of momentary recollection triggered by the interviewer's questions. Sometimes recollections are in fact 'suggested' memories, for example, when an inexperienced or particularly enthusiastic interlocutor suggests to the interviewee the 'correct' answer (usually by stating: 'is it true that …'). The survivor, not wishing to disappoint their interlocutor or to appear 'inauthentic', naturally agrees. Survivors were often eager to present themselves as reliable witnesses and frequently inserted *post facto* knowledge into their recollections.[67]

Frequently, the result was a 'tempered' memory, or a 'mis-memory' to employ the term coined by historian Tony Judt, as survivors sought to project 'authenticity', usually by relating a story where well-known perpetrators such as Joseph Mengele appear in their narrative.[68] Alberto Israel's memoir is a case in point of such 'mis-memory'. There is much to learn from his account about aspects of life in the *Juderia*, or the emotional turmoil of the deportation to Auschwitz and his arrival there, his internment in the camps, and his subsequent liberation. In his recollections, we learn, for instance, about the rare occurrence of mixed marriages between Jews and gentiles, a fact borne out by recent scholarship,[69] or where the family moved to during the aerial bombardments in 1944, or the unceremonious disposal of bodies on the side of the tracks to Auschwitz.[70] But there are also 'facts' remembered with great authority about events that simply did not occur, and others which are in all likelihood based on hearsay.[71]

Not only time and distance blur memories of the past. Life in the post-Holocaust world, with its new and different environments and its challenges, also served to shape the past, or at least, recollections of it. Former president Hizkia Franco's daughter Elisa, recalled in the mid-1990s how those friends who had been closest to her and with whom she had endured the journey through the camps, after liberation, took different paths through life that inevitably changed them. They thus became estranged from each other and only the memory (or a particular memory) of their past life served as the glue to bind them together.

I had the opportunity to meet some of them. But they founded their family there, in an English-speaking environment and, even if common memories still unite us very strongly, the different cultures in which we were immersed and the orientation of our lives, which shaped us differently, separate us now.[72]

For survivors, and later, their children and grandchildren in the Rhodesli Sephardi diaspora, establishing a connection to the *Juderia* served to anchor their own heritage in the Aegean.[73] Thus Giuseppe Gianotti, a second-generation survivor who was brought up as a Catholic in the Italian city of Genoa, 'returned' to Rhodes in 2022 for his bar mitzvah at the age of 60, 'the son of a survivor in the synagogue of his ancestors'.[74]

At various occasions, weddings or Rosh Hashanah or Pesach-Seder, survivors (and later their families) met together in their chosen exile and nostalgically evoked memories of their 'island of roses'. But few survivors journeyed back to Rhodes in the first years after resettling. And those that did, like Elisa Franco Hasson or Alice Tarica, did not remain long after touring their former neighbourhood and paying their respects to the dead at the Jewish cemetery. For the majority, returning to Rhodes meant too many painful memories, and to have walked the streets and lanes of the *Juderia* would have clashed with a remembered idyll. When asked if she returned to Rhodes, Clara Menascé declared, 'No, never, never, too many memories, we left our house .... I did go back in 1966 with my husband because he wanted to visit his parents' graves; we stayed for three days and never again!'[75] There were in Stella Levi's words too many ghosts.[76]

Eventually, the *Juderia* was relived in shared stories whenever survivors got together, but only a particular version of it was remembered, or, better said, remade. The second and third generations were particularly important in this enterprise. For example, Arthur Benveniste, born in 1934 in California, but whose parents had emigrated from Rhodes, uploaded a series of short video films to the popular platform YouTube, showing older members of the Rhodesli diaspora 'demonstrating' Sephardi culture of Jewish Rhodes. In one video, Rebecca Levy talks about the use of the Aruda herb and some women make Turkish coffee while preparing traditional Sephardi dishes of the type they or their mothers would have made.[77] In a second video, the same small group of Rhodesli women sing Ladino songs and dance (we are never told if these women are survivors or émigrés who left Rhodes prior to the deportation, or both). A third video made in 1984, shows Arthur's father, Harry Benveniste (b. 1901) who immigrated to the United States in the 1920s, together with a friend, Edward Amateau (Amato!), reading the Haggadah for Passover-Seder in Ladino.[78] Among other things, this sequence reinforces the depiction of Rhodes' Jews as being particularly pious. While some of its members were no doubt very religious, not all the community shared the same level of piety, as we saw in Chapter 2.

Later generations have been instrumental in the remaking of the *Juderia*. Notable in this remaking has been the Rhodes Jewish Historical Foundation (RJHF) and its museum established in 1997.[79] The RJHF has mobilized through its activism and its blog a lively interest in family heritage, with a particularly strong re-imagining of Sephardi life in which the everyday spoken language of Ladino has a key role.[80]

A visualization of this 'lost world' is the later rendering of the streets of the *Juderia* into Ladino – the vernacular domestic language of the community. In remembering the Jewish quarter, survivors and their progeny refer to the principal thoroughfare in Ladino as 'La Calle Ancha' or 'broad street' (one contemporaneous source writes 'Kay Ancha', not 'la Calle Ancha'). Very often, it is the only street remembered in this way. Nevertheless, the cartographic project of the RJHF recreates the quarter in its entirety, most of it framed in the Ladino vernacular, although the streets formally had Italian names by the 1930s (Map 9.1).[81]

Creating a walking tour for members of the Rhodesli diaspora of where their families once lived in the *Juderia* might be viewed as 'ancestor tourism', which is common to many diaspora communities.[82] But at the same time, the cartography is a work of memory-making, and allows the diaspora to spatially *imagine* the place of their forebears.

However, the cartographic representation of the *Juderia* raises questions in terms of historical verisimilitude when confronted by the archives. The first point to concede is that the area where the Jews of Rhodes were congregated, and this holds for Kos too, was a religio-ethnically diverse space, one shared with Turkish and Greek neighbours, and therefore multilingual, as we saw in Chapter 2. Perhaps they too had their own vernacular names for the streets and alleys that intersected the area. By the later 1930s, it had Italian street and

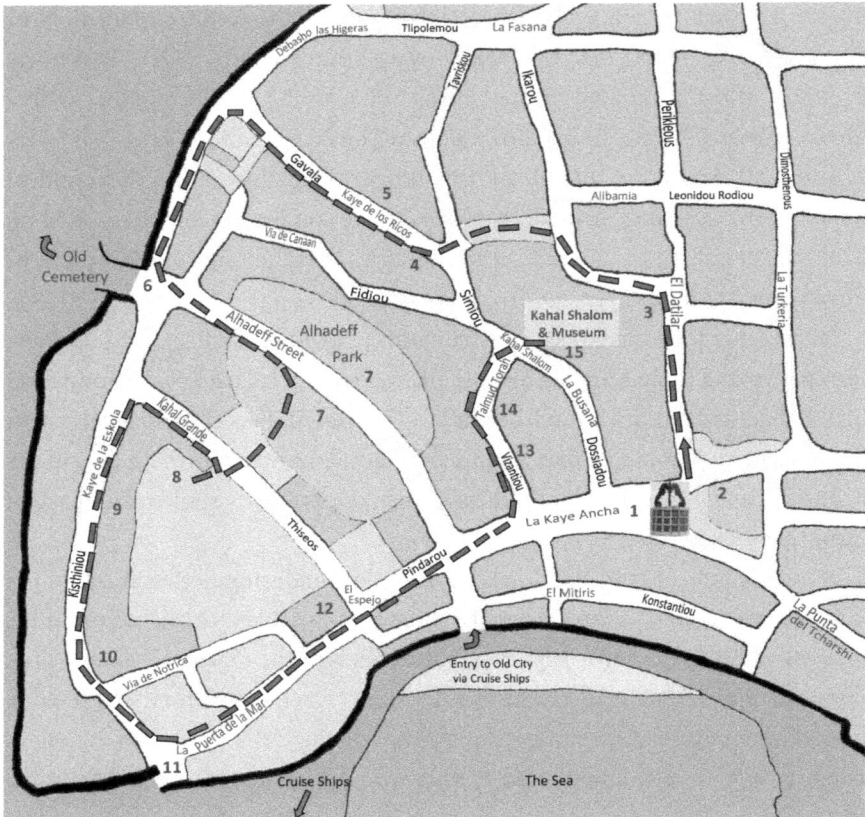

Map 9.1 Walking tour of the *Juderia* (excerpted)

Source: Courtesy Aron Hasson, *A Guidebook to the Jewish Quarter of Rhodes*, Rhodes Jewish Historical Foundation, Los Angeles (2012)

place names. The oft-cited 'Calle Ancha' where many of the festivities of Purim took place, was in those years called Via Principe di Piedmonte (today Plateia Evraion Martyron). The street where the Alliance Israélite Universelle was located, depicted as Calle de la Escola in the RJHF map, in fact at the time was called Via Elia del Bosco (today Kisthiniou). The Calle de los Ricos, where in the interwar years the Kahal Tikkun Hazot synagogue (or was it in fact a yeshiva?) had already vanished, was named by the Italians Via Antonio del Pozzo (today Leontos Gavala, usually abbreviated to Gavala).[83] Thus, official written sources from the mid-twentieth century do not always corroborate the Ladino renderings in the RJHF project, especially after 1938. Moreover, street and place names changed more than once under Italian rule (see Map 2.1 in Chapter 2), and each time without reference to the ethnic-linguistic character of the local community.[84]

It is not nit-picking to raise this issue of naming in memory-making and history; indeed, it goes to the heart of the argument throughout this book, namely that of seeking a greater alignment between archivally grounded lived experience and the memory of it.

However, the foregoing argument does not exclude the everyday usage of Ladino. Many survivors tell us how at home Ladino was commonly spoken, especially by parents and grandparents. Ladino was, therefore, a familiar or intimate tongue, and used between adults and children, such as in 'go to Mr Hasson in the Calle Ancha and buy beans', or greetings among relatives and neighbours. But it played no role in the public sphere. Indeed, by the later 1930s, Italian was the only language allowed in public places, as we saw in the episode with Ezra Hanan in Chapter 3.

As might be expected, the Jews who inhabited the *Juderia* used the Italian names in their communication with the authorities, and never Ladino. In a similar vein, those admitted into the Nazi camp system also gave their addresses in Italian, for example Piazza Piedmonte and not 'La Calle Ancha'. And the same is true of the post-war documentation in which survivors provided information to UNRRA and IRO officials. Nevertheless, Judeo-Spanish was used in correspondence between the representatives of the community and their counterparts from elsewhere, and Solitreo can be found in personal letter-writing, notably, albeit not exclusively, among older Jews. Thus, when Rebecca Alhadeff, born in 1870, wrote to her sons in the Congo, she used Judeo-Spanish, Solitreo, the cursive form of Hebrew common among Sephardi Jews.[85] As did 11-year-old Claire Barki when she wrote to her uncle in America. But we cannot be sure if this written form of Ladino was used exclusively among family and friends. For example, whereas León Leví in postcards sent to his brother Bohor in the Congo, referred to principal locations in Rhodes by their Ladino names, and wrote in Solitreo[86], Roberto Hasson's letters in 1945 to his sister in Brazil to inform her of the tragedy of the deportation and camps used both Judeo-Spanish and French.[87] A variety of language skills, both written and oral, is evident from post-war questionnaires, which survivors had to complete for refugee aid organizations. In these forms, survivors frequently answered they were fluent in Italian as a written and spoken language, Spanish (i.e. Ladino) as a spoken language, followed by French in a few cases and with an understanding of Greek and/or Turkish.[88]

The Jewish community was thus polyglot. But so too was its wider social environment. Jews may have been concentrated within the confines of a few streets and alleyways stretching from today's Dimosthenes/Perikleous to the old town walls,[89] but it was a shared space for much of the first half of the twentieth century. As noted already, Turks and Greeks also lived in this area, and it is unlikely they conversed in Ladino. As Alberto Israel told Marcello Pezzetti in the documentary film *The Longest Journey*, one spoke Italian with Italians, Greek with Greeks, Turkish with Turks, and Ladino at home. Thus, daily social intercourse occurred in a mix of languages, until the later 1930s when only Italian was permitted to be spoken in public spaces (as we saw in the case of Ezra Hanan in Chapter 3). Yet, an ever-expanding body of family histories conveys the Ladino peculiarity of this 'lost world', drawing from and adding to Hasson's rich cartographic landscape. This re-imagining of the *Juderia* as a specifically Ladino space is, in some respects, an interesting territorial appropriation, for it excludes the presence of other ethno-linguistic groups. However, focusing on Ladino exclusivity is in fact a way of forging a sense of community among the sprawling Rhodesli diaspora by emphasizing its Sephardi identity through the mother place.[90]

Similarly, the film *The Longest Journey – The Last Days of the Jews of Rhodes* (Italy, 2013), scripted by Marcello Pezzetti and directed by Ruggero Gabai – falls into the trap of romanticizing the Jewish community before its destruction in 1944. The three protagonists around which the documentary revolves, Alberto Israel, Stella Levi and Sami Modiano, each represent a different aspect of perceived island life: respectively youthful feistiness, romantic culture, childhood rupture with island innocence. Indeed, at one point Sami, sitting on a rock facing the Aegean Sea outside the old walls close to the Jewish quarter, tearfully states, 'It is difficult for you to understand … because we were innocent people. We hadn't committed any crime. Our crime was only that of having been born Jewish.'[91]

As well as films extolling Sephardi life on Rhodes, there has been a tradition of memoir and popular histories depicting Jewish life which lay emphasis on the uniqueness of its culture.[92] Only rarely do these accounts acknowledge that the 'unique' Sephardi culture in the Aegean, whether food or dances or music, was in fact part of a wider Ottoman and/or Levantine culture and not exclusive to Sephardim.[93] Thus, until the opening of the archives, accounts of life in the Jewish quarter of Rhodes were in fact re-imaginings based on snippets of information passed from one generation to the next in the tradition of family lore, or on ego-documents, such as discovered letters and diaries.[94] It is not possible to say if such nostalgic 'communities of memory' among Holocaust survivors and their progeny are any different to that of diaspora communities per se.[95]

The *Juderia* seen through the lens of archival records is absent in diasporic accounts. The explanation for this lies partly in the lack of awareness of the archives. As already mentioned in the preface, the sources documenting Jewish life in the Aegean are scattered across the globe and are in different languages: Turkish for pre-twentieth-century Aegean life; Italian for the period of its dominion over the Dodecanese (1912–47); French for some cultural aspects; English and German for the period of war; Greek (notably for restitution of stolen property post-1945). Transnational sources, such as those of the Jewish World Congress or the International Committee of the Red Cross, or the League of Nations are voluminous and have been digitized but require certain skills to navigate. The compensation claims lodged in the archives of the International Tracing Service are not readily accessible. Finally, it is only in the last decade that the most important sources for documenting Jewish life in Rhodes, namely, the *Carabinieri* files, have surfaced. And these too have now been closed. Circumnavigating these archives is a challenge, even for professional scholars.

As we noted in Chapter 1, Holocaust scholarship on the fate of the Jews in the Eastern Aegean in 1944 came late. Until recently, the story has been told in a clutch of publications for a Rhodesli diaspora audience.[96] These are frequently family histories and are not focused on Jewish life in the era of the Holocaust as part of a wider integrated history. Transplanted to an imagined world of the *Juderia*, the result is a history told in binaries of good/evil – light/ darkness, which we have explored in earlier chapters of this book.

There are, however, at least two considerations we need to reflect on. The first consideration is that when a survivor is remembering or a descendant is writing about their family, understandably, they wish to paint the picture in the best of tones. The deportation of the Aegean Jews to the gas chambers in Auschwitz is deeply engraved in the collective memory of the Rhodes Diaspora and has become part of its collective DNA. It is against this backdrop of the violent rupture that a reification of the community should be understood.

The second consideration is that family narratives of Jewish life in Rhodes, garnered from various sources by descendants of Holocaust survivors or émigrés, are sometimes based on [mis]interpretation of past events, or drawn from hearsay, and frequently are the result of conjecture where there are gaps in the storyline. These are the missing photographs, to again use Henderson's analogy. The result is a sort of 'memory fog' in which vague figures grace the historical landscape.

An example of 'memory fog' is offered by the experience of Henry F. His family narrative was told in terms of flight (emigration) from Rhodes in the late 1930s due to the German occupation. But as we know, there were no Germans on the island before the spring of 1943 (other than as individual tourists), and the German occupation of the island did not commence until 11 September. Did dates and events get jumbled up in telling the story of the family's departure from Rhodes as it passed from one generation to the next? Again, the key to resolving this question was in the *Carabinieri* file on his grandfather that the family did not know existed. The year of emigration was indeed 1939, and leaving appears to have been voluntary, not forced. Henry's grandfather, Hizkia, had a business selling various articles, including imported toy pistols with firing caps, and for which a special licence had to be obtained from the relevant office of the *Carabinieri*. Hence the police file. Henry recalled playing in his grandfather's garage that was stocked with similar toys. 'The story of Grandpa having imported cap guns took me to a memory. I was six years old, and playing in Grandfather's garage, which was a treasure trove of old WW2 uniforms, old appliances and many other vintage treasures. I recall playing Cowboys and Indians with a cap gun in that garage.'[97]

Grandfather Hizkia's file containing around sixty pages, also provided other information (as well as a passport photograph of the family in preparation for departure) that helped fill gaps in the family story. For example, for the first time, Henry was able to discover the exact address where the family had lived. And there was a surprise too. No one in the family, it would appear, ever heard Henry's grandfather talk about his sojourn in the United States at the beginning of the 1920s, before he married. This part of Hizkia's life was absent from the family narrative, which brings us back to Henderson's astute observation cited earlier, how some 'photographs' from the past (i.e. memories) are sometimes simply missing. The example of Henry's family is one of many similar cases where the discovery of documentation in the archives have helped to recast the family story. As Henry says of his own memory of playing in his grandfather's garage, '[I] will always remember this in a different light.'[98]

Before the opening of the archives, and notably before the discovery of the *Carabinieri* files, a picture of life in the *Juderia* was largely reliant on stories passed from one generation to the next. However, not just gaps in the information, or its accuracy, but also the passage of time occluded family memory. Moreover, the complex inter-relations of Jewish kinship in the Aegean added a further complication of confusing identities, as we can see in the following example.

In April 2015, Joseph Elkana (derivation of Alcana) contributed an interesting comment to the blogsite of the Rhodes Jewish Museum.

> Miru Alcana is my relative. I met her before she passed away few years ago. Both of her brothers escaped to Turkey. 1 [*sic*] of the brothers is my grandpa. My family shared their story [of] how they escaped Rhodes and they met Miru again in Israel. This is my family.[99]

The comment is interesting for the reference to Miru's brothers, Giuseppe and Nissim.

There is no record of either brother having escaped to Turkey before the deportation or of being among the few dozen Jews obtaining Turkish papers from the consul, Selahattin Ülkümen, and subsequently removed to Turkey in January 1945. According to the memorial book compiled by Jacqueline and Myriam Benatar, Miru's older brother Giuseppe (b. 1908) died in Mauthausen on 13 February 1945, shortly after arriving there on a 'death march'. Miru's younger brother Nissim perished in Bergen-Belsen in May. The Benatars' findings are corroborated by perpetrator sources, and confirmed by CDEC. Both brothers perished in the Holocaust along with Miru's parents and extended family.[100]

So the Giuseppe identified by Joseph Elkana in his quote cannot possibly have been his grandfather. This then raises the question of how Joseph is related to Miru.

There are eight households with the family name Alcana listed in the Racial Census of 1938. Two of these are single person households, namely that of Abramo Alcana (b. 1864), residing in Sinagoga della Pace 8, and that of Sara Alcana (b. 1867), living in Ammiraglio Bonaldi. There is one household comprising three persons, Isaaco Alcana (whose father was Celebi, below) and his wife Stella Galante, they were aged 27 and 28 respectively and had a baby daughter Matilde at the time of the Racial Census and lived in Sotto I Fichi (another child had been born by the time of the deportation). Another household composed of two persons was that of widow Rachele Alcana and her adult daughter, Stella. They too lived in the heart of the Jewish quarter of the walled town in Via della Turcheria 46 (renamed Via Sigismondo Malatesta). Then there is Miru's family who also lived in Via della Turcheria 20. There were five persons in her family resident at that address, her father Abramo, her mother Jovehet, and her brothers Giuseppe (1908) and Nissim (1917). Miru had a sister, also called Maria who was ten years her senior. She was married to Celebi Hasson and they had two children, a son Giuseppe (b. 1931) and a daughter Johevet (b. 1933). They lived at Turcheria (Sigismondo Malatesta) 24.

That leaves three other Alcana households; that of the widow Regina Alcana, an aunt of Miru, and her five children born between 1917 and 1932 (whose father's family name was Habib), this family also lived in the same street. The large family of Hizkia Alcana and his wife, Estrea Almeleh and their eight children lived next door to Miru's family. Finally, there is the family of Celebi Alcana and his wife, Rachele Behora Soriano and their four children: Nissim (1915), Violetta (1917), Giuseppe (1919) and Salvo (1921), who lived in Via Deodato Gozone 8, some of whom we have encountered in earlier chapters (see Illustration 9.1).

We now know from the *Carabinieri* files and from the 1940 household census that the brothers Joseph Elkana was referring to were in fact Giuseppe and Nissim from this last family. As we saw in Chapter 2, Celebi and Miru's father, Abramo, were brothers. Giuseppe survived the Holocaust but Nissim and his wife Maria Alhadeff and their two daughters, 4-year-old Rachele and 1-year-old Stella, did not. The older brother Salvo(tore) emigrated to Palestine after the census was taken. Giuseppe was not deported for he did indeed escape to Turkey in 1943, at the time of the Italian capitulation.[101]

Illustration 9.1 Celebi Alcana (inset, *c.* 1930s) and sons Salvatore and Giuseppe, with Giuseppe's bride, Esther (main photo, Palestine 1945)

Source: Courtesy family archive of Joseph Elkana

Thus Joseph got Miru's brothers and first cousins confused, which is easily done when tracing the complex kinship networks of Eastern Aegean Jewry so many years later. Families typically named their children after grandparents, and frequently, these cousins were close in age. Joseph's mixing-up of the families shows how easily the absence of hard details can lead to 'memory fog', especially when those who survived to answer questions themselves no longer could recall with clarity.

Possessing the correct information about family is important to descendants such as Henry and Joseph. As we saw above, Henry could re-imagine his own memory of his childhood in the light of the new information found in the *Carabinieri* files. In Joseph's case not only could he now correctly trace his lineage, but the family narrative also took on an even more powerful redemptive quality. Two of Celebi's six children had escaped the Holocaust and at least one of them, Salvatore, was mobilized in the British army's Jewish Brigade. Meanwhile, the story of his grandfather escaping from Rhodes in September 1943 had added a new aspect to the family lore, for the dark shadow of Holocaust is swept away by the story of escape and survival of his grandfather (albeit mistakenly believed to have been the younger brother of Miru).

In a similar vein of triumph over evil, the role of the Turkish consul Selahattim Ülkümen in saving fifty-four Jews from deportation discussed in Chapter 5 has been garnished in the subsequent telling and retelling as it transcended time and subsequent generations. The account of the Turkish consul's confrontation with Burger and his henchman in the *Aeronautica* offers a small triumph in the face of catastrophe in the folklore memory of Jewish Rhodes. And yet, as we saw in Chapter 5, two important and separate pieces of written testimony from the archives add an important dimension to this picture of triumph over adversity.[102]

*

The destruction of the community in the summer of 1944 opened up a space for its remaking in the memory of survivors and for its transformation in the imagination of later generations.

The survivors from the last transport were bearing witness to Jewish life in the Aegean before its destruction in the Holocaust. As the lived experiences of the *Juderia* receded, giving way to a remembered life, and as second and third generations discovered their Aegean identity through family stories, Jewish Rhodes became a *lieu de memoire*, a place of memorialization.[103] In this 'space memory' – detached from the written archive – survivors and following generations distilled the physical and lived 'lost world' into its nostalgic essence, enabling a counterfoil to the dark times of the Holocaust. In the process, it redefined the Jews of Rhodes and Kos, as a 'community of suffering', and as a 'community of survivors', who had populated a harmonious 'lost world'. The landscape of pre-deportation Jewish Rhodes, as refracted through the archive, remained unexplored. It is only when memory and archive are brought into alignment that the 'lost world' as it was lived can be rediscovered. The present study has offered merely an early reconnoitre of this terrain before it became transformed by the Holocaust.

Epilogue

Avec beaucoup de regret nous devons vous avouer que tout l'archive de notre Communauté lors de la déportation en masse de tous les members a été détruit, volé ou pillé et par consequent, aucune documentation n'y existe concernant la tragédie de nos coreligionnaires, sauf un aperçu redigé par nous mêmes exposant les circonstances tragiques de la deportation.

Maurice Soriano, President of the Jewish Community of Rhodes[1]

Maurice Soriano wrote these words in 1978. His remarks pertained to the archive of the community council; its correspondence with external bodies; assorted documents internal to the community; its finances. Soriano was unaware of the rich holdings of the state archive in Rhodes. But its holdings were housed in appalling conditions where they were exposed to the elements; they were poorly curated; the files left uncatalogued according to international standards and conventions, and they were shambolically shelved. With few exceptions, they remained out of bounds to the public.[2] Meanwhile, the richly detailed lives of the Jewish community (and others) in the hundreds of files of the *Carabinieri* archive had yet to surface from their tomb in the cellars of Rhodes police headquarters (formerly the headquarters of the *Carabinieri Reale*).

In lieu of documentation, memory took over.

By the late 1970s, some of the survivors, accompanied by their children, were returning on visits to Rhodes and Kos, touring the neighbourhoods where they had spent their earlier lives. As they did so, they remembered and told stories. We discussed in Chapter 9 how remembering can be complex, invariably incomplete and sometimes embellished with *post facto* knowledge. At the same time, the archives that surfaced a decade ago do not always provide information that might help to cast light on the past. It is thus a moot

point as to how much of the past we can know. This book makes no claim to
a total history of Jewish Rhodes or its destruction at the hands of the Nazis. It
merely opens a door onto a hidden interior. This brings us back to the boy in
the photograph.

In the Preface to this book, we noted that the boy in the doorway was
identified by Miru Alcana as Alessandro Angel. When donating the photograph
to Aron Hasson in March 1998, she was explicitly clear about the persons
in the image: the boy she identified as Alessandro Angel; the kneeling man
behind the boy she identified as 'Galanti'; 'Iju de Yomtov Galanti' (*sic*) – 'the
son of Yomtov Galante'. Miru was certain too, that he was not Isacco Galante,
but his younger brother, Abramo Galante.

At the time of the Race Census there were eight households with the name
Galante, but only one with brothers called Isacco (b. 1914) and Abramo
(b. 1917). Moreover, the father was called Yomtov. They lived at Via di Chenan
7. Abramo married Rosa Cordoval sometime after the Racial Census, and
they, like their parents and sisters, did not survive the Holocaust.[3] The Galante
brothers were not only friends of Isacco Alcana, their older sister Stella was
married to him.

In 1943, Alessandro would have been going on 17 years old, and this means
he cannot be the boy, unless the photograph is in fact wrongly dated. If that is
the case, then it would have to have been taken between 1932 and 1934 at the
latest, when Alessandro would have been between 8 and 10 years old. But if that
is the case, then the kneeling man appears too old to be either of the Galante
brothers. If Miru correctly identified Abramo, then in 1934 he would have been
just 17; in 1943, he would have been 26. The kneeling man in the photograph
also looks in his mid to later twenties. Even if Miru confused the brothers,
Isacco would have been 20 at the first date and 29 in 1943, also about the age
of the kneeling man. Thus, the ascribed dating of the photograph is likely to be
correct: 1943. In 1943 neither of the Galante brothers had children. We do not
know the relationship between the kneeling Abramo Galante and the boy. Nor
do we know the occasion on which the photograph was taken. But we do know
the location of the image, it is the entrance to the shop of Miru's cousin, Isacco
(the 32-year-old son of Celibe and Behora Soriano) at 38 Piazza Principe at the
heart of the *Juderia*. And we know from the records left behind by the Italians
in Rhodes that Isacco was married to Stella Galante.[4]

The boy is wearing a winter coat, and this suggests early 1943 when the winter months are coldest (and wettest). If this is correct, then the photograph coincides with the German order in Salonica (12 February) for Jews from the age of 5 to wear a 10x10 cm star made from yellow cloth next to the heart and across the right shoulder. There was no such requirement anywhere else in Greece or in the islands. The small star pinned to the boy's lapel thus possibly hints at solidarity. We also know that Isacco and his cousin Miru belonged to the Zionist group Menorah. Is this what the image is conveying? Solidarity and Jewish pride?

In the period covered by this book, taking a photograph was not a quotidian or mundane act, unlike today. The Dodecanesian archive has many small images of the Jews of Rhodes and Kos photographed for passports – either as individuals or as families. Commonly, people were often photographed in a studio. Having a photograph taken was reserved for special occasions, usually weddings, or festivities around Pesach, celebrating a gathering with a group of friends or family, whether in the Rodini park or at the beach, or capturing for posterity a group portrait of the community's elite, or indeed, the football club Macabee. Not everyone had a camera; and to develop a film's negative could be costly. Nonetheless, from surviving photographs (and there are many in the *Carabinieri* archive and in private collections) we can discern that possessing a camera was increasingly popular among families of the community.[5]

A photograph's purpose is to create a memory or memento.[6] But with the passage of time, and unless annotated in an album or verso if loose, the occasion and sometimes the identity of the characters can be forgotten or confused. Deciphering the photograph then becomes a question of inductive reasoning. And very often the conclusion is simply a speculation.

There is a boy on the list who *might* be the youngster Miru remembered. This is Leon Angel, the son of Signura Benveniste and Giuseppe Angel, a sailor, who apparently went missing at sea after the family's registration in the Racial Census in the spring of 1939.[7] Giuseppe was not on the deportation list. The family were poor and lived in Via delle Fasana, not far from the Alcanas. We know very little about this family. But we do know that like so many other poor families, Giuseppe as a boy of around 12 years (he was born in 1898) had gone to America but, because in his early life he had suffered from tuberculosis, he returned to Rhodes, in adult life becoming a sailor. His early biography thus bears similarities with that of Samuele Angel. In Rhodes he met Signuru

Benveniste, the daughter of Giacobbe and Sarota Benveniste, and the pair married in 1926, when she was 22 years old. The couple had four children, Sara (b. 1930), Giacomo (b. 1931), Leon (b. 1934) and Bulissa, born after the Racial Census. A grandmother, an uncle and two aunts were also part of the household. They were all deported and killed.

Illustration E.1 Who is the boy in the photograph?

Source: (main photograph) Rhodes Jewish Historical Foundation Archives (inset) Genika Archeia tou Kratous/Archeia Dodekanisou: Rodos, Ι.Δ.Δ. ΕΤΟΣ 1944 ΦΑΚ 293 ΤΜΗΜΑ 1/1

Could Leon be the boy in the photograph (Illustration E.1)? Because the only photograph in the archive of this family is of Giuseppe and not of his wife, nor of his children, we are left to speculate. We might never know the boy's name. Nevertheless, the image loses none of its power or symbolism because of this lack; if anything the mystery of the boy's identity possibly enhances both. For captured in this image is the innocence of a community so incomprehensibly destroyed by the Nazis as Sami Modiano recounted in *The Longest Journey*.

I would like to conclude by reconsidering the image in its totality and to think of it as a metaphor for the Jewish community of Rhodes and Kos. We know some facts about the people framed in the doorway. Miru's memory together with the *Carabinieri* files have allowed us to identify and reconstruct aspects of their lives. But we have also argued that sometimes memory plays tricks, to quote Mary Henderson again. Moreover, the memory as photograph (staying with Henderson's analogy) does not reveal everything when it is obscured, out of focus or blurred. The police files that have proven so valuable in offering up fragments from the past lives of the destroyed community do not always provide everything. And so, there are gaps in our knowledge, and as a result, the story is never complete.[8]

Let's look at the photograph again. In the reproduction that was circulating on the internet, the two figures standing to the rear of the boy and the kneeling man are barely discernible, they are partially obscured. Because the boy is in the foreground, our attention is directed at him, not least too, because of the star pinned to his coat's lapel. The smiling man kneeling next to the boy, whose identity would be unknown to most observers, might be assumed to be a proud relative, perhaps the boy's father. The two partially obscured figures are left out of consideration. The light is shed on the boy and kneeling man. The interior is cast in shadow. That this was the doorway leading into Isacco Alcana's shop at 38 Piazza Principe would not be known to a later generation of casual observers of the photograph (we need to delve into the archives for this information).

In many ways, how we view the image represents the story of the community writ large. Thus, testimony and the archive open the door into the interior of Jewish life. Indeed, we should also keep in mind that what happened in the Aegean is a microcosm of a larger historical event, and can thus reveal features that in a larger canvas might be obscured.[9] There is the immediate surface that we can see; when we probe deeper, aided by testimony or documentation, we begin to see more. Survivors left behind their memories of time and place, and of loved ones and friends. But the way scholars engage with their testimonies changes as methodologies change, sometimes offering up new insights in the process. It is not uncommon for scholars to look at the same document, but to interpret it differently. This produces debate and spurs researchers to look anew at the historical evidence. Eventually, we will discover more about Jewish Rhodes, but not everything. We might better understand its lived experience through different contexts, but not all of it. We can ask questions about its internal relationships and with other groups, and maybe answer some of these questions, but not all of them. And new questions will arise as new sources emerge. A lot of documentation and memories surfaced after Maurice Soriano wrote to Yad Vashem in 1978. There is no reason to think that in future more sources of information will not surface. Perhaps the boy's identity might become known. In this respect, the journey of this last transport from Greece is not over.

Notes

Preface

1   Imre Kertész, *The Holocaust as Culture*, English trans. Thomas Cooper (Seagull Books: London, 2011), p. 59.

2   Götz Aly, *Into the Tunnel: The Brief Life of Marion Samuel, 1931–1943*, trans. Anne Millin (Metropolitan Holt Paperbacks: New York, 2008), German original *Im Tunnel* (S. Fischer Verlag: Frankfurt am Main, 2004), reissued as *Eine von so vielen: Das kurze Leben der Marion Samuel 1931–1943* (Fischer Verlag: Frankfurt/Main, 2011).

3   On children's experiences in war, see Nicholas Stargardt, *Witnesses Of War: Children's Lives Under the Nazis* (Jonathon Cape: London, 2005).

4   Liliana Picciotto Fargon, *Il libro della memoria. Gli ebrei deportati dall'Italia (1943–1945)* (Mursia: Milan, 1991).

5   I was in fact looking in the wrong place. As I subsequently learned, the censuses were archived in the statistics office of the regional government.

6   They were eventually found again, and Professor Hirschon was able to secure funding to digitize the collection, thus making it searchable.

7   The equally interesting question, pursued in the Epilogue to this study, is how he came to be misidentified.

8   Yad Vashem Archives Item ID 10829188/9362, letter 1978.

9   Mauthausen KZ, Häftlings-Personal-Karte Nr 121818, It Jude (Alessandro Angio [*sic*]), www.http://db.yadvashem.org/names/imgPrint.html?imgSrc=http://namesfs.yadvashem.org/.

10 For a succinct overview see EHRI Online Course in Holocaust Studies, ch. 5: Sonja Schilcher 'Historiography' in https://training.ehri-project.eu/historiography.

11 Notably: Gerald Reitlinger, *The Final Solution: The Attempt to Exterminate the Jews of Europe 1939–1945* (Vallentine Mitchell: London, 1953); Raul Hilberg, *The Destruction of the European Jews* (Quadrangle Books: Chicago, 1961); Martin Gilbert, *Holocaust: The Jewish Tragedy* (Fontana: Glasgow, 1987).

12   Steven Bowman, *The Holocaust in Salonika: Eyewitness Accounts* (Sephardic
     House & Bloch Publishing Co.: New York, 2002); idem, *Jewish Resistance
     in Wartime Greece* (Vallentine Mitchell: London, 2006); idem, *The Agony
     of Greek Jews, 1940–1945* (Stanford University Press: Palo Alto, CA, 2009);
     Mark Mazower, *Inside Hitler's Greece: The Experience of Occupation, 1941–44*
     (Yale University Press: New Haven, CT, 1993); idem, *Salonica, City of Ghosts:
     Christians, Muslims and Jews, 1430–1950* (Harper Collins: London, 2004);
     Kathleen Fleming, *Greece: A Jewish History* (Princeton University Press:
     Princeton, 2008); Rena Molho, *Der Holocaust der griechischen Juden: Studien zur
     Geschichte und Erinnerung* translated Lulu Bail (J.H. Dietz: Berlin, 2016).
13   Hizkia Franco, *The Jewish Martyrs of Rhodes and Cos* (Harper Collins:
     Harare, Zimbabwe, 1994; orig. written in 1947 in French and translated by
     his son); Esther Fintz Menascé, *Gli ebrei a Rodi. Storia di un'antica comunità
     annientata dai* nazisti (Guerini e Associate: Milan, 2005); Esther Fintz Menascé,
     *Buio Nell'Isola del Sole: Rodi 1943–1945 I due volti di una tragedia quasi di
     metenticato: il martiro dell'ammarigalio Campioni* (Giuntina: Firenze, 2005).
14   Filippo Marco Espinoza, 'Fare gli Italiani dell'Egeo: Il Dodecaneso dall'Impero
     ottoman all'Impero del fascismo', Universita degli Studi Trento Scuola di
     Dottorato in Studi Umanistici (XXIX ciclo) Tesi di Dottorato (unpublished
     doctoral dissertation, 2017); Valerie McGuire, *Italy's Sea: Empire and Nation in
     the Mediterranean, 1895–1945* (Liverpool University Press: Liverpool, 2020);
     Andreas Guidi, *Generations of Empire. Youth from Ottoman to Italian Rule in the
     Mediterranean* (University of Toronto Press: Toronto, 2022); Marco Clementi,
     Storia della comunità ebraica di Rodi (1912–1947) (tab edizioni: Rome, 2022).
15   At the time of writing, public access to the *Carabinieri* archive has been
     restricted at the behest of the director of General State Archives of Greece
     (GAK) and the Greek minister of Education and Culture.
16   Saul Friedländer, 'An Integrated History of the Holocaust, Some Methodological
     Challenges', in Dan Stone (ed.), *The Holocaust and Historical Methodology*
     (Berghahn Books: New York, Oxford, 2012), p. 181; Guidi, *Generations of
     Empire*, p. 189.
17   Anthony McElligott, 'The Deportation of the Jews of Rhodes, 1944: An
     Integrated History', in Giorgos Antoniou and A. Dirk Moses (eds.), *The
     Holocaust In Greece* (Cambridge University Press: Cambridge, 2018), pp.
     58; Guidi, *Generations of Empire*, p. 85. A previous study had used the same
     methodological approach without referring to it as 'integrated history', Anthony
     McElligott, *Contested City: Municipal Politics and the Rise of Nazism in Altona,
     1917–1937* (University of Michigan Press: Ann Arbor, MI, 1997).

18   Anthony McElligott, 'Reflections on the *Juderia*: Remembering, Memory-
       making and History: Re-imagining the "Lost World" of Jewish Rhodes', in
       Aron Rodrigue and Valerie McGuire (eds.), *Italian Fascism in Rhodes and
       Dodecanese, 1923–1945* (Routledge: London and New York, 2024). For an
       uncritical treatment of Rhodes as the 'lost world' see Nathan Shachar, *Lost
       World of Rhodes: Greeks, Italians, Jews & Turks Between Tradition and Modernity*
       (University of Sussex Press: Brighton, 2013).
19   Two recent examples of the rich rewards reaped by adopting the former
       approach are the micro-studies by Mary Fulbrook and Omer Bartov: Mary
       Fulbrook, *A Small Town Near Auschwitz: Ordinary Nazis and the Holocaust*
       (Oxford University Press: Oxford, 2012); Omer Bartov, *Anatomy of a Genocide:
       The Life and Death of a Town Called Buczacz* (Simon and Schuster: New York,
       London, Toronto, Sydney, New Delhi, 2018). On the approach, see the essays in
       Claire Zalc and Tal Bruttmann, *Microhistories of the Holocaust* (Berghahn Books:
       New York & Oxford, 2017).
20   In conversations with the author in the 1980s.
21   United States Holocaust Memorial Museum, Exhibition Text: *The Holocaust in
       Greece*, pp. 13–14, https://www.ushmm.org/m/pdfs/20130305-holocaust-in-
       greece.pdf. On the benefits of micro-history see the classic essay by the Italian
       historian Carlo Ginzburg, 'Microhistory: Two or Three Things That I know
       about It', in *Critical Inquiry*, Vol. 20, No. 1 (Autumn 1993), pp. 10–35.
22   Saul Friedländer, *Nazi Germany and the Jews: The Years of Persecution,
       1933–1939* (HarperCollins: New York, 1997), and *The Years of Extermination:
       Nazi Germany and the Jews* (HarperCollins: New York, 2007).
23   Letter to the *International New York Times*, 1 April 2016.
24   Richard J. Evans, *In Defence of History* (Granta Books: London, 1997). Ian
       Kershaw, *The Nazi Dictatorship: Problems and Perspectives of Interpretation* 4th
       edition (Edward Arnold: London, 2000), p. 170 (pp. 152–153 in original edition)
       for his final comment on the moral role of the historian.

Chapter 1

1   *Die Verfolgung und Ermordung der europäischen Juden durch das
      nationalsozialistische Deutschland 1933–1945, Band 14: Besetztes Südosteuropa
      und Italien*, prepared by Sara Berger, Erwin Lewin, Sanela Schmid and Maria
      Vassilikou (De Gruyter: Oldenbourg, Boston/Berlin, 2017). Hereafter cited as
      VEJ Vol. 14.

2 Kathleen Fleming, *Greece – A Jewish History* (Princeton University Press: Princeton, NJ, 2010); Steven Bowman, *The Agony of Greek Jews, 1940–1945* (Stanford Studies in Jewish History and Culture) (Stanford University Press: Stanford, CA, 2009); Chryssoula Kambas and Marilisa Mitsou (eds.), *Die Okkupation Griechenlands im Zweiten Weltkrieg. Griechische und deutsche Erinnerungskultur* (Böhlau: Köln, Wien, Weimar, 2015); Rena Mohlo, *Der Holocaust der griechischen Juden: Studien zur Geschichte und Erinnerung*, trans. Lulu Bail (J.H. Dietz: Berlin, 2016). An exception is Martin Gilbert, *The Holocaust: The Human Tragedy* (Fontana Press: London, 1987), ch. 36, but its information on Rhodes and Kos is based largely on a single interview with a survivor and the post-war account by the former president of the Jewish Community of Rhodes Hizkia Franco and contains factual errors. See now: Valerie McGuire, 'The Jewish Communities of Rhodes and Kos: A transnational community between Ottoman Collapse and the Italian Empire', *Αρχειοτάξιο/Archeiotaxio Journal of Contemporary Social History Archives*, Vol. 19 (2017), pp. 141–159 (in Greek); Anthony McElligott, 'The Deportation of the Jews of Rhodes: An Integrated History', in Giorgos Antoniou and A. Dirk Moses (eds.), *The Holocaust in Greece* (Cambridge University Press: Cambridge, 2018), pp. 58–86. In Italian, Marco Clementi/Eirini Toliou, *Gli ultimi ebrei di Rodi. Leggi razziali e deportazioni nel Dodecaneso italiano (1938–1948)* (Derive Approdi: Rome, 2015), and Marco Clementi, *Storia della comunità ebraica di Rodi (1912–1947)* (tab edizioni: Rome, 2022).

For Corfu, see in part, Isaac Jack Lévy, with Rosemary Zumwalt, *The Sephardim in the Holocaust. A Forgotten People* (University of Alabama Press: Tuscaloosa, AL, 2020). For Crete, https://www.etz-hayyim-hania.org/the-jews-of-crete/the-history-of-the-jews-of-crete/.

3 Saul Friedländer, *The Years of Extermination: Nazi Germany and the Jews, 1939–1945* (Weidenfeld & Nicolson: London, 2007), p. 613. The small community of Cretan Jews was boarded on the Greek tanker, *Tanais*, that was subsequently sunk off Pireaus by a British submarine.

4 Bundesarchiv-Berlin Lichterfelde (hereafter: Barch-B) NS19/1577, Bl. 2–3, Himmler to Kaltenbrunner noting that he had instructed his chief statistician Richard Korherr to prepare a report for 'die Endlösung der europäischen Judenfrage', 1 January 1943. The sixteen-page report has subsequently become known as the 'Korherr Bericht', a copy can be found in NS19/1570, Bl. 12–28. See also Friedländer, *Nazi Germany and the Jews*, pp. 480–483.

5 TNA GFM 33/2518, Der Chef der Sicherheitspolizei und des SD IV B 4 – 2427/42g (1148) an das Auswärtige Amt, Berlin, 25. Januar 1943,

Betrifft: Massnahmen gegen Juden in Griechenland. See also the correspondence from 1942 between the German Foreign Office and the Security Police in the same file.

6   Eckart Conze, Norbert Frei, Peter Hayes and Moshe Zimmermann, *Das Amt und die Vergangenheit. Deutsche Diplomaten im Dritten Reich und in der Bundesrepublik* (Siedler: Munich, 2010), pp. 197–199, 252–259.

7   Reprinted in Norbert Frei and Wulf Kantsteiner (eds.), *Den Holocaust erzählen. Historiographie zwischen wissenschaftlicher Empirie und narrative Kreativität* (Wallstein Verlag: Essen, 2013), pp. 11–112. See the next chapter for a profile of the Jewish community.

8   Ian Kershaw, '"Working towards the Führer". Reflections on the Nature of the Hitler Dictatorship', *Contemporary European History*, Vol. 2, No. 2 (July 1993), pp. 103–118. Hans Safrian, *Eichmann's Men* translated by Ute Stargardt (Cambridge University Press: Cambridge, 2010).

9   Hans Mommsen, 'Cumulative Radicalisation and Progressive Self-destruction as Structural Determinants of the Nazi Dictatorship', in Ian Kershaw and Moshe Lewin (eds.), *Stalinism and Nazism Dictatorships in Comparison* (Cambridge University Press: Cambridge, 1997), pp. 75–87. Originally published as 'Der Nationalsozialismus. Kumulative Radikalisierung und Selbstzerstörung des Regimes' ('National Socialism: Cumulative Radicalization and the Regime's Self-Destruction'), in *Meyers Enzyklopädisches Lexikon* (1976). Donald Bloxham, 'Europe, the Final Solution and the Dynamics of Intent', *Patterns of Prejudice*, Vol. 44, No. 4 (2010), pp. 317–335. Richard Bessel, 'Functionalists vs. Intentionalists: the Debate Twenty Years on or Whatever Happened to Functionalism and Inentionalism?', *German Studies Review*, Vol. 26, No. 1 (Feb. 2003), pp. 15–20. See also, Mark Mazower, *Salonica, City of Ghosts: Christians, Muslims and Jews 1430–1950* (Harper Perennial: London, New York, Toronto and Sydney, 2004), pp. 303, 364.

10 As evidenced by Hitler's political testament written shortly before his suicide can be accessed at http://www.jewishvirtuallibrary.org/hitler-s-political-testament-april-1945. For an account of Hitler's 'last will and testament' see: Greg Bradsher, 'Hitler's Final Words. His Political Testament, Personal Will, and Marriage Certificate: From the Bunker in Berlin to the National Archives', available at https://www.archives.gov/files/publications/prologue/2015/spring/hitler-will.pdf. See also Nathan Eck, 'Hitler's Political Testament', http://www.yadvashem.org/yv/pdf-drupal/en/eichmann-trial/hitlers_political_testament.pdf.

11 Hans Mommsen, 'Hitlers Stellung im nationalsozialistischen Herrschaftssystem', in Gerhard Hirschfeld and Lothar Kettenacker (eds.), *Der Führerstaat. Mythos*

und Realität (Klett-Cotta: Stuttgart, 1981), pp. 43–72; idem, 'Die Realisierung des Utopischen: Die "Endlösung der Judenfrage" im Dritten Reich', *Geschichte und Gesellschaft*, Vol. 9 (1983), pp. 381–420 and in English '"The Realization of the Unthinkable" The "Final Solution of the Jewish Question in the Third Reich"', in Gerhard Hirschfeld (ed.), *The Policies of Genocide: Jews and Soviet Prisoners of War in Nazi Germany* (Unwin Hyman: London, 1986), pp. 93–144. And contrary to Mommsen, Gerald L. Weinberg, *Germany, Hitler, and World War II: Essays in Modern German and World History* (Cambridge University Press: Cambridge and New York. 1995), ch. 17.

12   Samuel M. Strong, 'The Future of the Jewish Populations of Europe', *Journal of Negro Education*, Vol. 10, No. 3, Racial Minorities and the Present International Crisis (Jul. 1941), p. 489. Strong's usage of 'holocaust' with a lower case was typical of the era in which he was writing. 'Holocaust' in upper case only emerged post-1945, and indeed did not gain wider currency in the Anglophone world until the 1960s, Peter Novick, *The Holocaust in American Life* (Houghton Mifflin: Boston and New York, 2000 (1999)), pp. 133–134, 144–145, 171–203. On post-First World War violence, see Robert Gerwarth and John Horne (eds.), *War in Peace: Paramilitary Violence in Europe after the Great War* (Oxford University Press: Oxford, 2012), and Robert Gerwarth, *The Vanquished. Why the First World War Failed to End* (Farrar, Straus and Giroux: New York, 2016). The classic text by Eric Hobsbawm, *The Age of Extremes. The Short Twentieth Century 1914–1991* (Penguin Random House: London, 1994), is largely silent on the Holocaust.

13   Raphael Lemkin, *Axis Rule in Occupied Europe: Laws of Occupation, Analysis of Government, Proposals for Redress* (Lawbook Exchange: Clark, NJ, 1943).

14   Steven Bowman, 'Jews', in Richard Clogg (ed.), *Minorities in Greece: Aspects of a Plural Society* (C. Hurst & Co.: London, 2002), pp. 64–80.

15   Mazower, *Salonica, City of Ghosts*, pp. 303, 364.

16   The World Jewish Congress Collection, Mss.Coll. 361, Box C265, File 5, The Central Board of Jewish Communities of Greece, 'List showing the losses of the Jewish population of Greece from the German persecutions of 1943 and 1944'. See the tables in Χρονίκα, April 1984, p. 3, and Steven Bowman, 'The Jews in Wartime Greece', *Jewish Social Studies*, Vol. 48, No. 1 (Winter 1986), pp. 45–62, here: 50–51, Table: Population of Jews in Greece 1904–1973.

17   Avraham Galante, *Histoire des Juifs de Turquie, Tome VII: 'Histoire des Juifs de Rhodes, Chio, Cos'* (Fratelli Haim: Istanbul, 1935); Renée Hirschon, 'The Jews of Rhodes: The Decline and Extinction of an Ancient Community', in M. Rozen

(ed.), *The Last Ottoman Century and Beyond: The Jews in Turkey and the Balkans* (Tel Aviv University: Tel Aviv, 2002), pp. 291–307.

18 Heinz Richter, *Griechenland im Zweiten Weltkrieg 1939–1941* 2nd expanded edition (Harrossowitz: Wiesbaden, 2015).

19 See also, *Dodecanese Handbook, Part 1: People and Administration* (HMSO, London, November 1943), Map 6.

20 Consisting of Rhodes, Kos, Leros, Samos, Scarpanto, Stampalia, Calino, Simi, Piscopi, Nisiro, Levita Alimnia. Luca Pignataro, *Il Dodecaneso italiano 1912–1947. 1: l'Occupazione Iniziale 1912–1922*, (Edizione Solfanelli: Chieti, 2011), p. 18.

21 TNA GFM 33/2518, (German Foreign Office Inl. Ii geheim, Bundle 55/2: Juden in Griechenland, Heft II, 1943–1944), LR v. Thadden Inl. II 1752 g Geheim an Gruppenleiter Inl. II, Dg. Pol.(report on the incident). In his own written statement of 21 June, Wisliceny pointed out that this incident referred to his deputy Alois Brunner who, with a detachment of *Sicherheitsdienst* and *Geheime Feldpolizei*, had flown to the port of Piraeus (German zone) in order to arrest Jews, but they found none because they had taken refuge in Athens, which was in the Italian zone. Ibid, Abschrift: Sonderkommando der Sicherheitspolizei für Judenangelegenheiten Saloniki-Ägäis, An das Deutsche Generalkonsulat Saloniki z.Hd.v.Herren Gneeralkonsul Dr Schönberg, 21.6.43.

22 *VEJ* Vol. 14, pp. 15–16, 50, 72–73, 483 fn. 8. Steven F. Sage, 'Bulgaria', *USHMM Encyclopedia*, Vol. 3, pp. 2–14.

23 Wiener Library, Nuremberg War Crimes Trial: Documents (hereafter: WL/NWCTD) 1655/1979 [NG4960], Luther to von Ribbentrop, 20 Feb. 1942; ibid, 1655/2134 [NG2198], Klingenfuss to Eichmann, 20 Aug. 1942. The other three key officials involved in the deportation of Jews were Karl Rademacher, Herbert Müller, Fritz-Gebhardt von Hahn, Christopher Browning, Susannah Heschel Michael R. Marrus, Milton Shain (eds.), *Holocaust Scholarship: Personal Trajectories and Professional Interpretations* (Palgrave Macmillan: London and New York, 2015), p. 52.

24 WL/NWCTD, 1655/1862, Telegram, Killinger to German Foreign Office reporting Marshall Antonescu's consent for deportation of Romanian Jews, 13 Nov. 1941; 1655/1971, Luther to von Weizsäcker, 11 Feb. 1942; Raul Hilberg, *Die Vernichtung der europäischen Juden* (Fischer Verlag: Frankfurt am Main, 1990 [1961]), pp. 810–811, and pp. 794–859 *passim*. Frederick B. Chary, *The Bulgarian Jews and The Final Solution, 1940–1944* (University of Pittsburgh Press: Pittsburgh, PA, 1972), p. 76.

25 Hilberg, *Die Vernichtung*, p. 727.

26 Ibid. Walter Manoschek, '*Serbien ist Judenfrei*'. *Militärische Besatzungspolitik und Judenvernichtung in Serbien 1941/42* (Oldenbourg Verlag: Munich, 1991), p. 195.

27 *VEJ* Vol. 14, Doc. 130. 'The purpose of the mission was to check on the spot whether the problem of the 8,000 Jewish agitators, whose deportation was demanded by the legation, could not be settled on the spot. … During the discussion, it emerged that from the outset it was not a question of 8,000 Jews, but only about 4,000, of whom, moreover, only 3,500 could be shot. The remaining 500 were needed by the state police and the health and order service to maintain the ghetto that was to be built.' These male Jews were shot by the time Rademacher made his report. A further 20,000 Jews comprising the elderly, women, and children, as well as 1500 Gypsies (whose men were also to be killed) were to be confined in the ghetto mentioned by Rademacher in the report.

28 Figures for Holocaust deaths in Greece, indeed for much of the Balkans, are problematic in that they are frequently compiled from different sources using different methods of calculation, see for instance the data cited by Hagen Fleischer, 'Griechenland', in Benz, *Dimension*, pp. 272–273. Mazower, *Salonica, City of Ghosts*, pp. 421–442. See now, Mark Levene, '"The Bulgarians Were the Worst!" Reconsidering the Holocaust in Salonika Within a Regional History of Mass Violence', in Antoniou and Moses (eds.), *The Holocaust in Greece*, pp. 36–57.

29 Liliana Picciotto Fargion, *Il libro della memoria. Gli Ebrei deportati dall'Italia (1943–1945)* (Mursia: Milano, 1991). Mark Mazower, *Inside Hitler's Greece: The Experience of Occupation 1941–44* (Yale University Press: New Haven and London, 1993).

30 Michael Wildt, *An Uncompromising Generation: The Leadership of the Reich Main Security Office*, trans. Tom Lampert, *The George L. Mosse Series in Modern European Cultural and Intellectual History* (University of Wisconsin Press: Madison Wisconsin, 2010).

31 *Dodecanese Handbook*, p. 7, Table: Population Statistics.

32 Joseph S. Roucek, 'The Legal Aspects of Sovereignty Over the Dodecanese', *The American Journal of International Law*, Vol. 38, No. 4 (Oct 1944), pp. 701–706, here: 705.

33 Karen Barkey and George Gavrilis, 'The Ottoman Millet System: Non-Territorial Autonomy and its Contemporary Legacy', *Ethnopolitics*, Vol. 15, No. 1 (2016), pp. 24–42, DOI: 10.1080/17449057.2015.1101845. Joseph R. Hacker, 'Jews in the Ottoman Empire (1580–1839)', *Cambridge History of Judaism. Volume Seven: The Early Modern Period* edited by Jonathon Karp, Adam Sutcliffe (Cambridge University Press: Cambridge, 2017), pp. 831–863.

34	See above all: Mia Fuller, *Moderns Abroad. Architecture, Cities and Italian Imperialism* (Routledge: London and New York, 2007).

35	Treaty of Peace with Italy, Part I, p. 318, 'Section V – Greece (Special Clause), Article 14', https://www.loc.gov/law/help/us-treaties/bevans/m-ust000004-0311.pdf. The Greek administration added little of architectural value after 1947, and many of the fine buildings left by both Ottoman and Italian occupiers have been left to decay.

36	*Dodecanese Handbook*, p. 19.

37	Richard Bosworth, *Italy: The Least of the Great Powers. Italian Foreign Policy before the First World War* (Cambridge University Press: Cambridge, 2005).

38	TNA FO 195/2486 (British Embassy, Angora), Telegram No. 1604 from Mr Helm, Ankara to Foreign Office, 16 September 1944, 'Top Secret'. Ibid, Telegram No. 1213 from Foreign Office to Mr Helm Ankara, 15 September 1944.

39	GAKR Ι.Δ.Δ ΕΤΟΣ 1944-45, ΦΑΚ 18, ΤΜΗΝΑ 11L.

40	Dr Skevos Zervos and Paris Roussos, *White Book: The Dodecanese. Resolutions and Documents Concerning the Dodecanese 1912–1919*, Second Edition with a Map of the Dodecanese (London, n.d. [1919]).

41	For instance, the Royal Geographical Society invited Zervos and Venizelos to address its annual meeting in March 1920. Reported in J. L. Myres, 'The Dodecanese I & II', in *The Geographical Journal*, Vol. 56, Nos. 5 & 6 (Nov. and Dec. 1920), pp. 329–347, 425–441.

42	Cited in Anthony McElligott, 'Dr Skevos Zervos and Greek Irredentism in the Dodecanese Islands: *Enosis* and Great Power Rivalry, 1912–1947', paper read to Security Studies Programme, Department of Mediterranean Studies, University of the Aegean, 4 May 2017.

43	Luca Pignataro, *Il Dodecaneso Italiano 1912–1947. Vol. 2: Il Governo Di Mario Lago 1923–1936* (Edizione Solfanelli: Chieti, 2011). McGuire, *Italy's Sea*, ch. 3: 'Belonging in the Archipelago: Nation, Race, and Citizenship'. See Filippo Espinoza, 'An Italian Nationality for the Levant: Citizenship in the Aegean from the Ottoman to the Fascist Empire (1912–1936)', in S. Berhe and O. De Napoli (eds.), *Citizens and Subjects of the Italian Colonies: Legal Constructions and Social Practices 1882–1943* (Routledge: New York, 2021), pp. 109–130, who argues that Italianization was preparatory to incorporating the Dodecanese as a province into metropolitan Italy. Davide Rodogno, *Fascism's European Empire: Italian Occupation During the Second World War* (Cambridge University Press: Cambridge, 2008), pp. 68–83.

44   Documented in TNA FO286/703, FO286/927, FO286/993, FO286/1024. Filippo
     Marco Espinoza, 'Fare gli Italiani dell'Egeo: Il Dodecaneso dall'Impero ottomano
     all'Impero del fascismo' (PhD Thesis, Università degli Studi di Trento Scuola di
     Dottorato in Studi Umanistici (XXIX ciclo) 2017), ch. 2 especially.
45   *Dodecanese Handbook*, p. 5.
46   On Lago's relations with Jews, see Pignataro, *Il Governo Di Mario Lago*, pp.
     523–547.
47   TNA 371/24963 Pag. 215 Secret: [R6937 G, 10 August 1940], E. R. Warner,
     report (untitled), Part II Italian Rule in the Dodecanese, para. 3.
48   Esther Fintz Menascé, *Buio Nell'Isola del Sole: Rodi 1943–1945 I due volti di una
     tragedia quasi di metenticato: il martiro dell'ammarigalio Campioni* (Giuntina:
     Firenze, 2005). See in general, Davide Rodogno, *Fascism's European Empire:
     Italian Occupation during the Second World War*, trans. Adrian Belton (New
     Studies in European History) (Cambridge University Press: Cambridge, 2006),
     pp. 63–83.
49   TNA FO/371/24963, for detail.
50   In the event, a rump force remained in Rhodes after it became logistically
     impossible to adhere to the timetable for their withdrawal.
51   Laurence Rees, *Auschwitz. The Nazis and the 'Final Solution'* (BBC Books:
     London, 2005), p. 298. Richard Breitman, *The Architect of Genocide: Himmler
     and the Final Solution* (Brandeis University Press: Chicago, 1991). Mark
     Mazower, *Hitler's Empire: How the Nazis Ruled Europe* (Penguin Press: New York
     & London, 2008), ch. 14.
52   Not least the revival of the notorious case of 'blood libel' from 1840. Olga
     Borovaya, 'The Rhodes Blood Libel of 1840: Episode in the History of Ottoman
     Reforms', *Jewish Social Studies*, Vol. 26, No. 3 (Autumn 2021), p. 35; Rees,
     Auschwitz, pp. 39, 63; Marc D. Angel, *The Jews of Rhodes: The History of a
     Sephardic Community* (Sepher-Hermon Press Inc.: New York, 1978), p. 37.
53   TNA FO 371/24963, Warner, report, Part II, para. 3.
54   Pierre Sintès, *Chasing the Past: Geopolitics of Memory on the Margins of Modern
     Greece* (Liverpool University Press: Liverpool, 2019).

Chapter 2

1   Alberto Israël, *Je ne vous ai pas oubliés*. Propos recueillis par Stipan Bosnjak with
    a preface by Simone Veil (Editions de l'institut Sepharade Européen: Brussels,
    2008), pp. 31–32.

2   For a good general introduction, Angel, *The Jews of Rhodes*. For general history, Paloma Díaz-Mas, *Sephardim: The Jews of Spain*, edited and translated by George H. Zucker (University of Chicago Press: Chicago, 1992).

3   Foreign Office, *Islands of the Northern and Eastern Aegean* (HMSO: London, 1920), p. 11.

4   See in Italian and based largely on the same sources but with a different approach, Marco Clementi, *Storia della comunità ebraica di Rodi (1912–1947)* (tab edizioni: Rome, 2022).

5   Sometimes also referred to as simply as 'Romiote'. Χρ. Ι., Παπαχριστοδούλου *Ιστορία Της Ρόδου Από Τους Προϊστορικούς Χρόνους Έως Την Ενσωμάτωση Της Δωδεκανήσου* (1948) (Παλαιοβιβλιοπωλείο: Αθήναι, 1972), pp. 401, 420.

6   Michael N. Triantafillou, *From Halicarnassus (Bodrum) to the Islands of the Dodecanese (Από την Αλικαρνασσό στα Δωδεκανησσα)* Vol. 3 (Rhodes, 2020), ch. 2. I am grateful to the author for making available this translated copy of the original Greek chapter.

7   Renée Hirschon, 'Reconstructing Life in the Old City 1939–44: The Value of the Italian Household Archive', contribution to The Deportation of the Jews of Rhodes & Cos: 1944–2014 A Commemorative International Symposium on the Holocaust in the Aegean, Rhodes, 22–24 July 2014. See also, Esther Benbassa and Aron Rodrigue, *Sephardi Jewry. A History of the Judeo-Spanish Community, 14th–20th Centuries* (University of California Press: Berkeley and Los Angeles, 2000), p. 39 and *passim*.

8   Luca Pignataro, *Il Dodecaneso Italiano 1912–1947: Vol. III, De Vecchi, Guerra e Dooguerra 1936–1947/50* (Edizioni Solfanelli: Chieti, 2018), p. 107. Pignataro claims the census of 1922 is unreliable and artificial; that the census of 1931 is imprecise; he accepts the 1936 census as more reliable.

9   British sources estimated a Jewish population of between 2,500 and 3,000 in 1920. Foreign Office, *Northern and Eastern Aegean*, pp. 11, 24.

10 More census information in Filippo Espinoza, 'Una cittadinanza imperial basata sul consenso: il caso delle isole italiane dell'Egeo (1924–1940)', in S. Lorozini and S.A. Bellezza (eds.), *Sudditi o cittadini? L'evoluzione delle appartenenze imperiali nella Prima guerra mondiale* (Vielle: Roma, 2018), pp. 189–204.

11 *Ke Haber Newsletter*, The Rhodes Historical Foundation, California, 2011, p. 9.

12 *Dodecanese Handbook* (HMSO: London, 1943), Part 1 People and Administration, p. 7 (Population Statistics), put the total populations of Rhodes and Kos in 1933 respectively at: 56,332 and 21,696.

13 Genika Archia tou Kratous/Archia Dodekanisou Rhodes (hereafter: GAKR) ΙΔΔ ΦΑΚ 1036 Π 1931 Censimento Della Populazione (1922), Governo delle

Isole Italiano dell'Egeo Populazione Complessiva del Possedimento (Dati desunti dal censimento numerico dell'anni 1922). At this census the total population of the island was given as 41,571 of which Greek Orthodox numbered 29,988 and 7,545 were Turks; however, in Rhodes town there were 5,654 Greeks and 6,461 Turks. Meanwhile, the population on Kos was as follows: 3,681 Greeks, 3,717 Turks, 31 Italians and 66 Jews. The original cards of the Racial Census 1938 can be found in the archive of the Jewish Community of Rhodes. I am grateful to Carmen Cohen for kindly allowing access to these. The later (1940) 'household' census originally located at the mayoralty offices in Rhodes has been digitized by Professor Renée Hirschon, St Peter's College, Oxford. I am grateful to Professor Hirschon for sharing her research.

14 I deal with their number in more detail in Chapter 4. The *leggi razziali* introduced in the Regio Decreto 17 Novembre 1938 Nr 1728. Joshua D. Zimmerman, *Jews in Italy Under Fascist and Nazi Rule, 1922–1945* (Cambridge University Press: Cambridge, 2005), chapter 8; Philip Morgan, *Italian Fascism, 1915–1945*, 2nd edition (Palgrave Macmillan: New York & London, 2004), pp. 193–204.

15 *Pinkus ha Kehillot, Encyclopedia of Jewish Communities from their Foundation till after the Holocaust: Greece*, ed. Bracha Rivlin (Jerusalem: Yad Vashem, 1998), pp. 347, 392. At the time of the armistice in September 1943, the figure was probably closer to 1,805. See also: Esther Fintz Menascé, *Gli ebrei a Rodi. Storia di un'antica comunità annientata dai* nazisti (Guerini e Associati: Milan, 2005), pp. 151–152, 275; Esther Fintz Menascé, *Buio Nell'Isola del Sole: Rodi 1943–1945 I due volti di una tragedia quasi di metenticato: il martiro dell'ammarigalio Campioni* (Giuntina: Firenze, 2005), p. 139. The data of Jewish families compiled by Benatar and Benatar, *Si je t'oublie*, is based largely on the Race Census.

16 *Dodecanese Handbook*, Part I, People and Administration, p. 7.

17 Ibid, Part II, Local Information, p. 3.

18 Karen Barkey and George Gavrilis, 'The Ottoman Millet System: Non-Territorial Autonomy and its Contemporary Legacy', *Ethnopolitics*, Vol. 15, No. 1 (2016), pp. 24–42.

19 *Dodecanese Handbook*, Part I, p. 9.

20 Ibid.

21 Ηλιαζ Β. Μεσσιναζ, *Κααλ Σαλωμ: Η Συναγωγή τηζ Κω* (Αστικη Εταιρεια Ἱπποκρατηζ, Κωζ, 2023), Ilias B. Messinas, *Kahal Shalom: The Synagogue of Kos* (Astiki Etaireia Ippocratis: Kos, 2023), pp. 44–52.

22 J.L. Myres, 'The Dodecanese I', *The Geographical Journal* Vol. 56, No. 5 (November 1920), pp. 329–347, here: p. 339.

23 Avraham Galante, *Histoire des Juifs de Turquie*, Tome VII: 'Histoire des Juifs de Rhodes, Chio, Cos' (Fratelli Haim: Istanbul, 1935, repr. Isis, 1985); idem, *Appendice a l'histoire des Juifs de Rhodes* (Editions Isis: Istanbul 1948). Rebecca Amato Levy, *I Remember Rhodes/Miakodro de Rhodes* (Sepher-Hermon Press: New York, 1987).

24 Professor Marco Clementi, University of Calabria, assisted in cataloguing the archive, an opportunity that allowed him to produce his own study, Clementi, *Storia della comunità ebraica di Rodi* as n. 4. While his research and mine converge in some aspects, our methodological approach, as well as some of our conclusions, differ from each other.

25 Henry Fanshawe Tozer, *The Islands of the Aegean* (Clarendon Press: Oxford, [1890] 2006), p. 207.

26 Charles Douglas Greaves Booth, *Italy's Aegean Possessions* (Arrowsmith: London, 1928), pp. 95–96.

27 TNA FO 371/24963, E.R. Warner, report, cited in Chapter 1.

28 https://collections.ushmm.org: RG-50.855.0040: Oral history interview with Michail Panagos, Summary.

29 Deutsches Historisches Museum, Fotosammlung: Hapag Grosse Orient Reise, 3 April 1939.

30 *Die Tagebücher von Joseph Goebbels, Teil 1 Aufzeichnungen 1923–1939, Band 6 August 1938–June 1939*, prepared by Jana Richter, ed. Elke Fröhlich (K.G. Sauer: Munich, 1998), p. 307: 3 April 1939. My translation.

31 Ibid, p. 371.

32 *Dodecanese Handbook*, Part II, p. 3.

33 'und man findet Gesichter, die sehr gut geschnitten sind'. *Ernst Jünger Drei Mal Rhodos. Die Reisen 1938, 1964 und 1981*, ed. Lutz Hagestedt and Luise Michaelsen (Aus dem Archiv Heft 2, 2010), p. 26. For a rebuttal of Jünger's alleged antisemitism, Marcus Bullock, 'Heiner Müller's Error, Walter Jens's Horror, and Ernst Jünger's Antisemitism', *Monatshefte*, Vol. 86, No. 2 (Summer 1994), pp. 152–171.

34 https://en.wikipedia.org/wiki/List_of_earthquakes_in_Greece#CITEREFNGDC. There was a smaller earthquake in 1926 that impacted Rhodes too, Μεσσιναζ, Κααλ Σαλωμ Η Συναγωγή τηζ Κω, p. 37.

35 http://www3.ogs.trieste.it/gngts/files/2017/S11/Riassunti/Kouskouna.pdf

36   Berro, Sylvia, Interview 5969. Tape 1. Visual History Archive, USC Shoah
     Foundation, 1995 (née Hasson, b. 1920). Accessed 10 January 2017.

37   Surmani Interview 53625, seg 25; see Amato Levy, *I Remember Rhodes*, p. 37.

38   For the Israel family, Benatar and Benatar, *Si je t'oublie*, p. 428.

39   Amato Levy, *I Remember Rhodes*, p. 39.

40   Francesca Veronese, 'Il Patrimonio Archeologico del Dodecaneso. E Il Suo
     Utilizzo Propagandistico: Spunti di Riflessione Sulla Politica Culturelle del
     Fascismo nel Mare Nostrum (ovvero 'Dell'Uso Publicco Della Storia')', in
     Massimo Peri (ed.), *La politica culturale del fascismo nel Dodecaneso. Atti del
     Convegno – Padova 16–17 November 2007* (Esedra editrice: Padua, 2009),
     pp. 137–150. Mia Fuller, *Moderns Abroad. Architecture, Cities and Italian
     Imperialism* (Routledge: London, New York, 2007), pp. 27–79, *passim*.

41   Raymond Matton, *Rhodes.Villes Et Paysages De Grèce* (Institut Francais
     D'Athenes: Athens, 1949); Lawrence Durrell, *Reflections on a Marine Venus. A
     Companion to the Landscape of Rhodes* (Faber & Faber: London, [1953] 2000).
     See in this respect the pertinent comment by Nathan Shachar, *The Lost Worlds of
     Rhodes*, p. 7. Kästner bore no relationship to the famous German author of *Emil
     and the Detectives*, Erich Kästner.

42   Valerie McGuire, 'Una faccia, una razza?: Italian citizenship and differentiation
     in the Dodecanese occupation', (paper presented at: 'The Deportation of the Jews
     of Rhodes & Cos: 1944–2014: A Commemorative International Symposium
     on the Holocaust in the Aegean', Rhodes, 22–24 July, 2014). Valerie McGuire,
     'Bringing the Empire Home: Italian Fascism's Mediterranean Tour of Rhodes',
     California Italian Studies, Vol. 8 (Dec. 2018), pp. 1–27. Peri (ed.), *La politica
     culturale del fascismo nel Dodecaneso.*

43   GAKR Box 827, File 225, 1938, ξενοδοχείο Θέρμες. *Dodecanese Handbook*,
     Part II, p. 13: Appendix E.

44   Figure quoted in McGuire, 'Bringing the Empire Home', p. 7, n. 26.

45   On the Jewish and Turkish quarters as 'oriental', McGuire, 'Bringing the Empire
     Home', pp. 17–18, 23. Valerie McGuire, *Italy's Sea: Empire and Nation in the
     Mediterranean, 1895–1945* (Liverpool University Press: Liverpool, 2020), ch. 2
     for a full discussion.

46   For the withdrawal of licences, see Chapter 3.

47   Miru was born in 1915. USHMM Interview Miru Alcana, 30 August 1992, Los
     Angeles, California, accessed at http://collections.ushmm.org, RG-50.233*0001,
     transcript, 5. I have left the transcription uncorrected.

48   Vittorio Alhadeff, *Le Chêne de Rhodes. Saga d'une grande famille sépharade* (Paris Méditerranée: n.p., 1998), p. 114.

49   Hanan, Rachel, Interview 13096. Tape 1. Visual History Archive, USC Shoah Foundation, 1996 (née Hugno, b. 1924). Accessed 12 January 2017. See also, "'It Was Paradise: Jewish Rhodes". Conversation with Prof. Richard Freund', in *Connecticut Jewish Ledger*, accessed at www.jewishledger.com /2015/09/it-was-paradise-jewish-rhodes-conversation-with-prof-richard-freund/.

50   Soriano, Clara, Interview 8852. Visual History Archive, USC Shoah Foundation, 1996 (née Avazaradel, b. 1926). Accessed 11 January 2017.

51   Isaac Jack Lévy, *Jewish Rhodes: A Lost Culture* (Judah L. Magnes Museum: Berkeley, 1989), p. 39. Laura Varon, *The Juderia: A Holocaust Survivor's Tribute to the Jewish Community of Rhodes* (Praeger: Westport, CO, London, 1999), pp. 1–2.

52   In the film documentary *The Longest Journey – The Last Days of the Jews of Rhodes*, dir. Ruggero Gabai (Italy, 2013).

53   Jerusalmi, Sara, Interview 8038. Tape 1. Visual History Archive, USC Shoah Foundation, 1996. (née Notrica, b. 1920). Accessed 9 January 2017.

54   Yad Vashem Archives (hereafter: YVA) 03/10423 Laura Varon, VD1390, interviewed by Yael Ben Schmuel, 14 November 1996, transcript p. 4.

55   Surmani, Eliezer, Interview 53625, seg. 1–7. Visual History Archive, USC Shoah Foundation, 2006. Accessed 12 January 2017. Surmani was interviewed on 29 March 2006, as part of the Bay Area Holocaust Oral History Project. Benatar and Benatar, *Si je t'oublie*, p. 616 for Surmani family photographs.

56   Her tombstone can be viewed at www.rhodesjewishmuseum.org/cemetery/plots/?letter=S, it is the last entry, with her name given in English translation of the Hebrew: Sara.

57   Three girls and three boys, including twins. One twin died before the war. As well as Eliezer, his sister Stella survived Auschwitz.

58   See the comments of Stella Levi, *The Longest Journey*, 12:00 min., and similar comments regarding family lineage and respectability by Gordon DeLeon, University Archives and Manuscripts Division, University of Washington, Seattle, Washington Digital Archives, Interview DeLeon ohc_324, transcript p. 5.

59   Surmani, Interview 53625, seg. 7, 171.

60   Fils, Flora, Interview 1423. Tape 1. Visual History Archive, USC Shoah Foundation, 1995 (née Hasson, b. 1928). Accessed 10 January 2017.

61   ALL'UFFICIO DELLO STATO CIVILE, Race Card Nr 288. The original registry cards are in an archive of the Jewish Synagogue of Rhodes.

62   The Jewish religious High Holidays in sequence are as follows: Rosh Hashanah; Yom Kippur; Sukkot; Simhat Torah; Hanukah Seder; Pesach; Purim.

63   In the Hebrew calendar Purim falls on the 14th of the month Adar and coincides in the Gregorian calendar around the same time as the Christian feast of Easter. Most of the survivors did not remember or talk about the festivals or feast days according to where they occurred in the Jewish calendar, but rather as they had experienced them as children. Hence the foregrounding of Purim.

64   Hasson, Jack [Giacomo], Interview 7687. Visual History Archive, USC Shoah Foundation, 1995. Accessed 11 January 2017.

65   Varon, Laura, Interview 26814. Tape 2. Visual History Archive, USC Shoah Foundation, 1997. Accessed 9 January 2017.

66   Amato Levy, *I Remember Rhodes*, pp. 55–56.

67   Levi, Stella, Interview 1701. Visual History Archive, USC Shoah Foundation, 1995. Accessed 9 January 2017. Stella was born in 1923.

68   Varon, Interview 26814. Tape 2. Sukkot commemorates the period the Jews spent in the desert en route to the Promised Land. In her interview with Yael Ben Schmuel (Yad Vashem) a year earlier, Varon says, 'My preferred holiday was Succot because the succa was my preferred refuge to go and dream and was very cosy and very nice place to be'. YVA 03/10423, Varon VD 1390, transcript p. 3.

69   Fils, Interview 1423, op cit. A photograph from 1934 of Rebecca together with Salvator Galante in the shop appears in The Rhodes Jewish Historical Foundation, *Rhodesli Jewish Calendar September 2018/September 2019–Elul 5778/Tishri 5780*, February 2019 facing page.

70   Hanan, Interview 13096, op cit.

71   On kinship, Renée Hirschon, 'The Jews of Rhodes: The Decline and Extinction of an Ancient Community', in Minna Rozen (ed.), *The Last Ottoman Century and Beyond: The Jews in Turkey and the Balkans* (Tel Aviv University: Tel Aviv, 2002), pp. 299–301.

72   Alberto Israel, *The Longest Journey*, 13:00 min. Alberto's family lived in Principe di Napoli and included his brothers: Elia (30.7.16), Aron (21.7.23), his sister Giovanna (1.4.25); his father Rahamin had been born in 1880, his mother Signoru in 1885. Three older brothers, Asher, Salvatore and Daniel and an older sister, Regine, had emigrated to the Congo by the time of the deportation. Only Alberto and Giovanna would survive to camps, Benatar and Benatar, *Si je t'oublie*, p. 428.

73   Amato Levy, *I Remember Rhodes*, p. 32.

74   Hirschon, 'The Jews of Rhodes', pp. 301, 303–304.

75   Judith Humphrey, 'Glimpses of Jewish Life in Crete at the Turn of the Century', in *Los Muestros* 6 (March 1992), p. 8.

76   Yad Vashem Archives (hereafter: YVA) 033c/3607, Regina Mazza né Palombo (22.05.22–05.01.95), interviewed by Jaqueline Benatar, 1988, transcript, p. 3.

77   Hanan, Interview 13096, tape 1.

78   Ibrahim Seyfullah, *Italien im östlichen Mittelmeer. Eine politische Studie über die Bedeutung der anatolischen Küsteninseln* (Kurt Vowinckel Verlag: Berlin, 1930), pp. 24–43, *passim*, p. 37. *Dodecanese Handbook*, Part 1, p. 8.

79   The semi-state company responsible for exports was Azienda tabacchi italiani S.p.A., established in 1927 with the participation of the Bank of Sicily and Bank of Naples. See Diana Giampietro, 'La storia del tabacco in Italia. III. Dalla formazione del Monopolio di Stato fino alla 2a guerra mondiale', accessed at http://www1.inea.it/ist/tab8pdf/storia3.pdf. By 1939, Italy was by far the most important trading partner with Rhodes, *Dodecanese Handbook*, Part 1, p. 7.

80   Fuller, *Moderns Abroad*, p. 178.

81   GAKR 2/42/18, Ogetto Dati statistici. 'Promenoria: Elenco delle principali industrie … Rodi, 8 Maggio 1940'. *Dodecanese Handbook*, Part 1, p. 8, cites the carpet manufacture of N.S. Modiano alongside the Italian conglomerate S.A. Italiane Tappeti Orientali.

82   Menascé a manufacturer of oriental rugs and also a director of the Alhadeff & fils business (department store). Benatar and Benatar, *Si je t'oublie*, p. 497.

83   Deported to Auschwitz together with his wife and two daughters. Only his younger daughter Lea (b. 1927) survived; she was liberated from Buchenwald. The property passed to her after the war. A son, Isaaco, disappeared (presumed dead) during the aerial bombardment of Rhodes in February 1944. Benatar and Benatar, *Si je t'oublie*, p. 632.

84   While many of the community's merchant class had substantial commercial property within the walls of the old city, several of the large manufacturing premises were located beyond the walls.

85   A photograph of Franco outside the house as it was being constructed can be found in Aron Hasson, *Rhodesli Jewish Calendar September 2020/September 2021–Ehd 5780/Tishri 5782*, March 2021/Adár & Nisán 5781, facing page.

86   World Jewish Congress Collection, Series C subseries 4: Indemnification 1939–1975, MSS Col No. 361, C266/1 Greece heirless property/Rhodes 1962/1963, Property list nos. 248, 259, 260, for example.

87   *Dodecanese Handbook*, Part II, p. 12.

88   Gini Alhadeff, *The Sun at Midday. Tales of a Mediterranean Family* (Random House: New York, 1997); Vittorio Alhadeff, *Le Chêne de Rhodes. Saga d'une grande famille sépharade* (Éditions Paris-Méditerranée: Paris, 1998); Esther Fintz Menascé, *Gli ebrei a Rodi. Storia di un'antica comunità annientata dai nazisti* (Guerini e Associati: Milan, 2005).

89   Hanan, Interview 13096, op cit., tape 2. Galante, *Histoire*, pp. 277–279. Alice Tarica-Israël, *Des ténèbres au soleil* (Clepsydre: Nivelles, 2015).

90   Μεσσιναζ, *Καα λ Σαλωμ*, p. 46.

91   Alhadeff, Nissim, Interview 1577. Tape 1. Visual History Archive, USC Shoah Foundation 1995. Accessed 10 January 2018. Alhadeff, *Le Chêne de Rhodes*, p. 22. The Salomon Alhadeff & Fils business is discussed in Chapter 7.

92   Present-day Square of the Jewish Martyrs. GAKR Carabinieri 6/P.S./346 (1932), Ufficio Centrale di P.S., 25 January 1934.

93   GAKR Carabinieri 6/P.S./390 (1932), Governo Delle Isole Italiane Dell'Egeo, Modiano, Mosé fu Saul. The following is based on this file.

94   *Messagario di Rodi* No. 98, April 1936. Nissim Tarica committed suicide in February 1939. See Chapter 3.

95   GAKR Carabinieri 15/P.S./53 (1932), Governo Delle Isole Italiane Dell'Egeo, Debito del Sig. Modiano, Mosé fu Saul verso il Governo.

96   These were in the Piazza Ibraim and in the Via del Ginnavio.

97   *Messagario di Rodi* No. 70, March 1936.

98   GAKR Carabinieri 20/P.S./2 (1932), 5.Fascicolo: Ufficio Centrale di Pubblico Sicurezza: Communita israelitica di Rodi – elenco elettori, 27 November 1935, lists 218 electors.

99   The evidence for the elite's social life can be gleaned from the applications to the authorities to stage dances and concerts, the sale of tickets (at prices that clearly targeted the well-off), and reports in the *Il Messaggero di Rodi* on funds raised and individual donations for charitable causes. These sources, however, are sporadic and can be mostly found spread throughout the *Carabinieri* files.

100 Soriano, Interview 8852, seg. 1.

101 According to Diamante, her father had been orphaned when 2 years old and subsequently brought up by his grandmother in 'modest' circumstances. He had had little schooling but had then been apprenticed as a tailor. Their house had a basement that was let to an Italian family, who later tried to help them during the deportation. Isaac was married to Perla né Alhadeff, they had seven children, two of whom emigrated to the Congo before the census of 1938 (Race Census, # 322). South African Holocaust and Genocide Foundation

Archive (hereafter: SAHGF), Diamante Franco, Interview 7 September 1986 interviewers: Dora Wynchank and Alan Fischer, Transcript, pp. 2, 4, 7.

102 Hanan, Interview 13096.

103 Benatar and Benatar, *Si je t'oublie*, p. 108.

104 Berro, Sylvia, Interview 5969 (née Hasson, b.15 Aug. 1920). The family lived at Giuseppe Notrica 6, Racial Census #301. Sylvia was the sole survivor of her family.

105 Hasson, Stella, Interview 1468, seg. 1. Visual History Archive, USC Shoah Foundation, 1995 (née Nachmias, b. 12 Oct. 1915). Accessed 9 January 2017.

106 Ruben and his wife Mazaltov had had seven children, but the first child died aged three years, and another child died in infancy. Ruben also owned some small properties in the *Juderia* and it is likely that he received a small income from rents. Berro, Interview 5969, segs. 1–2.

107 GAKR Carabinieri P.S. 2.40.37, 1933, Amato Sadih di Abramo, venditore ambulante. In 1934 they were living in Via di Chenan (renamed at the end of the 1930s Via Giovanni Parpaglia) in the poorer backstreets of the *Juderia*. The family comprised Giuseppe, 24 years old; Sara, 18 years old; Moses, 17 years old; Leon, 8 years old; Stella, 5 years old; Maria, 4 years old. The file ends in 1939.

108 GAKR Carabinieri P.S. 27.57.1, A., Bazzalel.

109 GAKR Carabinieri P.S. 1.52.8, H., Hannoch (*sic*) 1934.

110 GAKR Carabinieri P.S. 2.40.38, Oggetto Canan (*sic*) Abner di Moreno, lustrascarpe ambulante. We will return to Avner in Chapter 4. The street was renamed by late 1939 as Bernardo d'Airasca (present-day Odos Irinas).

111 GAKR Carabinieri P.S. 1.2.229, Levi, Elia di Isaaco. We will encounter Elia again in Chapter 5.

112 Aron Rodrigue, 'La mission éducative (1860–1939)', in André Kaspi (ed.), *Histoire de l'Alliance israélite universelle – De 1860 à nos jours* (Edition Armand Colin: Paris, 2010).

113 GAKR ΦAK 9, 1937-38, Scuola di Avviamento a Tipo Commerciale in Rodi, Anno Scolastico, 1937–38. Pignataro, *Il Dodecaneso Italiano*, Vol. II, p. 482.

114 *Dodecanese Handbook*, Part I, p. 17.

115 Nissim Alhadeff, Interview Nr 157: Seg. 13, 22–27. VHA, USC Shoah Foundation. GAKR Carabinieri, 2/P.S.19/123, Benatar Alessandro di Nissim, Pag. 31ff. Benatar was born in 1914, he went to Italy to study in 1933. Family papers of Alessandro Benatar. I am grateful to Bettina Benatar-Luetgerath for kindly sharing her family history.

116 Luca Pignataro, 'Il Collegio Rabbinica di Rodi', *Nuova storia contemporanea.*
     Bimestrale di ricerche e studi storici e politici sull'età contemporanea, Vol. 6
     (Milan, 2011), pp. 49–86. Luca Pignataro, *Il Dodecaneso Italiano 1912–1947:*
     II – Il Governo di Mario Lago 1923–1936 (Solfanelli: Chieti C.P., 2013), pp.
     523–547. Reported in *Bulletino Mensual de la Comunidad Israelitica de Rodes*,
     Kislev 5689, No.1 – November 1928 VII, 'En el Colegio Rabbinico'. See also
     Rabbi David Prato, *Cinque Anni di Rabbinato Alessandria d'Egitto 1933* (Rodi,
     n.d.), pp. 213–219. Prato was the Chief Rabbi of Alexandria, 1927–36 and had
     regular contact with the Community and with the Rabbinical College. See for a
     list of its students and their places of origin http://www.rhodesjewishmuseum.
     org/history/the-rabbis-of-rhodes.
117 Vittorio Buti, 'Il collegio rabbinico di Rodi e la missione dell'Italia', in *Oriente*
     Rivista delle Colonie italiane (Edita dal Ministero delle colonie: Rome, 1931),
     1–6; Aron Rodrigue, 'The Rabbinical Seminary in Italian Rhodes 1928–38:
     An Italian Fascist Project', *Jewish Social Studies*, Vol. 25, No. 1 (Autumn 2019),
     pp. 1–19. Simonetta della Seta Torrefranca, 'The Rabbinical Seminary of
     Rhodes 1926–1938', in Itzhak Bezalel (ed.), *Pe' Amim Studies in the Cultural*
     Heritage of Oriental Jewry (Ben-Zvi Institute of Yad Itzhak Ben-Zvi and Hebrew
     University Jerusalem: Jerusalem, 1988), pp. 78–112. Simonetta Della Seta,
     'Gli ebrei del Mediterraneo nella strategia politica fascista sino al 1938: il caso di
     Rodi', *Storia Contemporanea*, XVII/6 (Bologna, 1986), pp. 997–1032.
118 GAKR IΔΔ ΦAK 9, 1937/38, Movimento Collegio Rabbinico di Rodi – Anno
     1937–38.
119 The World Jewish Congress was founded in Geneva in August 1936 as a
     reaction to persecution and anti-Jewish measures in Nazi Germany and a rising
     tide of antisemitism elsewhere in Europe. At the same time by the mid-1930s,
     there was a sense among Sephardim that they had become cut-off from the
     wider world of Jewry. 'Abandoned to themselves, they had become preoccupied
     with local problems only, problems necessarily limited and confined.' (2ᵉ
     Conférence Universelle des communautés séphardites, Amsterdam 1938,
     Manifeste-Programme), p. 1. To overcome this isolation an international
     conference of Sephardim was organized in London in 1935 which also saw
     the establishment of the World Union of Sephardi Communities (WUSC).
     At its second conference held in Amsterdam in May 1938, the WUSC stated
     three aims that were its priority: the foundation of a Rabbinical University, the
     establishment of a trust fund, and the inauguration of research into the social
     and spiritual condition of Sephardi communities scattered across the globe.

John Menascé as president of the community was invited to take part in the second conference, Union Universelle des Communautés Séphardites to John Menasche (*sic*!), 8 Feb. 1938, GAKR Carabinieri 20.P.S.2 (1932), 6.Fascicolo: Ufficio Centrale di Pubblico Sicurezza: Communita israelitica di Rodi, copy of letter from Menashe (*sic*) to Union Universelle des communautés séphardites, 8 February 1938.

120 GAKR ΙΔΔ ΦΑΚ 9, 1937/38, Movimento Collegio Rabbinico di Rodi, plate 1120685, 14 February 1939 & plate P1120693. McGuire, *Italy's Sea*, pp. 214–215.

121 Rodrigue, 'The Rabbinical Seminary', *passim*.

122 We discuss this in Chapter 3.

123 Lucia Amato né Sciarcon, Interview 14687. Visual History Archive. USC Shoah Foundation, interviewed 1996, interviewer Rebecca Ziman, the daughter of another survivor Giuseppe Coné.

124 Diamante Franco, SAHGF, transcript, p. 6.

125 Amato, Interview 14687. This was probably the tobacco company TEMI.

126 We will return to these cohorts in Chapter 6. In the absence of pre-deportation data, the age-profile is based on the deportees. 'Children' as defined by the League of Nations.

127 Aron Rodrigues, *Jews and Muslims. Images of Sephardi and Eastern Jewries in Modern Times* (University of Washington Press: Seattle and London, 2003), chapters 10 and 12. Esther Benbassa and Aron Rodrigue, *Sephardi Jewry. A History of the Judeo-Spanish Community, 14th–20th Centuries* (University of California Press: Berkeley, CA, 2000 [orig. 1993]), pp. 83–89.

128 Andreas Guidi, *Generations of Empire: Youth from Ottoman to Italian Rule in the Mediterranean* (University of Toronto Press: Toronto, 2022), ch. 5.

129 As a corrective to this perception, see Nicholas Doumanis, *Myth and Memory in the Mediterranean Remembering Fascism's Empire* (Palgrave Macmillan: London and New York, 1997). On Italianization in Rhodes, Luca Pignataro, *Il Dodecaneso Italiano 1912–1947: II – Il Governo di Mario Lago 1923–1936* (Edizioni Solfanelli: Chieti, 2013), p. 442 and *passim*. See also Gini Alhadeff, *The Sun at Midday*, which captures this aspect brilliantly.

130 We do not know the occasion for this photograph, but it is possible that one of the sons (Yehuda who is not registered in the Racial Census) had returned to Rhodes to visit the family. A copy of the family photograph is in Benatar and Benatar, *Si je t'oublie*, p. 183. See also Rabbi Capuia's portrait photograph at the Jewish Museum of Rhodes, http://www.rhodesjewishmuseum.org/history/the-rabbis-of-rhodes and in a group photograph of rabbis and their wives, Angel, *The Jews of Rhodes*, p. 102.

131	Amato Levy, *I Remember Rhodes*, p. 6. See also photographs 11 and 12 in ibid.

132	Benatar and Benatar, *Si je t'oublie*, p. 185. Roberto perished in Mauthausen on 6 March 1945. His parents were gassed upon arrival in Auschwitz. His mother's younger half-sister by 28 years, Rachele Menascé, survived Auschwitz only to succumb in Bergen-Belsen barely a month after the ending of the war. The grandfather, Giacobbe (b. 1854) died in Rhodes in 1941 and is buried in the Jewish cemetery; his wife Miriam (b. 1857) died en route to Auschwitz. Two older sons, Giacomo and Giuseppe, left for the Belgian Congo before the beginning of the war. A similar generational contrast between Oriental and Occident can be found in the photograph of Isaac Amato and his grandson Isaac, in Aron Hasson, *Rhodesli Jewish Calendar September 2020/ September 2021 – Elul 5780/Tishri 5782*, January 2021, facing page.

133	Articles in *The American Sephardi* Vol. 78 (1975), pp. 84–91. Cynthia M. Crews, *Recherches sur le judéo-espagnol dans les pays balkaniques* (E. Droz: Paris, 1935). McGuire, *Italy's Sea*, p. 139. In fact, not modernization but Nazi genocidal policy ended the last vestiges of traditional Ottoman Jewry in the Aegean.

134	Amato Levy, *I Remember Rhodes*, p. 5.

135	Photographs in http://www.rhodesjewishmuseum.org/museum/family-photos. The Jewish Museum of Greece located in Athens, also has a large archive of contemporary photographs, some of which are from Rhodes and Kos. https:// www.jewishmuseum.gr/en/photograph-categories/

136	Benatar and Benatar, *Si je t'oublie*, p. 374.

137	And in appearance seems to have reversed the 'modernization' process. For the family: Racial Census (Card 301), Reuben and his wife Mazaltov (1884) married in January 1903. Mazaltov died a year before the deportation, 21 July 1943, and is buried in the Jewish Cemetery. Sylvia (also called Salva) was liberated from Theresienstadt in May 1945; she later moved to Salisbury, Rhodesia (present-day Harare, Zimbabwe), where she married. Benatar and Benatar, *Si je t'oublie*, p. 374.

138	Background discussion in: Benbassa and Rodrigue, *Sephardi Jewry*, pp. 72–82, 110–115.

139	Stella Levi, *The Longest Journey*, 16:08 min. Stella lived with her parents and sisters Felicia (6.5.12) and Renate (13.9.21) in Via Chenan; her father Juda (1879), who was blind, married her mother Maria Notrica (1889) in 1906. Stella and Renate would survive the Holocaust.

140	Christos I. Papachristodoulou, Παπαχριστοδούλου *Ιστορία Της Ρόδου Από Τους Προϊστορικούς Χρόνους Έως Την Ενσωμάτωση Της Δωδεκανήσου* (1948) *History*

of Rhodes from Prehistoric Times to the Integration of the Dodecanese (1948)
(Παλαιοβιβλιοπωλείο: Αθήναι, 1972) (Palaiovivliopoleio: Athens, 1972), p. 547.

141 GAKR Carabinieri CCRR 1-7-1 1933.

142 Pacifici came from Florence and arrived in Rhodes in August 1930. His wife
Wanda (Abenan) may have remained in Rome where she gave birth to their
son, Emanuele in 1931. A second child, Miriam, was born in Rhodes in late
February 1933, but died four years later in Genoa, where Pacifici was by now
the chief rabbi. Their third child, Raffaele Efraim, was born in Rome in July
1938. Pacifici and his wife were both deported from Genoa and killed in
Auschwitz in December 1943. Raffaele survived in hiding. Details: Fondazione
Centro Di Documentazione Ebraica Contemporanea http://digital-library.
cdec.it/cdec-web/persone/detail/person-5991/pacifici-riccardo.html and here
http://www.nomidellashoah.it/1scheda.asp?nome=Riccardo&cognome=P
acifici&id=5991. Further documents in *Die Verfolgung und Ermordung der
europäischen Juden durch das nationalsozialistische Deutschland 1933–1945,
Band 14: Besetztes Südosteuropa und Italien*, prepared by Sara Berger, Erwin
Lewin, Sanela Schmid and Maria Vassilikou (De Gruyter: Oldenourg, Boston/
Berlin, 2017), p. 276.

143 Menascé, *Gli ebrei a Rodi*, p. 280.

144 Israël, *Je ne vous ai pas oubliés*, pp. 31–32.

145 YVA 033c/3607, Regina Mazza né Palombo, transcript, pp. 4–5.

146 Stella Levi, *The Longest Journey*, 6:12 min.

147 According to Rebecca Levy there had been six synagogues while she was
growing up in the 1920s. Violette Maio Fintz also believed there had been
six synagogues, transcript of television interview in S. Africa. Varon in her
interview (YVA 03/10423 Laura Varon, VD1390, transcript p. 3) was quite clear
there had been just two synagogues in Rhodes.

148 GAKR Carabinieri, P.S. 20.2. 1932, Comunità Israelitica di Rodi, Gruppe
Carabinieri Reale – Ufficio Centrale Speciale nr 86/18-1933 di prov. div. I,
13 March 1940. M. Pariente, 'Les Israelites de Rhodes', *Bulletin de l'Alliance
Israelite Universelle* (Paris, 1888), Nr 13, pp. 101–110. Sintes, *Chasing the Past*,
p. 114 and pp. 106–116 *passim*. The street name changed after the census to Via
Antonio Del Pozzo.

149 YVA 033c/3606, Matilde Levy née Cohen, interviewed by Jaqueline Benatar,
10 October 1988, transcript p. 3. We discuss the Rabbinical College below.

150 GAKR Carabinieri, P.S. 20.2. 1932, Gruppo Carabinieri Reale – Ufficio Centrale
Speciale, No. 86/15-1933 di prot. Div. I, Ogetto: Comunicazione di dati,
13 March 1940.

151 Amato, Interview 14687. Guidi, *Generations*, p. 49.

152 Bruce Masters, 'Millet', in Ágoston, Gábor and Bruce Masters (eds.),
Encyclopedia of the Ottoman Empire (Facts on File: New York, 2009),
pp. 383–384. Idem, *Christians and Jews in the Ottoman Arab World: The Roots
of Sectarianism* (Cambridge University Press: Cambridge, 2001). Heather
J. Sharkey, *A History of Muslims, Christians, and Jews in the Middle East*
(Cambridge University Press: Cambridge, 2018).

153 GAKR Carabinieri 20/P.S./2, Communita Israelitica, Elenco degli
Elettori di Questa Communita per L'Anno in Corso (1932); https://www.
rhodesjewishmuseum.org/history/the-rabbis-of-rhodes/; Avram Galante,
Histoire des Juifs de Turquie Tome VII (Edition Isis: Istanbul, 1985, repr.),
pp. 270–271. *Dodecanese Handbook*, Part I, p. 16.

154 GAKR Carabinieri P.S. 20.2. 1932, Comunità Israelitica di Rodi, list from
27 March 1935 of 240 male heads of household eligible to vote.

155 GAKR Carabinieri, P.S. 20.2. 1932, for election to the council in 1933 and 1936.

156 Tarica-Israël, *Des ténèbres au soleil*, pp. 21, 25.

157 See for example, Clara Menascé née Gabriel, YVA 033C/86, 03/4318, transcript
p. 1. The interview took place in French, 19 October 1984. For the event itself,
Borovaya, 'The Rhodes Blood Libel of 1840', pp. 35–63.

158 GAKR Carabinieri, Onorevole Ufficio Centrale di Publica Sicurezza, letter
14 September 1936.

159 GAKR Carabinieri 1/1/264, Tarica, Nissim, contains various newspaper
clippings of such financial conflicts reported in Il Messagario di Rodi, 1936,
1937.

160 GAKR Carabinieri P.S. 6.27 (1932) Alcana, Giuseppe, di Abramo. The file opens
in 1932, the year Alcana first applied for a licence to trade as a shoemaker.

161 GAKR Carabinieri 1.47.1077 1934. Alcana Chaco (*sic*) di Celebi.

162 GAKR Carabinieri PS 1.2.837, Israele, Mose di Solomone.

163 The following account is based on this correspondence in Claire Barkey Flash,
*A Hug from Afar. One Family's Dramatic Journey through Three Continents to
Escape the Holocaust*, edited and compiled by Cynthia Flash Hemphill, trans.
Morris Barkey (Flash Media Services: Bellevue, WA, 2016 [orig. 2004]).

164 Letter, 5 August 1939, *Hug from Afar*, pp. 133–114. Claire's letter on behalf of
her parents to Ralph, 3 July 1939, informing him and his wife Rachel that they
had arrived in Tangier the previous day.

165 Ibid, letter, 10 August 1939, pp. 116–117.

166 GAKR Carabinieri 20/ P.S./2, 5.Fascicolo: p. 123, Promemoria (19 Nov. 1935), with entry stamp Grassini's office. Ibid, p. 124, Decree 26 November, stamped 29 November.

167 Ibid. Atti Ufficiali, Lago. For biographical details of Strumza see Chapter 3.

168 GAKR Carabinieri 20/P.S./2, 6.Fascicolo.

169 Ibid, Ufficio Centrale di P.I. Div. II, report 18 June 1936.

170 Guidi, *Generations*, pp. 51–54.

171 GAKR Carabinieri, 2.9.6, Associazione Ebraica 'Bene Berith'. On its origins in North America, Cornelia Wilhelm, *The Independent Orders of B'nai B'rith and True Sisters. Pioneers of a New Jewish Identity, 1843–1914* (Wayne State University Press: Detroit, MI, 2011). Wilhelm also shows its more social and gender aspects in the United States, which appears very different to its development into an elite organization in Rhodes.

172 GAKR Carabinieri 20.P.S.2, 6.Fascicolo: Unione delle Communita Israelitische Italiane requesting information on the position in Rhodes and letter from the President of the Community expressing loyalty to the Regime. For Pacifici' s loyalty, GAKR Carbinieri 1.2.17, Pacifici Riccardo (1935), Legione Territoriale dei Carabinieri Reali di Bari No. 2219, 26 January 1935 (Guido Grassini).

173 Varon, Interview 26814. Tape 2.

174 *El Boletin* 26 June 1936.

175 GAKR Carabinieri 20/P.S./2, 5.Fascicolo: Ufficio Centrale di P.S. Div. II to l'Ill/mo Signor Segretario Generale del Governatore, 12 May 1936.

176 GAKR Carabinieri 20.PS.2, 1.Fascicolo: Ufficio Centrale di P.S. Div. II (Capitano del CC.RR. Guido Grassini) to l'Ill/mo Signor Segretario del Governo, 13 September 1933.

177 GAKR Carabinieri 20.P.S./2 (1932), 1.Fascicolo: 15 April 1934 A.XII, Promemoria. Franco's obsession with authority and law and order is also reflected in his denunciation of Lola H., to the Carabinieri for alleged prostitution, in the same file. The following chapter provides a few examples of Jewish responses to antisemitism.

178 GAKR Carabinieri 20.P.S.2 (1932), 2.Fascicolo, pp. 69–71. Pro-Memoria: Il Brigadiere di piedi, f/to Ricci, Rodi di 11. August 1934. The incident occurred on 9 August 1934.

179 GAKR Carabinieri, P.S. 11.68, L., Stella fu Giuda. Her file has references to other young women from the *Juderia* likewise engaged in casual prostitution, and who came to the attention of the authorities after contracting gonorrhoea. Stella L. was granted permission to travel to Italy in April 1942. It is not known

if she survived the Holocaust in Italy. See also GAKR Carabinieri P.S. 11.71 (1932), Violetta B., fu Abramo, who lived in Via Ammiraglio Bonaldi. Violetta had arrived from Turkey in 1930. In spite of her Turkish citizenship, she was deported in 1944. At the time of coming under suspicion, she worked as a domestic servant in the household of Haco N.

180   GAKR Carabinieri 1/55/16, Ester C., b. 1901 (1934).

181   GAKR Carabinieri 1/47/10, Moise R., b. 1912 (1934), p. 11, letter from her father requesting permission for R., in the margin next to the pertinent sentence, an official has written an emphatic 'no! no! no!'. See same file p. 13, denying R. residence. Richetta was born in 1917, she and Moise met in 1934 while he was detained in prison (she appears to have been visiting her brother Menascé, serving a two-year sentence for drug dealing); the couple married in September 1937. Richetta's brothers Menascé (a fruiterer) and Salvo (a shoemaker) were born in 1909 and 1915. The family was described as propertyless and poor. Richetta was pregnant by Moise and thus the wedding was forced. Their daughter was born in late 1937, two years later, Moise left for Palestine and together with Menascé Levi and Giacobe Almeleh, joined the British army in 1940. He subsequently divorced Richetta. Clementi, *Storia della comunità ebraica di Rodi*, p. 331, is based on the same file. Their mother Stella Alcana (1887) was the sister of Hizkia Alcana (1889), who lived with his wife and eight children in Via Turcheria 19, see index cards of Race Census 1939, numbers 376 and 467.

182   GAKR Carabinieri PS 1/27/25, Israel H. (1934).

183   GAKR Carabinieri PS 1/47/1173, Boaz B., b. 1903 (1934). For instance, causing damage to the Sanatorium Road, although warned not to use this road (1936). Driving with only one wing mirror (1939).

184   GAKR Carabinieri PS 1/47/1173, Boaz B., b. 1903 (1934).

185   Myres, 'The Dodecanese I', pp. 340–341.

186   Fils, Interview 1423. Seg. 18.

187   See the interview of Gordon DeLeon about his father's and then his family's immigration to Seattle between 1909 and 1912, University Archives and Manuscripts Division, University of Washington, Seattle, Washington Digital Archives, Interview Gordon DeLeon, transcript, pp. 1–2.

188   According to his granddaughter, Bella Angel Restis, the former president of the Jewish Community of Rhodes.

189   Moise, 1908; Vittoria, 1910; Alberto, 1912; Rica, 1914; Caden (Ketty), 1918; Gioia, 1920(?).

190   In 1939, the street changed to Via Bonifacio Scarampi. We will return to this family in later chapters.

191   Alberto Israël, *The Longest Journey*, 15:00 min.

192   Alberto Israël, *Je ne vous ai pas oubliés*. Propos recueillis par Stipan Bosnjak with a preface by Simone Veil (Editions de l'institut Sepharade Européen: Brussels, 2008). A photograph of this wedding is reproduced in The Rhodes Jewish Historical Foundation, *Rhodesli Jewish Calandar September 2011/ September 2012–Elul 5771/Tishri 5773*, September 2011, facing page.

193   Interview DeLeon ohc_324, transcript p. 5.

194   Fintz, Violette Maio. Interview 5720. Seg. 2. Visual History Archive, USC Shoah Foundation, 1995. Accessed 9 January 2017. Violette later worked for Singer Sewing company; her father was a sweet maker.

195   Amato Levy, *I Remember Rhodes*, p. 10.

196   Sami Modiano, *The Longest Journey*, 18:51 min.

197   Alhadeff, *Le Chêne*, p. 113.

198   Stella Levi, *The Longest Journey*, 19:00 min. Her reference to 'foxtrot' and 'waltz' and popular Italian songs is another good example of the generational shift taking place we discussed earlier in the chapter.

199   De Leon, Stella, Interview 12055, seg. 8. Visual History Archive, USC Shoah Foundation, 1996. Accessed 10 January 2017. See also Fintz, Interview 5720, op cit.

200   https://www.timesofisrael.com/rhodeslis-make-annual-island-pilgrimage-to-remember-and-reboot/.

201   Alberto Israël, *The Longest Journey*, 19:57 min. In his memoir published a few years earlier, Alberto states that such mixed marriages were rare. Alberto Israël, *Je ne vous*, p. 26. Andreas Guidi found that over the period 1912–40 there were only seven marriages between Jews and Catholics. These related to civil marriages and not Church marriages, in stark contrast to 109 marriages between Catholic males and Orthodox women. Additionally, there are no figures for Jewish men marrying non-Jewish women. The reason for this imbalance is given as male emigration, Guidi, *Generations*, p. 196 (Table 5.2).

202   Amato, Interview 14687. Lucia explains Caden left Rhodes for Rome with her four children in 1942. Later in her interview she states that Caden died, whereas another sister, Gioia, also married to an Italian, survived the Holocaust.

203   GAKR Carabinieri 1.1.1042, Coll. Ufficio Centrale di Pubblica Sicurezza I/1, Da Fano. Achille survived the Holocaust and returned briefly to Rhodes after the war; Giuseppina was transferred to Bergen-Belsen in February or March

1945, after which we lose trace of her; the younger sisters with their mother were gassed on arrival at Auschwitz,http://digital-library.cdec.it/cdec-web/persone/detail/person-2338/da-fano-achille.html. Benatar and Benatar, *Si je t'oublie*, p. 231.

204 Benatar and Benatar, *Si je t'oublie*, p. 22.

205 GAKR Carabinieri 2.11.1987, 1937, Merolle, Rino di Luigi.

206 Haganah Archive, 'Breve Cenno sulla deportazione della colonia ebraica di Rodi', Statement by Rino Merolle, 23 May 1945 (in Italian). I am grateful to Professor Steven Bowman who kindly made this document available to me.

207 Michael Frank, *One Hundred Saturdays. Stella Levi and the Search for a Lost World* (Simon & Schuster: New York, 2022), p. 109.

208 IRO 'Care and Maintenance' Program/3.2.1.2 CM/1 Files originating in Italy. ITS Digital Archive. Arolsen Archives. We will return to Sara in Chapter 8.

209 Although, we cannot be certain that they were not subjected to persecution. Teresa Buciuk and her sister, Vittoria, for example, had to go into hiding and only emerged after the liberation of Rome.

210 We will encounter Da Fano again in Chapter 8.

211 Surmani, Interview 53625, seg. 80.

Chapter 3

1 Gilmore, Sara Hanan, Interview 439, Visual History Archive, USC Shoah Foundation 1994. Sara had turned 15 years old two months before the deportation.

2 Davide Rodogno, 'Italiani brava gente? Fascist Italy's Policy Toward the Jews in the Balkans, April 1941–July 1943', European History Quarterly Vol. 35, No. 2 (2005), pp. 213–240. Shira Klein, *Italy's Jews from Emancipation to Fascism* (Cambridge University Press: Cambridge, 2017), ch. 8 ('The Myth of the Good Italian'). See also: John Barruzza, 'The Good Italian, the Bad German, and the Survivor: Narratives and Counter-Narratives of the Shoah in Italy' (PhD Thesis, Syracuse University, 2020). *Dissertations – ALL.* 1187, accessed at https://surface.syr.edu/etd/1187. Diego Guzzi, 'The Myth of the "Good Italian", the Antisemitism and the Colonial Crimes', found at https://www.associazionemilgram.it/wp-content/uploads/2013/10/Materiali-Black-Box_The-Myth-of-the-Good-Italian-Antisemitism-and-Colonial-Crimes.pdf.

3 TNA HW12/295, Note of Irish Minister (ambassador) to the Vatican to Minister for Foreign Affairs, Dublin, 5 December 1943. In this note, the ambassador asked the Irish Foreign Minister to 'Please plead for justice, goodwill and clemency' for Italy's Jews. On memory and the 'good Italian' see: Nicholas Doumanis, 'Italians as "Good" Colonizers: Speaking Subalterns and the Politics of Memory in the Dodecanese', in Ruth Ben-Ghiat and Mia Fuller (eds.), *Italian Colonialism* (Palgrave Macmillan: New York, 2005), pp. 221–231. In general, Michele Sarfatti, *The Jews in Mussolini's Italy: From Equality to Persecution* (University of Wisconsin Press: Madison, 2006). On the role of Pius XII and the Vatican during the Holocaust, Carol Rittner and John K. Roth (eds.), *Pope Pius XII and the Holocaust* (Bloomsbury Academic Collections: London, 2016); David I. Kertzer, *The Pope at War: The Secret History of Pius XII, Mussolini, and Hitler* (Oxford University Press: Oxford, 2022).

4 TNA FO371/24963, cited in report by E.S. Wagner, 1940.

5 See Chapter 5 for the collaboration in relation to the deportation. Marco Clementi/Eirini Toliou, *Gli ultimi ebrei di Rodi. Leggi razziali e deportazioni nel Dodecaneso italiano (1938–1948)* (Derive Approdi: Rome, 2015), pp. 173–174, suggest that 10 per cent of the administration were members of the Italian Fascist Party (PNF). The remaining *Carabinieri* numbered among circa 450 Italian Fascists in the Italian administration after September 1943. According to British Intelligence sources, the majority of the circa 1,000-strong Carabinieri hailed from Sicily. *Dodecanese Handbook* Part 1, ch. 6.

6 No sooner had Admiral Campioni signed the unconditional surrender than several high-ranking officers of the Italian garrison and *Carabinieri*, among them Colonel Ferdinand Mittino, declared themselves as pro-Mussolini and pro-Axis. See Chapter 4.

7 RH26/1007/15, Bl. 43, Anlage 8, Sturmdiv. 1b/Br. B. Nr 411/44 g. Kdos. Lagebericht.

8 GAKR: Carabinieri Ufficio Centrale di Pubblica Sicurezza No. 1271/230-1932 di prot. Rodi, 18 Feb. 1938 xvi. Orgetto Comunita israelitica di Rodi. A sua Eccellenza il Governatore delle Isole Italiane dell'Egeo Rodi. Officially known as *Repubblica Sociale Italiana* (Italian Social Republic), the Republic of Salò was in fact a puppet regime created on 25 September by the Germans and headed by Mussolini after his dramatic release from confinement by German paratroopers. It stretched from the border to Tirol in the north to the German military zone encompassing Rome. Philip Morgan, *The Fall of Mussolini: Italy, the Italians,*

and the Second World War (Oxford University Press: New York, Oxford, 2007); MacGregor Knox, *Common Destiny: Dictatorship, Foreign Policy, and War in Fascist Italy and Nazi Germany* (Cambridge University Press: Cambridge, 2000); Jonathan Steinberg, *All or Nothing: The Axis and the Holocaust 1941–1943* (Routledge: London, 1990).

9   Davide Rodogno, *Fascism's European Empire: Italian Occupation during the Second World War* (Cambridge University Press: Cambridge, 2006). McGuire, *Italy's Sea.*

10   Vitalis Strumza, 'Alcuni Cenni Storici Sugli Ebrei di Rodi' (n.p.: Bologna, 1936). A copy is in Special Collections, University of Washington Libraries 3270 (Accession No. 3270-001). See also his cultural history of the Ottoman-era pirate Jan Janszoon van Haarlem aka Murad Reis, 'Il "Tecche" Di Murad Reis A Rodi', in *Rivista delle Colonie Italiane* (Capelli Editore: Bologna, 1934). For reference to Strumza's expertise on religious customs, Alexis Rappas, 'Mixed Marriages in the Fascist Aegean and the Domestic Foundations of Imperial Sovereignty', in Ulrike Lindner, Dörte Lerp (eds.), *New Perspectives on the History of Gender and Empire: Comparative and Global Approaches* (Bloomsbury: London, 2018), pp. 31–58, here: 42–43.

11   GAKR Governo delle Isole Italiane Dell'Egeo, Archivio Titolo: Piena Cittadinanza Strumza Vitalis, Fascicolo 1, contains documentation on his full citizenship from 19 February 1934. Grassini's comment in correspondence to All'ufficio centrale di publica sicurezza di Rodi, folio 1695, 19 Dec. 1934, XIII. Brief biographical details also in McGuire, *Italy's Sea*, p. 174.

12   'Italy's Fascist Jews: Insights on an Unusual Scenario', ed. Michele Sarfatti, *QUEST. Issues in Contemporary Jewish History. Journal of Fondazione CDEC*, Issue n. 11 (October, 2017); Alice Tarica-Israël, *Des ténèbres au soleil* (Clepsydre: Nivelles, 2015), pp. 18–19 (with photograph of Alice's twin brother Maurizio in his *Balilla* uniform).

13   Tracy H. Koon, *Believe, Obey, Fight: Political Socialization of Youth in Fascist Italy, 1922–1943* (University of North Carolina Press: Chapel Hill and London, 2012); Alessio di Ponzio, *Shaping the 'New Man'. Totalitarian Training Regimes in Fascist Italy and Nazi Germany* (University of Wisconsin Press: Madison, 2015) (paperback July 2017). An early account is by James W. Miller, 'Youth in the Dictatorships', *American Political Science Review*, Vol. 32, No. 5 (October 1938), pp. 965–970.

14   Unlike with youth, the surviving documentation of membership of adult Fascist organizations reveals little to nothing of Jewish membership.

15 Franco, Diamente Hugno, Shoah Foundation VHA Interview 48392, seg. 33. Visual History Archive, USC Shoah Foundation 1998. GAKR Carabinieri 1/47/1049 Hugno Nissim di Giuseppe.

16 GAKR, Carabinieri Files: Inventario Juderia 1932, 1,2/669. He was born in 1919 and emigrated to the Congo in 1939. Hizka Franco also left for Zimbabwe (then Rhodesia) before the deportation, probably after the death of his wife Sol Alhadeff in Kos on 27 November 1943. Their daughter Elisa was deported from Kos but survived the Holocaust; she was liberated from Theresienstadt, see Chapter 6. His son was not deported and he too survived the Holocaust.

17 GAKR Carabinieri 1/47/1054, Giacomo Alhadeff: Oggett Alhadeff Giacomo inscrizione al F[ederazione dei fasci].G[iovanale di].C[omattimento].

18 *The Longest Journey*, 21:45 min. *Dodecanese Handbook*, p. 20; Papachristodoulou, *Istoria tis Rodou*, pp. 562, 576; Alexander J. De Grand, *Fascist Italy and Nazi Germany: The 'Fascist' Style of Rule,* 2nd edition (Routledge: London and New York, 1997), p. 66.

19 Tarica-Israël, *Des ténèbres au soleil*, p. 18.

20 Hanan, Rachel Hugno, b. 22 October 1924. Interview 13096, seg. 16–17. Visual History Archive, USC Shoah Foundation.

21 Stella Levi in *The Longest Journey*, 21:37 min.

22 Hizkia M. Franco, *The Jewish Martyrs of Rhodes and Cos*, trans. from French by Joseph Franco (HarperCollins: Zimbabwe, 1954), p. 11. At the date of De Vecchi's arrival, the Jewish community numbered 3,134. On De Vecchi, see: Adolfo Mignemi, 'Il Governatorato di De Vecchi alla Vigilia Della Guerra', in Peri (ed.), *La politica culturale del fascismo*, pp. 107–121. An official summary of De Vecchi's career can be found at: http://notes9.senato.it/Web/senregno.NSF/a04d83b9abb14b3ec125711400382f82/b833a6591f828d4e4125646f005b1d2e?OpenDocument

23 Mignemi, 'Il Governatorato', p. 108.

24 The first settlement was established at Peveragno in 1929, today, Apo Kalamanos.

25 Avraham Galante, *Appendice a l'histoire des Juifs de Rhodes* (Editions Isis: Istanbul, 1948), p. 271, gives the turning point as 15 September 1938.

26 GAKR 2P.S. 2, Comunita Israelitica di Rodi (1932), Ufficio Centrale Pubblico di Sicurezza, No. 1271233-1932 di prot. 9 March 1938. Oggetto: Giornale Ebraica 'Israel', A Sue Excellenza il Governatore delle Isole Italiane dell'Egeo, Rodi. *Carabinieri* files translation of article 'Italy and Anti-Zionism: Information and Two Denials', *Israel*, 3 March 1938.

27 *Dodecanese Handbook*, Part I, People and Administration (HMO: London, 1943), p. 19.

28 *Messaggero di Rodi* No. 289, 19 December 1936. His mother, Teodolinda (b. 14.11.1853), died on 12 December 1936 in Turin, https://www.geni.com/people/Teodolinda-De-Vecchi/6000000075555294594

29 GAKR Carabinieri 20.P.S.2 (1932) Comunita Israelitica di Rodi 3.Fascicolo, Ufficio Centrale di Pubblica Sicurezza No. 1271/230-1932 di prot. Memorandum Guido Grassini, 18 February 1938.

30 Ibid, pag. 259: Promemoria (Il Commandante del Grupo CC.RR, capo del Ufficio Centrale Speziale. Maggiore F. Mittino), 27 September 1938.

31 Nicholas Doumanis, *Myth and Memory in the Mediterranean: Remembering Fascism's Empire* (Palgrave Macmillan: London, 1997), presents a more benign relationship between Greeks and Italians.

32 GAKR Carabinieri P.S. 2.20, Comunita Israelitica di Rodi, pag. 384 Prot. 798/40 Union Della Comunita Israeliche Italiane to Comunita Israelitica di Rodi, 11 June 1940 and response dated 21 June 1940, in same file.

33 Hanan, Interview 13096, seg. 17. Yom Kippur occurred mid-week from 4 to 5 October.

34 Isaac Jack Lévy, *Jewish Rhodes: A Lost Culture* (Judah L. Magnes Museum: Berkeley, CA, 1989), pp. 37–38. For the law: RD-L 5 settembre 1938, n. 1390, Provvedimenti per la difesa della razza nella scuola fascista (GU n. 209, 13 settembre 1938).

35 The decision to pass the law was taken by the Gran Consiglio del fascismo at its meeting of 6–7 October; it followed on the Manifesto of Race 14 July. The laws were approved on 11 November and came into effect on the 17th with their publication in the official gazette. Regio Decreto n. 1728, 17 novembre 1938-XVII sulla difesa della razza italiana. Galante, *Appendice a l'histoire*, 271–272. This newspaper was already presenting in its sports section highly antisemitic accounts of Jewish sport clubs. Eirini Toliou, 'Η φιλαναγνωσία ως εργαλείο προπαγάνδας μέσω της εφημερίδας Il Messaggero di Rodi, την περίοδο της Ιταλοκρατίας στα Δωδεκάνησα, 1923–1943' ('Literacy as a tool of propaganda through the newspaper Il Messaggero di Rodi, during the period of Italian rule in the Dodecanese, 1923–1943'), (MA Thesis University of Athens, 2019).

36 RD-L 17 novembre 1938, n. 1728, Provvedimenti per la difesa della razza italiana (GU n. 264, 19 novembre 1938). In most survivor accounts there is a conflation of the November laws and the earlier measures.

37 Michele Sarfatti, 'Characteristics and Objectives of the Anti-Jewish Racial Laws in Fascist Italy, 1938–1943', in Joshua D. Zimmerman (ed.), *Jews in Italy under Fascist and Nazi Rule, 1922–1945* (Cambridge University Press: Cambridge, 2005), pp. 71–80. The full text of the leggi razialli – R.D.L. Nr 1778, can be found at https://it.wikisource.org/wiki/R.D.L._17_novembre_1938,_n._1728_-_Provvedimenti_per_la_difesa_della_razza_italiana

38 GAKR ΙΔΔ ΕΤΟΣ 1938, ΦΑΚ 591/878, for annulment of religious courts 26 November 1938, and proscription of *shechitah*.

39 GAKR Carabinieri 20.P.S.2 1932, Comunita Israelitica di Rodi,. 3. Fascicolo, p. 30 'Promenoria' and report of military search of homes.

40 Tarica-Israël, *Des ténèbres au soleil*, p. 25.

41 Details in GAKR Governo della Isole Italiane Dell'Egeo, Strumza Vitalis, Fascicolo 1, as n. 11.

42 GAKR 1.1.136 (1933), Carabinieri: 'Strumza Vitalis'. The quote comes from his covering note to Mittino, letter 28 November 1938. Yet in a letter to Davide Prato, the chief rabbi of Rome, Strumza wrote: 'It's useless that I should describe to you our mood here. I am getting ready to leave, my heart heavy with bitterness at the thought of abandoning this island and this environment for which I have worked passionately and with love over the past eighteen years.' Letter to Davide Prato, 15 November 1938, in ibid.

43 GAKR 1.1.136, letter to Menascé, 22 May 1939. Luca Pignataro, *Il Dodecaneso Italiano 1912–1947: III – De Vecchi, Guerra E Dopoguerra 1936–1947/50* (Solfanelli: Chieti C.P., 2018), p. 472.

44 Alice Tarica, Interview, Fortunoff Archive, segs. 4, 7.

45 Ibid.

46 *Messaggero di Rodi*, Nr 276, 3 December 1938.

47 Tarica, Interview, Fortunoff Archives, seg. 4.

48 GAKR, ΙΔΔ ΕΤΟΣ 1939 Φακ 534 κγπο 975 ΤΜ1, report by Mancuso (Guardia di Finanza), 30 December 1938. For Alexandria see the 'family biography' Gini Alhadeff, *The Sun at Midday: Tales of a Mediterranean Family* (Pantheon Books: New York, 1997).

49 Alhadeff, Nissim, Interview 1577. Tape 1. Visual History Archive, USC Shoah Foundation 1995. Accessed 13 January 2017. Alhadeff, *Le Chêne de Rhodes*, p. 22.

50 GAKR ΙΔΔ ΕΤΟΣ 1939, ΦΑΚ: 534 κγπο 975 ΤΜ1, Governo delle isole italiane dell'Egeo. Archivio Titolo: Varie Informazioni, 1938. Secreto. Nota di servizio. Ogetto: Esportazione clandestine di capitali ebraica (Mancuso), 31 December 1938; also Mancuso's earlier report of 17 November 1938, and again of 19 May 1939 (Vendita fittizia di negozi da parte di guide) in the same file.

51   Giovanni Cecini, *La Guardia di Finanza Nelle Isole Italiane Dell'Egeo 1912–1945* (Gangermi Editore: Rome, 2014), p. 213.

52   Sami Modiano, *The Longest Journey*, 25:00 min.

53   Stella Levi, *The Longest Journey*, 24:35 min.

54   Ferrera, Rosa, Interview 44115, seg. 22. Visual History Archive, USC Shoah Foundation 1996. Accessed 22 June 2016.

55   Kantor, Lina, Interview 33706, seg. 13. Visual History Archive, USC Shoah Foundation, 1997. Her family name was Amato, she was born in 1936.

56   Hanan, Interview 13096, seg. 22. In her interview, Hanan recalls how she was told by the office manager she would not be able to continue working in the public sector; but the girls in the office threatened to leave unless she was reinstated, which happened unofficially.

57   USHMM, RG-50.233*0001, Alcana Transcript, p. 3.

58   GAKR Carabinieri Ufficio Centrale di P.S., 20.PS.2: Comunita Israelitica di Rodi (1932), Ufficio Centrale di Publica Sicurezza, No.1271/205-1932 di prot., Oggetto: Comunita israeilitca di Rodi, A S.E. il Governatore delle Isole Italiana dell'Egeo, 21 February 1937 (Il Maggiore Guido Grassini). The following is based on this account and a preliminary report. Gattegno was born in 1889 in Salonica and died at an early age in 1941. His four children Virginia, b. 1923, Lea, b. 1925, Alberto, b. 1927, and Michele, b. 1940, were deported with their 44-year-old mother Marcella Luzzatto (Deportation list nos. 962-966, GAKR I.Δ.Δ. ΦΑΚ 293, TMHMA 1/1). Virginia A24323 and Lea A24324 survived. Alberto B7333 perished in Mauthausen-Ebensee. Toddler Michele was gassed with his mother on arrival at Auschwitz. For family details (1939), see Race Card No. 235 and Benatar and Benatar, *Si je t'oublie*, p. 285.

59   Bension was born on 27 December 1924. Seven years after this event he would be deported to Auschwitz where he subsequently perished. His father, Giuseppe (b. 1899), was admitted to the camp but died sometime after 11 September. A sister Lucia (b. 1937), also was murdered, as too was his mother, Djoja-Gioia Levi. Another sister, Maria, born in 1930, survived. Benatar and Benatar, *Si je t'oublie*, p. 503.

60   GAKR Carabinieri Ufficio Centrale di P.S., 20.PS.2: Comunita Israelitica di Rodi (1932), Ufficio Centrale di Publica Sicurezza, No.1271/205-1932 di prot., Promemoria, 20 February 1937.

61   Report 21 February 1937. Grassini's actual words were: 'penso che un richiamo alla maestra potrebbbe sonore, senza chiasso l'incidente.' My translation.

62 GAKR Carabinieri 1.1.160 Politica razzista, No. 1271/224-1932 di prot. Appunti per Il Cav. Travani.

63 Ibid.

64 Details of individual members of this family can be found via the index in Pignataro, *Il Dodecaneso Italiano 1912–1947: III, passim.*

65 *Il Messaggero di Rodi* No. 236, 13 October 1937, PNF Fasci Giovanili die Combattimento Comando Federal dell'Egeo: Radiazione 11 October 1937.

66 GAKR 6/100, Protocollo n. 890/2 P.S. ufficio di igiene pubblica e sanità: venditore ambulante.

67 GAKR Carabinieri P.S. 6/110. The last reference in Ezra's file is in 1944 when he renewed his licence to polish shoes.

68 Clementi/Toliou, *Gli ultimi ebrei*, as n. 5. For Mittino: GAKR Carabinieri P.S. 1/2/117.

69 GAKR Carabinieri PS 6/27 (1932) Alcana, Giuseppe, di Abramo. The file opens in 1932, the year Alcana first applied for a licence to trade as a shoemaker.

70 Ibid, report of *Carabinieri* 5 November 1938.

71 GAKR Carabinieri P.S. 6.75, Alhanan, Celibi fu Natan. Interestingly, he was fined for 'innoservanza di calmiere', i.e. for sowing discord, presumably among other traders who he was undercutting.

72 GAKR Carabinieri: Inventaria Juderia, 2.40.84: Angel, Samuele, b. 1880.

73 Ibid, letter dated 27 April 1939.

74 Ibid.

75 GAKR Carabinieri P.S. 1.2.888, Avzaradel, Behor Baruh fu Isaco (*sic*). The following account is based on this file.

76 *Messaggero di Rodi*, No. 63, 18 March 1936.

77 GAKR Carabinieri P.S. 6.12/888, Avzaradel, Baruh.

78 GAKR Carabinieri P.S. 2.40.8/234 di Protocollo (1933). Gruppo Carabnieri Reali – Ufficio Centrale Speciale No. 234/20-1933 di prot.div. Ii°, Oggetto: Servizio delle guide autorizzate. A Il'Ufficio Finanza di Rodi, 28 February 1939. The guides whose licences were revoked were Nissim Benun, Giuseppe Cordoval, Giosue Coen, Leone Israel, Mose Levi, Mose Sciarcon and Marco Turiel. The file also contains the list of nine approved applicants for 1938 (22 June 1938); in addition to the aforementioned were Samuel Gattegno and Eliezer Israel.

79 For the family, see: Benatar and Benatar, *Si je t'oublie*, p. 593.

80 See for example, Flash, *A Hug from Afar,* p. 93. Her younger sister also mentions Claire's petitions to their Uncle Raphael, University Archives and Manuscripts Division, University of Washington, Seattle, Washington Digital Archives, Interview Regina Amira (Barkai), ohc_3137, transcript, p. 3.

81 *Dodecanese Handbook,* p. 14, where British observers noted that in general theft was 'mostly due to the extreme poverty of the inhabitants'.

82 GAKR Governo Delle Isole Italiane Dell'Egeo, Gruppo Carabinieri Reali Ufficio Centrale Speciale, Facicolo No. 53/1 A (1941).

83 Ibid, Procura de Re (Rodi), Richiesta di Notizie per Minorenne Delinquente O Traviato, 31 July 1941.

84 Ibid, Dispositivo di Sentenza, Il Tribunale Civile e Penale di Rodi, n. 254 Sentenza n. 271 R.P., 10 June 1942.

85 Ibid, Gruppo Autonomo Dei Carabiieri Reali Isole delle Isole Egee Ufficio Centrale Speciale, No.534/4-1941 di prot.div.3°, 13 July 1942 (S.Ten. Ettore Dalpiaz). One is tempted to think A. might be the 'friend' Eliezer Surmani mentions in his interview who stole money from a shop (Chapter 2).

86 The decree extended to all Italian colonies and possessions. On Italian colonialism and citizenship see above all: Filipo Espinoza, 'An Italian Nationality for the Levant: Citizenship in the Aegean from the Ottoman to the Fascist Empire (1912–1936)', in Simone Berhe and Olindo De Napoli (eds.), *Citizens and Subjects of the Italian Colonies: Legal Constructions and Social Practices 1882–1943* (Routledge: New York and London, 2022), pp. 109–130.

87 My calculation based on the Jewish Museum of Rhodes (JMR) Race Census cards. For the departures from September to December, GAKR Carabinieri 20.P.S.2. Comunita Israelitica, 3.Fascicolo, three lists, September, October and December together with a list of 64, totalling 161. An undated *Carabinieri* note in the same file mentions 104 passport applications for permament departure, ibid, p. 271.

88 Hirschon, 'The Jews of Rhodes', p. 297; Renée Hirschon, 'The Jews from Rhodes in Central and Southern Africa', in M. Ember, C. Ember and I. Skoggard (eds.), *Encyclopedia of Diasporas* (Kluwer Academic/Plenum Publishers: New York, 2005), pp. 925–934. Jacqueline Benatar and Myriam Pimienta-Benatar, *De Rhodes à Elisabethville: l'odyssée d'une communauté sépharade: essai historique illustré de 45 pages de photos et documents d'archives* (Editions SIIAC: Paris, 2000). Alhadeff, *Le Chêne de Rhodes,* pp. 231, 237–243. Andreas Guidi, 'Patterns of Jewish Mobility between Rhodes and Buenos Aires (1905–1948)', in

SüdosteuropäischeHefte, Vol. 4, No. 2 (2015), pp. 13–24. Individual examples at: http://www.rhodesjewishmuseum.org/history/emigration

89   GAKR Carabinieri Box102_1932_com.Israel_0002_0002E_2-PS_0002E_0174. jpg, p. 270.

90   Regio Decreto-Legge 17 novembre 1938 – XVII, n. 1728: Provvedimenti per la difesa della razza italiana, Art. 23 & 24.

91   GAKR Carabinieri 2.14.115, Varon, Salomone (passport application).

92   As in the case of the Jews who came from Halicarnassus (Bodrum) following the Lausanne Treaty.

93   GAKR Carabinieri 6.P.S.110, Hanan, Ezra di Moreno. Hanan's passport application letter, 22 June 1939. The photograph reproduced in Chapter 6 is the family passport photograph.

94   GAKR Carabinieri 20.P.S.2. Comunita Israelitica, 3.Fascicolo, letter to Grand Rabbi N. Ovadia, Paris, 9 December 1938, has the higher figure of 700. GAKR Carabinieri 20.P.S.2. Comunita Israelitica 5.Fascicolo. The file contains correspondence between Giacobbe Franco (incidentally which he signs off as 'vice president' of the Community and various international Jewish organizations). The figures of 300 persons is cited by Franco in his letter to the Union Universelle des Communautes Sephardites in Paris, 22 March 1939 (Prot. 456). The difference might be explained by departures between the racial laws and March. In 1939, John Menascé was still president of the Community but was in Italy when the war broke out and thus Franco acted on his behalf, ibid, No. 1271/377-1932, Gruppo Carabinieri Reale – Ufficio Centrale, Speciale 'Pro-Memoria', 13 November 1939; by the following year, Franco was signing off as president, ibid, Copy letter, Nr 877, Il Presidente, Comunita Israelitica Rodi to Unione delle Comunita Israelitiche Italiane, Roma, 21 June 1940. Meanwhile, the Jewish Telegraphic Agency in its bulletin 7 July, reported 450 refugees on the *Rim*. https://www.jta.org/archive/ship-taking-refugees-to-palestine-burns-passengers-rescued-by-italian-steamer. See also McGuire, *Italy's Sea*, p. 175.

95   It was now set for 12 March 1939. Details can be found in GAKR Carabinieri 20.P.S.2. Comunita Israelitica 5.Fascicolo.

96   GAKR Carabinieri 20.P.S. 2. 5.Fascicolo, letter from the American Consul General Naples, Foreign Service of the United States to President of the Jewish Community, 811.11 OH/LV, 12 June 1939.

97   GAKR Carabinieri, 20 P.S. 2. 3.Fascicolo translation of letter dated Giacobbe Franco to Saul Alhadeff, Salisbury, 27 December 1938. In this letter, Franco mentions 600–700 persons affected.

98 GAKR Carabinieri Cat.1/1/160 (1938), Oggetto: Politica Razzista: Elenco degli ebrei, già residenti a Rodi, partiti dal Possedimento dal 1. Septembre 1938.

99 Ibid. Looking at the the data it is not clear if some double-counting has occurred. Officials refer to Aegean Jews as well as Rhodian Jews; Turkish Jews are listed separately, as too are the *Rim* refugees and other foreign Jews. In mid-March and in mid-August, 137 and 166 Turkish Jews are listed; at the same dates 154 and 197 (or 192) Aegean Jews are listed as having or preparing to depart. In those two months alone – if the figures are correct – 1,511 Jews left, including circa 600 *Rim* and foreign Jews; the others comprised Turkish and Aegean as well as Rhodian Jews, i.e. around 911.

100 Triantafillou, *From Halicarnassus to the Dodecanese*, ch. 2.

101 GAKR 1.1.160 Governo delle Isole Italiane dell'Egeo, Gruppo CC.RR. Ufficio Centrale Speciale: Politica razzista, Elenco Nominativo degli ebrei, già residente a Rodi partito dal Possedimento dal 1. Settembre 1938. This is a five-page list with 200 entries – last ones here 19 February. We do not know if this is the complete list.

102 Ibid.

103 Ibid. Telepresso N. 6308/1465, Posizione A-71/6, Consolato Generale, Jersusalem, 13 November 1939: immigrazione clandestine di ebrei italiani.

104 Yad Vashem Archives (hereafter: YVA) 03/10423 Laura Varon, VD1390, interviewed by Yael Ben Schmuel, 14 November 1996, transcript, p. 17. The family were No. 11 on a list of sixty-four households due for expulsion, GAKR Carabinieri 20.P.S. 2. 3. Fascicolo, undated list but probably late spring 1939 – the Varons were present after the census in February/March was taken.

105 After France's surrender to Germany and Italy entered the war, Spain occupied the Free Zone of Tangier. Graham H. Stuart, *The International City of Tangier* (Stanford University Press: Stanford, 1931); Graham H. Stuart, 'The Future of Tangier', *Foreign Affairs. Council on Foreign Relations*, Vol. 23, No. 4 (July 1945). doi:10.2307/20029932. JSTOR 20029932.

106 GAKR Carabinieri 20.P.S. 2. 4. Fascicolo, letter Samuel M. Levy Haifa and Tel Aviv to Comunita Israelitica Rodi, 9 January 1939. An important contemporary assessment of the refugee crisis in the later 1930s, including defining a 'refugee', can be found in John Hope Simpson, 'The Refugee Crisis', in *International Affairs (Royal Institute of International Affairs 1931–1939)* Vol. 17, No. 5 (Sep.–Oct. 1938), pp. 607–628. More recently, Paul R. Bartrop, *The Evian Conference of 1938 and the Jewish Refugee Crisis* (Palgrave Macmillan: London, 2018). An accessible online introduction to the refugee crisis in Europe

resulting from Nazi anti-Jewish policies United States Holocaust Memorial Museum, 'The Evian Conference', *Holocaust Encyclopedia*, https://encyclopedia. ushmm.org/content/en/article/the-evian-conference. A critical study of the impact of the Italian Race Laws and expulsions resulting in a refugee crisis in the Mediterranean is a desideratum.

107 There was mention of 200 Jews affected by the expulsion order in a letter from the Jewish Community in Tangier, GAKR Carabinieri P.S. 2.20.1271 1932 6. Fascicolo, Comunidad Israelita de Tangier, Comité pro Refugiados to Comunita Israelitica Rodi, 11 July 1939. In 1945, there were 157 Aegean Jews in Tangier from a refugee population of 807 European Jews.

108 Levy [Amato], Rebecca, Interview 8750. Segs. 24-34. Visual History Archive, USC Shoah Foundation, 1996. Accessed January 2017. See the photograph of Rebecca in Moise's shop in Rhodes, reproduced in Rhodes Jewish Historical Foundation Calendar September 2018/September 2019 – Elul 5778/Tishri 5780, February 2019 facing page. Rebecca was a cousin of Stella Levi, whom we have cited several times in this chapter.

109 GAKR Carabinieri P.S. 2.20.1271, pag. 357f., letter from Hiskia Buenavida to Giacobbe Franco, dated 27 May 1939. The file has both a copy of the original handwritten letter and a typed copy in Italian.

110 GAKR Carabinieri P.S. 2.20.1271 Comunita Isrealitica di Rodi, pag. 376f, Gruppo Carabinieri Reale Nr 1271/355 copy of letter Refugee Committee Jewish Community Tangier to Jewish Community Rhodes, 8 August 1939. And GAKR Carabinieri P.S. 2.20.1271 1932, p. 355, copy of letter from Buenavida to Jewish Community Rhodes, 29 May 1939. Attached to the letter to Franco (n. 93) is another letter to Dr David Gaon in which Buenavida outlines the 'grave problems' facing all refugees in Tangier. See also British Foreign Office report on the influx of refugees into Tangier in 1939, TNA FO 371/4380 and FO 371/23117/13619.

111 GAKR Carabinieri P.S. 2.20.1271 1932 5. Fascicolo, Comunita Israelitica di Rodi, p. 372f. Gruppo Carabinieri Reale Nr 1271/271, 1 August 1939, copy of letter from Kewish Community of Salisbury Rhodesia to Jewish Community Rhodes, regarding the arrival of five families, 26 July 1939. See also p. 373 for a letter from the Jewish Community of Tangier to Rhodes, on the same theme of destitution among the Rhodes families.

112 Calculated from the prices given by Worldaround Transport and Shipping Company to Comunita Israelitica Rodi, 17 March 1939 in GAKR Carabinieri 20.P.S. 2. 1932 5. Fascicolo.

113   Ibid, letter from Giacobbe Franco to Dr Harry S. Tarica, President for the
      Committee Italian Jewish Refugee, Seattle, concerning Yanoulatos Bros.
      Shipping (China), Paris Office, Voyage en Palestine, 18 March 1939. See the
      offer from F. Pisante, Athens (£8 per person), to Comunita Israelitica Rodi,
      5 February 1939, in GAKR Carabinieri 20.P.S. 2. 1932 4. Fascicolo.

114   GAKR Carabinieri 20.P.S. 2. 1932 6. Fascicolo, letter dated 22 July 1939 from
      the vice president of the Sephardi Community Salisbury to Franco warning
      against a certain Viennese Dr Willy Perl who had previously 'mis-applied'
      Jewish emigration funds. The Rhodes community, however, had already entered
      a contract with Perl, ibid, Franco to Jewish Community Bucharest, Prot. 721,
      7 July 1939.

115   For example, see two surviving credit/debit loose sheets from 1939 of Robert
      Barcilon in Alexandria (Egypt) who appears to have acted as a broker between
      the community and donors in: GAKR Carabinieri 20.P.S. 2. 1932 6. Fascicolo.
      The main donors were from Salisbury, Elisabethville, Seattle and New York.
      See also the correspondence between Rhodes and donors relating to Barcilon's
      services in GAKR Carabinieri 20.P.S.2 1932 5. Fascicolo.

116   Rosemary Lévy Zumwalt, 'Stories, Food, and Place: Following a Sephardic
      Family to a New Home', *Sephardic Horizons*, Vol. 6, No. 1, https://www.
      sephardichorizons.org/Volume6/Issue1/Zumwalt.html. David Mussafir was
      also the president of the Etz Ahayem Congregation in Montgomery, GAKR
      Carabinieri P.S. 2.20.1271 1932 4. Fascicolo, letter David Mussafir to Giacobbe
      Franco, 5 January 1939.

117   Zumwalt, 'Stories, Food, and Place'.

118   Flash, *A Hug from Afar*, p. 115.

119   Ibid, p. 116.

120   Ibid, p. 130. At the time Claire was writing, Tangier was experiencing
      widespread social unrest; reports in TNA FO 371/31257 and FO 371/31256. For
      reports on the economic conditions in Tangier 1941-43, TNA FO 371/26937
      (1941), FO 371/31251 (1942); FO 371/34841 (1943).

121   It should be added here that the Nazis also monitored the Jews in Tangier, TNA
      GFM 33/2246/5197 (captured German documents).

122   Amato, Lucia Sciarcon, Interview 14687. Visual History Archive, USC
      Shoah Foundation, 1996. Accessed 23 June 2016. Lucia was born in 1921,
      née Sciarcon. Rachel Hanan in her testimony spoke of a mass exodus of 500
      young Jews who left. Although, in the interview, she gives 1938 as the year this
      occurred, it was in fact 1939. According to Galante, *Appendice a l'histoire*, 274,

the Racial Laws affected circa 103 families comprising 480 persons. The original data in the *Carabinieri* archive is sporadic. But if we calculate from the extant information, and include the refugees from the steamer *Rim*, then close to a thousand Jews were impacted by the laws.

123 Lucia Garzolini né Franco. USHMM Testimony RG-50.030*0452, June 4, 1997 (in Italian).

124 GAKR 1.1.160 Politica Razsista.

125 'As they hold Italian passports we should regard them as Italians, but for visa purposes it may be possible to treat them as friendly aliens if the consul general is satisfied that they are in fact friendly.' TNA 371/3444, Visas for British Territory for Rhode Island (*sic*) people (Italian Jews), 18 June 1942.

126 GAKR Carabinieri 20.P.S.2. 1932, 3 Fasicolo dal No. 216 et No. 286: Comunita Israelitica di Rodi. GAKR ΙΔΔ ΕΤΟΣ 1938 ΑΑ 889, ΦΑΚ 725, ΤΜ1, for individual queries regarding revocation of citizenship.

127 See Benatar and Benatar, *Si je t'oublie*, p. 272 for the family. All but one died in Auschwitz, Mauthausen and Bergen-Belsen.

128 GAKR Governo delle Isole Italiane Dell'Egeo, Ufficio Centrale di Pubblica Sicurezza, 2.20.25, 1933, Israel, Lea fu Nissim. Family details in Benatar and Benatar, *Si je t'oublie*, p. 322.

129 Benatar and Benatar, *Si je t'oublie*, pp. 27, 44.

130 GAKR Governo delle Isole Italiane Dell'Egeo, Ufficio Centrale di Pubblica Sicurezza 2.12.2292, (1833), Ricca (Ketty) Angel, di Samuele & GAKR Governo delle Isole Italiane Dell'Egeo, Ufficio Centrale di Pubblica Sicurezza, 2.12.802 (1934). Vittoria Angel applied for her passport in 1934.

131 Elsewhere in her file, a 'certificate of good conduct' gives her birth date as 21 March 1906 (!).

132 Benatar and Benatar, *Si je t'oublie*, p. 403. Bulissa was 55 years old at the time of the deportation.

133 Benatar and Benatar, *Si je t'oublie*, p. 273. Rebecca was 47 years old in 1944.

134 Benatar and Benatar, *Si je t'oublie*, p. 73; describes 45-year-old Estrea as widow. There is no record of Marco Amato in the Jewish cemetery of Rhodes, www.rhodesjewishmuseum.org/cemetery/plots?letter=A-Tombstones

135 Benatar and Benatar, *Si je t'oublie*, p. 587. Mazaltov was 42 years old when deported.

136 We will return to Mazaltov and her husband Marco Scemaria in Chapter 7.

137 It is not clear from her interview why this should be the case, especially given the expulsion clause in the decree of 7 September 1938, and incorporated into the Law for the Defence of the Italian Race, 17 November.

138 Bowman, *Agony*, p. 37. Papachristodoulou, *Istoria tis Rodou*, p. 576.

139 GAKR Carabinieri 1.1.264 1934, Tarica, Nissim.

140 GAKR Carabinieri 1.1.264, Tarica, Nissim.

141 Ibid, Governatore Telepresso Nr 6678, 15 February 1939. Tarica was told that
     no exceptions could be made. Meanwhile, he started the process for obtaining
     the passport for himself and his Turkish-born wife Lina Ferrera (1907 in Izmir)
     and their 10-year-old son Sami, by requesting from the *Carabinieri* a statement
     of 'good conduct'. The passport was to be valid for Italy, France, Cypress,
     Palestine and Egypt, ibid, p. 21.

142 GAKR Carabinieri 1.1.124.

143 He is buried in the Jewish cemetery in Rhodes.

144 As well as Rodogno, 'Italiani brava gente?' and Klein, *Italy's Jews from
     Emancipation to Fascism* cited in n. 2, see Paolo Fonzi, 'Beyond the Myth
     of the "Good Italian": Recent Trends in the Study of the Italian Occupation
     of Southeastern Europe during the Second World War', *Südosteuropa*, Vol. 65
     (2017), pp. 239–259.

145 Moreover, these measures against the islands' Jews cannot be equated with
     Italian cooperation in the Holocaust more generally. See Michele Sarfatti, *The
     Jews in Mussolini's Italy: From Equality to Persecution*, trans. John and Anne
     C. Tedeschi (Wisconsin University Press: Madison Wisconsin, 2006), ch. 5
     especially.

146 See the abovementioned studies by Clementi/Toliou, *Gli ultimi ebrei*
     (critical),and Pignataro, *Il Dodecaneso Italiano: III* (apologetic).

147 GAKR 20.P.S. 2, Comunita Israelitica di Rodi (1932), Ufficio Centrale
     Pubblico di Sicurezza, No. 1271/233-1932 di prot., 9 March 1938. Oggetto:
     Giornale Ebraica 'Israel', A Sue Excellenza il Governatore delle Isole Italiane
     dell'Egeo, Rodi. Carabinieri files translation of article 'Italy and Anti-Zionism:
     Information and Two Denials', *Israel*, 3 March 1938.

148 Garzolini,Testimony RG-50.030*0452, as n. 123.

149 Hanan, Interview 13096, seg. 22, testimony.

150 Various reasons have been given for his recalling, the most cited is that Rome
     feared his abrasive manner would alienate further the Greek population driving
     it into the hands of the British.

151 GAKR ΙΔΔ ΕΤΟΣ 1942,ΦΑΚ 1616M 1a 236, has various requests from the
     Jewish community for religious observance – all granted by Campioni.

152 Esther Fintz Menascé, *Buio nell'isola del sole: Rodi 1943–1945. I due volti di una
     tragedia quasi dimenticata: il martirio dell'ammiraglio Campioni e dei militari
     italiani in Egeo, e lo sterminio degli ebrei di Rodi e Coo* (Giuntina: Firenze, 2005).

153 GAKR Ufficio Centrale Speciale (Carabinieri) 5755 Fascicolo di Angel, Gioia (1942).

154 GAKR, IDD FAK 17/2 (1944), miscellaneous compensation lists.

155 ACICR B Sec. CG56, B-03403 (28.11.1944–29.03.1945), Rapport de M. Raymond Courvoisier, 23 March 1945, p. 17.

156 BA-MA RH26/1007/12, Bl. 9, for report of February bombardment.

157 BA-MA RH26/100725 Anl. 8. Kdt. Ost Aegaeis Abt. 1c Br.B. Nr 4930/44 geh. 5.7.44/Di. Betr. 1c Beitrag zum 1a Lagebericht pp. 4/5 Bl. 21 Anlage 1 zu kdt. Ost.A. Abt. 1c Nr 941/44 g.kdos. Einzelheiten über feindl. Luftangriffe von 1.6.44–7.7.44.

158 While it is unlikely the British stepped down their attacks against Rhodes, the Dodecanesian archive nonetheless fall silent after this date. The attacks were mostly nocturnal; from early July a squadron of German fighters was sent to Rhodes.

159 Popular lore wrongly has it that the Germans bombed his house in retaliation for his intervention preventing the deportation of Jews holding Turkish papers. See Chapters 5 and 9 of this study. Also, Clementi and Toliou, *Gli ultimi ebrei*, pp. 186–187, 190–191, 283, n.699. Clementi, *Storia della comunità*, pp. 419–420.

160 GAKR I.Δ.Δ. ΕΤΟΣ 1944, ΦΑΚ 195, unordered invoices and receipts for repairs to their property in Via Duca degli Abruzzo, Impresa Eligio Pagani, 8 May 1944; Telepresso 174, Ente Governativo Case Economiche e Popolari, 27 November 1944 and Telepresso N.308, Direzione dei Lavori Pubblici Rodi, 7 December 1944.

161 GAKR Governo Delle Isole Italiane Dell'Egeo Archivio R.14: Elenco nominativo delle famiglie sinistrate dai bombardamenti aerei dell'8-9-10 Aprile 1944.

162 Franco, *The Jewish Martyrs*, p. 58; Benatar and Benatar, *Si je t'oublie*, p. 641.

163 RH26/1007/14, Kommandant Ost-Ägäis, Abt. 1a Br. B.N. 933/44, g.Kdos. Betr. Lagebeurteilung, Dem Oberkammondo der Heeresgruppe E, Abt. 1a, 8 July, Anlage 24/25.

164 The British airforce was deterred by the arrival of a squadron of Stukas; until that point, British bombers had had a free run of the skies over Rhodes.

165 ACICR B Sec. CG56, B-03403 (28.11.1944-29.03.1945), Rapport de M. Raymond Courvoisier, 23 March 1945, p. 17.

166 BA-MA RH26-1007/14, Anlage 24 & 25, Bl. 24-37, Kdt. Ost-Ägäis Abt. 1a Br. B.N. 933/44, g.Kdos. Betr. Lagebeurteilung Dem OberKdo. Der Hgr. E Abt. 1a, 8 July 1944, Anlage 24-25, 1.7. –27.9.44.

167   Matilde had converted to Catholicism in November 1943. We will meet her
      again in Chapter 8.

168   GAKR I.Δ.Δ. ΦAK 293: Carabinieri, 'Elenco degli Ebrei Deportati dai Tedeschi
      il 16.7.1944', sequential list: 1269, Guiseppe; 1270, Rachele; 1271, Stella.
      Photograph of the family in Benatar and Benatar, *Si je t'oublie*, p. 253. Another
      daughter, Maria, had left the island at the time of the census in 1938. The family
      entry in *CDEC* wrongly gives the children and both parents as having been
      deported to Auschwitz. Stella was transferred to Dachau at the end of October,
      and from there to the Flossenburg sub-camp of Wilischthal and finally to
      Theresienstadt, where she was liberated. See Chapter 8 for more detail.

169   The couple had married at the end of March 1928, their daughter Matilde
      was born in November. They also had a 13-year-old son Giuseppe (1931) and
      a second daughter, 11-year-old Yohevet who was named after her maternal
      grandmother. The family was said to live in miserable conditions (*versa in
      miseria*). See Benatar and Benatar, *Si je t'oublie*, p. 327.

170   GAKR Elenco, as n. 161.

171   We will come across this dimension of official files again in Chapter 8 when we
      discuss the sequestration of Jewish property.

172   Tracey Loughram, 'Shell Shock, Trauma, and the First World War: The Making
      of a Diagnosis and Its Histories', *Journal of the History of Medicine and Allied
      Sciences*, Vol. 67, No. 1 (1 January 2012), pp. 94–119.

173   Michael Roper, 'From the Shell-shocked Soldier to the Nervous Child:
      Psychoanalysis in the Aftermath of the First World War', *Psychoanalysis and
      History* Vol. 18, No. 1 (2016), pp. 39–69. See also generally, Nicholas Stargadt,
      Witnesses of War: Children's Lives Under the Nazis (Vintage Books: New York,
      2006).

174   Tarica-Israël, Interview Fortunoff Archive, seg. 7.

175   Tarica-Israël, *Des ténèbres au soleil*, pp. 30–31.

176   Ull'Ufficio Dello Stato Civile Rodi: Racial Census Card (Nr 242). Allegra was
      the daughter of Abramo Alcana and Sigura Hugno, Benatar and Benatar, *Si je
      t'oublie*, p. 15.

177   GAKR Carabinieri P.S. 2.40.10, Lustracarpe ambulante (1933); details also in
      his personal file: GAKR Carabinieri P.S. 2.40.38, Canan Abner (*sic*) di Moreno,
      Lustracarpe ambulante (1933).

178   Ibid, two page report 21 June 1944, Capo dell'Off. Locale di Polizia (Romeo
      Tinarelli).

179   Sara's siblings were Amelia, Violetta, Bellina, Giacobbe and Salva.

Chapter 4

1 Bundesarchiv-Militärarchiv Freiburg (hereafter: BA-MA) RH26/1007/15, Bl. 157, KTB Anlage 253.

2 BArch NS19/1806 fol. 1–33, report to OKW 14 June 1943.

3 Lucy Dawidowicz, *The War Against the Jews 1933–1945* (Viking Penguin Inc.: New York, 1975).

4 Discussion in Steven Bowman, 'Could the Dodekanesi Jews Have Been Saved?', Newsletter *of The Jewish Museum of Greece*, Vol. 26 (Winter 1989), pp. 1–2. See also Chapter 5 of the present study.

5 Hagen Fleischer, *Im Kreuzschatten der Mächte Griechenland 1941–1944* (Peter Lang: Frankfurt am Main, Bern, New York, 1986), p. 306.

6 On British oil interests in the Near East, Fiona M. Venn, 'The Wartime "Special Relationship"? From Oil War to Anglo-American Oil Agreement, 1939–1945', *The Journal of Transatlantic Studies*, Vol. 10, No. 2 (2012), pp. 119–133, and more generally: Fiona M. Venn, *Oil Diplomacy in the Twentieth Century* (Palgrave: London & New York, 1986).

7 These can be found in TNA FO371/24963.

8 TNA FO371/24963, p. 2–5, Minute Sheet: G. L. McDermott, 27 February 1940, here, p. 3.

9 The island would be later retaken by British forces and used as a launchpad for clandestine commando operations in the Eastern Aegean.

10 TNA FO/371/24963 for details.

11 Martin van Creveld, 'Prelude to Disaster: The British Decision to Aid Greece 1940–41', *Journal of Contemporary History* IX (3) (July 1974), pp. 65–92.

12 TNA FO371/24963, p. 476 Foreign Office 6 January 1940; cf p. 377goede, 380, minutes; Sheila Lawlor, 'Greece, March 1941: The Politics of British Military Intervention', *Historical Journal* XXV (4), (December 1982), pp. 439–464.

13 FO 954/11A/93, 'Most Secret Cypher Telegram' from Mideast to Air Ministry (Chiefs of Staff), CC 176, 12 January 1943. As well as references in FO371/24963, see FO286/1180 (1946 Dodecanese).

14 See the various reports of naval engagements in the Eastern Aegean documented in the German naval war diary and reproduced at www.wlb-stuttgart.de/seekrieg/.

15 From 1943 on Rhodes, these activities were conducted by Force 133 led by Major D. A. Riddle. Force 292 operated on Leros; Force 281 was a much larger force and from late 1944, operated throughout the Dodecanese. TNA HS5/585,

SOE Greece (September 1943–February 1945). Peter C. Smith and Edwin R. Walker, *War in the Aegean: The Campaign for the Eastern Mediterranean in WWII*, Stackpole Military History Series (Stackpole Books: Mechanicsburg, PA, [1974] 2008). Anthony Rogers, *Churchill's Folly: The Battles for Kos and Leros, 1943*, Foreword by Lord Jellicoe (The History Press: Stroud, [2003] 2017). Peter Schenk, *Kampf um die Ägäis: Die Kriegsmarine in Griechischen Gewässern 1941–1945* (E. S. Mitler & Sohn: Hamburg, Berlin, Bonn, 2000).

16   The *Deutsches Afrika Korps* was established in February 1941 under the command of General, later Fieldmarshal, Erwin Rommel.

17   Barch NS19/240 fol.1-10, 'Niederschrift' (Himmler's account of the meeting of 11 Oct 1942). Barch NS19/1972, microfiche: folio 1-3, RF-SS, Feldk[omman]do[stelle], 22 October 1942, correspondence between Himmler and Ribbentrop.

18   Barch NS 19/1951, Mikrofiche, Fol. 1-3, Der RFSS Chef der SS-Hauptamtes Tgb. Nr 1492/42 geh. 2.4.43, Betr. Schreiben des Hptm.d.R., Siebel.

19   Josef Schröder, *Italiens Kriegsaustritt 1943. Die deutschen Gegenmaßnahmen im italienischen Raum: Fall 'Alarich' und 'Achse'* (Musterschmidt Verlag: Göttingen, Zürich, Frankfurt, 1969), pp. 245ff.

20   Percy E. Schramm (ed.), *Kriegstagebuch des Oberkommandos der Wehrmacht 1943 Teilband II, Zusammengestellt und erläutert von Walther Hubatsch* (Manfred Pawlak, Verlagsgesellschaft: Herrsching, 1982), pp. 829–845, cited hereafter: KTB OKW. Timothy D. Saxon, 'The German Side of the Hill: Nazi Conquest and Exploitation of Italy, 1943–45' (PhD Thesis, University of Virginia, 1999), pp. 196ff. Jens Petersen, 'Deutschland und Italien 1939 bis 1945', in Wolfgang Michalka (ed.),*Der Zweite Weltkrieg: Analysen, Grundzüge, Forschungsbilanz, Im Auftrag des Militärgeschichtlichen Forschungsamtes* (Seehamer Verlag: Munich, 1989), pp. 108–119.

21   Robert Citino, 'Drive to Nowhere: The Myth of the *Afrika Korps*, 1941–43', https://www.nationalww2museum.org/war/articles/drive-nowhere-myth-afrika-korps-1941-43

22   Mazower, *Hitler's Empire*.

23   BA-MA RH26/1007/15, Bl. 157, KTB Anlage 253.

24   BA-MA RH26/1007/1 Anlage 11a, Bl. 27: Abschrift Fernschreiben vopn OKW/WF St. An OB Südost v. 19.5.43.

25   Wilhelm Deist, *Militär, Staat und Gesellschaft: Studien zur preußisch-deutschen Militärgeschichte* (Beiträge zur Militärgeschichte, Band 34) (De Gruyter/Oldenbourg: Berlin, 1991), pp. 385–430.

26 Barch Pers.6/223, Heeresleitung Personalamt. Personalakten f. Kleemann, Ulrich (BA-MA, Gs-Bestand Nr 6 Archiv Nr 223 Koblenz 'B', Nr 305, 21994 (BDC)).

27 Ibid. See also http://www.lexikon-der-wehrmacht.de/Personenregister/K/KleemannU-R.htm. According to internet sources, Kleemann commanded the 90th Light Africa Division from the end of April until mid-June 1942, https://www.feldgrau.com/WW2-German-90th-Light-Africa-Division. The *Führerreserve* was the designation given to officers currently inactive and awaiting new assignments.

28 In September 1944, Kleemann was redeployed to Bulgaria as General der Panzer. His Panzer division, *Feldherren*, was utterly destroyed the following spring and he was taken into American captivity. He remained as a prisoner of war until the end of June 1947.

29 BA-MA RH26/1007/1, Bl. 12, Kriegsrangliste, Sturmdivision Rhodos. Staff headquarters on Rhodes would eventually number around eighty men.

30 BA-MA RH26/1007/3, Sturmdivision Rhodos, Abt.1a Nr 66/43 g.Kdo. 16, Juli 1943, Mussolini Lagebeurteilung, III. Eigene taktische Lage und Absichten b) Eigene taktische Lage.

31 BA-MA RH26/1007/1, Bl. 27, Anlage 11a: Abschrift: Fernschreiben von OKW/WFSt. an OB. Südost vom 19.5.43

32 According to Schenk, *Kampf*, p. 78, Lieutenant-Colonel Müller led the successful assault against Simi, 7–8 October.

33 BA-MA RH26/1007/26, Heeres-, Luftwaffen- und Kriegsmarine-Einheiten und Dienststellen mit Stellenbesetzung im Befehlsbereich Kommandant Ost-Ägäis 28. März 1943 bis 8. Mai 1945 (Müller-Mangeot). This nine-page document was compiled by First Lieutenant Müller who was First Ordnance Officer from 16.7.43 to 22.9.44; he compiled it from memory and using the surviving documents and war diary of the Division. The foregoing is based on this document. For Wagener, Otto Wagener, *Hitler aus nächster Nähe. Aufzeichnungen eines Vertrauten 1929–1932*, ed. Henry Ashby Turner (Ullstein Verlig: Berlin, 1985), also translated as *Hitler: Memoirs of a Confidant* edited and introduced by Henry Ashby Turner (Yale University Press: New Haven, CT, 1985).

34 BA-MA RH26/1007/6, Bl.39, KTB Rhodes Ib, Anlage 164: 15.9.43, Personalstârke vom 31.8.43; ibid, Anlage 166: Auf der Insel Rhodos befindliche [Italian] Truppen. The total Italian force included 8,250 sailors, a large part of which would have been stationed at the naval base on Leros.

35 We return to this point below.

36 BA-MA RH26/1007/3, Bl. 57, Sturmdivision Rhodos Abt.1a Nr 66/43, g.kdos. Div.Gef.Std., Betr. Lagebeurteilung, 16 Juli 1943.

37 BA-MA RH26/1007/3, Bl. 82, Kommandeur-Besprechung am 25 Juli 1943.

38 BA-MA RH26/1007/3, Bl. 84-86, Anl. 52. The Legion was a voluntary force composed of civilian Fascists which formed the paramilitary wing of the PNF.

39 Ibid, Bl.110. Sturmdiv. Rhodos, Abt. 1a Nr 90/43 g. Kdos, 29 July 1943 (Zusatz).

40 See for example, BA-MA RH26/1007/3, Bl. 104, Captain Bayer handwritten notes on Peretti's second visit to Kleemann on 28 July.

41 BA-MA RH26/1007/3, Bl. 85-86, Bayer, handwritten notes Nr 4, 26 July 1943 (Besuch des Div. K[omman]deurs beim General Scaroina).

42 BA-MA RH26/1007/3, Bayer, handwritten notes, Nr 5, 26 May 1943.

43 BA-MA RH26/1007/3, Bl.105, Gespräch mit Lt. De Luca von der Division 'Regina'. Captain Bayer, handwritten notes, 28 July 1943.

44 BA-MA RH26/1007/4, Bl. 12, Kommandierenden General- und Befehlshaber Süd-Griechenland [Speidel], 31 July 1943.

45 BA-MA RH26/1007/4, Bl. 50, 55-56, Tagesbefehl Nr 14/43, 14 Aug. 1943. Ibid, Bl.103, Kleemann, 27 July 1943.

46 Ibid, Bl.103, Kleemann, 27 July 1943.

47 BA-MA RH26-1007/4, copies of correspondence.

48 BA-MA RH26/1007/1, Bl. 61-64, Geheim: 1c-Beitrag zum Taetigkeitsbericht der Sturmdivision Rhodos fuer den Zeitabschnitt 1.1.43-30.6.43, Abt. 1c, 22.11. Nr 1001/43 gd., here: Bl. 64 (p.4 of report). This is a good example of successful misinformation/intelligence designed to dupe the Germans.

49 KTB OKW 6, 1943 Teilband II, p. 868. The original codenames for this operation were *Alarich* and then *Konstantin*, ibid, pp. 829–845.

50 BA-MA RH26/1007/3, Bl. 82-83, Anl. 51, Kommandeur-Besprechung am 25. Juli 1943. KTB OKW 1943 Teilband II, August, p, 1038.

51 Supplement to the *London Gazette* of Friday 8 October 1948: 'Naval Operations in the Aegean Between 7th September, 1943 and 28th November, 1943', p. 5372, col. 1.

52 BA-MA RH26/1007/2, Bl. 28 [27], Darstellung der Ereignisse.

53 Schenk, *Kampf*, p. 52, omits to mention that Kleemann did in fact agree, but retracted after he saw Italian reserve troops mobilizing at Campochiaro.

54 BA-MA RH26/1007/9, Capt. Goedeckemeyer, Erlebnisbericht ueber die Kampftage v.8. –11.9.43. The preceding and following account is based on this source as well as that cited in n. 52. Each of the divisional units produced their own report.

55 BA-MA RH26/1007/4, Bl. 21-24, Anlage 98, Stichwort 'Achse'. Schenk, *Kampf*, pp. 51–54.

56 This was probably the 50th Artillery Regiment of the Division. The three infantry regiments were the 9th, 309th and 331st.

57 Nathan Shachar attributes the eventual capitulation of the superior Italian force to technical inferiority – this is not the case. If anything, the *Sturmdivision* was less well-equipped than the Italian garrison when it came to artillery and it lacked heavy armoured vehicles. The explanation for Campioni's decision to accept Kleemann's terms for surrender lay in both the poor quality and lack of fighting spirit of his troops.

58 BA-MA RH26/1007/7, Bl. 53, Geheim! IV./Art.-Regt.(mot.) 999, Abt. 1a, Br.Tgb.Nr 433/43 geh. Betr. Verwendung der IV./Art.-Regt.(mot.) 999 an der Front in Italien. An das Oberkommando des Heeres Chef. H. Rüst u. B.d.E (Maj. Winter, Abt. Kdr.).

59 BA-MA RH26/1007/5, Bl. 80-88, for events leading to Campioni's surrender. BA-MA RH26/1007/2, 'Darstellung der Ereignisse' Bl. 28-42, here: Bl. 37, states the capitulation was signed in the building of the International Red Cross in Afandou; other reports refer to the *Carabinieri* station. See also, BA-MA RH26/1007/9 Sturmdiv. Rhodos Abt. 1a Nr 111/44. G.kdos. Gefechtsberichte über den Kampf um die Insel Rhodos vom 8.–11.9.43, Nr 1: Goedeckemeyer, Erlebnisbericht, 31 Oct 1943, Bl. 2-4.

60 Panagiotis Gartzonikas, 'Amphibious and Special Operations in the Aegean Sea 1943–1945. Operational Effectiveness and Strategic Implications' (MA Thesis, Naval Postgraduate School, Monterey, CA, 2003), p. 21.

61 Jürgen Rohwer with Gerhard Hümmelchen, *Chronik des Seekrieges 1939–1945, Herausgegeben von der Bibliothek für Zeitgeschichte, Württembergische Landesbibliothek* (Stuttgart 2007 bis 2018) at: http://www.wlbstuttgart.de/seekrieg/43-09.htm.

62 Richard C. Hall (ed.), *War in the Balkans: An Encyclopedic History from the Fall of the Ottoman to the Breakup of Yugoslavia* (ABC-CLIO: Santa Barbara, CA, etc., 2014), p. 97.

63 Cited by Fleischer, *Im Kreuzschatten*, p. 306.

64 Ibid, p. 307.

65 Gartzonikas, 'Amphibious and Special Operations', pp. 21–24. Winston S. Churchill, *The Second World War: Closing the Ring* (Houghton Mifflin Co: Boston, 1951), pp. 134–137, 210–211.

66   IWM Catalogue Nr 13039, George Patrick John Rushworth Jellicoe, interviewed
     4 February 1993, Reel 5. Jellicoe commanded the Special Boat Service in the
     Mediterranean and Aegean, 1942–1943. The following is based on Jellicoe's
     interview.

67   'Dolbey' was in fact the SOE alias for the Polish Count Dobriski. The Earl Lord
     Jellicoe, 'Foreword', in Rogers, *Churchill's Folly*, p. 5.

68   BA-MA RH26/1007/2, Bl. 39, the German report mentions the presence of
     British officers in Rhodes but showed no knowledge that they were in the
     Knights' Castle at the same time as the German delegation.

69   BA-MA RH26/1007/6, Bl. 33-38, KTB 163, [undecipherable] September 1943,
     'Entwurf Lagebeurteiling'.

70   Jellicoe, Interview.

71   Jeffrey Holland, *The Aegean Mission: Allied Operations in the Dodecanese, 1943*
     (Greenwood Press: New York, 1988); Rogers, *Churchill's Folly*. Saxon, 'The
     German Side of the Hill', p. 332.

72   Gartzonikas, 'Amphibious and Special Operations', p. 22 and *passim*.

73   TNA FO 954/11A/113-114, (Cypher) Foreign Office to Washington, No. 6732,
     7 October 1943, this is a copy of a letter sent by Prime Minister Churchill
     (No. 438) to President Roosevelt, same day. FO 954/32B/338-339, for Roosevelt's
     response.

74   Fleischer, *Im Kreuzschatten*, p. 307.

75   *London Gazette*, 'Naval Operations' p. 5372, col. 2, nos. 10, 11. For tension
     with Eisenhower, see Winston Churchill, *The Second World War Vol. 5: Closing
     the Ring* (Cassell: London, 1952), Book 1: Italy Won, pp. 237–261, especially
     pp. 258–261.

76   KTB OKW 1943 Teilband II, pp. 1138-1139. Smith and Walker, *War in the
     Aegean*, pp. 40–41.

77   KTB OKW 1943 Teilband II, pp. 1068–1069.

78   *London Gazette*, 'Naval Operations', p. 5378, col. 2, no. 72.

79   *London Gazette*, 'Naval Operations', p. 5373, col. 2, no. 20.

80   Jellicoe, 'Foreword', p. 6. The meeting would have taken place after 1 December
     when Churchill was returning from the Teheran Conference (28 November–1
     December 1943).

81   Ian Gooderson, 'Shoestring Strategy: the British Campaign in the Aegean, 1943',
     Journal of Strategic Studies, Vol. 25, No. 3 (2002), pp. 1–36.

82   BA-MA RH26/1007/2, Bl. 42 KTB 17 September 1943, Darstellung der
     Ereignisse, Anlage 267 in ibid, RH26/1007/15, Bl. 145. BA-MA RH26/1007/15,
     Bl. 267 [145], Verlustmeldung des Kampftages vom 9.–13. Sept. 1943.

83 Aldo Levi, *Avvenimenti in Egeo dopo l'armistizio (Rodi, Lero e isole minori)* (La Marina italiana nella seconda guerra mondiale, Vol. 16), (Rome, 1972), p. 80.

84 Gerhard Schreiber, *Die italienischen Militärinternierten im deutschen Machtbereich 1943 bis 1945: Verraten – verachtet – vergessen* (R. Oldenbourg Verlag: Munich, 1990), pp. 157–159; Richard Lamb, *War in Italy, 1943–1945: A Brutal Story* (Da Capo Press: Boston, MA, 1996), pp. 134–135.

85 The *Acqui* Division on Cephalonia refused to relinquish the island to the 1st Mountain Division, led by 31-year-old Colonel Harald Hirschfeld. Hirschfeld, promoted to Major-General on 15 January 1945, was severely wounded three days later at the Battle for Dukla Pass, Sáros County, Hungary (today Prešov, Slovakia), and died. Somewhat sanitized biographical details in: https://www.lexikon-der-wehrmacht.de/Personenregister/H/Hirschfeld-R.htm. See his army personal file in BArch Pers. 6/2555.

86 Schreiber, *Die italienischen Militärinternierten*, pp. 179–180, for the summary execution of the commander of Italian forces on Kos, Col. Felice Leggio and eighty-one of his officers. See also Isabella Insolvibile, *Kos 1943–1948: La strage, la storia* (Edizioni scientifiche italiane: Naples, 2010), who gives a slightly higher figure. Isabelle Insolvibile, 'The island of Kos under German Occupation and British Military Administration (1943–1947)', paper delivered to 'The Deportation of the Jews of Rhodes & Cos: 1944–2014', paper read at 'A Commemorative International Symposium on the Holocaust in the Aegean' July 2014. On Leros, the victory of Müller's 22nd Infantry Division came at a heavy price: 41% of the force was killed or wounded, KTB OKW 1943, Teilband II, p. 1299, see also ibid, p. 1289 for Italian and British prisoners taken in the Battle for Leros.

87 Menachem Shelah, 'Die Ermordung italienischer Kriegsgefangener, September–November 1943', in Hannes Heer and Klaus Neumann (eds.), *Vernichtungskrieg. Verbrechen der Wehrmacht 1941 bis 1944* (Hamburger Editionen: Hamburg, 1995), pp. 191–207, here: p. 198 and *passim*. See Schreiber, *Die italienischen Militärinternierten*, p. 175. Both authors cite two Italian studies: Levi, *Avvenimenti*, op cit., and Mario Torsiello, *Le operazioni delle unita italiane nel settembre-ottobre 1943* (Ministero della difesa, Stato maggiore dell'Esercito, Ufficio storico: Rome, 1975), p. 542. Neither latter author provides contemporary sources for these figures. The German sources (notably the Division's War Diary) does not mention these events. For Kleemann's interrogation: United States National Archives and Records Administration (NARA), RG238 M1019 Roll 35. I am grateful to Kaan Turgay for sharing this source. A particularly crass and misleading account of German treatment of prisoners, is given in the novel

by Patricia Wilson, *Island of Secrets* (Bonnier Books: London, 2017), where she states the Germans on Rhodes killed all the Italian prisoners. It is possible she has taken the massacre of Italian troops on Kos and transposed this to Rhodes. The novel, with the fate of Jews at its centre, is replete with historical inaccuracies.

88 Levi, *Avvenimenti*, pp. 80–81.

89 The internees comprised 43 officers, 118 non-commissioned officers and 3,885 soldiers. 'Il Naufragio dell'Oria', http://www.dodecaneso.org/tragedie.htm. This source also has information on the sinking of the Donizetti. At the time of the battle for Rhodes, there had been 3,172 air and 8,250 naval personnel stationed on the island. BA-MA RH26/1007/6, Bl. 41, Anlage 166, 'Auf der Insel Rhodos befindliche Truppen'. Schreiber, *Die italienischen Militärinternierten*, pp. 177, 274: Tabelle 5.

90 BA-MA RH26/1007/12, Bl.6, R.S. von Heeresgruppe E 1a Nr 292/44 geh. 29.1.44.

91 KTB OKW 1943, Teilband II, p.1107. Schreiber, *Die italienischen Militärinternierten*, pp. 259–260.

92 BA-MA RH26/1007/12, Bl.7, R.S. von Heeresgruppe E 1a Nr 292/44 geh. 1.2.44 and Kleemann's response.

93 Schreiber, *Die italienischen Militärinternierten*, p. 258. Kleemann's concern was proven correct as we saw above in the case of the *SS Oria*.

94 Germany does not appear as a signatory to the Geneva Convention of 27 July 1929, relative to the Treatment of Prisoners of War, Treaty Series No. 846, between the United States and other Powers, 1923–1937, Volume 5224. Text available at https://avalon.law.yale.edu/20th_century/geneva02.asp. Nonetheless, as is well known, German military personnel faced charges after the war for crimes committed against POWs: https://avalon.law.yale.edu/imt/judwarcr.asp. Neville Wylie, 'The 1929 Prisoner of War Convention and the Building of the Inter-war Prisoner of War Regime', in Sibylle Scheipers (ed.), *Prisoners in War* (Oxford University Press: Oxford, 2010), pp. 91–108, 102.

95 Schreiber, *Die italienischen Militärinternierten*, pp. 258–259, 465.

96 BA-MA RH26/1007/5, Bl. 184f. Anl. 274, Der Gouvernuer der Ital. Insel der Aegaeis to Kleemann (translation into German of original letter in Italian).

97 Ibid, Bl. 151, Anl. 278, 'Der Befehlshaber der Insel Rhodos gibt bekannt.' Schreiber, *Die italienischen Militärinternierten*, pp. 258–259, 465. Also, Esther Menascé-Fintz, *Buio nell'isola del sole: Rodi 1943-1945. La tragedia dei militari italiani e l'annientamento degli ebrei* (Passato Prossimo: Florence, 2014). Partial information can be found at https://en.wikipedia.org/wiki/Inigo_Campioni#Imprisonment_and_execution

98   Anthony McElligott, '"German Servicemen see Europe": Cultural Mobilization of Troops on the Aegean "Quiet Front"', in Catriona Pennell and Filipe Ribeiro de Meneses (eds.), *A World at War, 1911–1949: Explorations in the Cultural History of War*, History of Warfare Vol. 124 (Brill: Leiden, Boston, 2019), pp. 61–80.

99   Verordnungen des Befehlhabers, Verordnung Nr 2, 17 September 1943.

100   Verordnungen des Befehlhabers, Verordnung Nr 8, 23 September 1943.

101   On 17 September, BA-MA RH26/1007/2, Bl. 41, 'Darstellung'.

102   BA-MA RH26/1007/15, Anl. 218, Sturmdiv. Rhodos, Abt. IIa, [Meynier]: Bericht über die Erlebnisse in der Zeit 9. –11.9.43.

103   BA-MA RH26/1007/27, Rhodes, 31.12.43. It is likely these were civilians, possibly Italian colonists or Italian levantines.

104   BA-MA RH26/1007/7, Bl.90, KTB 359, Geheim! Sturmdivision Rhodos, Abt.1a Nr 734/43 geh. 22 October 1943.

105   BA-MA RH29/1007/14, Bl. 398, report Abt. Iva Intendant Sturmdiv. (Bismarck), Ausstattung (Kos), 24 June 1944.

106   Further details in McElligott, '"German Servicemen See Europe"', pp. 61–80. BArchB NS7/98, Bl. 4, on imposing exemplary death penalty for desertion, defeatism etc., among Italian auxiliaries.

107   BA-MA RH26/1007/15, Bl.182, Anl. 273, M.V.S.M. kdo der 201 Schwarzhemden-Legion Az. 2366/2-A di Prot. Betrifft Mitteilung dem Herrn General Kleemann Militärbefehlhaber der Insel, F.P.550, 18 September 1943.

108   BA-MA RH26/1007/2, Bl. 42, Celebrano to Kleemann, 18 Sept. 1943. In a note to Kleemann, Celebrano is reported to have said the Legion was imploding ('fällt in sich zusammen'), BA-MA RH26/1007/15, Bl. 182: M.V.S.M. Kdo der 201 Schwarzhemden-Legion, Az:2366/2-A di Prot. Gen. Kleemann, Betr. Mitteilung, 18.9.43, German translation of RH26/1007/6 Bl. 183, Milizia Volontaria Per la Sicurezza Nazionale Comando della 201 Legione CC.NN. d'Assalto.

109   BA-MA RH26/1007/27, KAWI, HIWI and POW/MI, 31.12.43, for the islands of Skarpanto, Kos, Leros and Samos.

110   BA-MA RH26/1007/14, Bl. 24, Kommandant Ost-Aegaeis Abt. 1a, Br.B, No.933/44, g.kdos. Betr. Lagebeurteilung, 8 Juli 1944, report to OKH E Abt.1a.

111   BA-MA RH26/1007/8, Sturmdiv. Rhodos, Abt. 1a, Nr 263/43 g. kdos. Anlage 446, report to Heeresgruppe E. Abt. 1a, 12.12.43.

112   BA-MA RH26/1007/25, Kommandant Ost-Aegaeis Abt. 1c, Br.B.Nr 1167/44 g. Kdos. 11.8.44/Li. Anl. 11, Bl. 27.

113 BA-MA RH26/1007/16, Kreiskommandantur Rhodos, Tgb.Nr 357/44 geh. To Sturmdivision Rhodos, Abt. 1c, 4 Aug. 44, Betr. Zusätze für die Lagebeurteilung (Herpich).

114 BA-MA RH26/1007/6, Anlage 1 zu Sturmdiv. Rhodos 1a Nr 734/43 geh. Abschrift betr. Abt. 1a Nr 713/43 geh. Einsatz der Faschisten-Kompanie. Ibid. Bl. 90, KTB 359.

115 BA-MA RH26/1007/16, Bl. 131, Anl. 109, Kdt. Ost Ägäis Abt. 1a Br.B. Nr 1140/44, g. kdos. Lagebeurteilung, 7 August 1944. BA-MA RH26/1007/25, Kdt. Ost-Aegaeis Abt. 1c, Br.B.Nr 4930/44 geh. Anlage 8, 5.7.44/Di. Ic Beitrag zum 1a Lagebericht. The problems besetting the Italian Fascists as a coherent force persisted into the autumn 1944, when an attempt was made by Antonio Coccheri to unify all Italians – not so much to fight the Allies but to counteract Dodecanesian enosis, BA-MA RH26/1007/16, Bl. 42, Kommandant Ost-Aegaeis Militaerverwaltung Br.B.Nr 436/44 geh. 2.9.1944: Betr. Lagebeurteilung.

116 McElligott, "'German Servicemen See Europe'", pp. 61–80.

117 See Schreiber, *Die italienischen Militärinternierten*, pp. 168–187, for a comprehensive account of operations in the Dodecanese islands. For the end phase of Hitler's 'empire' see: Mark Mazower, *Hitler's Empire, Nazi Rule in Occupied Europe* (Penguin Books: London, 2008), ch. 16.

118 Hans H. Hildebrand/Walter Lohmann, *Deutsche Kriegsmarine 1939–45* (Podzun: Bad Nauheim, 1956–64), Vol. II, ch. 163.

119 BA-MA RH 26-1007/15, Anlage zu St.Div.Rh. 1a Nr 1093/44 g. Rhodos, Meldung vom 1 August 1944. The exact shortfall of men is given as 947 in the report. Ibid, Anlage zu Kommandant Ost-Ägäis 1a, Nr 1140/44, g.Kdos v 7.8.44, Bl. 139–141.

120 BA-MA RH26/1007/25, Bl. 17 Anl.9, Kommandant Ost-Aegaeis Abt. 1c Br.B.Nr 694/44, geh. 8.7.44, 1c Beitrag zum 1a Lagenericht Anl. 1, Bl.21–22. Ibid. Bl. 32, Anl. 1 zu Kammandant Ost-Aegaeis 1c Nr 1167/44 g. Kdos. 11.8.44.

121 BA-MA RH26/1007/5, Bl. 80-88, Standesrechtliche Erschiessungen, 20.9.43 and 22.9.43. BA-MA RH26/1007/6, Anl. 316, 4 October 1943 (order to shoot Italians considered as escapees under curfew); ibid, Bl. 45 for the arrest and execution of a group of Italian soldiers led by Lieutenant Vece and Greek civilians in December 1943.

122 BA-MA RH26/1007/5, Anlage 3a, Verordnungen des Befehlhabers der Insel Rhodos, Verordnung Nr 1 and Verordnung Nr 3.

123 BA-MA RH26/1007/5, Bl. 207-209, Anl. 291, Div. Tagesbefehl Nr 21/43, 24.9.43.

124 Tarica, *Des ténèbres*, p. 33.

125 Erhart Kästner, *Griechische Inseln. Aufzeichnungen aus dem Jahre 1944* (Insel Verlag: Frankfurt/Main, 1975).

126 McElligott, "'German Servicemen See Europe'", pp. 61–80, for the example of Sergeant Otto Stenker.

127 Michael Frank, *One Hundred Saturdays. Stella Levi and the Search for a Lost World* (Simon & Schuster: New York, 2022), p. 105.

128 Ibid, pp. 96–97. It is difficult to date this encounter, but it must have been in 1944. Kleemann arrived on Rhodes in June 1943. The girlfriend of Stella was the younger of two sisters whose birthdays occurred on 18 February and 14 April, suggesting the encounter could not have taken place that year. The older sister whose birthday was in February, had married Ernesto Licitri (and thereby converted to Catholicism) in his home town of Caltanissetta in Sicily in 1937, when she was 24 years old.

129 Frank, *One Hundred Saturdays*, p. 109. Licitri, was eventually removed to Germany in April 1944. In recounting this episode, Stella says 'Kleemann, … stepped outside of his office to listen to their request. He wrote down the name of the soldier, and then went back to work.' Michael Frank, to whom Stella Levi told this story found it 'astonishing' (p. 108) that she could so easily obtain an audience with Kleemann (albeit only for all of three minutes). I do too. From the description, it is more likely she met the military administrator, Hans zur Nedden. Kleemann did not have an office in the Grand Master's Palace, but had moved his staff headquarters after the Italian capitulation to General Forgiero's former residence close to Profitis Ilias (known today as 'Mussolini's villa'). BA-MA RH26/1007/2 Bl. 39, KTB Div.Gef. Peveragno, 15 Sept. 1943, Darstellung der Ereignisse.

130 Frank, *One Hundred Saturdays*, p. 105.

131 BA-MA RH26/1007/13, Anlage 44.

132 Michael Matsas, *The Illusion of Safety: The Story of the Greek Jews During the Second World War* (Pella Publishing Company: Athens, 1997).

133 The abstract to Lucia Garzolini's interview erroneously states 'German troops arrived on Rhodes and Kos in September 1943, and soon began strictly enforcing racial laws.' GARZOLINI, Lucia Franco, USHMM [The Jeff and Toby Herr Oral History Archive] RG-50.030*0452, 4 June 1997, in Italian. Transcript, p. 4. A similar belief can be found in Michael Molho and Joseph

Nehama, *In Memoriam: hommage aux victimes juives des Nazis en Grèce*
[Imp. N. Nicolaidès], (Salonique, 1949, 2nd edn, 1973), German translation
by Peter Katzung, Essen 1981, and found at YVA Record Group p. 26, Heiner
Lichtenstein Collection, File 156, p. 287. https://collections.ushmm.org/searc
h/?utf8=%E2%9C%93&q=Garzolini&search_field=all_fields. Cf. Benatar and
Benatar, *Si je t'oublie*, p. 274 for biographical details of the family.

134   McElligott, "'German Servicemen See Europe'", pp. 61–80, for Stenker. Erhart
      Kästner, *Griechische Inseln. Aufzeichnungen aus dem Jahre 1944* (Insel Verlag:
      Frankfurt/Main, 1975), pp. 66–77.

135   In a similar vein after the war, Lawrence Durrell, *Reflections on a Marine Venus:
      A Companion to the Landscape of Rhodes* (Faber and Faber: London, 1953).

136   See Chapter 7 for their role in the dispersal and acquisition of Jewish property
      after the deportation.

137   Omer Bartov, *The Eastern Front, 1941–45: German Troops and the Barbarisation
      of Warfare*, 2nd edition (Palgrave: London & New York, 2001).

138   BA Ludwigsburg B162/1515 Bl. 483-84. Testimony Hermann Neeff.

139   Garzolini, Lucia Franco, RG-50.030*0452, 4 June 1997, in Italian. Transcript,
      p. 10.

140   Ibid, pp. 5, 7.

141   BA-MA, Gs-Bestand Nr 6 Archiv Nr 223 Koblenz 'B', Nr 305, 21994 (BDC).
      Interrogated in Nuremberg in 1947, Kleemann denied he had been a Party
      member. His military personal file has no reference to membership. In the
      1950s and again in the 1960s Kleemann, who had retired to Oberusel in
      Taunus, was twice investigated for war crimes, including the deportation of the
      Jews from Rhodes. These accusations were dropped for lack of evidence, BA
      Ludwigsburg, B162/1513, Bl. 27.

142   Luca Pignataro, *Il Dodecaneso italiano 1912–1947. Vol. III: De Vecchi,
      Guerra E Dopoguerra 1936–1947/50* (Solfanelli: Chieti, 2018), pp. 423–438,
      gives 70 nautical miles. I have used the maritime calculator https://www.
      sailgreeceyachts.com/sailing-distances-greece.html.

143   Yad Vashem Archives, O.3/2680 – Testimonies Department Item ID 3556194
      Testimony of Sidney Simcha Fahn, 19 pp., here: pp. 6–7.

144   John Bierman, *Odyssey* (Simon and Schuster: New York, 1984), pp. 209–210.

145   However, we should note that the brothers' privileged position did not protect
      them and their families from deportation, Fahn, 'Testimony', p. 8.

146   Amato, Lucia Sciarcon, Interview 14687. Seg. 13. Visual History Archive. Shoah
      Foundation 1996.

147 Rebecca Franco né Hazan, 33394, interviewed 1997, tape 2, segs. 38. VCA Shoah Foundation.

148 Shoah Foundation 1701, Levi, Tape 2, interviewed by Yitchak Kerem, 27 March 1995. See also, Stella's recollections in Frank, *One Hundred Saturdays*, p. 96.

149 Tarica-Israël, Interview Fortunoff Archive, seg. 7.

150 There is no study that I am aware of that examines sexual relations or liaisons between German occupation troops and local women, although as we have been noting here, such relationships existed. For a different context entirely, but on the subject of relationships between German occupiers and local women, see Richard Cobb, *French and Germans, Germans and French: A Personal Interpretation of France under Two Occupations, 1914–1918/1940–1944* (Penguin Modern Classics: London, New York, 2018), and the novel by the Jewish author Irène Némirovsky, *Suite française* (Denoël: Paris, 2004). The manuscript was discovered sixty years after her murder in Auschwitz.

151 Julia Hiller von Gaertringen, '*Meine Liebe zum Griechenland*': Studien zum literarischen Werk Erhart Kästners (Wolfenbütteler Forschungen, Harrassowitz Verlag: Wiesbaden, 1994), pp. 121–128.

152 Andreas Kunz, 'Junge Soldaten in der Wehrmacht. Struktur- und organisationsgeschichtliche Betrachtungen', in Ulrich Herrmann and Rolf-Dieter Müller (eds.), *Junge Soldaten im Zweiten Weltkrieg. Kriegserfahrungen als Lebenserfahrungen* (Juventa Verlag: Weinheim, Munich, 2010), pp. 81–112, here: pp. 110–111, Tables 2 and 3.

153 This was Camp 379, where Kästner spent a period of eighteen months. Erhart Kästner, *Das Zeltbuch von Tumilat* (Suhrkamp Verlag: Frankfurt am Main, 1967), pp. 156–180, here: 157–158. Gaertringen, '*Meine Liebe zum Griechenland*', p. 267.

154 McElligott, '"German Servicemen See Europe,"' p. 72.

155 BA Ludwigsburg, B162/1513 Bl. 61-63, testimony Oberstlt. A. D. Hermann Wröndel.

156 Foregoing based on TNA FO208/4645, Report No. PWIS (H)/LDC/903 HAG Ref: MD/JAG/FS/55/29B, Secret: Consolidated Report on Investigation of all Rhodes PsW: 'Character Sketches of PsW'. Wagenführ had a successful academic career after the war, publishing studies of statistics on the war economy.

157 The other three groups were 611, 621 and 640; 510 was the only unit to remain active in Greece until end of the war; the other three were in Croatia. See: Robert Winter, *Die geheime Polizei* (Melchior Verlag: Wolfenbüttel, 2013), ch. 3 *passim*.

158 BA-MA Freiburg RH26-1007-25, Bl. 125, Abschrift: Oberkommando Heeresgruppe E Gruppe 1c/ Nr 10431/44 geh. 23.Juli 1944: Betr.: Ausweise fuer GFP-Angehoerige (gez. Warnstorff).

159 BA-MA Freiburg RH26-1007-25, Bl. 131, Gruppe Geheime Feldpolizei 510, Sektretariat IV (Rhodes), 22.8.44: Feldpolizeiinspektor: 'Besetzung des Sekretariats vor und nach dem 1.4.1944'.

160 Barch-Lg, B162/1512, Bl. 538. BArch, RH48/2, Geheime Feldpolizei, Stammtafeln (1941). Manshausen was never investigated or prosecuted for his role in the deportation of Jews from Crete or Rhodes. After the war he became head of the fraud squad in Hamburg.

161 Winter, *Die geheime Feldpolizei*, p. 71. Klaus Gessner, *Geheime Feldpolizei. Die Gestapo der Wehrmacht* (Militärverlag: Berlin, 2010), pp. 132–150 for duties etc. Gessner surprisingly ignores Greece and Italy.

162 Winter, *Die geheime Feldpolizei*, p. 72–73, 79–81, in part not entirely accurate.

163 WL 1655/2518 NOKW 1801: Memorandum of Commandant East Aegaeis, signed KLEEMANN, concerning the attitude of the *Wehrmacht* commander to the Jewish Question in Rhodes, 16 July 1944.

164 Kleemann later claimed not to have had direct jurisdiction over the fate of the Jews.

165 *Dodecanese Handbook* Part I, p. 7.

166 Another point to consider is the climate within the *Wehrmacht* following the 20 July plot to assassinate Hitler, BA-MA RH26/1007/15, Bl. 81, Kommandant Ost-Ägäis StQu 4 August 1944/kr.

167 Kleemann, and his counterpart in Crete, General Bruno Bräuer, were accorded greater jurisdictional powers in August 1943 and again in June 1944, a sign of the importance of their roles in holding the islands. *'Führer-Erlasse' 1939–1945*, Zusammengestellt und eingeleitet von Martin Moll (Franz Steiner Verlag: Stuttgart 1997), Documents 264, 327. KTB 1943 Teilband II, pp. 1068–1069.

168 See Chapter 5. The building where Eichmann's office was located was demolished in 1961.

Chapter 5

1 Sami Modiano in *The Longest Journey – The Last Days of the Jews of Rhodes*, Dir. Ruggero Gabai (Italy, 2013).

2 Already under discussion in 1942 following the Wannsee Conference, see n. 11 below.

3   *Die Verfolgung und Ermordung der europäischen Juden durch das
    nationalsozialistische Deutschland 1933–1945, Band 14: Besetztes Südosteuropa
    und Italien*, prepared by Sara Berger, Erwin Lewin, Sanela Schmid and Maria
    Vassilikou (De Gruyter: Oldenbourg, Boston/Berlin, 2017), Docs. 227,
    229. Mark Mazower, *Salonica, City of Ghosts: Christians, Muslims and Jews,
    1430–1950* (Penguin Random House: New York, 2004); Giorgos Antoniou
    and A. Dirk Moses (eds.), *The Holocaust in Greece* (Cambridge University
    Press: Cambridge, 2019). Jonathan Steinberg, *All or Nothing: The Axis and the
    Holocaust, 1941–1943*, 2nd edition (Routledge: London and New York, 2002).

4   There were two further transports the following spring, and the final 23rd
    transport taking the Aegean Jews to Auschwitz in July.

5   TNA GFM/2518, the incident took place in June 1943. Memorandum from
    von Thadden, Inl.II 1752 g to Gruppenleiter Inl. II, June 17, 1943. See also the
    correspondence between Consul Dr Schönberg and German foreign office, and
    Wisliceny's own account in the same file. See also his testimony in StBr, 4,89/3-
    863, Bl. 61–66.

6   After Mussolini's escape from custody, the Germans installed him as head of a
    puppet-state in the north of Italy *Repubblica Sociale Italiana*, or Italian Social
    Republic – known as *Repubblica di Salò* – that lasted from September 1943 until
    May 1945.

7   TNA HW12/295, Intercept No. 12874, 8 Dec. 1943: Irish Minister Vatican City
    to Foreign Secretary Dublin, No. 127, 5 Dec. 1943. He was of course, referring to
    the eighteen-point Manifesto di Verona (14–16 November) which declared Jews
    a separate race and enemies of the Italian fascist Social Republic (Point 7),
    retrieved at http://www.storiologia.it/apricrono/storia/a1943u.htm. It is likely
    that Kiernan was connected through his wife Delia Murphy to Monsignor Hugh
    O'Flaherty who had a diplomatic function in the Vatican, and who used his
    position to aid Allied combatants and Jews, Stephen Walker, *Hide & Seek: The
    Irish Priest In The Vatican Who Defied The Nazi Command* (Harper Collins:
    London, 2011).

8   Gilbert, *The Holocaust: The Jewish Tragedy*, p. 632, confuses the date of arrest
    with that of the deportation. See the brief and inconclusive entry in www.
    jewishvirtuallibrary.org/jsource/judaica/ejud_0002_0015_0_15312.html.

9   CDEC Digital Library, http://digital-library.cdec.it/cdec-web/persone/detail/
    person-5991/pacifici-riccardo.html and http://digital-library.cdec.it/cdec-web/
    persone/detail/person-9/abenaim-wanda.html. Liliana Picciotto Fargion, 'Italien',
    in Wolfgang Benz (ed.), *Dimension des Völkermords: Die Zahl der jüdischen*

Opfer des Nationalsozialismus (dtv Wissenschaft: Munich, 1996 [1991]),
pp. 220–221, Table 2.

10   Liliana Picciotto, 'Italy', in Benz (ed.), *Dimension*, p. 216. According to Picciotto's
data: 8,564 were deported of which 1,009 survived. The deportees included non-
Italians, *Die Verfolgung 14*, pp. 33–37.

11   The Wannsee Conference took place on 20 January 1942, but it was not where
the decision to comb all of Europe was taken. The purpose of the meeting in
Berlin was to assert RSHA 'ownership' of the so-called 'Jewish Question' and to
coordinate the implementation of mass murder. Mark Roseman, *The Villa, the
Lake, the Meeting: Wannsee And the Final Solution* (Penguin: Harmondsworth,
2003); Peter Longerich, *Wannsee-Konferenz: Der Weg zur Endlösung* (Pantheon
Verlag: Munich, 2016).

12   Eric Joseph Epstein and Philip Rosen, *Dictionary of the Holocaust Biography,
Geography, and Terminology* (Greenwood Press: Westport, CT, 1997), p. 264.

13   TNA GFM33/2518, RSHA to AA, July 11, 1942. Suhr was a senior officer in the
so-called Eichmann *Judenreferat* IV B4 *Reichssicherheitshauptamt*.

14   Ibid. Tel[egram]. 325 v. 18 Feb. 1943 Leg.Rat.Wagner to v. Thadden.

15   TNA GFM33/2518, Wagner note, 15 May 1943.

16   On hatred of Jews as motivation: Leon Poliakov, *Brévaire de la haine* (1951)
translated as *Harvest of Hate: The Nazi Program for the Destruction of the Jews
of Europe* (Syracuse University Press: New York, 1954). Raul Hilberg, on the
other hand, writes of the bureaucratic mentality of German officials that made
genocide a systemized and inexorable administrative process, Hilberg, *Politics of
Memory: The Journey of a Holocaust Historian* (Ivan R. Dee: Chicago, IL, 1996),
p. 70. Of course, neither visceral hate nor bureaucracy are mutually exclusive.
Jürgen Matthäus, 'Holocaust als angewandter Antisemitismus? Potential und
grenzen eines Erklärungsfaktors', in idem, Frank Bajohr and Andrea Löw (eds.),
Der Holocaust: Ergebnisse und neuen Fragen der Forschung (Fischer Verlag:
Frankfurt am Main, 2015), pp. 102–123.

17   Staatsarchiv Bremen (hereafter: StBr.) 4.89/3-863, Bl. 121–144, here 132–133.
The phrase 'war against the Jews' is taken from Lucy Davidowicz's classic
study, *The War Against the Jews, 1933–1945*. For the idea of antisemitism
as zealotry, Saul Friedländer, 'Erlösungsantisemitismus: Zur Ideologie der
"Endlösung"', in *Nachdenken über den Holocaust* (C.H. Beck: Munich, 2007),
pp. 28–53, and 'Der Judenhass steckt tiefer, als man denkt. Gespräch mit Martin
Doerry', in ibid, pp. 177–178. Dan Stone, *Histories of the Holocaust* (Oxford
University Press: Oxford, 2010), pp. 242–244.

18 Bowman, *Agony*, pp. 80, 92–93. Hans Safrian, *Eichmann's Men*, trans. Ute Stargardt (Cambridge University Press: Cambridge, 2010 [orig. 1993]), pp. 181–193.

19 Other areas included Albania, Istria Peninsula and the French Mediterranean coastal region of Menton and neighbouring Nice. The deportations from Salonica and Macedonia had been completed by this date.

20 Christoph U. Schminck-Gustavus, *Winter in Griechenland. Krieg – Besatzung – Shoah 1940–1944* (WallsteinVerlag: Göttingen, 2011), pp. 157–158, 162–163, 165 for the deportation from Ioannina. Mazower, *Inside Hitler's Greece*, p. 252; Bowman, *Agony*, pp. 68–69. The term 'night and fog' is based on the so-called Night and Fog Decree of 7 December 1941 and applied initially to France.

21 TNA GFM33/2518, Graevenitz to AuswärtigesAmt, 20 April 1944, addendum to report 3 April, overestimated the number of Jews on Crete (600) and underestimated the size of the community on Corfu (1,000–1,500). According to post-war Greek data, the communities numbered 2,000 on Corfu; 350 on Crete; 275 on Xanthi and 1900 on Rhodes-Kos, 'Table showing losses of Jewish population after German occupation 1943–1944', *Xronika* (April 1984), 3. The Jews of Xanthi and Zakynthos escaped deportation. Denes Seder, *Miracle at Zakynthos: The Only Greek Jewish Community Saved in its Entirety from Annihilation* (Philos Press: Lacey, WA, 2014). Meanwhile, the destruction of the communities of Corfu and Crete await their histories.

22 Götz Aly, *Hitlers Volksstaat: Raub, Rassenkrieg und nationaler Sozialismus* (Fischer Verlag: Frankfurt am Main, 2005), English trans. *Hitler's Beneficiaries: Plunder, Racial War, and the Nazi Welfare State* (Holt: New York, 2008), p. 300.

23 Discussed in Bowman, 'Could the Dodekanesi Jews Have Been Saved?', pp. 1–2. See: Isaac Jack Lévy with Rosemary Lévy Zumwalt, *The Sephardim in the Holocaust: A Forgotten People* (University of Alabama Press: Tuscaloosa, 2020), p. 14.

24 Fortunoff Archive Elisa Franco Hasson, Interview, seg. 4 and 5.

25 Excerpt of United States Office of Strategic Services (OSS) report on the arrest of the Jews of Hania, 25 May 1944, reproduced in Central Board of Jewish Communities in Greece: Etz Hayyim Synagogue Commemorative Album, 2nd edn (Jewish Museum of Greece: Athens, 2008), accessed at http://greekjewishlegacy.org/hania/arrestCommunityEN.html. See also https://www.etz-hayyim-hania.org/the-jews-of-crete/the-history-of-the-jews-of-crete/; and https://www.timesofisrael.com/greek-jews-honor-crete-community-drowned-in-entirety-en-route-to-auschwitz/

26 The British were able to intercept enemy signals, but the first indication that Jews were being deported only occurred during the actual transportation from the

islands, but was not recognized. Walter Eytan, 'The Z Watch in Hut 4, Part II', in F.H. Hinsley and Alan Stripp (eds.), *Codebreakers: The Inside Story of Bletchley Park* (Oxford University Press: Oxford, 1993), p. 60.

27   Safrian, *Eichmann's Men*, p. 187.

28   Bundesarchiv Aussenstelle Ludwigsburg (hereafter: BA-Ludwigsburg), Zentrale Stelle der Landesjustizverwaltungen, StB162/1513, Bl. 32–37.

29   BarchB R70/III, Der Befehlshaber der Sicherheitspolizei und des SD für Griechenland in Athen, Personalliste (15.7.1944), Bl. 20 (p. 21), Aussenstelle Joannina. Manowsly reported to both Loos and Blume in Athens.

30   Wisliceny's claim that Eichmann had been dissatisfied with his lack of progress in dealing with the remaining Jews of Greece/Macedonia is disingenuous and should be treated with scepticism. In fact, he was assigned only to oversee the deportations from Salonica. Having completed that task, he was subsequently recalled to Bratislava after seeking permission to marry a Slovakian woman, BarchB SS0-001c frame1356, Der Chef des Heiratsamtes im Rasse- und Siedlungshauptamtes-SS, HA.III Sip.Nr 139 170 Th./Fi., Betr. Heiratsgenehmigung des SS-Hstuf. Dieter Wisliceny, geb. 13.1.1911, An den Chef der Sicherheitspolizei und des SD SS-Obergruppenführer Dr Kaltenbrunner, 12.2.1943. Mazower, *Inside Hitler's Greece*, p. 351.

31   StABr. 4.89/3-863, Bl. 135; ibid, Bl. 65 for Burger as his replacement.

32   StBr. 4,98/3-882, Dez[ernat] Stengelmann, StA Bremen Ermittlungsakten I 29Js 1/70, Envelope 3, 'Lebenslauf'. Burger remained an unreconstructed Nazi and antisemite to the end of his life.

33   Bundesarchiv Berlin-Lichterfelde (hereafter: BarchB) SSO – 122, SS-Führerpersonalakten, Anton Burger, frames 771-775; see also Landesarchiv Berlin (hereafter: LAB) B Rep 057-01/731 Anton Burger, 'Lebenslauf'. BarchB R70/III, Der Befehlshaber der Sicherheitspolizei und des SD für Griechenland in Athen, Personalliste der Dienststelle des Befehlhabers der Sicherheitspolizei und des SD für Griechenland in Athen Stand vom 15.7.1944. There is a vague but unsubstantiated reference that Burger had assisted Wisliceny in the deportations from Salonica. Certainly, Burger led the action in Athens in March 1944. Safrian, *Eichmann's Men*, p. 183.

34   BarchB PKD238 (formerly Berlin Document Center: Personalkartei), Anton Burger, microfilm 680-771. A scholarly biography of Burger is lacking, although there are some details in Safrian, *Eichmann's Men*. Otherwise the account by journalist Karla Müller-Tupath, *Verschollen in Deutschland: Das heimliche Leben von Anton Burger: Lagerkommandant von Theresienstadt* (Konkret Literatur

Verlag: Hamburg, 1994), is in part useful. On Theresienstadt, H.G. Adler, *Theresienstadt 1941–1945: The Face of a Coerced Community*, trans. Belinda Cooper, 2nd rev. edition (Cambridge University Press: Cambridge, 2017 [orig. 2004]). The first edition was published in 1955 and later revised in 1960 by the author with additional material. The English translation is based on this second revised edition.

35   BarchB R70/III, Personalliste der Dienststelle des Befehlhabers der Sicherheitspolizei und des SD für Griechenland in Athen Stand vom 15.7.1944. His superiors in Athens Walter Blume and Roman Loos both with a police background, had also served in leading roles for a period in *Einstazgruppe* B. Burger was the only member of the six-man department in Athens not to have a police background, the rest were regular police officers. Yad Vashem (www.yadvashem.org) incorrectly ascribes to Burger the leadership of Section IV B4 the 'Jewish Desk' in Athens. On Böhm's previous role in Jewish persecution: Andrzej Żbikowski, 'Pogroms in Northeastern Poland – Spontaneous Reactions and German Instigations', in Elazar Barkan, Elizabeth A. Cole and Kai Struve (eds.), *Shared History, Divided Memory: Jews and Others in Soviet-occupied Poland 1939–1941*. Leipziger Beiträge zur judische Geschichte und Kultur Bd.5 (Leipziger Universitätsverlag: Leipzig, 2007), pp. 315–354, here: 327.

36   StABr. 4,89/3-886, Ermittlungsakten StA Bremen (20 Js) 29Js 403/72, Bl. 223.

37   BA-Ludwigsburg, B162/1517, Bl. 1170–1186, statement by Friedrich Linnemann, 11 December 1969. LABr 4,89/3-862 Bl. 40–42, Statement by Friedrich Linnemann, 12 August 1948 and Bl. 43–44, Der Senator für Politische Befreiung 31872/48 Hch/Sl., Klageschrift, 9 Sept. 1948, and sentence against him, 12 Oct. 1948.

38   Sidney Fahn in his 1965 testimony, states that because he was fluent in German, he was asked to act as translator. If he did so, then this was not in any official capacity. Yad Vashem Archives, O.3 – Testimonies Department Item ID 3556194 Testimony of Sidney Simcha Fahn, transcript, p. 8.

39   http://www.yadvashem.org/yv/en/about/institute/deportations_catalog_details. asp?country=Greece.

40   BA-Ludwigsburg, B162/1512, Bl. 538. Barch, RH48/2, Geheime Feldpolizei, Stammtafeln (1941). Like so many frontline perpetrators, Manshausen was never investigated or prosecuted for his role in the deportation of Jews from Crete or Rhodes. After the war he became head of the fraud squad in Hamburg.

41   WL 1655/2399 NOKW1915 Correspondence between the XXII Mountain Corps and the Secret Field Police concerning the deportation of Jews from Corfu on

Himmler's orders. WL 1655/2440 NOKW1985 Report from Joannina Corps
Group to Army Group E Ic, concerning the solution of the Jewish Question in
Corfu and preparatory measures for the deportation of Jews. WL1655/2789 Lanz
138, Affidavit by Ulrich Bürker concerning the deportation of Jews from Corfu
on Himmler's orders (2 October 1947).

42   Testimonies in BA-Ludwigsburg B162/1513, Bl. 32–37, Kleemann's adjutant,
Klaus Goedeckemeyer, Bl. 65–67, testimony of the Divisional military
administrator, Robert Roddewig. Cf., StABr. 4,89/3-862, Staatsanwaltshaft beim
Landgericht Bremen, Handakten zu der Strafsache gegen Linnemann u.a. wegen
Mordes; Der leitende Oberstaatsanwalt bei dem Landgericht 10Ja 156/64, 29 Feb.
1963. See also, Safrian, *Eichmann's Men*, pp. 188–192.

43   BA-Ludwigsburg B162/1514, Bl. 298 for testimony of Gädecke's predecessor Otto
Stavenhagen, who believed that Gädecke in his capacity as port commander
must have known about the deportation. This is corroborated by Karl
Würmseher, formerly adjutant to Gädecke, who confirmed in his testimony that
Burger had liaised secretly with the port commander, ibid, Bl. 302, testimony
27.1.1964.

44   BA-Ludwigsburg B162/1513, different eyewitness statements. For Blume and the
security police, Michael Wildt, *Generation des Unbedingten. Das Führungskorps
des Reichssicherheitshauptamtes* (Hamburger Edition: Hamburg, 2003), pp. 184,
239–259.

45   The order to cooperate was conveyed to Kleemann via Army Group E
headquarters in Belgrade.

46   BA-MA RH26/1007/14, Bl. 99, Kommandant Ost-Ägäis, Verordnung Nr 30:
Meldepflicht auf der Insel Rhodos, 13 Juli 1944; Bl. 98, Kommandant Ost-
Ägäis, Abt. 1a, Betr. Meldepflicht auf Rhodos, Der erste Generalstabsoffizier,
13.7.1944. Those families and individuals who had moved to other villages
such as Koskinou or Asguro and even further south, had to move to one of
the designated areas. The list that was compiled of Jewish households had to
provide details of family name, first name, age, sex, occupation, marital status
and nationality. The deportation list in the Dodecanese archives in Rhodes is
a different compilation made by the Italian authorities and with names and
patrimony only.

47   BA-Ludwigsburg B162/1513, Bl. 34, Goedeckemeyer testimony.

48   This chain of communication has led to speculation about the role of Austria's
former president Kurt Waldheim, who was a desk officer in military intelligence.

49   This was the position adopted by assistant prosecuting counsel Walter Rapp
      in Nuremberg in 1947, NARA RG 238 M1019 Roll 35 Office of US Chief of
      Counsel for War Crimes APO 696-A Evidence Division Interrogation Branch,
      17 June 1947. I am grateful to Turguy Kaan, Stuttgart, for sharing this document.
      Ascribing sole responsibility to Kleemann is also in Shachar, *The Lost World of
      Rhodes*, p. 224; Stella Hasson, *Du Paradis à l'Enfer* (Éditions Clepsydre: Nivelles,
      2007), p. 13. See Safrian, *Eichmann's Men*, pp. 191–192, 283 n. 83 for a partial
      correction.

50   BA-Ludwigsburg, StB162/1513, Bl. 47–49, Testimony Curt Kronbein.

51   BA-MA, Gs-Bestand Nr 6 Archiv Nr 223 Kobra 'B', Nr 305, 21994 (BDC).

52   BA-Ludwigsburg, B162/1514, Bl. 269–271, testimony Matthes.

53   Rino Merolle, 'Breve Cenno Sulla Deportazione della Colonia Ebraica di Rodi',
      typescript. I am grateful to Professor Steven Bowman who kindly provided
      a copy of this document. The individual cards have been annotated in what
      looks like a German hand/symbols. I am grateful to Professor Renée Hirschon,
      St Peter's College, Oxford, for sharing her research.

54   I am indebted to Professor Marco Clementi, who helped to catalogue the
      Carabinieri archive, for bringing these documents to my attention. The list is
      also referred to by Brenner, the Division's intelligence (Ic) officer in the German
      military files.

55   Organizational details of Athens office in Barch R70/II, Bl. 38, and Barch R70/
      III, Dienststelle Walter Blume. StABr. 4,89/883, Ermittelungen gegen Friedrich
      Linnemann wegen Beihilfe zum Mord. Staatsanwalt beim Landgericht Bremen,
      Handakten zu der Strafsache gegen Linnemann u.a., wegen Mordes. Der
      Leitende Oberstaatsanwalt bei dem Landgericht 10.Ja. 156/64, 29 February 1968,
      p. 2. Ibid, Staatsanwalt Bremen, Bericht (undated), report, p. 9. Details of the
      GFP in Rhodes also in BA-Ludwigsburg B162/1516, Bl. 722–725, 774.

56   See the correspondence in Barch NS7/98, Bl. 3–6, Der höchste SS- und
      Polizeiführer in Italien, Befehlshaber der Ordnungspolizei, 111-32 51, 9
      January 1944; Abschrift (Telegram) Berlin-Köpenick, 16 November 1943;
      Der Reichsführer-SS Hauptamt Ia 130 Nr 28, 16 February 1944.

57   We should also note that the first round-ups and deportations from Italy to
      Auschwitz, including the ones that transported rabbi Pacifici and his wife,
      were carried out by the Italian authorities working closely with the Germans.
      Bridget Kevane, 'A Wall of Indifference: Italy's Shoah Memorial', *The Jewish
      Daily Forward* (29 June 2011), at https://forward.com/news/139293/a-wall-of-
      indifference-italy-s-shoah-memorial/

58   GAKR, ΙΔΔ ΦΑΚ 293 ΤΜΗΝΑ1/1, Deportation list. I am grateful to Professor
     Renée Hirschon, St Peter's College, Oxford, for allowing me access to her copy of
     the 1940 household census. On the summons to the *Aeronautica*, Franco, *Jewish*
     Martyrs, p. 62. Miriam Novitch, *The Passage of the Barbarians: Contribution to*
     the History of the Deportation and Resistence of Greek Jews translated from the
     French by Mrs P. Senior (The Wilberforce Council: Hull, 1989), interview with
     Maurice Soriano, p. 132.

59   We have no record who this officer may have been, possibly the aforementioned
     First Lieutenant Sommer or someone from the Secret Military Police.

60   Levi, Interview 1701, seg. 41. Stella De Leon, Interview 12055, Visual History
     Archive, USC Shoah Foundation, seg. 26–28. Fortunoff Archives, Elisa Franco
     Hasson, Interview, seg. 4.

61   BA-Ludwigsburg, B162/1515, Bl. 614–615, Testimony Recanati.

62   Yad Vashem Archives 03/10423, Laura Varon Interview transcript, p. 13. The
     SS-team was not interested in local currency (in this case, the Italian lirette), but
     instead took with them coins and jewellery.

63   USHMM RG-50.030.0452_trs_en.pdf, Garzolini, trasnscript, p. 11 (my
     pagination).

64   BA-Ludwigsburg, B162/1513, Bl. 29. According to Kleemann, the GFP was
     not under his command, but that of Main Army Group E. See details of
     members of the Feldgendarmerie in StBr., 4,89/3-486, Bl. 1066–1076; and
     StBr., 4,89/3-876.

65   BA-MA RH26/1007/25, Bl. 131–132, Sturmdivision Abt. 1c Br. B. Nr
     4668/44geh., Betr. Verstaerkung der GFP, An Oberkommando Heeresgruppe E
     Gr. 1c/AO, 28 June 1944. Ibid, Gruppe Geheime Feldpolizei 510 Sekretariat IV
     (Rhodos) 22 August 1944. BA-Ludwigsburg, B162/1516, Bl. 984–987, Testimony
     Ruschmeier (*sic*). He would again serve in the police in Dortmund after the war
     was over, TNA WO311/373.

66   Merolle, Breve Cenno Sulla Deportazione della Colonia Ebraica di Rodi,
     p. 2. We should not discount the possibility that Merolle was seeking to
     cast the Italian administration as press-ganged helpers, rather than active
     perpetrators.

67   BA-Ludwigsburg, B162/1515, pp. 470–481, Landeskriminalamt, Baden-
     Württemberg, Sonderkommission Zentrale Stelle, z.Zt. Mannheim, 20.7.64,
     Vernehmungsniederschrift: Constantin Recanati, p. 9. Cf. Levi, Interview 1701,
     seg. 41. The former barracks today houses the Rhodes campus of the University
     of the Aegean. See also the account in Berman, *Odyssey*, pp. 217–219.

68 Accounts by Germans during the post-war investigations into Burger and
    Linnemann do not refer to Jewish elders carrying out this task. Meanwhile in
    parts of the testimony, Recanati confuses details of the round-ups in Athens and
    Corfu with that in Rhodes.

69 BA-Ludwigsburg, B162/1515, Bl. 400. BA-MA RH26/1007/25, Bl. 51–54,
    Lagebericht, Teil II (undated report for month July), p. 3, section 8,
    Judenabschub.

70 BA-MA RH26/1007/14, Bl. 156, Anlage 43, 16 July 1943, Stellungnahme
    Div. Kdr., zur Judenfrage. Also available in WL 1655/2518, Memorandum of
    Commandant East Aegaeis, signed KLEEMANN, concerning the attitude of the
    Wehrmacht commander to the Jewish Question in Rhodes. NOKW1801.

71 https://www.yadvashem.org/righteous/stories/ulkumen.html. Clementi and
    Toliou, *Gli ultimi ebrei*, pp. 186–187, 190–191. Clementi, *Storia della comunità*,
    pp. 419–420.

72 After the war, Recanati was sentenced to death by a Greek court, but his
    sentence was commuted to life imprisonment. He was subsequently released
    and, contrary to the conditions of his release, left Greece and made his way to
    Mannheim in Germany. By the time the German authorities were investigating
    the deportation from Rhodes, Recanati had moved to Ludwigshafen-
    Friesenheim where he managed a tavern, 'Balkanstube', and drew a small
    pension for his war-time services. BA-Ludwigsburg, B162/1513, Bl. 431–432,
    State Prosecutor Zeug to Landeskriminalamt Nordrheinwestfalen, 24 April 1964.
    Ibid, B162/1515, Bl. 614–615.

73 BA-Ludwigsburg, B162/1515, Bl. 615, Recanati, Vernehmungsniederschrift, p. 8.

74 Laurence Rees, *Auschwitz: The Nazis and the Final Solution* (BBC Books:
    London, 2005), pp. 299–301 for a similar case involving Hungarian Jews.

75 World Jewish Congress Records, MS-361, Box H178, Folder 13. American
    Jewish Archives, Cincinnati, Ohio. Affidavit Bension Menashe [sic], 24 February
    1945, Marmaris (in French and with English translation).

76 Frank, *One Hundred Saturdays*, p. 109. For Bulissa Cugno see Chapter 8.

77 Kantor, Interview 33706, Visual History Archive, USC Shoah Foundation, seg. 18.

78 This is indicated in the heading of the *Carabinieri* list of deportees showing
    18 July as the day of their removal from the island.

79 StABr. 4,89/3-876, has photograph of the index files of the Feldgendarmerie in
    Rhodes, complete with names of members of the force.

80 *Longest Journey*, 34:51–35:09 min. At the time, no one in the community knew
    to where they were being taken.

81   Jerusalmi, Sara, Interview 8038, seg. 5. Visual History Archive, USC Shoah Foundation, 1996. Accessed 10 January 2017.

82   ITS Digital Archive, Arolsen Archives. CM/1 Files originating in Italy/Matilde Alhadeff, 3.2.1.2/80912936.

83   BA-MA RH26/1007/13, Bl. 15, KTB entry for 23 July. Lenz was interviewed twice; the first time in 1947, and the second time in 1963, by when it became clear to investigators that he had not been an eyewitness but had heard from others. He also claimed that he saw the ships taken out to sea and sunk.

84   Lucia Capelluto, *Testimony: My Life in Auschwitz & Bergen Belsen* (Levant Imprimeurs: Marseille, 1997), p. 12.

85   USHMM RG-50.030*0452, Garzolini, Lucia Franco interviewed 4 June 1997, transcript, p. 11.

86   Maurice Soriano, in Novitch, *The Passage of the Barbarians*, p. 133.

87   Varon, Laura, Interview 26814, tape 1. Visual History Archive, USC Shoah Foundation, 1997. Accessed 9 January 2017.

88   Perpetrators, Linnemann for example, also used this fiction of temporary displacement in his post-war interrogations to exculpate himself.

89   Alberto Israel in *The Longest Journey*, 30 mins.

90   Varon, Interview 26814, seg. 10. Jerusalmi, Interview 8038, seg. 5.

91   BA-MA RH26/1007/16, Bl. 103, report 1 August 1944.

92   In his recollection to his daughter, Vittorio Hasson remembered stopping at Nisiros and then Kos for the embarkation of Jews, including his uncle and aunt Haim Capelluto and Zimbul Sciarcon and their three children. At Leros, a single Jew joined the convoy. Hasson, *Du Paradis*, pp. 62–63.

93   Elisa Franco Hasson, *Il Était une fois l'Île des Roses* (Éditions Clepsydre: Nivelles, 1996), p. 49.

94   Varon, Interview 26814, tape 1. In other accounts he is described as Hungarian. It might be that he was ethnic German from Hungary.

95   Fintz, Violetta Maio, Interview 5720, seg. 6. Visual History Archive, USC Shoah Foundation, 1997. Accessed 20 June 2016.

96   Capelluto, *My Life*, 13.

97   Hasson, *Du Paradis*, p. 63.

98   Hanan, Rachel, Interview 13096. Tape 2. Visual History Archive, USC Shoah Foundation, 1996 (née Hugno, b. 1924). Accessed 12 January 2017.

99   Levi, Interview 1701, tape 2. Lévy and Zumwalt, *The Sephardim*, p. 15 for the journey.

100 So Sami Modiano in *The Longest Journey*, 39:04 min.

101 According to the Race Census 1938, Clara Gabriele, 10 June 1923, lived with her parents and two siblings, Giacomo, 22 June 1918, and Eleanora, 18 December 1920, and an elderly uncle, Gabriel Mizrahi, 11 July 1861, in Maria P. di Savoia Nr 7. ALL'Ufficio dello Stato Civile Rodi, card 227.

102 Levi, Interview 1701, tape 2.

103 Levi, Interview 1701, tape 2.

104 Jerusalmi, Interview 8038, seg. 6.

105 Hanan, Interview 13096.

106 Varon, Interview 26814, seg 12.

107 As well as Varon, ibid, see her brothers' recollections, Varon, Asher, Interview 43798, Visual History Archive, USC Shoah Foundation, 1998, tape 1. Accessed 20 June 2016; Varon, Josef, Interview 34396, tape 1. Visual History Archive, USC Shoah Foundation, 1997. Accessed 20 June 2016. Fintz, seg. 7. Fintz also recalled this episode in a television interview in 1992 for the South African Holocaust & Genocide Foundation, Cape Town Holocaust Memorial Council, Television Interview with Violette Fintz, transcript.

108 De Leon, Stella, Interview 12055, seg. 34. Visual History Archive, USC Shoah Foundation 1996. Accessed January 2017.

109 StABr. Staatsanwaltshaft beim Landgericht Bremen Handakten zu der Strafsache gegen Linnemann u.a. wegen Mordes, 29 Js. 1/70, Der leitende Oberstaatsanwalt bei dem Landgericht 10 Js. 156/64, Bremen, 29 February 1968, Anklageschrift, p. 20.

110 Fils, Flora, Interview 1423, tape 1. Visual History Archive USC Shoah Foundation, 1995, tape 1. Accessed 21 June 2016. See also Jerusalmi, Interview 8038, tape 1 (25 min.).

111 Capelluto, *My Life*, p. 14.

112 Alice Tarica-Israël, *Des ténèbres au soleil* (Éditions Clepsydre: Nivelles, 2007), p. 42.

113 Sara Gilmore (née Hanan), was 16 years old at the time of the deportation; she later spoke of the guards carrying out vaginal searches of the girls and older women. See also the testimony of Laura Hasson, Sara Benatar and others cited in Galante, *Appendice a l'histoire*, p. 290 and in n. 116 below. Ronit Lentin, 'Expected to Live: Women Shoah Survivors' Testimonials of Silence', *Women's Studies International Forum*, Vol. 23, No. 6 (2000), pp. 689–700; Helene Sinnreich, '"And It Was Something We Didn't Talk about": Rape of Jewish Women During the Holocaust', *Holocaust Studies*, Vol. 14, No. 2 (2008),

pp. 1–22. Also, Steven T. Katz, 'Thoughts on the Intersection of Rape and *Rassen[s]chande* during the Holocaust', *Modern Judaism*, Vol. 32, No. 3 (2012), pp. 293–322.

114 ACICR B G 0017 05-150, Prisonniers en Grèce, 1942–1947: Correspondence avec la crois-rouge hellenique, les autorités hellenique, les délégues, janvier 42–janvier 47: Note pour le Bureau de M. de Graffenried-Villars, 18 Mars 1944, Concerne: Prisons et camps de concentrations d'internés civile et d'otages.

115 StABr. 4.89/3-865, Bl. 19–21, witness statement Nikoloas Androulakis.

116 http://digital-library.cdec.it/cdec-web/storico/detail/IT-CDEC-ST0026-000224/34-laura-hasson-sara-benatar-anna-cohen-giovanna-hasson-34.html, transcript, 2.

117 Capelluto, *My Life*, p. 14.

118 Cited in Galante, *Appendice a l'histoire*, p. 300. Giacomo had immigrated to Buenos Aires shortly before the war began.

119 See testimony of his niece, Lucia Garzolini, née Franco, USHMM RG Number: RG-50.030.0452, transcript, p. 14. Also Fintz, Interview 5720, seg. 8; Levi, Interview 1701, seg. 54. Menascé had been a merchant of crystal and glass. The couple had lived at delle Feritoie 28. Benatar and Benatar, *Si je t'oublie*, p. 512.

120 BarchB R70/III Griechenland, Bl. 1–28, Der Befehlshaber der Sicherheitspolizei und des SD für Griechenland in Athen, 'Personalliste der Dienststelle des Befehleshabers der der Sicherheitspolizei und des SD für Griechenland in Athen Stand vom 15.7.1944', here, Bl. 5, Durchgangslager Chaidari. The contingent of guards was possibly higher, according to another earlier list, BarchB R40/I, Bl. 39–43, Durchgangslager Chaidari, 15 April 1944 (Fischer): An den Befehlshaber der Sicherheitspolizei und des SD für Griechenland Abt. I in Athen, Betr.: Familienunterstützung der im Lager diensttuenden SS-Männer, Anlage. This file and R70/II contains details of the [police] officers posted to the Athens department of the Sipo. Thomas Casagrande, *Die Volksdeutsche SS-Division 'Prinz Eugen': Die Banater Schwaben und die nationalsozialistischen Kriegsverbrechen* (Campus Verlag: Frankfurt/New York, 2003), pp. 327–330. Valdis O. Lumans, *Himmler's Auxiliaries: The Volksdeutsche Mittelstelle and the German National Minorities of Europe, 1933–1945* (UNC Press: Chapel Hill and London, 1993), pp. 222–232.

Mazower, *Inside Hitler's Greece*, p. 229, cites a reference from Walter Blume's office in Athens casting some doubt on the racial credentials of the guards.

121 Christopher Browning, *Ordinary Men. Police Battalion 101*; Harald Welzer, *Täter. Wie aus ganz normalen Menschen Massenmörder werden* (Fischer Verlag: Frankurt am Main, 2005), paperback edition, 2007.

122 Lumans, *Himmler's Auxiliaries*, p. 230. Casagrande, *Volksdeutsche*, p. 329. Rolf-Dieter Müller, *An der Seite der Wehrmacht. Hitlers ausländische Helfer beim "Kreuzzug gegen den Bolschewismus" 1941–1945* (Fischer Taschenbuch: Frankfurt/Main, 2014 [orig. Chr. Links Verlag, 2007]).

123 Perahia Margosch, Rachelle, United States Holocaust Memorial Museum Collection, courtesy of the Jeff and Toby Herr Foundation. Oral History. Accession Number: 2004.303. RG Number: RG-50.030.0486 2004.

124 BarchB R70/II, Bl. 26, Bl. 53, Begl. Abschrift, Berlin Nue 195 162, 20.10.43 An den BDS Athen.

125 Kostas Birkas cited by Fleischer, *Im Kreuzschatten*, p. 548.

126 Ibid. Mazower, *Inside Hitler's Greece*, pp. 228–230.

127 StABr., 4,89/3-865, Beweismittel Fischer u. a. wegen Mordes. Staatsanwaltschaft Berlin 3p [k] Js. 298/40.

128 BarchB R70/I, Durchgangslager, Chaidari. See witness statements in StABr. 4.89/3-865, Bl.1–3, and ibid, Bl. 96, witness statement Paritsis.

129 BarchB R70/I Durchgangshaftlager, Chaidari 15 April 1944 An den Befehlshaber der Sicherheitspolizei und des SD für Griechenland Abt. I in Athen, Betr. Familienunterstützung der im Lager diensttuenden SS-Männer. Lumans, *Himmler's Auxiliaries*, pp. 225–226.

130 BA-Ludwigsburg B162/1517, Bl. 1017–1019, 1021–1022.

131 Barch NS19/370, Der Reichsführer, Tgb.Nr 36/154/4 3g. Feldkommandostelle, 11 Juni 1943. Rolf-Dieter Müller, *An der Seite der Wehrmacht. Hitlers ausländische Helfer beim 'Kreuzzug gegen den Bolschewismus' 1941–1945*, 22nd edition (Fischer Verlag: Frankurt/Main, 2014).

132 In Varon's memoir the families stayed together in Haidari, *The Juderia*, pp. 48-49; see ibid, pp. 50–53 on the guards' use of violence in the camp.

133 Danuta Czech, *Danuta Czech, Kalendarium der Ereignisse im Konzentrationslager Auschwitz-Birkenau 1939–1945*, trans. Jochen August with a foreword by Walter Laqueur (Rowohlt: Reinbek, 1989), gives the figure of 2,500 arrivals on Transport Nr 44.

134 South African Holocaust and Genocide Foundation Archive, Jack Hasson, Interview Transcript 2004, p. 1. Jack Hasson Interview 7687, seg. 4. Visual History Archives. USC Shoah Foundation.

135   Ibid, p. 2. Jack believed his father and two uncles buried her in the adjacent field, although this would not have been possible given the circumstances.

136   Perahia Margosch, Rachelle, United States Holocaust Memorial Museum Collection, courtesy of the Jeff and Toby Herr Foundation. Oral History. Accession Number: 2004.303. RG Number: RG-50.030.0486 2004. Czech, *Kalendarium*, p. 851, gives an approximate figure of 2,500. She also states that of those gassed, 1,202 were men.

137   Surmani, Interview 53625, seg. 80.

138   Fintz, Interview 5720, seg. 8.

139   For the rail network in the so-called Greater Reich including the Generalgouvernement (occupied Poland), Deutsche Reichsbahn Generalbetriebsleitung Ost, Übersichtskarte zum 15. Verzeichnis der SF-Züge (1943), http://maps.mapywig.org/m/German_maps/various/Bahn/Uebersichtskarte_zum_15._Verzeichnis_der_SF_Zuege_Mai_1943.jpg. Background in, Alfred Gottwaldt, *Julius Dorpmüller, Die Reichsbahn und die Autobahn. Verkehrspolitik und Leben des Verkehersministers bis 1945* (Argos Verlag: Berlin, 1995).

140   An overview of the route can be found at Yad Vashem, https://deportation.yadvashem.org/index.html?language=en&itemId=10991997&ind=-1

141   Gottwaldt, *Julius Dorpmüller*, pp. 100–111 for the Ostbahn. Raul Hilberg's forensic account of those involved in transporting Jews to Auschwitz is told to Claude Lanzmann in the latter's film, *Shoah* (1985) and can be watched in part at https://www.youtube.com/watch?v=H-aAwsJjJxY.

142   Giuseppe (Joseph) Coné, Interview 27 September 1986, South African Union of Jewish Students.

143   Bierman, *Odyssey*, pp. 222–223. See Fahn's own testimony in YVA Record Group O.3 – Testimonies Item ID 7838793 Tape NumberVT/10513 Protokoll Sidney Simcha Fahn. For Bresova's geographical location, https://www.jewishgen.org/communities/community.php?usbgn=-841043.

144   For the halt at Budapest, Fintz, Interview 5720. For a discussion of the role of the ICRC and with a link to literature on the subject, https://www.icrc.org/en/document/icrc-wwii-holocaust.

145   Capelluto, *My Life*, p. 15.

146   Salomon Galante, interview in Novitch, *The Passage of the Barbarians*, p. 131. Varon, Interview 26814, seg. 13.

147   Galante, *Appendice a l'histoire*, p. 300.

148   Hanan, Interview 13096. testimony, tape 2.

149 Hasson, *Du Paradis*, p. 66. Alice Tarica also recalled the silence in her wagon, *Des ténèbres*, p. 44.

150 Capelluto, *My Life*, p. 15.

151 Fintz Interview 5720, seg. 8.

152 Varon, Interview 26814, seg. 13. Varon, *The Juderia*, p. 60.

153 Ibid.

154 A fascinating study of the experiences of deportees during transports to Auschwitz and other camps, is that by Simone Gigliotti, *The Train Journey: Transit, Captivity and Witnessing in the Holocaust* (Berghahn Books: New York & Oxford, 2010), especially p. 113.

155 Levi, Interview 1701, seg. 54.

156 Varon, Asher, Interview 43798, seg. 13. Visual History Archive, USC Shoah Foundation, 2006. Accessed 20 June 2016.

157 On this aspect, see the groundbreaking study by Gigliotti, *The Train Journey*.

158 Yad Vashem Archives (hereafter: YVA) 03/10423 Laura Varon, VD1390, interviewed by Yael Ben Schmuel, 14 November 1996, transcript, p. 17.

159 GAKR Carabinieri 2.40.12 (1933), Sabetai, Nissim fu Salomone. Benatar and Benatar, *Si je t'oublie*, p. 578.

160 Fortunoff Archives, Tarica, Interview, seg. 12. See also, Hanan, Interview 13096, tape 2 (25.56 mins). Soriano, Clara, Interview 8852, seg. 8. Visual History Archive, USC Shoah Foundation 1996. Accessed 9 January 2017.

161 Alberto Israel, *The Longest Journey*, 43:00 min.

162 Surmani, Interview 53625, seg. 101. There are inconsistencies in the documentation: the deportation list includes his entire family including his brother Mosé (nos. 494–98), who, according to CDEC did not survive; but according to his testimony, his older sister Stella survived (CDEC data shows her as having not survived), while his brother Mosé had previously escaped the island in a boat, eventually arriving in Palestine where he ultimately fought for and was killed during the creation of the Israeli state. Mosé is now honoured in its pantheon of heroes. See the photographs of Mosé submitted by Eliezer to Yad Vashem, archival signature: 8630/2, http://collections.yadvashem.org/photoarchive/en-us/7316335.html; Benatar and Benatar, *Si je t'oublie*, p. 616 for correct information and photographs.

163 Alberto Israel, *The Longest Journey*, 56:53 min.

164 Sami Modiano, *The Longest Journey*, 44:07 min.

Chapter 6

1   Robert Collis and Han Hogerzeil, *Straight On* (Routledge Library Editions:
    Responding to Fascism, Vol. 12, repr., London, 2010, originally published 1947),
    p. 90. Collis, an Irish paediatrician, was describing Bergen-Belsen where he had
    joined a medical team after liberation.

2   https://www.auschwitz.org/en/history/auschwitz-and-shoah/the-unloading-
    ramps-and-selections/.

3   Franco, *Jewish Martyrs*, pp. 64–66. According to Isaac Benatar, *Rhodes and
    the Holocaust: The Story of the Jewish Community from the Mediterranean
    Island of Rhodes* (iUniverse Inc.: New York and Bloomington, 2010), p. 36,
    his grandfather, Isaac Hanan, was among those who died en route although
    his name does not appear in Franco's list. Cf. Bierman, *Odyssey*, p. 221.

4   Danuta Czech, *Kalendarium der Ereignisse im Konzentrationslager Auschwitz-
    Birkenau 1939–1945*, trans. Jochen August with a foreword by Walter Laqueur
    (Rowohlt: Reinbek, 1989), p. 851. Those admitted received the numbers B-7159 to
    B-7504 (males) and A-24215 to A-24468 (females). Czech cites the quarantine list.

5   Hasson, Interview 7687. Visual History Archive. USC Shoah Foundation, seg. 4.
    Jack believed his father and two uncles (Salomon and Giacobbe) buried her in a
    field next to the tracks before passing through Zagreb.

6   Giuseppe Coné, Interview 27 September 1986, The South African Union of
    Jewish Students, The Student Holocaust Interviewing Project Cape Town.

7   Violetta Fintz, Interview 5720, seg. 8–9. VHA. USC Shoah Foundation.

8   Primo Levi, *If this is a Man/The Truce*, trans. Stuart Woolf, with an introduction
    by Paul Bailey (Penguin Books: London, 1979), p. 26. Levi gives a graphic
    account in his memoir-cum-report of his arrival on 26 February on the transport
    from Fossoli among 650 Jews, of these ninety-five 'young and apparently able-
    bodied men' and 'also young – a meagre group made up of only' twenty-nine
    women were admitted to the camp, the rest 'the most numerous of all, of the
    children, the infirm and the old' numbering 526 were gassed, ibid, pp. 34–35. See
    Czech, *Kalendarium*, p. 730.

9   Surmani, Eliezer, Interview 53625, seg. 92. Visual History Archive, USC Shoah
    Foundation, interviewed in 2006. Eliezer lived with his widowed father (15
    March 1900), paternal grandmother (7 September 1869) and his four siblings:
    Rachele, 12 February 1924, Stella, 6 September 1926, Moses, 14 August 1931,
    and Maria, 7 December 1933, at Via delle Feritoie 24–26, ULL'Ufficio dello Stato
    Civile Rodi, card no. 504. According to his testimony his mother Giovanna

Hasson died giving birth to Salva in 1938, the baby also appears to have died. Eliezer apparently passed away in 2011, www.rhodesjewishmseum.org/ genealogy/family-trees Blog entry Jack Surmani (son) 10 December 2013.

10   Charlotte Delbo, *Auschwitz and After*, 22nd edition, trans. Rosette C. Lamont with a new foreword by Lawrence L. Langer (Yale University Press: New Haven and London, 1995), p. 4.

11   Fintz, Interview 5720, seg. 9. Visual History Archive. USC Shoah Foundation. Transcript is verbatim and mistakes uncorrected. Miriam died just after the liberation of Bergen-Belsen, ibid, seg. 16. See also Fintz's interview, South Africa Holocaust and Genocide Foundation, interviewed in 1992, transcript p. 5.

12   Details in https://digital-library.cdec.it/cdec-web/persone/detail/person-3421/ hanan-ezra.html.

13   Gilmore Sara, Interview 439. Visual History Archive. USC Shoah Foundation, interviewed in 1994. It is unclear if her older sister Amalie/Amelia was included among those admitted to the camp, or if she joined her mother, grandparents and younger siblings. For Ascer/Asher Hanan and his siblings, ITS Digital Archive. Arolsen Archives, 1.1.5.3, Personal file of Ascer Hanan, Sig. 8800370, frame 0139 – Ascer returned to Rhodes exactly one year after the deportation, on 23 July 1945. We return to the Hanan children in Chapter 8.

14   Sub-Collection, 3.2.1.2/80912936, CM/1 Files originating in Italy/Matilde Alhadeff, ITS Digital Archive, Arolsen Archives.

15   GAKR, Carabinieri file: 293 TMHNA1/1, Deportation list numbers: 625, 627, 628. Isaaco would have turned 9 in September.

16   Details in http://digital-library.cdec.it/cdec-web/persone/detail/person-4617/ levi-elia.html. Stella Levi in the *Longest Journey*, mentions a woman 'over 100 years old'. It is possible that she had Fassana in mind. From anecdotal evidence, it appears that many if not most of this cohort did not survive the conditions of the transport.

17   See the introduction to Jordan Goodman, Anthony McElligott and Lara Marks (eds.), *Useful Bodies: Humans in the Service of Medical Science in the Twentieth Century* (Johns Hopkins University Press: Baltimore, 2003).

18   CDEC Coll. Fond Massimo Adolfo Vitale, unità archivistica b. 3, fasc. 82, Testimonianza di Rachele Cugno (1) deportata ad Auschwitz nell'agosto 1944. It is not clear if Rachel (Hugno) was reporting something she saw with her own eyes, or if she had heard of this alleged event. I will return to this issue of remembering in the final chapter.

19   Laura Varon, Interview 26814, seg. 14. Visual History Archive. USC
     Shoah Foundation. Stella De Leon, Interview 12055, seg. 50–51. VHA
     Shoah Foundation. Such violent imagery has become an enduring trope
     when describing arrivals at Auschwitz. Elie Wiesel, *Night* translated from the
     French by Marion Wiesel (Penguin Books: Harmondsworth, 2006 [orig. 1972]),
     p. 30, also gives a stylized account of the use of violence on arrival in Auschwitz.
     In contrast to Wiesel (and others), both Primo Levi and Nyiszli make reference
     to the calm, 're-assuring' tone of the guards during disembarkation and the
     selection that followed.

20   Max Mannheimer, *Spätes Tagebuch. Theresienstadt-Auschwitz-Warschau-
     Dachau*, with a Foreword to this edition by Wolfgang Benz, expanded paperback
     edition (Piper: München, [2000] 2010), pp. 66–67. For an English translation
     of Mannheimer's experience, 'Theresienstadt-Auschwitz-Warsaw-Dachau.
     Recollections', in *Dachau Review* 1 (n.p. and n.d.), pp. 55–92, and 57–68 for the
     selection. His memoir is based on three interviews made in 1956 and originally
     published in German in *Dachauer Hefte* 1 (Dec. 1985).

21   Miklós Nyiszli, *Auschwitz: A Doctor's Eyewitness Account* (Arcade: New York,
     2011 [orig. 1946]), p. 3.

22   Levi, *If this is a Man*, pp. 19–20, 22–27. The quotation is from p. 26.

23   Shlomo Venezia, *Inside the Gas Chambers*, p. 36. It is probable that this was the
     same transport that carried Erikos Sevillias and his cousins and nephews. See
     the following quote.

24   The last transport comprised *c.* 2,500 deportees of which 346 males and 254
     females were admitted; of those gassed: 1,202 were males and 698 females.
     Czech, *Kalendarium*, p. 831.

25   Fintz, Interview 5720, seg. 8 and 9.

26   Leni Yahil, *The Holocaust: The Fate of the European Jewry, 1932–1945: The Fate of
     European Jewry, 1932–1945*, trans. from the Hebrew by Ina Friedman and Haya
     Galai (Oxford University Press: New York, Oxford, 1991), pp. 559–572.

27   Erikos Sevillias, *Athens-Auschwitz*, trans. and introduced by Nikos Stavroulakis
     (Lycabettus Press, Athens, 1983), pp. 21–23.

28   Levi, *If this is a Man*, for the increasingly arbitrary and inconsistent character of
     the selection process and also for the factor of 'luck' in surviving Auschwitz.

29   Joseph D. Alhadeff, *The Jewish Community of Rhodes: A Short History*
     (Publication of the Jewish Community: Rhodes: n.d.), p. 28. Elsewhere in his
     book, Alhadeff appears to resort to pure fantasy, or simply confuses stages
     in the genocide, as on page 31 when he claims that gold teeth were extracted

from the deportees while held at Haidari. There is no evidence either from survivor testimony or in official documentation to support this claim.

30 The CDEC data is incomplete. The actual number of survivors was higher according to post-war reports, see Chapter 8.

31 Namely, Giacomo (Jack) Hasson, Alberto Israel, Ascer Varon, Sami Modiano, Eliezer Surmani.

32 Stella was born on 14 August 1931, Sub-Collection 3.2.1.4/80912936 CM/1 Files originating in Switzerland – UNHCR/Stella Berun (*sic*), ITS Digital Archive, Arolsen Archives. We discuss Stella's subsequent fate in Chapter 8.

33 He was born on 20 August 1927. His family lived at Principe di Napoli no. 50; father Rahamin (1880) was a baker; his mother Signorù (1885); they married in December 1924. His three siblings were all older: Elia, 30 July 1916; Aronne, 21 July 1923; Giovanna, 1 April 1925. All'UFFICIO DELLO STATO CIVILE Rodi Racial Census, # 353. Data on those entering the camp from Czech, *Kalendarium*, p. 851.

34 Alberto Israel, *The Longest Journey*, 42:18 min.

35 Elisa Franco Hasson, *Il Était Une Fois l'Île Des Roses* (Éditions Clepsydre: Nivelles, 1996, repr. 2012), p. 60.

36 Alice Tarica-Israël, *Des ténébres au soleil* (Éditions Clepsydre: Nivelles, 2007), p. 46.

37 For example the indispensable chronic *Kalendarium* compiled by Danuta Czech, as n. 4.

38 https://www.yadvashem.org/yv/de/exhibitions/album_auschwitz/index.asp. Tal Bruttman, Stefan Hördler and Christoph Kreutzmüller, *Die fotografische Inszenierung des Verbrechens. Ein Album aus Auschwitz. Bildanalyse des Lili-Jacob-Albums* (Wissenschaftliche Buchgesellschaft: Darmstadt, 2019). For the transports from Hungary, Randolph L. Braham, *The Politics of Genocide: The Holocaust in Hungary*. Vol. 1 (Columbia University Press: New York, 2016), pp. 771, 774–775.

39 Nyiszli, *Auschwitz: A Doctor's Eyewitness Account*, p. 3. A good description of this standardized procedure is found in Lucy Dawidowicz, *The War Against the Jews*, p. 148.

40 The fact that the family also were fluent in German helped. Erika Kounio-Amarilio, *From Thessaloniki to Auschwitz and Back: Memories of a Survivor from Thessaloniki* (Vallentine Mitchell: London, 2000).

41 See Robert J. Büchler's account of telling the doctor at the selection that he was 16 years old (and not 14 years old) when he arrived in summer 1944, 'Unter den Kindern von Auschwitz', *Dachauer Hefte* 12 (Nov. 1996), pp. 169–195, here: 170.

42 De Leon, Interview 12055, seg. 37–39, 89; seg. 69 for Gianette's death. For the family, Benatar and Benatar, *Si je t'oublie*, p. 358.

43 Fils, Interview 1423, seg. 37 and following.

44 Jerusalmi, née Notrica, Interview 8038, seg. 7. Visual History Archive. USC Shoah Foundation. However, Salvo[Salvatore] was admitted to the camp, see below. See also, Soriano, Clara, Interview 8852. Visual History Archive. USC Shoah Foundation 1996. Accessed 9 January 2017.

45 Hasson, Interview 7687, seg.4, 5. Benatar and Benatar, *Si je t'oublie*, p. 362.

46 For example, Anna Almeleh, née Cohen, Interview 6738. Visual History Archive. USC Shoah Foundation.

47 Lucia Amato, née Sciarcon, Interview 14687. Visual History Archive. USC Shoah Foundation.

48 Surmani, Interview 53625, seg. 99, 102.

49 BA-Ludwigsburg, B162/1515, Bl.520-21. In her testimony she gives her date of birth as 20 October 1928, in Benatar and Benatar, *Si t'oublie*, p. 595, it appears as 21 October 1927.

50 JMR Racial Census, Card #486.

51 Benatar and Benatar, *Si t'oublie*, p. 527. Samuele's brother Saul Modiano died before the deportation aged 26.

52 Giamila's brother Samuele was married to Reina Alcana, the daughter of Hizkia Alcana, an uncle of Miru Alcana whom we have cited elsewhere in this study.

53 Gedenstaette Mauthausen, Die Toten des KZ Mauthausen, Saul Alhadeff 1920–1945.

54 Benatar and Benatar, *Si je t'oublie*, p. 49. Ruben was the older brother of Bulissa Alhadeff (b. 1897) also murdered in Auschwitz, who was the mother of Matilde Alhadeff, the wife of Rino Merolle. We discuss Matilde in Chapter 8. See Benatar and Benatar, *Si je t'oublie*, pp. 22, 544.

55 We discuss Mauthausen below.

56 Varon, Interview 26814, seg. 17. Varon, *The Juderia*, pp. 68–71. Neither of her uncles, Rahamin and Samuel survived.

57 De Leon, Interview 12055, seg. 49.

58 Stella Hasson (née Nachmias), Interview 1468, Visual History Archive. USC Shoah Foundation. Tape 1, at 17 mins. Stella (Esther) was born 12 October 1915.

59 Yad Vashem Archives, 03/10423, Laura Varon, Interview transcript, p. 25.

60 Miru Alcana, Testimony 129, Visual History Archive. USC Shoah Foundation, seg. 9. Stella Levi, Interview 1701, seg. 62. Visual History Archive. USC Shoah Foundation.

61 Surmani, Interview 53625, seg. 158.

62 Alcana, Interview 129, seg. 9.

63 WJC MSS. Col. No. 361 H178/13, Albert Hanan, appeal to the PCIRO 9 January 1950. '[…] plusiers de mes compatriots furent a l'occasion elimines.'

64 Hasson, Interview 7687, seg. 7. It is probable he was sent to the gas chambers at the end of the two-week quarantine period.

65 Hanan, Interview 13096. Tape 4, 5.28 minutes, 12 minutes. Visual History Archive. USC Shoah Foundation. Rachel's older brothers also did not survive the Holocaust; Aaronne (22.4.16) died in Auschwitz and Giacomo (25.3.18) died in Dachau in December. Rachel's sister Diamente (21.10.13) survived. Benatar and Benatar, *Si je t'oublie*, p. 396.

66 Fintz, Interview 5720, seg. 12. See Benatar and Benatar, *Si je t'oublie*, p. 491, who give Miriam's date and place of death as 14 May 1945 in Bergen-Belsen.

67 Benatar and Benatar, *Si je t'oublie*, p. 428. Reference to the winding down of selections at Auschwitz, Primo Levi with Leonardo De Benedetti, *Auschwitz Report* (orig. 1945) trans. by Judith Woolf and edited by Robert S. C. Gordon (Verso: London, New York, 2006), pp. 72–73. Danuta Czech noted that gassings after selections continued until 2 November, after this date, prisoners were shot in the gas chamber, Czech, *Kalendarium*, pp. 920–921.

68 We discuss Mauthausen below.

69 As well as the reference to this process in nearly all the survivor testimonies cited in this chapter, Primo Levi, *If This Is a Man*, trans. by S. Woolf, (Abacus: London, [1958] 1987), pp. 45–46; and Paul Steinberg: *Speak You Also: A Survivor's Reckoning* (Henry Holt: New York, 2000), p. 46. The procedure of registration was uniform throughout the camp system: exhibition of the Gedenkstätte Dachau https://www.kz-gedenkstaette-dachau.de/stop06.html.

70 Jersusalmi, Interview 8038, seg. 8–9.

71 Varon, Interview 26814, seg. 15.

72 Czech, *Kalendarium*, p. 851. For a vivid description of this process, Hanan, Interview 13096, tape 3, 2 min.

73 Surmani, Interview 53625, seg. 98; Benatar and Benatar, *Si je t'oublie*, p. 616, has a photograph of his registration card from Mauthausen, also showing his Auschwitz number.

74 De Leon, Interview 12055, seg. 44, 45.

75 Jerusalmi, Interview 8038, seg. 8.

76 Levi, Interview 1701, seg. 60.

77   Franco, Rebecca, Interview 33394, seg. 68. Visual History Archive, USC Shoah Foundation, 1997. Accessed 12 January 2016.

78   She also lost her sight in one eye because of beatings. Alcana, Interview 129, seg. 9.

79   http://www.jpost.com/Magazine/Features/Its-time-they-knew-our-names. De Leon, Interview 12055, seg. 47.

80   Soriano, Interview 8852, seg. 8.

81   Tony Alhadeff, *The Family Treasure* (n.p., 2020), p. 79. Alhadeff is the grandson of Gella.

82   Fintz, Interview 5720, seg.10.

83   Fintz, Interview 5720, seg. 11.

84   As recalled by Jack Hasson, Interview 7687, seg. 7. See Benatar and Benatar, *Si t'oublie*, p. 273 for details of David Galante, born 15 July 1925, and his family. The brother is Mosé, born 22 June 1923. He, like the three sisters, did not survive the camps.

85   De Leon, Interview 12055, seg. 47, Varon, Interview 26814, seg. 18–20, Berro, Interview 5969, seg. 11, for examples.

86   Tarica-Israël, *Des ténèbres au soleil*, p. 55.

87   Alcana, transcript, 1. See, Jerusalmi, Interview 8038, seg. 5 and Capelluto, *My Life*, p. 16.

88   Stella Levi, 'It's time they knew our names', *The Jerusalem Post*, April 16, 2009, https://www.jpost.com/magazine/features/its-time-they-knew-our-names. Fintz, Interview 5720, seg. 10.

89   Almeleh, Interview 6738, seg. 8. Cf. Büchler, 'Unter den Kindern', p. 181, who talks about the importance of potatoes for survival.

90   Fintz, Interview 5720, seg. 11.

91   On scavenging, Fils, Interview 1423, seg. 50; Levi, Interview 1701, seg. 67. Jerusalmi, Interview 8038, seg. 13. On its debilitating impact on some of the women, Franco Hasson, *Il Était Une Fois*, p. 73, and Levi and De Benedetti, *Auschwitz Report*, pp. 49–51.

92   Franco Hasson, *Il Était Une Fois*, p. 68. My translation.

93   Hanan, Interview 13096, Tape 4, 13:00 min.

94   Levi, Interview 1701, seg. 63, 69. Alcana, Interview 129, seg. 10–11. Amato, Interview 1468, tape 1, at 17:25 min.

95   Joan Ringelbaum, 'Women and the Holocaust: A Reconsideration of Research', *Signs*, Vol. 10, No. 4, 'Communities of Women' (Summer 1985), pp. 741–761. Falk Pingel, 'Social Life in an Unsocial Environment', in Jane Caplan and Nikolaus Wachsmann (eds.), *Concentration Camps in Nazi Germany: The New Histories* (Routledge: London and New York, 2009), pp. 58–81, here: 70–72.

96   Fils, Interview 1432, seg. 50.

97   Jerusalmi, Interview 8038, segs. 13, 18, 61.

98   Surmani, Interview 53625, seg. 104. Hasson, Interview 7687, seg. 5. Varon, Interview 43798, seg. 30–32.

99   Czech, *Kalendarium*, p. 883. In their later interviews, survivors invariably refer to Rydułtowy by its German name, Rideltau.

100 Ibid. Franciszek Piper, 'Die Rolle des Lagers Auschwitz', in Ulrich Herbert, Karin Orth and Christoph Dieckmann (eds.), *Die nationalsozialistischen Konzentrationslager* 2 vols. (Fischer: Frankfurt am Main, 2002), pp. 390–414, here: 408.

101 Cited in Franciszek Piper, *Voices of Memory 9: Jews in Auschwitz* (Auschwitz-Birkenau State Museum: Oswiecim, 2019), p. 157. There were in fact more than 100 Aegean Jews working in the mines.

102 Personal data for nineteen of the fifty-four guards at the mine show that they were in their late forties or fifties. http://www.tenhumbergreinhard.de/1933-1945-taeter-und-mitlaeufer/personal-charlottengrube.html

103 Hasson, Interview 4687, seg. 5.

104 Varon, Ascer Interview 43798, seg.30–32. Visual History Archive. USC Shoah Foundation, interviewed in 1998.

105 On hierarchy and violence in the camp system, Wolfgang Sofsky, *Die Ordnung des Terrors: Das Konzentrationslager* (Fischer Verlag: Frankfurt am Main, 1997).

106 *Manchester Guardian*, 19 April 1945, 'Cannibalism in Prison Camps: British Medical Officer's Visit to "Most Horrible Place"', https://www.theguardian.com/world/1945/apr/19/secondworldwar.fromthearchive. The standard work on Bergen-Belsen is Joanna Reilly, *Belsen: The Liberation of a Concentration Camp* (Routledge: London, 1997).

107 Paul Peachey, 'Cannibalism "rampant" at Nazi concentration camp, new documents reveal', *The Independent*, 31 March 2016, accessed at https://www.independent.co.uk/news/uk/home-news/cannibalism-rampant-nazi-concentration-camp-new-documents-reveal-a6960876.html

108 Berro, Interview 5969. See also, http://edition.cnn.com/2011/WORLD/europe/06/24/holocaust.rape/

109 Iakovos Kambanellis, *Die Freiheit kam im Mai* (Ephelant Verlag: Vienna, 2010), pp. 20–21.

110 ITS Digital Archive. Arolsen Archives, 1.1.26.0 (Mauthausen), Lageplan des KL Mauthausen und Berichte über das Lager vom November 1945, 'Extraits de la Traduction du rapport du Chef de Camp Mauthhausen', p. 8.

111 Tarica-Israël, *Des ténèbres au soleil*, pp. 54, 55, 66, and her interview Fortunoff Archive, seg. 14 and 15. The description of Magda as a monster comes from Elisa Franco Hasson, *Il Était Une Fois l'Île Des Roses*, p. 80. For abuse in the camp, including sexual abuse, ibid, pp. 82, 84, 92.

112 Renee Ghert-Zand, 'Groundbreaking study exhumes untold Nazi brutalization of women's bodies', *The Times of Israel*, 5 May 2016. See the award-winning book, Beverley Chalmers, *Birth, Sex and Abuse: Women's Voices Under Nazi Rule* (Grosvenor House Publishing Ltd: Guildford, 2015), and its limitations: Michelle Mouton, Review of Chalmers, Beverley, *Birth, Sex and Abuse: Women's Voices under Nazi Rule*. H-German, H-Net Reviews. August, 2017, http://www.h-net.org/reviews/showrev.php?id=46348; Selma Leydesdorff, 'Birth, Sex and Abuse: Women's Voices under Nazi Rule, by Beverley Chalmers', *Women's History Review*, Vol. 26, No. 3 (2017), pp. 504–506, DOI: 10.1080/09612025.2016.1248044.

113 Dorota Glowacka, 'Sexual Violence against Men and Boys during the Holocaust: A Genealogy of (Not-So-Silent) Silence', *German History*, Vol. 39, No. 1 (March 2021), pp. 78–99, published online: May 2020; Tommy J. Curry, 'Thinking through the Silence: Theorizing the Rape of Jewish Males during the Holocaust through Survivor Testimonies', *Holocaust Studies: A Journal of Culture and History*, Vol. 27 (2021), Special Issue: Buried Words: Sexuality, Violence and Holocaust Testimonies, pp. 447–472. Laura Jule Landwehrkamp, 'Male Rape in Auschwitz?: An Exploration of the Dynamics of Kapo-*Piepel* Sexual Violence in KL Auschwitz during the Holocaust' (Masters Thesis, University of Uppsala, Faculty of Arts, Department of History, The Hugo Valentin Centre, 2019).

114 Kerstin Steitz, 'No "Innocent Victim"?: Sexual Violence Against Jewish Women During the Holocaust as Trope in *Zeugin aus der Hölle*', *Women in German Yearbook*, Vol. 33 (2017), pp. 101–127. I do not exclude the possibility that there were in fact no occurrences of sexual abuse of men or boys from Rhodes and Kos.

115 They remained in what Imre Kertész referred to as the 'hidden recesses' of memory, Imre Kertész, *The Holocaust as Culture*, English trans. Thomas Cooper (Seagull Books: London, 2011), p. 59.

116 Varon, Interview 43798, seg. 27, 30–32. Hasson, Interview 7687, seg. 5.

117 Hanan, Interview 13096, Tape 4. Rachel only learned of her father's death after the war – that he had 'disappeared', apparently a victim of typhus along with the rest of the inmates of his barrack.

118 Hasson, Interview 7687, seg. 7. Jerusalmi, Interview 8038, seg. 14. Salvatore died in Mauthausen, as we shall see below. Varon, Interview 43798, seg. 26.

119 Surmani, Interview 53625, seg. 98.

120 Piotr Setkiewicz, 'Häftlingsarbeit im KZ Auschwitz III-Monowitz. Die Frage nach der Wirtschaftlichkeit der Arbeit', in Herbert, Orth and Dieckmann (eds.), *Konzentrationslager*, pp. 584–605.

121 Czech, *Kalendarium*, p. 916.

122 Wolfgang Benz and Hans Brenner, *Frauen in den Aussenlagern des KZ Flossenbürg* (Arbeitsgemeinschaft ehem. KZ Flossenbürg e.V.: Regensburg, 1999).

123 Amato, Interview 14687, seg. 70. Pascal Cziborra, *KZ Wilischthal: Unter 'Hitlerauges' Aufsicht: Die Außenlager des KZ Flossenbürg* (Lorbeer-Verlag; 2nd edition: Bielefeld, 2015), reproduces the list of names.

124 Ringelbaum, in a reappraisal of her earlier research, is now critical of such gendered-specific networks, 'Women and the Holocaust'.

125 https://www.gedenkstaette-flossenbuerg.de/en/history/satellite-camps/ wilischthal. Ulrich Fritz, 'Wilischthal', in Wolfgang Benz, Barbara Distel and Angelika Königseder (eds.), *Der Ort des Terrors. Geschichte der nationalsozialistischen Konzentrationslager. Bd. 4: Flossenbürg, Mauthausen, Ravensbrück* pbk. (C.H. Beck: Munich, 2018), pp. 267–270.

126 https://collections.ushmm.org/search/catalog/irn47548, USHMM Oral History interview with Miru Alcana, Accession Number: 1999.A.0122.1297: RG-50.477.1297, 22 December 1988, Tape 2: 11.26 mins.

127 Fritz, 'Wilischthal', p. 268. https://www.gedenkstaette-flossenbuerg.de/en/ history/satellite-camps/wilischthal

128 Amato, Interview 14687, seg. 70 and 78.

129 The *kapos* made frequent use of their whips 'without cause', Büchler, 'Unter den Kindern', pp. 181–182.

130 Sara learned of his death after liberation. Salvatore was among the 123 male Jews from Rhodes and Kos known to have been admitted to Mauthausen in January, ITS Digital Archive. Arolsen Archives 1.1.26 Mauthausen Concentration Camp, Reference Code: 01012608073.

131 Jerusalmi, Interview 8038, seg. 11.

132 Fintz, Interview 5720, seg. 11 and 13.

133 Jerusalmi, Interview 8038, seg. 9 and 16.

134 Levi, Interview 1701, seg. 82–84.

135 Marc Buggeln, *Arbeit & Gewalt: Das Außenlagersystem des KZ Neuengamme* (Wallstein Verlag: Göttingen, 2009), pp. 106–111.

136 See the first-hand account in Nyiszli, *Auschwitz*, pp. 149–152. Daniel Blatman, 'The Death Marches and the Final Phase of Nazi Genocide', in Caplan and Wachsmann, *Concentration Camps*, pp. 167–185, and *Die Verfolgung und Ermordung der europäischen Juden durch das nationalsozialistische Deutschland 1933–1945* Band 16, Das KZ Auschwitz 1942–1945 und die Zeit der Todesmärsche 1944/45, Bearbeitet von Andrea Rudorff (De Gruyter/ Oldenbourg: Berlin, Boston, 2018), Einleitung, pp. 81–83. Also, Daniel Goldhagen, *Hitler's Willing Executioners: Ordinary Germans and the Holocaust* (Vintage Books: New York, 1996), chapter 14, *passim*.

137 Varon, Interview 43798, seg. 26.

138 Czech, *Kalendarium*, pp. 968, 977.

139 Heinz Kounio, *Ein Liter Suppe*, p. 136, gives 18 January as the date they left, making the journey a week in length. It is possible that each of the witnesses cited here was on a different march; it is no longer possible to determine this with any accuracy. There were at least two major transports in January, one on the 18th, of 5,000 prisoners to Gross-Rosen, and the second on 26 January to Buchenwald of 3,935; a third transport took place on 22 January, this may have been the transport that Eliezer was on; but not Nyiszli, if his account is accurate. Two smaller transfers of three and thirty-one Italian prisoners took place on 18 and 21 January: http://www.tenhumbergreinhard.de/transportliste-der-deportierten/transportliste-der-deportierten-1945/index.html. On the death marches, Daniel Blatman, *The Death Marches: The Final Phase of Nazi Genocide*, trans. Chaya Galai (Harvard University Press: Cambridge, MA, 2010).

140 Hans Maršálek, *Die Geschichte des Konzentrationslagers Mauthausen. Dokumentation* (edition Mauthausen: Vienna, 2006); reprint 2016), p. 149, states 5,714 prisoners arrived from Auschwitz.

141 Nyiszli, *Auschwitz*, pp. 151–152.

142 WJC MSS. Col. No. 361 H178/13, Albert Hanan, appeal to the PCIRO 9 January 1950:

> Mauthausen dans un etat des plus lamentables, on nous aurait pris pour des ombres, nous fumes laisses sans aucun abri sur la neige pendant 40 heures pour passer a la disinfection. Je fus garde a Mauthause jusqu'au debut du mois de fevrier et puis transfere a Gusen I, a 7 km plus loin, ou je travaillai dans la fabrique des appareils 'Messerschmidt', cache dans les entrailles de la montagne. – Par contre, mes trois freres furent conduits a Eben-Zee [*sic*] et Dachau ou ils trouverent une mort horrible.

143 Florian Freund and Bertrand Perz, 'Mauthausen – Stammlager', in Wolfgang Benz, Barbara Distel and Angelika Königseder (eds.), *Der Ort des Terrors: Geschichte der nationalsozialistischen Konzentrationslager*, Bd. 4 (C.H. Beck: Munich, 2006), pp. 293–346.

144 ITS Digital Archive, Arolsen Archives (Mauthausen) 1.1.26.0, Ref. 2127003: Arrivals and Discharges March 1943–April 1945. The following numbers of Jews were registered at the camp: 31 May 1943: 11 (majority between 20 and 30 years old); 30 June 1943: 10; 31 July 1943: 9; September 1943: 15; 31 December 1943: 3; January 1944: 1.

145 Benz, Distel and Königseder, *Der Ort des Terrors*, n. 143. Stanisław Dobosiewicz, *Vernichtungslager Gusen: Mauthausen-Studien. Schriftenreihe der KZ-Gedenkstätte Mauthausen Band 5* (Bundesministerium für Inneres, Abt. IV/7: Vienna, 2007). This is a translation of the Polish original from 1977. On the guards, Gregor Holzinger, 'Kurzbiografien von Angehörigen des Kammandaturstabs', in idem (ed.), *Die Zeite Reihe. Täterbiografien aus dem Konzentrationslager Mauthausen: Mauthausen-Studien. Schriftenreihe der KZ-Gedenkstätte Mauthausen Band 10* (new academic press: Vienna, 2016), pp. 45–200 *passim*, especailly pp. 184–191 for Ziereis.

146 Stefan Hördler, *Ordnung und Inferno: Das KZ System im letzten Kriegsjahr* (Wallstein Verlag: Göttingen, 2015), p. 381. Stefan Hördler, 'Mauthausen', in Geoffrey P. Megargee (ed.), Foreword by Elie Wiesel, *The United States Holocaust Memorial Museum Encyclopedia of Camps and Ghettos, 1933–1945*, Volume I: Early Camps, Youth Camps, and Concentration Camps and Subcamps under the SS-Business Administration Main Office (WVHA) Wagener, pp. 899–964.

147 Hördler, *Ordnung und Inferno*, pp. 380–381. Cf. Jakowas Kambanellis, 'Mauthausen', *Dachauer Hefte*, Vol. 12 (Nov. 1996), pp. 81–103, who estimates that 200 Greek Jews were in Mauthausen in July 1945; the Aegean Jews would have been counted as Italians.

148 Sub-Collection 1.1.26.3, Individual Documents Regarding Male Detainees Mauthausen /Isacco Alcana, ITS Digital Archive, Arolsen Archives. All following data on male deaths has been collated from Mauthausen: Case No. 000-50 (Vol. X – Folder III List of Victims): US vs. Hans Altfuldich, et al. N.d. RG 153, Records of the Office of the JAG (Army), War Crimes Branch, Entry 149, Concentration Camp Trials. National Archives (U.S.). Archives Unbound. Web. 8 Nov. 2019. http://go.gale.com/gdsc/i.do?&id=GALE%7CSC5106350329 &v=2.1&u=353lime&it=r&p=GDSC&sw=w&viewtype=fullcitation

149   Dieter Pohl points out, 'annihilation through labour' was only in reference to building the so-called 2,000-km-long Durchgangsstrasse IV (Transit Road IV) in Ukraine, to supply Germany's southern sector of the Eastern Front. Pohl, 'The Holocaust and the Concentration Camps', in Caplan and Wachsmann (eds.), *Concentration Camps*, pp. 149–166, here, p. 161.

150   Varon, Interview 43798, seg. 27, 30-32. In the interview, it appears that Ascer is confusing conditions in *Charlottengrube* and Mauthausen. He was in fact, sent to Mauthausen's satellite camp Ebensee.

151   Florian Freund, *Arbeitslager Zement: Das Konzentrationslager Ebensee und die Raketenrüstung* (Verlag für Gesellschaftskritik: Vienna, 1989). From 12 May 1944, the US Air Force began to target and destroy the German fuel industry. The first targets were the huge refineries of Leuna, Brüx, Böhlen, etc. Shortly afterwards, the US Air Force also began to destroy the oil industry in Austria, which was particularly felt in places such as Moosbierbaum and Floridsdorf. The German leadership recognized the danger and, on 30 May, Hitler appointed Edmund Geilenberg, managing director of 'Stahlwerke Braunschweig', as General Commissioner for Immediate Measures. His task was to secure the Third Reich's fuel production – a practically impossible task, as was soon to become apparent: http://www.geheimprojekte.at/info_geilenberg.html.

152   Maršálek, *Geschichte des Konzentrationslagers Mauthausen*, p. 75.

153   Florian Freund, *Konzentrationslager Ebensee: Ein Außenlager des KZ-Mauthausen* (New Academic Press: Vienna, 2016). Robert G. Waite, 'Ebensee', in Megargee (ed.), *Encyclopedia of Camps and Ghettos*, pp. 911–913.

154   Solomon J. Salat, March 10, 1998, in *betrifft widerstand* Nr 66, Februar 2004, pp. 23-26, here: 23. https://web.archive.org/web/20130329090413/http://www.memorial-ebensee.at/de/index.php?view=article&catid=1%3Akz-ebensee&id=27%3Azeitzeugenbericht-die-letzten-wochen-im-lager-ebensee-englisch&option=com_content&Itemid=15.

155   Waite, 'Ebensee', in Megargee (ed.), *Encyclopedia of Camps and Ghettos*, pp. 911–913, here: 912.

156   The figures were as follows: February: 704; March: 1,752; April: 3,102; 1–6 May: 1,116, Florian Freund, 'Die Toten von Ebensee', in Bundesministerium für Inneres (ed.), *KZ- Gedenkstätte Mauthausen/Mauthausen Memorial 2010* (Bundesministerium für Inneres: Vienna, 2010), pp. 21–30, here: pp. 22–23.

157   ITS Digital Archive, Arolsen Archives, 1.1.26.1 Concentration Camp Mauthausen Death Books, 07.01.1939–29.04.1945; my calculation. Unless otherwise stated, all references to deaths are from this source.

158 Buggeln, *Arbeit & Gewalt*, pp. 83–84, 89.

159 See: Bertrand Perz, 'Der Arbeitseinsatz im KZ Mauthausen', in Herbert, Orth and Dieckmann (eds.), *Konzentrationslager*, pp. 533–557, and Florian Freund, 'Häftlingskategorien und Sterblichkeit in einem Außenlager des KZ Mauthausen', in ibid, pp. 874–886. See also Hördler, *Ordnung und Inferno*.

160 Arolsen Archives, Ref. 738000, 1.1.26.1, Death Book of CC Mauthausen, infirmary, Jewish hospital Block 6, 1945, for the death entries of those cited here. On trials of injecting with lethal chemical compounds into prisoners as a way of killing them, see: http://auschwitz.org/en/history/camp-hospitals/selections-and-lethal-injections/. Paul Weindling, 'Medizinische Gräueltaten in Mauthausen und Gusen: Die Opfer erzwungener medizinischer Forschung im Nationalsozialismus', in Bundesministerium für Inneres (ed.), *KZ-Gedenkstätte Mauthausen, Mauthausen Memorial 2011* (Bundesministerium für Inneres: Vienna, 2011), pp. 41–54.

161 Dr Zoltan Klar was a Jewish inmate and director of the hospital and compiled the lists between June 1944 and May 1945 in six books. Among those also admitted around the same time as Alessandro were 34-year-old Alberto Cugnio (Hugno), 21-year-old Giuseppe Capelluto, and 16-year-olds Abramo Levi and Nissim Berro, 'Zugangsbuch' Solvek 6 Book 3, pp. 65–66, 248, accessed at https://collections.yadvashem.org/en/documents/7935178

162 Maršálek, *Geschichte*, p. 321 and *passim*. The data varies slightly.

163 Levi and De Benedetti, *Auschwitz Report*, p. 72.

164 Ibid.

165 Before 1944, prisoners were frequently sent to the Hartheim euthanasia centre where they were murdered either by lethal injection or gas. ITS Digital Archive, Arolsen Archives, 1.1.26.1, Mauthausen: Bericht über Genesungslager: Aufstellung über die Art der Ermordung von Häftlingen im KL Mauthausen (Zeugenprotokolle Martin). For the use of gasoline as a method for killing prisoners, see Hans Maršálek, *Geschichte des Konzentrationslagers Mauthausen* (Österreichische Lagergemeinschaft Mauthausen: Vienna, 1980), p. 174, who cites trial documents. Most of the camp's doctors were later tried and sentenced to death in 1946 and executed a year later in Landsberg an der Lech. Maršálek, *Geschichte*, pp. 217–228. As well as Weindling, 'Medizinische Gräueltaten', see Florian Schwanninger, 'Die "Sonderbehandlung 14 f 13" in den Konzentrationslagern Mauthausen und Gusen. Probleme und Perspektiven der Forschung', in Bundesministerium für Inneres (ed.), *KZ-Gedenkstätte Mauthausen*, pp. 55–67.

166 Arolsen Archives, 1.1.26.0 Mauthausen Report Kanthack, pp. 73–78. Kanthack's report also names the doctors and orderlies involved in these murders. For Kanthack see Jens Dobler, 'Täteropfer. Der Berliner Kriminalkommissar Gerhard Kanthack im KZ Mauthausen', in Bundesministerium für Inneres (ed.), *Jahrbuch Mauthausen KZ- Gedenkstätte Mauthausen/Mauthausen Memorial 2015: Justiz, Polizei und das KZ Mauthausen* (Bundesministerium für Inneres: Vienna, 2015), pp. 57–68.

167 ITS Digital Archive. Arolsen Archives Personal Files (male) – Concentration Camp Mauthausen, Ref. Code 0101260305/1328391 – SADOK ALCHADEW (*sic*).

168 https://collections.arolsen-archives.org/G/SIMS/01012603/0049/109129771/00 1.jpg.

169 Kambanellis, *Die Freiheit*, p. 51.

170 Gedenstaette Mauthausen, Die Toten des KZ Mauthausen, Saul Alhadeff 1920–1945.

171 JDC Archives, Istanbul Office of the American Jewish Joint Distribution Committee, IST 37-49/4/16/IS.228, Jews from Rhodes, List of Survivors, 17 August 1944.

172 Freund and Perz, 'Mauthausen – Stammlager', in Benz, Distel and Königseder (eds.), *Der Ort des Terrors*, pp. 312–324.

173 Buggeln, *Arbeit & Gewalt*, p. 91.

174 Foregoing data based on Mauthausen: Case No. 000-50 (Vol. X – Folder III List of Victims). For Gusen, see: Stanisław Dobosiewicz, *Mauthausen/Gusen: obóz zagłady* [*Mauthausen/Gusen: the Camp of Doom*] (Ministry of National Defence Press: Warsaw, 1977), p. 78, cited in https://en.wikipedia.org/wiki/Mauthausen-Gusen_concentration_camp_complex

175 Florian Freund, 'Die Toten von Ebensee', p. 22.

176 Surmani, Interview 53625, seg. 138.

177 Alberto Israël, Je *ne vous ai pas oubliés* (Institut sépharade européen: Brussels, 2008), p. 124: 'les plus belles années de mon adolescence furent englouties par l'angoisse du néant'.

178 ITS Digital Archive, Arolsen Archives, 1.1.26.1, Mauthausen.

179 Benatar and Benatar, *Si je t'oublie*, p. 542. IST Digital Archive. Arolsen Archives, 1.1.26.8 Mauthausen Prisoners Personal Cards.

180 1.1.26.3 Mauthausen Concentration Camp, Personal file Benun Elia, 01012603 079.371. ITS Digital Archive, Arolsen Archives.

181 Benatar and Benatar, *Si je t'oublie*, p. 108.

182 Hasson, Interview 7687, seg. 10. Details of family, Benatar and Benatar, *Si je t'oublie*, p. 362.

183 Levi, *If This is a Man*, p. 15. Nyiszli in his memoir, *Auschwitz*, p. 137, also records its significance when he mentions how an SS guard told him on 17 November, that killings had been suspended.

184 Stella Hasson, *Du Paradis à l'Enfer* (Éditions Clepsydre: Nivelles, 2007), p. 74, cites Alberto Israel who mentions Block B, barrack 21. On the association of Jews with disease during the Holocaust, Paul Weindling, *Epidemics and Genocide in Eastern Europe, 1890–1945* (Oxford University Press: Oxford, New York, 2000), pp. 271–321. Also, Dan Michman, *The Emergence of Jewish Ghettos during the Holocaust*, trans. Lenn J. Schramm (Cambridge University Press: New York, 2011).

185 Reproduced in Alhadeff, *The Family Treasure*, pp. 77–81, the quote is on p. 79.

186 Novitch, *The Passage of the Barbarians*, p. 131. Novitch does not provide Galante's biographical details, but she describes him as being in his forties when she meets him in 1952. It is likely that he is the same person as Salomon Galante in Benatar and Benatar, *Si je t'oublie*, p. 277. His brothers Nissim and Aronne also entered the camp, both died there. His widowed mother was gassed on arriving; a sister, Vittoria, appears not to have been on the deportation list. According to the Benatars' research, she was last known to have been on Kos in late March 1941.

187 ITS Digital Archive, Arolsen Archives Doc. ID. 71180581. See also his personal file: ibid, 3.2.1.5 Personal File Alhadeff Ruben.

188 Sami Modiano, *Per questo ho vissuto. La mia vita ad Auschwitz-Birkenau e altri esili* (BUR Rizzoli: Milan, 2013), pp. 128–129. As well as the 234 youth, there were 416 children under the age of 13 years, Helen Kubica, 'Kinder und Jugendliche im KZ Auschwitz 1940–1945', in Wacław Długoborski and Franciszek Piper (eds.), *Auschwitz 1940–1945 – Studien zur Geschichte des Konzentrations- und Vernichtungslagers Auschwitz* (5 vols.), translated from Polish (Auschwitz-Birkenau State Museum, 1995), vol. 2, pp. 255, 349, 351. There is also an English-language edition of the five volumes: *Auschwitz 1940–1945: Central Issues in the History of the Camp*, trans. William Brand (Auschwitz-Birkenau State Museum, 2000). I have consulted the German edition. Laura Fontana provides a list of youngsters liberated at Auschwitz, but her information diverges from that found in the individual files of the International Tracing Service (ITS). Laura Fontana, *Gli Italiani ad Auschwitz (1943–1945). Deportazioni – 'Soluzione finale' – Lavoro forzato – un osaico di vittime* (Museo Statale die Auschwitz-Birkenau, 2021), p. 374.

189 ITS Digital Archive, Arolsen Archives, 1.1.26.3, Personal file Giuseppe Coné. Benatar and Benatar, *Si je t'oublie*, p. 220 cite two children, 5-year-old Matteo and 1-year-old Lucia. WJC MSS. Col. No. 361 H178/13, Albert Hanan, appeal to the PCIRO 9 January 1950.

190 ITS Digital Archive. Arolsen Archives CM/1 files from Italy A-Z Ref. Code: 03020102 oS: Coen, Moses, Slides 80342455-80342461.

191 Two sisters were also listed: Diamante Hugno and Rachel Hugno. AJDC, IST 37-49/4/16/15 228-867525, 63B: Jews from Rhodes – List of Survivors from Mauthausen (Austria) Concentration Camp 8/17/1944 [Collection: 1937-1949: Istanbul Office of the American Jewish Joint Distribution Committee].

192 Barbara Distel and Wolfgang Benz (eds.), *Die Befreiung*, Dachauer Hefte Nr 1: Die Befreiung (Verlag Dachauer Hefte: Dachau, 1985).

193 Alice's father Leone Yehuda was a director of one of the four Jewish-owned banks in Rhodes; the family lived in the prosperous Maria Pia di Savoia. Benatar and Benatar, *Si je t'oublie*, p. 626.

194 Stella was also called Ester and was born on 14 August 1931. Her Dachau file gives her birth year as 1930. This might have been a subterfuge at the time. Copies in ITS Digital Archives Arolsen Archives, 1.1.6.2 Dachau: 01010602012.067 Stella Benun and n. 30 in this chapter. For her family, Benatar and Benantar, *Si je t'oublie*, p. 123.

195 Cziborra, *KZ Wilischthal*, pp. 172–176. See Czech, *Kalendarium*, p. 918, gives the total number of women transferred to KL Flossenbürg as 504.

196 ITS Digital Archive, Arolsen Archives 1.1.5.3 Concentration Camp Buchenwald, Personal file Ascer Hanan. We come back to Ascer's post-war story in chapter 8.

197 *Die Verfolgung und Ermordung*: Band 16, Einleitung, pp. 60–96, Docs. 161–289, *passim*.

198 Levi with DDDe Benedetti, *Auschwitz Report*, pp. 43, 49–50, 65.

199 Reilly, *Belsen*, ch. 1. Ben Shephard, *After Daybreak. The Liberation of Belsen 1945* (London: Pimlico, 2006). Dan Stone, *The Liberation of the Camps: The End of the Holocaust and Its Aftermath* (Yale University Press: New Haven, CT, 2015).

200 IWM Collections, Oral History, Dick Williams IWM SR 15437. In 1945, Williams was a staff captain in the Supplies and Transport branch of VIII Corps Headquarters and was part of the small force sent ahead to assess conditions in the camp. As well as the literature cited in n. 173, see Paul Kemp, 'The British Army and the Liberation of Bergen-Belsen April 1945', in Jo Reilly, David

Cesarani, Tony Kushner and Colin Richmond (eds.), *Belsen in History and Memory* (Routledge: London, 1997), pp. 134–148.

201 https://www.theguardian.com/world/2005/apr/14/secondworldwar.germany. See the testimonies of former British soldiers at Bergen-Belsen, including Major Williams, at the IWM Oral History Project, https://www.iwm.org.uk/history/the-liberation-of-bergen-belsen.

202 Her mother Gioia Arditti and her three younger sisters, 14-year-old Maria, 11-year-old Elsa and 7-year-old Annetta were gassed on arrival.

203 ITS Digital Archive, Arolsen Archives 1.1.6.2, Personal File Da Fano, Giuseppina. Her registration cards showing the dates of arrival in Dachau (Kaufering) and Bergen-Belsen are the only extant records. For Kaufering, see: Edith Raim, 'Unternehmen Ringeltaube'. Dachaus Außenlagerkomplex Kaufering, in *Dachauer Hefte*, Nr 5, Die vergessenen Lager (Dachau, 1989), pp. 193–213.

204 ITS Digital Archive, Arolsen Archives 1.1.6.2, Personal file Capelluto, Sara.

205 Alcana, Interview 129, segs. 9, 11. Visual History Archive. USC Shoah Foundation.

206 ITS Digital Archive, Arolsen Archives 1.1.41.2 Stutthof, Personal File, Israel, Christian Leon.

207 Florian Freund, *Concentration Camp Ebensee: Subcamp of Mauthausen*, trans. Max R. Garcia (Dokumentationsarchiv des Österreichischen Widerstandes: Vienna, 1990), p. 46.

208 A contemporary account of the dangers of typhus among the camp population in wartime and post-war Europe is provided by a New York medical doctor J.C. Snyder, 'Typhus Fever in the Second World War', *California Medicine*, Vol. 66, No. 1 (January 1947), pp. 3–10, here: 5–7. Snyder, using USA Typhus Commission records, gives 18,000 cases in Germany, 14,000 in Poland and 8,244 in Romania. Of the countries surveyed, only Egypt and Morocco had comparable cases. In addition to the danger posed by typhus epidemic, there was also that of venereal disease spreading as populations criss-crossed the continent. At particular risk from solicited and unsolicited sexual activity were children and young adults: Lisa Haushofer, 'The "Contaminating Agent" UNRRA, Displaced Persons, and Venereal Disease in Germany, 1945–1947', *American Journal of Public Health*, Vol. 100, No. 6 (June 2010), pp. 993–1003.

209 WJC MSS. Col. No. 361 H178/13, Albert Hanan, appeal to the PCIRO 9 January 1950. See below for Hanan's story.

210   Lucia Franco, USHMM Collections, Acc. No. 1997.A.0431/RG-50.030.0452,
      Tape 3, Side A. She and the other women from Rhodes and Kos were among
      about fifty women transferred in late October 1944 to Dachau's sub-camp at
      Landsberg; after 5 months she and her compatriots were transferred to the sub-
      camp at Allach, where she remained until liberation.

211   The photograph can be viewed on the website of the Jewish Museum Rhodes:
      https://www.rhodesjewishmuseum.org/history/holocaust/

212   Σαμουελ Μοντιάνο: Η Αποστολή. Από τη Ρόδο στο Άουσβιτς', Cine Chevalier
      Workshop of Rhodes Scholarship Foundation Em. & M. Stamatiou, Greece
      2019. Subtitles translation from the Greek by Theoni Chantziara. See also
      Modiano's account of this episode in *Per Questo Ho Vissuto*, pp. 128–133.

213   Ibid, pp. 133–145.

214   Before arriving there, she recalled in one interview passing through Ebensee,
      where her uncle Samuele died. Yad Vashem Archives, 0.3 Testimonies, File
      10423, VT 1390 Laura Varon, interview 01.09.1996.

215   Laura Varon, *The Juderia: A Holocaust Survivor's Tribute to the Jewish
      Community of Rhodes* (Praeger: Westport, CT; London, 1991), pp. 105–106.

216   Arolsen Archives Postwar Card Files (A–Z) Ref. Code 030101010S: 69601853
      Laura Varon: A.E.F. D.P. Registration Record; Varon, Interview 26814, VHA
      Shoah Foundation, seg. 30. Varon, *Juderia*, pp. 107–132 *passim*. Avraham
      Galante, *Histoire des juifs vol.7*, p. 315, incorrectly gives her location in 1946/47
      as Switzerland.

217   UNRRA S-1252-0000-0278-0002 (DP Divisional Reports), Frames 83–95:
      Division of Displaced Persons Quarterly Report for the Quarter Ending
      30 September 1945, Frame 86: 'B': Special situation of Interest, 26 July 1945.

218   AJDC (Paris), Paris List #1,280 (16 October 1945).

219   Arolsen Archives Online 3.1.1.3: Signatur 8806870: Listen betr. Personen,
      die 1944/46 in Italien, Rhodos, Türkei, Koos Islands (*sic*), Schweden und
      Deutschland lebten. The documents in this file are copies of originals provided
      by the AJDC Athens & Compagnia Singer per Macchine da Cucire SAI Rhodes,
      through AJDC Paris & CLI New York. These radically challenge the popular
      belief that only 152 deportees survived. See Chapter 8.

220   South African Holocaust & Genocide Foundation, Cape Town Holocaust
      Memorial Council, Television Interview with Violette Fintz, 1992,
      Transcript, p. 15.

221   Benatar and Benatar, *Si je t'oublie*, p. 185 for photographs. We discussed this
      family in Chapter 2.

222 Soriano, Interview 8852, seg. 9, 11.

223 Ministero degli Affari Esteri to Dir. Gen. Italiani All'Estero-Serv.Affari Privati. Telepresso N.19/25793, Roma, 8 Nov. 1945, ITS Digital Archive, Arolsen Archives. For Oretta: 1.1.6 Dachau, ibid, Benatar and Benatar, *Si je t'oublie*, p. 614.

224 Hasson, Interview 7687, seg. 10. Heinz Kounio, who was liberated from Ebensee together with Jack, weighed around the same, Kounio, *Ein Liter Suppe*, p. 132, photograph. Kounio's sister and mother were liberated after escaping a final 'death march' from the woman's camp of Ravensbrück, 90 km north of Berlin, as the Russians approached. Erika Kounio Amariglio, *From Thessaloniki to Auschwitz and Back. Memories of a Survivor from Thessaloniki*, Library of Holocaust Testimonies (Vallentine Mitchell: London, Portland, OR, 2000), pp. 120–139, *passim*, here: 132–133.

225 This aspect of memory and mis-memory is explored in Chapter 9. On the question of remembering events, see Jorg Semprun, *Schreiben oder Leben* (orig. L'écriture ou la vie, Editions Gallimard, 1994) trans. Eva Moldenhauer (Suhrkamp: Frankfurt am Main, 1995), pp. 38–39.

226 https://encyclopedia.ushmm.org/content/en/oral-history/abraham-klausner-1. Klausner's biography can be found here: https://collections.ushmm.org/search/catalog/irn559428 and https://collections.ushmm.org/search/catalog/pa1119574 (with a contemporary portrait photograph).

227 Gary Barker, driver with the US 685th Ordnance Ammunition Company cited in Anthony S. Pitch, *Our Crime was Being Jewish: Hundreds of Holocaust Survivors Tell their Stories*, Foreword by Michael Berenbaum (Skyhorse Publishing: Delaware, 2015), p. 237. For Klausner's testimony, Robert H. Abzug, *Inside the Vicious Heart: Americans and the Liberation of Nazi Concentration Camps* (Oxford University Press: Oxford and New York, 1987), p. 94, also with a photograph showing a guard or possibly a *kapo* being beaten (to death?) by former prisoners.

228 Kambanellis, *Die Freiheit*, p. 19.

229 Lucia Franco Amato, USHMM Collections, Acc. No. 1997.A.0431/RG-50.030.0452, Tape 2, Side A. 'Magda' appears in a number of the female Aegean survivors' testimonies; her nationality is unclear, possibly she was Polish, not Hungarian.

230 Kounio, *Ein Liter Suppe*, pp. 233–235.

231 Freund, *Concentration Camp Ebensee*.

232 Czech, *Kalendarium*, p. 851.

233 Pingel, 'Social Life', p. 69.

234 TNA FO371/57851, War Organization of the British Red Cross Society and
     Order of St John of Jerusalem, Foreign Relations Department to Miss Horsfield,
     The Foreign Office, 6 March 1949, with enclosures (three lists of Rhodes and
     Kos survivors with some overlap of names). See Franco, *Jewish Martyrs*, who
     gives the lower figure of 151 survivors, pp. 103–105, and pp. 80–105 *passim*
     for slight discrepancies between the two lists of deportees and survivors.
     On gender-specificity and survival see: Gabriele Pfingsten and Claus
     Füllberth-Stolberg, 'Frauen in Konzentrationslagern – geschlechtsspezifische
     Bedingungen des Überlebens', in Herbert, Orth and Dieckmann (eds.),
     Konzentrationslager, pp. 911–938. Buggeln, *Arbeit & Gewalt*, pp. 508–518,
     597–603, for emphasis on structural conditions.

Chapter 7

1 Eyewitness Charalambos Anamourlis in *The Longest Journey*, 45:21 min.

2 Lawrence Durrell, *Reflections on a Marine Venus: A Companion to the
   Landscape of Rhodes* (Faber and Faber: London, 1953), pp. 123–124. Raymond
   Mills, 'Lawrence Durrell on Rhodes, 1945–47', *Twentieth Century Literature*,
   Vol. 33, No. 3, Lawrence Durrell Issue, Part I (Autumn 1987), pp. 312–316.

3 See the chapters by Maria Kavala, Stratos Dordanas and and Kostis Kornetis,
   in Giorgos Antoniou and A. Dirk Moses (eds.), *The Holocaust in Greece*
   (Cambridge University Press: Cambridge, 2018). Neither Bowman, *Agony*, nor
   Fleming, *Greece*, nor Molho, *Der Holocaust*, tackle this aspect of the persecution
   in their otherwise important studies. For Italy, Michael A. Livingston, *The
   Fascists and the Jews of Italy Mussolini's Race Laws, 1938–1943* (Cambridge
   University Press: Cambridge, 2014).

4 GAKR I.Δ.Δ. ΕΤΟΣ 1944, ΦΑΚ 195, Governo delle Isole Italiane Dell'Egeo
   Archivio Verbale Denuncianti, VI Sottocommissione, list of items retrieved
   from the property of Talie C., 20 September 1944; report of Bono Remigio,
   31 October 1944.

5 Moreover, it is doubtful if wealthy Greeks or Italians would have had the need
   to trade their furniture.

6 In his post-war testimony, Recanati claimed the looted items ended up in their
   private possession to be used as bribes to buy their escape after Germany's
   defeat. Note 8 below.

7   SAHGF Interview Diamante Franco, 7 September 1986, interviewers Dora
     Wynchank and Alan Fischer, transcript p. 13.

8   Bundesarchiv Zentrale Stelle der Landesjustizverwaltungen Ludwigsburg
     (hereafter: BA-Ludwigsburg), B162/1515, pp. 470–481, Landeskriminalamt,
     Baden-Württemberg, Sonderkommission Zentrale Stelle, z.Zt. Mannheim,
     20.7.64, Vernehmungsniederschrift: Constantin Rekanatis (*sic*), p. 8.

9   Hanan, Rachel, Interview 13096. Visual History Archive, USC Shoah
     Foundation, 1996, tape 2.

10 Alice Tarica-Israël, Interview, Fortunoff Archive, seg. 9.

11 Her paternal grandmother was on the *Mas* that sailed for Turkey on 13 January
     1945. Alberto and his wife Renate and Lina are not listed, so it is possible that
     some documentation has been lost. GAKR I.Δ.Δ. ΕΤΟΣ 1944/45, ΦΑΚ18
     TMHNA 1/L, Elenco Nominativo delle Persone Trasferiti in Turchia il Giorno
     13.1.1945 Barca Diverse 'MAS'.

12 Kantor, Lina, Interview Code 33706. Visual History Archive USC Shoah
     Foundation, 1997, tape 2. See the Italian Race Card for members of the extended
     family in 1938. All'Ufficio dello Stato Civile, Rodi, card 62. This family, Uncle
     Davide (brother of Lina's father), his wife Eleonara and their daughter Rebecca
     (same age as Lina) emigrated prior to the deportation. The brothers' mother
     Rachele (b. 1874) also lived with them.

13 Livingston, *The Fascists*, for examples of this. For Germany see, Christoph
     Kreutzmüller, *Ausverkauf. Die Vernichtung der jüdischen Gewerbetätigkeit in
     Berlin 1930–1945* (Berlin: Metropol, 2012), pp. 324–334. On the other hand,
     many émigrés secretly sent back remittances to support their families and
     parents. GAKR I.Δ.Δ. ΕΤΟΣ 1939, ΦΑΚ534 TMHNA 1, Governo Delle Isole
     Italiane Dell'Egeo, Archivio: Titolo Varie informazione Anno 1938, Riservato.
     Nota di servizio 14 December 1938 (Mancuso).

14 GAKR Carabinieri, Gruppe Carabinieri Reali – Ufficio Centrale Speciale,
     No. 1577/2-1944 prot. Div.III, Oggetti, Sequestro beni immobili e mobile
     appartementi ad ebrei (Mittino report).

15 Jewish survivors returning to the islands after 1945 proved to be an
     uncomfortable reminder of this complicity, as we shall see in Chapter 8.

16 'Governo delle Isole Italiane dell'Egeo, Decreto Governatoriale 21 Juglio 1944-
     XXII, n. 94 – Divieto di alienazione die beni di ebrei' (signed: Faralli), printed
     in *Il Messaggero di Rodi* 23 Juglio 1944-XXII. See, Marco Clementi, *Storia della
     comunità ebraica di Rodi (1912–1947)* (tab edizioni: Rome, 2022), pp. 425–441.

17 Merolle, 'Breve Cenno Sulla Deportazione della Colonia Ebraica di Rodi',
     p. 2. The idea that the administration took Jewish property into its care for

safekeeping for later restitution is also asserted by the pre-eminent Italian historian of the Italian administration of the Dodecanese Luca Pignataro, *Il Dodecanese*, vol. III, p. 475. As we shall see in this chapter, this is not the case.

18   WL 1655/200, PS154, Letter from Lammers to the supreme Reich authorities concerning Hitler's order to Rosenberg to fight the Jews as instigators of the war, and to confiscate their property. For Mussolini, chapter 5, n. 7.

19   GAKR I.Δ.Δ. ΕΤΟΣ 1944, ΦΑΚ 19, Governo delle isole Italiane dell'Egeo, Archivio Titolo 1142. D.G. no. 160A – Suddivisione in gruppi dei beni appartenenti agli ebrei ed istituzione di un da commissione vigilanza. Chaired by Faralli, its members were: Antonio Coccheri, an engineer; Michele Tura the chief accountant of the Governatore (he would also head-up the 3rd sub-committee dealing exclusively with the Alhadeff company); also members were two local businessmen, Giovanni Economidis and Hadja Mahmit, and Vincenzo Cipolla a reserve lieutenant from the Guardia di Finanza and Cesare Cerati, a lieutenant from the *Carabinieri*. The chairs and members of these *sottocommissioni* were mostly also members of the *federazione dei fasci di combattimento dell'Egeo* and its ancillary organizations in the Dodecanese. See Pignataro, *Il Dodecanese*, vol. III, p. 221, n. 608, p. 318, n. 1130. for some names of PNF members, including Dante Zarli chair of the V Sottocommissione, Antonio Coccheri (Sottocommissione III), Prof Giuseppe Scandol and Vito Zichittella (Sottocommissione VI). Giovanni Cecini, *La guardia di finanza delle isole Italinae dell'Egeo 1912–1945* (Gangemi Editore: Rome, 2014), pp. 271, 283, 285–286, for biographical details for Cipolla and Cerati. Like so many of their fascist fellow-travellers in the Italian administration, these men were repatriated to Italy in the course of 1946 and never called to account for their roles in the persecution of Rhodes' Jews.

20   Decreto governatoriale 21 luglio 1944, No. 94: Divieto di alienazione di beni di ebrei, also published in *Il Messaggerio di Rodi*, 23 July 1944.

21   GAKR I.Δ.Δ. ΕΤΟΣ 1944, ΦΑΚ 19, Governo delle isole Italiane dell'Egeo, Archivio Titolo 1142. Decree 102, 3 Aug. 1944, created a sub-committee chaired by Arturo Morreale to ascertain the assets of traders; members were Dr Stelio Cottiadi, Abdulla Cumaniagi, and a secretary, Strato Tuagioglu. Cottiadi resigned soon after and was replaced by Dr Giorgio Papanichita, ibid, D.G. n. 173A, (Il Governatore – Faralli, dated 25 September 1944, signed by P.C.C. Il Segretario A. Voiagi). And various notes: GAKR I.Δ.Δ. ΕΤΟΣ 1943, ΦΑΚ 162, TM: 1.

22   GAKR I.Δ.Δ. ΕΤΟΣ 1944, ΦΑΚ 19, Governo delle isole Italiane dell'Egeo, Archivio Titolo 1142. D.G. no. 165A Visto il D.G. 30 agosto 1944, no. 159A

(Il Governatore – Faralli, dated 15 September 1944, signed by P.C.C. Il Segretario A. Voiagi). Pignataro, *Il Dodecanese*, vol. III, p. 221, n. 608.

23 The following discussion focuses on Rhodes. The *Carabinieri* files dealing with the sequestration of Jewish-owned property do not extend to Kos.

24 https://collections.ushmm.org/search/catalog/irn517208. See also Kreutzmüller, *Ausverkauf*, especially pp. 218–241.

25 The inventories dating from July are mostly handwritten; typed copies of these early lists date from September and October, with final reports appearing in November. This three-tier process is not necessarily consistent in every case. For the process in Salonica, see the chapter by Dordanas, in Antoniou and Moses (eds.), *Holocaust in Greece*, as n. 4. Photostat copies and notes on Salonica's shopkeepers deposited by historian Mark Mazower in the Wiener Library London also document the process of spoliation of Jewish property in Salonica. WL 692/1 List of Jewish shop owners in Salonica in March 1943.

26 According to a member of the official government commission created to investigate spoliation in Italy, the estimated sum of spoliation between September 1943 and 1944 was believed to be in the region of US$1 billion in 2010 values: https://www.nytimes.com/2010/11/05/nyregion/05italians.html

27 Values calculated in 2021, https://www.in2013dollars.com/us/inflation/1944?amount=11421. The lira was devalued against both sterling and the dollar between 1943 and 1949, when it settled at $1=625I£. From June 1943 until 1947/49, it was fixed at $1=120I£ https://www.dollartimes.com/inflation/inflation.php. Our difficulty is that wartime official exchange rates are masked. It is probably safer to accept the 1949 rate as closer in providing us with some indication of values in 1944. During the war and occupation, the Italian £ was exchanged for 10RM. But the German policy was to use occupation currency, rendering any meaningful exchange rate void. For background see, William D. Grampp, 'The Italian Lira, 1938–45', *Journal of Political Economy*, Vol. 54, No. 4 (Aug. 1946), pp. 309–333.

28 GAKR Governo dell IsoleItaliane Delle'Egeo N. 1577 di Protocollo 1944, Oggetto sequestro di beni appartenenti ad ebrei.

29 Kantor, Lina, Interview 33706, seg. 15. Visual History Archive, USC Shoah Foundation, 1996. Accessed January 2017. Alhadeff, Nissim, Interview 1577, seg. 1. Visual History Archive, USC Shoah Foundation, 1996. Accessed January 2017.

30 He was spared the deportation allegedly through his wife, Batami's, Turkish military connections. Ibid.

31 Ibid, Alhadeff, tape 1. It is not certain if this recollection is accurate. As we
    shall see below, the house was rented to a family; again, it is not clear from the
    documents if this was before or after their departure. According to his cousin,
    Gini Alhadeff, after the war, Jack returned to Rhodes with Batami and their
    10-year-old son, Isacco, and recovered most of the family's assets, Gini Alhadeff,
    The Sun at Midday: Tales of a Mediterranean Family (Random House: New York,
    1997), pp. 92, 96–97.
32 Calculated in 2021 from https://www.dollartimes.com/inflation/inflation.php?.
33 A few rents appeared to have been backdated to June, in, GAKR I.Δ.Δ. ΦΑΚ
    53. This file contains receipts and invoices relating to post-deportation Jewish
    properties. An in-depth study of the role of the Bank of Sicily in the spoliation of
    Jewish property during the era of the Holocaust is a desideratum.
34 GAKR I.Δ.Δ. ΕΤΟΣ 1944, ΦΑΚ 195, Governo delle Isole Italiane Dell'Egeo
    Archivio Verbale Denunciati (Statements). Benatar and Benatar, *Si je t'oublie*,
    p. 316. The family had lived at No. 29.
35 GAKR I.Δ.Δ. ΦΑΚ 53, Governo delle Isole Italiane Dell'Egeo Gestione Falascati
    di Ebrei, Banco di Sicilia servizio di tesoreria. Elenco Duca di Savoia 17.
36 GAKR I.Δ.Δ. ΦΑΚ 53, Ordine di Riccosione No. 1, No. 159 and No. 160.
    (deposito 1 mensilita fitto dell'alloggia). GAK IΔΔ 1936-1944 ΦΑΚ 17 THM.
    1/1, Governo delle Isole Italiane Dell'Egeo, Archivo Titolo R. 14, fascio 6: Elenco
    nominative delle famiglie sinistrto dai bombardimento aereo del 28 Giugno 1944.
37 Assorted receipts in GAKR I.Δ.Δ. ΦΑΚ 53.
38 GAKR I.Δ.Δ. ΦΑΚ 53, Ordine di Ricossione N. 152. For Franco's family, Benatar
    and Benatar, *Si je t'oublie*, p. 250.
39 GAKR I.Δ.Δ. ΦΑΚ 53, Ordine di Ricossione. No. 106 (October).
40 BA-MA RH26/1007/16, Bl. 63, Militärverwaltung Rhodos, 29 August 1944. See
    also WL 655/1416 NOKW1795 for earlier report (4 August 1944) concerning,
    amongst other matters, the activities of the 'Commission for the Seizure of
    Jewish Property'. The inventory's three volumes can be found here: GAKR I.Δ.Δ.
    ΕΤΟΣ 1944 ΦΑΚ 19, 3. Sottocommissione: Accertamento Beni Ebrei Magazzino
    Ferramenta Salomon Alcadeff (*sic*) in Rodi, Inventario; 3. Sotto-Commissione
    (*sic*) A.B.E., Elenco delle fattura di merci, materiali e mobili effettuate durante I
    lavori di accertamento in case a fattura inviate per la ricossione alla G.A.G.B.M.E.;
    3. Sotto Commissione (*sic*), Inventario dei mobile e materiali accertati nei
    magazzini e nei depositi della Ditta Salomon Alcadeff (*sic*) e figli, Rodi.
41 At the time of writing in 2021. The two-volume inventory is in GAKR I.Δ.Δ. Etos
    1944 ΦΑΚ 19. https://www.dollartimes.com/inflation/inflation.php for currency
    conversions.

42 Vittorio Alhadeff, *Le Chêne de Rhodes: Saga d'une grande famille sépharade* (Éditions Paris-Méditerranée: Paris, 1998), pp. 43ff., and Alhadeff, *The Sun at Midday*, pp. 77ff., for the following account. Both authors' accounts are almost verbatim of each other, barring the foregrounding in the family history of their respective fathers (Joseph=Vittorio) and grandfather (Isaac=Gini).

43 Alhadeff, *The Sun at Midday*, pp. 80–82. The author is Isaac's (Haco) granddaughter. Her account is idiosyncratic but also fun to read. See also Vittorio Alhadeff's account of the bank, Alhadeff, *Le Chêne de Rhodes*, pp. 156–161.

44 Shoah Foundation USC, interview with Yitzhak Kerem, 26 March 1995, tape 1.

45 Jack would return to Rhodes after the war with his wife Batami and their son Isacco (Izzie) and was able to recover most of the family business and property. Jack's older son, Nissim, settled in New York. Benatar and Benatar, *Si je t'oublie*, p. 28.

46 GAKR I.Δ.Δ. ΕΤΟΣ 1943 ΦΑΚ 162/1, Governo Dele Isole Italiane Dell'Egeo, Archivio Titolo Rodi, Anno 1943-, Salomon Alhadeff Figli, Dettaglio. GAKR I.Δ.Δ. ΕΤΟΣ 1943 ΦΑΚ 397: Governo Delle Isole Italiane Dell'Egeo, Archivio Titolo Calchi, Anno 1941-43, Hassan [Hazan] Boaz, Tessuti – e glieri alimentari. Hazan had a haberdashery business on the small neighbouring island of Calchi (Halki, in Greek, Xalki). In some of the correspondence, Hazan signs his name as 'Giuseppe', e.g., letter 27 October 1942 to Uffico dell'Economica Corporativa.

47 GAKR I.Δ.Δ. ΕΤΟΣ 1944 ΦΑΚ 19, Verbale 6, 10 August 1944.

48 Ibid, Verbale 7, 11 August 1944.

49 Ibid, Verbale 8, 12 August 1944, with reference to various items acquired on 7 and 8 August.

50 These files provide in detail household possessions and inter alia provide graphic corroboration of the poverty among the families of the *Juderia* acknowledged in the files of administration dealing with compensation for victims of the repeated aerial bombardments.

51 Decreto governatoriale 21 luglio 1944, No. 94: Divieto di alienazione di beni di ebrei, Art. 3.

52 GAKR I.Δ.Δ. ΕΤΟΣ 1944, ΦΑΚ 195, Governo delle Isole Italiane Dell'Egeo Archivio Verbale Denunciati, Verbale, 27 July and statement of VI Sottocommissione, 1.12.1944.

53 Ibid, statement of Iggide P., 28 July 1944. The Capellutos' daughter was not registered in the 1938 Racial Census, indicating she was born after that date (early 1939), making her a rising 4 or younger (Racial Census, # 173). Ester's brothers were jewellers in the Piazza Brusciata (del Fuocco). Biographical details in Benatar and Benatar, *Si je t'oublie*, p. 173.

54 GAKR I.Δ.Δ. ΕΤΟΣ 1944, ΦΑΚ 195, Governo delle Isole Italiane Dell'Egeo Archivio Verbale Denunciati, (no pagination) commissione beni gia appartementi gli Ebrei Ufficio Coordinmento, Rodi, 1 September, 3 October 1944 and warehoused on 11 October.

55 As well as Benatar and Benatar, *Si je t'oublie*, p. 173, see her details in https://digital-library.cdec.it/cdec-web/persone/detail/person-3845/halfon-clara.html.

56 GAKR I.Δ.Δ. ΕΤΟΣ 1944, ΦΑΚ 195, VI Sottocommissione, verbale 30 October 1944.

57 GAKR I.Δ.Δ. ΕΤΟΣ 1944, ΦΑΚ 195, Governo delle Isole Italiane Dell'Egeo, VI Sottocommissione R.D.F.C.V., verbale 23 August 1944, signed off 28 October 1944, Vito Zichittella, Bono Remgio, Tartaglia Generoso.

58 Dora b. 3 August 1920, Esther b. 9 February 1922, Giovanna b. 1924, Giacomo b. 20 September 1926. Marco's father, Giacobbe, b. 1855, was living with them at the time of the Racial Census but does not appear on the deportation list (Nos. 536–540). Dora was the only one of this family to survive the Holocaust. Benatar and Benatar, *Si je t'oublie*, p. 587.

59 GAKR I.Δ.Δ. ΕΤΟΣ 1944, ΦΑΚ 195, Governo delle Isole Italiane Dell'Egeo Archivio Verbale Denunciati statement by Dott. Ing. Mario Lanari, 5 August 1944, and 11 September 1944.

60 Ibid.

61 Ibid, VI Sottocommissione, Allegato verbale originale di consegna, 31 October 1944.

62 GAKR Carabinieri, Telepresso N.1577/7-1944- 3.Div.: Beni gia appartenenti agli ebrei internati, Mittino report, 28 August 1944.

63 GAKR ΕΤΟΣ 1944 ΦΑΚ 195, Telepresso 23463 al Sig. Vito Zichitella Presidente 6. Sotto-Commissione, 22 August 1944, Oggetto, Regina Capelluto.

64 GAKR I.Δ.Δ. ΕΤΟΣ 1944, ΦΑΚ 195, Governo delle Isole Italiane Dell'Egeo Archivio Verbale Denunciati, statement by Carmelo C., 28 July 1944.

65 GAKR I.Δ.Δ. ΕΤΟΣ 1944, ΦΑΚ 195, Governo delle Isole Italiane Dell'Egeo Archivio Verbale Denunciati, Direzione C/A.B.E. Ufficio Coordinamento, Telepresso N. 23468, Indrizzato a Al Sig. Vito Zichitetella Presidente 6 Sotto-Commissione Rodi, 22 Ago. 1944: Oggetto Regina Capelluto. The street on which the family had lived had been renamed from Porto a Mare to Ammiraglio Legnani.

66 Benatar and Benatar, *Si je t'oublie*, p. 352; her sister Allegra, (b. 1896). Marco does not appear on the deportation list, nor is he registered in the Jewish cemetery, but suggesting he may have left the island before the deportation is difficult to confirm, not least because among the possessions was his passport.

67 GAKR I.Δ.Δ. ΕΤΟΣ 1944, ΦΑΚ 195, Governo delle Isole Italiane Dell'Egeo Archivio Verbale Denunciati, VI Sottocommissione, 30 November 1944.

68 GAKR Carabinieri Pratica n. 277 di Prot. anno 1933 – I-46-I., Matteo E. The family was repatriated to Italy in 1946.

69 GAKR I.Δ.Δ. ΕΤΟΣ 1944, ΦΑΚ 195, hand-scrawled note, la Sottocommissione, 30 November 1944, and typed version signed by Zichittella.

70 BA-MA RH26/1007/16, Bl. 63, Militärverwaltung Rhodos, report on popular opinion by Kleemann's Ic (intelligence) officer, 29 August 1944.

71 GAKR Carabinieri, Telepresso N.1577/4-1944- 3.Div. Mittino to Dir. C.A.B.E.: Nazahat Daracchiali loan to Abramo Amiel, report 30 August; ibid, Lucia Cavura (Tadocchia) furniture left with Alessandro Habib, n.d.; ibid, Bicicletta gia di Israel, Sara, report 31 August 1944.

72 GAKR Gruppo Carabinieri Reali – Ufficio Centrale Speciale, No. 1557/2-1944, prot. Div. III, Oggetto: sequestro beni immobili e mobile appartenenti ad ebrei, reports by local Carabinieri Antonio Salvate.

73 GAKR Carabinieri, Telepresso N.1577/7-1944- 3.Div.: Beni gia appartenenti agli ebrei internati, Mittino report, 28 August 1944.

74 *The Longest Journey*, 45:21 min.

75 https://collections.ushmm.org: RG-50.855.0039: Oral history interview with Michail Zaraftis, Summary. The single quotations indicate a paraphrasing of the original Greek.

76 Cited in https://collections.ushmm.org: RG-50.855.0040: Oral history interview with Michail Panagos, Summary. The single quotations indicate a paraphrasing of the original Greek.

77 GAKR I.Δ.Δ. ΕΤΟΣ 1944, ΦΑΚ 195, undated handwritten list of Benun family possessions, with the name of a member of the commission, Dr Raffaele, scrawled across.

78 GAKR Governo delle Isole Italiane Dell'Egeo, Oggetti, Furti nelle case degli ebrei internati (1944), Ufficio Centrale di Polizia, 1589/7-1944-3 di prot. Div.III, Oggetto: Alienazione beni appartementi all famiglia internata Benun (Mittino report), 30 August 1944.

79 GAKR Governo delle Isole Italiane Dell'Egeo, Oggetti, Furti nelle case degli ebrei internati (1944), Ufficio Centrale di Polizia, 1589/9-1944-3 div., Mittino, report, 6 September 1944. The address is not given in the reports. The Sciami family Racial Card is also missing thus rendering cross-checking difficult, Benatar and Benatar, *Si je t'oublie*, p. 590 and p. 416 for a photograph of Sciami's 33-year-old wife, Diana/Desiree.

80 Governo delle Isole Italiane Dell'Egeo, Oggetti, Furti nelle case degli ebrei internati (1944), Ufficio locale Polizia di Rodi S. Giovanni, Capo dell'Ufficio Locale di Polizia, Andrea Tinacci, n. 46/191 del rapports, 3 September 1944.

81 GAKR I.Δ.Δ. ΕΤΟΣ 1944, ΦΑΚ 195, Governo delle Isole Italiane Dell'Egeo Archivio Verbale Denunciati, statements by Ali S. 2 October 1944 and VI Sottocommissione, Bono Remigio and Tartaglia Generoso. Alcana's wife, Estrea had died in 1941 at the age of 42 years and is buried in the Jewish cemetery in Rhodes. The children were Renata (Reina), b. 1921 and married to Samuele Alhadeff, they had two children, Estrella (Estrea) b. 1942 and Ruben; the next eldest child was Elia b. 1922, followed by Vittorio b. 1926, Isacco b. 1929, Sara b. 1932, Rachele b. 1934, Salvo b. 1936, Racial Census Card. 7 and in Benatar and Benatar, *Si je t'oublie*, p. 10.

82 Ibid. Given that Ali had suffered 4 months' shortfall in rental income, it is tempting to think he might have been involved in the mysterious disappearance of Alcana's belongings. As he put it: 'because the Jew was already in debt for two months, and now [the house is] closed for two months with his belongings, the undersigned has not received the rent for four months already.'

83 GAKR Governo delle Isole Italiane Dell'Egeo, N.1577 di Protocollo 1944, Oggetti, Sequestro dei beni appartanenti ad ebrei, Sottocommissione 5, Rodi to Presidenza della Commissione di Coordinamento beni Ebraica. P.C. Comando Carabinieri, Telepresso 41, 25 August 1944, Verbal 83. It is possible that the Donna Hasson referred to was Donna Hasson the widow of Giacomo Hasson, 20 years her senior. They had married in 1927 when she was 17 years old. She is the only person listed in the census with that name; at the time he was still alive. Racial Census # 275.

84 GAKR Governo delle Isole Italiane Dell'Egeo, N.1577 di Protocollo 1944, Oggetti, Sequestro dei beni appartanenti ad ebrei, Ufficio Centrale di Polizia al Governo delle Isole Italiane Dell'Egeo, Telepresso N.1577/7-1944- 3.Div.: Beni gia appartenenti agli ebrei internati, Mittino report, 28 August 1944 (Mittino). Rosa Masliah was the widow of Isaac Hanan who died in 1940, of their three children, only Gella survived the Holocaust. Benatar and Benatar, *Si je t'oublie*, p. 312. There is only one entry in the Racial Census for Sarina Hanan but the address is given as G. Notrica No. 5, ibid, p. 315. Benatar and Benatar, *Si je t'oublie*, pp. 315, 320.

85 GAKR Governo delle Isole Italiane Dell'Egeo, N.1577 di Protocollo 1944, Oggetti, Sequestro dei beni appartanenti ad ebrei, Ufficio Centrale di Polizia al

Governo delle Isole Italiane Dell'Egeo, Telepresso N.1577/7-1944- 3.Div.: Beni
gia appartenenti agli ebrei internati, Mittino report, 28 August 1944.

86   Ibid.

87   GAKR Carabinieri 20.PS.2 (1932) Comunita israelitica di Rodi 6.Volume, pag.
394-395: Ufficio Centrale di Policia-Terza Divisione- No. 1300/8-1941 di prot.
19 August 1944, with witness statements. The pair do not appear to have been
related.

88   The road name changed in 1939 and became either Bernardo d'Airasca or Via
Bonifacio Scarampi.

89   GAKR Carabinieri files: Ufficio Centrale di Polizia No, 1589-4/1944 di prot.,
23 agosto. 1944-XXII, OGGETTO/: Furte nell'abitazione dell'ebreo internate
BERRO Boas (Mittino report), and report by Carabinieri iajunte capo G.N.R.
Andrea Tinacci in same file.

90   GAKR Carabinieri, Telepresso No. 66, 1 March 1945.

91   GAKR Carabinieri, Telepresso No. 1589/13-1944 di prot. Div. 3 (Cesare Ceruti,
VI Sottocommissione) response to Telepresso No. 79, Governatori, 13 March
1945.

92   GAKR Carabinieri, report 9 March 1945, vice Brigata Guido Alessandro.

93   Raffaelli previously had been the representative of the *Governatore* on the
island of Simi, and Director of Civil Affairs in the Dodecanese, Pignataro,
Il Dodecanese, vol. III, pp. 228, 241, 269.

94   Governo delle Isole Italiane Dell'Egeo, Oggetti, *Furti nelle case degli ebrei
internati* (1944), Carabinieri Il Direttore no. 1589/1-1944 di prot. 19 August
1944, and 1589/2-1944 Asportazione oggetti preziosi abitazione Benveniste al.
N.22528 dell'Il corr. 11 August 1944.

95   Brief biographical details in Benatar and Benatar, *Si t'oublie*, p. 135.

96   GAKR Governo delle Isole Italiane Dell'Egeo, Oggetti, *Furti nelle case degli ebrei
internati* (1944), Carabinieri Il Direttore no. 1589/1-1944 di prot. 19 August
1944, and 1589/2-1944 Asportazione oggetti preziosi abitazione Benveniste al.
N.22528 dell'Il corr. 11 August 1944.

97   GAKR I.Δ.Δ. ΕΤΟΣ 1944, ΦΑΚ 19, 3. Sotto-Commissione A.B.E., Verbale,
12 March 1945.

98   GAKR Governo delle Isole Italiane Dell'Egeo, Oggetti, *Furti nelle case degli ebrei
internati* (1944), Sottocommissione 5, Verbale No. 98, 26 August 1944, report by
Zarli.

99   Ibid.

100   Violetta Hionidou, *Famine and Death in Occupied Greece, 1941–1944* (Cambridge University Press: Cambridge, 2012), chs. 2, 9–11.

101   McElligott, 'German Soldiers See the World', p. 73.

102   *Dodecanese Handbook*, Part III, p. 6.

103   Götz Aly, *Hitlers Volksstaat. Raub, Rassenkrieg und nationaler Sozialismus* (Fischer Taschenbuch Verlag: Frankfurt am Main, 2005), pp. 299–308. The entire section is unreliable, mixing up the sequence of events to fit his argument. On p. 307, Aly cites the report referenced in n. 104. This report is also cited in Bowman, *Agony*, p. 74. If one reads the document carefully, then it becomes clear that the reference is *post facto* to the deportation. Aly's thesis has been roundly dismissed by Saul Friedländer.

104   An example of this in the reports from Corfu dealing with the local population's attitude towards deportation of that island's Jewish community, which was comparable in size to that of Rhodes. IMT NOKW 1916, undated report 1c Aussenstelle Korfu Wr. 6/44 Geheim Kdos. See also WL 1655/2399.

105   BA-MA RH26 1007/26, Kommandant Ost-Aegaeis Anlage 10: Abt. 1c Br.B. Nr 5733/44 geh. Betr. 1c – Beitrag zum 1a – Lagebericht, St.Qu., 2 August 1944/ Kr., p. 2.

106   Ibid, p. 2.

107   An agreement was reached in 1963 between the Jewish community Rhodes and the Jewish Board of Deputies of Greece allowing so-called 'heirless' property in Rhodes to pass to the Board. See correspondence in World Jewish Congress, MSS Col. 361, C266/1, Greece Heirless Property, 1962–1963.

Chapter 8

1   Virginia Gattegno, Interview in the *FT Weekend* 28/29 May 2016.

2   Karl Schleunes, *The Twisted Road to Auschwitz: Nazi Policy Toward German Jews, 1933–1939* (University of Illinois Press: Champaign, IL, 1970).

3   Haganah Archive 14/491, report by Mezkevet, Ha'mosad LeAliya Beit (Ha'Mossad LeAliyah Bet), 4 July 1945. I am grateful to Dr Maayan Hillel, Northwestern University, for obtaining this document for me. The Ha'mosad LeAliya Beit was the precursor to the Israeli intelligence service, Mossad, and at that time an underground organization. Some background information on the organization can be found at http://www.palyam.org/English/HaMossad/ mainpage.php

4   JDC Archives. Istanbul Office of the American Jewish Joint Distribution
    Committee, IST 37-49/4/16/IS.228, NYAR 194554/4/44/3/647-702354, The
    American Joint Distribution Committee c/o American Embassy, Israel Jacobson
    to Moses A. Leavitt, AJDC, New York, 22 November 1945, 'Rhodes Jewish
    Population'. Jacobsen listed 204 survivors in Italy, 34 Aegean in Rhodes, 12 in
    Kos and 16 in Turkey. See also ITS Digital Archive. Arolsen Archives 3.1.1.3:
    Listen betr. Personen, die 1944/46 in Italien, Rhodos, Türkei, Kos Islands,
    Schweden und Deutschland lebten.

5   ITS Arolsen Archives, 3.1.1.3: Listen betr. Personen, die 1944/46 in Italien,
    Rhodos, Türkei, Kos Islands, Schweden und Deutschland lebten, Signatur
    311300017, Deputy Director M. S. Ellis (Special Administrative Team Lübeck),
    'Evacuation of sick Displaced Persons to Sweden, 23 June–25 July 1945'.

6   Frequently with the help of relatives, a new beginning in either North or South
    America, or the Belgian Congo, or Southern Rhodesia or Mandate Palestine (from
    1948, Israel) beckoned, with de-colonization Belgian Congo became the Democratic
    Republic of the Congo, 1964; Rhodesia was renamed as Zimbabwe, 1979.

7   TNA FO371/42890, WR1098/1098/48: 'Deportation of Jews of Rhodes', Harrison
    to de Lantsheere. It is likely that the information was transmitted by SOE from
    the island contemporaneous to the deportation itself.

8   TNA FO371/42890, intercepted letter, Censor's Office.

9   TNA WR1202/1098/48, Chief Rabbi's Emergency Council, Rabbi
    Solomon Schonfeld to Mr Randall, Refugee Department of Foreign Office,
    21 September 1944.

10 TNA FO 371/42980, letter Foreign Office (Refugee Department), Paul Mason to
    Vicomte de Lantsheere, 9 October 1944.

11 JDC Archives, NYAR 194554/4/44/3/647-702439, Leo Gallin to Donald B.
    Hurwitz, 3 January 1945.

12 TNA FO371/181726 for details and n. 10 above.

13 TNA DO35/1168, file 'Miscellaneous enquiries on behalf of Southern Rhodesia
    Govt., Jewish Community of Rhodes Island concerning disappearance of them'.
    The enquiries stretched into September 1945. By August there was information
    about those members of the community who were not deported and who had
    left for Turkey in January.

14 JDC Archive. G 45-54/4/17/2/Tk.1-2660416, letter from Harold Trobe
    to Mr Arthur Fishzohn, 19 February 1945. Trobe to Fishzohn, February
    1945. And Reuben Resnick to Lewis Waddilove, Documents\Geneva45-54\
    G45-54_Count\G45-54_MISC_010\G45-54_MISC_010_1034.pdf in JDC

Collection: 1945–54: Records of the Geneva Office of the American Jewish Joint
Distribution Committee – G 45–54 | Sub Collection: Countries and Regions – G
45–54 / 4 | Record Group: Greece – G 45–54 / 4 / 9 | Series: Greece: Localities –
G 45–54 / 4 / 9 / 13.

15 JDC NYAR (New York Office) 1945–54/4/44/3/647-702426, letter Morris
N. Capouya to Donald Hurwitz, 27 April 1945. This file has a small number of
correspondences relating to Capouya's enquiry.

16 JDC IST (Istanbul Office) 37–49 4/16/228, NYAR 194554/4/44/3/647-702419,
Correspondence from Jeannette Robbins Personal Inquiries Department to
Dr Morris Capouya (Capuia), May–July 1945.

17 JDC NYAR 1945-54/4/44/3/647-702421, letter from Norman Fresco to
Mr Hyman (JDC, New York), 15 May 1945. Correspondence from Jeannette
Robbins Personal Inquiries Department letter to JDC 15 May 1945.

18 A son, Mauritzio, does not appear to have been deported and thus may have
emigrated. There was one other family of the same name (also originally from
Smyrna) and possibly related. Three daughters of this family survived; two
of these Gaon sisters were among the survivors who found their way to Italy
Benatar and Benatar, *Si je t'oublie*, pp. 281 and 282 (separate entries).

19 Trobe to Fishzohn, 19 February 1945.

20 JDC Documents\Geneva45-54\G45-54_Count\USHMM-GENEVA_00042\
USHMM-GENEVA_00042_00527.pdf, Letter from Harold Trobe to Mr
Arthur Fishzohn, Re: Celebi Elkana and Family Rhodes (Dodecanese) Via
Granvimaestro (*sic*) Deodato Gozzone 8, 16 February 1945.

21 I would like to thank Joseph Elkana of Florida who graciously shared with me
information about his family. See Chapter 9 for discussion of his family.

22 JDC Documents\Geneva45-54\G45-54_Count\USHMM-GENEVA_00042\
USHMM-GENEVA_00042_00523.pdf: Letter from Harold Trobe to Mr
Arthur Fishzohn, Re: Mazaltob B. Hasson Rhodes, 21 February 1945. There is
a Mazaltov Hasson né Alhadeff (b. 1888) married to Haim Hasson and listed
in the Racial Census (card #276), who had a daughter Gianetta (Giovanna)
(b. 1922). Mazaltov's daughter Rebecca was married to survivor Giuseppe Mallel.
According to the family entry in CDEC none of Mazaltov's family survived.
Thus, it remains uncertain who is referred to here.

23 https://collections.arolsenarchives.org/en/archive/85977023/?p=1&s=capeluto&
doc_id=85977024; Benatar and Benatar, *Si je t'oublie*, pp. 29 and 525.

24 There is no documentation in the WJC files indicating where the enquiry for
information originated.

25 http://www.nomidellashoah.it/1scheda.asp?id=5470 (Mizrahi family) and http://www.nomidellashoah.it/1scheda.asp?id=99 (Alhadeff family).

26 https://collections.arolsen-archives.org/en/search/person/85977023?s=matilde%20capelluto&t=0&p=0

27 JDC Archives. S-508, JDC from Rome, 'Survivors from Rhodes now in Italy looking for Relatives' CLI, 17 August 17 1945 (fifteen persons).

28 Surmani, Interview 53625, seg. 198. Visual History Archive. USC Shoah Foundation. Eliezer was 78 years old at the time of his interview. Benatar and Benatar, *Si je t'oublie*, p. 616. At the time of liberation of Auschwitz, Soviet troops found 416 children under the age of 13 and 234 boys and girls aged between 14 and 17 years. Helen Kubica, 'Kinder und Jugendliche im KZ Auschwitz 1940-1945', in Wacław Długoborski and and Franciszek Piper (eds.), *Auschwitz 1940–1945 – Studien zur Geschichte des Konzentrations- und Vernichtungslagers Auschwitz* (5 vols.), trans. from Polish (Auschwitz-Birkenau State Museum: Auschwitz, 1995), Vol. II, pp. 255, 349, 351.

29 Bollettini di informazione del Comitato ricerche deportati ebrei (CRDE) di Roma, dal n. 1 al n. 36. (1), https://digital-library.cdec.it/cdec-web/storico/detail/IT-CDEC-ST0018-000008/bollettini-informazione.html

30 Miru Alcana, Interview 129, seg. 17. Visual History Archives. USC Shoah Foundation.

31 *Longest Journey*, 43:42 min.

32 *Longest Journey*, 46:30 min. Sami Modiano in the same sequence of the film, tells Pezzetti, 'I chose Italy because I felt Italian and I will die an Italian. Jewish but Italian.'

33 https://www.zwangsarbeit-archiv.de/en/zwangsarbeit/zwangsarbeit/zwangsarbeit-hintergrund/index.html for forced labour. Yasmin Khan, 'Wars of Displacement: Exile and Uprooting in the 1940s', in Michael Geyer and Adam Tooze (eds.), *The Cambridge History of the Second World War* Vol. 3, Total War: Economy, Society and Culture (Cambridge University Press: Cambridge, 2015), pp. 277–297, here p. 278. Contemporaries described the war as 'the costliest and most destructive war in history' (*The World Almanac*, 1946). The University of Berkeley economist, Robert A. Brady, put the cost of military operations at $1,154 billion, and that for war damage at $230 billion. These figures underestimate the long-term financial costs; nor do they consider the cost of lost human life: estimated at 52 million dead (nearly four times the dead of the First World War). In general, Mark Mazower, *Dark Continent: Europe's Twentieth Century* (Knopf: New York, 1999), chs. 6 and 7; Richard Vinen, *A History In*

Fragments: Europe in the Twentieth Century (De Capo Press: Boston, MA, 2001), part 3, ch. 1.

34 On the racial re-ordering of Eastern Europe, see: Mechthild Rössler and Sabine Schleiermacher, *Der 'Generalplan Ost': Hauptlinien Der Nationalsozialistischen Planungs- Und Vernichtungspolitik* (Schriften der Hamburger Stiftung für Sozialgeschichte des 20. Jahrhunderts) (Akademie-Verlag: Berlin, 1993). Bruno Wasser, *Himmlers Raumplanung im Osten: Der Generalplan Ost in Polen 1940–1944 (SPG – Stadt – Planung – Geschichte, Band 15)* (Birkhäuser Verlag: Basel, 1994), English edition. Elizabeth Harvey, *Women and the Nazi East: Agents and Witnesses of Germanization* (Yale University Press: New Haven, CT, 2003), ch. 10.

35 Gerard Daniel Cohen, *In War's Wake: Europe's Displaced Persons in the Postwar Order* (Oxford University Press: New York, Oxford, 2011), p. 37. Ruth Balint, *Destination Elsewhere:. Displaced Persons and Their Quest to Leave Postwar Europe* (Cornell University Press: Ithaca and London, 2021), pp. 20–40 *passim*.

36 UN Archives (hereafter: UNRRA) S-1252-0000-0278-00002 (DP Divisional Reports), Frames 191–194: Displaced Persons in Germany and Austria, 27 Feb. 1945, Frame 191.

37 Mark Wyman, *DPs: Europe's Displaced Persons, 1945–1951*. With a New Introduction (Cornell University Press: Ithaca and London, [1989] 1998), pp. 61–85.

38 Discussed below. See for a contemporary pre-war definition of refugees, John Hope Simpson, 'The Refugee Problem', *International Affairs* (Royal Institute of International Affairs 1931–1939), Vol. 17, No. 5 (Sep–Oct 1938), pp. 607–628.

39 Dan Stone, *The Liberation of the Camps: The End of the Holocaust and Its Aftermath* (Yale University Press: New Haven, CT, 2015), p. 19, for the lower figure or about one-quarter of the total number of concentration camp prisoners in May 1945. The higher figure is from https://encyclopedia.ushmm.org/content/en/article/displaced-persons. The anomaly might lie in the inclusion of non-camp displaced persons in the figure given by USHMM. See also Ben Shephard, *The Long Road Home: The Aftermath of the Second World War* (Alfred A. Knopf: New York, 2011), p. 102, who also quotes the higher figure of 200,000.

40 The classic account of the return journey from Auschwitz to Italy remains that by Primo Levi originally published in Italian in1963, *The Truce* translated from Italian by Stuart Woolf (The Bodley Head: London, 1965).

41 Jessica Reinisch, 'Old Wine in New Bottles? UNRRA and the Mid-Century World of Refugees', in Matthew Frank and Jessica Reinisch (eds.), *Refugees*

in Europe, 1919–1959: A Forty Year Crisis? (Bloomsbury: London, 2017), pp. 147–175.

42 The DELASEM was established in 1933 as a Jewish-run aid organization providing support for Jewish refugees and was officially recognized by the fascist government. After Italy's armistice with the Allies and the creation of the Salò Republic in the north, it went underground. Rabbi Riccardo Pacifici, the former director of the rabbinical school in Rhodes, led the Genoa branch until his deportation in 1943; the Bologna branch was led by Mario Finzi. The synagogue and communal buildings became, after the passing of the racial laws in 1938, a centre of Jewish aid and resistance through the DELASEM. https://resistenzamappe.it/bologna/bo_razzismo/via_de_gombruti_9_comunita_ebraica. Laura Bava, 'Aiding gli Ebrei' – DELASEM under fascism, 1939 to 1945 (MA Thesis, University of Notre Dame, Australia, 2016), retrieved at https://researchonline.nd.edu.au/theses/124.

43 UNRRA S-1253-0000-0604-00001, frame 5: Report of Standing Technical Committee on Displaced Persons, Restricted T.D.P. (45)9, 7 July 1945, p. 3. Also: UNRRA, S-1451-0000-0032-00001.PDF, UNRRA European Region DP 38/13, various reports on estimates of DPs in Italy. For post-war conditions, Paul Ginsborg, *A History of Contemporary Italy: Society and Politics, 1943–1988* (Penguin: London, 1990).

44 Miru Alcana Interview 129, seg. 12–14. Visual History Archive. USC Shoah Foundation. Sylvia Berro, Interview 5969, seg. 17–18. VHA. USC Shoah Foundation.

45 USHMM, RG- RG-50.233.0001_trs_en.pdf, interviewed 30 August 1992, transcript, p. 14.

46 Soriano, Interview 8852, seg. 9, Visual History Archive. USC Shoah Foundation.

47 Tony Alhadeff, *The Family Treasure* (n.p., 2020), pp. 80–81.

48 Alhadeff, *The Family Treasure*, pp. 74–76.

49 Lucia Franco (Garzolini), USHMM Collections, Acc. No. 1997.A.0431/RG-50.030.0452, Tape 3, Side A. They married and immigrated to the Congo, but eventually moved to Brussels in Belgium in 1974.

50 Andrea Sciarcon and Fabrizio Nurra, *Io desidero la pace. Vita di Morris Sciarcon, ebreo di Rodi sopravvissuto alla Shoà* (Edizioni Angelo Guerni E Associati: Milan, 2017), pp. 113–125.

51 Lubica, 'Kinder und Jugendliche'.

52 Sami Modiano, *Per questo ho vissuto, La mia vita ad Auschwitz-Birkenau e altri esili* (Rizzoli: Milan, 2013), pp. 133–145, 147. The following is based on this account.

53   Modiano does not give any personal details about Limentani. There are just
     three entries for Settimio Limentani in the Arolsen Archives, each with different
     birth dates: 26/5/1907, 29/4/1919 and 23/10/1891. Of these three entries, it is
     tempting to speculate that the second one is Modiano's travel companion.

54   Modiano, *Per questo*, pp. 135, 140–145.

55   Ibid.

56   UNRRA S-1479-0000-0047-00001, frames 81–82. Susanna Kokkonen, 'Jewish
     Displaced Persons in Postwar Italy, 1945–1951', in *Jewish Political Studies Review*,
     Vol. 20, No. 1/2 (Spring 2008), pp. 91–106.

57   https://encyclopedia.ushmm.org/content/en/article/displaced-persons.

58   UNRRA S-1479-0000-0047-00001, frames 40–48, 102–108 (report by DELASEM,
     7 January 1946); UNRRA S-1372-0000-0004-00001: DP Operations Italy, 405
     AJDC November 1946–December 1946, frames 207–215 (report by DELASEM,
     November 1946). A particularly ugly incident took place in March 1947 in Rivoli
     DP camp between Jewish activists of the Betar Group and other Jewish DPs,
     UNRRA S-1479-0000-0084-00001.PDF, frames 9–13. See also, Monty Noam
     Penkower, *After the Holocaust* (Touro University Press: New York, 2021).

59   For example, UNRRA S-1479-0000-0095-00001.PDF, an incident in November
     1946 where Yugoslav guards at Cinecittà beat a DP (also Yugoslav) suspected of
     theft.

60   UNRRA, S-1479-0000-0047-00001, frame 133, report from DELASEM to
     Mr Keeny, UNRRA, Rome, 31 October 1945.

61   Diamante Hugno Franco, Interview 48392, tape 2, Visual History Archives. USC
     Shoah Foundation. In a WJC source, the sisters were listed among those Aegean
     Jews liberated from Mauthausen, when according to Diamante's testimony,
     they were liberated from Auschwitz. Benatar and Benatar, *Si je t'oublie*, p. 396,
     also give Auschwitz as the place of liberation. It is possible that forty years later
     interviewed in South Africa, Diamante mixed up Mauthausen for Auschwitz.
     Interview with Diamante Franco, Cape Town, 7 August 1986, South African
     Holocaust and Genocide Foundation Archive.

62   See the photograph of six young women of Rhodes in Bologna *c.* 1945 at the
     Rhodes Jewish Museum website: https://www.rhodesjewishmuseum.org/history/
     holocaust/. Stella is the last on right in the second row. The soldiers are from the
     Jewish Brigade as indicated by the insignia on their truck door.

63   The Jewish Brigade Group had been formed in September 1944 and its members
     strongly Zionist, https://encyclopedia.ushmm.org/content/en/article/jewish-
     brigade-group. See the review article 'We proved to the world that we can fight'

by Joanna Paraszczuk of Chuck Olin's documentary film of the Brigade, 'In Their Own Hands: The Hidden Story of the Jewish Brigade in World War II', 85 mins ([orig. 1998] general release 2010) in *The Jerusalem Post*, 12 March 2010; available online: https://www.jpost.com/Local-Israel/Tel-Aviv-And-Center/We-proved-to-the-world-that-we-can-fight. The documentary itself can be accessed here: https://sites.google.com/view/olinfilms/in-our-own-hands. One if its members was Celebi Alcana's son, Salvatore.

64 As far as I am aware, there is no scholarly study of post-war ad hoc Jewish out-of-camp centres.

65 Its full name was (is) Via dei Condotti – with the 'dei' dropped in common usage.

66 GAKR Carabinieri 1.47.1025, Coen, Sipora (*sic*) fu Mose, 1934. She had been married to Giacomo Calavreso, who had died by the time of the Racial Census. Benatar and Benatar, *Si je t'oublie*, p. 147.

67 There was a total of sixteen Jews on the *Mas* that day, six were described as Turkish, five as Aegean citizens and five as Catholic. GAKR Carabinieri 1/1/160, 1938 Politica razzista, Partito il giorno, 13.1.1945 Barche diverse 'Mas': Egei Cattolici. While Teresa and Sipura Coen appear in the Race Census, Vittoria does not. In Benatar and Benatar, *Si je t'oublie*, p. 147, Teresa appears as Violetta, and her father is given as Giacomo Calavreso; it appears the sisters came by the name Buciuk, after their mother remarried Giacobbe Buciuk, but then subsequently divorced. According to the Benatars' editorial note, 'Violetta' was commonly known as Zimbul and changed her name to Maria upon converting to Catholicism when she married Giovanni Cavalli in 1935. In the ITS files, she appears as Teresa, also with her married name Cavalli. Three brothers with the name Buciuk, Moses (b. 1910 in Smyrna), Vittorio (b. 1912) and Alberto (b. 1919) both born in Rhodes, lived a few doors away at Nr 3005, they immigrated to the Belgian Congo after the census was taken. Their parents, Menachem Buciuk and Stella Benaderet had died by the time of the census. Their relationship to Vittoria and Teresa is unclear. A Mosè Benaderet originally from Smyrna left with his wife and a daughter on the steamship *Erzorum* on 25 January 1939 bound for Smyrna (Izmir), GAKR Carabinieri 1/1/160, 1938 Politica razzista.

68 Vittoria is referred to as Mrs Castrucci in Joint correspondence to Morris Alhadeff of the Rhodes Survivors Aid Committee in New York (3 April 1946), adding to the mystery surrounding her biography. For reference to her former life as a dressmaker on Rhodes, Arolsen Archives affidavit Caterina Sciarcon,

Arolsen Archives CM/1 files from Italy A-Z, Reference Code: 03020102 oS: Document ID: 80489786.

69   World Jewish Congress Records, MS-361, Box H178, Folder 13. American Jewish Archives, Cincinnati, Ohio: letter from Fritz Becker to Kurt Grossman, 31 October 1947 and related correspondence.

70   Sami Modiano, *Per questo*, p. 155 (my translation). Vittoria Buciuk was in her mid-30s in 1945.

71   The centres were outside the official apparatus of UNRRA and later IRO but received financial aid from these organizations as well as being supported by the Joint and by donations from the diaspora. UNRRA S-1253-0000-0620-00001. PDF for reports and analyses of out-of-camp populations (mostly 1946).

72   My thanks to Bettina Benatar Luetgerath, Hamburg, for sharing this information on her father.

73   World Jewish Congress Records, MS-361, Box H178, Folder 13. American Jewish Archives, Cincinnati, Ohio, ms0361.h178.013.pdf, p. 33 of 89: Rhodes Survivors Aid Committee (Rome), Elenco dei Profughi di Rodi rientrati dai campi di concentramento gia in posseso degli affidavit in attesa di aver il passaporto, 26 August 1946. The list cites eight other survivors: Stella and Ricca Nahmias, Stella and Eliezer Surmani, Matilda and Regina Menascé, Stella Hasson and Dora Capuya (mentioned above).

74   The New York committee was chaired by Solomon Moise Alhadeff; it is not clear if the Rome group was ever formally affiliated to the RSACNY. Its board comprised well-known family names. In Seattle the chair was Dr Harry Tarica, vice chair was Morris D. Hanan, secretaries were Albert A. Alhadeff and Joseph De Leon. The treasurer was Harry Franco.

75   Klaus Voigt, *Villa Emma: Jüdische Kinder auf der Flucht 1940–1945* 2nd edition (Metropol-Verlag: Berlin, 2016).

76   Thus Nico Bachas (or Arizo Bachar) and Matilda Capuleto (sic) at Via Settembrini 45, also in Milan, took in fellow survivor Ascer Hanan.

77   JDC Archives Documents\NY_AR_45-54\NY_AR45-54_Count\NY_AR45-54_00074\NY_AR45-54_00074_00896.pdf. The early estimates of killed or survivor Jews in Greece do not include Rhodes or Kos, at that time, technically, still not part of Greece. See TNA FO 371/42900, summary report: Jews in Greece.

78   JDC Archives Documents\NY_AR_45-54\NY_AR45-54_Count\NY_AR45-54_00074\NY_AR45-54_00074_00854.pdf, 3 Dec. 1945, Israel G. Jacobson to Moses A. Leavitt, 'Report on Visit to Rhodes (Nov. 1945)'. The attached lists

are found in: JDC Archives Documents\NY_AR_45-54\NY_AR45-54_Count\
NY_AR45-54_00074\NY_AR45-54_00074_00862.pdf. Copies are also available
here: ITS Digital Archive. Arolsen Archives, 3.1.1.3, Listen betr. Personen, die
1944/46 in Italien, Rhodos, Türkei, Kos Islands, Schweden und Deutschland
lebten. Einer ging von Rhodos über Alexandria nach Palästina, https://
collections.arolsen-archives.org/de/archive/3-1-1-3_8806870. In addition to
these camp survivors in Italy, the report listed those who were not deported,
namely thirty-four persons who had returned to Rhodes, another eight adults
and four children who had returned to Kos, and sixteen persons in Turkey. This
means of the original community numbering *c.* 1,800 in 1939 and of the *c.* 1,754
deported, 261 or 266 survived post-deportation (the data is slightly unclear), and
thus a much higher figure than the 152 usually cited in the literature, and less
than the *c.* 303 believed by the British Military Administration (Dodecanese)
to have survived. Marco Clementi/Eirini Toliou, *Gli ultimi ebrei di Rodi. Leggi
razziali e deportazioni nel Dodecaneso italiano (1938–1948)* (Derive Approdi:
Rome, 2015), pp. 184–185, 282, n. 682 & 683 for differing (inaccurate) figures.
Repeated in greater detail in: Marco Clementi, *Storia della comunità ebraica di
Rodi (1912–1947)* (tab edizioni: Rome, 2022), pp. 407–419.

79 TNA FO 371/561, Refugees 1946, War Organization of the British Red Cross
Society and Order of St John of Jerusalem, S. J. Warner to Miss Horsfield,
Foreign Office, 6 March 1946. (Duplicated in TNA FO 371/57851). Lists
compiled by the Rhodes Survivors Committee.

80 We know very little about the day-to-day operations of these centres.
Documentation is sparse and there has been little to no in-depth study,
apart from Bava cited above (n. 42). Klaus Voigt's study of Villa Emma deals
principally with German-speaking Jewish refugee children mainly during the
war years. I have not been able to determine if Voigt completed the collection
and editing of the papers of the DELASEM, see the notice in *La Rassegna mensile
di Israel* terza serie Vol. 69, No. 1, Saggi sull'ebraismo italiano del Novecentocin
onore chi Luisella Montana Ottolenghi, Tomo 1 (Gennaio-Aprile 2003), xiv.

81 De Sica's contemporary Roberto Rosselini also took the theme of post-war
displacement and renewal in his masterpiece *Stromboli: Terra di Dio* (Italy, 1950).

82 JDC Archives, Documents\NY_AR_45-54\NY_AR45-54_Count\NY_AR45-
54_00074\NY_AR45-54_00074_00557.pdf, Blanco Sussidi Pagati Nel Mese Di
Giugno 1945.

83 UNRRA S-1480-0000-0025-00001.PDF, frame 57, report, 6 February 1947.
See also the six-page report from Maurice Rosen UNRRA Italian Mission

Memorandum, to S.M. Keeny, 'Jewish Displaced Persons in Italy', 24 February 1946, in UNRRA S-1479-0000-0047-00001.PDF, frames 75–80, frame 79 especially.

84 UNRRA S-1479-0000-0047-00001, frame 82, Zvi Leiman (Jewish Soldiers Welfare Centre) to Department for Displaced Persons, UNRRA Rome, 5 September 1945 (stamped: received October 1945).

85 World Jewish Congress Records, MS-361, Box H178, Folder 13. American Jewish Archives, Cincinnati, Ohio: undated letter from Buciuk to WJC New York, in response to letter from Kurt Grossmann, 15 August 1947.

86 UNRRA S-1481-0000-0012-00001.PDF, Jewish Vocational Training Centre, 51-B/0 L14, 113, and S-1480-0000-0026-00001.PDF, 71 B9 L14: Hachshara Policy and Administration. I am not aware of any full-length study of the operation of *Hachsharoth* in Italy, or European-wide, for that matter. A start can be found in 'Training for Aliyah: Young Jews in Hachsharot across Europe between the 1930s and late 1940s', Verena Buser and Chiara Renzo (eds.), *Quest: Issues in Contemporary Jewish History. Journal of the Fondazione CDEC*, Vol. 21, No. 1 (2022), pp. 75–102.

87 UNRRA S-1450-0000-0089-00001.PDF, UNRRA European Region, WR 12/13, frame 5, UNRRA Italian Mission Bureau of Relief Services, Jewish Displaced Persons Receiving UNRRA Assistance in Towns, Hachsharoth and UNRRA Operated Camps.

88 World Jewish Congress Records, MS-361, Box H178, Folder 13. American Jewish Archives, Cincinnati, Ohio: letter Buciuk to WJC, 21 December 1947.

89 JDC Archives, Department of State Incoming Cable, Division of Central Services Telegraph Section, Rome, to Secretary of State Washington for Moses Leavitt AJDC New York from Reuben Resnik, AJDC Rome, 2 August 1945. See also, Resnik's letter 28 February 1945 to American Joint Distribution Committee, New York, in ibid, Documents\NY_AR_45-54\NY_AR45-54_Count\NY_AR45-54_00074\NY_AR45-54_00074_00960.pdf.

90 JDC Documents\NY_AR_45-54\NY_AR45-54_Count\NY_AR45-54_00074\NY_AR45-54_00074_00858.pdf, Henrietta K. Buchman AJDC New York to AJDC Paris, 30 November 1945. The enquiry mentions Capelluto was staying in Room 7, Roulef House. Roulef House was in the Jewish DP camp in Bergen-Belsen. Thomas Rake, 'Bergen-Belsen Main Camp', in Geoffrey P. Megargee (ed.), *Encyclopedia of Camps and Ghettos 1933–1945*. Vol. I: *Early Camps, Youth Camps, and Concentration Camps and Subcamps under the SS-Business Administration Main Office (WVHA)* (Indiana University Press: Bloomington,

IN, 2009), pp. 278–281; Habbo Knoch (ed.), *Bergen-Belsen: Wehrmacht POW Camp 1940–1945, Concentration Camp 1943–1945, Displaced Persons Camp 1945–1950: Catalogue of the permanent exhibition* (Wallstein Verlag: Göttingen, 2010).

91   JDC Archives NY_AR45-54_00074_00890.pdf, NLT Jointfund, Rome, Telegram 17 October 1945.

92   JDC Archives NYAR 194554/4/44/3-/627, Outgoing Cable Rome 14 November 1945. JDC Archives IST 37-49/4/16/IS.228, incoming cable 17 November 1945.

93   JDC Archives NYAR 194554/4/44-647, Isidore Freiberg & Sons, Invoice Bo. 336, 22 October 1945. Of the eight bales, three bales each to Rome and Milan and two to Florence. See also the numerous cable references to material and financial support in JDC Archives IST 37-49/4/16/IS.228.

94   For example, JDC Archives NYAR 194554/4/44/3-/627, Henrietta Buchman to Rhodes Survivors Aid Committee, 25 October 1945, and Henrietta Buchman to Rhodes Aid Committee New York, 5 November 1945. On the cost of living, see Ginsborg, *A History of Italy*, p. 80.

95   JDC Archives, Documents\NY_AR_45-54\NY_AR45-54_Count\NY_AR45-54_00074\NY_AR45-54_00074_00825.pdf, Letter from Henrietta K. Buchman to Mr Maurice Alhadoff (*sic*), 3 April 1947. This sum equated to barely 15 dollars in May 1947 when the exchange rate was I£909 to the dollar, Ginsborg, *A History of Italy*, p. 113.

96   World Jewish Congress Records, MS-361, Box H178, Folder 13. American Jewish Archives, Cincinnati, Ohio, letter AJC Los Angeles Women's Division (Mrs Fred Pollock) to Dr Kalman Stein, WJC New York, 26 November 1945.

97   JDC NY AR194554 / 4 / 44 / 3 / 647, Folder: Italy, Island of Rhodes, 1945, United Jewish Appeal, New York, Memorandum 19 November 1945 Isidor Coons to Louis Sobel, with attached extract of letter to Isidor Coons from Arthur Adams (JDC), 16 November 1945. In previous years the Jewish Federation of Montgomery had contributed to the United Jewish Appeal, but Adams claimed these were sums that did not reflect its wealth. Ibid, Memorandum 19 November 1945, Isidor Coons to Louis Sobel. In this memorandum Coons described the community as one known to Sobel 'through its complacency and easy going way'.

98   JDC Archives NY_AR45-54_00074_00890.pdf, NLT Jointfund, Rome, Telegram 17 October 1945.

99   Pollock to Stein, letter 26 November 1945.

100 UNRRA S-1480-0000-0072-00001.PDF, frames 19–20, Organization of Jewish Refugees in Italy to Maj.-Gen. Lowell Rooks, Director General UNRRA, Ref. 1147, 7 April 1947.

101 In February 1947, UNRRA was assisting 6,999 out-of-camp DPs and expected to cut this case load by 50 per cent through changing eligibility criteria. UNRRA S-1480-0000-0025-00001.PDF, Out of Camp Assistance Policy and Administration, frames 29–30, 33, 36, 45.

102 Ibid, frames 9, 17, 46: 'Nationality Breakdown/Out of Camp', May, April, February. The number had been reducing slightly before the policy change: at the beginning of 1947, it had been 31, in October 35, ibid, frames 64 and 76.

103 World Jewish Congress, Series H: Subseries 1: Box H178 File 13, undated letter Vittoria Buciuk to Kurt Grossmann and his response referring to her letter of 21 December 1947.

104 UNRRA S-1372-0000-0004-00001 DP operations Italy, 40s AJDC, November 1946–December 1946, frame 3. Letter from the IRO to Buciuk, 7 January 1947.

105 World Jewish Congress, Series H: Subseries 1: Box H178 File 13, Letter Vittoria Buciuk to WJC (undated, presumably end of summer early autumn 1947), in response to letter 15 August 1947. Grossman wrote to the Unione in mid-August requesting financial support for the group, eventually, the Unione acknowledged his letters, but it too was strapped for cash.

106 UNRRA S-1479-0000-0047-00001, AG 018-018 Dodecanese Mission/AG018-009: Italy Mission, frames 40–43. There were repeated calls to close the largest of the UNRRA camps, Cinecittà, a few kilometres south of Rome, because of persistent sewage problems and squalid conditions. There were also reports of corruption, and frequent drunkenness and fights among the DPs, in this and in other camps, UNRRA S-1479-0000-0046-00001, and UNRRA S-1479-0000-0047-00001.PDF various reports.

107 As well as sources in n. 58, see UNRRA S-1479-0000-0046-00001.PDF, frame 30, UNRRA Italian Mission, Director, Displaced Persons Division to Deputy Chief of Mission, Ref. DP/ADM/5/16, Subject, Reported Disturbances at NIDP camp, Bari, 11 October 1946.

108 UNRRA S-1479-0000-0046-00001.PDF, frames 105–109, Department for Displaced Persons, UNRRA Rome, report by Z. Leimann, 10 September 1945. Wiener Library, MF Doc 54/Reel 8, Doc. 525: N. Katzenstein, 'Report of Jews in Liberated Countries, July 1945'. For Poland, Jan Gross, *Fear: Anti-Semitism in Poland After Auschwitz: An Essay in Historical Interpretation* (Princeton University Press: New Jersey, 2006). For German antisemitic attacks

on DPs near Stuttgart in Germany, see Penkower, *After the Holocaust*, ch. 4. Social/welfare reports on the Stuttgart Jewish DP camp can be found here: UNRRA S-0436-0043-0004-00001 UC.tif, Team 502 Stuttgart (Jewish Camp).

109 https://encyclopedia.ushmm.org/content/en/article/displaced-persons-administration. The question of repatriation of civilians was codified in Article 134: Repatriation and Return to Last Place of Residence (1) of the Convention (IV) relative to the Protection of Civilian Persons in Time of War, Geneva, 12 August 1949, https://ihl-databases.icrc.org/applic/ihl/ihl.nsf/Comment.xsp?documentId=8EAF8444731529F5C12563CD0042E350&action=OpenDocument

110 Based on (i) Convention (IV) respecting the Laws and Customs of War on Land and its annex: Regulations concerning the Laws and Customs of War on Land. The Hague, 18 October 1907; (ii) Convention (IV) relative to the Protection of Civilian Persons in Time of War. Geneva, 12 August 1949, both at ICRC https://ihl-databases.icrc.org/applic/ihl/ihl.nsf/vwTreaties1949.xsp. The standard work on international approaches to refugees/DPs is Tommie Sjöberg, *The Powers and the Persecuted: The Refugee Problem and the Intergovernmental Committee on Refugees (IGCR), 1938–1947* (Lund University Press: Lund, 1991). The year 1938 was chosen because of the subsequent changed borders following Germany's annexation and later occupation policies.

111 UNRRA S-1253-0000-0604-00001, Frame 4: Report of Standing Technical Committee on Displaced Persons, Restricted T.D.P. (45)9, 7 July 1945, p. 2. Resolutions 40 and 90 are discussed in two outgoing cables from the Eelfare division of UNRRA dated 12th and 13th April 1946 (albeit concerning Jewish refugees still in Germany/Austria) in UNRRA Series 138, Box 33, File 68–69, S-1536-0000-0226-00001 UC.tif, frame 66. UNRRA (European Region), WR 17, frames 13-15, UNRRA Policy Directive, 'UNRRA's responsibility with regard to resettlement of Displaced Persons', 4 December 1946. See for the Earl Harrison mission in 1945, Penkower, *After the Holocaust*, chs 2 and 3.

112 Greece's sovereignty over the Dodecanese was ratified in Article 14 of the Treaty of Paris (February 1947) that took effect in March 1948. Background in Joseph S. Roucek, 'The Legal Aspects of Sovereignty over the Dodecanese', *The American Journal of International Law*, Vol. 38, No. 4 (Oct. 1944), pp. 701–706. The nationality issue continued to be an issue for survivors wishing to be resettled; they in turn argued that they were 'subjects' rather than 'citizens'.

113 UNRRA S-1302-0000-5097-00001, Frames 19-20, UNRRA Incoming Message, No. 3921 Rome (Sorieri) to Paris 142, 8/5/47, DP Statistics as of 30 April 1947, Section D.

114   Laura J. Hilton, 'The Experiences and Impact of the Stateless in the Postwar
      Period', in Rebecca Boehling, Susanne Urban, Elizabeth Anthony and Sizanne
      Brown-Fleming (eds.), *Freilegungen. Spiegelungen der NS-Verfolgung und ihrer*
      'zen, Jahrbuch der Internationalen Tracing Service Vol. 4 (Wallstein Verlag:
      Göttingen, 2015), p. 159. Referring to the figure of Peter Schlemihl, the protagonist
      in Adelbert von Chamisso's fantasy tale of that title about a man without a shadow,
      Hilton describes the DP as 'a person without shadow; a non-person; non-
      belonging searching for a place in war's wake', ibid, p. 160. IRO treatment of DPs/
      refugees was on the basis of nationality, which did not always work for Jews.

115   Sara Jerusalmi, Interview 8038, seg. 21.Visual History Archive USC Shoah
      Foundation. Sara was the daughter of Maslia Notrica and Rosa Franco. We
      encountered her and her brother Salvo in Chapter 6. ITS Digital Archive.
      Arolsen Archives, 1.1.6.2 and 1.1.6.7 Personal office files, Dachau. Benatar and
      Benatar, *Si je t'oublie*, p. 542.

116   Benatar and Benatar, *Si je t'oublie*, pp. 314 (with photograph of Rosa and
      Giuseppe (Joseph)), 493.

117   ITS Digital Archive. Arolsen Archives. 3.2.1.2 CM/1 Files originating from
      Italy, IRO Questionnaire Case No. RC/2296/RIC/628/49, 3 March 1949. Mallel,
      Josef (*sic*).

118   Ibid.

119   ITS Digital Archive. Arolsen Archives. 3.2.1.2 CM/1 Files originating from
      Italy, IRO Eligibility Office to Rome Intake Center (copy), HQL/DEC/3134,
      7.4.49 1 April 1949, ds/1907/E-142.

120   ITS Digital Archive. Arolsen Archives. 3.2.1.2 CM/1 Files originating from
      Italy, IRO International Refugee Organization. Decision of the Review Board
      RP/340, 21 February 1950.

121   ITS Digitial Archive. Arolsen Archives, 1.1.26.3 Individual Files Mauthausen,
      Josef (*sic*) Mallel; ibid., 3.2.1.2. CM1/ Files from Italy A-Z. International Refugee
      Organization Decision of the Review Board, Geneva 17231 25 May 1951.

122   The synagogue and communal buildings became, after the passing of the
      racial laws in 1938, one of the centres of Jewish aid and resistance. For more
      information on Jewish resistance in Bologna, https://resistenzamappe.it/
      bologna/bo_razzismo/via_de_gombruti_9_comunita_ebraica

123   World Jewish Congress Records, MS-361, Box H178, Folder 13. American
      Jewish Archives, Cincinnati, Ohio, Albert Hanan, letter of appeal to the PCIRO,
      9 January 1950. See his incarceration file in ITS Digital Archive. Arolsen
      Archives, 1.1.26.3. Individual Files Mauthausen, Hanan, Alberto.

124 Hanan, letter of appeal, 9 January 1950 as n. 116. Letter is written in French, my translation.

125 World Jewish Congress Records, MS-361, Box H178, Folder 13. American Jewish Archives, Cincinnati, Ohio, Vittoria Buciuk to Kurt R. Grossman, Acting Head, Relief & Rehabilitation Dept, World Jewish Congress New York, undated letter.

126 ITS Digital Archive. Arolsen Archives, 3.2.1.4, CM/1 Files Originating in Switzerland, Personal file of Albert Hanan, Vittoria Buciuk to Dr Liban, 27 January 1950. Liban then wrote to the IRO in Geneva in early February requesting they review the case, correspondence in same file. See also Liban's 'Aktenvermerk' 24 January 1950, in World Jewish Congress Records, MS-361, Box H178, Folder 13. American Jewish Archives, Cincinnati, Ohio and the correspondence from Grossman to Gerhard Riegner, WJC Geneva, 24 January 1950, in ibid.

127 ITS Digital Archive. Arolsen Archives, 3.2.1.5, CM/1 Opposition proceedings. IRO Bureau Geneva. Reference Code 1763000 018.308, Personal file Hanan, Alberto. IRO Decision of the Review Board, No. 17017, 15 February 1950. DocID: 81281871 (ALBERTO HANAN). Capitalized emphasis in original.

128 AJDC Rome HQ D #1107 Paris General #636, Attn. Mr Beckelman from Jacob L. Trobe, 11 August 1947, AJDC G45-54_IT_004_0598.pdf.

129 Simpson, 'The Refugee Problem'.

130 ITS Digital Archive. Arolsen Archives. 3.2.1.5 CM/1 Opposition Proceedings. IRO Bureau Geneva. Reference Code 03020102025.055, Personal file Levi Balsamo, Vittoria. The following account is based on this file. Vittoria married Balsamo after the Racial Census, when she was living with her parents; her two older brothers, Haim and Giuseppe left Rhodes after the census was taken, JCR, Racial Census, card 366. Benatar and Benatar, *Si je t'oublie*, p. 442.

131 Formerly Via Sinagoga dell Pace where the Kahal Grande was located. In the application for resettlement, Vittoria also gives her address between 1936 and 1945 as Enrico Duce; it has not been possible to determine the location of this street, or, indeed, if it actually existed under this name. Her brothers Giuseppe (b. 1909) and Haim (b. 1915) and another brother Bension together with his wife and son subsequently immigrated to the Belgian Congo. Her parents were deported and perished in Auschwitz.

132 ITS Digital Archive. Arolsen Archives. 3.2.1.5 CM/1 Opposition Proceedings IRO Bureau Geneva. Reference Code 03020102025.055. Questionnaire, 13 September 1950. GAKR IΔΔ ETOΣ 1944-45, ΦAK 18 TMHMA 112, 13 Jan.

Barche Diverse: Mas. There is no mention of Israel Levi on this transport. Only Vittoria's name is listed and not that of the children. She is also listed as a 'Catholic', as was Teresa Buciuk who was on the same boat. Between 9 December and 25 January thirty-six Jews and their families were repatriated to Turkey. Of these, the status for twenty-seven was given as Aegean Jews, eight as Catholic and six as Turkish. Among those listed as Catholic, were the prominent Jews saved as Turkish nationals by the Turkish Consul Selahattin Ülkümen.

133 ITS Digital Archive. Arolsen Archives. 3.2.1.5 CM/1 Opposition Proceedings IRO Bureau Geneva. Reference Code 03020102025.055. Application for IRO Assistance, Israel Levi, ICR/und/F/89/50, 23 February 1950. There is just one Israel Levi born on 3 November 1906 listed in the Racial Census (Card # 386). He had resided with five siblings at della Turcheria 15.

134 Ibid, Rome Intake Center Questionnaire 24 February 1950.

135 ITS Digital Archive. Arolsen Archives. 3.2.1.5 CM/1 Opposition Proceedings IRO Bureau Geneva. International Refugee Organization Geneva No. 2541, Decision of the Review Board, 13 December 1950.

136 ITS Digital Archive, Arolsen Archives 3.2.1.2, CM/1 Files originating in Italy A-Z, Personal file Hanan, Ascer. IRO Field Welfare Office Rome, Karl D. Feller, to Welfare Division, Subject: Hanan, Ascer, Ref. RFWS 4, 28 November 1949. DocID: 80385251. In this document, Feller states that assistance to Lina was discontinued in March 1948 when she went missing, and that Ascer's brother Alberto Hanan told IRO officers on 28 May 1948 that Ascer had left for Palestine, information that was confirmed by Vittoria Buciuk. There are no individual files for his two siblings in the ITS Archive. The following account is based on information in this file and in ITS Digital Archive. Arolsen Archives, 1.1.5.3. Concentration camp Buchenwald. Personal File of Hanan, Ascer.

137 ITS Digital Archive. Arolsen Archives, 3.2.1.2.CM/1 Files Originating in Italy, Personal file of Hanan, Ascer. IRO, Questionnaire Ref. ICR 2565/49, Interviewed 23 September 1949. DocID: 80385243, 13 December 1949.

138 The information in CDEC stating Avner was deported and killed in Auschwitz is incorrect: https://digital-library.cdec.it/cdec-web/persone/detail/person-3379/hanan-abner.html

139 As n. 128, and same details for Lea and Alberto.

140 Ibid.

141 UNRRA Series 138, Box 33, File 6, S-1536-0000-0226-00001 UC.tif, frame 66, note from Dudley Ward, General Counsel (UNRRA) to Undersecretary of State, Foreign Office, 21 May 1946.

142 Hilton, 'Experiences' p. 169, has examples of disagreement over status. On the question of what constituted 'legitimate' refugee status see Ruth Balint, 'The Use and Abuse of History: Displaced Persons in the ITS Archive', in Boehling, Urban, Anthony and Brown-Fleming (eds.), *Freilegungen Spiegelungen der NS-Verfolgung und ihrer Konsequenzen*, pp. 173–186, here: p. 176.

143 Fortunoff Archive, Alice Tarica. Interview seg. 24.

144 Ibid. See also list of Rhodes Jews helped by the Jewish Community, Modena: JDC Archives, Documents\NY_AR_45-54\NY_AR45-54_Count\NY_AR45-54_00074\NY_AR45-54_00074_00912.pdf, Memorandum from B. Sapir to Mr L.H. Sobel and Mr D.Z. Hurwitz, Re: Refugees from Rhodes, 23 August 1945.

145 Stella was born on 14 August 1931, Sub-Collection 3.2.1.4/80912936 CM/1 Files originating in Switzerland – UNHCR/Stella Berun (*sic*), ITS Digital Archive, Arolsen Archives 3.2.1.4, Personal file of Berun (*sic*), Stella. Cf., Benatar and Benatar, *Si je t'oublie*, p. 123.

146 Stella appears as Esther in the Racial Census, and her mother's maiden name as Fiss, JCR Racial Census #102 (or 109). CDEC gives her names as Fis, https://digital-library.cdec.it/cdec-web/persone/detail/person-2622/fis-rachele.html. There are no details for Esther/Stella in CDEC. In her IRO narrative, Stella gives her mother as Finz, as n. 132. To IRO Summary Declaration (Stella Benun), 20 September 1950 (certified translation of Italian original, also in file).

147 ITS Digital Archive, Arolsen Archives 3.2.1.4, Personal file of Berun (*sic*), Stella. IRO Headquarters Bagnoli Naples Resettlement Placement Service to Resettlement Placement Unit, Geneva Subject: Reclassification of IHC cases, Ref. PB/2829, 26 January 1951. Ibid, note from C.G. de Poret, Chief Africa-Europe Branch for Director of Resettlement and Repatriation to IRO Oslo Norway, RPS. 11148-11461, 5 May 1951, and response IRO Director of Field Services (R.F. Lent), Bagnoli to Poret's office, 17 May 1951.

148 Ibid, C.G. de Poret, Chief Africa-Europe Branch for Director of Resettlement and Repatriation to IRO Calo., RPS. 11461, 26 June 1951, Subject: Stella Benun.

149 It is possible that he had been placed there under the *Hachsharoth* programme, see for example: UNRRA S-1481-0000-0012-00001.PDF, frame 30.

150 Ibid. IRO policy towards Jewish orphans is as yet an unwritten dimension of child survivors of the Holocaust that possibly bears some similarity to many Jewish children saved from Nazi Germany who arrived in Britain on the *Kindertransport* in 1938/39, and who subsequently found themselves *quasi* indentured to farmers or confined as domestic servants. Andrea Hammel and Bea Lewkowicz (eds.), *The Kindertransport to Britain 1938/39: New Perspectives: 13* (Yearbook of the Research Centre for German and Austrian Exile Studies)

(Rodopi: Amsterdam, New York, 2012). Wolfgang Benz, Claudia Curio and Andrea Hammel (eds.), *Die Kindertransporte 1938/39: Rettung und Integration* (Die Zeit des Nationalsozialismus) (Fischer Verlag: Frankfurt am Main, 2003). The uplifting story of child rescue is presented in Mark Harris Jones and Deborah Oppenheimer (eds.), *Into the Arms of Strangers: Stories of the Kindertransport* (Bloomsbury: London, 2000). For the Levi family, see Benatar and Benatar, *Si je t'oublie*, p. 204. Moses had a half-sister from his father's previous marriage to Amelia Hasson, Rebecca, b. 1909, who was not on the deportation list. We have no information for her and she does not feature in Moses' interview notes from 1947.

151 ITS Digital Archive. Arolsen Archives CM/1 Files originating in Italy A-Z, Ref. Code: 03020102 oS: Coen, Moses, Slides 80342455-80342461. Hilton, 'Experiences', p. 159.

152 Joseph A. Berger, 'Displaced Persons. A Human Tragedy of World War II', in *Social Research*, Vol. 14, No. 1 (March 1947), pp. 45–58.

153 UNRRA S-1345-0000-0031-00001: Dodecanese Mission, frames 78, 85–90. It also meant that they would eventually escape having to answer for their part in the persecutory measures against Jews, their collaboration in the deportation and their spoliation of Jewish property. An exploration of the Arolsen Archives reveals hundreds of Italians displaced from the Dodecanese. UNRRA archives also contain individual petitions for repatriation, for example: UNRRA Master file: S-1345-0000-0117-00001.PDF Displaced Persons.

154 Cooperation between the two organizations was sometimes marred by tension over demarcation of responsibilities. Pamela Ballinger, *The World Refugees Made: Decolonization and the Foundation of Postwar Italy* (Cornell University Press: New York, 2020).

155 UNRRA S-1345-0000-0117-00001: frame 213: Repatriation of Italians. The figures were as follows: from a total of 1,472 persons, 679 were administrators and overwhelmingly former members of the PNF; 509 refugees; 125 'undesirables' and 159 medical cases.

156 UNRRA S-1345-0000-0117-00001: frame 214: Repatriation of Dodecanesian Refugees.

157 Ibid. It is likely that these Jews were from those expelled to Turkey at the beginning of 1945, or who had escaped from the islands and thus avoided the deportation. At war's end, they were located on the islands of Simi, Casos and Cyprus, or were in Marmaris on mainland Turkey.

158 https://search.archives.jdc.org/multimedia/Documents/NY_AR_45-54/NY_
AR45-54_Count/NY_AR45-54_00074/NY_AR45-54_00074_00854.pdf#search
Letter Israel G. Jacobsen to Moses A. Leavitt, AJDC New York, 3 December
1945, Enclosure 22 November 1945: 'Jewish People Living in Rhodes'. There
were a further sixteen Jews from Rhodes and Kos in Turkey at that time.

159 UNRRA S-1345-0000-0031-00001: Frame 77, Report January 1946, p. 8, and
Frame 214, Return of Dodecanesians, from December 1945 to August 1946.
They were among the 4,302 repatriates to the Dodecanese over that period.

160 UNRRA S-1345-0000-0117-00001: frames 211-212: Jewish Refugees (file.
5.19.D./4). This is a two-page background report on the Aegean Jews from the
mid-1930s to post-war. According to the report, the information was supplied
by 'Mr. Alhadeff', presumably Solomon Alhadeff, in New York. However, the
information in the UNRRA report is not entirely accurate where the number
and names of the returnees are concerned. The most accurate report, in my
view, is that by Jacobson.

161 UNRRA S-1345-0000-0113-00001: frame 84; ibid, frame 30 for Rachele
Alhadeff, Vittorio Hasson and Ascer Cordoval.

162 UNRRA S-1345-0000-0113-00001: frame 77, Jewish Community Rhodes to
Major Miles Bailey, 1 April 1946.

163 Galante cites 146 persons with their locations, but undated: Rome: 66; Milan:
38; Bologna: 18; Florence: 6; and one each in Treviso and Sassari. There were
a further sixteen in Belgium (1), France (6), Switzerland (5) and Rhodes (4),
Galante, *Histoire des Juifs*, pp. 309–315.

164 ACICR: CICR Geneva: B SEC CGSG B-034 I, Courvoisier Report May 1945,
p. 12.

165 UNRRA European Region, DG 25/55, various reports, S-0523-0020-0016-
00001.pdf.

166 Report by Chief of UNRRA Dodecanese Mission to Deputy Director General,
European Office (London), 22 December 1945, UNRRA European Region
DG25/55, S-0523-0020-0016-00001.pdf.

167 Helen Nussbaum, 'One "Sunshine" Spot in Greece', *American Journal of Nursing*,
Vol. 49, No. 1 (Jan. 1949), pp. 11–12. She also noted the severe shortage of shoes
and clothing for children.

168 Courvoisier Report May 1945, p. 16. According to the report, the Germans
ate the dogs, the Italians ate the cats, and the rats were trapped and eaten by
Greeks. See also reference to eating cats and dogs in the report by Chief of
UNRRA Dodecanese Mission to Deputy Director General, European Office

(London), 22 December 1945, UNRRA European Region, DG 25/55, S-0523-0020-0016-00001.pdf. Also, Col. Toby, Outgoing Cable No. 7630, 19 December 1945, in same file.

169 *Longest Journey*, 46:41–47:15 min. Stella De Leon, née Hasson, Interview 12055, seg. 76. Visual History Archive. USC Shoah Foundation, returned to Rhodes in the early 1990s but stayed a mere 48 hours; 'that was enough for me' was her response when asked why the visit was so short.

170 While, as we saw, not everyone who applied to the BMA to return to Rhodes was successful, Soriano was informed at the beginning of August that his wife Vittoria Soriano and their two children, Elio (13) and Rita (5) had been given permission to join him in Rhodes, UNRRA S-1345-0000-0117-00001: frame 140. Dodecanese Mission, Assistant Chief Welfare Officer to Mr Moise Soriano, Ref. 15/19/O/3, 1 August 1946.

171 UNRRA S-1345-0000-0031-00001: Frame 89, Report August–November 1945, p. 5. Of the 204 listed Jews in Italy in November 1945, 69 were male survivors.

172 UNRRA S-1345-0000-0117-00001: frame 261. HIAS is the acronym for Hebrew Immigrant Aid Society.

173 UNRRA S-1345-0000-0117-00001.PDF, frames 77–78.

174 Ibid, UNRRA Rome to UNRRA Rhodes and to BMA requesting Demontis to be granted permission to enter Rhodes, 12 and 17 August 1946. See UNRRA S-1345-0000-0116-00001: frame 204. October 1946. 'No reason for refusal' stated in the file.

175 This was notable in the case of those Greeks who had been exiled by the Italians and who were either known Dodecanesian nationalists or suspected communists.

176 Unpublished obituary Moishe (*sic*) Sulam 06/03/1922–11/02/1982. I would like to thank Carmen Cohen for providing me with Sulam's biographical details. See also: Race Census card #500 for his family: parents, Reuben Sullam (*sic*) and Bulissa Hasson, and their three children: Mosé, Amelia and Nissim, and more fully in Benatar and Benatar, *Si je t'oublie*, p. 613. His brother Nissim (b. 1927) was killed during the aerial bombardment in February 1944, his parents were killed in Auschwitz, but his sisters Amelia and Rachel survived the Holocaust. Amelia was liberated from Theresienstadt and Rachel from Dachau.

177 JDC Archives, NY_AR_194545/4/44/3/647, Item ID 702350, letter from Israel G. Jacobsen to Moses A. Leavitt, Subject: Report on visit to Rhodes (19–21 November), 3 December 1945. The islands suffered an infestation of rats in the post-war period because allegedly Italians had eaten the cats, while the

German garrison ate the dogs during the famine in the final months of the war, according to Jacobsen's report. However, the Red Cross delegation noted that the civilian population had also hunted and eaten the rats.

178 As well as sources in n. 101, see Koppel S. Pinson, 'Antisemitism in the Post-War World', *Jewish Social Studies*, Vol. 7, No. 2 (Apr. 1945), pp. 99–118.

179 US Department of State, The JUST Act Report: Greece: Emergency Law 846/1946 on Heirless Jewish Property, accessed at https://www.state.gov/reports/just-act-report-to-congress/greece/#:~:text=Emergency%20Law%20846%2F1946%20on,no%20heirs%20to%20claim%20it.

180 Fortunoff Archive, Mathilde Cohen Interview, seg. 26, 30. Matilde b. 1927 had been liberated from Bergen-Belsen. A sister, Caden, emigrated to the Belgian Congo before the Racial Laws. The rest of the family (parents and three siblings) perished in the Holocaust, Benatar and Benatar, *Si je t'oublie*, p. 198. See also her entry in CDEC, http://digital-library.cdec.it/cdec-web/audiovideo/detail/IT-CDEC-AV0001-000013/matilde-cohen.html.

181 Fortunoff Archive, Tarica Interview, seg. 30.

182 See his entry in the register in Liliana Picciotto, *Il libro della memoria. Gli Ebrei deportati dall'Italia (1943–1945)* (Mursia: Milano, 1991), pp. 66–71, 77–80.

183 Galante, *Histoire de Juifs*, p. 310. Benatar and Benatar, *Si je t'oublie*, p. 495, gives her date of birth as 1914, possibly either a mis-transcription from the Racial census card: or the entry on her Kaufering concentration camp registration card is wrong. ITS Digital Archive. Arolsen Archives 01010602 131.142 Document I.D. 10201082 (FORTUNEE MENASCHE).

184 In a post-war group photograph taken in Rhodes, Fortunée has her hand on Da Fano's shoulder, and she is described as 'Mrs. Menashe Dafano'. The dating of the image (August 1945) is wrong, however. Da Fano only arrived in Italy in September 1945. It is possible that the actual dating is from 1947 when the first survivors from the camps appeared in Rhodes. It is likely that this group were the first returnees, since they were also among the survivors listed in Italy in the autumn of 1945. They are pictured with the president of the community, Maurice Soriano. The photograph is reproduced in The Rhodes Jewish Historical Foundation (California), Rhodesli Jewish Calendar September 2018/September 2019 – Elul 5778/Tishri 5780, compiled by Aron Hasson.

185 http://digital-library.cdec.it/cdec-web/persone/detail/person-2338/da-fano-achille.html. Benatar and Benatar, *Si je t'oublie*, p. 231.

186 See for instance the reference to repatriating Italians on the SS *Princess Catherine*, 26 June 1946, in UNRRA S-1345-0000-0117-00001.PDF, Displaced Persons, frame 42, Copy, Memorandum for Col. Batterby; Ibid, frames 86–93: Internal Memorandum to Chief of Mission from Asst. Chief Welfare Officer, DPs-Refugees, Ref. 5.19.0/3, 16 August 1946, Repatriation of Italians (Copy), August 1945–August 1946: 1,472; of this number 125 were classified as undesirables and 679 as government officials. This memorandum also includes a brief history of the deported Jewish community based on information received from Salomon Alhadeff (Egypt).

187 ITS Digital Archive. Arolson Archives, CM/1 files from Italy A-Z Reference Code 03020102 oS: Reference Code: 03020102-009.035. The following is based on this file unless otherwise stated.

188 Ibid, IRO Questionnaire, March 1950. Initially, the supervising officer Streeter, deemed her ineligible for resettlement, but this decision was overturned on appeal three months later in March 1950. Record of Interview CM/4, 3 April 1951. The file ends here.

189 See https://en.wikipedia.org/wiki/List_of_converts_to_Christianity_from_Judaism.

190 WJC Inter-Governmental Committee on Refugees, Headquarters Allied Commission Rome, AJDC Rome to American Joint Distribution Committee Lisbon, Naples, Athens: Dodecanese Islands, 22 April 1945. Her father and sister also were spared deportation. They had lived in the Sinagoga Grande No. 29, Benatar and Benatar, *Si je t'oublie*, p. 397. For Amato, see ibid, p. 77.

191 Bad Arolsen, Digital copy: Doc. No. 78779949#1 (3.1.1.3/0001-0197/0045/0177) in conformity with the ITS Archives, 11.07.2013, Archivnummer: 4186 'Turkish Jews forced to leave Rhodes 1945'.

192 World Jewish Congress Records, MS-361, Box 195, Folder 14. American Jewish Archives, Cincinnati, Ohio, for exchange of letters on this issue from early 1960s between Nehemiah Robinson (WJC) and law firm Simon S. Nessim, New York. Further cases in World Jewish Congress Records, Mss-361 Box C265, Folder 5 (Greece restitution correspondence, 1944–1946).

193 The total number of survivors in Greece was itself barely one-tenth of its pre-invasion total. Richard Clogg, 'Introduction', in Bowman, 'Jews', in Clogg (ed.), *Minorities in Greece*, p. xiv.

194 National Statistical Service of Greece, Population Census 1951, 7 April (Athens, 1958), pp. 240–241, 248–249. Roderick Beaton, *Greece: Biography of a Modern Nation* pbk. edition (Penguin Books: Harmondsworth, 2020 [orig. 2019]), p. 302.

Chapter 9

1   Mary Henderson, *Xenia – A Memoir. Greece 1919–1949* (Weidenfeld and MacMillan: London, 1988), p. xv.

2   http://collections.ushmm.org: RG Number: RG-50.233.0001 Interview Miru Alcana, Interviewer Kenneth Fleisch, 30 August 1992, Transcript, p. 16, 'Some they went to South Africa and some they went to Congo Belgium, some they went to United States and some they stay in Milan. Some they went to Buenos Airs [*sic*] but we are in touch with everyone and some they are in Israel.'

3   Laura Varon, Interview 26814, seg. 13. Visual History Archives. USC Shoah Foundation. Interviewed 1997, interviewer Felicia Fowler. See also Yad Vashem Archives, Interview 03/10423 Laura Varon, transcript p. 39. For Jack Hasson, Interview 7687, seg. 4. Visual History Archives. USC Shoah Foundation.

4   Tarica-Israël, *Des ténèbres au soleil*, pp. 85, 107, 111.

5   Israël, *Je ne vous ai pas oubliés*, p. 124.

6   Pothiti Hantzaroula, *Child Survivors of the Holocaust in Greece. Memory, Testimony and Subjectivity* (Routledge: London and New York, 2021), p. 145.

7   Lawrence L. Langer, *Holocaust Testimonies: The Ruins of Memory* (Yale University Press: New Haven, CO, 1991).

8   Henderson, *Xenia*, p. xv.

9   Franco Hasson, *Il Était Une Fois*, p. 79. For further evidence, *Die Verfolgung und Ermordung der europäischen Juden durch das nationalsozialistische Deutschland, 1933–1945: Band 16: Das KZ Auschwitz 1942–1945 und die Zeit der Todesmärsche 1944/45*, compiled by Andrea Rudorff (De Gruyter: Oldenbourg, Berlin and Boston, 2018), Einleitung, pp. 75–76, and Dok. 201. The sixteen-volume series is currently being translated into English.

10 Henderson, *Xenia*, p. xv.

11 Stella Levi, Interview 1701, seg. 19. Visual History Archives. USC Shoah Foundation. Stella never witnessed this, but her account is based on hearsay and rumours circulating after the war.

12 *The Longest Journey*, 34:51 min.

13 Other than the Italian Race Laws and the German Occupation as pre-history to the deportation, the event that has received common attention is the shipwreck of the *Pentcho* and less so the arrival of the refugee ship *Rim*.

14 Berman, *Odyssey*, p. 216. Burger held the rank of SS-Captain. The author's description is based on Sidney Fahn's testimony in Yad Vashem Archives 03/2680.

15 Alcana Interview 129, seg. 18. Varon, Interview 26814, seg. 11.

16   Ibid, seg. 14. Hasson, Interview 7687, seg. 6.

17   Yad Vashem Archives 03/10423, Interview Varon, pp. 27, 46 (Grese) and pp. 31–32 (Anne Frank).

18   Esther Fintz Menascé, *Buio Nell'Isola del Sole: Rodi 1943–1945 I due volti di una tragedia quasi di metenticato: il martiro dell'ammarigalio Campioni* (Giuntina: Firenze, 2005).

19   Among these are the references to encountering the notorious camp doctor Joseph Mengele at the ramp at Auschwitz, or the belief that Kurt Waldheim (the later president of Austria) personally oversaw the deportation from Rhodes.

20   This phenomenon is discussed in Milena Callegari Cosentino, 'Remembering Rhodes and the Holocaust: Intergenerational Trauma, Nostalgia and Identity' (PhD Thesis, University of Limerick, 2021). The thesis is currently being prepared for publication with Vallentine Mitchell, London.

21   Our interest in this chapter is not to negate or privilege one approach in preference for the other, but to show how memory and archive can complement each other.

22   https://www.cdec.it/ricerca-storica-e-progetti/aree-di-ricerca/la-deportazione-degli-ebrei-dallitalia/

23   Rüdiger Fleiter: 'Die Ludwigsburger Zentrale Stelle – eine Strafverfolgungsbehörde als Legitimationsinstrument? Gründung und Zuständigkeit 1958 bis 1965', *Kritische Justiz*, Vol. 35, Jg., (2002), pp. 253–272. Annette Weinke, *Eine Gesellschaft ermittelt gegen sich selbst: Die Geschichte der Zentralen Stelle in Ludwigsburg 1958–2008* (Wissenschaftliche Buchgesellschaft: Darmstadt, 2008).

24   StABr 4,89/3-863 Beweismittel, Band 1: Eichmann Dokumente.

25   Merten returned to Greece on vacation in 1957(!) and was recognized, arrested and subsequently tried and sentenced to twenty-five years in prison for his part in the persecution of Greek Jews. He was released after only thirty months in prison thanks to the intervention of German chancellor Konrad Adenauer. Susanne-Sophia Spiliotis, 'Der Fall Merten und die deutsch-griechische "Aufarbeitung" der Besatzungsherrschaft in Griechenland während des Zweiten Weltkrieges', in Karl Giebeler (ed.), *Versöhnung ohne Wahrheit? Deutsche Kriegsverbrechen in Griechenland im Zweiten Weltkrieg* (Biblipolis: Mannheim, 2001), pp. 68–77. Wisliceny was tried in Bratislava (where he had been active during the war) in February 1948, sentenced to death and executed on 4 May 1948. The focus of his trial was not so much the murder of Jews, as that of partisans and the civilian population per se.

26 NARA RG 238 M1019 Roll 35 Office of US Chief of Counsel for War Crimes APO 696-A Evidence Division Interrogation Branch, 17 June 1947. The transcript of the 45-minute interrogation is worthy of a separate study but cannot be pursued here, other than to say, Rapp was pursuing Kleemann on a faulty piece of evidence provided by Erwin Lenz, a former member of the Penal Battalion 999.

27 BA-Ludwigsburg B162/19595, fol 1, Bl. 1–19, copies of investigating prosecutors, 16 March 1960. In the following decade, the focus turned more broadly to the Athens office of the security police and Gestapo (including the Secret Field Police). It was only during these investigations that in 1963 the names of Anton Burger and Friedrich Linnemann, the two SS officers who carried out the deportation, came to light, as well as the role of the military police in Rhodes and Kos. The story of this investigation is worthy of a study in itself. The book on Burger by the journalist Müller-Turpath only scratches the surface of the rich seam of evidence.

28 BA-Ludwigsburg B162/1513, Bl. 9, Staatsanwalt Dr Zeug to Major Dr Eytan Otto Liff, Tel Aviv, 8 November 1963. See further correspondence among others, with Lt.Col. Dr Eytan Otto Liff, Leiter der Untersuchungsstelle für NS-Gewaltverbrechen, BA-Ludwigsburg B162/1515, Der Leitende Oberstaatsanwalt be dem Landgericht -10-Js 156/1964 Bremen, 18 January 1965, Bl. 634. See also StABr 4,89/3-883, various correspondence.

29 BA-Ludwigsburg B162/1514, Bl. 307 correspondence and Bl. 250–251, 309–391 Zeug to Daniel Turiel, New York, and to Sephardi Hebrew Organization of Rhodesia, Zeug requesting help with tracing survivors, 1964. StABr 4,89/3-883.

30 Hantzaroula, *Child Survivors*, p. 144. On the inability (reluctance) of post-war Germans to confront what they had inflicted upon their victims: see the famous work by German psychoanalysts Alexander Mitscherlich and Margarete Mitscherlich, *Die Unfähigkeit zu trauern: Grundlagen kollektiven Verhaltens* (Piper Taschenbuch: Munich, 1977 [orig. 1967]) trans. Beverly R. Placzek *The Inability to Mourn: Principles of Collective Behavior* (Grove Press Inc.: New York, 1984).

31 Varon, Interview 26814, seg. 29.

32 Stella De Leon né Hasson, Interview 12055, seg. 31–33. Visual History Archive. USC Shoah Foundation. Interviewed 1996, interviewer Janice Engelbart. See also the transcript of her interview in University Archives and Manuscripts

Division, University of Washington, Seattle, Washington Digital Archives, Hasson_ohc_11.pdf.

33 Stella Hasson, née Nachmias, Interview 1468. Visual History Archives. USC Shoah Foundation. Interviewed 1995, interviewer Yitzhak Kerem. Stella ends the interview abruptly with the words: 'I Think it's enough.'

34 Diana E. Greenway, 'Dates in History: Chronology and Memory', *Historical Research*, Vol. LXXII, No. 178 (June 1999), pp. 127–139, here: p. 139.

35 Clara Soriano née Avzaradel, Interview 8852, seg. 11.

36 Greenway, 'Dates in History', p. 138.

37 Yad Vashem Archives, Interview 03/10423, Laura Varon, transcript, p. 32.

38 An example is that of Clara Avzaradel Soriano's 'blink of an eye' mentioned above.

39 Notable among the many spurs to this change must be the powerful and probing documentary produced by Claus Lanzmann, *Shoah* (1985) and Steven Spielberg's box office film, *Schindler's List* (1994). The earlier controversial American TV mini-series *Holocaust* (1978), written by Gerald Green and telling the story of the Weiss family of Berlin, also signalled a turning point and is one of the earliest examples of portraying the Holocaust from the perspective and experience of the Jews, as too is the East German DEFA film *Jakob der Lügner* (Jacob the Liar) 1974, directed by Frank Beyer and based on the best-selling novel of the same name by Jurek Becker, a survivor of the Łódź ghetto and published in 1964.

40 Imre Kertész, *The Holocaust as Culture*, English trans. Thomas Cooper (Seagull Books: London, 2011), p. 590. And in a similar vein, Langer, *Holocaust Testimonies*.

41 Yad Vashem Archives, Interview 03/8591, Rebecca Capelluto Franco, transcript, p. 4. Rebecca was deported from Kos.

42 Clara Soriano, Interview 8852, VHA Shoah Foundation, 1 February 1996, seg. 13, 15. Clara was born in 1926. As we saw in Chapter 6, her younger sister Renée was killed in Auschwitz. Her father was the butcher Baruch/Behor Avzaradel mentioned in Chapter 3, and who, together with her mother Esther Russo, 'disappeared' on disembarkation at Auschwitz (Chapter 5).

43 Franco Hasson, *Il Était Une Fois*, p. 78.

44 Langer, *Holocaust Testimonies*, p. 15. Langer's conclusions are not that far removed from those observed by the psychologist David P. Boder in his 1946 interviews of Holocaust survivors. For Boder 'traumatic experience cannot be fully known or assimilated but rather belatedly invades the victim's life by means

of flashbacks and nightmares'. Alan Rosen, *The Wonder of Their Voices: The 1946 Holocaust Interviews of David Boder* (Oxford University Press: Oxford, 2010), p. 198. In this case, there is no natural coherence to memory but it is imposed through the creation of narrative.

45 The original concept 'the non-simultaneity of the simultaneous' dates from the mid-1920s but was applied by Bloch in his famous analysis of Nazism as irrational revolt against the Enlightenment. Ernst Bloch, *Heritage of our Times*, trans. Neville Plaice and Stephen Plaice (Polity Press: Cambridge, 1991).

46 Amato, Lucia Sciarcon, Interview 14687. Visual History Archive. Shoah Foundation 1996. Rebecca Ziman is second generation Rhodesli diaspora, her father was survivor Giuseppe Coné.

47 *Longest Journey*, 12:00 min.

48 Zoë Vania Waxman, *Writing the Holocaust: Identity, Testimony, Representation* (Oxford University Press: Oxford, 2006), chs. 3 and 5 in particular.

49 RG-50.233.0001, Alcana, Interview transcript, p. 16. Stella Levi also spoke of going through a difficult period settling down to a new life, Visual History Archives. Interview 1701, seg. 99/100.

50 http://collections.ushmm.org, RG-50.233.0001, Alcana, Interview transcript, p. 16.

51 The full quote is in Chapter 2. '"It Was Paradise: Jewish Rhodes". Conversation with Prof. Richard Freund', in *Connecticut Jewish Ledger*, accessed at www.jewishledger.com/2015/09/it-was-paradise-jewish-rhodes-conversation-with-prof-richard-freund/.

52 An early essay on the difficulty of finding words after the Holocaust, Saul Friedländer, *Probing the Limits of Representation: Nazism and the Final Solution* (Harvard University Press: Cambridge, MA, 1992).

53 http://collections.ushmm.org, Garzolini, Lucia Franco RG-50.030*0452, interview 4 June 1997, tape 3, side B, transcript p. 19.

54 'Quand mes camarades me questionnent sur le chiffre tatoué sur mon bras, ils ne croient rien de mes récits. Je passe pour une menteuse, qui tente d'attirer l'attention en racontant des histoires. Alors, je decide de ne plus en parler.' Tarica-Israël, *Des ténèbres au soleil*, pp. 82–83. Alice recounted this episode in the present tense, for the purpose of narrative style, I have rendered it into the past tense.

55 Ibid.

56 Levi, Interview 1701, seg. 60, 109.

57 Frank, *One Hundred Saturdays*, p. 207.

58 South African Holcoaust and Genocide Foundation Cape Town, Interviewed by Michele Greek and Dalya Goldberg, 15.09.1987, transcript, p. 12. See also Stella Levi, Interview 1701, seg. 99–100, on difficulty of adjusting to post-Holocaust life.

59 Laura Jockusch (ed.), *Collect and Record! Jewish Holocaust Documentation in Early Postwar Europe* (Oxford University Press: Oxford and New York, 2012), pp. 191–192. For a compelling case of the 'past in hiding', see Mark Roseman, *The Past in Hiding. Memory and Survival in Nazi Germany* (Allen Lane, The Penguin Press: Harmondsworth, 2000).

60 Cipolato, Virginia Gattegno, Interview 44692. Visual History Archive. Shoah Foundation 1998.

61 Virginia Gattegno, 'I survived due to will and instinct', interviewed by Hannah Roberts, *Financial Times Weekend*, 28/29 May 2016.

62 Jockusch (ed.), *Collect and Record!*, p. 187. An example of imposing chronological order on 'scattered' memories, see the interview of Matilde Levy né Cohen, Yad Vashem Archives 033c/3606, interviewed by Jacqueline Benatar 10 October 1988. Transcript p. 2.

63 Yad Vashem Archives Interview 03/4318, Clara Menascé, 19 October 1984, transcript, p. 1.

64 Franco Hasson, *Il Était Une Fois*, p. 42. Elisa Franco, Interview Fortunoff Archive, seg 3.

65 Surmani, Interview 53625, seg. 40.

66 Esther Fintz Menascé, *A History of Jewish Rhodes* (Rhodes Jewish Historical Foundation: California, 2014), pp. 11–18, states Rhodes derives its name from the ancient Greek ρόδον.

67 Anthony McElligott, 'Reflections on the *Juderia*: Remembering, Memory-making and History: Re-imagining Jewish Rhodes', in Valerie McGuire and Aron Rodrigue (eds.), *Italian Fascism in Rhodes and Dodecanese, 1923–1945* (Routledge: New York, London, 2024).

68 Greenway, 'Dates in History', p. 130.

69 Andreas Guidi, *Generations of Empire. Youth from Ottoman to Italian Rule in the Mediterranean* (University of Toronto Press: Toronto, Buffalo, London, 2022), p. 196.

70 Isräel, *Je ne vous ai pas oubliés*, pp. 26, 45, 54–55.

71 Ibid, p. 49 (arrest and murder of Italian officers by Germans), 64 (baby thrown into furnace in Auschwitz), p. 78 (the killing of Rhodian compatriot 'H' found hiding in the toilets in *Charlottengrube*), p. 107 the account of the liberation of Ebensee – where he was in 1945, but in fact is based on the French communist

resister, Jean Lafitte's memoir, *Ceux qui vivent* (Éditions Hier et Aujourd'hui, 1947). The memoir was re-issued in 1970 by Livre club Diderot, 1970. Alberto quotes from the later edition.

72 Franco Hasson, *Il Était Une Fois*, p. 115.

73 A particularly good example of a journey of discovery is provided in Hannah Pressman, "'I'd like to Become a Bird": My great-great-grandmother's letters – in Ladino – paint a portrait of the Sephardic community on the Isle of Rhodes, moments before it was destroyed in the Holocaust', in *The Tablet*, 21 August 2017, https://tabletmag.com/jewish-life-and-religion/242352/ladino-letters-from-rhodes. On this theme, see Sintès, *Chasing the Past*, *passim*.

74 https://www.timesofisrael.com/rhodeslis-make-annual-island-pilgrimage-to-remember-and-reboot/.

75 Menascé, YVA Interview 03/4318, transcript, p. 10.

76 Stella Levi, *Longest Journey*, 46:41–47:15 min. See also Chapter 8 for the full quote.

77 Zumwalt, 'Stories, Food, and Place'.

78 Both Harry and his wife, R., gave their place of birth as Italy, meaning Rhodes and Kos. They had three children, Rashell the oldest was 11 years old at the time of the 1940 US Census and had been born in Oregon, indicating the Benvenistes had immigrated already in the 1920s. Arthur aged 6 and a younger sister, Jeannette aged 4, were both born in California. At the time of the census, the family were living in their own house in Los Angeles, where Harry worked as a leather goods salesman – a typical occupation for Rhodesli Jewish men. 1940 United States Federal Census, California, Los Angeles, 60-572. Copy of their entry can be found here: https://www.ancestry.com/imageviewer/collections/2442/images/m-t0627-00424-00216?ssrc=&backlabel=Return&pId=74057427. On the Haggadah, Marc D. Angel, *The Rhythms of Jewish Living: A Sephardic Exploration of Judaism's Spirituality* (Jewish Lights Publishing; Woodstock, Vermont, 2015), pp. 33–35, p. 34.

79 https://www.rhodesjewishmuseum.org/museum/establishment-of-the-museum/.

80 On the distinction between spoken Ladino and written Solitreo, D.M. Bunis, 'Soletreo: Writing the Ladino Script with Prof. David Bunis' (University of Washington: Seattle, WA, 2015), https://jewishstudies.washington.edu/sephardic-studies/how-to-write-soletreo-ladino-alphabet-with-david-bunis/. Carlos Yebra López, 'A Simplified Guide to Reading and Writing Ladino in Rashi and Solitreo', in *Ladinar Estudios sobre la literatura, la música y la historia de los sefardíes* Vol. XIII (2023), pp. vii–xxvi.

81 Further maps can be found at https://www.rhodesjewishmuseum.org/juderia/

82 Pierre Sintès, 'Providing a Context: Remembering Jews of the Mediterranean', paper read at Testimony, memory, and history: Remembering Jewish Rhodes. Rhodes Workshop, 19 July 2023. A fuller and astute discussion can be found in idem, *Chasing the Past: Geopolitics of Memory on the Margins of Modern Greece*, trans. Jenny Money, Samantha Eddiso and Caroline Stephens (Liverpool University Press, Provence University Press, 2019), pp. 87–134.

83 Ibid. For Jewish space in an Islamic context: Emily Gottreich, 'Rethinking the "Islamic City" from the Perspective of Jewish Space', *Jewish Social Studies*, Vol. 11, No. 1 (Autumn 2004), pp. 118–146.

84 The renaming of place names itself was part of the Italianization campaign, combining references to the (Roman-Genoa-Knights) past and the Italian present as a Fascist and imperial project.

85 Hannah Pressman, 'I'd like to become a Bird', *The Tablet Magazine*, 21 August 2017, accessed at https://www.tabletmag.com/sections/community/articles/ladino-letters-from-rhodes.

86 Rhodes Jewish Calendar September 2016–September 2017, August 2017 facing page; Rhodes Jewish Calendar September 2021–September 2022, February 2022 facing page; Rhodes Jewish Calendar September 2022–September 2023, August 2023 facing page.

87 Yad Vashem Archives (YVA) YVA/O.75/7130. See also the carnet of postcards sent by (?) Alhadeff to his brother as a momento of the 'land of his birth', Rhodes Jewish Calendar September 2022–September 2023, November 2022 facing page.

88 Arolsen Archives. There are few references to place/street-names in the popular version.

89 Dimosthenes was formerly named Via Gran Maestro de Gozone Deodato and Perikleous was Via Sigismondo Malatesta.

90 Benedict Anderson, *Imagined Communities: Reflections on the Origin and Spread of Nationalism* (Verso: London, 1983).

91 Sami Modiano, *The Longest Journey*, 44:00 min. Of course, being born Jewish is not a crime, but murdering Jews is.

92 Esther Fintz Menascé, *A History of Jewish Rhodes* (Rhodes Jewish Historical Foundation; Los Angeles, CA, 2014), ch. 5 passim.

93 As well as Zumwalt, 'Stories, Food, and Place' as n. 77, see the insightful account by Hannah Pressman, 'My Sephardic Inheritance: a Spoonful of Salt, a Spoonful of Sugar', in *The Tablet*, February 2017 (online), and here: https://hannahpressman.com/selected-writing/

94 As well as Pressman (n. 73), see the collection of letters in Flash, *A Hug from Afar* Stella Hasson, *Du Paradis à l'Enfer* (Clepsydre: Nivelles, 2007) and Tony Alhadeff, *The Family Treasure* (n.p., 2020) use family interviews as well as ego-documents.

95 Sintès, *Chasing the Past*, pp. 94–101. On the subject of trauma and nostalgia and their intergenerational transmission, Cosentino, 'Remembering Rhodes and the Holocaust', as n. 20.

96 Commencing with Hizkia Franco, *The Jewish Martyrs of Rhodes and Cos* (Harper Collins: Harare, Zimbabwe, 1994, a report originally written in 1947 in French and trans. by his son and republished). An exception is the Sephardi scholar Avraham Galante, *Appendice a l'histoire des Juifs de Rhodes* (Editions Isis: Istanbul 1948).

97 Email communication Henry F., 12 July 2022.

98 Ibid. On how memory can alter as a consequence of changing knowledge, see the review by Hannah Pressman of a lecture by Professor Aron Rodrigue, 'Sephardim, Memory, and the Holocaust', accessed at https://jewishstudies.washington.edu/blog/Sephardic-holocaust-memory-rhodes-jewish-community/.

99 www.rhodesjewishmuseum.org/history/holocaust#comment-34403-Holocaust, comment left 2 April 2015. I have corrected typographical errors in the original blog.

100 In all, the family and its extended members totalled fifty-seven adults and children.

101 1941 Italian Household Census, entry for Alcana, Celebi. This is from a digital copy made available to me by Professor Renée Hirschon. Professor Hirschon has since donated her research materials to Yad Vashem Archives Record Group 0.77 File 539.

102 S-1098-0004-08-00008 Turkish Consul.pdf. For Ülkümen see the recent biography, Yücel Güçlü, *Selahattin Ülkümen, the Turkish Righteous among the Nations* (Cambridge Scholars: Newcastle Upon Tyne, 2022).

103 Pierre Nora (ed.), *Les Lieux de mémoire* 3 vols. (Gallimard: Paris, 1997).

Epilogue

1 YVA 031/144, Letter ΑΡΙΘ ΠΡΡΩΤ. 126, 18 May 1978, Maurice Soriano to Yad Vashem.

2   This situation only began to change with the appointment of a new head archivist in 2010. The regional government of Rhodes and the Ministry of Education and Culture in Athens have for decades failed to provide either adequate funds to maintain the collections, or a proper purpose-built environment for the archive. The files are mostly in a state of decay despite the efforts by the head archivist to protect them. This neglect by the authorities is neither recent nor exclusive to Rhodes. Mazower, *Inside Hitler's Greece*.

3   Benatar and Benatar, *Si je t'oublie*, pp. 227, 280.

4   Racial Census #8.

5   Aron Hasson, *Jewish Life in Rhodes: Family Portraits. A Photographic Collection of the Jews of Rhodes 1880s–1940s* (The Rhodes Jewish Historical Foundation: Los Angeles, CA, 2022). The Jewish Museum of Greece, Athens, also has a vast photographic archive covering mainland Greece, but also the islands.

6   See for example CDEC Giuseppe Mallel portrait image with its inscription of 'the two brothers' Achille Da Fano. The dedication 'the two brothers' possibly refers to their common experience through the camps, and if it does, is suggestive of their mutual support in order to survive. https://digital-library.cdec.it/cdec-web/persone/detail/person-5646/mallel-giuseppe.html

7   By the date of the deportation, Signura is described as a widow, https://digital-library.cdec.it/cdec-web/persone/detail/person-400/benveniste-signora.html

8   Christopher R. Browning, *Collected Memories: Holocaust History and Post-War Testimony* (University of Wisconsin Press: Madison, WI, 2003).

9   Carlo Ginzburg, 'Microhistory: Two or Three Things That I Know about It', *Critical Inquiry*, Vol. 20, No. 1 (Autumn 1993), pp. 10–35.

Primary Sources

Genika Archia Tou Kratous/
Archia Dodekanisou Rhodos (GAKR I.Δ.Δ.)

A: Governo delle isole Italiane dell'Egeo

GAKR I.Δ.Δ. ΕΤΟΣ 1937/38 ΦΑΚ 9 Movimento Collegio Rabbinico di Rodi
GAKR I.Δ.Δ. ΕΤΟΣ 1944 ΦΑΚ19 Salomon Alhadeff & Fils
GAKR I.Δ.Δ. ΕΤΟΣ 1939 ΦΑΚ 534
GAKR I.Δ.Δ. ΕΤΟΣ 1938 827, ΦΑΚ 225
GAKR I.Δ.Δ. ΦΑΚ 293 ΤΜΗΝΑ1/1
GAKR I.Δ.Δ. ΕΤΟΣ 1931 ΦΑΚ 1036 Π Censimento Della Populazione (1922)
GAKR I.Δ.Δ. ΦΑΚ 293 Elenco degli Ebrei Deportati dai Tedeschi il 16.7.1944
GAKR I.Δ.Δ. ΕΤΟΣ 1944 ΦΑΚ 17/2
GAKR I.Δ.Δ. ΕΤΟΣ 1944 ΦΑΚ 19
GAKR I.Δ.Δ. ΕΤΟΣ 1944/45, ΦΑΚ 18 ΤΜΗΝΑ 1/L/112
GAKR I.Δ.Δ. ΦΑΚ 53
GAKR I.Δ.Δ. ΕΤΟΣ 1943 ΦΑΚ 162/1
GAKR I.Δ.Δ. ΕΤΟΣ 1944 ΦΑΚ 195
GAKR I.Δ.Δ. ΕΤΟΣ 1943 ΦΑΚ 397
GAKR I.Δ.Δ. ΕΤΟΣ 1939 ΦΑΚ 534 ΤΜΗΝΑ 1
GAKR I.Δ.Δ. ΕΤΟΣ 1944 ΦΑΚ 778
GAKR BOX 056_0001-0040_DR_0001, Strumza Vitalis, Fascicolo 1

B: Carabinieri Reale – Ufficio Centrale di Pubblica Sicurezza

GAKR Carabinieri P.S. 2.20.1271 (Fascicolo Nos. 1–6), Comunita Israelitica di Rodi
GAKR Carabinieri P.S. 2.19/123 Benatar Alessandro di Nissim
GAKR Carabinieri P.S. 1.47.1049 Hugno Nissim di Giuseppe
GAKR Carabinieri P.S. 1.47.1054 Giacomo Alhadeff
GAKR Carabinieri P.S. 6.346
GAKR Carabinieri P.S. 6.390 Modiano, Mosé fu Saul
GAKR Carabinieri P.S. 15.53 Modiano, Mosé fu Saul verso il Governo

GAKR Carabinieri P.S. 2.40.37 Amato Sadih di Abramo

GAKR Carabinieri P.S. 27.57.1 A., Bazzalel

GAKR Carabinieri P.S. 1.52.8 H., Hannoch [*sic*]

GAKR Carabinieri P.S. 2.40.38 Canan [*sic*] Abner di Moreno

GAKR Carabinieri P.S. 1.2.229 Levi, Elia di Isaaco

GAKR Carabinieri P.S. 6.27 Alcana, Giuseppe, di Abramo

GAKR Carabinieri P.S. 1.47.1077 Alcana Chaco [*sic*] di Celebi

GAKR Carabinieri P.S. 1.2.837 Israele, Mose di Solomone

GAKR Carabinieri P.S. 1.27.25 H., Israel

GAKR Carabinieri P.S. 11.68 L., Stella fu Giuda

GAKR Carabinieri P.S. 11.71 Violetta B., fu Abramo

GAKR Carabinieri P.S. 1.55.16 Ester C.

GAKR Carabinieri P.S. 1.47.10 Moise R.

GAKR Carabinieri P.S. 1.1.1042 I/1, Da Fano, Achille

GAKR Carabinieri P.S. 2.11.1987 Merolle, Rino di Luigi

GAKR Carabinieri P.S. 1.1.160 Politica Razsista

GAKR Carabinieri P.S. 6.110

GAKR Carabinieri P.S. 1.2.117 Mittino, Ferdinand

GAKR Carabinieri P.S. 6.27 Alcana, Giuseppe, di Abramo

GAKR Carabinieri P.S. 6.75 Alhanan, Celibe fu Natan

GAKR Carabinieri P.S. 2.40.84 Angel, Samuele

GAKR Carabinieri P.S. 1.2.888 Avzaradel, Behor Baruh fu Isaco [*sic*]

GAKR Carabinieri P.S. 2.40.0123

GAKR Carabinieri P.S. 1.1.264 Tarica, Nissim

GAKR Ufficio Centrale Speciale (Carabinieri) 5755 Fascicolo di Angel, Gioia

GAKR Carabinieri P.S. 2.40.10

GAKR Carabinieri P.S. 2/40/38 Canan (Hanan) Abner di Moreno

GAKR Carabinieri P.S. 1.47.1025 Coen, Sipora [*sic*] fu Mose

GAKR Carabinieri P.S. 1.1.136 Strumza, Vitalis

Bundesarchiv Berlin-Lichterfelde (BarchB)

NS4-MA/57 (Mauthausen)

NS7/ SS-und Polizeigerichtsbarkeit

/85 Besprechung

/98-1-3 Strafrechtliche Behandlung italienischer Freiwillige

/99-1 Gerichtsbarkeit

NS19/ Perönlicher Stab Reichsführer SS

/240

/370 Der Reichsführer

/1570

/1577

/1644

/1806 RFSS

/1951 Italien (1942)

/1972 Himmler/Ribbentrop

/2121 Auslandsamt (AA)

/2289

/2410 Himmler

/2967 Schimana

/3911 RFSS

NS34 SS-Personalhauptamt

/31 Beförderungen

/82 Lebensläufe Höherer SS-Führer

Parteikanzlei (formerly Berlin Document Center, PK) VBS1 PK/Parteikorrespondenz

DO238 Günther

H0161 Linnemann

G0186 Korherr

RS A5385

RS B0158

R19/ Chef der Ordnungspolizei

/135 BdO Griechenland

/322 Bd 3

/333 Befehlshaber Ordnungspolizei

/370 Chef der Ordnungspolizei

R34/12 Führer beim Stab SS-Personalhauptamt

R34/82 Lebensläufe Höhere SS-Führer

R43/ Stab Rosenberg

/386

/844 (Judenfrage Italien)

/898

RH48/2 Geheime Feldpolizei, Stammtafeln (1941)

R58/ Reichssicherheitshauptamt
/296
/528
/1124
Pers.6/223, Heeresleitung Personalamt. Personalakten f. Kleemann, Ulrich (BA-MA, Gs-Bestand Nr 6 Archiv Nr 223 Koblenz 'B', Nr 305, 21994 (BDC))

R70 Griechenland
/I Durchgangslager Chaidari
/II Griechenland
/III Der Befehlshaber der Sicherheitspolizei und des SD für Griechenland

SSO SS-Führerpersonalakten der SS-Führer
SSO-07B
SSO-122 (Anton Burger)
SSO-180B
SSO-201A (Richard Korherr)
SSO-001c Personalakten der Rasse- und Siedlungshauptamtes-SS (Dieter Wisliceny, Anton Burger)

Bundesarchiv-Militärarchiv Freiburg Im Breisgau (BA-MA)

RH26/1007/-Kommandant Ost-Aegaeis/KTB Sturnmdivision Rhodos
/1
/2
/3
/4
/5
/6
/7
/8
/9
/10
/11
/12
/13
/14

/15
/16
/17
/18
/19
/20
/21
/22
/23
/24
/25
/26
/27
/28
/29
/30
/31
/32
/33
/34

Bundesarchiv-Außenstelle Ludwigsburg Zentrale Stelle Der Landesjustizverwaltungen Zur Aufklärung Nationalsozialistischer Gewaltverbrechen Ludwigsburg (BA-Ludwigsburg)

B162/1512
B162/1513
B162/1514 (Unbekannt, Rhodos)
B162/1515 Friedrich Linnemann
B162/1516 Friedrich Linnemann
B162/1517 Friedrich Linnemann u.a.
B162/19595 fol. 1 Kleemann

Staatsarchiv Bremen (StABr)

Staatsanwaltschaft Bremen Ermittlungsverfahren 4,89/3-

841 Ermittlungsverfahren gegen Dr Walter Blume, u.a. (Friedrich Linnemann, Anton Burger)

842 Ermittlungsverfahren gegen Dr Walter Blume, u.a. (Friedrich Linnemann, Anton Burger)

844 Ermittlungsverfahren gegen Dr Walter Blume, u.a. (Friedrich Linnemann, Anton Burger)

845 Ermittlungsverfahren gegen Dr Walter Blume, u.a. (Friedrich Linnemann, Anton Burger)

846 Augenzeugen (witnesses)

858 Augenzeugen (witnesses)

860 Augenzeugen (witnesses)

861 Augenzeugen (witnesses)

862 Ermittlungsverfahren Linnemann

863 Beweismittel (evidence)

864 Beweismittel (evidence)

865 Fischer/Radomski

869 Fischer/Radomski

871 Fischer/Radomski

876 Kartei Feldgendarmerie Trupp A B (Mot) 999

881 Ermittlingsverfahren Burger

882 Ermittlingsverfahren Burger

883 Ermittlingsverfahren Linnemann

884 Ermittlingsverfahren Linnemann

885 Ermittlingsverfahren Linnemann

886 Ermittlingsverfahren Linnemann

966 Ermittlingsverfahren Linnemann

Landesarchiv Berlin (LAB)

B Rep 057-01/731 Anton Burger
B Rep 057-01/1172 Rolf Günther

The National Archives Kew, London (TNA)

AIR 23/899 1943
AIR 29/469
AIR41/53 Dodecanese 1943
AIR51/288/285 1944
DO35/1168 Correspondence Rhodesia 1945

Foreign Office FO/
/195/2486/573 British Embassy Angora
/195/2479 Dodecanese, 1943
/195/2486 Political reports Dodecanese 1944
/208/4645
/286/703 Minorities Dodecanese
/286/850 Dodecanese
/286/927 Nationality Issues, 1925
/286/961 Turkish subjects Rhodes, 1926
/286/993 Nationality Issues, 1927
/286/1024 Dodecanes Miscellaneous
/286/1180 Dodecanese 1946
/286/1267 Consular Reports Dodecanese
/371/181726
/371/23117/13619
/371/24963
/371/26937 (1941)
/371/31251 (1942)
/371/31257
/371/31256
/371/34841 (1943)
/371/42890
/371/57851
GFM 33/2246/5197 (captured German documents)
GFM 33/2518 (captured German documents)
HS5/227 SOE Operations
HS5 496 SOE Operations (Force 133)
HS5/584 SOE Operations
HS5/585 SOE Operations
HS5/715 SOE Operations
HW1/2118 S-E Europe, Greece, Crete, Rhodes, 1943

HW1/2145 Intercepted signals 1943
HW1/2260 BONIFACE Summaries
HW1/2263 BONIFACE Summaries
HW1/2267 BONIFACE Summaries
HW1/2263
HW1/2145
HW1/2449 Sinking of Oria 1944
HW1/3076 Intercepted signals, Rhodes, Simi, July 1944
HW12/295

War Office WO/
/106/3145 (Cos)
/106/6106
/170/4012
/201/736
/208/4645 (POW 1945/1947)
/218/89-95
/218/97
//218/104 (SBS)
/218/212
/310/190 (Wagener)
/311/373 (Wagener)
/311/612
/32/11430 (Battle for Rhodes)
WR1098/1098/48
WR1202/1098/48

International Committee of the Red Cross (ACICR) Geneva

B Sec. CGSG B-034.01 (Courvoisier Report May 1945)
B Sec. CGSG B-034.02
B Sec. CGSG B-034.03
B Sec. CGSG B-034.04
B Sec. CGSG B-034.05
B Sec. CGSG B-034.06
B Sec. CGSG B-035
B Sec. CGSG B-036

B Sec. CGSG B-037

BG 003 27-26 (1945, Correspondence)

BG 003 27-29 i–iv (Rhodes Correspondence, 1946)

BG 003 60/1 (Mission de Raymond Courvoisier, 1945)

BG 0017 05-150 Prisonniers en Grèce, 1942–1947

BG 0017 05-198 Prisonniers à Rhodes

G59-2/147-31 Rhodes, 1941–1944

G59-3/147-77 Rhodes Camps

G59-3/53-69 Grèce Camps

G59-7/184

G59-7/213.01 (Rapport)

G59-7/279 (Leopoldville)

International Tracing Service Bad Arolsen

A: Bad Arolsen Archive, Ou5

DE IST 1.2.7.25 Verfolgungsmassnahmen Griechenland

1.2.7.25 ONr 1 Varia

1.2.7.25 ONr 2 Salonica

1.2.7.25 ON3. 3 Wiedergutmachung

1.2.7.25 ONr 4 Politisches Archiv Auswärtiges Amt

DE IST 3.1.1.3 GR Registrierungen von ehemaligan Verfolgten Griechenland

Sig. 708000

Sig. 8805350

Sig. 8800370

Sig. 8800390

Sig. 8800880

Sig. 8802790

Sig. 9023400

Sig. 988000

Sig. 990000

DE IST 1.1.47.1 Listen Material– Griechenland

Sig. 3796000 No. 119

Sig. 3669000 No. 0109

B: /ITS Digital Archive, Arolsen Archives

1.1.41.2 Stutthof Personal File

1.1.5.3. Concentration camp Buchenwald

1.1.6.2 Dachau

1.1.6.7 Personal office files, Dachau

1.1.26.3 Individual Files Mauthausen

1.1.26.0 Mauthausen

1.1.26.1 Mauthausen

1.1.26.8 Mauthausen Prisoners Personal Cards

3.1.1.3 Listen betr. Personen, die 1944/46 in Italien, Rhodos, Türkei, Kos Islands, Schweden und Deutschland lebten

3.2.1.2 CM/1 Files originating in Italy A–Z

3.2.1.4, CM/1 Files Originating in Switzerland

3.2.1.5, CM/1 Files Opposition Proceedings

United Nations Archives (UNRRA) New York (Online)

S-0523-0020-0016-00001

S-1252-0000-0278-00002

S-1253-0000-0604-00001

S-1302-0000-5097-00001

S-1345-0000-0031-00001

S-1345-0000-0113-00001

S-1345-0000-0116-00001

S-1345-0000-0117-00001

5-1372-0000-0004-00001

S-1372-0000-0004-00001

S-1450-0000-0089-00001

S-1451-0000-0032-00001

S-1479-0000-0046-00001

S-1479-0000-0047-00001

S-1480-0000-0025-00001

S-1480-0000-0072-00001

S-1536-0000-0226-00001

United States Holocaust Memorial Museum (USHMM) Archives

RG-45.003*03 Statements of camp survivors
RG-45.003*04 Search for Deportees 1945–46
RG-45.003*06 Repatriations
RG-45.003*08 Relief 1946–47
RG-45.003*14 Immigration to Palestine 1946–49
RG-45.003*15 Properties of Dodecanesian Jews 1941–51
RG-45.003*16 Jewish Property in Greece 1941–51
RG-45.003*18 Miscellaneous

Fondazione Centro Di Documentazione Ebraica Contemporanea (CDEC) Massimo Vitale Collection

https://digital-library.cdec.it/cdec-web/storico/detail/IT-CDEC-ST0026-000020/Massimo+Adolfo+Vitale.html

University of Limerick, Gale Primary Sources, Archives Unbound Collection

Mauthausen: [Case No. 000-50] (Vol. X – Folder III List of Victims): US vs. Hans Altfuldich, et al. N.d. RG 153, Records of the Office of the JAG (Army), War Crimes Branch, Entry 149, Concentration Camp Trials. National Archives (U.S.) http://go.gale.com/gdsc/i.do?&id=GALE%7CSC5106350329&v=2.1&u=353lime&it=r&p=GDSC&sw=w&viewtype=fullcitation

United States National Archives and Records Administration (NARA), College Park, Maryland

Record Group (RG)238 M1019 Roll 35 (Kleemann)

Wiener Holocaust Library London (WL)

1655 Nuremberg War Crimes Trial: Documents

World Jewish Congress Cincinnati (WJC), The Jacob Rader Marcus Center of the American Jewish Archives

MSS. Col. No. 361 C195/14
MSS. Col. No. 361 H178/13

American Joint Distribtution Committee Archives (JDC)

G 45-54/4/9/13
G 45-54/4/17/2/Tk1
IST 37-49/4/16/IS.228
NYAR 194554/4/44/3/647

Online Resources

https://www.auschwitz.org/en/
https://avalon.law.yale.edu/20th_century/geneva02.asp
https://www.gedenkstaette-flossenbuerg.de/en/history/satellite-camps/wilischthal
https://www.kz-gedenkstaette-dachau.de/stop06.html
https://ihl-databases.icrc.org/applic/ihl/ihl.nsf/vwTreaties1949.xsp
https://encyclopedia.ushmm.org/en
http://www.jewishvirtuallibrary.org/
https://www.loc.gov/law/help/us-treaties/bevans/m-ust000004-0311.pdf
http://www.lexikon-der-wehrmacht.de/Personenregister/K/KleemannU-R.htm
https://www.rhodesjewishmuseum.org/history/holocaust/
https://www.rhodesjewishmuseum.org/genealogy/
http://www.rhodesjewishmuseum.org/history/the-rabbis-of-rhodes
http://www.storiologia.it/apricrono/storia/a1943u.htm
http://www.tenhumbergreinhard.de/transportliste-der-deportierten/transportliste-
    der-deportierten-1945/index.html

http://www.tenhumbergreinhard.de/1933-1945-taeter-und-mitlaeufer/personal-
　charlottengrube.html
https://it.wikisource.org/wiki/R.D.L._17_novembre_1938,_n._1728_-_
　Provvedimenti_per_la_difesa_della_razza_italiana
http://www.yadvashem.org/yv/en/about/institute/deportations_catalog_details.
　asp?country=Greece
https://www.yadvashem.org/research/research-projects/deportations/deportation-
　catalog.html
https://www.yadvashem.org/yv/de/exhibitions/album_auschwitz/index.asp

Jewish Community Rhodes

Jewish Community Register (heads of household and family, undated ledger)
Ull'Ufficio Dello Stato Civile Rodi: Racial Census (pagination of the individual
　registration cards was added after 1945)
Unpublished mss. obituary Moishe Sulam 06/03/1922–11/02/1982

Interviews & Transcripts

A: Fortunoff Video Archives

Alice Tarica-Israel (6027)
Alberto Israel (5302)
Elisa Franco (5342)
Mathilde Capelluto (5287)
Lea Gattegno (5317)
Mathilde Israel (5323)
Rosa or Ferera (4256)
Gabriel, Clara (5296)

B: Imperial War Museum Oral History (IWM)

13039, George Patrick John Rushworth Jellicoe
15437 William Richard 'Dick' Williams
https://www.iwm.org.uk/history/the-liberation-of-bergen-belsen

C: South African Holocaust and Genocide Foundation (SAHGF) Archive

Giacomo (Jack) Hasson
Giuseppe (Joseph) Coné
Fintz Violette
Ascer Varon
Lucia Amato
Matilde Hasson
Sara Jerusalmi
Stella Israel
Diamante Franco

D: United States Holocaust Memorial Musem USHMM Collections (The Jeff and Toby Herr Oral History Archive)

RG-50.030*0452 Lucia Franco (Garzolini)
RG-50.855*0040 Michail Panagos.
RG-50.233*0001 Miru Alcana
RG-50.477*1297 Miru Alcana
RG-50.855*0039 Michail Zaraftis
RG-50.030*0486 Rachelle Perahia Margosch

E: University Archives and Manuscripts Division, University of Washington, Seattle, Washington Digital Archives

Barkai ohc_3137 (Regina Barkey Amira)
Capelluto ohc_399 (Victoria Israel)
DeLeon ohc_324 (Gordon DeLeon)
Hasson ohc_11 (Stella DeLeon)
Menasce ohc_2339 (Matilde Menasche)
Varon ohc_267 (Laura Varon)

F: Visual History Archive USC Shoah Foundation

Amato, Lucia 14687
Alcana, Miru 129

Alhadeff, Nissim 1577
Almeleh, Anna, 6738
Avzaradel, Clara 8853
Berro, Sylvia 5969
Cipolato, Virginia 44692
De Leon, Stella 12055
Ferrera, Rosa 44115
Fils, Flora 1423
Fintz, Violetta Maio 5720
Franco, Diamante 48392
Franco, Rebecca 33394
Gilmore, Sara 439
Hanan, Rachel 13096
Hasson, Jack 7687
Hasson, Stella 1468
Jerusalmi, Sara 8038
Kantor, Lina 33706
Levi, Stella 1701
Levy, Rebecca 8750
Surmani, Eliezer 53625
Soriano, Clara 8852
Soriano, Maurice 45045
Soriano, Vittoria 45055
Varon, Asher 43798
Varon, Josef 34396
Varon, Laura 26814

G: Yad Vashem Archives (YVA) 0.3 Testimonies Department

2680 Sidney Simcha Fahn
8016 Matilde Levy née Cohen
8017 Regina Mazza née Palombo
4318 Clara Menascé née Gabriel
8591 Rebecca Capelluto
10423 Laura Varon

Newspaper Interviews

Virginia Gattegno, 'I survived due to will and instinct', interviewed by Hannah Roberts, *Financial Times Weekend*, 28/29 May 2016

Stacey Menchel, 'It's time they knew our names', *The Jerusalem Post*, 16 April 2009: interview with Stella Levi, http://www.jpost.com/Magazine/Features/Its-time-they-knew-our-names

Gavin Rabinowitz, 'Rhodeslis make annual island pilgrimage to remember and reboot', *Times of Israel*, 21 August 2015: interview with Giuseppe Giannotti (second generation survivor) and Carmen Cohen https://www.timesofisrael.com/rhodeslis-make-annual-island-pilgrimage-to-remember-and-reboot/

Film

Island of Roses: The Jews of Rhodes in Los Angeles, dir. Gregori Viens (USA, 1995)

In Their Own Hands: The Hidden Story of the Jewish Brigade in World War II, dir. Chuck Olin (USA, [orig. 1998] 2010)

Il viaggio più lungo. Rodi-Auschwitz, in English, *The Longest Journey*, dir. Ruggero Gabbai (Italy, 2013)

Σαμουελ Μοντιάνο: Η Αποστολή. Από τη Ρόδο στο Άουσβιτς (Samuel Modiano: The Mission: From Rhodes to Auschwitz) Cine Chevalier Workshop of Rhodes Scholarship Foundation Em. & M. Stamatiou (Greece, 2019)

Memoirs & Family Histories

Alhadeff, Gini, *The Sun at Midday: Tales of a Mediterranean Family* (Random House: New York, 1997)

Alhadeff, Joseph, *The Jewish Community of Rhodes: A Short History* (Publication of the Jewish Community: Rhodes, n.d.)

Alhadeff, Tony, *The Family Treasure* (n.p., 2020)

Alhadeff, Vittorio, *Le Chêne de Rhodes: Saga d'une grande famille sépharade* (Éditions Paris-Méditerranée: Paris, 1998)

Amariglio, Erika Kounio, *From Thessaloniki to Auschwitz and Back. Memories of a Survivor from Thessaloniki*: Library of Holocaust Testimonies (Vallentine Mitchell: London, Portland, OR, 2000)

Benatar, Isaac, *Rhodes and the Holocaust: The Story of the Jewish Community from the Mediterranean Island of Rhodes* (iUniverse Inc.: New York and Bloomington, 2010)

Capelluto, Lucia, *Testimony: My Life in Auschwitz & Bergen Belsen* (Levant Imprimeurs: Marseille, 1997)

Flash, Claire Barkey, *A Hug from Afar: One Family's Dramatic Journey through Three Continents to Escape the Holocaust*, edited and compiled by Cynthia Flash Hemphill, trans. Morris Barkey (Flash Media Services: Bellevue, WA, 2016 [orig. 2004])

Franco Hasson, Elisa, *Il Était Une Fois l'Île Des Roses* (Éditions Clepsydre: Nivelles, 1996, 2012 repr.)

Frank, Michael, *One Hundred Saturdays: Stella Levi and the Search for a Lost World* (Simon & Schuster: New York, 2022)

Hasson, Stella, *Du Paradis à l'Enfer* (Éditions Clepsydre: Nivelles, 2007)

Israël, Alberto, *Je ne vous ai pas oubliés*. Propos recueillis par Stipan Bosnjak with a preface by Simone Veil (Éditions de l'institut Sepharade Européen: Brussels, 2008)

Kounio, Heinz, *Ein Liter Suppe, A Liter of Soup and Sixty Grams of Bread: The Diary of Prisoner Number 109565* (Bloch Publishing: Jacksonville, FL, 2003)

Lévy, Isaac Jack, *Jewish Rhodes: A Lost Culture* (Judah L. Magnes Museum: Berkeley, 1989)

Levy, Rebecca Amato, *I Remember Rhodes/Miakodro de Rhodes* (Sepher-Hermon Press: New York, 1987)

Mannheimer, Max, 'Theresienstadt-Auschwitz-Warsaw-Dachau. Recollections', in *Dachau Review* 1 (n.p. and n.d.), pp. 55–92, originally published in German in *Dachauer Hefte* 1 (Dec. 1985)

Mannheimer, Max, *Spätes Tagebuch. Theresienstadt-Auschwitz-Warschau-Dachau*, mit einem Vorwort zur aktuellen Ausgabe von Wolfgang Benz, expanded paperback edition (Piper: München, [2000] 2010)

Modiano, Sami, *Per questo ho vissuto. La mia vita ad Auschwitz-Birkenau e altri esili* (BUR Rizzoli: Milan, 2013)

Novitch, Miriam, *The Passage of the Barbarians: Contribution to the History of the Deportation and Resistence of Greek Jews*, trans. from the French by Mrs. P. Senior (The Wilberforce Council: Hull, 1989)

Pressman, Hannah, 'My Sephardic Inheritance: A Spoonful of Salt, a Spoonful of Sugar', in *The Tablet*, February 2017, retrieved at: https://hannahpressman.com/selected-writing/

Pressman, Hannah, '"I'd like to Become a Bird": My great-great-grandmother's letters – in Ladino – paint a portrait of the Sephardic community on the

Isle of Rhodes, moments before it was destroyed in the Holocaust', in *The Tablet*, 21 August 2017, retrieved at: https://tabletmag.com/jewish-life-and-religion/242352/ladino-letters-from-rhodes

Sevillias, Erikos, *Athens-Auschwitz* translated and introduced by Nikos Stavroulakis (Lycabettus Press: Athens, 1983)

Tarica-Israël, Alice, *Des ténèbres au soleil* (Éditions Clepsydre: Nivelles, 2007)

Varon, Laura, *The Juderia: A Holocaust Survivor's Tribute to the Jewish Community of Rhodes* (Praeger: Westport, CO, London, 1999)

Venezia, Shlomo, *Inside the Gas Chambers: Eight Months in the Sonderkommando of Auschwitz* (Polity Press: Cambridge, 2009)

Printed & Miscellanous Sources

El Boletin, newspaper of the Rhodes Sephardi community: various

Benatar, Jacqueline and Benatar, Myriam, *Si je t'oublie, Rhodes … Mémorial de la Communauté de Rhodes de 1939 à 1945* (Editions JEM et Erez: Jerusalem, 2012)

British Foreign Office, *Islands of the Northern and Eastern Aegean* (HMSO: London, 1920)

Χρονίκα (Chronika) April 1984

Deutsches Historisches Museum Berlin, Fotosammlung: Hapag Grosse Orient Reise, 3 April 1939

Dodecanese Handbook, Part 1: People and Administration (HMSO: London, November 1943)

'*Führer-Erlasse*' *1939–1945*, Zusammengestellt und eingeleitet von Martin Moll (Franz Steiner Verlag: Stuttgart 1997)

Haganah Archive 14/491, report by Mezkevet, Ha'mosad LeAliya Beit [Ha'Mossad LeAliyah Bet], 4 July 1945

Hasson, Aron, *Rhodesli Jewish Calendar September 2020/September2021 – Ehd 5780/ Tishri 5782*, March 2021/Adár & Nisán 5781

Hasson, Aron, *Rhodesli Jewish Calendar September 2020/September2021 – Ehd 5780/ Tishri 5782*, January 2021/Tivét & Shevát 5781

leggi razziali Regio Decreto 17 Novembre 1938 Nr 1728

Merolle, Rino, 'Breve Cenno Sulla Deportazione della Colonia Ebraica di Rodi' typed mss. affidavit, Jerusalem (copy in author's possession) RD-L 5 settembre 1938, n. 1390, Provvedimenti per la difesa della razza nella scuola fascista (GU n. 209, 13 settembre 1938)

Il Messaggero di Rodi No. 63, 18 March 1936

Il Messaggero di Rodi No. 70, March 1936

Il Messaggero di Rodi No. 98, April 1936

Il Messaggero di Rodi No. 289, 19 December 1936

Il Messaggero di Rodi No. 276, 3 December 1938

Pariente M., 'Les Israelites de Rhodes', *Bulletin de l'Alliance Israelite Universelle* (Paris, 1888), Nr 13, pp. 101–110

Pinkus ha Kehillot, *Encyclopedia of Jewish Communities from their Foundation till after the Holocaust: Greece*, ed., Bracha Rivlin (Yad Vashem: Jerusalem, 1998)

La Rassegna mensile di Israel terza serie Vol. 69, No. 1, Saggi sull'ebraismo italiano del Novecento inonore chi Luisella Montana Ottolenghi, Tomo 1 (Gennaio–Aprile 2003), xiv

Schramm Percy E., (ed.), *Kriegstagebuch des Oberkommandos der Wehrmacht 1943 Teilband II, Zusammengestellt und erläutert von Walther Hubatsch* (Manfred Pawlak, Verlagsgesellschaft: Herrsching, 1982)

Die Tagebücher von Joseph Goebbels, Teil 1 Aufzeichnungen 1923–1939, Band 6 August 1938–June 1939, prepared by Jana Richter, ed. Elke Fröhlich (K.G. Sauer: Munich, 1998)

Die Verfolgung und Ermordung der europäischen Juden durch das nationalsozialistische Deutschland 1933–1945, Band 14: Besetztes Südosteuropa und Italien, prepared by Sara Berger, Erwin Lewin, Sanela Schmid und Maria Vassilikou (De Gruyter: Oldenbourg, Boston/Berlin, 2017)

Die Verfolgung und Ermordung der europäischen Juden durch das nationalsozialistische Deutschland, 1933–1945: Band 16: Das KZ Auschwitz 1942–1945 und die Zeit der Todesmärsche 1944/45, prepared by Andrea Rudorff (De Gruyter: Oldenbourg, Berlin and Boston, 2018)

The World Almanac, 1946

Secondary Sources

Abzug, Robert H., *Inside the Vicious Heart: Americans and the Liberation of Nazi Concentration Camps* (Oxford University Press: Oxford and New York, 1987)

Adler, H. G., *Theresienstadt 1941–1945: The Face of a Coerced Community*, trans. Belinda Cooper 2nd rev. edition (Cambridge University Press: Cambridge, 2017 [orig. 2004])

Aly, Götz, *Hitlers Volksstaat: Raub, Rassenkrieg und nationaler Sozialismus* (Fischer Verlag: Frankfurt am Main, 2005), English trans. *Hitler's Beneficiaries: Plunder, Racial War, and the Nazi Welfare State* (Holt: New York, 2008)

Angel, Marc D., *The Jews of Rhodes: The History of a Sephardic Community* (Sepher-Hermon Press Inc.: New York, 1978)

Angel, Marc D., *The Rhythms of Jewish Living: A Sephardic Exploration of Judaism's Spirituality* (Jewish Lights Publishing: Woodstock, Vermont, 2015)

Antoniou, Giorgos, and A. Dirk Moses (eds.), *The Holocaust in Greece* (Cambridge University Press: Cambridge, 2018)

Auschwitz 1940–1945: Central Issues in the History of the Camp, trans. William Brand (Auschwitz-Birkenau State Museum, 2000)

Balint, Ruth, 'The Use and Abuse of History: Displaced Persons in the ITS Archive', in Rebecca Boehling, Susanne Urban, Elizabeth Anthony and Suzanne Brown-Fleming (eds.), *Freilegungen Spiegelungen der NS-Verfolgung und ihrer Konsequenzen*, Jahrbuch des Internationalen Tracing Service Vol. 4 (Wallstein Verlag: Göttingen, 2015), pp. 173–186

Balint, Ruth, *Destination Elsewhere: Displaced Persons and Their Quest to Leave Postwar Europe* (Cornell University Press: Ithaca and London, 2021)

Barkey, Karen, and George Gavrilis, 'The Ottoman Millet System: Non-Territorial Autonomy and its Contemporary Legacy', *Ethnopolitics*, Vol. 15, No.1 (2016), pp. 24–42

Barruzza, John, 'The Good Italian, the Bad German, and the Survivor: Narratives and Counter-Narratives of the Shoah in Italy' (PhD Thesis, Syracuse University, 2020). *Dissertations – ALL*. 1187, retrieved at https://surface.syr.edu/etd/1187

Bartov, Omer, *The Eastern Front, 1941–45: German Troops and the Barbarisation of Warfare* 2nd edition (Palgrave: London & New York, 2001)

Bartrop, Paul R., *The Evian Conference of 1938 and the Jewish Refugee Crisis* (Palgrave Macmillan: London, 2018)

Bava, Laura, 'Aiding gli Ebrei' – DELASEM under fascism, 1939 to 1945 (MA Thesis, 2016) University of Notre Dame, Australia, retrieved at https://researchonline. nd.edu.au/theses/124

Benatar, Jacqueline, and Myriam Pimienta-Benatar, *De Rhodes à Elisabethville: l'odyssée d'une communauté sépharade: essaihistoriqueillustré de 45 pages de photos et documents d'archives* (Editions SIIAC: Paris, 2000)

Benbassa, Esther, and Aron Rodrigue, *Sephardi Jewry: A History of the Judeo-Spanish Community, 14th–20th Centuries* (University of California Press: Berkeley and Los Angeles, 2000)

Benz, Wolfgang, *Dimensionen des Völkermords: Die Zahl der jüdischen Opfer des Nationalsozialismus* (dtv Verlagsgesellschaft: Frankfurt, 1996)

Benz, Wolfgang, and Hans Brenner, *Frauen in den Aussenlagern des KZ Flossenbürg* (Arbeitsgemeinschaft ehem. KZ Flossenbürg e.V.: Regensburg, 1999)

Benz, Wolfgang, Claudia Curio and Andrea Hammel (eds.), *Die Kindertransporte 1938/39: Rettung und Integration* (Die Zeit des Nationalsozialismus) (Fischer Verlag: Frankfurt am Main, 2003)

Berger, Joseph A., 'Displaced Persons. A Human Tragedy of World War II', *Social Research*, Vol. 14, No. 1 (March 1947), pp. 45–58

Bessel, Richard, 'Functionalists vs. Intentionalists: the Debate Twenty Years on or Whatever Happened to Functionalism and Inentionalism?', *German Studies Review*, Vol. 26, No. 1 (Feb. 2003), pp. 15–20

Bierman, John, *Odyssey* (Simon and Schuster: New York, 1984)

Bloch, Ernst, *Heritage of our Times*, trans. Neville Plaice and Stephen Plaice (Polity Press: Cambridge, 1991)

Bloxham, Donald, 'Europe, the Final Solution and the Dynamics of Intent', *Patterns of Prejudice*, Vol. 44, No. 4 (2010), pp. 317–335

Booth, Charles Douglas Greaves, *Italy's Aegean Possessions* (Arrowsmith: London, 1928)

Borovaya, Olga, 'The Rhodes Blood Libel of 1840: Episode in the History of Ottoman Reforms', *Jewish Social Studies*, Vol. 26, No. 3 (Autumn 2021), pp. 35–63

Bosworth, Richard, *Italy: The Least of the Great Powers. Italian Foreign Policy before the First World War* (Cambridge University Press: Cambridge, 2005)

Bowman, Steven, 'The Jews in Wartime Greece', *Jewish Social Studies*, Vol. 48, No. 1 (Winter 1986), pp. 50–51

Bowman, Steven, 'Could the Dodekanesi Jews Have Been Saved?', *Newsletter of The Jewish Museum of Greece* 26 (Winter 1989), pp. 1–2

Bowman, Steven, 'Jews' in Richard Clogg (ed.), *Minorities in Greece: Aspects of a Plural Society* (C. Hurst & Co.: London, 2002), pp. 64–80

Bowman, Steven, *The Agony of Greek Jews, 1940–1945* Stanford Studies in Jewish History and Culture (Stanford University Press: Stanford, CA, 2009)

Bradsher, Greg, 'Hitler's Final Words. His Political Testament, Personal Will, and Marriage Certificate: From the Bunker in Berlin to the National Archives', retrieved at https://www.archives.gov/files/publications/prologue/2015/spring/hitler-will.pdf.

Braham, Randolph L., *The Politics of Genocide: The Holocaust in Hungary*, Vol. 1 (Columbia University Press: New York, 2016)

Browning, Christopher, *Ordinary Men: Reserve Police Battalion 101 and the Final Solution in Poland* (HarperCollins: New York, 1992)

Browning, Christopher, Susannah Heschel, Michael R. Marrus and Milton Shain (eds.), *Holocaust Scholarship: Personal Trajectories and Professional Interpretations* (Palgrave Macmillan: London and New York, 2015)

Browning, Christopher, *Collected Memories: Holocaust History and Post-War Testimony* (University of Wisconsin Press: Madison, WI, 2003)

Bruttman, Tal, Stefan Hördler and Christoph Kreutzmüller, *Die fotografische Inszenierung des Verbrechens. Ein Album aus Auschwitz. Bildanalyse des Lili-Jacob-Albums* (Wissenschaftliche Buchgesellschaft: Darmstadt, 2019)

Büchler, Robert J., 'Unter den Kindern von Auschwitz', *Dachauer Hefte*, 12 (Nov. 1996), pp. 169–195

Bullock, Marcus, 'Heiner Müller's Error, Walter Jens's Horror, and Ernst Jünger's Antisemitism', *Monatshefte*, Vol. 86, No. 2 (Summer 1994), pp. 152–171

Buti, Vittorio, 'Il collegio rabbinico di Rodi e la missione dell'Italia', in *Oriente Rivista delle Colonie italiane* (Edita dal Ministero delle colonie: Rome, 1931), pp. 1–6

Casagrande, Thomas, *Die Volksdeutsche SS-Division 'Prinz Eugen': Die Banater Schwaben und die nationalsozialistischen Kriegsverbrechen* (Campus Verlag: Frankfurt/New York, 2003)

Cecini, Giovanni, *La guardia di finanza delle isole Italinae dell'Egeo 1912–1945* (Gangemi Editore: Rome, 2014)

Chary, Frederick B., *The Bulgarian Jews and The Final Solution, 1940–1944* (University of Pittsburgh Press: Pittsburgh, PA, 1972)

Chalmers, Beverley, *Birth, Sex and Abuse: Women's Voices Under Nazi Rule* (Grosvenor House Publishing Ltd: Guildford, 2015)

Churchill, Winston, *The Second World War Vol. 5: Closing the Ring* (Cassell: London, 1952)

Citino, Robert, 'Drive to Nowhere: The Myth of the *Afrika Korps*, 1941–43', retrieved at https://www.nationalww2museum.org/war/articles/drive-nowhere-myth-afrika-korps-1941-43

Clementi, Marco / Eirini Toliou, *Gli ultimi ebrei di Rodi. Leggi razziali e deportazioni nel Dodecaneso italiano (1938-1948)* (Derive Approdi: Rome, 2015)

Clementi, Marco, *Storia della comunità ebraica di Rodi (1912-1947)* (tab edizioni: Rome, 2022)

Clementi, Marco, 'The End of the Rhodes Jewish Community' in Giovanni Orsina and Andrea Ungari (eds.), *The 'Jewish Question' in the Territories Occupied by Italians 1939-1943* (Viella: Rome, 2019), pp. 215-230

Clogg, Richard (ed.), *Minorities in Greece: Aspects of a Plural Society* (C. Hurst & Co.: London, 2002)

Cobb, Richard, *French and Germans, Germans and French: A Personal Interpretation of France under Two Occupations, 1914-1918/1940-1944* (Penguin Modern Classics: London, New York, 2018)

Cohen, Gerard Daniel, *In War's Wake: Europe's Displaced Persons in the Postwar Order* (Oxford University Press: New York, Oxford, 2011)

Collis, Robert and Han Hogerzeil, *Straight On* (Routledge Library Editions: Responding to Fascism, Vol. 12, reprint, London, 2010, originally published 1947)

Conze, Eckart, Norbert Frei, Peter Hayes and Moshe Zimmermann, *Das Amt und die Vergangenheit. Deutsche Diplomaten im Dritten Reich und in der Bundesrepublik* (Siedler: Munich, 2010)

Cosentino, Milena Callegari, 'Remembering Rhodes and the Holocaust: Intergenerational Trauma, Nostalgia and Identity' (PhD Thesis, University of Limerick, 2021)

Creveld, Martin van, 'Prelude to Disaster: The British Decision to Aid Greece 1940-41', *Journal of Contemporary History*, Vol. IX, No. 3 (July 1974), pp. 65-92

Curry, Tommy J., 'Thinking Through the Silence: Theorizing the Rape of Jewish Males during the Holocaust through Survivor Testimonies', *Holocaust Studies: A Journal of Culture and History*, Vol. 27 (2021) Special Issue: Buried Words: Sexuality, Violence and Holocaust Testimonies, pp. 447-472.

Czech, Danuta, *Kalendarium der Ereignisse im Konzentrationslager Auschwitz-Birkenau 1939-1945*, trans. Jochen August with a foreword by Walter Laqueur (Rowohlt: Reinbek, 1989)

Cziborra, Pascal, *KZ Wilischthal: Unter 'Hitlerauges' Aufsicht: Die Außenlager des KZ Flossenbürg* (Lorbeer-Verlag: 2nd edition, Bielefeld, 2015)

Dawidowicz, Lucy, *The War Against the Jews 1933-1945* (Viking Penguin Inc.: New York, 1975)

Dawidowicz, Lucy, *Holocaust and Historians* (Harvard University Press: Cambridge, MA, 1983)

Deist, Wilhelm, *Militär, Staat und Gesellschaft: Studien zur preußisch-deutschen Militärgeschichte* (Beiträge zur Militärgeschichte, Band 34) (De Gruyter/ Oldenbourg: Berlin, 1991)

Delbo, Charlotte, *Auschwitz and After*, 2nd edition, trans. Rosette C. Lamont with a new foreword by Lawrence L. Langer (Yale University Press: New Haven and London, 1995)

Díaz-Mas, Paloma, *Sephardim: The Jews of Spain*, edited and translated by George H. Zucker (University of Chicago Press: Chicago, 1992)

Distel, Barbara, and Wolfgang Benz (eds.), Die Befreiung, *Dachauer Hefte* Nr 1 (Dachau, 1985)

Dobler Jens, 'Täteropfer. Der Berliner Kriminalkommissar Gerhard Kanthack im KZ Mauthausen' in Bundesministerium für Inneres (ed.), *Jahrbuch Mauthausen KZ-Gedenkstätte Mauthausen/Mauthausen Memorial 2015: Justiz, Polizei und das KZ Mauthausen* (Bundesministerium für Inneres: Vienna, 2015), pp. 57–68

Dobosiewicz, Stanisław, *Vernichtungslager Gusen: Mauthausen-Studien. Schriftenreihe der KZ-Gedenkstätte Mauthausen Band 5* Bundesministerium für Inneres, Abt. IV/7 (Vienna, 2007), German translation of: *Mauthausen/Gusen; obóz zagłady* [*Mauthausen/Gusen; the Camp of Doom*] (Ministry of National Defence Press: Warsaw, 1977)

Doumanis, Nicholas, *Myth and Memory in the Mediterranean Remembering Fascism's Empire* (Palgrave Macmillan: London and New York, 1997)

Doumanis, Nicholas, 'Italians as 'Good' Colonizers: Speaking Subalterns and the Politics of Memory in the Dodecanese', in Ruth Ben-Ghiat and Mia Fuller (eds.), *Italian Colonialism* (Palgrave Macmillan: New York, 2005), pp. 221–231

Durrell, Lawrence, *Reflections on a Marine Venus: A Companion to the Landscape of Rhodes* (Faber & Faber: London, [1953] 2000)

Eck, Nathan, 'Hitler's Political Testament', retrieved at http://www.yadvashem.org/yv/ pdf-drupal/en/eichmann-trial/hitlers_political_testament.pdf

Espinoza, Filippo, 'Una cittadinanza imperial basata sul consenso: il caso delle isole italiane dell'Egeo (1924–1940)', in S. Lorozini and S. A. Bellezza (eds.), *Sudditi o cittadini? L'evoluzione delle appartenenze imperiali nella Prima guerra mondiale* (Vielle: Roma, 2018), pp. 189–204

Espinoza, Filippo, 'An Italian Nationality for the Levant: Citizenship in the Aegean from the Ottoman to the Fascist Empire (1912–1936)' in S. Berhe and O. De Napoli (eds.), *Citizens and Subjects of the Italian Colonies: Legal Constructions and Social Practices 1882–1943* (Routledge: New York, 2021), pp. 109–130

Eytan, Walter, 'The Z Watch in Hut 4, Part II', in F.H. Hinsley and Alan Stripp (eds.), *Codebreakers: The Inside Story of Bletchley Park* (Oxford University Press: Oxford, 1993)

Favez, Jean-Claude, *The Red Cross and the Holocaust* (Cambridge University Press: Cambridge, 1999)

Fleischer, Hagen, *Im Kreuzschatten der Mächte Griechenland 1941–1944* (Peter Lang: Frankfurt am Main, Bern, New York, 1986)

Fleischer, Hagen, 'Griechenland' in Wolfgang Benz, *Dimension des Völkermords: Die Zahl der jüdischen Opfer des Nationalsozialismus* (dtv Verlagsgesellschaft: Frankfurt, 1996), pp. 272–273

Fleiter, Rüdiger, 'Die Ludwigsburger Zentrale Stelle – eine Strafverfolgungsbehörde als Legitimationsinstrument? Gründung und Zuständigkeit 1958 bis 1965', *Kritische Justiz*, 35. Jg., 2002, pp. 253–272

Fleming, Kathleen, *Greece – A Jewish History* (Princeton University Press: Princeton, NJ, 2010)

Fontana, Laura, *Gli Italiani ad Auschwitz (1943–1945). Deportazioni – 'Soluzione finale' – Lavoro forzato – un osaico di vittime* (Museo Statale die Auschwitz-Birkenau: Auschwitz, 2021)

Franco, Hizkia, M., *The Jewish Martyrs of Rhodes and Cos*, trans. from French by Joseph Franco (HarperCollins: Zimbabwe, 1994 [orig. (1947) 1954])

Frei, Norbert, and Wulf Kantsteiner(eds.), *Den Holocaust erzählen. Historiographie zwischen wissenschaftlicher Empirie und narrative Kreativität* (Wallstein Verlag: Essen, 2013)

Freund, Florian, *"Arbeitslager Zement". Das Konzentrationslager Ebensee und die Raketenrüstung* (Verlag für Gesellschaftskritik: Vienna, 1989)

Freund, Florian, *Concentration Camp Ebensee: Subcamp of Mauthausen* (Austrian Resistance Archives: Vienna, 1990)

Freund, Florian, 'Mauthausen: Zu Strukturen von Haupt- und Außenlagern', *Dachauer Hefte*, Vol. 15 (1999), pp. 254–272

Freund, Florian, and Bertrand Perz, 'Mauthausen – Stammlager', in Wolfgang Benz, Barbara Distel and Angelika Königseder (eds.), *Der Ort des Terrors: Geschichte der nationalsozialistischen Konzentrationslager*, vol. 4 (C.H. Beck: Munich, 2006), pp. 293–346

Freund, Florian, 'Häftlingskategorien und Sterblichkeit in einem Außenlager des KZ Mauthausen' in Wolfgang Benz, Barbara Distel and Angelika Königseder (eds.), *Der Ort des Terrors: Geschichte der nationalsozialistischen Konzentrationslager*, vol. 4 (C.H. Beck: Munich, 2006), pp. 874–886

Freund, Florian, 'Die Toten von Ebensee', in Bundesministerium für Inneres (ed.), *KZ- Gedenkstätte Mauthausen/Mauthausen Memorial 2010* (Bundesministerium für Inneres: Vienna, 2010), pp. 21–30

Friedländer, Saul, *Probing the Limits of Representation: Nazism and the Final Solution* (Harvard University Press: Cambridge, MA, 1992)

Friedländer, Saul, *Nazi Germany and the Jews, The Years of Persecution 1933–1939* (Harper Perennial: New York, 1998)

Friedländer, Saul, *Nazi Germany and the Jews: The Years of Extermination 1939–1945* (HarperCollins: New York, 2007)

Friedländer, Saul, *Nachdenken über den Holocaust* (C.H. Beck: Munich, 2007)

Fritz, Ulrich, 'Wilischthal', in Wolfgang Benz, Barbara Distel and Angelika Königseder (eds.), *Der Ort des Terrors: Geschichte der nationalsozialistischen Konzentrationslager. Bd. 4: Flossenbürg, Mauthausen, Ravensbrück* pbk. (C.H. Beck: Munich, 2018), pp. 267–270.

Fuller, Mia, *Moderns Abroad: Architecture, Cities and Italian Imperialism* (Routledge: London, New York, 2007)

Gaertringen, Julia Hiller von, *'Meine Liebe zum Griechenland': Studien zum literarischen Werk Erhart Kästners* (Wolfenbütteler Forschungen: Harrassowitz Verlag, 1994)

Galante, Avraham, *Appendice a l'histoire des Juifs de Rhodes* (Editions Isis: Istanbul, 1948)

Galante, Avraham, *Histoire des Juifs de Turquie*, Tome VII: 'Histoire des Juifs de Rhodes, Chio, Cos' (Fratelli Haim: Istanbul, 1935, repr. Isis, 1985)

Gartzonikas, Panagiotis, 'Amphibious and Special Operations in the Aegean Sea 1943–1945. Operational Effectiveness and Strategic Implications' (MA Thesis, Naval Postgraduate School, Monterey, CA, 2003)

Gerwarth, Robert, *Hitler's Hangman, The Life of Heydrich* (Yale University Press: New Haven, 2011)

Gerwarth, Robert, and John Horne (eds.), *War in Peace: Paramilitary Violence in Europe after the Great War* (Oxford University Press: Oxford, 2012)

Gerwarth, Robert, *The Vanquished: Why the First World War Failed to End* (Farrar, Straus and Giroux: New York, 2016)

Gessner, Klaus, *Geheime Feldpolizei. Die Gestapo der Wehrmacht* (Militärverlag: Berlin, 2010)

Giampietro, Diana, 'La storia del tabacco in Italia. III. Dalla formazione del Monopolio di Stato fino alla 2a guerra mondiale', retrieved at http://www1.inea.it/ist/tab8pdf/storia3.pdf

Gigliotti, Simone, *The Train Journey: Transit, Captivity and Witnessing in the Holocaust* (Berghahn Books: New York & Oxford, 2010)

Gilbert, Martin, *The Holocaust. The Human Tragedy* (Fontana Press: London, 1987)

Ginsborg, Paul, *A History of Contemporary Italy: Society and Politics, 1943–1988* (Penguin, London, 1990)

Ginzburg, Carlo, 'Microhistory: Two or Three Things That I Know about it', *Critical Inquiry*, Vol. 20, No.1 (Autumn 1993), pp. 10–35

Glowacka, Dorota, 'Sexual Violence against Men and Boys during the Holocaust: A Genealogy of (Not-So-Silent) Silence', *German History*, Vol. 39, No. 1 (March 2021), pp. 78–99

Goldhagen, Daniel, *Hitler's Willing Executioners. Ordinary Germans and the Holocaust* (Vintage Books: New York, 1996)

Gooderson, Ian, 'Shoestring Strategy: the British Campaign in the Aegean, 1943', in *Journal of Strategic Studies*, Vol. 25, No. 3 (2002), pp. 1–36

Goodman, Jordan, Anthony McElligott and Lara Marks (eds.), *Useful Bodies: Humans in the Service of Medical Science in the Twentieth Century* (Johns Hopkins University Press: Baltimore, 2003)

Gottwaldt Alfred, *Julius Dorpmüller, Die Reichsbahn und die Autobahn. Verkehrspolitik und Leben des Verkehersministers bis 1945* (Argos Verlag: Berlin, 1995)

Grampp, William D., 'The Italian Lira, 1938–45', *Journal of Political Economy*, Vol. 54, No. 4 (Aug. 1946), pp. 309–333

Grand, Alexander J. De, *Fascist Italy and Nazi Germany: the 'Fascist' Style of Rule* 2nd edition (Routledge: London and New York, 1997)

Greenway, Diana E., 'Dates in History: Chronology and Memory', in *Historical Research*, Vol. LXXII, No. 178 (June 1999), pp. 127–139

Guidi, Andreas, 'Patterns of Jewish mobility between Rhodes and Buenos Aires (1905–1948)', in *SüdosteuropäischeHefte*, Vol. 4, No. 2 (2015), pp. 13–24

Guidi, Andreas, *Generations of Empire: Youth from Ottoman to Italian Rule in the Mediterranean* (University of Toronto Press: Toronto, 2022)

Guzzi, Diego, 'The Myth of the "Good Italian", The Antisemitism and the Colonial Crimes', retrieved at https://www.associazionemilgram.it/wp-content/uploads/2013/10/Materiali-Black-Box_The-Myth-of-the-Good-Italian-Antisemitism-and-Colonial-Crimes.pdf

Hacker, Joseph R., 'Jews in the Ottoman Empire (1580–1839)', in Jonathon Karp and Adam Sutcliffe (eds.), *Cambridge History of Judaism. Volume Seven: The Early Modern Period* (Cambridge University Press: Cambridge, 2017), pp. 831–863

Hackett, David (ed. & trans.), *The Buchenwald Report* (Westview Press: Boulder, CO, 1995)

Hagestedt, Lutz, and Luise Michaelsen (eds.), *Ernst Jünger Drei Mal Rhodos. Die Reisen 1938, 1964 und 1981* (Aus dem Archiv Heft 2: Neckar, 2010)

Hall, Richard C. (ed.), *War in the Balkans: An Encyclopedic History from the Fall of the Ottoman to the Breakup of Yugoslavia* (ABC-CLIO: Santa Barbara, CA, etc., 2014)

Hammel, Andrea, and Bea Lewkowicz (eds.), *The Kindertransport to Britain 1938/39: New Perspectives: 13* (Yearbook of the Research Centre for German and Austrian Exile Studies) (Rodopi: Amsterdam, New York, 2012)

Hantzaroula, Pothiti, *Child Survivors of the Holocaust in Greece: Memory, Testimony and Subjectivity* (Routledge: London and New York, 2021)

Harvey, Elizabeth, *Women and the Nazi East: Agents and Witnesses of Germanization* (Yale University Press: New Haven CT, 2003)

Haushofer, Lisa, 'The "Contaminating Agent" UNRRA, Displaced Persons, and Venereal Disease in Germany, 1945–1947', *American Journal of Public Health*, Vol. 100, No. 6 (June 2010), pp. 993–1003

Heberer, Patricia, *Children During the Holocaust: Documenting Life and Destruction. Holocaust Sources in Context* (AltaMira Press: Plymouth, UK, 2011)

Henderson, Mary, *Xenia – A Memoir. Greece 1919–1949* (Weidenfeld and MacMillan: London, 1988)

Hilberg, Raul, *Die Vernichtung der europäischen Juden* (Fischer Verlag: Frankfurt am Main, 1990 [1961])

Hilberg, Raul, *Politics of Memory: The Journey of a Holocaust Historian* (Ivan R. Dee: Chicago, IL, 1996)

Hildebrand, Hans H., and Walter Lohmann, *Deutsche Kriegsmarine 1939–45* (Podzun: Bad Nauheim, 1956–64)

Hilton, Laura J., 'The Experiences and Impact of the Stateless in the Postwar Period', in Rebecca Boehling, Susanne Urban, Elizabeth Anthony and Suzanne Brown-Fleming (eds.), *Freilegungen. Spiegelungen der NS-Verfolgung und ihrer Konsequenzen*, Jahrbuch der Internationalen Tracing Service Vol. 4 (Wallstein Verlag: Göttingen, 2015)

Hionidou, Violetta, *Famine and Death in Occupied Greece, 1941–1944* (Cambridge University Press: Cambridge, 2012)

Hirschon, Renée, 'The Jews of Rhodes: The Decline and Extinction of an Ancient Community', in Minna Rozen (ed.), *The Last Ottoman Century and Beyond: The Jews in Turkey and the Balkans* (Tel Aviv University: Tel Aviv, 2002), pp. 291–307

Hirschon, Renée, 'The Jews from Rhodes in Central and Southern Africa' in M. Ember, C. Ember and I. Skoggard (eds.), *Encyclopedia of Diasporas* (Kluwer Academic/Plenum Publishers: New York, 2005), pp. 925–934

Hirschon, Renée, 'Reconstructing Life in the Old City 1939–44: The Value of the Italian Household Archive', contribution to The Deportation of the Jews of Rhodes & Cos: 1944–2014 A Commemorative International Symposium on the Holocaust in the Aegean, Rhodes, 22–24 July 2014

Hobsbawm, Eric, *The Age of Extremes. The Short Twentieth Century 1914–1991* (Penguin Random House: London, 1994)

Holland, Jeffrey, *The Aegean Mission: Allied Operations in the Dodecanese, 1943* (Greenwood Press: New York, 1988)

Holzinger, Gregor, 'Kurzbiografien von Angehörigen des Kammandaturstabs', in idem (ed.), *Die Zweite Reihe. Täterbiografien aus dem Konzentrationslager Mauthausen, Mauthausen-Studien. Schriftenreihe der KZ-Gedenkstätte Mauthausen Band 10* (new academic press: Vienna, 2016)

Hördler, Stefan, *Ordnung und Inferno. Das KZ System im letzten Kriegsjahr* (Wallstein Verlag: Göttingen, 2015)

Hördler, Stefan, 'Mauthausen', in Geoffrey P. Megargee (ed.), Foreword by Elie Wiesel, *The United States Holocaust Memorial Museum Encyclopedia of Camps and Ghettos, 1933–1945, Volume I: Early Camps, Youth Camps, and Concentration Camps and Subcamps under the SS-Business Administration Main Office* (WVHA) (Indiana University Press: Bloomington, IN, 2009), pp. 899–964

Humphrey, Judith, 'Glimpses of Jewish Life in Crete at the Turn of the Century', *Los Muestros*, Vol. 6 (March 1992), pp. 10–11

Insolvibile, Isabella, 'The Island of Kos under German Occupation and British Military Administration (1943–1947)', paper delivered to 'The Deportation of the Jews of Rhodes & Cos: 1944–2014', A Commemorative International Symposium on the Holocaust in the Aegean' July 2014

Insolvibile, Isabella, *Kos 1943–1948: La strage, la storia* (Edizioni scientifiche italiane: Naples, 2010)

Jockusch, Laura (ed.), *Collect and Record! Jewish Holocaust Documentation in Early Postwar Europe* (Oxford University Press: Oxford and New York, 2012)

Jones, Mark Harris, and Deborah Oppenheimer (eds.), *Into the Arms of Strangers: Stories of the Kindertransport* (Bloomsbury: London, 2000)

Kambanellis, Jakowas (Iokovas), 'Mauthausen', *Dachauer Hefte* 12 (Nov. 1996), pp. 81–103

Kambanellis, Jakowas, *Die Freiheit kam im Mai* translated into German by Elena Strubakis (Ephelant Verlag: Vienna, 2010)

Kambas, Chryssoula, and Marilisa Mitsou (eds.), *Die Okkupation Griechenlands im Zweiten Weltkrieg. Griechische und deutche Erinnerungskultur* (Böhlau Verlag: Cologne, Weimar, Vienna, 2015)

Kassow, Samuel D., *Who Will Write Our History? Emanuel Ringelblum, the Warsaw Ghetto, and the Oyneg Shabes Archive* 2nd edition (Indiana University Press: Bloomington, IN, 2018)

Kästner, Erhart, *Das Zeltbuch von Tumilat* (Suhrkamp Verlag: Frankfurt am Main, 1967)

Kästner, Erhart, *Griechische Inseln. Aufzeichnungen aus dem Jahre 1944* (Insel Verlag: Frankfurt/Main, 1975)

Katz, Steven T., 'Thoughts on the Intersection of Rape and *Rassen[s]chande* during the Holocaust', *Modern Judaism*, Vol. 32, No. 3 (2012), pp. 293–322

Kemp, Paul, 'The British Army and the Liberation of Bergen-Belsen April 1945', in Jo Reilly, David Cesarani, Tony Kushner and Colin Richmond (eds.), *Belsen in History and Memory* (Routledge: London, 1997), pp. 134–148

Kershaw, Ian, '"Working towards the Führer". Reflections on the Nature of the Hitler Dictatorship', *Contemporary European History*, Vol. 2, No. 2 (July 1993), pp. 103–118

Kershaw, Ian, *The Nazi Dictatorship: Problems and Perspectives of Interpretation*, 4th edition (Bloomsbury: London, 2000)

Kertész, Imre, *The Holocaust as Culture English*, trans. Thomas Cooper (Seagull Books: London, 2011)

Kevane, Bridget, 'A Wall of Indifference: Italy's Shoah Memorial', *The Jewish Daily Forward* (29 June 2011), retrieved at https://forward.com/news/139293/a-wall-of-indifference-italy-s-shoah-memorial/

Klein, Shira, *Italy's Jews from Emancipation to Fascism* (Cambridge University Press: Cambridge, 2017)

Kokkonen, Susanna, 'Jewish Displaced Persons in Postwar Italy, 1945–1951', in *Jewish Political Studies Review*, Vol. 20, No. 1/2 (Spring 2008), pp. 91–106

Koon, Tracy H., *Believe, Obey, Fight: Political Socialization of Youth in Fascist Italy, 1922–1943* (University of North Carolina Press: Chapel Hill and London, 2012)

Králová, Katerina, Marija Vulesica and Giorgos Antoniou (eds.), *Jewish Life in Southeast Europe: Diverse Perspectives on the Holocaust and Beyond* (Routledge: London, 2021)

Kreutzmüller, Christoph, *Ausverkauf. Die Vernichtung der jüdischen Gewerbetätigkeit in Berlin 1930–1945* (Metropol: Berlin, 2012)

Kubica, Helen, 'Kinder und Jugendliche im KZ Auschwitz 1940–1945', in Wacław Długoborski and Franciszek Piper (eds.), *Auschwitz 1940–1945 – Studien zur Geschichte des Konzentrations- und Vernichtungslagers Auschwitz* (5 vols.), trans. from Polish (Auschwitz-Birkenau State Museum: Auschwitz, 1995)

Kunz, Andreas, 'Junge Soldaten in der Wehrmacht. Struktur- und organisationsgeschichtliche Betrachtungen', in Ulrich Herrmann and Rolf-Dieter Müller (eds.), *Junge Soldaten im Zweiten Weltkrieg. Kriegserfahrungen als Lebenserfahrungen* (Juventa Verlag: Weinheim, Munich, 2010), pp. 81–112

Lamb, Richard, *War in Italy, 1943–1945: A Brutal Story* (Da Capo Press: Boston, MA, 1996)

Landwehrkamp, Laura Jule, 'Male Rape in Auschwitz?: An Exploration of the Dynamics of Kapo-*Piepel* Sexual Violence in KL Auschwitz during the Holocaust', (Master's Thesis, University of Uppsala, Faculty of Arts, Department of History, The Hugo Valentin Centre, 2019), retrieved at https://www.diva-portal.org/smash/get/diva2:1325746/FULLTEXT01.pdf

Langer, Lawrence L., *Holocaust Testimonies: The Ruins of Memory* (Yale University Press: New Haven, CO, 1991)

Langer, Lawrence L., *Admitting the Holocaust: Collected Essays* (Oxford University Press: Oxford, 1996)

Lawlor, Sheila, 'Greece, March 1941: The Politics of British Military Intervention', *Historical Journal*, Vol. XXV, No. 4 (December 1982), pp. 439–464

Lemkin, Raphael, *Axis Rule in Occupied Europe: Laws of Occupation, Analysis of Government, Proposals for Redress* (Lawbook Exchange: Clark, NJ, 1943)

Lentin, Ronit, 'Expected to Live: Women Shoah Survivors' Testimonials of Silence', *Women's Studies International Forum*, Vol. 23, No. 6 (2000), pp. 689–700

Levene, Mark, '"The Bulgarians Were the Worst!" Reconsidering the Holocaust in Salonika Within a Regional History of Mass Violence', in Giorgos Antoniou and A. Dirk Moses (eds.), *The Holocaust in Greece* (Cambridge University Press: Cambridge, 2018), pp. 36–57

Levi, Aldo, *Avvenimenti in Egeo dopo l'armistizio (Rodi, Lero e isole minori)* (La Marina italiana nella seconda guerra mondiale, Vol. 16), (Rome, 1972)

Levi, Primo, *If This Is a Man/The Truce*, trans. Stuart Woolf, with an introduction by Paul Bailey (Penguin Books: London, 1979)

Levi, Primo, *If This Is a Man*, trans. Stuart Woolf (Abacus: London, [1958] 1987)

Levi, Primo with Leonardo De Benedetti, *Auschwitz Report* trans. Judith Woolf, edited by Robert S.C. Gordon (Verso Books: London, New York, 2006 [orig. 1946])

Lévy, Isaac Jack with Rosemary Lévy Zumwalt, *The Sephardim in the Holocaust: A Forgotten People* (University of Alabama Press: Tuscaloosa, 2020)

Livingston, Michael A., *The Fascists and the Jews of Italy Mussolini's Race Laws, 1938–1943* (Cambridge University Press: Cambridge, 2014)

Longerich, Peter, *Wannsee-Konferenz: Der Weg zur Endlösung* (Pantheon Verlag: Munich, 2016)

Loughram, Tracey, 'Shell Shock, Trauma, and the First World War: The Making of a Diagnosis and Its Histories', *Journal of the History of Medicine and Allied Sciences*, Vol. 67, No. 1, 1 January 2012, pp. 94–119

Lumans, Valdis O., *Himmler's Auxiliaries. The Volksdeutsche Mittelstelle and the German National Minorities of Europe, 1933–1945* (UNC Press: Chapel Hill and London, 1993)

Marcuse, Harold, *Legacies of Dachau: The Uses and Abuses of a Concentration Camp, 1933–2001* (Cambridge University Press: Cambridge, 2001)

Marsalek, Hans, *Geschichte des Konzentrationslagers Mauthausen* (Österreichische Lagergemeinschaft Mauthausen: Vienna, 1980)

Matsas, Michael, *The Illusion of Safety: The Story of the Greek Jews During the Second World War* (Pella Publishing Company: Athens, 1997)

Matton, Raymond, *Rhodes: Villes Et Paysages De Grèce* (Institut Francais D'Athenes: Athens, 1949)

Mazower, Mark, *Inside Hitler's Greece: The Experience of Occupation 1941–44* (Yale University Press: New Haven and London, 1993)

Mazower, Mark, *Dark Continent: Europe's Twentieth Century* (Knopf: New York, 1999)

Mazower, Mark (ed.), *After the War Was Over: Reconstructing the Family, Nation, and State in Greece, 1943–1960* (Princeton University Press: Princeton, NY, 2000)

Mazower, Mark, *Salonica City of Ghosts: Christians, Muslims and Jews 1430–1950* (Harper Perennial: London, New York, Toronto and Sydney, 2004)

Mazower, Mark, *Hitler's Empire: How the Nazis Ruled Europe* (Penguin Press: New York & London, 2008)

McElligott, Anthony, 'Dr Skevos Zervos and Greek Irredentism in the Dodecanese Islands: *Enosis* and Great Power Rivalry, 1912–1947', unpublished paper, Security Studies Programme, Department of Mediterranean Studies, University of the Aegean, 4 May 2017

McElligott, Anthony, 'The Deportation of the Jews of Rhodes: An Integrated History', in Giorgos Antoniou and A. Dirk Moses (eds.), *The Holocaust in Greece* (Cambridge University Press: Cambridge, 2018), pp. 58–86

McElligott, Anthony, '"German Servicemen see Europe". Cultural Mobilization of Troops on the Aegean "Quiet Front"', in Catriona Pennell and Filipe Ribeiro de Meneses (eds.), *A World at War, 1911–1949. Explorations in the Cultural History of War, History of Warfare* Vol. 124 (Brill: Leiden, Boston, 2019), pp. 61–80

McElligott, Anthony, 'Reflections on the *Juderia*: Remembering, Memory-making and History: The "Lost World" of Jewish Rhodes', in Valerie McGuire and Aron Rodrigue (eds.), *Italian Fascism in Rhodes and the Dodecanese Islands, 1912–44* (Routledge: New York, 2024)

McGuire, Valerie, 'Arcadian histories: Italian Encounters in the Eastern Mediterranean', *New Perspectives in Italian Cultural Studies* (2012), pp. 231–258

McGuire, Valerie, 'Una faccia, una razza?: Italian citizenship and differentiation in the Dodecanese occupation' (paper presented at: 'The Deportation of the Jews of Rhodes & Cos: 1944–2014: A Commemorative International Symposium on the Holocaust in the Aegean', Rhodes, 22–24 July 2014)

McGuire, Valerie, 'The Jewish Communities of Rhodes and Kos: A Transnational Community between Ottoman Collapse and the Italian Empire', Αρχειοτάξιο/ *Archeiotaxio* (*Journal of Contemporary Social History Archives*) (2017), pp. 141–159 (in Greek)

McGuire, Valerie, 'Bringing the Empire Home: Italian Fascism's Mediterranean Tour of Rhodes', *California Italian Studies*, Vol. 8 (Dec. 2018), pp. 1–27

McGuire, Valerie, *Italy's Sea: Empire and Nation in the Mediterranean, 1895–1945* (Liverpool University Press: Liverpool, 2020)

McGuire, Valerie, and Aron Rodrigue (eds.), *Italian Fascism in Rhodes and the Dodecanese Islands, 1912–44* (Routledge: New York, 2024)

Menascé, Esther Fintz, *Gli ebrei a Rodi. Storia di un'antica comunità annientata dai nazisti* (Guerini e Associati: Milan, 2005)

Menascé, Esther Fintz, *Buio Nell'Isola del Sole: Rodi 1943–1945 I due volti di una tragedia quasi di metenticato: il martiro dell'ammarigalio Campioni* (Giuntina: Florence, 2005)

Menascé, Esther Fintz, *Buio nell'isola del sole: Rodi 1943–1945. La tragedia dei militari italiani e l'annientamento degli ebrei* (Passato Prossimo: Florence, 2014)

Menascé, Esther Fintz, *A History of Jewish Rhodes* (Rhodes Jewish Historical Foundation: Los Angeles, CA, 2014)

Michman, Dan, *The Emergence of Jewish Ghettos during the Holocaust*, trans. Lenn J. Schramm (Cambridge University Press: New York, 2011)

Mignemi, Adolfo, 'Il Governatorato di De Vecchi alla Vigilia Della Guerra' in Massimo Peri (ed.), *La politica culturale del fascismo nel Dodecaneso. Atti del Convegno – Padova 16–17 November 2007* (Esedra editrice: Padua, 2009), pp. 107–121

Miller, James W., 'Youth in the Dictatorships', *American Political Science Review*, Vol. 32, No. 5 (October 1938), pp. 965–970

Mills, Raymond, 'Lawrence Durrell on Rhodes, 1945–47', *Twentieth Century Literature*, Vol. 33, No. 3, Lawrence Durrell Issue, Part I (Autumn 1987), pp. 312–316

Mitscherlich, Alexander and Margarete Mitscherlich, *Die Unfähigkeit zu trauern: Grundlagen kollektiven Verhaltens* (Piper Taschenbuch: Munich, 1977 [orig. 1967]), English *The Inability to Mourn* (New York, 1984)

Molho, Michael, and Joseph Nehama, *In Memoriam: hommage aux victimes juives des Nazis en Grèce* (Imp. N. Nicolaidès: Salonique, 1949; 2nd edition, 1973), German translation by Peter Katzung, Essen, 1981

Molho, Rena, *Der Holocaust der griechischen Juden: Studien zur Geschichte und Erinnerung*, trans. Lulu Bail (J.H. Dietz: Berlin, 2016)

Mommsen, Hans, 'Cumulative Radicalisation and Progressive Self-destruction as Structural Determinants of the Nazi Dictatorship', in Ian Kershaw and Moshe Lewin (eds.), *Stalinism and Nazism Dictatorships in Comparison* (Cambridge University Press: Cambridge, 1997), pp. 75–87

Morgan, Philip, *Italian Fascism, 1915–1945* 2nd edition (Palgrave Macmillan: New York & London, 2004)

Müller, Rolf-Dieter, *An der Seite der Wehrmacht. Hitlers ausländische Helfer beim „Kreuzzug gegen den Bolschewismus" 1941–1945* (Fischer Taschenbuch: Frankfurt/Main, 2014 [orig. Chr. Links Verlag, 2007])

Müller-Tupath, Karla, *Verschollen in Deutschland: Das heimliche Leben von Anton Burger: Lagerkommandant von Theresienstadt* (Konkret Literatur Verlag: Hamburg, 1994)

Némirovsky, Irène, *Suite française* (Denoël: Paris, 2004)

Nora, Pierre (ed.), *Les Lieux de mémoire* 3 vols. (Gallimard: Paris, 1997)

Nussbaum, Helen, 'One "Sunshine" Spot in Greece', *American Journal of Nursing*, Vol. 49, No. 1 (Jan. 1949), pp. 11–12

Nyiszli, Miklós, *Auschwitz: A Doctor's Eyewitness Account* (Arcade: New York, 2011 (1946))

Orth, Karin, *Die Konzentrationslager-SS. Sozialstrukturelle Analysen und biographische Studien, Göttingen 2000* (Taschenbuchausgabe: Munich, 2004)

Orth, Karin, *Das System der nationalsozialistischen Konzentrationslager. Eine politische Organisationsgeschichte, Hamburg 1999* (Taschenbuchausgabe: Zürich/ Munich, 2002)

Papachristodoulou, Christos I., Παπαχριστοδούλου *Ιστορία Της Ρόδου Από Τους Προϊστορικούς Χρόνους Έως Την Ενσωμάτωση Της Δωδεκανήσου* (1948) History of Rhodes from Prehistoric Times to the Integration of the Dodecanese (1948) (Παλαιοβιβλιοπωλείο: Αθήναι, 1972) (Palaiovivliopoleio: Athens, 1972)

Pelt, Robert van Deborah Dwork, *Auschwitz* (W.W. Norton & Company: New York, 2002)

Penkower, Monty Noam, *After the Holocaust* (Touro University Press: New York, 2021)

Peri, Massimo (ed.), *La politica culturale del fascismo nel Dodecaneso. Atti del Convegno – Padova 16–17 November 2007* (Esedra editrice: Padua, 2009)

Perz, Bertrand, *Projekt Quarz. Steyr-Daimler-Puch und das Konzentrationslager Melk* (Verlag für Gesellschaftskritik: Vienna, 1991)

Perz, Bertrand, 'Der Arbeitseinsatz im KZ Mauthausen', in Herbert Ulrich, Karin Orth and Christoph Dieckmann (eds.), *Die nationalsozialistischen Konzentrationslager* 2 vols. (Fischer: Frankfurt am Main, 2002), pp. 533–557

Petersen, Jens, 'Deutschland und Italien 1939 bis 1945', in Wolfgang Michalka (ed.), *Der Zweite Weltkrieg: Analysen, Grundzüge, Forschungsbilanz, Im Auftrag des Militärgeschichtlichen Forschungsamtes* (Seehamer Verlag: Munich, 1989), pp. 108–119

Pfingston, Gabriele, and Claus Füllberth-Stolberg, 'Frauen in Konzentrationslagern – geschlechtsspezifische Bedingungen des Überlebens', in Herbert Ulrich, Karin Orth and Christoph Dieckmann (eds.), *Die nationalsozialistischen Konzentrationslager* 2 vols. (Fischer: Frankfurt am Main, 2002), pp. 911–938

Picciotto Fargion, Liliana, *Il libro della memoria. Gli Ebrei deportati dall'Italia (1943–1945)* (Mursia: Milano, 1991)

Picciotto Fargion, Liliana, 'Italien' in Wolfgang Benz (ed.), *Dimension des Völkermords. Die Zahl der jüdischen Opfer des Nationalsozialismus* (dtv Wissenschaft: Munich, 1996 [1991])

Pignataro, Luca, 'Il Collegio Rabbinica di Rodi', *Nuova storia contemporanea. Bimestrale di ricerche e studi storici e politici sull'età contemporanea*m, Vol. 6 (Milan, 2011), pp. 49–86

Pignataro, Luca, *Il Dodecaneso Italiano 1912–1947. Vol. 1: l'Occupazione Iniziale 1912–1922* (Edizione Solfanelli: Chieti, 2011)

Pignataro, Luca, *Il Dodecaneso Italiano 1912–1947. Vol. 2: Il Governo Di Mario Lago 1923–1936* (Edizione Solfanelli: Chieti, 2013)

Pignataro, Luca, *Il Dodecaneso Italiano 1912–1947: Vol. 3, De Vecchi, Guerra e Dopoguerra 1936–1947/50* (Edizioni Solfanelli: Chieti, 2018)

Piper, Franciszek, 'Die Rolle des Lagers Auschwitz' in Ulrich Herbert, Karin Orth, Christoph Dieckmann (eds.), *Die nationalsozialistischen Konzentrationslager* 2 vols. (Fischer: Frankfurt am Main, 2002), pp. 390–414

Piper, Franciszek, *Voices of Memory 9: Jews in Auschwitz* (Auschwitz-Birkenau State Museum: Oswiecim, 2019)

Pitch, Anthony S., *Our Crime was Being Jewish Hundreds of Holocaust Survivors Tell their Stories*, Foreword by Michael Berenbaum (Skyhorse Publishing: Delaware, 2015)

Poliakov, Leon, *Brévaire de la haine* (1951) translated as *Harvest of Hate: The Nazi Program for the Destruction of the Jews of Europe* (Syracuse University Press: New York, 1954)

Ponzio, Alessio di, *Shaping the 'New Man': Totalitarian Training Regimes in Fascist Italy and Nazi Germany* (University of Wisconsin Press: Madison, WI, 2015; paperback July 2017)

Prato, David, *Cinque Anni di Rabbinato Alessandria d'Egitto 1933* (Rodi, n.d.), pp. 213–219

Raim, Edith, 'Unternehmen Ringeltaube', Dachaus Außenlagerkomplex Kaufering, in *Dachauer Hefte*, Nr 5, Die vergessenen Lager (Dachau, 1989), pp. 193–213

Rappas, Alexis, 'Mixed Marriages in the Fascist Aegean and the Domestic Foundations of Imperial Sovereignty', in Ulrike Lindner and Dörte Lerp (eds.), *New Perspectives on the History of Gender and Empire: Comparative and Global Approaches* (Bloomsbury: London, 2018), pp. 31–58

Reilly, Joanna, *Belsen: The Liberation of a Concentration Camp* (Routledge: London, 1997)

Reinisch, Jessica, 'Old Wine in New Bottles? UNRRA and the Mid-Century World of Refugees', in Matthew Frank and Jessica Reinisch (eds.), *Refugees in Europe, 1919–1959: A Forty Year Crisis?* (Bloomsbury: London, 2017)

Richter, Heinz, *Griechenland im Zweiten Weltkrieg 1939–1941* 2nd expanded edition (Harrossowitz: Wiesbaden, 2015)

Ringelbaum, Joan, 'Women and the Holocaust: A Reconsideration of Research', *Signs*, Vol. 10, No. 4, 'Communities of Women' (Summer 1985), pp. 741–761

Rodogno, Davide, *Fascism's European Empire: Italian Occupation during the Second World War*, trans. Adrian Belton (New Studies in European History) (Cambridge University Press: Cambridge, 2006)

Rodrigue, Aron, *Jews and Muslims: Images of Sephardi and Eastern Jewries in Modern Times* (University of Washington Press: Seattle and London, 2003)

Rodrigue, Aron, 'La mission éducative (1860–1939)', in André Kaspi (ed.), *Histoire de l'Alliance israélite universelle – De 1860 à nos jours* (Edition Armand Colin: Paris, 2010)

Rodrigue, Aron, 'The Rabbinical Seminary in Italian Rhodes 1928–38: An Italian Fascist Project', *Jewish Social Studies*, Vol. 25, No. 1 (Autumn 2019), pp. 1–19

Rogers, Anthony, *Churchill's Folly: The Battles for Kos and Leros, 1943*, Foreword by Lord Jellicoe (The History Press: Stroud, [2003] 2017)

Rohwer, Jürgen, with Gerhard Hümmelchen, *Chronik des Seekrieges 1939–1945*, *Herausgegeben von der Bibliothek für Zeitgeschichte, Württembergische Landesbibliothek* (Stuttgart, 2007–2018) retrieved at: http://www.wlb-stuttgart.de/seekrieg/43-09.htm

Roper, Michael, 'From the Shell-shocked Soldier to the Nervous Child: Psychoanalysis in the Aftermath of the First World War', *Psychoanalysis and History*, Vol. 18, No. 1 (2016), pp. 39–69

Roseman, Mark, 'Surviving Memory: Truth and Inaccuracy in Holocaust Testimony', *Journal of Holocaust Education*, Vol. 8, No. 1 (1999), pp. 1–20

Roseman, Mark, *The Past in Hiding. Memory and Survival in Nazi Germany* (Allen Lane, The Penguin Press: Harmondsworth, 2000)

Roseman, Mark, *The Villa, the Lake, the Meeting: Wannsee and the Final Solution* (Penguin edn: Harmondsworth, 2003)

Rosen, Alan, *The Wonder of Their Voices: The 1946 Holocaust Interviews of David Boder* (Oxford University Press: Oxford, 2010)

Rössler, Mechthild, and Schleiermacher, Sabine, *Der 'Generalplan Ost': Hauptlinien Der Nationalsozialistischen Planungs- Und Vernichtungspolitik* (Schriften der Hamburger Stiftung für Sozialgeschichte des 20. Jahrhunderts) (Akademie-Verlag: Berlin, 1993)

Roucek, Joseph S., 'The Legal Aspects of Sovereignty Over the Dodecanese', *The American Journal of International Law*, Vol. 38, No. 4 (Oct. 1944), pp. 701–706

Safrian, Hans, *Eichmann's Men*, trans. Ute Stargardt (Cambridge University Press: Cambridge, 2010 [orig. 1993])

Sarfatti, Michele, 'Characteristics and Objectives of the Anti-Jewish Racial Laws in Fascist Italy, 1938–1943', in Joshua D. Zimmerman (ed.), *Jews in Italy under Fascist and Nazi Rule, 1922–1945* (Cambridge University Press: Cambridge, 2005), pp. 71–80

Sarfatti, Michele, *The Jews in Mussolini's Italy: From Equality to Persecution* (University of Wisconsin Press: Madison, WI, 2006)

Saxon, Timothy D., 'The German Side of the Hill: Nazi Conquest and Exploitation of Italy, 1943–45' (PhD Thesis, University of Virginia, 1999)

Schenk, Peter, *Kampf um die Ägäis: Die Kriegsmarine in Griechischen Gewässern 1941–1945* (E.S. Mitler & Sohn: Hamburg, Berlin, Bonn, 2000)

Schleunes, Karl, *The Twisted Road to Auschwitz: Nazi Policy Toward German Jews, 1933–1939* (University of Illinois Press: Champaign, IL, 1970)

Schminck-Gustavus, Christoph U., *Winter in Griechenland. Krieg – Besatzung - Shoah 1940–1944* (Göttingen: WallsteinVerlag, 2011)

Schreiber, Gerhard, *Die italienischen Militärinternierten im Deutschen Machtbereich 1943–1945: Verachtet – Verraten – Vergessen* (De Gruyter/Oldenbourg Verlag: Munich, 1990)

Schröder, Josef, *Italiens Kriegsaustritt, 1943. Die deutschen Gegenmaßnahmen im italienischen Raum: Fall 'Alarich' und 'Achse'* (Verlag: Göttingen, Zürich, Frankfurt, 1969)

Schwanninger, Florian, 'Die "Sonderbehandlung 14 f 13" in den Konzentrationslagern Mauthausen und Gusen. Probleme und Perspektiven der Forschung', in Bundesministerium für Inneres (ed.), *KZ-Gedenkstätte Mauthausen, Mauthausen Memorial* 2011 (Bundesministerium für Inneres: Vienna, 2011), pp. 55–67

Seder, Denes, *Miracle at Zakynthos: The Only Greek Jewish Community Saved in its Entirety from Annihilation* (Philos Press: Lacey, WA, 2014)

Semprun, Jorge, *Schreiben oder Leben* (orig. *L'écriture ou la vie*, Editions Gallimard, 1994) translated Eva Moldenhauer (Suhrkamp: Frankfurt am Main, 1995)

Seta Torrefranca, Simonetta della, 'The Rabbinical Seminary of Rhodes 1926–1938', in Itzhak Bezalel (ed.), *Pe' Amim Studies in the Cultural Heritage of Oriental Jewry* (Ben–Zvi Institute of Yad Itzhak Ben-Zvi and Hebrew University: Jerusalem, 1988), pp. 78–112

Seta, Simonetta Della, 'Gli ebrei del Mediterraneo nella strategia politica fascista sino al 1938: il caso di Rodi', *Storia Contemporanea* XVII/6 (Bologna, 1986), pp. 997–1032

Setkiewicz, Piotr, 'Häftlingsarbeit im KZ Auschwitz III-Monowitz. Die Frage nach der Wirtschaftlichkeit der Arbeit', in Ulich Herbert, Karin Orth and Christoph

Dieckmann (eds.), *Die nationalsozialistischen Konzentratiosnlager* (Fischer: Frankfurt am Main, 2002), pp. 584–605

Seyfullah, Ibrahim, *Italian im östlichen Mittelmeer. Eine politische Studie über die Bedeutung der anatolischen Küsteninseln* (Kurt Vowinckel Verlag: Berlin, 1930)

Shachar, Nathan (Mats Erik Ahnlund), *The Lost Worlds of Rhodes: Greek, Italians, Jews and Turks between Tradition and Modernity* (Sussex Academic Press: Brighton, Portland, Toronto, 2013)

Shelah, Menachem, 'Die Ermordung italienischer Kriegsgefangene, September–November 1943', in Hannes Heer and Klaus Neumann (eds.), *Vernichtungskrieg. Verbrechen der Wehrmacht 1941 bis 1944* (Hamburger Editionen: Hamburg, 1995), pp. 191–207

Shephard, Ben, *After Daybreak. The Liberation of Belsen 1945* (Pimlico: London, 2006)

Shephard, Ben, *The Long Road Home: The Aftermath of the Second World War* (Alfred A. Knopf: New York, 2011)

Simpson, John Hope, 'The Refugee Problem', *International Affairs (Royal Institute of International Affairs 1931–1939)*, Vol. 17, No. 5 (Sep.–Oct. 1938), pp. 607–628

Sinnreich, Helene, ""It Was Something We Didn't Talk about": Rape of Jewish Women During the Holocaust', *Holocaust Studies*, Vol. 14, No. 2 (2008), pp. 1–22

Sintès, Pierre, *Chasing the Past: Geopolitics of Memory on the Margins of Modern Greece*, trans. Jenny Money, Samantha Eddison and Caroline Stephens (Liverpool University Press, Provence University Press: Liverpool, 2019)

Sjöberg, Tommie, *The Powers and the Persecuted: The Refugee Problem and the Intergovernmental Committee on Refugees (IGCR), 1938–1947* (Lund University Press: Lund, 1991)

Smith, Peter C., and Walker, Edwin R., *War in the Aegean: The Campaign for the Eastern Mediterranean in WWII*, Stackpole Military History Series (Stackpole Books: Mechanicsburg, PA, [1974] 2008)

Snyder, J.C., 'Typhus Fever in the Second World War', *California Medicine*, Vol. 66, No. 1 (January 1947), pp. 3–10

Stargadt, Nicholas, *Witnesses of War: Children's Lives Under the Nazis* (Vintage Books: New York, 2006)

Steitz, Kerstin, 'No "Innocent Victim"?: Sexual Violence Against Jewish Women During the Holocaust as Trope in *Zeugin aus der Hölle*', *Women in German Yearbook*, Vol. 33 (2017), pp. 101–127

Steinberg, Paul,: *Speak You Also: A Survivor's Reckoning* (Henry Holt: New York, 2000)

Stone, Dan, *Histories of the Holocaust* (Oxford University Press: Oxford, 2010)

Stone, Dan, *The Liberation of the Camps: The End of the Holocaust and Its Aftermath* (Yale University Press: New Haven, CT, 2015)

Strong, Samuel M., 'The Future of the Jewish Populations of Europe', *Journal of Negro Education*, Vol. 10, No. 3, Racial Minorities and the Present International Crisis (July 1941)

Strumza, Vitalis, 'Il "Tecche" Di Murad Reis A Rodi' in *Rivista delle Colonie Italiane* (Capelli Editore: Bologna, 1934)

Strumza, Vitalis, *Alcuni Cenni Storici Sugli Ebrei di Rodi* (n.p.: Bologna, 1936)

Stuart, Graham H., *The International City of Tangier* (Stanford University Press: Stanford, 1931)

Stuart, Graham H., 'The Future of Tangier', *Foreign Affairs*, Vol. 23, No. 4 (July 1945)

Suleiman, Susan Rubin, 'Problems of Memory and Factuality in Recent Holocaust Memoirs: Wilkomirski/Wiesel', *Poetics Today*, Vol. 21, No. 3 (Autumn 2000), pp. 543–559

Tolios, Irini, 'Η φιλαναγνωσία ως εργαλείο προπαγάνδας μέσω της εφημερίδας Il Messaggero di Rodi, την περίοδο της Ιταλοκρατίας στα Δωδεκάνησα, 1923–1943' ('Literacy as a tool of propaganda through the newspaper Il Messaggero di Rodi, during the period of Italian rule in the Dodecanese, 1923–1943') (MA Thesis, University of Athens, 1991)

Torsiello, Mario, *Le operazioni delle unita italiane nel settembre–ottobre 1943* (Ministero della difesa, Stato maggiore dell'Esercito, Ufficio storico: Rome 1975)

Tozer, Henry Fanshawe, *The Islands of the Aegean* (Clarendon Press: Oxford, 2006 [orig. 1890])

Triantafillou, Michael N., *From Halicarnassus to the Dodecanese* Vol. 3 (Rhodes, 2023)

Venn, Fiona M., *Oil Diplomacy in the Twentieth Century* (Palgrave: London & New York, 1986)

Venn, Fiona M., 'The Wartime "Special Relationship"? From Oil War to Anglo– American Oil Agreement, 1939–1945', *The Journal of Transatlantic Studies*, Vol. 10, No. 2 (2012), pp. 119–133

Veronese, Francesca, 'Il Patrimonio Archeologico del Dodecaneso. E Il Suo Utilizzo Propagandistico: Spunti di Riflessione Sulla Politica Culturelle del Fascismo nel Mare Nostrum (ovvero 'Dell'Uso Publicco Della Storia')', in Massimo Peri (ed.), *La politica culturale del fascismo nel Dodecaneso. Atti del Convegno – Padova 16–17 November 2007* (Esedra editrice: Padua, 2009), pp. 137–150

Vinen, Richard, *A History In Fragments: Europe in the Twentieth Century* (De Capo Press: Boston, MA, 2001)

Voigt, Klaus, *Villa Emma: Jüdische Kinder auf der Flucht 1940–1945* 2nd edition (Metropol-Verlag: Berlin, 2016)

Wagener, Otto, *Hitler aus nächster Nähe. Aufzeichnungen eines Vertrauten 1929–1932*, edited Henry Ashby Turner (Ullstein Verlig: Berlin, 1985), also translated as *Hitler: Memoirs of a Confidant* edited and introduced by Henry Ashby Turner (Yale University Press: New Haven, CT, 1985)

Waite, Robert G., 'Ebensee', in Geoffrey P. Megargee (ed.), *The United States Holocaust Memorial Museum Encyclopedia of Camps and Ghettos, 1933–1945*, Vol. I (Indiana University Press: Bloomington, IN, 2009), pp. 911–913

Walker, Stephen, *Hide & Seek: The Irish Priest In The Vatican Who Defied The Nazi Command* (HarperCollins: London, 2011)

Wasser, Bruno, *Himmlers Raumplanung im Osten: Der Generalplan Ost in Polen 1940–1944 (SPG – Stadt – Planung – Geschichte, Band 15)* (Birkhäuser Verlag: Basel, 1994)

Waxman, Zoë Vania, *Writing the Holocaust: Identity, Testimony, Representation* (Oxford University Press: Oxford, New York, 2006)

Weindling, Paul, *Epidemics and Genocide in Eastern Europe, 1890–1945* (Oxford University Press: Oxford, New York, 2000)

Weindling, Paul,'Medizinische Gräueltaten in Mauthausen und Gusen: Die Opfer erzwungener medizinischer Forschung im Nationalsozialismus', in Bundesministerium für Inneres (ed.), *KZ-Gedenkstätte Mauthausen, Mauthausen Memorial 2011* (Bundesministerium für Inneres: Vienna, 2011), pp. 41–54

Weinke, Annette, *Eine Gesellschaft ermittelt gegen sich selbst: Die Geschichte der Zentralen Stelle in Ludwigsburg 1958–2008* (Wissenschaftliche Buchgesellschaft: Darmstadt, 2008)

Welzer, Harald, *Täter: Wie aus ganz normalen Menschen Massenmörder werden* (Fischer Verlag: Frankurt am Main, 2005, paperback edition, 2007)

Wiesel, Elie, *Night* translated from the French Marion Wiesel (Penguin Books: Harmondsworth, 2006 [orig. 1972])

Wildt, Michael, *An Uncompromising Generation: The Leadership of the Reich Main Security Office*, trans. Tom Lampert, The George L. Mosse Series in Modern European Cultural and Intellectual History (University of Wisconsin Press: Madison, WI, 2010)

Wilhelm, Cornelia, *The Independent Orders of B'nai B'rith and True Sisters. Pioneers of a New Jewish Identity, 1843–1914* (Wayne State University Press: Detroit, MI, 2011)

Winter, Robert, *Die geheime Polizei* (Melchior Verlag: Wolfenbüttel, 2013)

Wyman, Mark, *DPs: Europe's Displaced Persons, 1945–1951*. With a new Introduction (Cornell University Press: Ithaca and London, [1989] 1998)

Yahil, Leni, *The Holocaust: The Fate of the European Jewry, 1932–1945*: *The Fate of European Jewry, 1932–1945* translated from the Hebrew by Ina Friedman and Haya Galai (Oxford University Press: New York, Oxford, 1991)

Żbikowski, Andrzej, 'Pogroms in Northeastern Poland – Spontaneous Reactions and German Instigations', in Elazar Barkan, Elizabeth A. Cole and Kai Struve (eds.), *Shared History, Divided Memory: Jews and Others in Soviet-occupied Poland 1939–1941*. Leipziger Beiträge zur judische Geschichte und Kultur Bd.5 (Leipziger Universitätsverlag: Leipzig, 2007)

Zervos, Dr Skevos, and Paris Roussos, *White Book: The Dodecanese. Resolutions and Documents Concerning the Dodecanese 1912–1919*, 22nd edition with a map of the Dodecanese (London, n.d. [1919])

Zimmerman, Joshua D., *Jews in Italy Under Fascist and Nazi Rule, 1922–1945* (Cambridge University Press: Cambridge, 2005)

Zumwalt, Rosemary Lévy, 'Stories, Food, and Place: Following a Sephardic Family to a New Home', *Sephardic Horizons*, Vol. 6, No. 1 (9/2/2021), retrieved at https://www.sephardichorizons.org/Volume6/Issue1/Zumwalt.html

Index